TRUSTS:
CASES AND MATERIALS

AUSTRALIA
Law Book Co.
Sydney

CANADA and USA
Carswell
Toronto

HONG KONG
Sweet & Maxwell Asia

NEW ZEALAND
Brookers
Wellington

SINGAPORE and MALAYSIA
Sweet & Maxwell Asia
Singapore and Kuala Lumpur

TRUSTS:
CASES AND MATERIALS

James P. Chalmers, LL.B., LL.M., Dip.L.P.

Lecturer in Scots Law, University of Aberdeen

EDINBURGH
W. GREEN/Sweet & Maxwell
2002

Published in 2002 by W. Green & Son Ltd
21 Alva Street
Edinburgh EH2 4PS

Typeset by LBJ Typesetting Ltd, Kingsclere
Printed and bound in Great Britain by Ashford Colour Print, Hants

No natural forests were destroyed to make this product;
only farmed timber was used and replanted

A CIP catalogue record for this book is available from
the British Library.

ISBN 0 414 01337 9

PREFACE

This book was originally to have been written by Roderick Paisley, but he had to relinquish the project due to other commitments. I am very grateful to him for his guidance and support in getting the project off the ground. The finished product deliberately retains the same structure as was employed in Professor Paisley's *Trusts LawBasics* book. While some may wish (perhaps justifiably) to attribute this to a lack of imagination on the part of the present author, it is hoped that it will enable students (and other readers) to use the two books in conjunction efficiently.

Nicola McKibben, whilst working as a research assistant for Roderick Paisley, collected various materials which helped to speed up the book's eventual production, while David Carey Miller brought some useful materials on constructive trusts to my attention. The staff of the Taylor Library, including Mike Gordon, Lin Masson, Julie Oates and Elaine Shallcross, displayed more tolerance than could reasonably have been expected. Most importantly, the support of the staff of W. Green, including Philippa Blackham, Neil McKinlay and Lyn Minay, without which this book would never have been published, must be recognised.

I am very grateful to all of these people (and others), but none of them, of course, bears any responsibility for such errors, infelicities and omissions as the reader may notice. (An earlier draft of this preface described these as "inevitable", but it is probably bad practice to announce the fallibility of a text before the reader has even reached the opening page of the first chapter.) If readers draw such matters to the author's attention, it would be of great assistance in improving any future editions.

James Chalmers
Aberdeen
July 2002

CONTENTS

TABLE OF CASES

References are to paragraph numbers. **Bold** paragraph numbers refer to extracts of cases.

TABLE OF STATUTES

References are to paragraph numbers. **Bold** paragraph numbers refer to legislation reproduced in full.

TABLE OF STATUTORY INSTRUMENTS

References are to paragraph numbers

Scottish Statutory Instruments

LIST OF ABBREVIATIONS

(excluding standard law reports and journals)

Bell, *Commentaries*	George Joseph Bell, *Commentaries on the law of Scotland and on the Principles of Mercantile Jurisprudence* (7th ed. by John McLaren, 1870)
Bell, *Principles*	George Joseph Bell, *Principles of the law of Scotland* (10th ed. by William Guthrie, 1899)
Delany	Hilary Delany, *Equity and the Law of Trusts in Ireland* (2nd ed., 1999)
Erskine, *Inst.*	John Erskine, *An Institute of the Law of Scotland* (1871)
Gloag and Henderson	Gloag and Henderson, *An Introduction to the Law of Scotland* (11th ed., 2001)
Hanbury and Martin	Hanbury and Martin, *Modern Equity* (16th ed. by Jill E. Martin, 2001)
Johnston, *Prescription and Limitation*	David Johnston, *Prescription and Limitation* (1999)
Keeton and Sheridan	George Williams Keeton and L.A. Sheridan, *The Law of Trusts* (12th ed., 1993)
Macdonald, *Succession*	D.R. Macdonald, *Succession* (3rd ed., 2001)
McKenzie Skene, *Insolvency*	Donna W. McKenzie Skene, *Insolvency Law in Scotland* (1999)
Mackenzie Stuart	A. Mackenzie Stuart, *The Law of Trusts* (1932)
McLaren	John McLaren, *The Law of Wills and Succession as Administered in Scotland, Including Trusts, Entails, Powers and Executry* (3rd ed., 1894)
Norrie and Scobbie	Kenneth McK. Norrie and Eilidh M. Scobbie, *Trusts* (1991)
Pearce and Stevens	Robert A. Pearce and John Stevens, *The Law of Trusts and Equitable Obligations* (2nd ed., 1998)
Reid, *Property*	Kenneth G.C. Reid, *The Law of Property in Scotland* (1996)
Stair	James Dalrymple Stair [1st Viscount], *The Institutions of the Law of Scotland* (2nd ed., 1693)
Stewart, Restitution	William J. Stewart, *The Law of Restitution in Scotland* (1992)
Tudor on Charities	*Tudor on Charities* (8th ed., 1995 by Jean Warburton, assisted by Debra Morris)
Walker, *Civil Remedies*	David M. Walker, *The Law of Civil Remedies in Scotland* (1974)

Walker, *Principles*   David M. Walker, *Principles of Scottish Private Law* (4th ed., in 4 Vols, 1988/1989)

Walkers on Evidence   *Walker and Walker: The Law of Evidence in Scotland* (2nd ed., 2000 by Margaret L. Ross with James Chalmers)

Wilson and Duncan   W.A. Wilson and A.G.M. Duncan, *Trusts, Trustees and Executors* (2nd ed., 1995)

Chapter 1

Introductory Concepts

1. What is a Trust?

The creation of a trust involves three parties—or, at least, three roles, for one person may fulfil more **1.01** than one of those roles.

These three roles are the truster (the person who creates the trust and is the owner of the trust property before its creation), the trustee (who is the owner of the trust property after the trust is created), and the beneficiary (the person for whose benefit the trust property is held by the trustee).

The trust is created when the property passes from the truster to the trustee, accompanied by a declaration of the trust purposes for which it is to be held by the trustee. (For the specialities of trusts where the truster and trustee are the same person, and trusts which are implied by law, see Chapter 2).

A trust may, in principle, have any number of trusters, trustees or beneficiaries, although it is often thought desirable for there to be more than one trustee (*cf.* the special rules relating to charitable trusts, *infra* paras 4.09 and 4.13).

The same person may fill more than one of these roles. However, a sole trustee cannot also be the sole beneficiary, or the trust will be extinguished by the doctrine of confusion.

How exactly is the concept of "trust" to be defined? It might be naively thought that it would not be too difficult to find a definition. An obvious starting point would be the Trusts (Scotland) Act 1921, which codifies some (but only some) aspects of the Scottish law of trusts. Indeed, that statute does define "trust", stating in section 2:

> "Trust" shall mean and include—
> (a) any trust constituted by any deed or other writing, or by private or local Act of Parliament, or by Royal Charter, or by resolution of any corporation or public or ecclesiastical body, and
> (b) the appointment of any tutor, curator, guardian or judicial factor by deed, decree or otherwise

Such a definition is unlikely to be of much assistance to the student, or indeed to any other person. "Trust" includes "any trust". (A rose is a rose is a rose). And, indeed, the statutory definition is over inclusive, for it seems that the scenarios covered in part (b) are not really trusts at all, but were simply included in the 1921 Act for "administrative convenience", in order to give tutors etc. certain powers which are conferred upon trustees by the Act. (See *Inland Revenue v. McMillan's C.B.*, 1956 S.C. 142, *infra*, para. 1.08).

A second port of call might be W.A. Wilson and A.G.M. Duncan's *Trusts, Trustees and Executors*, the standard work on the Scottish law of trusts, the second edition of which was published in 1995. And that work does indeed include a detailed section headed "Definitions of trust" (1–54 *et seq.*). Firstly, we are told that "definitions propounded by English writers are of little assistance because they include the word 'equitable'." That seems correct, given that Scots law has not accepted the English division between law and equity, although it marks an interesting contrast between Wilson and Duncan's book and its predecessor as the standard text on the Scottish law of trusts, Mackenzie Stuart's *The Law of Trusts* (1932), where the very first sentence does in fact define a trust in such terms.

Thereafter, Wilson and Duncan turn to the definitions found in the Scottish writers, informing the reader that a four-part definition given by Bell in his *Principles* does not apply to all examples of trusts.

A description of a "typical trust" given by Lord Normand in *Camille and Henry Dreyfus Foundation Incorporated v. Inland Revenue*, 1955 S.L.T. 335, at 337, "is a satisfactory description but it is too narrow as a definition". McLaren's definition is "narrow" and Menzies' is "unsatisfactory". The authors then quote without criticism a definition found in the American Law Institute's Restatement, but presumably do not mean to endorse it, given that it includes the word "equitable". Finally, the following definition is suggested (at 1–63):

> "A trust then is a legal relationship in which property is vested in one person, the trustee, who is under a fiduciary obligation to apply the property to some extent for the benefit of another person, the beneficiary, the obligation being a qualification of the trustee's proprietary right and preferable to all claims of the trustee or his creditors."

Even this definition is, however, open to criticism. The suggestion that the trustee's obligations to the beneficiary are "preferable to all claims of the trustee or his creditors" implies that, if the trustee is able to satisfy the trust purposes without exhausting the trust property, he is then entitled to apply the property to his own ends, or that his creditors may then claim that property in satisfaction of his debts. But that is quite clearly not the case. Neither the trustee nor his creditors has any such right. (See *infra* paras 2.29 *et seq.* on the application of the doctrine of resulting trusts to cases where the trust purposes are satisfied without exhausting the trust property). Secondly, this definition does not account for the fact that the trustee is entitled to claim reimbursement from the trust estate for expenditure properly incurred in the administration of the trust—a claim which is not automatically postponed to the rights of the beneficiaries.

Defining the trust in this way, however, does focus attention on the most important feature of the trust—the "insolvency effect". The trustee owns the trust property, but if he becomes insolvent, his creditors have no claim against the trust property. Gretton has highlighted the importance of this doctrine:

George L. Gretton, *Constructive Trusts*
(1997) 1 E.L.R. 281, 287–288

1.02 "What is a trust? Not an easy question to answer. It lies at the meeting-point of three divisions of law: obligations, persons and property. In many respects it could be subsumed under the law of obligations. Much could be done purely through contract. For instance, a contract between a quasi-truster and a quasi-trustee could confer rights on the quasi-beneficiaries *stipulatio in favorem tertii*, or *jus quaesitium tertio*. But trust does more than contract can do. It can confer rights upon a party without his consent or even knowledge. It can confer rights upon the incapax and upon the unborn. It can not only confer rights but also divest them, even sometimes non-consensually. But with these aspects of the trust we are not much concerned. Constructive trusts tend not to raise such issues. So in what other respect does the institution of trust manifest itself? The answer is that it manifests itself in insolvency law. Whether this is a defining feature of the trust as such is a difficult question, but at all events in the modern Scots trust, it can be said the insolvency aspect is central.

It is a curious phenomenon. The general principle of insolvency law is that the rights of unsecured creditors—whether operating through diligence or through the collective processes of sequestration or liquidation—are subject to third-party real rights but prevail over third party personal rights. For example, if the debtor has already granted a heritable security, the unsecured creditors take subject to that security, but if the debtor has merely contracted to grant a heritable security, the unsecured creditors prevail. Since the right of a beneficiary in a trust is a personal right one would expect that it would be subject to the claims of the unsecured creditors. But it is not. Though a personal right, it is an enhanced personal right. So enhanced, indeed, that some people have felt a temptation to call it a real right, but that view, quite properly, has not prevailed. The right of a trust beneficiary is, in our law, not a real right which in some ways is like a personal right, but a personal right which in some ways is like a real right.

It is this quality which takes the trust wholly out of the law of obligations. I said above that trust can do some things which contract cannot. But contract has never really tried very hard. All we would have to do is make contract law do some callisthenics, and it could nearly do anything a trust can do—but not protection against creditors. That is something quite different, something that is the true mark of a genuinely separate and distinct legal institution."

NOTE:

Whether the concept of a trust can be reduced to a simple, unarguable, one-paragraph definition is **1.03** perhaps doubtful (as Wilson and Duncan (at 1–54) acknowledge). In some important recent work, however, Reid and Gretton have suggested that "patrimony" should properly be regarded as the defining feature of the trust. This concept is explained by Reid in the following extract:

Kenneth G.C. Reid, *Patrimony not Equity: the trust in Scotland*
(2000) 8 E.R.P.L. 427, 432–33

"4. Two patrimonies
The idea of patrimony is familiar enough. A patrimony is an aggregate of rights and **1.04** liabilities. Usually patrimony and personality coincide, so that a person has one patrimony only, comprising the totality of his assets and liability. In a trust, however, there are two patrimonies held by one person. A trustee, like everyone else, has his own private (or general) patrimony. But in addition he also has the trust patrimony. The two patrimonies are distinct in law, and should also be kept distinct in practice, by proper labelling and accounting. The assets of one patrimony cannot normally be transferred to the other. And if an asset is sold from one patrimony, the proceeds of the sale are paid into the same patrimony, each patrimony thus operating its own real subrogation.

Much the same is true of liabilities. A trustee may incur liabilities either in a private capacity or in the capacity as trustee, and a creditor is thus either a private creditor or a trust creditor. The difference is crucial. Leaving aside the case where a creditor has a right in security over a particular asset, a creditor is, in principle, restricted to a single patrimony. A private creditor must claim from the private patrimony and a trust creditor from the trust patrimony. If that patrimony is empty, he must go without, for the other patrimony is not available. In this principle lies the most convincing explanation of a beneficiary's protection against insolvency. The reason why a beneficiary prevails against the private creditors of the trustee is, quite simply, that each has a claim in respect of a different patrimony. But the rule is even-handed, and could be re-stated as being that the personal creditors prevail against the beneficiary. For the fact that the private creditors have no claim against the trust patrimony is balanced by the fact that the beneficiaries have no claim against the private patrimony. One claim is not better than the other. They are merely different.

Of course, the economic realities are otherwise. Since trusts do not normally trade, the trust patrimony will rarely become insolvent. Only the private patrimony is at risk, and if insolvency strikes the beneficiaries are protected. It is this practical protection which is being hinted at in Honoré and Cameron's 'protected right in personam'. But the expression tends to mislead. As a matter of legal doctrine, the position of the beneficiary is actually inferior to the position of an ordinary creditor. Both have personal rights, it is true, but the personal right of the beneficiary is postponed to the personal rights of all other creditors *in the trust patrimony*. If trust debts are incurred which exceed the value of the estate, the beneficiaries will get nothing. But this is so unusual in practice as to go almost unnoticed.

In one sense the division of patrimonies is imperfect, for occasionally a claim is allowed against the 'wrong' patrimony. But this is always a claim by the creditor of the trust. (It is a cardinal rule that a private creditor is never able to take from the trust patrimony.) There are two cases. One is the rule that a creditor of the trust can take from either patrimony unless the contract was made on the basis that the trust patrimony only was to be available. This resolves into the proposition that the trustee has personal liability for trust debts. The other is the rule that damages for breach of trust can be recovered (by the beneficiary) from the private patrimony of the trustee.

5. Detached patrimonies

In the case of a trust, the attachment of patrimony to person is provisional and likely to change. Suppose, for example, that a trust is set up in which Andrew is sole trustee. In that case Andrew has both a private patrimony and the trust patrimony. But if Andrew assumes Betty as a new trustee (as he is usually entitled to do), there are now two trustees and the patrimony is shared by both. If Colin is further assumed as a trustee, the patrimony is shared three ways. Betty, of course, might already be a trustee in two other trusts. In that case she has her private patrimony as well as a share in three trust patrimonies. Andrew might now decide it is time to resign as trustee. Resignation terminates ownership, without the need for any transfer process, and the patrimony is then held by the remaining trustees (Betty and Colin). In Scotland this rule has been incorporated into statute:

> 'Where a trustee entitled to resign his office shall have resigned. . . such trustee shall be thereby divested of the whole property and estate of the trust, which shall accrue to or devolve upon the continuing trustees or trustee without the necessity of any conveyancing or other transfer by the resigning trustee.' [Trusts (Scotland) Act 1921, s.20]

What happens if all the trustees die or resign? There is then a patrimony but no person. This does not bring the trust to an end. A trust patrimony has a life of its own, which does not depend upon the accident of the existence, or non-existence, of trustees. A trust without trustees is like a ship in which all the crew have perished. There is no one to sail the ship. But the ship remains a ship, and, if a new crew is found, it can take to the seas once more. So it is with trusts. If the trustees have died, the court will appoint new ones. The integrity of the patrimony is unaffected."

NOTE:

1.05   See also George L. Gretton, *Trusts Without Equity* (2000) 49 I.C.L.Q. 599, and the discussion of the nature of the beneficiary's right *infra* paras 3.15 *et seq.*, where part of that article is excerpted.

2. WHY CREATE A TRUST?

1.06   The trust is a versatile device and its uses are not restricted to any one particular concept. Seven useful features of the trust may be noted, as follows:

1) It can divorce the right to benefit from property from the right of ownership of the property. (In this respect, it may be significant that a right of ownership in heritable property in Scotland must be made a subject of public record, in the Land Register or the Register of Sasines—whereas a right to benefit from such property need not be publicly registered).
2) It can divorce the right to benefit from property from the control and administration of that property.
3) It can split the right to benefit from property between two or more individuals.
4) It can place restrictions on the right to benefit from trust property, or lay down conditions which must be fulfilled before an individual is entitled to become owner of that property.
5) It can be used to postpone a decision on who is to benefit from the property.
6) It can be used to place property in the hands of persons who are regarded as more appropriate to administer it than the trustee—perhaps because they are better qualified to do so, or are able to devote more time to the role.
7) As noted earlier (*supra* para. 1.02), trust property is protected from the insolvency of either the truster (subject to the law regarding gratuitous alienations— *infra* para. 13.06) or the trustee.

Not all of these features are unique to the trust, but the trust may be regarded as a convenient way of achieving these results. Some examples of the use of trusts are as follows:

A. Protecting the incompetent or the vulnerable

1.07   Features (1) and (2) provide a means whereby a truster may allow an individual to benefit from that property without giving them the ownership of that property. There are two principal situations in which a truster might wish to follow this course:

(a) the beneficiary is legally incapable of managing property (because they are a child or mentally incapable).

(b) the beneficiary is legally capable of managing property, but the owner considers it unwise to give them ownership—perhaps because they are a spendthrift and would squander the property, or because the management of the property requires specialist skills which the beneficiary does not possess (such as where the trust property comprises shares in a business, or investments).

In scenario (b), one special option which is open to the truster is the creation of an alimentary liferent. An alimentary liferent has two special characteristics:

- Once accepted, it cannot be renounced by the beneficiary. The beneficiary may, however, seek permission from the court for a variation or revocation of an alimentary liferent: Trusts (Scotland) Act 1961, s.1(4) (*infra* paras 12.05 *et seq.*).
- The beneficiary cannot assign the liferent to a third party, nor can it be attached by his creditors, except as regards alimentary debts (debts necessarily incurred for the maintenance of the beneficiary).

Any excess in the liferent (*i.e.* beyond that which is reasonably required for the beneficiary's maintenance) is both assignable and attachable by creditors. On alimentary liferents generally, see Wilson and Duncan, paras 8–26 *et seq.*

Where a person is incapable of managing his own affairs, a *curator bonis* may be appointed to administer his property. This does not create a trust, because ownership of the property remains with the incapax (the incapable individual) and the curator simply administers his property. There are, however, some similarities between the position of a curator and a trustee, and a curator is included in the definition of "trustee" given in section 2 of the Trusts (Scotland) Act 1921 (and is therefore subject to part of the law of trusts). The significance of this provision was explained in the following case:

Inland Revenue v. McMillan's C.B.
1956 S.C. 142; 1956 S.L.T. 67

LORD PRESIDENT (CLYDE): "It is quite true that in order to enable a *curator bonis* to carry **1.08** out his duty of management he is included in the definition section of the Trusts (Scotland) Act 1921, within the term 'trustee', and the decree of Court appointing him is included within the term 'trust deed'. But this is no novelty. A similar provision is to be found in the earlier Trusts Acts in Scotland. The object of these provisions was to confer on a curator certain powers in connection with the management of the estate of the *incapax* which these Acts conferred upon trustees.

But the respondent founded upon the Trusts Acts as making the *curator bonis* a trustee, as converting the estate by implication into a trust estate, and therefore as converting the *incapax* into a mere beneficiary entitled to a net payment from the trustee out of the estate in the hands of the trustee. In my view this is to read into the Acts far more than they have provided. The Acts do not either expressly or impliedly convert the estate into a trust estate, nor convert the *incapax* into a beneficiary of a trust. So to construe the Acts is to confuse a mere question of title with a question of substantive right. For administrative convenience the Acts conferred on a *curator bonis* certain powers conferred on trustees. They conferred on a *curator bonis* power in certain circumstances to sell the estate of the *incapax* (*Marquess of Lothian's C.B.*, 1927 S.C. 579). But they did not convert the curator into a trustee for all purposes. He still remained as he always was the manager of the estate, the whole income of which is still the ward's income."

B. Trusts for the benefit of the public

The special features of the trust may be used to set up a fund to be applied to specified public purposes **1.09** (which may, but need not, be charitable purposes). The use of the trust to achieve this end has several advantages, including:

- A truster may refrain from putting his money to these uses during his lifetime, but instead appoint trustees under his will to undertake this task with property forming part of his estate on death.

- The trust property need not be used immediately, but may be held by the trustees to be distributed as appropriate at a later date (for example, in response to applications for support, or in response to certain events specified by the truster).
- The truster may use the trust to delegate decision-making on questions of benefit to specified trustees. The trustees may be able to bring specialist knowledge to the question of how the property should be applied, or may simply be able to relieve the truster of the administrative burden which he would have to undertake in administering the funds himself.
- Although a trust is not, strictly speaking, a legal person in itself, it may function much like a corporation and engage in fund-raising to solicit donations from members of the public. (Members of the public might, for obvious reasons, happily donate money to a trust where they would not donate money to a private individual for the same purposes).

C. Collective investment purposes

1.10 Trusts provide a convenient means of administering collective investment schemes. Such schemes have two principal advantages over individual investment: firstly, they allow for diversification of investment in a fashion which would not be available to the individual investor and, secondly, they allow for professional investment management of a standard which would not be affordable to most persons acting on an individual basis. By far the most common types of collective investment are pension funds and unit trust schemes.

D. Holding property for unincorporated associations and partnerships

1.11 Under Scots law, unincorporated associations do not have legal personality and cannot hold property. The office-bearers of the association can, however, hold the property as trustees for the purposes of the association. (See, for discussion, Christine R. Barker, *Charity Law in Scotland* (1996), paras 3.2.9 and 3.3.31–3.3.39)

Although partnerships have legal personality under Scots law, it is generally accepted that they cannot hold heritable property. (See G.L. Gretton, "Who Owns Partnership Property?" 1987 J.R. 163; S.C. Styles, "Why can't Partnerships Own Heritage?" (1989) 34 J.L.S.S. 414; George L. Gretton, "Problems in Partnership Conveyancing" (1991) 36 J.L.S.S. 232). As a matter of practice, therefore, property is normally held in the names of some or all of the partners as trustees for the firm. This will become unnecessary when the Abolition of Feudal Tenure etc. (Scotland) Act 2000 comes into force, as section 70 of that statute provides that "a firm may, if it has a legal personality distinct from the persons who compose it, itself own land". It will therefore be possible to take title in the name of the partnership.

E. Tax efficiency

1.12 Although this book does not attempt to deal with the law of taxation in relation to trusts, it should be noted that the manipulation of ownership and control by means of the trust device may be used by a truster in order to minimise liability to taxation. (For a useful summary of the law, see Pearce and Stevens, pp. 140–145).

In particular, there is a special exception for "accumulation and maintenance trusts" under section 71 of the Inheritance Tax Act 1984. Broadly speaking, in an accumulation and maintenance trust, property is put in trust for a child, or children under the age of 25, and the income from the property is either accumulated or applied for the "maintenance, education or benefit" of a beneficiary. One or more persons must become entitled to either the trust property or a liferent of the property before the age of 25. Such trusts attract favoured treatment in respect of the inheritance tax and income tax regimes.

F. Executors

1.13 The executors in a deceased's estate are included within the definition of "trustee" under section 2 of the Trusts (Scotland) Act 1921 (which is extended by section 20 of the Succession (Scotland) Act 1964 to include executors-dative).

The position of an executor has been described as follows:

> "An executor is not a trustee in the sense of being a depositary. A trustee has to hold as a depositary; not so an executor, who has to administer, not to hold. An executor must pay legacies and debts within a certain time, and is liable in interest if he does not. An executor is nothing else than a debtor to the legatees or next of kin. He is a debtor with a limited liability; but he is nothing else than a debtor; and the creditors of the deceased and the legatees who claim against him do so as creditors." (*Jamieson v. Clark* (1872) 10 M. 399, *per* the Lord President (Inglis) at 405).

This should not be taken as suggesting that an executor is not to be regarded as a trustee. Executors do not *merely* "administer" the deceased's estate, but are the owners of it: under section 14(1) of the Succession (Scotland) Act 1964, "every part" of the deceased's estate, whether heritable or moveable, vests "for the purposes of administration" in the executor. Lord Inglis's comments simply reflect the limited nature of the executor's role, which is to distribute the deceased's estate among the beneficiaries, and not to hold it for any further purposes.

For further discussion of the (limited) distinction between executors and trustees generally, see Wilson and Duncan at 31–08 *et seq.*, where it is noted (at 31–13) that "the modern tendency is to reduce the significance of the distinction between trustees and executors".

G. Sequestration

Where a person's estate is sequestrated, an interim and a permanent trustee will be appointed. The **1.14** responsibilities of the interim and permanent trustee are laid down in statute (Bankruptcy (Scotland) Act 1985, ss.2–3).

Chapter 2

CLASSIFICATION AND CREATION OF TRUSTS

1. CLASSIFICATION OF TRUSTS

Trusts may be classified into various categories, the most common of which are noted in this section. A trust may fall into more than one of these categories.

A. Discretionary trusts

2.01 It is commonly said that Scots law does not recognise a special category of "discretionary trusts" (*e.g.* Norrie and Scobbie, p. 23). Nevertheless, a truster:

> "may, in the disposition of his property, select particular classes of individuals and objects, and then give to some particular individual a power, after his death, of appropriating the property, or applying any part of his property, to any particular individuals among that class whom that person may select and describe in his will." (*Crichton v. Grierson* (1828) 3 W. & S. 329, *per* Lord Lyndhurst L.C. at 338–339).

Although Lord Lyndhurst refers to the truster's "will", these comments are equally applicable to an *inter vivos* trust. Such action necessarily involves conferring a discretion upon the trustee (or trustees) as to how they will choose to apply the property.

Two issues arise from this principle: first, how broad a discretion may the truster validly confer on the trustees?

Secondly, it is generally thought that a truster may not validly confer a discretion upon his trustees without also selecting particular individuals to act as trustees. It is, of course, impossible to establish an *inter vivos* trust without the truster selecting trustees, but this is not the case with a *mortis causa* trust where there are legal rules designed to establish who has a right to administer the estate where the testator has not selected an executor (or where his choice is ineffective for whatever reason). In such a case, the testator may not simply confer a discretion on "anyone who may anyhow acquire a title to administer the estate" (*Angus's Exrx v. Batchan's Trs*, 1949 S.C. 335, *per* the Lord President (Cooper) at 367).

These issues are discussed in more detail *infra*, paras 5.03 *et seq.*

B. *Inter vivos* and *mortis causa* trusts

2.02 An *inter vivos* trust takes effect during the truster's lifetime; a *mortis causa* (or "testamentary") trust takes effect on the truster's death. A person who is appointed executor under a will may therefore be regarded as a trustee (for further discussion, see *supra* para. 1.13 and Wilson and Duncan, Chapter 31).

C. Public and private trusts

2.03 The distinction between public and private trusts is of considerable importance, and has been summarised as follows:

Kenneth McK. Norrie and Eilidh M. Scobbie, *Trusts* (1991), pp. 17–18

"A private trust is a trust designed to benefit a specified individual or a specified group of individuals . . . A public trust on the other hand is one that is set up for the benefit of the public in general, or of a specified class of the public in general."

Two questions arise from this. Firstly, why does the distinction matter? Secondly, how is it to be drawn? Each of these questions will be dealt with in turn.

(a) *Why does the distinction matter?*

Norrie and Scobbie (at pp. 19–20) suggest that there are four principal consequences which result from **2.04** drawing the distinction. They are as follows:

(i) The radical right of appointment

In a private trust, if all the original trustees fail, the truster always has a "radical right" to appoint new trustees. In a public trust, the truster has no such right unless he has expressly reserved such a right in the trust deed. See further *infra* paras 4.10–4.11.

(ii) Enforcement of the trust purposes

Where the trust is a public one, a wider class of persons may be entitled to enforce the trust purposes. It has sometimes been suggested that any member of the public may seek to enforce the purposes of a public trust by way of an *actio popularis*. Whether or not this is strictly correct has been doubted (see the cases cited by Wilson and Duncan at 14–03), but as Norrie and Scobbie point out (at p. 20), "the search for a precise answer is probably vain. With a public trust as with a private trust those who may benefit may sue to enforce it; with public trusts that class by definition will be large and will include any person who may receive benefit, of whatever nature, from the carrying out of the trust purposes." Furthermore, the Lord Advocate may act in the public interest to enforce the purposes of a public trust (*Aitken's Trs v. Aitken*, 1927 S.C. 374, *per* Lord Ashmore at 387). The Lord Advocate also has a specialised supervisory role in relation to charitable trusts (see Chapter 11).

(iii) "Benignant construction"

The Scottish courts have traditionally adopted an approach of "benignant construction" towards public trusts (see generally, Wilson and Duncan, paras 14–47 *et seq.*). This has two principal consequences. Firstly, the courts are prepared to accept relatively vague phrases as a sufficiently specific statement of trust purposes for the public benefit (principally, "charitable purposes" is sufficient). See *infra* paras 5.07 *et seq.* Secondly, where a truster has directed that his property is to be applied for specified public purposes, but has failed to provide machinery for that direction to be given effect, the Court of Session can provide machinery in the exercise of its *nobile officium*. See *infra* paras 12.10 *et seq.*

(iv) The supervisory jurisdiction of the Court of Session

This is perhaps the most important consequence of the distinction between public and private trusts. The Court of Session has the power to vary the purposes of both public and private trusts in appropriate cases, but the rules vary considerably as between the two types of trust. See Chapter 12.

(b) *Drawing the distinction*

Glentanar v. Scottish Industrial Musical Association
1925 S.C. 226

Lord Glentanar presented a silver shield to the Scottish Industrial Musical Association for **2.05** an annual brass band competition. A few years later, the Association went into liquidation. The liquidator proposed to sell the shield. Lord Glentanar argued that the shield was not the property of the Association, but was held on trust by the Association for the purpose of the competition. He purported to appoint new trustees, who accepted office. He and the new trustees sought a declarator that the shield was held on trust, and should be delivered to the newly appointed trustees.

LORD ANDERSON [after holding that the shield was trust property]: "Finally, the defenders contended that they were entitled to retain until new trustees have been properly appointed. It was urged that Lord Glentanar had no right to appoint new trustees, but that that right was solely in the Court by way of an exercise of the *nobile officium*. I do not see that the defenders have any higher title to urge this contention than that of *amici curiae*, as our decision on the other points in the case deprives them of all interest in the future of the shield. The defenders, however, profess to be anxious to retain the shield till this suggested judicial appointment has been made, for what reason I am unable to surmise. I should have thought that the liquidator, now that it has been decided that he cannot turn the shield into money, would have been glad to get rid of the responsibility of keeping it, with, I presume, the incidental cost of insuring it, and would not have resisted a decree ordaining him to deliver it to Lord Glentanar. I have reached the conclusion, however, that the judgment of the Sheriff-substitute on this part of the case is right, and the contention of the defenders wrong. If this were a public trust, in the full and proper sense of the term, then the appointment of new trustees would undoubtedly have to be made by the Court in virtue of the *nobile officium*—*Anderson*, 1914 S.C. 942. But I do not regard the trust as being of that character. There are no funds which have to be administered for public ends. In such a case the matter of the personnel of the trustees is of importance. Here the only patrimonial interest involved is the annual possession of a corporeal moveable which does not produce any revenue. The only interest which the beneficiaries—the juvenile brass bands—have is to be assured that the contests for the shield will be conducted under fair conditions. Now the trustees who have been appointed are prepared, as I have already pointed out, to conduct the contests in the future on the same conditions as applied to contests in the past. This being so, it does not seem to concern the beneficiaries who are to be custodiers of the shield. The trust seems to me to be more akin to a private trust than to a public trust in the proper sense of that term. Now, in the case of a private trust, a living truster may appoint new trustees to take the place of those who have failed—*Lindsay*, 9 D. 1297; *Tovey*, 16 D. 866; *Newlands*, 9 R. 1104. I am therefore of opinion that Lord Glentanar was entitled to make the appointment which has been made."

The Lord Justice-Clerk (Alness), Lords Hunter and Ormidale delivered concurring opinions.

NOTES:

2.06
1. Wilson and Duncan say (at 14–07) that "[i]t is not easy to follow this argument. The trust would clearly appear to be a public one. The court was probably influenced by its desire to overcome a procedural difficulty in a matter of small value."
2. Lord Anderson appears to place reliance on two facts in particular. Firstly, that the trust assets were not revenue-generating. It is not easy to see why this is of importance, but perhaps the argument is that (a) public trusts are subject to a greater degree of court supervision and (b) the need for such supervision is less where there can be no duty of investment upon the trustees and they are only responsible for the safekeeping of an item of moveable property.
   It is even more difficult to see how the fact that the new trustees were prepared to conduct future contests on the same conditions as earlier ones could have any bearing whatsoever on whether the trust was public or private, and yet Lord Anderson appears to also place reliance on this fact.

D. Charitable trusts

2.07 In English law, trusts for the public benefit are generally not regarded as valid unless their purposes qualify as "charitable" (see, *e.g. Re Astor's Settlement Trusts* [1952] Ch. 454). No such rule applies in Scotland, however, and the validity of a public trust does not depend on whether or not its purposes can be described as charitable. However, public trusts may also be considered "charitable trusts" depending on the purposes for which they are established, a status which has various consequences in terms of taxation, administration and supervision. For further discussion of these issues, see Chapter 11.

E. Trusts created voluntarily and those created by legal implication

The remainder of this chapter explores how trusts may be created in two ways: first, by the voluntary **2.08** act of the truster, and secondly, by operation of law.

2. CREATION OF TRUSTS: VOLUNTARILY CREATED TRUSTS

Two requirements must be satisfied for the creation of a voluntary trust. There must be (a) a declaration of trust and (b) a transfer of property from the truster to the trustee.

A. The declaration of trust

(a) The intention to create a trust

A transfer of property is clearly insufficient to create a trust. There must have been an intention on the **2.09** part of the truster to create a trust; *i.e.* to bind the recipient of the property to apply it for specified purposes. The intention of the truster must be determined from the terms of the trust deed (see, *e.g.* *Wilson v. Lindsay* (1878) 5 R. 539, *per* the Lord President (Inglis) at 541).

The law will only recognise certain purposes as being valid, an issue which forms the subject of Chapter 6. But the fact that A transfers property to B with a reference to B applying the property for specified purposes is not of itself sufficient to create a trust. The question is this: did A (i) intend to make an outright gift of the property to B coupled with a recommendation as to how the property should be applied, but ultimately leaving it up to B as to what he chose to do with the property—in which case no trust is created—or (ii) intend to bind B to apply the property to specified purposes, thus creating a trust? The following cases illustrate the distinction which is being drawn here:

Barclay's Exr v. McLeod
(1880) 7 R. 477

Mr Barclay died, leaving all his property to his wife. His will directed as follows: **2.10**

> "But while it is my wish that my said spouse shall enjoy the free and undisturbed use of my said means and estate, if she should survive me, it is my anxious desire that, as soon after my death as is convenient, she will execute a testament bequeathing one-half of the means and estate which may pertain and be resting owing to her at the time of her decease to be divided amongst certain of my relatives to be named by me in a separate writing containing my wishes on that subject."

He left a separate probative writing listing certain relatives for this purpose. His wife subsequently died intestate. The Court of Session (without delivering opinions) held that her executor was not bound or entitled to give effect to the request in his will.

Macpherson v. Macpherson's C.B.
(1894) 21 R. 386

Robina Young died in 1893, leaving a will which contained the following provision: **2.11**

"Also I give and bequeath to Katherine Alexandrina Macpherson, for the benefit of herself and her sister Jane Macpherson, both daughters of the aforesaid Alice Young or Macpherson, all the cash moneys, securities for money, books, wardrobe and all the rest, remainder and residue of my estate which I may be possessed of at the time of my decease."

Jane Macpherson "had been all her life weak mentally, and incapable of doing anything to earn a livelihood, and was entirely dependent on those with whom she resided for ordinary personal comfort."

The parties were in some doubt as to whether the provision in Miss Young's will (a) left the property to Katherine absolutely, giving her an absolute right to use the property as she saw fit (leaving it purely in her discretion as to whether or not she wished to use the property to benefit her sister), or (b) created a trust for the benefit of both Katherine and Jane, with Katherine as trustee. Accordingly, a special case was presented to the Court of Session.

LORD McLAREN: "The question raised is whether the gift imports an absolute gift to Katherine, or whether it is in a trust for her for the benefit of herself and her sister. It was suggested, as the result of recent decisions in England, that the court should construe the expression used very critically, and that if its meaning is of a doubtful character should not construe it as importing a trust. I do not think it is necessary in this case to consider very carefully the law of England, which I have always supposed to be in this matter the same as that of Scotland, but I would point out that our law requires no special or technical words in order to constitute a trust. If there is an appointment of a beneficiary, and if some person is charged with the administration of the funds beneficially destined, we have the essentials of a trust. If there is a clear indication of a trust to be constituted it is immaterial whether the words 'in trust for' or 'for the benefit of', or 'for behoof of', or other similar words be used. Of all expressions other than 'in trust for' I should have thought the words 'for the benefit of' A the clearest, because it is equivalent to a declaration that A is a beneficiary in the estate given to B. In this case no distinction is drawn between the extent of the interest to be taken by the two nieces. Katherine, it is true, was not constituted an executor; another executor is named at the end of the will. The executor would cease to act when the estate was realised. The testator did not continue him as trustee probably because she did not expect to leave a large fortune. No trust was therefore constituted in the normal way, but as Jane was unable to attend to business or to administer her share, an informal trust was constituted in the person of Katherine to administer it for her.

It is impossible to maintain that there was not here a qualified gift, and the result is that Katherine holds as trustee for herself and her sister."

The Lord President (Robertson) and Lord Kinnear delivered concurring opinions.

The Court answered the questions in the special case accordingly.

Reid's Trs v. Dawson
1915 S.C. (H.L.) 47

2.12   Robert Reid died, having left the following letter addressed to his law-agent, who was also one of his trustees under his will:

"Recognising as I do, the necessity, in the event of my death, of making some provision for Miss Christina Dawson and her son Robert, 113 Comiston Road, Edinburgh, I hereby instruct you to pay to her, on the 1st of each month after my death, the sum of ten shillings, being at the rate of £150 a year. But in lieu of this I would prefer that as soon as you conveniently can, that the sum of £3000, say Three thousand pounds, should be taken from my life insurance funds, and paid over to her law adviser, Mr Maitland, or her brother, Mr William Dawson . . ."

Doubt having arisen as to the effect of these directions, a special case was presented to the Court of Session, the decision of which was appealed to the House of Lords:

EARL LOREBURN: ". . . this letter was a letter written by a layman, and I think that in construing letters written by laymen those who are familiar with the law and its difficulties are sometimes apt—as I feel myself sometimes apt—to overthink the meaning of the particular expressions, and therefore to overstrain the language. I desire to avoid that danger, if I can. I read this will myself as having the following effect: It is a bequest of a monthly payment of £12, 10s. without any period as to the duration of that payment being named in the document, but it is evidently meant to be terminable upon the payment of a capital sum of £3000, which at five per cent yields the same sum annually, namely £150. It is evident to my mind, from the scheme of the document itself, that Mr Young was intended to pay the capital sum, and then to discontinue the payment of the monthly sum. I think that in substance he was directed to pay that capital sum. The document, I need hardly say, it not skilfully expressed, but the £3000 is spoken of in it as a bequest, and that seems to me to settle any doubt that might have existed as to whether there was a direction to pay that sum or not. The monthly payment and that capital payment do not appear to me to have been intended, or expressed, as being alternative payments at the option either of the trustee or of the lady herself, but the one is to follow the other as soon as convenient, and that is the only thing it seems to me that is left to the discretion of the trustees. The use of the word 'prefer' indicates not an alternative for selection by the trustee, but that there has been an alternative in the mind of the testator, which he proceeds to resolve in the document before your Lordships. The trustee is bound to pay this money—he is bound and entitled to pay it at a time that he thinks convenient, but he is, of course, to do so in good faith, and in the same way as in the case of all other trust funds . . ."

LORD ATKINSON: "I concur. I agree with my noble and learned friend on the woolsack that the word 'prefer' *prima facie* means a choice between two alternatives, but at the same time I think that in this particular will this clause providing for payment 'as soon as you conveniently can' is absolutely inconsistent with any discretion being given to Mr Young as to whether he should pay or should never pay. I think they indicate clearly that he is to pay, and therefore I construe the words 'I prefer' as if they were 'I wish.' . . ."

Lords Kinnear and Sumner concurred.

Lords Dunedin and Parker of Waddington delivered concurring opinions.

Their Lordships answered the questions in the stated case accordingly.

NOTES:

1. It is clear that no special form of words is required to create a trust. Nevertheless, the form **2.13** of words used by the truster must clearly demonstrate an intention to create a trust. See *Richards v. Delbridge* (1874) L.R. 18 Eq. 11, *per* Jessel M.R. at 14: "It is true he need not use the words, 'I declare myself a trustee', but he must do something which is equivalent to it, and use expressions which have that meaning; for however anxious the court may be to carry out a man's intention, it is not at liberty to construe words otherwise than according to their proper meaning." See further Wilson and Duncan, paras 2–04 *et seq.*

2. Language such as "for behoof of", "on behalf of", etc., will usually be considered sufficient to create a trust. But just as there is no magic about the word "trust" (*Gillespie v. City of Glasgow Bank* (1879) 6 R. (H.L.) 104, *per* Lord Cairns L.C. at 107), there is no magic about these formulae either.

   In *Style Financial Services Ltd v. Bank of Scotland (No. 2)*, 1998 S.L.T. 851, Goldberg (a large retail company) established Style as a subsidiary company to run an in-house credit card system. They subsequently sold Style to the Royal Bank of Scotland. Goldberg regularly collected payments to Style accounts within their stores and, with Style's agreement, paid these into their (overdrawn) bank account. A mandate granted by Style entitled them to do this even where cheques were made payable to Style rather than Goldberg. They calculated the sums which were due to Style and regularly settled accounts with Style. They were not required to remit funds until around 30 days after their receipt, however, effectively giving them a substantial interest-free loan. Goldberg subsequently went into insolvency, owing a substantial sum of money to Style. Style argued that the payments received by Goldberg were held on trust for Style, and pointed to a clause in the Trading Agreement between the two parties, which referred to sums received by Goldberg "on behalf of or for the account of" Style (clause eighth (5)). Lord Gill rejected the argument that this language indicated the existence of a trust. In the course of a detailed judgment, he observed (at 865):

> "The expression "on behalf of" may signify the existence of a trust if the circumstances of the case are consistent with that interpretation (cf *Gillespie v. City of Glasgow Bank* (1879) 6 R. (H.L.) 104, Lord Cairns L.C. at pp. 106–107; *cf. Re Ross, ex p Att. Gen. for Northern Territory* (1979) 54 A.L.J.R. at p. 149); but in my view that expression ought not to be given that interpretation in this case. Where an agent has collected moneys on behalf of his principal, he may in a sense be considered to hold the moneys on behalf of his principal; but where other detailed contractual provisions between them have the effect that the agent is obliged only to remit funds of an equivalent amount at a postponed date, the suggested trust qualification may be excluded, notwithstanding the use of the expression "on behalf of". That, in my view, is the effect of the agreements between the pursuers and Goldberg in this case, whether or not the mandate is taken into account.
>
> Moreover, in the present case the words "on behalf of" must be interpreted in the context of the provision in which they occur and of the other provisions of the agreement. Clauses Eighth (4) and (5) have not been devised for the purpose of creating a trust. On the contrary, in my view, these provisions are typical of an agreement regulating a system of running accounts based on a multiplicity of transactions with periodic settlements either way. They are not concerned in any way with title to property. In the absence of any provision restricting Goldberg's use of the Style collections and in particular in the absence of any provision that they should be held as a discrete fund in a designated account (*cf. Royal Bank of Scotland v. Skinner*, 1931 S.L.T. 382), I consider that cll Eighth (4) and (5) are not sufficient to create, by necessary implication, a trust over the relevant receipts."

(b) The formalities of the declaration

Requirements of Writing (Scotland) Act 1995, s.1

Writing required for certain contracts, obligations, trusts, conveyances and wills

2.14   **1.**—(1) Subject to subsection (2) below and any other enactment, writing shall not be required for the constitution of a contract, unilateral obligation or trust.

(2) Subject to subsection (3) below, a written document complying with section 2 of this Act shall be required for—

    (a) the constitution of—

        (i) a contract or unilateral obligation for the creation, transfer, variation or extinction of an interest in land;

        (ii) a gratuitous unilateral obligation except an obligation undertaken in the course of business; and

        (iii) a trust whereby a person declares himself to be sole trustee of his own property or any property which he may acquire;

    (b) the creation, transfer, variation or extinction of an interest in land otherwise than by the operation of a court decree, enactment or rule of law; and

    (c) the making of any will, testamentary trust disposition and settlement or codicil.

(3) Where a contract, obligation or trust mentioned in subsection (2)(a) above is not constituted in a written document complying with section 2 of this Act, but one of the

parties to the contract, a creditor in the obligation or a beneficiary under the trust ("the first person") has acted or refrained from acting in reliance on the contract, obligation or trust with the knowledge and acquiescence of the other party to the contract, the debtor in the obligation or the truster ("the second person")—

(a) the second person shall not be entitled to withdraw from the contract, obligation or trust; and

(b) the contract, obligation or trust shall not be regarded as invalid, on the ground that it is not so constituted, if the condition set out in subsection (4) below is satisfied.

(4) The condition referred to in subsection (3) above is that the position of the first person—

(a) as a result of acting or refraining from acting as mentioned in that subsection has been affected to a material extent; and

(b) as a result of such a withdrawal as is mentioned in that subsection would be adversely affected to a material extent.

(5) In relation to the constitution of any contract, obligation or trust mentioned in subsection (2)(a) above, subsections (3) and (4) above replace the rules of law known as *rei interventus* and homologation.

(6) This section shall apply to the variation of a contract, obligation or trust as it applies to the constitution thereof but as if in subsections (3) and (4) for the references to acting or refraining from acting in reliance on the contract, obligation or trust and withdrawing therefrom there were substituted respectively references to acting or refraining from acting in reliance on the variation of the contract, obligation or trust and withdrawing from the variation.

(7) In this section "interest in land" means any estate, interest or right in or over land, including any right to occupy or to use land or to restrict the occupation or use of land, but does not include—

(a) a tenancy;

(b) a right to occupy or use land; or

(c) a right to restrict the occupation or use of land, if the tenancy or right is not granted for more than one year, unless the tenancy or right is for a recurring period or recurring periods and there is a gap of more than one year between the beginning of the first, and the end of the last, such period.

(8) For the purposes of subsection (7) above "land" does not include—

(a) growing crops; or

(b) a moveable building or other moveable structure.

NOTE:

The 1995 Act repeals the Blank Bonds and Trusts Act 1696–which had given rise to considerable difficulties in interpretation—with retrospective effect, except with regard to proceedings commenced before the 1995 Act came into force (see section 14(4)). For the law on proof of trust prior to 1995, see Wilson and Duncan, Chapter 5.

(c) "Secret" and "half-secret" trusts

It will be noted that, in accordance with s.1(2)(c) of the Requirements of Writing Act 1995, a **2.15** testamentary trust cannot be created except by writing. English law (in common with certain other systems) allows for an important qualification to this rule via the concept of the "secret trust". The doctrine is succinctly explained by Delany:

Hilary Delany, *Equity and the Law of Trusts in Ireland* (2nd ed., 1999), pp. 95–96
"A fully secret trust usually arises where a testator makes a gift of property to a named person in his will without expressly stating that the latter is to hold it on trust. If either

before or after making his will, but during his lifetime, he informs the legatee that he wishes him to hold the property on trust for a third party or a particular purpose and the legatee either expressly or by his silence impliedly agrees to do so, he will be bound by the trust. A half secret trust on the other hand is said to exist where it is clear from the will that the legatee is to hold the property on trust but neither the terms of the trust nor the identity of the beneficiaries are disclosed in the will.

Historically, the reason for the creation of such trusts was to allow a testator to make provision for a mistress or an illegitimate child or another person whom he wished to benefit for some reason without his family or the world at large being aware of the gift. While this is rarely necessary today, a testator may still employ this device, often to prevent having to specify with precision at the time of making a will how he intends his property to be distributed. This practice of giving effect to secret trusts created for such a purpose has been criticised as it effectively allows a testator to bypass the statutory requirements laid down in relation to the execution of wills where the need for secrecy is not present."

Testators may also, of course still wish to employ this device to prevent publicity being given to their testamentary intentions. The question of whether Scots law recognises "secret trusts" was considered in the following case:

Shaw's Trs v. Greenock Medical Aid Society
1930 S.L.T. 39

2.16 LORD MACKAY: "This multiplepoinding is raised for the distribution of the estate of Mrs Christina Campbell or Shaw, who died at Wemyss Bay in February 1924. With the exception of one somewhat novel claim (the claim for John Thomson) the facts do not appear to be in any way in dispute. I shall deal with this claim in the sequel.

Mrs Shaw left three testamentary documents: (1) A formal trust disposition, 3rd December 1917; (2) a codicil thereto, 23rd January 1922; and (3) a second codicil, 1st February 1923. The principal testament took the now usual form of a complete conveyance to trustees of her whole estate, heritable and moveable, and was indubitably intended to be exhaustive in its beneficiary parts of her whole means, containing as it did a residue clause around which the principal controversy turns. Had the original deed stood there would have been no controversy, because the rest, residue and remainder, were given simply to a certain Christian Rodger, a cousin once removed, who appears to have survived. But by the first codicil she revoked that residual bequest for reasons assigned, and, accordingly, had she died between January 1922 and February 1923 her will would have been incomplete as far as exhausting her estate, and the residue would have fallen into intestacy. By her second codicil she purported to amend this state affairs. After referring to her previous revocation, she endeavoured to dispose of the residue thus:

> 'I now desire to leave it, to my husband in trust firstly for his own liferent use, and secondly for behoof of sundry religious or benevolent institutions to be selected by him, and regarding which he knows my mind, and therefore may be assured of my absolute approval thereof.'

The first controversy which must be decided is therefore whether this substituted residue clause is a valid bequest in law. [Lord Mackay considered the question of whether a bequest to 'religious or benevolent institutions' was sufficiently precise to be valid, and concluded that it was too wide to be valid. (See further on this issue, *infra* paras 5.07 *et seq.*), and continued:]

What was in the end argued was a somewhat special and novel view upon the construction of this clause—namely, that a description of the intended class of beneficiaries which would admittedly be much too wide, and incapable of being saved by the mere addition of a power of selection from out of that wide class, is nevertheless saved by the following words, 'regarding which he knows my mind, and therefore may be assured of my absolute approval thereof'. Now it was said that in the testamentary law both of England and of Scotland could be found illustrations of a doctrine whereby secret or private trusts communicated verbally to an executor or trustee may be rendered effectual, the true intentions of the testator being proved by parole evidence received by the Court on oath or affidavit, and, if properly and sufficiently ascertained by such means, being thereby set up. A large number of English cases in support of the doctrine I have thus sketched were cited, the series ending in, and being summed up in, the very recent House of Lords case of *Blackwell v. Blackwell* ([1929] A.C. 318). I ventured to question, and still feel bound to question, whether the development of the English testamentary law, and particularly of this doctrine, enables one with any safety to appeal to a foreign law for aid in the construction of a Scottish testamentary instrument, but the residuaries, as I understood, contended to the end that the case of *Blackwell* and its antecedents were receivable and illustrated a doctrine which found expression, although very spasmodically, in Scottish decisions. Their opponents strenuously disputed that this somewhat intricate English doctrine found place in Scots law at all. In these circumstances, unless the matter in controversy as to the English doctrines be capable of being resolved on a mere consideration of the formulation in ordinary English terms of the doctrine, without pretence to any understanding of the intricacies or technical terms and modes of expression of a foreign law, I should refuse, as a judge unfamiliar with that law, to interpret the cases, but should confine myself for my decision to such authority as exists in Scotland. Nevertheless, lest I should be wrong in that view, I have endeavoured with such help as I got from both sides of the Bar to understand the alien analogy, and I think I can, without overstepping the bounds set, sufficiently satisfy myself that the English doctrine takes origin in a state of testamentary law entirely alien to Scottish thought in the matter, and develops along lines which have never been, even approximately, received in Scotland. In the recent case of *Blackwell* the history of this doctrine in England is interestingly given by Lord Sumner. He makes it plain that the doctrine was regarded as almost immutably imbedded in the English law by the cases of *Pring v. Pring* (1689, 2 Vern. 99) and *Crook v. Brooking* (1688, 2 Vern. 50, 106), and as applied to a residuary whose secret trust was mentioned on the face of the will by *In re Fleetwood* (1880, 15 Ch. D. 594) and *In re Huxtable* ([1902] 1 Ch. 214; [1902] 2 Ch. 793), but that nevertheless it remained still, in 1929, very open to question whether such an ancient doctrine should be affirmed by the highest Court when there was considerable doubt as to whether it was not self-evident that it conflicted with section 9 of the Wills Act, 1837.

The decision appears to me to turn on very narrow grounds—namely, that for reasons given the older decisions were not amended away by section 9, but could still be held to stand side by side with it. Accordingly the origin of the doctrine is inevitably found in a state of the law which permitted of verbal proof of testamentary intentions in a degree wholly alien to the ancient law of Scotland. Lord Sumner says: 'I recoil from interfering with decisions of long standing which reject this anomaly unless constrained by statute.' In another passage he says: 'The Wills Act is an amending Act of which it may be said in no merely theoretical sense that the Legislature was acquainted with the existing state of the law as enacted and decided... The extent to which parole evidence was admissible under existing practice for various purposes and the evils thereout arising were known.' And the argument proceeds to demonstrate that the Wills Act should be construed in light of the view that the Legislature were well aware of the cases of *Pring*, *Smith v. Attersoll* (1826, 1 Russ. 266), and *Jones v. Nabbs* (1718, Gilb. Eq. Rep. 146), and as they had not expressly repealed that law the cases in equity might stand. 'The Wills Act made no attempt to correct this quaint way of regarding a statute.' Perhaps this might be enough, but I think that I should add (secondly) that, according to the best of my ability to grasp them, the whole series of cases depends upon a special doctrine of the Equity Courts, which Lord Westbury in the case of *M'Cormick v. Grogan* (1869, L.R., 4 H.L. 82) thus explains:

'It is a jurisdiction by which a Court of Equity, proceeding on the ground of fraud, converts the party who has committed it into a trustee for the party who is injured by that fraud.'

2.17 In the third place, it appears sufficiently clear to me that the whole doctrine reposes on an erection of what is called conscience, by which a party, to whom verbally was committed a trust which is variously described as 'a secret trust', 'an unspecified trust', or 'an undisclosed trust', may be, under the safeguards of an oath, put upon his conscience to disclose that secret trust on the ground that to do anything other than disclose upon the compulsitor of oath would be a fraud on the testator. In my judgment, all that *Blackwell* (and *Fleetwood*, which it approved) decided was that it was sufficient to admit such a doctrine that there should have been a fraud in the sense of a breach of conscience against the testator, and that it was not required to shew that there was a definite fraud against any particular beneficiary. The ratio, in short, is not materially different in such a special case, and the nature of the doctrine is otherwise unaltered.

Now if that be right, I am satisfied, as I shall shew, that no such doctrine of charging the conscience with a 'fraud' has ever been received in our law of wills. I do not think we ever had, in the sense of the English law, a common law of wills controlled by a Court of Equity for the prevention of frauds on the testator. It might also be enough to point out that, so far as authority goes, such secret trusts are not provable by writings of the trustee alone; they must be put to his conscience while he lives, and upon the sanction of an oath taken in Court. There seem to be two apparent exceptions, but both are explained in Fleetwood itself as depending on admissions in pleading.

Lastly, Lord Sumner ([1929] A.C. at p. 339) makes it clear that there are strict rules of limitation of this doctrine, among which he cites and approves of *In re Hetley* ([1902] 2 Ch. 866), decided after Farwell J.'s decision in *Huxtable*, which (on this point) was affirmed by the Court of Appeal. Now the facts in *Hetley* seem to me to be indistinguishable from the present, the alleged trustee being given, not the reversion or fee, but only the tenancy for life of the fund. The decision was adverse to the competency of proving the alleged 'secret' trust. And so, even if the general doctrine were received with us, the established limitation of it would exclude its application here. *In re Hetley* was not cited to me.

Four cases in Scotland were said to incorporate or illustrate the same, or at least an analogous, doctrine: *Warrender v. Anderson* (1893, 1 S.L.T. 304); *Smellie's Trs v. Glasgow Royal Infirmary* (1905, 13 S.L.T. 450); *Miln's Trs v. Drachenhauer* (1921, 1 S.L.T. 152); and *Mitchell's Trs v. Fraser* (1915 S.C. 350). I have carefully examined these cases and listened to the arguments upon them, but I remain without any conviction that they embody any hint of the alleged doctrine of 'secret' or 'unspecified' trusts.

Mitchell's Trs is the only Inner House decision, a decision which, therefore, would be binding upon me. The somewhat special gift which was there held valid and not void can only be considered by being cited at length. I therefore refrain from quoting the clause. I am satisfied that in the Division it was treated in its context as a clause which might be construed as charitable (Lord Guthrie at p. 359; Lord Salvesen at p. 356). In this they express a different view from that of Lord Skerrington (Ordinary). The Lord Ordinary reached the same conclusion upon a different set of authorities, but these are authorities perfectly familiar to the law of Scotland and not connected with the English doctrine of fraud. They depend merely upon a clause sufficiently limited to ascertainable beneficiaries with an interior power of selection. Thus the principal sentence in his opinion is this:

'The beneficiaries contingently interested in the residue are a limited and ascertainable class, *viz.* the testator's children and grandchildren.' This brings the decision into simple line with decisions as old as *Crichton v. Grierson* (1828, 3 W. & S. 329).

Coming to the Outer House decisions, in *Smellie's Trs*, Lord Dundas (the Lord Ordinary) expressly proceeded to apply the rules of law laid down in *Crichton* and later well-known cases. It is only in relation to this doctrine that he says on reaching the last member of the class: 'Some difficulty, however, is occasioned by the words which follow "or others whom my trustees shall consider that I would wish to remember."' He then sustains the clause, with difficulty, on the footing that it may fairly be read as meaning other persons so similarly circumstanced as to permit of ready assimilation to, or inclusion in, one or other of the already defined classes. So understood, the decision neither illustrates the English doctrine nor aids in the present case.

Miln's Trs was a very special case. It also turned on the same doctrines to which I have referred. A formal codicil directed payment of residue to such charitable or benevolent purposes as the trustees thought fit. 'Charitable or benevolent', being read conjunctively, was held to constitute a good class. So far the case was entirely within the authorities. A letter of five months later, addressed to the law agent, which was treated as testamentary in its nature, expressed a hope that a portion of his residue should be applied to certain missionary associations. The argument (rather far-fetched) appears to have been that the gift in this testamentary letter should be read into the broad class 'charitable or benevolent' purposes, and, so read, demonstrated that the testator intended objects under that class which, being religious, the law did not treat with exceptional favour. The argument was plainly open to criticism, as no Court had ever laid down that every religious purpose formed a bad bequest, but only that religious purposes with a scope as wide as the world formed too indefinite a class. In any event, the case seems to have no relevant bearing.

Warrender is a decision of Lord Kyllachy apt to cause a little more trouble. It is very **2.18** shortly reported indeed, and only in one set of reports. No one at the Bar, I think, was quite able to offer a satisfactory suggestion as to what Lord Kyllachy's more fully reasoned opinion may have been. The clause was, 'give the residue to those whom you know respect me'. His Lordship held that a gift to those who respected the testator would be bad, because there would be no workable definition, but he held it good owing to the presence of the words 'you know,' because, as he put it, 'the trustee has the means of defining the beneficiaries'. For my part I should not be prepared to affirm what seems a startling doctrine on a case so slightly reported. I make sure that had Lord Kyllachy treated the case as one of high principle, illustrating in Scots law something of the nature of 'secret trusts' in the neighbouring system of law, the matter would have received fuller attention.

If I must treat it as it stands, however, I can neither follow the reasoning in principle, nor do I think it consists with the later expositions of the law whereby not merely the repository of the power to select must be enabled to select, but the Court also must be enabled to control that repository if he or she should for good or bad reason exceed the scope of his power.

In the result I am prepared to hold (1) that neither the doctrine of secret trusts nor any analogue of it has ever been admitted in Scots law; (2) that our law has uniformly retained and enforced the simple rule that, with the exception of small monetary legacies, no testamentary gift can be set up by anything else than authentic writ; and (3) that the supposed illustrations referred to are no more than illustrations of a particular small class being defined with a limited power of selection within it.

Mr Wark, it appears to me, was right in submitting that the law of Scotland, starting from an almost diametrically different standpoint, that the legal expression of a testator's will is solely his written instrument, has consistently adhered to that. A doctrine sometimes stated as if it added somewhat to the law of nuncupative legacies is entirely confined to the following two cases: *Legatars of Hannah v. Guthrie* (otherwise *Phin v. Guthrie*) (1738, Mor. 3837, and Elchies, *Legacy*, No. 5); *Forsyth's Trs v. M'lean* (1854, 16 D. 343). Now, as explained in the latter case by Lord Cowan at p. 345, and approved by the Inner House, *Phin* does not deviate from the law of nuncupative settlements at all. Lord Ivory, he points out, in his Note to Erskine (III. ix. 7), explains *Phin* as depending entirely upon the ordinary doctrine of trust. A party who is not merely executor but intromitter and general disponee, with right to the residue, is truly a trustee, and his oath is admissible evidence to prove the condition of the trust. That is, he may be made liable for a trust by proving that trust by his writ or oath under the Act. The report of *Phin* in Morison incorporates in the decision the words 'who by the will hath right to the residue of the effects, if any be, after payment of the legacies'; and Lord Kilkerran's note of the case (5 Bro. Supp. 203) brings that out clearly as the ground of the decision. In *Forsyth*, in these circumstances, the Court very naturally refused to apply the ratio of the decision to a case in which it was sought to refer a nuncupative legacy of over £100 Scots to the oath of the executor, who had not such a beneficial interest in the estate. These cases are found summarised in M'Laren on Wills (para. 1033), but I may say I prefer the formulation just given from Lord Cowan to the collocation in which the matter is placed in Lord M'Laren's book. In any event it does not justify the present contentions. I shall accordingly, in the first place, pronounce an interlocutor repelling the claim for the residuaries..."

NOTES:

2.19

1. Wilson and Duncan cite this decision (at para. 2–30) as authority for the proposition that "[a] verbal or secret trust is not recognised by Scots law". That statement (which the authors qualify heavily in a footnote) should be treated with great care. Scots law quite clearly *does* recognise verbal trusts, except in a few fairly narrowly defined (but important) cases, as the Requirements of Writing Act 1995 makes clear.

2. Secret trusts are a means of avoiding the formalities required in a will (for which, in England, see the Wills Act 1837, s.9), but that does not mean that the terms of a secret trust must be "verbal". Indeed, this would present considerable difficulties of proof, and the following recommendation of the (English) Law Society is of interest:

> "Occasionally, a testator may wish to leave all or a substantial part of his or her estate to a solicitor to be dealt with in accordance with the testator's wishes as communicated to the solicitor either orally or in a document, or as a secret trust. The Council consider that where a solicitor in such circumstances will not benefit personally and financially, there is no need to ensure the testator receives independent advice. However, solicitors should preserve the instructions from which the will was drawn and should also see that the terms of such secret trust are embodied in a written document signed or initialled by the testator." (*Guide to the Professional Conduct of Solicitors* (7th ed., 1996), p. 279).

Although Norrie and Scobbie (at p. 51) also equate "secret" and "verbal" trusts, it is submitted that the equation is misleading and should be avoided.

3. Standing the decision in *Shaw*, resort may not be had to the doctrine of secret trusts in order to cure a provision in a will which would otherwise be void from uncertainty. But if A leaves property to B in his will without even purporting to create a trust, but enters into a separate agreement with B (possibly, but not necessarily, verbal) that B is to hold that property on trust, is there any reason why Scots law should not give effect to such an arrangement? That situation might be analysed as a combination of (a) an unqualified bequest from A to B and (b) a contractual agreement binding B to declare himself trustee of the bequest when he receives it. (See *infra* paras 2.25 *et seq.* on the creation of trusts where the truster and the trustee are the same person, as B would be in this case).

A half-secret trust should be unproblematic under Scots law, provided the trust purposes are reduced to writing, because Scots law allows a testator to incorporate informal writings (past or future) into his will by an appropriate direction in the will itself. (See *Stair Memorial Encyclopaedia*, Vol. 25, para. 727). It is not thought that the Requirements of Writing Act 1995 affects this position (Rennie and Cusine, *The Requirements of Writing Act 1995* (1995), para. 2.39, but *cf. Currie on Confirmation of Executors* (8th ed., 1995 by Eilidh M. Scobbie), paras 4.18 *et seq.*). Whether such directions can in fact be kept secret is, however, another question, given that testamentary writings must be exhibited to the commissary department of the appropriate sheriff court in order to obtain confirmation, and an interested party is presumably then entitled to obtain an extract copy of the relevant writing from the sheriff court books (see *Walkers on Evidence*, para. 19.21.1).

See also *Edmond v. Lord Provost of Aberdeen* (1898) 1 F. 154, where a Mr Edmond conveyed heritable property to his son in liferent and to trustees in fee "for the uses, end, and purposes specified or to be specified by me, in any writing under my hand." He left, on his death, a sealed envelope which appeared to contain such directions. It was held that the trustees were entitled to have the envelope opened to see if it made provision regarding the fee, and it appears to have been assumed that his son (who, as heir-at-law, would have taken the property if it had not contained such instructions) was also entitled to know what was contained within the envelope.

B. The transfer of property

(a) The requirement of transfer of property

A trust will not be effective until the trust property is vested in the trustee.

Bell, *Commentaries on the Laws of Scotland* (7th ed., 1870), p. 34

"The trust-estate cannot be considered as fully created, until the right is so vested in the **2.20** trustee as to denude the maker of the trust, and so prevent his creditors, or others deriving right from him, from attaching anything but the reversionary interest, after the purposes of the trust are fulfilled. This, in land estates, can be accomplished only by the same feudal act of sasine by which the trustee's right, if a real creditor or purchaser, would have been completed and rendered effectual against all deriving right from the granter."

NOTES:

1. It appears that it is competent to create the trust by transferring the property to only one of the trustees. According to Bell (*Commentaries*, p. 34) "[t]he trust estate may be vested, and very conveniently so, in one person, subject to the administration of several trustees. A numerous body is fitter to deliberate than to act."
2. It is common to say that "delivery" of property is required to create the trust, and while that is perfectly correct it may be more appropriate to say that a "transfer of property" is required, for two reasons. First, some types of property which may be the subject of a trust (heritable and incorporeal property) are generally considered incapable of *actual* delivery, although such property can obviously be transferred. Second, it is possible for a person to declare himself trustee of his own property. In such a case, there is no question of "delivery", but there must be some act which transfers the property from his personal patrimony to his trust patrimony. Both these issues are discussed further below.

(i) Why does the transfer of property matter?

In *Connell's Trs v. Connell*, 1955 S.L.T. 125, C, immediately prior to his marriage, executed an ante- **2.21** nuptial bond of provision. The bond purportedly bound himself and his representatives to convey certain property after his death to trustees. The property was to be held in trust for his wife in liferent and for the children of the marriage in fee. The bond was not delivered to the trustees until after his death. It was accepted that the bond could not have effect as a testamentary writing. The Inner House therefore had to consider whether it could be regarded as an effective bond notwithstanding the absence of delivery. In holding that it could not be, Lord Hill Watson made the following observations (at 132–133):

"It was suggested that since, in the present deed, payment could only be exacted after the granter's death there was no necessity to deliver the deed during his lifetime. In my view, this argument is fallacious if the deed was to be a valid and effectual provision in favour of the children. While it would not create in the children a *jus crediti* which could compete with the father's creditors, yet during the father's lifetime there were certain rights which could be enforced by the trustees against him. In my opinion, the deed if valid and effectual was a deed of the nature described in Bell's Principles, paragraph 1987, which, dealing with the effect of marriage contract provisions, says: 'Where the obligation is not prestable during the father's life, the children, although they have no *jus crediti* against onerous creditors of the father, may pursue the father's representative for implement, and challenge gratuitous deeds as *contra fidem tabularum nuptialium*'. If in the present case Mr Connell had threatened to divest himself of his whole estate during his lifetime, in my opinion, the trustees, if the deed had been delivered to them, would have been entitled to interdict him from so doing, which demonstrates the necessity for delivery during the granter's lifetime."

Conversely, if delivery (or some equivalent) were unnecessary, it could encourage the fraudulent creation of trusts in order to shield property from creditors. As Lord Reid stated in *Allan's Trs v. Inland Revenue*, 1971 S.L.T. 62, at 64:

"I reject the argument . . . that a mere proved intention to make a trust coupled with the execution of a declaration of trust can suffice. If that were so it would be easy to execute such a declaration, keep it in reserve, use it in case of bankruptcy to defeat the claims of creditors, but if all went well and the trustee desired to regain control of the fund simply suppress the declaration of trust."

(ii) What is delivery?

2.22   At first sight, the concept of delivery appears rather elementary. We are naturally inclined to interpret "delivery" as involving the physical handing over of an item of property. However, that is not the only form of delivery recognised by Scots law. See, as an example, the following case:

Milligan v. Ross
1994 S.C.L.R. 430

In 1972, Mrs Milligan executed a deed of trust. The deed stated that she irrevocably disponed certain corporeal moveable property (furnishings and household goods), specified in a schedule to the deed, to certain persons as trustees. The trustees were directed to allow Mrs Milligan (and her husband, if he survived her) a liferent of the trust estate. They were directed that, upon the death of Mr and Mrs Milligan, they were to make over the trust estate to her daughter, Mrs Ross. The deed contained a clause consenting to registration for preservation and execution, and was duly delivered to the trustees and registered in the Books of Council and Session. The property remained in Mrs Milligan's possession and she continued to pay all relevant insurance premiums.

LORD CLYDE: "The pursuer now seeks a declarator that she has the sole and exclusive right of ownership in the corporeal moveable property described in the schedule to the trust settlement. She avers that these corporeal moveables were never delivered to the trustees, that she has remained in possession of them and accordingly remains the owner of them. It is accepted that they were never physically handed over to the trustees and the question which was argued before me was whether there had been an effective transfer of these assets into a trust so as to divest the pursuer.

The debate before me was conducted on a narrow front. It was not disputed that the necessity for actual delivery in order to achieve a transfer of property in corporeal moveables was not an absolute rule. Constructive delivery and equivalents to delivery could be admitted. Reference was made to Hume's Lectures for his statement of the position in volume 3 of the Stair Society edition between pp. 246 and 251 and to Erskine's Institute II.1.18. Reference was also made to the more recent work by Professor Gordon entitled *Studies in the Transfer of Property by Traditio* and in particular chapter 12 of that work.

The trust deed in the present case is expressed to be irrevocable and given its delivery and its recording it would be difficult to deny that the deed was irrevocable. No argument before me, however, was developed along that basis nor was any discussion opened regarding the nature or enforceability of any rights which the daughter or her assignees might have acquired in such circumstances apart from the question whether there had been a transfer effected to the trustees. Reference was made incidentally to the case of *Cameron's Trustees v. Cameron*, 1907 S.C. 407 and more fully to *Tennent v. Tennent's Trustees* (1869) 7 M. 936 and to *Scott v. Scott*, 1930 S.C. 903. These cases were concerned principally with questions of revocability but it was observed that in the case of *Tennent* Lord President Inglis (at p. 948) stated that the effect of registration in the Books of Council and Session was to put the deed beyond the power of recovery by the granter and that registration was a significant fact in the question of the delivery of the deed. He observed that when the grantees obtained the deed into their possession, they would be entitled to demand instant delivery of the assets in the hands of the granter and that they were entitled to enter into possession and to administer the estate for the benefit of the beneficiaries. But in the present case it is delivery of the trust estate which is under challenge not simply delivery of the deed.

The problem whether property in corporeal moveables has been transferred often arises in the situation where the alleged transferor has become financially embarrassed and his creditors or his trustee in bankruptcy are making a claim to the property allegedly transferred. There is no suggestion that the present case arises out of any such problem. In that situation, however, the court has always been careful to see that there has not been some attempt to evade the rule of delivery by attempting to disguise what is intended to be a means of giving security without possession by adopting a different form for the transaction, as, for example, a fictitious sale to the creditor with a fictitious lease back to the debtor. Thus one consideration in determining the problem of the transfer of ownership has been that of the bona fides of the parties in making the particular transaction. But the matter is essentially one to be determined in the circumstances of each case. Without attempting any exhaustive definition it seems to me that where the transaction has been honest and open and the circumstances are such as to make it evident to or at least reasonably discoverable by third parties that there has been a change in ownership, then it may be accepted that that change has occurred even though the goods have not been physically transferred from the transferor to the transferee. The significance of the element of public knowledge is noted by Professor Gordon where he observes (*op. cit.*, p. 218) that the test for recognising delivery is not the existence of a *causa detentionis* but

> 'whether it is, or ought to be, clear to third parties that there has been a change of ownership, despite the fact that there is no change in the physical situation of the goods'.

Erskine puts the matter in this way (Institute II.1.18):

> 'But that the will of the owner to transfer may be known with the greater certainty, and that consequently property may be the better secured, the Romans, and other nations, have reasonably required, in all cases which can well admit of it, the delivery of possession for completing the conveyance; or at least some public act, by which it may appear that the former proprietor has given up his right: so that he who gets the last conveyance with the first tradition, is preferred to the property, according to the rule, *traditionibus et usucapionibus, non nudis pactis, transferuntur rerum dominia.*'

Where the goods remain in the possession of the transferor, it may not be necessary to resort to an analysis of what constitutes constructive delivery or what may serve as equivalent to delivery. At least in the case where the goods remain in the possession of a third party, Erskine rejects the analysis of a *ficta traditio* and takes the robust view (II.1.19) that: **2.23**

> 'the plain reason why tradition is not required in that case is, because there is no room for it; for no subject can be delivered to one who hath it already in his custody'.

The views which I have expressed seem to me to be borne out by the various cases to which I was referred and I now simply refer to these in their chronological order . . . . [His Lordship reviewed the case law, and continued:]

Counsel for the pursuer argued that not enough had been done in the present case to achieve delivery. He did not require that the furniture should have been moved from the pursuer's house to the trustees and then returned to the pursuer and replaced in its former position. What he did submit, however, was that the trustees should have inspected the alleged trust estate, checked its location and in those and other ways asserted their control.

Looking to the facts of the present case, it seems to me that what was done was sufficient to divest the pursuer of the furniture in question. There is no suggestion of anything in the transaction which was not in *bona fide*. It appears in every respect to have been open and honest. No question of attempting to create a security is raised and there is no question of any financial embarrassment. The terms of the trust and the specification of the trust estate were set out fully and formally in writing. The deed which was expressed as an irrevocable trust was delivered to the trustees and registered in the Books of Council and Session. It was thus published and put beyond the pursuer's control. The fiar knew of it and exercised her rights under it. The pursuer remained in possession of the trust estate but that was precisely what she intended should happen. It seems to me that after granting and delivering the deed, that possession should be attributed to her right as liferentrix and no longer to her right as owner. The payment of the insurance premiums in respect of the trust estate over the long period since 1972 until the present time seems to me to be a particular acting relating to that estate and reflects the obligations which she had under the trust. In these circumstances, where the retention of the estate by the truster was a purpose of the trust and the detail of that estate and of the provisions of the trust were formally recorded, accepted by the trustees and published and where all of this was carried out openly and honestly, it seems to me that there was no further particular act required of the trustees to complete a conveyance in trust to themselves. This was not a case which, to use Erskine's phrase, could well admit of delivery of possession and there was a public act which could show that the pursuer had given up her right. In my view a trust was effectively constituted here and the pursuer has been divested of her exclusive right of property. I shall, accordingly, in terms of the motion made to me, sustain the first plea-in-law for the defenders and repel the second plea for the pursuer, both of which are pleas to the relevancy, and dismiss the action."

NOTES:

2.24
1. *Milligan v. Ross* illustrates two points: first, that it is inappropriate to take an overly simplistic view of the concept of "delivery" in the creation of a trust, and second, that this is not really a question of trust law at all, but rather a question of the general law of property. On transfer of ownership generally, see Reid, *Property*, Chapter 13.
2. Heritable property can, obviously, not be physically transferred from the truster to the trustee. The transfer of ownership is effected by registration:

> "if A, infeft in land, disposes gratuitously that land to B, and then registers the disposition in the Register of Sasines, the donation is perfected, not, I think, because of the publication in the register of A's deed, but because by the constructively effected sasine the land itself, the subject of the gift, has been delivered by A to B in the only way in which land can be delivered." (*Cameron's Trs v. Cameron*, 1907 S.C. 407, *per* the Lord President (Dunedin) at 413).

Such registration might nowadays be in the Land Register rather than the Register of Sasines, but this does not affect the principle involved.

(b) The problem of the truster as trustee

2.25 Where a truster appoints himself sole trustee of his own property, there can obviously be no question of delivery between the truster and trustee. Some equivalent to delivery is therefore necessary. It appears that this equivalent is found in intimation to the beneficiaries of their rights under the trust.

Allan's Trs v. Inland Revenue
1971 S.L.T. 62

LORD REID: "Miss Allan was a wealthy woman. When aged 77 and in failing health she was concerned about the amount of duty which would have to be paid on her death. So a scheme was devised to diminish the amount of estate duty. In her will she had provided for legacies of £20,000 each to Mrs Jeffrey and Miss Marr free of estate duty. Miss Ramsay who was a close friend and adviser was residuary legatee. In pursuance of this scheme she revoked the legacies to Mrs Jeffrey and Miss Marr by codicil of 17th October 1963, and in December 1963, made a proposal to an insurance company with a view to taking an endowment policy under which she was to be a trustee for these ladies and to have no beneficial interest in the policy or its proceeds. The arrangements were made by her solicitor and the strange nature of the insurance is explained by the fact that the solicitor and Miss Ramsay knew that Miss Allan could not survive for long although she herself did not know that.

In a letter to the insurance company of 12th December 1963, Miss Allan said: 'I intend that the policy shall from the moment of its commencement be held upon an irrevocable trust for the benefit of the beneficiary or beneficiaries aftermentioned.' The policy was for a sum of £1,345,164 payable on the survivance of Miss Allan until 27th December 1973, the annual premium being £120,000, but in the event of her death before that date the company agreed to pay £117,000 in respect of each year's premium paid. Miss Allan died on 3rd December 1964, when only one year's premium had been paid and the company paid to the appellants as her trustees and executors the sum of £117,000.

The appellants contend that this sum should not be aggregated with Miss Allan's estate on the ground that she never had an interest in the policy, so they must show that from the moment of its commencement she never had an interest in it. They can do that if they can show that from that moment she held it on irrevocable trust. I think there is no doubt that that was her intention, but the respondents maintain that that is not enough—there must also be something in the nature of delivery to constitute an irrevocable trust.

The policy contained a declaration that the only interest of Miss Allan under it should be as trustee. The sum assured was to be payable to Miss Allan as trustee and the receipt of the trustee for any sum payable was to be a full and sufficient discharge to the company which should not be concerned to see to the application of any such sum. The declaration in the policy further provided that the policy should be held in trust for the benefit of Mrs Jeffrey to the extent of £20,000, of Miss Marr to the extent of £20,000 and of Miss Ramsay to the extent of the remainder.

Miss Ramsay had full knowledge of the negotiations and was aware of the terms of the trust set out in the policy. But neither Mrs Jeffrey nor Miss Marr had any knowledge of this. The respondents admit that this 'intimation to Miss Ramsay of the trust in her favour effected notional delivery to her of the rights conferred upon her by the said policy from the moment when these rights came into existence to the entire exclusion of the deceased'. But they contend that because there was no intimation or notional delivery to the other beneficiaries Miss Allan could validly and effectively have caused the terms of the policy to be altered so as to deprive those other beneficiaries of any benefit under the policy. Admittedly if she could have done that she had an interest in the two sums of £20,000 sufficient to require aggregation of these two sums.

The idea that a person can make himself a trustee of his own property is something of a novelty in the law of Scotland and there is little authority as to whether this is possible or as to how it can be done. On such a matter we cannot seek enlightenment from the law of England because the origin of trusts in Scotland is very different from its origin in England. Trusts were well known in Scotland by the seventeenth century, but I need not explore the early history. For present purposes it is I think sufficient to refer to Lord McLaren's work on Wills and Succession, published in 1895, from which it appears (p. 824) that the institutional writers regarded trust as akin to a combination of the contracts of deposit and mandate so that in early days the truster and trustee must have been different persons.

Then Lord McLaren says: 'A trust may properly be defined as an interest created by the transfer of property to a trustee, in order that he may carry out the truster's directions, respecting its management and disposal. This definition includes the two essentials of a trust, viz., the conveyance or transfer of the legal estate to a trustee, and the constitution of a trust purpose.' Clearly it never occurred to him that a person could make himself a trustee for trust purposes.

The earliest reference to this which counsel were able to discover is in Menzies on Trustees, published in 1913. That author says (p. 30): 'The truster may himself be one of the trustees, or even the sole trustee; and in the latter case, by treating the truster qua truster as a different legal persona from the truster qua trustee, the above classification holds good.' The only authority cited is an English case which does not support this explanation. I do not see how any individual can convert himself into two different legal personae.

But by 1934 there seems to have been some development. Professor Mackenzie Stuart says (Trusts, p. 8): 'Delivery may be made by a third party on the truster's instructions or it may be by the donor as truster to himself as trustee.' He gives no authority for this. But on the next page he says: 'Where there is no delivery there must be its equivalent. There must be something done by the truster to take the subject effectually out of his control and to put it into the control of the trustee or beneficiary.' As authority for that he cites *Cameron's Trustees v. Cameron*, 1907 S.C. 407. That was a case where a lender took the bond and disposition in security in favour of himself as trustee for his daughter but did not inform the daughter. The question arose on his death. The case was treated as raising a question of donation, and the rule was applied that to make a perfected donation there must be delivery from the donor to the donee. The bond and disposition in security had been registered in the Register of Sasines but that was held to be insufficient. Lord Kinnear said (p. 422): 'I think the father has done nothing equivalent to delivery as between himself and the children, because he has done nothing to take the deed out of his own control and put it into his children's control.' There was no suggestion that it made any difference that the father had declared himself to be a trustee.

Later (p. 12) Professor Mackenzie Stuart returned to the present question: 'Where the granter has appointed himself sole trustee delivery in the ordinary sense is impossible and equivalents to it are more easily presumed than in the case of the trustees being independent of the granter. But there must be something equivalent to delivery so as to operate divestiture.'

2.26 I think that we can now accept the position, as a reasonable development of the law, that a person can make himself a trustee of his own property provided that he also does something equivalent to delivery or transfer of the trust fund. I reject the argument for the appellants that mere proved intention to make a trust coupled with the execution of a declaration of trust can suffice. If that were so it would be easy to execute such a declaration, keep it in reserve, use it in case of bankruptcy to defeat the claims of creditors, but if all went well and the trustee desired to regain control of the fund simply suppress the declaration of trust.

The appellants founded on *Carmichael v. Carmichael's Executrix*, 1920 S.C. (H.L.) 195. That is in some respects a difficult case to interpret. It dealt with *jus quaesitum tertio*, and the appellants presented an alternative argument that here Miss Allan and the insurance company had by their contract created such rights in the beneficiaries. I have no hesitation in rejecting this alternative argument. To have a *jus quaesitum tertio* the third party must have been given by the contract of the contracting parties a right to get something from one or both of them. But here the proceeds of the policy were to be paid to Miss Allan. The beneficiaries were given no right against the company: on the contrary the company having paid Miss Allan were freed from all liability to see that she paid the money to the beneficiaries. Any benefit to the beneficiaries flowed from the declaration of trust not from the terms of the contract.

But the appellants also founded on *Carmichael's* case (*supra*) as one where intention without more was sufficient. But that was not the question for decision. The policy there provided for the payment of the sum assured in certain events to a third party, the executors or assigns of a son of the father who made the contract with the insurance company. As Lord Dunedin pointed out (p. 201) the real question was whether it was intended that the son's right given by the contract should be irrevocable. Normally the parties who make a contract can, if they choose, cancel or alter it. But if they have chosen to give to a third party a right which they intended to be irrevocable then they cannot do that. The question is what they intended and *Carmichael's* case deals with the means by which that intention can be proved. I do not think that Lord Dunedin meant to say that this intention to make the provision in favour of the third party irrevocable can never be established by the terms of the contract itself. Generally it cannot and then other evidence of intention is required. But that seems to me to be very far removed from the present case and I cannot read *Carmichael's* case as lending any support to the argument that there is no need for any equivalent of delivery of the trust fund to establish a trust.

I shall not examine in detail the other authorities cited. They deal with donation or *donatio mortis causa* and they show that fine distinctions have been made as to what in addition to intention is necessary to establish donation. None appears to question the general rule that delivery or some equivalent is necessary.

So I come to the question what was the effect of intimation to Miss Ramsay—did it merely set up the gift to her or did it bring the whole trust into operation? There are many cases, particularly where the donor reserves a liferent for himself, where a trust, though properly constituted by conveyance of the fund to trustees for specific trust purposes, is nevertheless revocable and only confers rights in the beneficiaries if unrevoked when the donor dies. That must be because on a proper interpretation of the deed it was the intention of the truster to create a revocable trust. I can well understand that in such a case intimation to one beneficiary might create a new irrevocable right in him though leaving the rest of the rights conferred subject to revocation. But this case is quite different. Here the intention was to create an irrevocable trust, but there was no operative trust at all until something equivalent to delivery occurred. I find it difficult to understand how such an inchoate trust can be set up in part. What is required to create an effective trust is some bona fide physical act of the truster equivalent to conveyance, transfer or delivery of the subject of the trust. Suppose the truster declares himself a trustee for A in liferent and B whom failing C in fee and then intimates the trust to B but not to A. It seems unreal to say that he has transferred the trust fund to himself as trustee in a question with B but has made no such transfer in a question with A. If he has transferred it as regards B then he must during the life of A hold the property in trust until it is seen whether the fiar survives to take a vested interest. So as the property has been earmarked as trust property I do not see why all the trust purposes should not take effect.

I have already quoted the respondents' contention that intimation to Miss Ramsay effected notional delivery of the rights conferred upon her. But I think that is wrong. One cannot deliver rights. What is required is delivery of the trust property.

It cannot be said that when the trust was intimated to Miss Ramsay that set up an irrevocable right in her but revocable rights in the other two ladies. There never was any intention to set up a revocable trust. As regards the other two ladies it must be all or nothing.

There is a further difficulty if intimation only sets up that part of the trust which benefits the person to whom it has been intimated. What if there are unborn beneficiaries? The trust cannot be intimated to them. So the law would have to be that a truster can only make himself a trustee as regards persons to whom intimation can effectively be made.

If we accept the position that a person can now create a valid trust by declaring himself a trustee of certain property and giving intimation to a beneficiary, I think we must follow that to its logical conclusion. That intimation is equivalent to delivery of that property and therefore brings the whole trust into operation.

I would allow this appeal."

LORD GUEST (*dissenting*): "I can see no reason in logic or in principle why intimation to one beneficiary is equivalent to intimation of the trust to the other beneficiaries. I should have thought if intention had any bearing on the matter, the opposite result would follow and because Miss Allan intimated to Miss Ramsay her interest it showed that she did not intend the other interests to be irrevocable. If the argument be sound it would mean that if an illusory benefit say of £1 was intimated to one beneficiary the whole complicated provisions of a trust deed would be valid and irrevocable. I consider that the interests of Mrs Jeffrey and Miss Marr were revocable, as no valid trust had been created in their favour. To hold otherwise would, in my view, strain to breaking point the Scots doctrine of trusts."

Lords Morris of Borth-y-Gest, Upjohn and Donovan concurred with Lord Reid.

NOTES:

    1. The case of *Cameron's Trs v. Cameron*, 1907 S.C. 407, referred to by Lord Reid, appears to **2.27** have held that where a deed is registered in the Register of Sasines, declaring that A holds

property in trust for B, this is not sufficient to constitute a trust. Why not? Should publication in the Register of Sasines or the Land Register—public registers—not be regarded as intimation to B? In rejecting that argument, Lord Low observed (at 425):

> "It is said, however, that whatever may have been Cameron's intention the registration of the bonds published to all the world that the sums of money for which they were granted belonged to his children, for whom he was trustee. That being so, it was argued, it would be inconsistent with the reliance which the public are entitled to place upon all entries in the public registers to hold that Cameron was entitled to repudiate the trust and claim the trust funds as his own.
>
> At first sight that appeared to me to be a formidable argument, but I think that a sufficient answer is this—the Register of Sasines is a register of land rights, and its object is to enable anyone interested in a particular property to ascertain what is the state of the title of that property and what are the burdens upon it. Therefore, when each of the bonds in question and its disposition in security was recorded, it seems to me that the fact which was thereby published, and upon which the public were entitled to rely, was, not that Cameron had as trustee for his children lent a certain sum of money to the borrower, but that the property of the latter, which he had disponed to Cameron in security of the debt, was validly burdened with the debt. No doubt an examination of the register would disclose that the bonds were granted to Cameron as trustee for his children, but that is not a matter which falls within the scope and purpose of the register, and therefore, in my judgment, it is not a matter in regard to which the public are entitled to rely upon the faith of the records."

The situation may, however, be different where B has provided the funds for A to purchase the property. It appears that this fact, combined with registration, may be sufficient to constitute the trust. See *Gilpin v. Martin* (1869) 7 M. 807, as interpreted by Lord Kinnear in *Cameron's Trs* at 420–421.

For a detailed criticism of the decision in *Cameron's Trs*, see Wilson and Duncan, paras 3–34 to 3–45.

2. *Multiple beneficiaries and multiple trusts.* In *Allan's Trs*, there was one single endowment policy to be held for the benefit of three beneficiaries, and it was held that intimation to one of these beneficiaries sufficed. Compare this with *Clark's Trs v. Inland Revenue*, 1972 S.L.T. 190, where C took out seven assurance policies which he purported to hold for seven different beneficiaries. There was a single proposal form and the first premiums were paid by one single cheque. It was argued that this was one single trust, and that following *Allan's Trs*, intimation to one of the beneficiaries was sufficient to bring the trust into existence. The Inner House rejected this argument, holding that there were seven separate and distinct trusts.

3. *Intimation to whom?* The *Clark's Trs* court did, however, accept C's argument that intimation to the accountant (a friend of C's) who had advised him as to taking out the policies and was subsequently assumed as a trustee, should be regarded as intimation to the beneficiaries. The court accepted that the accountant had become an agent for the beneficiaries. (Nothing is said about any conflict of interest which might arise from the remarkable position of being the truster's agent, a trustee, *and* the beneficiaries' agent.) In *Kerr's Trs v. Inland Revenue*, 1974 S.L.T. 193, Lord Fraser considered to whom intimation might properly be given (at 201–202):

> "in the case of one of the families, the so-called intimation was given to a person whose receipt of the information was not, in my opinion, sufficient to divest the settlor of the beneficial right in the estate. Intimation to a beneficiary himself would, of course, be sufficient for that purpose; so, I think, would intimation to his agent, such as his solicitor or accountant, or to a person authorised by the general law to act on behalf of the beneficiary, such as his curator or guardian. In *Clark's Trustees v. Inland Revenue* this Division held that these categories could be extended and that intimation had been effectively given to the truster's accountant, whom the truster had originally intended to appoint as a trustee. Lord Wheatley referred to this accountant as the agent for the truster, which he plainly was, and held that he was at the same time acting as 'agent' for the beneficiaries, 'in the sense that although not appointed by them as such, he was

placed in that position by the truster himself'. Later in his opinion Lord Wheatley referred to the accountant as a person whom the truster had wanted to be a trustee and added 'there was no change in the truster's intentions so far as [the accountant] was concerned. He all along wanted [the accountant] to be a trustee . . .'. The context appears to me to show that the word 'agent' in the former passage was not used in its ordinary sense, and I think that must be so, because it would be impossible for the truster to appoint an agent for someone else unless he had authority, either specifically or under the general law, to act for that other person. Suppose the 'agent', appointed by the truster, had called upon the beneficiary as his principal to pay his professional fees, I do not see how the beneficiary could have been liable to pay them. It seems to me that his Lordship regarded the accountant as being a trustee, or at least a quasi-trustee, for the beneficiaries. That was also, I think, the view of Lord Milligan, as appears from the last five paragraphs of his opinion on p. 197. On that view of the matter, intimation to him would, of course, be sufficient. But intimation to a stranger or to a person with no right or duty to act on behalf of the beneficiaries, would, in my opinion, not be effective. In the present case the intimation relied upon, so far as the Cook family is concerned, was intimation by the settlor's accountant, Mr Lindsay, to Mrs Cook, the settlor's niece, who was the mother of six of the beneficiaries. At the date of the intimation two of these beneficiaries were of full age, being more than 21 years old, and so far as Mrs Cook's four younger children were concerned, she was not their tutor or curator. It was argued by counsel for the appellants that, although Mrs Cook had no legal standing to act for her children, she was nevertheless an appropriate person to whom an intimation of some benefit to be conferred upon the children could be made. I do not agree. In my opinion, intimation to Mrs Cook as representing her children who were of full age could not be effective or equivalent to intimation to the children themselves. The position with regard to the minor and pupil children is perhaps less clear, but, in my opinion, intimation to the mother was not equivalent to intimation to those children themselves. Accordingly, for this reason also, I am of opinion that the so-called intimation, so far as the Cook family is concerned, was not effective. The position of the Reid-Kerr family is different, because the intimation which is relied upon was given to their father, Sheriff Reid-Kerr, and he was the curator or tutor of the children, all of whom were in minority. Accordingly he was, in my opinion, a person to whom intimation could properly have been given on their behalf."

(On whether intimation to a trustee or co-trustee may suffice, see *Cameron's Trs v. Cameron*, **2.28** 1907 S.C. 407, *per* the Lord President (Dunedin) at 413).

4. *Intimation when?* In *Kerr's Trs*, it was held that the intimation must take place simultaneously with, or subsequent to, the execution of the declaration of trust (which itself requires the trust fund to be in existence—see *Clark Taylor, infra.*). Lord Fraser observed (at 200–201):

"Looking at the matter apart from authority, it appears to me that anything said by an intending settlor to an intended beneficiary, before the settlor has executed a declaration of trust, cannot be more than an expression of intention and the intention could be changed at any time before the declaration is executed. The only exception would be where there is some contractual obligation by the settlor towards the beneficiary, but there is nothing of that sort here. Counsel for the appellants argued that for a trust to be constituted two steps were required, viz., first, an intention by the truster expressed in a form habile to constitute a trust, and, second, an overt act by the truster equivalent to delivery, and that it was immaterial in which order the steps were taken. I reject that argument, not only for the reasons I have already stated, but because of the practical difficulties that it would create. If the intimation can precede the expression of intention, how long can the interval of time between them be, and how widely can they differ in their terms? If a rich uncle says to his nephew 'I intend to declare myself to be sole trustee of £1,000 or 1,000 shares in Company A in trust for you', and he later executes a declaration of trust in favour of the nephew for £10,000 or 1,000 shares in Company B or a house worth £50,000, is the declaration effective to constitute an irrevocable trust immediately and without further intimation? And would it make any difference if an interval of a year or 10 years had elapsed since he expressed the intention? Such questions would I think be bound to arise if an expression of intention to execute a trust in the future were to be treated as equivalent to an intimation of the fact that a trust had been executed, and I would regard that as undesirable."

In *Clark Taylor & Co. Ltd v. Quality Site Development (Edinburgh) Ltd*, 1981 S.C. 111, C sold bricks to Q under a contract which included the following term (11(b)):

"In the event of the buyer reselling or otherwise disposing of the goods or any part thereof before the property therein has passed to him by virtue of Clause 11 (a) hereof then the buyer will, until payment in full to the seller of the price of goods, hold in trust for the seller all his rights under such contract of resale or any other contract in pursuance of which the goods or any part thereof are disposed of or any contract by which property comprising the said goods or any part thereof is or is to be disposed of and any money or other consideration received by him thereunder".

The Inner House held that this attempt to create a trust was ineffective, *inter alia* because the contractual term was at most a declaration of intention to create a trust (*i.e.*, as in *Kerr's Trs*, it preceded the trust fund coming into existence) and not an intimation. The decision was accompanied by considerable hostility to the use of such a device. The Lord President (Emslie) observed (at 116):

"if a condition such as condition 11 (b), designed only to freeze assets of a debtor and to keep them out of other creditors' hands until a particular creditor's debt is paid in full, were to be regarded as constituting a proper trust in accordance with the law of Scotland, and were to be adopted widely by sellers of goods, the damage which would be done to the objectives of the law of bankruptcy and of liquidation would be incalculable. Other interesting complications can easily be figured, and a person creating more than one such 'trust' in favour of his creditors could readily find himself in trouble under the criminal law."

The decision was met with considerable criticism at the time. For discussion, see George L. Gretton, "Using Trusts as Commercial Securities" (1988) 33 J.L.S.S. 53; W.A. Wilson, "Romalpa and Trust", 1983 S.L.T. (News) 106; John M. Halliday, "Romalpa Again—The Trust Device", 1984 S.L.T. (News) 153; Kenneth G.C. Reid, "Trusts and Floating Charges", 1987 S.L.T. (News) 113; D.P. Sellar, "Trusts and Liquidators—Further Thoughts", 1988 S.L.T. (News) 194; Kenneth G.C. Reid, "Trusts and Liquidators—A Reply", 1988 S.L.T. (News) 365 and Wilson and Duncan, Chapter 4. (See also George L. Gretton, "Constructive Trusts" (1997) 1 Edin L.R. 281, 304–305: "In my younger days I attacked the decision of the First Division in *Clark Taylor v. Quality Site Development*. In my older and, I hope, wiser middle age I wish to repent. While not everything in that case may be right, its heart was in the right place.")

5. An exception to the rule that intimation is required for a person to be regarded as sole trustee of his own property may be found in section 2 of the (perhaps misleadingly titled) Married Women's Policies of Assurance (Scotland) Act 1880:

"A policy of assurance effected by a man or woman on his or her own life, and expressed upon the face of it to be for the benefit of his or her spouse or children, or his or her spouse and children, or any of them shall, together with all benefit thereof, be deemed a trust for their benefit; and such policy, immediately on its being so effected, shall vest in him or her and his or her legal representatives in trust for the purpose or purposes so expressed, or in any trustee nominated in the policy, or appointed by separate writing, duly intimated to the assurance office, but in trust always as aforesaid, and shall not otherwise be subject to his or her control, or form part of his or her estate, or be liable to the diligence of his or her creditors, or be revocable as a donation, or reducible on any ground of excess or insolvency; And the receipt of such trustee for the sums secured by the policy, or for the value thereof, in whole or in part, shall be a sufficient and effectual discharge to the assurance office;

> Provided always, that if it shall be proved that the policy was effected and premiums thereon paid with intent to defraud creditors, or if the person upon whose life the policy is effected shall be made bankrupt within two years from the date of such policy, it shall be competent to the creditors to claim repayment of the premiums so paid from the trustee of the policy out of the proceeds thereof."

For a full discussion, see Wilson and Duncan, paras 6–22 to 6–39.

3. CREATION OF TRUSTS: INVOLUNTARILY CREATED TRUSTS

A. Resulting trusts

(a) General

Where trust purposes fail, the trustees may be deemed to be holding the trust property in a "resulting **2.29** trust" for the benefit of the truster or his representatives. This concept, which has been described as "the last resort to which the law has recourse when the draftsman has made a blunder or failed to dispose of that which he has set out to dispose of" (*Re Cochrane* [1955] Ch. 309, *per* Harman J. at 316), is neatly summarised by Lord Young in *Edmond v. Lord Provost of Aberdeen* (1898) 1 F. 154, at 163–164:

> "I quite assent to the argument that, when anyone creates a trust and expresses no trust purposes, or the purposes which he expresses fail, then there is a resulting trust for himself if he continues in life, or if not, for those who after his death come in his place. If a man makes a trust of any part of his estate, or of the whole of it, to take effect in his lifetime, and either declares no trust purposes, or the purposes which he has expressed fail, there is a resulting trust for himself, and the trustees will have to convey the property back to him, although he has given them possession of it; and so here if there are no trust purposes, then the trustees to whom there is, according to my opinion, a good conveyance, will hold the estate upon the legal title which is given to them as a resulting trust, the beneficial estate being in the heir of the truster—the disponer."

How is the doctrine of resulting trusts to be justified? The matter does not appear to have received much attention in Scotland, but the English textbooks generally take the view that it is "founded on the unexpressed but presumed intention of the settlor" (Delany, 133). In other words, the law presumes that the truster would wish the trust property to be returned to him if the trust purposes fail. It would follow, therefore, that the truster can exclude the operation of the doctrine (a view accepted by Norrie and Scobbie, p. 58).

But if the trust purposes have failed and the truster has excluded the possibility of a resulting trust, what is to happen to the property? The truster may, of course, when specifying purposes, make clear what is to happen if those purposes fail. For example, Wilson and Duncan suggest (at 6–40) that "[t]here may be a question as to whether the beneficial interest was given to the trustees themselves". While this is undoubtedly correct as a practical point, if the truster's intention was that the trustees were to benefit if the trust purposes *otherwise* failed, then the benefit to the trustees is clearly itself a trust purpose. The trust purposes have therefore not failed and there is no question of a resulting trust being created. Similarly, it will be normal for a will to contain a clause disposing of the residue of the estate. In that case, if specific purposes which apply to part of the estate fail, that property will normally become subject to the residue clause—and so, again, the trust purposes have not failed and there is no need for the doctrine of resulting trust to operate.

But what if the truster has both excluded the possibility of a resulting trust and the trust purposes genuinely fail? There appears to be no Scottish authority on the point, but it may be that the only logically possible answer in this scenario is that the property falls to the Crown as *bona vacantia* (see *Westdeutsche Landesbank Girozentrale v. Islington LBC* [1996] A.C. 669, *per* Lord Browne-Wilkinson at 708). It is, of course, unlikely that a truster would seek to exclude the operation of the doctrine, although it may be noted that resulting trusts can have unpleasant consequences in terms of taxation in certain circumstances.

(b) The circumstances in which a resulting trust may arise

Mackenzie Stuart categorises the situations in which a resulting trust may arise as follows:

A. Mackenzie Stuart, *The Law of Trusts* (1932), p. 42

2.30   "A resulting trust may arise where estate has been conveyed under trust but the trust purposes have never been declared, or where a trustee has been given discretionary powers personal to him and he has not accepted or has died without exercising them. It may arise where for any reason the trust purposes, whether as originally constituted or through the failure of beneficiaries or in any other way, do not exhaust the trust estate. It is also found where the trust purposes have failed from vagueness, illegality or the like."

NOTES:

2.31
1. *Purposes never declared*. In *Thomas v. Tennent's Trs* (1868) 7 M. 114, the truster (in July 1864), conveyed heritable property (in Scotland) to his wife in liferent and to trustees in fee. The trustees were directed that, upon his wife's death, the property should be sold and the proceeds should form part of his residuary estate, which was to be applied in the manner set forth in his (English) will of May 1864. However, he revoked that will in 1866 and destroyed the earlier one. The Court of Session held that the trustees held the property in a resulting trust for his heir-at-law. The Lord Justice-Clerk (Patton) observed (at 119):

    > "So far as relates to the fee of the Scotch property, the case is that of a trust constituted in favour of trustees with a direction in favour of parties whose names it is impossible to conjecture. The reference to the prior cancelled deed failing, and there being no purposes pointed out except to carry out a distribution, the result in law is, that the trust purposes are undeclared—a case in which trustees must be held to hold for the heir-at-law of the granter."

    Although the Lord Justice-Clerk refers to the trust purposes as "undeclared", this is somewhat artificial and should not be taken to suggest that the trustees were *always* holding for the heir-at-law. As Lord Neaves pointed out in the same case (at 126), the revocation of the earlier will "converted the trust into a trust for the heir at law". Prior to that point, the trustees were holding the property in favour of the parties named in the first will, odd as that may seem given that they could no longer be identified.
2. *Discretionary powers not accepted*. Trust purposes which purport to confer discretion upon trustees will generally not be effective unless the truster has selected named trustees to exercise that discretion. See *infra* para. 5.11.
3. *Trust purposes void from vagueness, illegality etc.* See *infra* Chapter 5 for the rules governing validity of trust purposes.
4. *Trust purposes which do not exhaust the trust estate*. See the following case:

Anderson v. Smoke
(1898) 25 R. 493

2.32   LORD YOUNG: "This case appears to me very clear. Mr Anderson created a trust for behoof of his son Archibald, about whom there seems to have been—at least in his father's opinion—some peculiarity which is not explained to us. Mr Anderson placed in the hands of his two daughters, Victoria and Alicia, as trustees, a sum of about £2000, to be administered 'for behoof of my son Archibald.' Then he directed them to pay to or for behoof of Archibald this money and any interest on it 'at such times and in such ways and sums as I may direct, and failing direction from me at such times and in such ways and sums as they, or the survivor of them, may think proper.' It is a typical trust direction, the immediate trust beneficiary being Archibald. The trustees might in their administration have exhausted the trust by giving the whole to Archibald if they had thought that proper or expedient. In point of fact they expended for him part of the fund, and when he died in July 1897 there remained £1000. Now the direction of the writing constituting the trust as to that case is, 'should the whole not be disposed of in the lifetime of Archibald, my said daughters may dispose of the balance in any way they should think proper.' We had a contention on that on the daughters' part. They said, 'that is equivalent to saying that if any balance remain after the purpose for Archibald is executed, I (the father) make a gift of it to Victoria and Alicia.' But he made no gift to them. He said to them, as trustees, that they were to dispose of it as they 'think proper'.

On the other hand, the executor of Archibald maintained that the 'disposal' belonged to the daughters but not the money, and that it belonged to him as representing Archibald, for whose behoof the daughters had it. I cannot so read the trust. It makes no gift to Archibald, but only says that the daughters are to pay to him as they think proper, and if any balance remains at his death they are to dispose of it as they think proper. This is no more a gift to Archibald than it is a gift to them. There is good authority, some of which was quoted to us, for the proposition that such a direction to dispose as they think proper is not a good and enforceable trust direction, and that the consequence is a resulting trust for the truster's heirs in intestacy or the residuary legatee under his will, if he has one. In this case these persons are designed in the will of Mr Anderson.

On these grounds I think that the balance of £1000 referred to in the case must be delivered over to the third parties, and that we should answer the question accordingly."

The Lord Justice-Clerk (Macdonald), Lord Trayner, and Lord Moncreiff concurred.

The Court found that the trustees whom Mr Anderson had appointed under his will were entitled to the £1000.

NOTES:

1. This decision may, perhaps, be open to question—or at least quibbling. It is well settled that **2.33** a direction to trustees to dispose of property "as they may think proper" is invalid (*Sutherland's Trustees v. Sutherland's Trustee* (1893) 20 R. 925, and see *infra* paras 5.04 *et seq.*). This is because it is inconsistent with the notion of trusteeship to confer such a wide discretion upon trustees. But do decisions such as *Sutherland* really apply to this scenario? Might Mr Anderson's directions not be interpreted as meaning that Victoria and Alicia— who were undoubtedly trustees before Archibald's death—were to cease to be trustees upon that event and take full ownership of the property themselves? To interpret them otherwise leaves his directions as incomplete, or a blunder, which is perhaps to be avoided. If, as was suggested earlier, the doctrine of resulting trust is based upon an assumption as to the truster's intention, is it fair to conclude that Mr Anderson would have intended the property to revert to his estate in this way? In any case, it should be clear that the problem which arose here can be avoided by better drafting.

2. Compare *Anderson* with the English case of *Re Foord* [1922] 2 Ch. 519, where the testator's will included the following direction: "All my effects including rubber and all other shares I leave absolutely to my sister Margaret Juliet on trust to pay to my wife per annum (three hundred pounds) with income tax, 100l. (one hundred pounds) to be free of income tax." Sargant J. held that this direction did not create a resulting trust for the balance of the estate after the annuity was paid, concluding that the will (just barely) indicated an intention on the part of the testator that the balance should go to the testator's sister. In doing so, he relied upon three factors: (1) the use of the word "absolutely"; (2) the reference to "my sister Margaret Juliet" rather than "Miss Foord", indicating a recognition of the relationship between them; and (3) the fact that the effects included property which would not produce income. See also *Croome v. Croome* (1888) 59 L.T. 582; (1889) 61 L.T. 814.

3. *How is it to be determined when trust purposes which have not exhausted the trust estate have failed?* The English courts have, on a number of occasions, been faced with trusts established for the education of children, who have gone on to complete their education without exhausting the trust funds. Is a resulting trust created in such a situation? They have consistently taken the view that a resulting trust is not created and that the children remain entitled to the balance of the trust funds. While this can perhaps be justified on a wide construction of the term "education" (*Re Andrew's Trust* [1905] 2 Ch. 48), such an approach

was more difficult in *Re Osoba (Deceased)* [1979] 1 W.L.R. 247, where the trust deed specifically referred to "the training of my daughter Abiola up to university grade". The Court of Appeal nevertheless held that no resulting trust had been created, with Goff L.J. describing the father's directions as (at 253) "a provision for her benefit, which ought to be treated as a gift with a superadded purpose, which should be disregarded". In such cases, a generous interpretation of the truster's intention is employed in order to avoid resort to the doctrine of resulting trust.

4. See also *Templeton v. Burgh of Ayr*, 1910 2 S.L.T. 12, where Templeton (who died in 1879) directed that his estate should be left to his sisters in liferent, and in fee to the "Provost and Town Council in trust, in order that they, or their successors in office, may use the whole thereof in rebuilding the Old Bridge of Ayr, when such a thing may be required". The last survivor of his sisters died in 1904 and the property was passed to the officers of the Burgh. The Town Council resolved in 1905 to take down the Old Bridge and renew it, but this plan met with public opposition and a Preservation Committee raised £10,000 by public subscription to restore and preserve the bridge. Mr Templeton's next of kin then raised an action against the Burgh, claiming that the trust purposes had failed and a resulting trust had been created in their favour. Lord Skerrington rejected their claim, observing (at 14) that:

"Seeing that it is admitted, and is indeed part of the pursuer's case, that the Old Bridge of Ayr was not rebuilt by the Preservation Committee, but on the contrary was only restored, I am unable to appreciate the argument that the trust for rebuilding the bridge has lapsed. No doubt the testator did not anticipate the course of events which has actually happened and which has postponed the necessity for rebuilding the bridge to an indefinite date, but the words of the will seem to me to apply and include the actual state of matters, and accordingly I assoilzie the defenders from the leading conclusion of the summons."

(c) The problem of public subscriptions

2.34 A problem may arise where individuals contribute money to a fund set up for charitable or similar purposes, and (a) the purposes are achieved without exhausting the fund; or (b) the purposes are rendered impossible, either because insufficient money is raised or for some other reason. In some circumstances, it may be possible to utilise the procedures for variation of trust purposes (see Chapter 12). However, that raises two questions: first, is it actually necessary to invoke these procedures? Second, if they are unavailable for whatever reason, what is to happen to the monies remaining in the fund? Consider the following two *dicta*:

Connell v. Ferguson
(1857) 19 D. 482

Lord Deas: "Where parties join in a subscription to effect a particular object, and place the money subscribed in the hands of certain persons to carry out that object, I think the *quasi* trust thereby created, is for the alternate purpose of either carrying out the object of the subscription, or, if that cannot be done, of paying back the money."

Trustees of Falkirk Certified Industrial School v. Ferguson Bequest Fund
(1899) 1 F. 1175

Lord McLaren: "I think it is consistent with the general understanding regarding subscriptions to societies for public purposes that money paid by a subscriber does not constitute a trust, but is a gift under conditions. That is a material difference, because if it did constitute a trust, then on the failure of the objects of the society the subscription would fall to be returned to the donor or to his representatives. But if such a subscription is a gift under conditions, then on the failure of the purposes of the society or the impossibility of giving effect to the conditions, the gift vests absolutely. I am far from saying that a gift may not be made in such terms as to constitute a trust, but I think that there are few societies which would be willing to accept subscriptions on a footing which would make every individual subscriber a truster, entitled to call the society to account, and would put upon the society the burden of discovering the donor or his heirs, if its objects became impossible. But as I have always thought the common law to be the quintessence of the common sense of mankind applied to the ordinary affairs of life, I can well understand that with regard to subscriptions to societies the general understanding that they are mere gifts may be taken to be the rule of law applicable to all cases where there is no special bargain."

NOTES:

1. Are these views reconcilable? Wilson and Duncan (at 6–54 to 6–56) suggest that they are, **2.35** drawing a distinction between a freestanding fund (where the subscriptions must be returned, assuming variation is unavailable) and subscriptions received by an existing society (which may be retained without resort to variation). It is not clear, however, why this should make any difference in principle and neither the authors nor—it is submitted—the cases which they cite offer any justification for such a distinction.

2. One might view the concepts which Lord Deas and Lord McLaren resort to with some suspicion. What, precisely, is a "*quasi* trust"? The term has been used from time to time in the case law, but it is not clear what (if anything) it denotes. (One might be mischievous—if, as has been suggested, liability for breach of a trust may be "*ex quasi delicto*", is liability for breach of *quasi* trust "*ex quasi quasi delicto*"?) Presumably either a trust exists, or it does not. And what is a "gift under conditions" in the sense that Lord McLaren uses that term?

3. It is suggested that the better view is that the matter is governed by the intention of the truster. Lord McLaren, it will be recalled, suggested that if the subscription "did constitute a trust, then on the failure of the objects of the society the subscription would fall to be returned to the donor or to his representatives". That proposition is incorrect once it has been accepted that the truster may exclude the operation of the doctrine of resulting trust, which is why the consequences of accepting that public subscriptions may constitute trusts may not be as far-reaching as Lord McLaren appears to fear. As has been observed in the English courts:

   > "It is inconceivable that any person paying for a concert ticket or placing a coin in a collecting-box presented to him in the street should have intended that any part of the money so contributed should be returned to him when the immediate object for which the concert was given or the collection made had come to an end. To draw such an inference would be absurd on the face of it." (*Re Welsh Hospital (Netley) Fund* [1921] 1 Ch. 655, *per* P.O. Lawrence J. at 660. See also *Re West Sussex Constabulary's Widows, Children and Benevolent (1930) Fund Trusts* [1971] Ch. 1, *per* Goff J. at 12.)

   It should be clear that the truster's intention in such a case is unlikely to vary according to whether he is contributing to a free-standing fund or an organisation which is already extant. The consequences may, however, differ. If the contribution is to an existing organisation, the fair conclusion is likely to be that the truster intended the money to vest absolutely in that organisation in the event of the specified purposes failing or the fund being over-subscribed. That result is consistent with Lord McLaren's comments in the *Falkirk Certified Industrial School* case, but it is based on giving effect to the truster's intention rather than the concept of a "gift under conditions" which his Lordship invokes. If the contribution is to a free-standing fund, then the consequence is likely to be that the funds fall to the Crown as *bona vacantia* (*Re West Sussex Constabulary's Widows, Children and Benevolent (1930) Fund Trusts* [1971] Ch. 1).

   However, where the gift is a larger one (or perhaps a smaller one for a particular purpose that is specifically recorded in a society's books), it will probably be both (a) easier to infer that the truster intended it should be returned in the event of the trust purposes failing, and (b) easier, as a practical matter, to return it.

4. The law is hardly in a clear and satisfactory state, however. The following recommendation of the Scottish Charity Law Review Commission should be noted:

CharityScotland:
The Report of the Scottish Charity Law Review Commission (2001)
para. 5.51

2.36 "Difficulties can arise when funds have been raised by way of public subscription or as a result of a public collection for purposes which either do not exhaust the fund or which cannot for any reason be carried out. For example, a collection may be mounted to purchase a specialist piece of equipment for disabled children. Once the purchase price of the equipment has been collected, any additional money is theoretically surplus to requirements. Normally, we would expect the Scottish Charity to use additional funds to purchase other equipment that might be required or provide another service for disabled children. There may be instances where this is not possible, for example if funds were raised to extend a cat and dog home and in the meantime, the home was left a legacy which made specific provision for the necessary building extension. In some cases, the funds can be applied to a different charitable purpose through use of the cy pres jurisdiction of the Court of Session but this may not be practical or possible. In such cases, it can be unclear what should happen to small or anonymous donations which cannot readily be returned to the owners. Where the funds have been raised for charitable or public benefit purposes, we consider that CharityScotland should have powers to authorise their transfer to a Scottish Charity with similar purposes."

The possibility of authorising a transfer to a charity with similar purposes would avoid the unsatisfactory solution of *bona vacantia*.

(d) The nature of the resulting trust

2.37 Although the resulting trust has been dealt with here under the heading of "legally implied trust", in common with the approach which is taken generally in the Scottish textbooks, it is far from clear that it is any such thing. If the view which has been taken here—that the doctrine is based upon giving effect to the intention of the truster—is accepted, then it would seem that a resulting trust is simply a voluntarily created trust like any other. That may involve invoking certain presumptions as to the truster's intention—which is why resulting trusts deserve special consideration—but it would probably be wrong to treat them as a distinct *form* of trust:

> "I think that in modern Scots usage a resulting trust is not a kind of trust but rather a term implied by law into all trusts, or at least all private trusts, whereby a contingent beneficial right is established in favour of the truster, the contingency being purified in the event of the failure of the trust purposes at a time when there are still trust assets. Thus it is not a type of trust but a term of a trust." (George L. Gretton, "Constructive Trusts" (1997) 1 Edin L.R. 281, 309–310).

B. Fiduciary fees

2.38 In considering involuntarily created trusts, a brief mention should be made of the oddity that is the "fiduciary fee".

George Gretton, *Trusts*, in Reid and Zimmerman (eds.),
A History of Private Law in Scotland, Vol. I (2000), p. 481, at 513:

"Curiously, one situation which perhaps should be classified as constructive trust has always been treated as a special doctrine. This is the doctrine in *Frog's Creditors v. His Children* [(1735) Mor. 4262] and *Newlands v. Newlands' Creditors* [(1794) Mor. 4289] in 1794. Some background is needed, and a curious background it is. In the eighteenth century—and perhaps before—it was often desired to convey property to X for his lifetime and then to his children. How could this be done? To convey to X with a destination (*i.e.* a *substitutio* to the children) was possible but capable of being defeated by 'evacuation'. A tailzie (entail) was possible but cumbersome, expensive and inflexible. The obvious solution, to a modern conveyancer, would be to dispone to trustees to hold for X in liferent (usufruct) and to the children in fee. What is curious and instructive is that this solution seems simply not to have occurred to eighteenth-century conveyancers. They attempted a direct conveyance to X in liferent and to his children in fee. But that obviously could not work, since the owners were at the time of the conveyance indeterminate. When I write 'obviously' I hope I am not being anachronistic, but surely even at that period the impossibility was clear enough. What happened if the attempt was made? In the leading case of *Frog's Creditors v. His Children* it was held that the effect was to give ownership to X. Undeterred, and rather like lemmings, conveyancers continued, but now added the word 'allernally' [meaning 'only'] to the liferent. The courts decided that the word had to be given effect to. But it was still obvious that 'a fee cannot be *in pendente*' to use the traditional maxim. So in *Newlands* it was held that the effect would be to give *dominium* to X (and to that extent following *Frog*) but subject to what was a sort of trust to hold for himself in liferent and his children in fee. This was called the doctrine of the 'fiduciary fee'. One might argue that this was best classed as implied *fideicommissum*. But nobody did. I speak in the past tense, because such conveyances are never now used, but the rule in *Newlands* in fact eventually received statutory blessing and is in substance still law."

NOTES:

1. The statutory provision referred to by Gretton is section 8 of the Trusts (Scotland) Act 1921, **2.39** which provides as follows:

   "Where, in any deed, whether *inter vivos* or *mortis causa*, heritable or moveable property is conveyed to any person in liferent, and in fee to persons who, when such conveyance comes into operation, are unborn or incapable of ascertainment, the person to whom the property is conveyed in liferent shall not be deemed to be beneficially entitled to the property in fee by reason only that the liferent is not expressed in the deed to be a liferent allernaly; and all such conveyances as aforesaid shall, unless a contrary intention appears in the deed, take effect in the same manner and in all respects as if the liferent were declared to be a liferent allernaly."

2. It should be noted that this not only gives "statutory blessing" to *Newlands*, but also overrules *Frog* so that a fiduciary fee is created whether or not the word "allernaly" is used. It is slightly defective in this respect, however, as Sheriff Dobie has pointed out:

   "The section is limited, however, to cases in which, on the liferent opening, the fiars are unborn or incapable of ascertainment, and thus it does not affect a conveyance to a woman in liferent and her unnamed children in fee, if, when the liferent opened, she has a family but is past the age of child-bearing, and nothing precludes the ascertainment at that date of the fiars. This presents the anomaly that, if at the commencement of the liferent, the fiars are not ascertainable, a fiduciary fee will be held for them by virtue of this section, under the rule in *Newlands*, but if the fiars are ascertained but unnamed the case falls back into the rule in *Frog*, and the liferenter takes the full fee, the children having only a *spes successionis*." (Wm. Jardine Dobie, *Manual of the Law of Liferent and Fee in Scotland* (1941), p. 34).

3. As with resulting trusts, the status of a fiduciary fee as a "legally implied" trust may be doubted—although it is generally treated as such in the textbooks. It might be argued that the fiduciary fee is really a voluntarily created trust which arises from construing the truster's intention so as to avoid the impossibility of the fee being *in pendente*.

4. For a detailed treatment of the law governing fiduciary fees, see Wilson and Duncan, paras 6–01 to 6–21. See also Mackenzie Stuart, pp. 38–42.

C. Constructive trusts

(a) To what extent does Scots law recognise constructive trusts?

2.40   "There is a great deal to be proud of in Scots law, but also, alas, much not to be proud of. One may be proud of the way in which Scots law has been able to absorb and develop the trust without damage to the basic principles of property law, and without adopting English conceptions of equity. But when one turns to the constructive trust, all is confusion." (George L Gretton, "Constructive Trusts and Insolvency" (2000) 8 E.R.P.L. 463, at 466).

One might, at first sight, wonder whether the picture is really so confused. A glance at Wilson and Duncan (para. 6–61) suggests that the situation is quite straightforward:

"The situations in which a constructive trust arises fall into two main categories:

     (i)   where a person in a fiduciary position gains an advantage by virtue of that position;

     (ii)   where a person who is a stranger to an existing trust is to his knowledge in possession of property belonging to the trust."

Norrie and Scobbie (at p. 54) also adopt this classification, and note that is has been "accepted by the courts", citing *Black v. Brown*, 1982 S.L.T. (Sh. Ct) 50. There is, perhaps, also some implicit acceptance of the classification in *Raymond Harrison & Co's Tr. v. North West Securities Ltd*, 1989 S.L.T. 718, *per* Lord Clyde at 722. But both of these authorities simply refer in passing to Wilson and Duncan's classification, rather than analysing it in any way. It may be useful to consider whether these two categorisations can be justified by reference to the cases which are generally cited to support them.

(i) Where a person in a fiduciary position gains an advantage by virtue of that position

Cherry's Trs v. Patrick
1911 2 S.L.T. 313

2.41   LORD ORMIDALE: "That the defender supplied goods as a wholesale dealer to the Coatbridge and Main Street businesses just as he had done in Mr Cherry's lifetime is admitted. That he charged 'management expenses' is not disputed.

     The defender avers and maintains that this was done with the knowledge and approval of his fellow-trustees, and in accordance with an arrangement come to with them at a meeting held on 4th January 1907. Whether such an arrangement could be enforced against a trust estate it is not necessary, in the view I take of the evidence, to consider, for I am unable to hold that any such arrangement is proved. But it seems to me that if any beneficiary, or any one else having an interest to do so, were to challenge an arrangement according to which one of several trustees was enabled to make a profit on the sale of goods to the trust, it would be no answer for him to say that he had the consent of his co-trustees to his doing so, and that the profit he made was less than what any other trader would be content to make. His primary duty as a trustee is to the trust, and the law will not permit him to place himself in such a position that his duty as a trustee may conflict with his self-interest. For him to manage the businesses of the trust and to take payment for so doing, either directly or indirectly, when he might have employed others to manage it, also offends against a well-established rule of trust law. He would probably be entitled to recover actual outlays, but he could not charge anything more against the trust estate unless he had the warrant of the truster for so doing. If the defender here had been appointed the paid manager or factor by the trustees in terms of the power conferred upon them by Mr Cherry's trust disposition, then no one could have challenged his taking payment for his management, but he has, in my opinion, failed altogether to prove that he was so appointed. . ."

On the whole matter, my view is that the defender has so conducted the affairs of the trust in relation to his own dealings with it, viz. the supplying of goods, as to take a benefit to himself, that he was not warranted in doing so, and that he must communicate the benefit to the trust. The actual figure in money has been adjusted by the parties, and is £291, 9s. 6¹/₂d. And, further, he took payment for doing work for the trust which, being a trustee, he was not entitled to charge against the trust estate."

George L. Gretton, "Constructive Trusts"
(1997) 1 Edin L.R. 281, 294

"Another case frequently cited as one of constructive trust is *Cherry's Trs v. Patrick*, where a **2.42** trustee who had traded with the trust was held liable to pay the trust the profits he had made. I would not question the decision, but where is the trust? What is the fund which is constructively held in trust? Indeed, there is no mention of constructive trust in the case at all. Finally, there is no insolvency. The case seems a very simple one of breach of fiduciary duty with a consequent obligation to pay. That is not a trust. (Of course, it all depends on what you mean by trust. "Trust" is indeed a word which has been used in a multitude of senses. But it is generally taken to imply a separate estate or asset fund with its own group identity, separate from the general assets of the trustee, and which is in principle exempt from the attentions of the ordinary creditors of the trustee, in his private capacity. I do not offer this as a definition, but as a sketch I hope it would be regarded as uncontroversial.)"

NOTES:

1. For similar treatments of some of the other cases commonly cited as examples of this type of constructive trust, see *ibid.* at pp. 292–299, and George Gretton, "Constructive Trusts and Insolvency" (2000) 8 E.R.P.L. 463, at 467–469.
2. A person in a fiduciary position will normally be liable in damages if he breaches his fiduciary duty. But cases such as *Cherry's Trs* (of which there are many), although they are clear examples of such liability, do not establish that such liability arises in the form of a constructive trust. Whether or not the liability takes such form will generally be irrelevant, except where the fiduciary has become insolvent. In that situation, if the liability is in trust, then the beneficiary's right is protected from the claims of other creditors. If it is not a liability in trust, then the beneficiary must compete with the other creditors for satisfaction of his claim. As noted earlier (*supra* para. 1.01), it is this protection from insolvency more than anything else which is the defining feature of the trust.
3. Perhaps the only clearly valid example of a constructive trust of this type can be found in the following case:

Sutnam International Inc. v. Herbage
Outer House, August 2, 1991, *unreported*
(noted at 1991 G.W.D. 30–1772)

Heritable property in Inverness-shire was in 1984 disponed to a husband and wife (the first **2.43** and second defenders in this action). The husband and wife had been appointed directors of Sutnam in 1981. Sutnam and its liquidator now alleged that the husband and wife had bought the Inverness-shire property with funds which had been embezzled from Sutnam. The husband was now insolvent.

Sutnam and the liquidator brought an action against the husband and wife and the husband's trustee in bankruptcy in the Court of Session. They sought a declarator that they were the "true beneficial owners" of the Inverness-shire property, and a decree ordaining the defenders to transfer the property to them.

LORD CULLEN: "As regards the relevancy and specification of the pursuers' case, counsel for the second defender submitted that the pursuers had failed to set out facts and circumstances on the basis of which it could be concluded that the subjects were truly the property of Sutman and hence were held by the first and second defenders under a constructive trust. The mere fact that money of Sutman had been used to purchase them was not enough. The pursuers did not aver that the transactions were ultra vires of Sutman by reference to its memorandum of association. It was not self evident that any question of breach of fiduciary duty arose. Further explanation was required. If the sole directors were in agreement as to what was done, this was evidence of Sutman's agreement. The pursuers had not made a frank response to the second defenders' averment that the first and second defenders at the material time 'held the whole beneficial interest in the whole shareholding in' Sutman and 'the whole beneficial interests in the whole shareholdings of the other companies in the group'.

As regards the mode of proof, counsel submitted that the Act 1696 c25 [the "Blank Bonds and Trusts Act"] applied. The action was in substance a declarator of trust. Each of [the] dispositions was a 'deed of trust'. Further it fell to be inferred that absolute title had been taken with the consent of Sutman, the alleged trustee. On the last point, the fact that the first and second defenders were the sole directors and had sole management and control of Sutman indicated prima facie that Sutman consented, at least in the absence of any proposition to the contrary. There was no averment of any fraud on Sutman. Even if there were adequate averments of breach of fiduciary duty it was disputed that their existence would be adequate to elide to application of the statute.

In reply counsel for the pursuers submitted that the second defender had not shown that if the pursuers established all their averments they would be bound to fail, which was the appropriate test to be applied. In the light of the pursuers' averments as to the drawing of the cheques on Sutman's account, the purchase of the subjects by means of them, the taking of title in name of the first and second defenders; and their averments that the second defender had shown two of the cheques in Sutman's books and had not contributed any value to the purchase price of the subjects, the Court was entitled to conclude that this was a case in which there was an invalid application of company funds in circumstances giving rise to a constructive trust.

As regards the mode of proof, counsel for the pursuers submitted that the statute did not apply in respect that the present action was not a declarator of trust. It arose out of the abuse of the fiduciary duties owed by the first and second defenders to Sutman. Further the Act did not apply to a case such as the present where the defender had acted in breach of his duty to the pursuer and accordingly it could not be said that the pursuer had agreed to the property being taken in name of the defender. A number of cases were referred to in this connection, including *Horne v. Morrison* (1877) 4 R. 977. In that case the pursuer alleged that the defender, his co-adventurer, had, contrary to instructions, taken the title to heritage belonging to the joint adventurers in his own name. It was held that in respect that the pursuer averred that he had not trusted the defender to take the title in his own name, the Act 1696, c25 did not apply and that the pursuer was entitled to prove his averments *prout de jure*. At page 979 Lord President Inglis said 'The statute only applies when one man alleges that he has trusted another to take a title in his own name'. He went on to say: 'As to necessity for alleging fraud, I do not see that fraud is required. The missive might have been taken carelessly, foolishly, in good faith, and yet there might be a relevant allegation that it was taken in the agent's name instead of in the joint name of the pursuer and defender. Having taken the disposition in his own name the fraud would consist in the defence of this action.' Lord Deas observed that the case did not raise the question of trust but an ordinary question of mandate 'Just as if a law-agent were verbally authorised to go to a public sale and purchase an estate for a client, and nothing was said as to the name in which the purchase should be made. The agent might, in such a case, purchase the estate in his own name, and afterwards become a consenting party to a disposition being granted to his client. That is a very common mode of acting. But if the agent should take it into his head to say that he had made the purchase for himself, that would raise a mere question of verbal mandate, which might be proved *prout de jure*'. A constructive trust fell to be clearly distinguished from what was merely a matter of personal obligation. Reference was made on this point to *Bank of Scotland v. Liquidators of Hutchison, Main and Company Limited* 1914 S.C. (H.L.) 1, per Lord Shaw of Dunfermline at page 15. Having regard to the separate persona of the company the pursuers' averments should not be read as indicating that Sutman had consented. As regards the use of the funds of Sutman, reference was made to *Ridge Securities Limited v. Inland Revenue Commissioners* [1964] 1 All E.R. 275, [1964] 1 W.L.R. 479 in which so-called 'interest' payments which in fact represented a gratuitous disposition of a company's assets were held to be *ultra vires*. At page 495 Pennycuick J said: 'A company can only lawfully deal with its assets in furtherance of its objects. The corporators may take assets out of the company by way of dividend or, with leave of the Court, by way of reduction of capital, or in a winding up. They may, of course, acquire them for full consideration. They cannot take assets out of the company by way of voluntary disposition, however described, and, if they attempt to do so, the disposition is ultra vires the company'. It would follow that it would be a breach of their fiduciary duty for directors to apply the assets of the company in this way. If there were special circumstances which justified title being taken in the name of directors, this would require particular authorisation and the Act might then apply. It was pointed out that in connection with a call which the pursuers had made on the second and third defenders, they had denied that Sutman had authorised the first and second defenders to take title to the subjects in their names.

I am of opinion that the pursuers have set out averments which prima facie would, if proved, entitle them to the remedy which they seek. From their averments it appears that the first defender, with the knowledge and co-operation of the second defender, appropriated substantial funds of Sutman and applied them in the purchase of heritable property in the names of the first and second defenders absolutely. Against the background of the law as to the proper application of company assets, the pursuers are, in my opinion entitled to treat these averments as founding more than a mere speculation that the assets of Sutman have been misapplied. I accept that they are sufficient to instruct the inference that such misapplication has occurred, in the absence of any good explanation to the contrary, and accordingly that the pursuers are the true beneficial owners of the subjects. In these circumstances I am satisfied that the pursuers have averred sufficient to justify inquiry. As regards the mode of proof on any inquiry I reject the second defender's argument that the Act 1696, c25 applies. I am satisfied that the Act does not apply to the one and only case which the pursuers seek to make."

Proof before answer allowed.

NOTES:

1. The language of this case is confusing, particularly the suggestion that Sutnam might be the **2.44** "true beneficial owners" of the property—a concept which might be considered alien to Scots law (but *cf.* the almost identical—and probably equally objectionable—use of terminology in Enid Marshall, *General Principles of Scots Law* (7th ed., 1999), para. 15–01). In substance, however, the pursuers appear to have been seeking a declarator that they were the beneficiaries in a constructive trust of which the first two defenders were trustees, and that the trust asset was the Inverness-shire property.

2. Even those who dispute the existence of the constructive trust in Scots law would not dispute that Sutnam should (and would) have a remedy against the two directors, assuming that their averments could be substantiated at proof. That much is uncontroversial. It is the *nature* of the remedy that is important, given the insolvency of one of the directors. For if the remedy is based upon the general law of obligations, Sutnam would have to compete with his other creditors for satisfaction of their claim. But if the remedy is by way of constructive trust, then their claim will be satisfied in full (to the detriment, it will be observed, of all the other creditors). So a constructive trust gives the pursuers priority in insolvency, while other remedies do not. But what is the justification for granting such priority? Why should Sutnam be regarded as more deserving than other creditors?

(ii) "Where a person who is a stranger to an existing trust is to his knowledge in possession of property belonging to the trust."

2.45 In the brief discussion of this type of constructive trust in Wilson and Duncan (paras 6–65 to 6–68), it is instructive that only two Scottish decisions are cited, and in one of those (*Raymond Harrison & Co's Tr. v. North West Securities Ltd*, 1989 S.L.T. 718) it was held that no constructive trust existed. That leaves the following case:

Huisman v. Soepboer
1994 S.L.T. 682

Roelof Huisman raised an action seeking decree for payment jointly and severally against (first) Taekele Soepboer and (second) Highland Holidays (Strathnairn) Ltd of his share of the profit of a joint venture involving himself and two other individuals, Soepboer and Kooistra. The joint venture had involved the purchase of a farm and its subsequent resale with the profit being shared equally. The pursuer averred that Soepboer had concealed part of the price achieved on the resale and that it had been understood that Soepboer would take the title to the farm in his own name but that, unknown to Kooistra and the pursuer, title had been taken by the second defenders, a company with 150,000 issued shares of which Soepboer owned 149,999, and of which he was the sole director. The pursuer further averred: "The second defenders thus took title to the farm in the knowledge that it was the subject of the said agreement among the pursuer, Kooistra and the first defender and in the knowledge of the terms of that agreement. They thus held it on behalf of those parties and are liable to make payment in terms of that agreement."

In seeking dismissal of the action on procedure roll the defender argued that there was no basis for a joint and several decree against both defenders. The defenders argued that the pursuer's pleadings, and in particular his plea in law, perilled his case on an agreement but the agreement averred was an agreement involving the pursuer, Kooistra and Soepboer to which there was no plea or averment linking the company. In repelling that argument and allowing a proof before answer the Lord Ordinary (Coulsfield) said:

> "The pursuer's reply to this argument was, in my opinion, clear and convincing. It was pointed out that the case was that there was a joint venture and that, if the first defender had taken the title in his own name, he would have done so on a fiduciary basis, on behalf of the joint venture. In fact the second defenders had acquired title, but the first defender was their only director and they acquired the title in the knowledge that it was subject to the joint venture agreement. Their acquisition was not, therefore, in good faith. Where a partner handed over partnership property to another who did not take it in good faith both were liable. Reference was made to Wilson and Duncan on Trusts, p. 77, Stair Memorial Encyclopaedia, Vol 24, para. 30 and *Soar v. Ashwell* [1893] 2 QB 390. In my view, these submissions are well founded. There are ample averments that the second defenders took the title in the knowledge that it was subject to the conditions of the joint venture. It is clear, in particular from the opinions in Soar, that in such a case there may be a constructive trust and the constructive trustee may be liable jointly and severally with the partner."

George L. Gretton, "Constructive Trusts"
(1997) 1 Edin L.R. 281, 300

2.46 "*Huisman v. Soepboer* was a case in which it was held that there was a constructive trust, and it has been regarded as a case which arose from the alienation of trust assets to a person taking in bad faith and thus as a constructive trustee. But that analysis strikes me as doubtful, and indeed I doubt whether trust of any sort was involved in this case. A, B and C agreed to buy and later sell a property, sharing any profit made. Title was to be taken in the name of A, but in fact A took title in the name of A Ltd, a company he controlled. A Ltd resold at a profit. B successfully sued A and A Ltd jointly and severally for his share of the profit. I cannot see from the report that there existed at any stage any express trust. A Ltd was thus not a bad faith recipient of trust property. Moreover, no attempt was made to claim any trust property, and so far as I can see there was no trust property to claim. The action was purely for payment of a debt. Hence I do not regard this case as one of constructive trust arising out of bad faith receipt of trust property. It is true that the learned Lord Ordinary uses the term 'constructive trust', but it seems to me that he does not mean 'trust'. There was no insolvency and therefore no proper contradictor to challenge any finding of trust. There is no suggestion that there was any trust fund. The liability here was, it seems to me, exclusively part of the law of obligations. But the case is an alarming one, for it illustrates forcibly the precipice at the edge of which we stand. The learned Lord Ordinary relied much on *Soar v. Ashwell*, a case which has indeed been too frequently cited in Scotland. In *Soar* trustees gave trust funds to their solicitor to invest. He failed to return part of the funds, and after his death they sued his executor for the balance. It was held that the solicitor was to be regarded as a constructive trustee. But why? The decision seems to emerge from the Delphic mysteries of the equity/law divide. For some reason the trustees had no action 'in law', so they had to sue 'in equity'. The obligation to repay was not a legal obligation but an equitable one, and so the truster was bound to 'account as a trustee'. I am baffled as to how a case like *Soar*, relevant only to a system which divides law and equity, could have acquired any sort of currency here. But as I have said, the story illustrates the dangers. A few more cases like *Huisman* and we can turn out the lights. Of course, the fault lies with us, the academics. We have failed to give the needed guidance."

(b) The expansionist view of the constructive trust

It has occasionally been argued that the constructive trust could be used to accord rights to cohabiting **2.47** couples. For the detail of this argument, the reader is referred to Alida Wilson, "The Constructive Trust in Scots Law", 1993 J.R. 99, and the article by Norrie excerpted below. The authority for such use of the constructive trust in Scots law is slim if not non-existent (although *cf. McDougall v. McDougall*, 1947 S.N. 1102), although that is not to say that it would not be open to the courts to develop the law along these lines. The following excerpts are concerned more with the desirability of such a development in principle.

Kenneth McK. Norrie, "Proprietary Rights of Cohabitants"
1995 Jur.Rev. 209, 225

"To the above argument [in favour of such a use of constructive trusts], there are at least **2.48** two counter-considerations, but neither, it is submitted, is strong enough to fully answer its thrust. First, some couples deliberately choose cohabitation to avoid the proprietary consequences of marriage. To this we may answer that such couples are unlikely to be fiduciaries to each other and in any case the availability of cohabitation contracts will remain to those who want to control the consequences of their own relationships. Secondly, Scots law has always placed high importance on the security of property transactions, and to recognise that the court has the common law right to alter property ownership by means of constructive trust clearly compromises that security. Whether that price is worth paying is a debate that this article is designed to stimulate."

George L. Gretton, "Constructive Trusts and Insolvency"
(2000) 8 E.R.P.L. 463, 473

"In the common law world there has been a strong tendency to say that if two people **2.49** cohabit in a sexual relationship—married or unmarried, heterosexual or homosexual—and one of them is the owner of the shared home, then that home may be (depending on the circumstances) deemed to be held in constructive trust for the other, in some proportion, such as 50%. The issue is one which arises on the breakdown of the relationship. It is less likely to be pled if the parties are married, for in that case divorce law will (usually) bring about a fair sharing of property. But here, as so often in the field of constructive trusts, two different issues are muddled up. The first issue is whether, on the failure of a sexual relationship, one party should be entitled to money (or property) from the other. The second is whether that claim should be privileged in the event of the insolvency of the second party. Many people would agree that the first is reasonable. But the first does not imply the second. In the common law world it implies the second only by a mere accident, namely that the only mechanism identified for the first result is the constructive trust. It leads to the strange result that the ex-lover is likely to be in a *better* position than the spouse who is claiming money (or property) in a divorce action, for the claims of a spouse are subject to the claims of creditors. Thus, whilst both ex-lover and spouse will be subject to a debt secured over the defendant's house, if the debt is unsecured the ex-lover is likely to prevail (because she may be the beneficiary of a constructive trust) whereas the spouse will not. As a matter of public policy this is absurd.

Happily Scots law has not, so far at least, turned ex-lovers into constructive trustees."

NOTES:

2.50
    1. Would such a use of constructive trusts really put an ex-lover in a better position than the divorcing spouse? If an ex-lover can claim that a constructive trust exists for his benefit, then presumably the divorcing spouse is equally entitled to do so (and, indeed, would probably have a stronger case). That, of course, does not explain why *either* the ex-lover or the divorcing spouse should be accorded a priority in insolvency, but it is, with respect, not clear that the use of the constructive trust in this way would lead to the absurdity which Gretton claims.
    2. The objection raised by Gretton does not, of course, apply to non-trust remedies. For a recent example of the use of unjustified enrichment remedies in this context, see *Shilliday v. Smith*, 1998 S.C. 725, discussed by Janeen Carruthers, "Unjustified Enrichment and the Family: Re-visiting the Remedies" (2000) 5(1) S.L.P.Q. 58; W.D.H. Sellar, "*Shilliday v. Smith*: Unjust Enrichment through the Looking Glass?" (2001) 5(1) Edin L.R. 80.

(c) Does Scots law recognise or need the constructive trust?

2.51 Two propositions should be clear from the above discussion of constructive trusts. Firstly, the device is problematic in that it creates a priority in insolvency without any apparent justification for doing so. Secondly, the authority for the existence of the constructive trust in Scots law is scant indeed.

Does Scots law actually *need* the constructive trust? Gretton, on the basis of extensive research, has suggested that there may only be four decisions of the Scottish courts which are genuine cases of constructive trust. (George L. Gretton, "Constructive Trusts" (1997) 1 Edin L.R. 281, 302–303). Two of these cases (*Macadam v. Martin's Tr.* (1872) 11 M. 33 and *Jopp v. Johnston's Tr.* (1904) 6 F. 1028) involve solicitors who had received client funds for investment, but had in fact banked the funds in their own name instead. The solicitors died insolvent. It was held that the clients were entitled to the funds in full. Gretton suggests that these cases might be examples of constructive trust, or perhaps an implied voluntary trust. But it is not clear that it is necessary to rely on either of these concepts, for one might argue that when a solicitor who accepts money for a client for the purposes of investment, there is quite clearly an express voluntary trust. Indeed, Lord Ardmillan in particular in *Macadam* appears to accept as much. *Jopp*, however, is less clear, and the Lord Justice-Clerk (Macdonald) makes the rather confusing statement that "[i]t is no doubt true that Mr Johnston was not in the strict sense of the word Mrs Jopp's trustee. He was undoubtedly, while he held the money, under the obligations of trust, the obligation to hold it for another and to deal with it solely for that other's interest." But what is this supposed to mean? How can someone who is not a trustee come "under the obligations of trust"? And if these cases are not cases of express voluntary trust, what are the policy arguments for according such clients a priority over other creditors in the event of their solicitor's insolvency, particularly given the modern protections of the Guarantee Fund and professional indemnity insurance? (Solicitors (Scotland) Act 1980, ss.43–44).

That leaves us with two other cases: *Smith v. Liquidator of James Birrell Ltd*, 1968 S.L.T. 174–a case where the facts giving rise to the trust are unclear and the point was not fully argued—and *Sutnam International Inc v. Herbage*, 1991 G.W.D. 30–1772 (*supra*, para. 2.43), which is perhaps the only clear case of constructive trust in Scots law. And as noted earlier, the argument for recognising a constructive trust in the *Sutnam* scenario is weak indeed. All of which, perhaps, points towards the conclusion (reached by Gretton) that Scots law should abolish the constructive trust rather than extend it.

Chapter 3

PARTIES AND PROPERTY

1. WHO MAY BE A TRUSTER?

This is essentially a question of capacity to deal with property, rather than of any special rule of the law of trusts.

A. Mackenzie Stuart *The Law of Trusts* (1932), p. 49

3.01 "Every person who has a right in property of which he can dispose, may constitute a trust in respect of such property to the extent of his right. The test of power to make a trust is the extent of the power of disposal."

NOTES:

1. Why should the "extent of the power of disposal" be the test of "power to make a trust"? At first sight, this seems logical—A cannot convey property to B in trust unless A has the power to dispose of that property. But it must be remembered that a truster does not have to convey property to another person to create a trust, because it is perfectly competent for a person to declare himself as trustee of his own property (see *supra* paras 2.25 *et seq.*). This is a minor point, but it may be of importance where a person wishes to make himself trustee of property which he cannot assign (such as non-assignable contractual rights). This issue is discussed later in the context of the property which may be subject to a trust. (See *infra* paras 3.07 *et seq.*)

2. Both legal and natural persons may create a trust.

3. *Children*. A child under the age of 16 has no legal capacity to enter into any transaction, unless it is a transaction "of a kind commonly entered into by persons of his age and circumstances", "on terms which are not unreasonable". (Age of Legal Capacity (Scotland) Act 1991, ss.1(1)(a) and 2(1)). Children under 16 cannot, therefore, generally be trusters. It should be noted that where a child over the age of 16 but under the age of 18 enters into a transaction, they may apply to the court to have that transaction set aside for so long as they remain under the age of 21 (1991 Act, s.3).

    However, children over the age of 12 do have testamentary capacity, and a child over that age may therefore write a will and be truster in a *mortis causa* (testamentary) trust (1991 Act, s.2(2)).

4. *The Crown*. The Crown can convey property into a trust (Crown Private Estates Act 1862, s.6).

5. *Disabilities*. Wilson and Duncan note (para. 2–01) that "No disability now attaches to married women, bastards, aliens or criminals."

2. WHO MAY BE A TRUSTEE?

John McLaren (Lord McLaren),
Law of Wills and Succession (3rd ed., 1894), Vol. II, para. 1618

"It may be affirmed as a general principle that the law of Scotland imposes no restrictions **3.02** on the power of the subject to accept a trust and to execute its purposes, excepting such as arise from the incapacity of the grantee, or the illegality of the purposes of the conveyance. It is no disqualification that the trustee takes a beneficiary interest under the instrument declaring the trust; indeed, if beneficiaries were held to be disqualified from acting as trustees, it would be impossible in many cases to obtain the services of persons willing to undertake the responsibilities of the office."

NOTES:

1. This reflects a principle enunciated by Chitty J. in *Tempest v. Lord Camoys* (1888) 58 L.T. **3.03** (N.S.) 221, at 223 (curiously, far more often quoted in the Scottish literature than the English) to the effect that where a truster selects a trustee "he is first of all free from every rule which operates on a court of justice. He can select any person he chooses of whatever character." Note, however, that specific restrictions do exist in relation to charitable trusts (*infra* para. 11.11) and pension trusts (Pensions Act 1995, ss.3–6 and 29–30). See also Finance Act 1989, Sched. 5, para. 3(3)(c) (employee share ownership trusts) and Inheritance Tax Act 1984, Sched. 4, para. 2(ii) (maintenance funds for historic buildings where exemption from inheritance tax is sought).

2. Lord McLaren's general principle is question-begging. If Scots law recognises such restrictions "as arise from the incapacity of the grantee", then what restrictions are these? A number of (possible) restrictions fall to be considered, as follows:

3. *Children.* At common law, a pupil (a male under fourteen or a girl under twelve) could not be a trustee, but a minor child (a person under the age of eighteen but above the age of a pupil) could. See *Hill v. City of Glasgow Bank* (1879) 7 R. 68, *per* the Lord President (Inglis) at 74–75. The matter is now regulated by the Age of Legal Capacity (Scotland) Act 1991. The provisions noted *supra*, para. 3.01, which regulate the capacity of children under 18 to enter into transactions apply equally to acting as a trustee (1991 Act, s.9(f)). Accordingly children under 16 cannot normally be trustees and, while a child between the ages of 16 and 18 can be a trustee, this would be subject to the court's power to set aside as prejudicial any transactions which they enter into during that period. (As to whether these provisions preclude a court from holding that a child is a trustee on a resulting or constructive trust, *cf. Re Vinogradoff* [1935] W.N. 68).

   If it is intended to appoint a person as executor under a will, and that person is still a child when the will is drawn up, it may be desirable for their appointment to be stated as being conditional upon their having attained the age of legal capacity (or the age of eighteen) at the time of the testator's death. See Barr *et al.*, *Drafting Wills in Scotland* (1994), paras 3.13 and 3.27.

4. *Insolvency.* Bankruptcy or insolvency does not render a person incapable of acting as a trustee, nor is it (in itself) sufficient ground for removal of a trustee by the court. (See Menzies, paras 77 and 913 and cases cited there). Note, however, that an undischarged bankrupt may not act as a trustee in a charitable trust: Law Reform (Miscellaneous Provisions) (Scotland) Act 1990, s.8, *infra* para. 11.11.

5. *Criminal guilt.* Conviction of a criminal offence does not affect a person's capacity to be a trustee. It is commonly stated that a conviction for high treason forms a "definite disqualification for trusteeship" (Wilson and Duncan, para. 18–14 and McLaren, para. 1628), but that rule may rest on the now superseded sentence of forfeiture of property in treason cases, whereby a person convicted of high treason was rendered incapable of holding property (see *McKenzie v. McDonald* (1736) 1 Elch. "Trust", No. 4). It should be noted, however, that a person convicted of an offence of dishonesty may not act as a trustee in a charitable trust: Law Reform (Miscellaneous Provisions) (Scotland) Act 1990, s.8, *infra* para. 11.11.

   The fact that someone is serving a sentence of imprisonment may, as a practical matter, prevent them from accepting office as a trustee. (See Menzies, para. 70, but *cf.* Wilson and

Duncan, para. 18–14, note 40 where, it is submitted, Menzies' use of the word "convict" is misinterpreted). A conviction for a criminal offence may be a ground for applying to the court for removal of a trustee. On removal generally, see *infra* paras 4.22 *et seq.*

6. *Residence abroad or foreign nationality.* These are not disqualifications, although foreign nationals may be disqualified from holding certain property (ships and aircraft) in the U.K., which would make it impossible to act as a trustee. See Wilson and Duncan, paras 18–15 and 18–16. Residence abroad is not generally a disqualification but may be a ground for removal of a trustee by the court. See *infra* para. 4.22. It may, however, be made a ground of disqualification in certain special types of trust: see Bankruptcy (Scotland) Act 1985, s.24(2)(d) (permanent trustee in bankruptcy); Finance Act 1989, Sched. 5, para. 3 (employee share ownership trusts).

7. *The Crown.* It is accepted that the Crown may be a trustee. (See McLaren, II, para. 1619; *McKenzie v. McDonald* (1736) 1 Elch. "Trust", No. 4; *Civilian War Claimants Association Ltd v. R.* [1932] A.C. 14, *per* Lord Atkin at 27). There are two particular problems here, however. Firstly, there is the difficulty of enforcing the trust due to the Crown's immunity in legal proceedings. This difficulty has, however, been at least partly removed by the Crown Proceedings Act 1947, although it remains impossible for the court to interdict the Crown or order specific performance. Secondly, it may be difficult as a practical matter to prove that the Crown has accepted a legally enforceable obligation. The English courts have accepted that, even where the Crown declares that it acts as trustee, a distinction must be drawn between "trusts in the lower sense" and "trusts in the higher sense". While the former is a true trust and enforceable by the courts, the latter is a governmental obligation and is not enforceable. For discussion, see *Tito v. Waddell (No. 2)* [1977] Ch. 106.

8. *Foreign governments.* It appears that a foreign government may be a trustee: *Re Robinson* [1931] 2 Ch. 122.

9. *Insanity.* An insane person cannot accept the office of trustee. In *Laidlaw* (1882) 10 R. 130, a *curator bonis* was granted authority to resign two trusteeships on behalf of his ward, who had become incapable after accepting office. Insanity is a ground for removal of a trustee by the court: see *infra* para. 4.22.

10. *The truster.* It is perfectly competent for a truster to also hold the office of trustee. (See, for examples, the cases on how a trust is to be created where the truster and trustee are the same person, cited at paras 2.25 *et seq. supra*). If, however, a sole trustee becomes sole beneficiary, the trust will become extinguished by the doctrine of confusion.

11. *Ex officio trustees.* Rather than nominating a particular individual as trustee, the truster may nominate the holder of a specified office as trustee. In such a case, the position of trustee attaches to the office and not to the individual. However, because no-one can be obliged to accept the position of a trustee (see *infra* para. 4.06), it may be that the original or subsequent office-holders refuse to accept the position. This will not, however, bar their successors in office from assuming the trusteeship (*Mags. of Edinburgh v. McLaren* (1881) 8 R. (H.L.) 140). The need to re-convey any heritable property held by the trust each time the office-holder changes may be avoided by reliance on certain statutory provisions (Conveyancing (Scotland) Act 1874, s.45 and Titles to Land Consolidation (Scotland) Act 1868, s.26).

12. *Mortis causa trusts and the "unworthy heir".* It has been held that a person who has killed the deceased cannot be appointed executor on his estate: *Smith, Petr*, 1979 S.L.T. (Sh. Ct) 35. This is an application of the "unworthy heir" rule whereby a person who has killed the deceased is barred from taking any benefit, subject to the possibility of relief under the Forfeiture Act 1982: see generally the Stair Memorial Encyclopaedia, Vol. 25, paras 668 *et seq.*

13. *Legal persons.* While legal persons are capable of being trustees, the Scottish courts have not always been favourably disposed to them. Compare the following two decisions:

Leith's Exr, Petr
1937 S.L.T. 208

3.04 In his will, John Leith, of Aberdeen, established a trust for the relief of poverty. After the last of the appointed trustees died, the executor-nominate of the last surviving trustee applied to the court for the appointment of a new trustee.

LORD JAMIESON: "In these circumstances the executor-nominate of the last surviving trustee applies for the appointment of a new trustee, and suggests the Aberdeen Association for

Improving the Condition of the Poor. That body is incorporated under the Companies Act, 1929, and a print of its memorandum and articles of association has been lodged in process. It acts as administrators and managers of a number of charitable funds or agencies, and amongst its purposes set forth in its memorandum of association are the following: 'To give assistance to, or to or for the dependants of any persons of either sex irrespective of their nationality, domicile, or ordinary place of residence who may while in the city of Aberdeen be, by reason of poverty, in temporary need, and that' (*inter alia*) '(i) by grants of money, (ii) by the provision of food, clothing, shelter, or other necessaries.' The memorandum also provides that the association may undertake any trusts which may be deemed requisite or useful for any of the objects of the association. The appointment of such a body is unusual, but it would in this case have the advantage of ensuring continuity of the trust and also facilitating its administration. The petition has been intimated to the Lord Advocate for the public interest and he has not thought it necessary to intervene. In the circumstances I think I would be in safety to make the appointment."

Ommanney, Petr
1966 S.L.T. (Notes) 13

OPINION OF THE COURT: "This is an application for approval of an arrangement [a variation **3.05** under s1 of the Trusts (Scotland) Act 1961] in an *inter vivos* trust set up by the petitioner in 1938. Two points arise for consideration in connection with this case; the first of these is that in the arrangement there is a provision entitling the trustees to 'assume as a trustee any Bank or Trust Corporation who shall be entitled to be remunerated and to act in accordance with their published terms and conditions in force for the time being'. This provision is not contained in the original *inter vivos* trust. It is not a provision which we regard with favour, particularly in a case such as the present where a discretion is conferred by the arrangement on the trustees as to the way in which the fund or part of the fund may be distributed among the beneficiaries. An impersonal body such as a Bank or a Trust Corporation is not a suitable party to exercise such a discretion involving personal and family considerations for its proper exercise. We shall, accordingly, not approve of an arrangement which includes such a provision."

NOTES:

1. As Lord Jamieson observes in *Leith's Exr*, a corporation may in some respects have certain **3.06** advantages over private individuals in fulfilling the office of trustee. A corporation provides (or, at least, can provide) continuity, professionalism and security in the management of a trust-fund. But what of the disfavour shown to such corporations in *Ommanney*? A number of observations may be made. Firstly, it is not clear why a trust corporation should be capable of exercising discretion as to who should be entitled to benefit from a charitable trust (as in *Leith*) but not as regards the administration of a family trust (as in *Ommanney*). Indeed, one might argue that a corporate body is highly appropriate as a trustee in a case such as *Ommanney* because it could be regarded as more objective and impartial than a private individual. Secondly, *Ommanney* seems to reflect a view of trust corporations as cold, impersonal and insensitive; unable and unwilling to listen or respond to family considerations. It may be objected, however, that this view is entirely unwarranted:

   "A corporation is likely to be suspect *a priori* of lacking any such warmth of individual sentiment. But experience has shown that the 'organs' of the corporation, not necessarily the Public Trustee himself, nor the directors of the companies, but the individual officers who make personal contact with beneficiaries, can supply it, or something closely approaching it. In so far as the individual officers cannot do so they are in like case with the private individual trustee, and that their 'personal relationships' in such matters are bounded by their office hours and need not come home to their innermost concerns can be in some ways as advantageous as the contrary. It is a commonplace to remark that, paraphrasing Bacon, counsel too much drenched in affection is not of the best." (D.R. Marsh, *Corporate Trustees* (1952), p. 193).

> Provided that the trust deed gives some guidance (as it should do) as to how the trustees' discretion is to be exercised, it might be thought that there is no practical reason why a corporate body should not act as a trustee.

2. It may be noted that the scepticism regarding corporate trustees which was demonstrated in *Ommaney* does not appear to extend to England, where "trust corporations" are given a special status by statute provided they fulfil certain requirements as to connection with England and Wales and share capital (see the Trustee Act 1925, s.68(18) and the Public Trustee (Custodian Trustee) Rules 1975 (S.I. 1975 No. 1189)). In particular, a trust corporation which fulfils these requirements is entitled in certain cases to act alone where two trustees would normally be necessary.

3. Companies can, of course, only act as trustees if they are constitutionally empowered (by the terms of their Memorandum of Association) to do so. Companies may be set up specifically for this purpose. On corporate trustees, see generally D.R. Marsh, *Corporate Trustees* (1952) and G.W. Keeton, *Modern Developments in the Law of Trusts* (1971), pp. 18–26.

4. Local authorities can also act as trustees. (See Wilson and Duncan, para. 18–20.)

3. WHAT PROPERTY MAY BE SUBJECT TO A TRUST?

A. Mackenzie Stuart
The Law of Trusts (1932), p. 65

3.07 "The general rule is that any property corporeal or incorporeal which can be conveyed or assigned may be made the subject of a trust. A right may be so purely personal that it cannot be assigned. Thus a right to a peerage cannot be held subject to a trust express or implied that it shall be transferred from the existing peer and his heirs to a new holder on the peer for the time succeeding for another peerage, and the patent to that extent is invalid. [*Buckhurst Peerage* (1876) 2 App. Cas. 1] Similarly rights which cannot legally be assigned, such as alimentary rights, are not possible subject-matter of trusts except within the limits to which they can be transferred.

NOTE:

Mackenzie Stuart's statement that "any property corporeal or incorporeal which can be conveyed or assigned may be made the subject of a trust" is broadly similar to Wilson and Duncan's assertion (at 2–18) that "any property which can be alienated can be the subject of a trust". Both statements seem broad, inclusive and unproblematic, but that is not in fact the case. Why should property require to be capable of alienation in order to be the subject of a trust? Consider the matter in this way. If A holds property which he is incapable of alienating, he clearly cannot convey that property to B in trust. That much is obvious. But why should he be prevented from declaring *himself* to be trustee of that property? Two recent English decisions, *Don King Productions Inc. v. Warren* [1999] 3 W.L.R. 276 and the following case, bear on the matter:

Smith v. Dairywise Farms Ltd
[2000] 1 W.L.R. 1177

3.08 JACOB J.: "This is another case involving the juridical nature of milk quota. It particularly involves the extent to which quota can by some legal machinery be treated as security for a loan. The applicants are the joint liquidators of Dairywise Ltd. ("the company"), which went into a creditor's voluntary liquidation in June 1999. The company's business was moneylending to farmers. Over £2m. remains outstanding. Those debts are the company's only significant assets.

The farmers were required to provide security for the loans made to them. Machinery was set up whereby quotas were to be used as security. However, quota is not the same as other sorts of property often offered by way of security. Its legal nature is unique. It gives the holder who produces milk an exemption from a levy which would otherwise be payable. There is a fundamental principle that 'quota follows the land.' Quota can only be attached to a holding of appropriate land—called 'a euroholding'—from which milk can be produced. A detailed examination of the position is to be found in the judgments of Chadwick J. in *Faulks v. Faulks* [1992] 1 E.G.L.R. 9 and the Court of Appeal in *Harries v. Barclays Bank Plc.* [1997] 2 E.G.L.R. 15. Chadwick J. noted that quota was widely perceived as being an independent asset having an economic value but his judgment makes it clear that the special nature of quota means that it cannot always simply be treated in the same way as other assets. The nature of quota and how it can be 'traded' was elegantly explained by Rattee J., in a passage quoted by Morritt L.J. in *Harries v. Barclays Bank Plc.* [1997] 2 E.G.L.R. 15, 18. He said:

> "However, it is clear that a market has developed in quota as a valuable commodity apart from the holding to which it relates, in the following way. It has become common practice that, where farmer A has quota in respect of his holding but no longer wishes to carry out a dairy farming business and, therefore, wishes to dispose of his quota without the land, he will grant a short lease for, say 11 months, of his holding to farmer B, who wishes to acquire farmer A's quota. It will be a term of the arrangement that the land let by farmer A to farmer B shall not be used for dairy production. On taking the lease farmer B will be registered as the holder of what was farmer A's quota in respect of the holding comprised in the lease. Farmer A's land and farmer B's land will thereafter during the continuance of the lease form one holding for the purposes of the quota regulations. As a result, when the lease in respect of farmer A's land terminates, an apportionment will have to be made of the quota enjoyed during the term of the lease in respect of the composite holding, and that apportionment will fall to be made according to the use made of the two parts of that composite holding. Since farmer A's land will not have been used during the lease for dairy farming, the whole of the quota will be apportioned to farmer B's land, which will have been used for dairy farming. Thus farmer A recovers his land, leaving farmer B with the quota previously enjoyed by farmer A in respect of that land. By such artifical means permanent transfers of quota are apparently frequently made. It follows that by this means a permanent transfer can be effected of quota without the land comprised in the holding to which that quota was originally attached, whereas no permanent transfer can be made of the land, leaving the quota in the original owner's enjoyment."

Now in this case the company did not have a euroholding. So it could not itself adopt the machinery described by Rattee J. to take quota by way of assignment from the borrowing farmer. What was done was to use a sister company, Dairywise Farms Ltd. ("Farms"), as the vehicle for holding the quota. Farms did have a euroholding in the shape of an agricultural tenancy agreement. [Jacob J. explained the nature of the loan agreements which the company entered into, followed by the argument of the liquidators that Farms held the quota in trust for the company, and continued:]

   The first question therefore is whether quota can be the subject of a trust. The respondents submit that it is not by its nature capable of forming the subject matter of a trust. They say this follows because it is not a free standing and freely marketable asset. Because it is merely an exemption from a levy and must be attached to a producer's holding, it cannot be held by a producer on trust.

   I reject those submissions. Quota has commercial value and a legal effect. Merely because there are limitations on how it may be held or conveyed is not a reason for equity to refuse to impose a trust where conscience so requires. Take a simple case. A asks B, who has a euroholding, to acquire quota for him and to hold it on trust. He pays B to do so and B duly acquires quota. It seems to me elementary that A can call upon B to deal in that quota in any manner permitted by the rules applicable to quota. A, assuming he has no euroholding, could not require B to transfer the quota to him but he could require B to realise the quota and transfer the proceeds to him. And if A acquired a euroholding he could call upon B to set in train the machinery described by Rattee J. for transfer to A's euroholding.

I do not think this conclusion is inconsistent with *Faulks v. Faulks* [1992] 1 E.G.L.R. 9. In that case the question was whether quota was a partnership asset. The partnership did not own the holding. The quota, being attached to the holding, was likewise not an asset owned by the partnership. As Chadwick J. put it, at p. 16, the conclusion was 'a necessary consequence of the bargain which the brothers made in relation to the tenancy of the farm.'

There are other species of 'property' in respect of which the law may put fetters or specific rules preventing or controlling assignment or transfer. It does not follow that the law cannot impose a trust. Lightman J. held in *Don King Productions Inc. v. Warren* [1999] 3 W.L.R. 276, 304:

> 'in principle I can see no objection to a party to contracts involving skill and confidence or containing non-assignment provisions from becoming trustee of the benefit of being the contracting party as well as the benefit of the rights conferred. I can see no reason why the law should limit the parties' freedom of contract to creating trusts of the fruits of such contracts received by the assignor or to creating an accounting relationship between the parties in respect of the fruits.'

It seems to me that a trust of quota or the fruits of quota is a complete analogy with a trust of non-assignable contracts. Lightman J.'s decision was upheld in the Court of Appeal: it is noticeable that Morritt L.J., at p. 315a, explained the decision in *Faulks v. Faulks* [1992] 1 E.G.L.R. 9 as depending on the terms of the partnership.

I am reinforced in my conclusion by the reasoning in *In re Celtic Extraction Ltd.* [2000] 2 W.L.R. 991, where the Court of Appeal was concerned with whether a waste management license was 'property' as defined by section 436 of the Insolvency Act 1986, which provides:

> '"property" includes money, goods, things in action, land and every description of property wherever situated and also obligations and every description of interest, whether present or future or vested or contingent, arising out of, or incidental to, property.'

The court held that such a licence was indeed 'property' within that definition. Morritt L.J., at p. 1003, applied a threefold test on the point:

> 'there must be a statutory framework conferring an entitlement on one who satisfies certain conditions even though there is some element of discretion exercisable within that framework. . . the exemption must be transferable. . . the exemption or license will have value . . .'

All of those tests are satisfied by quota. It is 'property' within the statutory definition. I can see no reason why equity, by analogy, should not also treat 'quota' as 'property' capable of being the subject of a trust and every reason as to why it should. The fact that quota must be attached to land merely means that the trustee (who necessarily will also hold the land) cannot deal in his land as though the trust was non-existent. But that is a consequence of his being a trustee, not a reason for equity to say there cannot be a trust. And there really is no hardship—after all he can free any particular parcel of land from the quota by use of the established methods by which farmers deal in quota."

NOTES:

3.09   1. On the general problem of whether milk quotas can be characterised as "property", see Michael Cardwell, "Milk and Livestock Quotas as Property" (2000) 4 Edin L.R. 168.
2. In *Don King Productions Inc. v. Warren* [1999] 3 W.L.R. 276, the boxing promoters Don King and Frank Warren entered into a partnership agreement. The initial partnership agreement

purported to assign to the partnership all the promotional and management agreements that each of the promoters held. This would, however, have been legally impossible for three reasons, as Lightman J. observed (at 285):

> "(a) an assignment of the burden was legally impossible (save indirectly by novation); (b) the benefit (at any rate) of the promotion and management agreements was not assignable because they were contracts based on the personal mutual confidence of the boxer and the promoter and manager. The management agreements involved the right to manage and the promotion agreements involved the right to require the boxer to fight the specified bout or bouts and to sell rights in respect of it; (c) all the management agreements and some of the promotional agreements (including the Hamed agreements) and (it may be) some of the associated agreements contained express prohibitions against assignment."

The parties' legal advisers appear to have (belatedly) appreciated this difficulty, and a second partnership agreement (which superseded the first) provided instead that King and Warren would instead hold these agreements "for the benefit of the partnership absolutely". Such language would normally be sufficient to create a trust, but when a dispute arose following the dissolution of the partnership, it was argued that the benefit of the contracts could not be the subject of a trust because they were non-assignable. Lightman J. rejected that contention, observing (at 303–304):

> "If one party wishes to protect himself against the other party declaring himself a trustee, and not merely against an assignment, he should expressly so provide . . . A declaration of trust cannot prejudice the rights of the obligor. If the contract requires any judgment to be exercised whether by the obligor or the obligee, an assignment cannot alter who is to exercise it or how that judgment is to be exercised or vest the right to make that judgment in the court."

Lightman J.'s decision was affirmed by the Court of Appeal. It is thought that, Mackenzie Stuart and Wilson and Duncan's broad statements notwithstanding, the reasoning of the English courts in *Smith v. Dairywise Farms* and *Don King* would be followed in Scotland. (For a valuable discussion of the practical issues involved, see David Cabrelli, "Can Scots Lawyers Trust Don King? Trusts in the Commercial Context" (2001) 6 S.L.P.Q. 103, who points to the usefulness of such arrangements in cases involving the sale of all or part of a firm's assets.)

It might be objected that to recognise a trust of a non-assignable right would be inconsistent with the special status of alimentary liferents under Scots law. An alimentary liferenter cannot assign his liferent interest, since to do so would defeat the purpose of an alimentary liferent. If he were able to declare that he held his liferent interest in trust for a third party, this would equally defeat the purpose of the liferent. That objection, however, is not fatal. A declaration that a liferent is alimentary should be regarded both as making it non-assignable and as barring the liferenter from declaring himself trustee of his own liferent interest. Such a principle does not, however, have any wider implications.

4. WHO OWNS TRUST PROPERTY?

3.10 The institutional writers were quite clear in their view that the trustees were the owners of the trust property. So, for example, Stair states that "the property of the thing intrusted, be it land or moveables, is in the person of the intrusted, else it is not proper trust" (I, 13, 7), while Bell observes that "In order to make an available trust, the subject of it must be legally vested in the trustee", and that the vesting of the estate in the trustee "completes the constitution of the trust, with purpose to preserve it as a separate estate in the person of the trustees for the uses and purposes intended; guarding it at once against the truster himself, and his creditors or representatives, and against the trustee and his creditors." (*Principles*, ss.1992 and 1994).

This principle (hereafter referred to as the "trustee-as-owner theory"), however, was thrown into some confusion around the end of the nineteenth century by attacks on two fronts.

The first attack was the suggestion that *both* the trustee and the beneficiary had rights of ownership in the trust estate. In two cases, Lord McLaren suggested (in a rather offhand, and certainly *obiter* fashion) that, although the trustee was indeed the owner of the trust property, the beneficiary might also be regarded as an owner. So, in *Hay's Trs v. Hay* (1890) 17 R. 961, he opined that "the beneficiary has a concurrent estate or *jus crediti* which he may vindicate by action", and in *Govan New Bowling-Green Club v. Geddes* (1898) 25 R. 485, he referred to "both sets of owners—the owners of the legal and the owners of the beneficial estate". (Mackenzie Stuart, it may be noted, expresses a similar view on the very first page of his text: "a trust may be defined as the legal relationship which arises when estate is owned by two persons at the same time, the one being under an obligation to use his ownership for the benefit of the other.")

At first glance, this seems unintelligible, or even dangerous, and possibly both. The law of property in Scotland is normally (and correctly) thought of as unititular, recognising only one right of ownership in a thing at any one time. That is not to say that the right of ownership cannot be shared (as in the case of joint or common property), but two separate rights of ownership in the same thing cannot co-exist at the same time. Some clarification can, however, be gained from reading these *dicta* alongside McLaren's extrajudicial work on trusts, where, in a section headed "Estate of the Beneficiary", it is argued:

> "The beneficiary interest has been defined as a *jus crediti* affecting the trustee; a definition which, if accurate at all, is only accurate when applied to the case of a beneficiary interest arising under an *ex facie* absolute disposition, qualified by a separate declaration. The beneficiary interest under deeds of settlement, conveying the estate ostensibly for uses and purposes, may be more correctly defined as a personal right of property in the estate which is the subject of disposition." (McLaren, II, s.1527).

McLaren, therefore, appears to have been attempting to avoid the terminology of *jus crediti* (right of credit) which had been used by earlier writers such as Bell (*Principles*, s.1996) to describe the beneficiary's right. And in doing so, he clearly had some justification. To characterise the beneficiary's right as a *jus crediti* suggests that a beneficiary is a mere creditor of the trustee, when in actual fact he is in a much stronger position than a creditor, because the trust estate is not available to satisfy the personal debts of the trustee, and the creditors of the trustee cannot attach it for this purpose. If a trustee becomes insolvent and is sequestrated, his creditors must compete with each other for payment of their debts. A beneficiary is not, however, put in the position of a competitor. Indeed, sequestration of the trustee does not (in itself) prevent the trustee from continuing to administer the trust-estate as before.

This is not, of course, to say that Bell did not understand this point. He understood it very well, as McLaren acknowledges in a footnote. But the terminology may still be objected to as confusing. However, McLaren's terminology is equally objectionable. "Concurrent estates" simply do not make sense in Scots law; nor does the notion of a "personal right of property". As Reid has explained:

> "while in general a real right is a right to use, or to prevent others from using, a thing, a personal right is a right to make a person perform some act, or alternatively to prevent him from performing some act." (Reid, *Property*, para. 3).

To refer to a "personal right of property" is very odd indeed. One could, of course, say that the beneficiary has a personal right to require the trustee to apply the trust property in accordance with the trust deed, but that is no better than asserting that the beneficiary has a *jus crediti*. Neither concept explains the special nature of the beneficiary's right.

We will return to the precise nature of the beneficiary's right later (*infra* para. 3.15). For the moment, we must consider, the second, more serious attack on the trustee-as-owner principle—that is, the suggestion that the trust property is not the property of the trustee *at all*.

Heritable Reversionary Co. Ltd. v. Millar
(1892) 19 R. (H.L.) 43

3.11 LORD WATSON: "I think it may be useful to consider the nature of the relations existing between a solvent trustee who is feudally vested in the heritable estate of the trust by a title *ex facie* absolute, and his *cestui que* trust, whose right rests upon a latent back-bond. As between them there can, in my opinion, be no doubt that according to the law of Scotland the one, though possessed of the legal title, and being the apparent owner, is in reality a bare trustee; and that the other, to whom the whole beneficial interest belongs, is the true owner. Upon that point the opinions expressed by noble and learned Lords in *Union Bank of Scotland v. National Bank of Scotland*, 12 App. Cases, 53, [(1886) 14 R. (H.L.) 1] and by those learned Judges of the Court of Session with whom their Lordships in that case agreed, appear to me to be conclusive. But in that state of the title the trustee, though his action may be in breach of duty, or even grossly fraudulent, can communicate a valid right to a purchaser or a lender on the security of the trust-estate, who transacts with him for value and without notice of the interest of the beneficiary. That rule, which alike applies to moveable and heritable estate, was finally settled in the law of Scotland by the judgment of this House in *Redfearn v. Somervail*, 1 Dow's App. 53, an authority which seems to have been regarded by the Lord President as practically decisive of the present case. It must, however, be kept in view that the validity of a right acquired in such circumstances by a *bona fide* disponee for value does not rest upon the recognition of any power in the trustee which he can lawfully exercise, because breach of trust duty and wilful fraud can never be in themselves lawful, but upon the well-known principle that a true owner who chooses to conceal his right from the public, and to clothe his trustee with all the *indicia* of ownership, is thereby barred from challenging rights acquired by innocent third parties for onerous considerations under contracts with his fraudulent trustee."

NOTES:

1. See also *Bank of Scotland v. Liquidators of Hutchison Main & Co Ltd*, 1914 S.C. (H.L.) 1, *per* **3.12** Lord Shaw at 15–16.
2. The most serious problem for the beneficiary-as-owner theory suggested by Lord Watson is this. If a trustee is not the owner of the trust property, why is it that a third party who purchases trust property from a trustee, in good faith and for value, acquires ownership of the trust property? (*infra* para. 10.10). Scots law adheres to the principle of *nemo dat quod non habet* ("no one can give what he does not have"), and if the beneficiary-as-owner theory were adopted, then it would be impossible for the trustee to confer ownership on a third party.

   Lord Watson appreciates this difficulty, and attempts to explain the protection which the law accords to *bona fide* third parties as an application of the rule of personal bar. But that will not do, for two reasons. Firstly, as Wilson and Duncan point out (at 11–47), the decision in *Redfearn v. Somervail* was not founded upon personal bar. Secondly, expressing the rule in this way would mean that no third party who acquires property from a trustee (and such transactions will frequently take place, for perfectly legitimate reasons) would ever acquire a real right of ownership in that property by virtue of the transaction alone. While the third party would have a good defence to any attempt by the beneficiary to vindicate his "ownership", he would have no right to vindicate the property in question himself if it fell into the hands of a fourth party—and that surely cannot be correct. Apart from the problem of principle with this approach, it would make third parties extremely reluctant to enter into transactions with trustees.

   The issue was revisited by the First Division recently in *Sharp v. Thomson*, where the trustee-as-owner theory was re-asserted.

Sharp v. Thomson
1995 S.C. 455
(reversed 1997 S.C. (H.L.) 66)

LORD PRESIDENT (HOPE): "I do not find it necessary to say much in this chapter about **3.13** *Heritable Reversionary Co Ltd v. Millar* (1892) 19 R. (H.L.) 43 and *Bank of Scotland v. Liquidators of Hutchison Main & Co Ltd* 1914 S.C. (H.L.) 1, or *Union Bank of Scotland Ltd v. National Bank of Scotland Ltd* (1886) 14 R. (H.L.) 1 to which we were also referred. These cases were grouped together by senior counsel for the second defenders as dealing in various respects with the doctrine of apparent ownership. The *Union Bank* case was concerned with a right in security constituted by a disposition which was *ex facie* absolute together with a back letter which was not recorded. *Millar* was concerned with the question whether heritable property vested in a bankrupt, which was subject to a latent trust, passed to the trustees in his sequestration free of that trust to be held for distribution among his personal creditors. *Hutchison Main* was concerned with a claim by the bank in the liquidation of the company under a debenture in its favour which the company was under a contractual obligation to assign to it but which had not yet been assigned to the bank. In the *Union Bank* case there was a discussion of the nature of the transaction by which heritable property was disponed absolutely in security, especially in regard to the nature of the right of the disponer in a question with the disponee. Lord Watson said at p 4 that, apart from considerations of feudal law, the radical right remained with the disponer in the sense that, according to the reality of the transaction, she was the only person who had a proprietary interest in the subjects of the security. In *Millar* the relationship was that between a bare trustee, formally vested in the heritable estate of the trust under a title *ex facie* absolute, and the beneficiaries under the estate. It was held that the heritable estate did not belong to the bare trustee, as the beneficiaries were the true and beneficial owners of the property, so it did not pass to the trustee in his sequestration as his 'property' within the meaning of the Act. A distinction was drawn both by Lord Herschell at p 44 and by Lord Watson at p 51 between the case of a latent trust by which the owner appearing on the register is a bare trustee, and that where the owner is under a contractual obligation, or mere personal contract, to convey the property to another. In *Hutchison Main* the personal obligation to assign the debenture to the bank was held to be nothing more than an unfulfilled promise which did not have the effect of depriving the company of its beneficial interest in the property. . .

It is true that there are *dicta* in all three cases which may be used to support the view that a distinction can be drawn between the apparent title and the beneficial interest in the property where questions arise as to who is owner of it. But here again the analogy which the second defenders seek to draw from these *dicta* seems to me to break down on closer analysis. In the *Union Bank* case Lord Watson at p 4 recognised that in form the right of the disponer under the back letter was a personal right, and he made it clear, in his description of the radical right, that he was not proceeding upon feudal principles. I do not think that one can, with safety, draw any conclusion from his observations in that case in support of the arguments which the second defenders wish to advance about the effect of the delivery of the disposition to the disponee by a person who was undoubtedly the owner of the property on entering into the transaction which he was thereby implementing. In *Millar* the only question which required to be decided was whether the heritable property was the 'property' of the debtor, within the meaning of that expression as used in sec 102 of the Bankruptcy Act 1856. The decision that it was not his property in the sense of the Act was based on *dicta*, endorsed in *Hutchison Main* by Lord Shaw of Dunfermline, which may seem to have a wider significance. But in *Inland Revenue v. Clark's Trs* 1939 S.C. 11, Lord President Normand said at p 22 that the right of a beneficiary under a trust was 'nothing more than a personal right to sue the trustees and to compel them to administer the trust in accordance with the directions which it contains'. This observation was referred to with approval by Lord Keith of Avonholm in *Parker v. Lord Advocate* 1960 S.C. (H.L.) 29 at p 41. Lord Moncrieff in *Clark's Trs* at p 26 said that he had difficulty in seeing how the right of a beneficiary could properly be defined, as McLaren had defined it in *Wills and Succession*, Vol II, p 832, as 'a personal right of property in the estate which is the subject of disposition', and then said: 'In my view, the right of property in the estate of the trust is vested in the trustees to the exclusion of any competing right of property, and the right of the beneficiary. . . is merely a right *in personam* against the trustees to enforce their performance of the trust.'

In this matter I agree with the views expressed in Wilson and Duncan, *Trusts, Trustees and Executors* [1st ed. 1975] at pp 14 and 15, contrary to the *dicta* in the cases about apparent ownership, that the preponderance of authority is to the effect that the property, in the normal sense, is vested in the trustee. This is consistent with the basis structure of the law of Scotland as already discussed, which draws a distinction between the law of property and the law of obligations, and with the statement in Bell, *Commentaries*, i, 36 that the beneficial interest gives only a *ius crediti* or personal action against the trustee. In my opinion it is not part of the law of Scotland that there exist in the trustee and the beneficiary concurrent rights of ownership in the property which is subject to the trust. The argument that there can be a separation of interests of ownership according to what was described as the reality of the situation is contrary to principle."

NOTES:

1. Although the decision of the First Division in *Sharp v. Thomson* was subsequently reversed **3.14** by the House of Lords (1997 S.C. (H.L.) 66), it is thought that Lord Hope's observations remain valid.
2. The trustee-as-owner principle is reflected in section 31(1) of the Bankruptcy (Scotland) Act 1985, which provides that "the whole estate of the debtor shall vest as at the date of sequestration in the permanent trustee for the benefit of the creditors". Property held on trust by the debtor for any other person is, however, excluded (s.33(1)(b)).

5. THE NATURE OF THE BENEFICIARY'S RIGHT

It was noted earlier that the exact nature of the beneficiary's right in the trust property has been **3.15** considered problematic. Bell (*Principles*, s.1996) considered the beneficiary's right to be a personal right of credit ("*jus crediti*") against the trustee, an approach which is approved by Lord Hope in *Sharp v. Thomson* (*supra* para. 3.13). Various writers, however, have objected to this characterisation as obscuring the special nature of the beneficiary's right. For example, Norrie and Scobbie observe (at 4):

"This is however a very peculiar personal right since it is one that can, in some circumstances, defeat a real right. The trustee's right to the property is strictly constrained by the law of trusts, and by the right which that law confers upon the beneficiaries. So the right of the trustee does not transmit on his death to his successors, nor is it available for the satisfaction of the trustee's personal debts."

Similarly, Gretton has observed that:

"The rights of beneficiaries do not behave like ordinary personal rights, but at the same time they do not behave like real rights either. Functionally, they are something in-between. But if the law is to aspire to coherence, matters cannot be left thus. Conceptual analysis is needed." (*Trust and Patrimony*, in MacQueen (ed.), *Scots Law into the 21st Century: Essays in Honour of W.A. Wilson*, p. 182, at 184)

Gretton has provided that conceptual analysis, initially in the essay from which the quote is taken, and more recently, in a more developed form, in "Trusts Without Equity" (2000) 49 I.C.L.Q. 599. The answer, Gretton suggests, can be found by resorting to the concept of "patrimony". Every individual has a patrimony, meaning the totality of his assets and liabilities. And normally, no person has more than one. A trustee, however, has a "special patrimony", a separate fund, segregated from his "general patrimony". This special patrimony is the trust fund. Where there is more than one trustee, the trustees own the special patrimony jointly, while their general patrimonies remain separate and individual. Gretton explains the consequences of this analysis as follows:

George L. Gretton, "Trusts Without Equity"
(2000) 49 I.C.L.Q. 599, 612–614

"With the explanation of trust as patrimony everything falls into place. The rights of **3.16** beneficiaries are personal rights. They are personal rights against the trustee, enforceable against the special patrimony. (And sometimes, depending on the legal system and the circumstances of the case, against the general patrimony also.) Conversely, personal rights enforceable against the trustee in his personal capacity are not (in general) enforceable against the special patrimony. *There is thus no need to seek to classify the right of beneficiaries as being in some way privileged as quasi-real or as in some way 'trumping' the rights of the creditors of a trustee in his personal capacity.* There is no need to resort to duality of ownership. Instead of duality of ownership, there is duality of patrimony. As for the fact that a trust estate is a 'fund' the constituent items of which may change without changing the identity of the fund, this is of the essence of the idea of a patrimony. It is also essential to the trust concept. . .

Far from beneficial trust rights having *priority*, they are in fact *postponed* claims. For if a trust becomes insolvent, the claims of the beneficiaries are postponed to the claims of those who are creditors of the trust. If anything needs to be explained, it is *this* fact. But the explanation is not difficult. It is the explaining of priority which is difficult—very difficult indeed unless one invokes the idea of a real right. But explaining postponement is unproblematic. (And no one would seek to argue that ordinary creditors of a trustee all have real rights.) The conception is simple: a beneficial right is a personal right which is to be met only when creditors have been provided for. (Indeed, in commercial transactions subordinated debt is common and can be created purely by contract.)

The patrimonial conception of the trust also explains, or at least underlines the explanation of, other features. It helps to explain why a trust will not fail for want of a trustee, so that even if all the trustees die the trust continues, and new trustees can be appointed. It helps to explain how it is that a court can take a trust out of the hands of the existing trustees and place it in the hands of new trustees. It explains why a trust estate, as such, can be made bankrupt, at any rate in Scots law and in South African law."

NOTE:

As an ordinary personal right, the right of the beneficiary can be assigned to a third party. See Wilson and Duncan, paras 10–38 *et seq.*

Chapter 4

APPOINTMENT, ASSUMPTION AND RESIGNATION OF TRUSTEES

---

1. APPOINTMENT OF ORIGINAL TRUSTEES

Bell, *Commentaries on the Laws of Scotland* (7th ed., 1870), p. 32

"Trustees may effectually be appointed, not only by name, but by descriptive reference, and **4.01** such reference may be either to office, as in nominating the trustees of a public charity, or to an assumption, or appointment, by those expressly named, or to nomination by a stranger; or to the legal line of succession of the trustees named."

NOTE:

There is no formula which must be followed in the naming of a trustee, and the sole test is whether the truster has sufficiently identified the person who is to be appointed as trustee. This is made clear by *Martin v. Ferguson's Trustees* (1892) 19 R. 474, where the Inner House had to consider the validity of a clause which stated "I wish my estate to be managed by the same trustees as my brother." The Lord President (Robertson) held that the direction was valid, stating (at 478) that:

"A man may quite competently appoint trustees or executors if he designates the persons sufficiently so as to identify them, even if the criterion of identification be another man's settlement."

Another example is provided by the following case:

Murdoch v. Magistrates and Ministers of Glasgow
(1827) 6 S. 186

In his will, James Murdoch left £5,000 "to be laid out in lands for the maintenance of a **4.02** school for boys for reading and writing and arithmetic, to be under the management of the Magistrates and the Ministers of the established church." His next of kin argued that this was ineffectual as it did not sufficient identify who was to manage the sum of £5,000. The Lord Ordinary rejected this argument, and in his interlocutor he "found, that, from the terms of the settlement and codicil executed by James Murdoch, and from the admitted facts that he was born and resided in Glasgow, and carried on business there till the period of his death, it must be inferred that he intended the school in question to be under the management of the Magistrates of Glasgow and the Ministers of the established church in that city." On appeal to the Inner House:

LORD PRESIDENT (HOPE): "In addition to the circumstances noticed in the interlocutor, it is to be observed that the deed is dated at Glasgow; and therefore we must presume that the testator had reference to the Magistrates and Ministers of that city, and not of any other, and consequently effect must be given to his intention."

Appeal refused.

NOTES:

4.03
1. According to Mackenzie Stuart (p. 53), if a description "applies to one person at the date of the deed and to another at the opening of the trust, the former is presumed to be the person intended by the truster unless there is evidence in the deed of a contrary intention." So, for example, if a testator states in his will that his "eldest son" is to be his executor, but his eldest son predeceases him, a younger son who has now become the eldest at the time of death will not automatically be entitled to be the executor (*Amyot v. Dwarris* [1904] A.C. 268). Similarly, if a testator were to state in his will that his "sister-in-law" was to be his executor, but his brother were to divorce and remarry before his death, this provision would be interpreted as referring to his *former* and not his *current* sister-in-law.
2. Sometimes, trustees will be appointed *ex officio* (as the holder of an office). For example, the trust deed in *Parish Council of Kilmarnock v. Ossington's Trs* (discussed below) stated that one of the trustees would be "the chairman of the Parochial Board of the parish of Kilmarnock, and his successor in office for the time being, so long as such board shall exist". *Ex officio* trustees are, like all other trustees, personally liable for any breach of trust they might commit. The body in which they hold office is not itself liable (*Ministers of Edinburgh v. Lord Provost of Edinburgh* (1849) 6 Bell's App. 509). What happens if there is some change in the body, such as an amalgamation with another body? Do the holders of positions in this new body become *ex officio* trustees? This problem arose in the following case:

Mailler's Trs v. Allan
(1904) 7 F. 326

4.04 James Whyte Mailler, a minister of the United Presbyterian Church, died in 1869. His will appointed several persons as trustees, including several ministers and a clerk of the United Presbyterian Church. The will stated that they "and their successors in their several charges [or, in the case of the clerk, the clerkship] shall be trustees *ex officio*." In 1900, the United Presbyterian Church and the Free Church of Scotland entered into a union and became the United Free Church of Scotland. The trustees presented a petition to the Court of Session seeking *inter alia* a declaration that they were entitled to act as trustees.

LORD TRAYNER: "The second head of the proposed scheme sets forth that the following parties shall be the trustees. Now, it is upon that point that the trustees first applied to us. The difficulty they had was this, that the truster named two personal friends as trustees and several others who may be called *ex officio* trustees—that is to say, they were not selected in respect of the truster's predilection for them, but because they were incumbents of certain Churches there described, all belonging to the United Presbyterian Church in Perth or in that district. These *ex officio* members who were incumbents of these particular Churches, thought their trusteeship might be disputed because they were no longer members of the United Presbyterian Church, but of the United Free Church. The change on the name, to my mind, makes no difference whatever in their character. The name may be right or the name may be wrong, but there is no doubt they are the persons indicated by the truster as the persons whom he desired to carry on and administer the trust. They are the incumbents of certain Churches well defined and their successors. I think the present incumbents of these Churches (the petitioners), though called ministers of the United Free Church, are in fact ministers of the United Presbyterian Church, and are the persons to whom the truster committed the administration of the trust. And, accordingly, I think the second article may be approved."

NOTE:

4.05 Compare this decision with *Parish Council of Kilmarnock v. Ossington's Trs* (1896) 23 R. 833, where the truster nominated "the chairman of the Parochial Board of the parish of Kilmarnock, and his successor in office for the time being, so long as such board will exist". The Parochial Board was later abolished and replaced with a Parish Council by the Local Government (Scotland) Act 1894. Section 22 of that Act provided that "a parish council shall, subject to the provisions of this Act, come in place of a parochial board and shall be deemed to be a continuance thereof; and a parish council shall have and may exercise all the powers and duties, and shall be subject to all the liabilities, of a parochial board". The Inner House subsequently had to decide whether the chairman of the new Parish Council was entitled to act as an *ex officio* trustee. Lord Trayner said (at 835) that:

> "In [the] sense, that the parish council in future should represent the parochial board in its rights and obligations, the one is deemed to be a continuance of the other, but only in this sense. As the trust in question was one with which the parochial board had no concern, so I think the parish council has nothing to do with it. And accordingly, I am of opinion that the chairman of the parish council cannot claim *ex officio* to be a trustee."

The judgments in *Mailler's Trs* make no reference to *Ossington's Trs*, and the two cases are rather difficult to reconcile. It might be argued that the Parish Council in the latter case was an entirely new body, whereas the United Free Church was not, but was simply an amalgamation of one existing body with another—but that is an extremely fine distinction.

2. ACCEPTANCE OF ORIGINAL TRUSTEES

4.06 It is a generally accepted principle that no person may be compelled to accept the office of trustee. However, there are three exceptions. Firstly, in the case of *ex officio* trustees, it may be a condition of accepting the office that the person also accept the position of trustee. The principle remains, however, that "no *ex officio* trustee can be forced to accept office against his will" (*Vestry of St Silas Church v. Trustees of St Silas Church*, 1945 S.C. 110, *per* the Lord Justice-Clerk (Cooper) at 121).

Secondly, it is possible that a person might enter into a binding contract in which they undertake to accept the office of trustee. Most writers are sceptical about this second possibility, arguing that such promises should, where possible, be interpreted as a statement of intent rather than as a legally binding obligation (McLaren, s.2077). It is generally not disputed, however, that it is possible to legally bind oneself to accept the office of trustee. Wilson and Duncan (para. 18–41) see this possibility as unimportant, arguing that the trustee would be "under no obligation to retain office after his acceptance", as all trustees have a statutory power to resign (Trusts (Scotland) Act 1921, s.3(a)). However, trustees only have this power where it is not excluded by the trust deed, and a binding and effective obligation to accept the office of trustee is therefore conceivable.

Thirdly, certain trusts may arise by operation of law (see *supra* paras 2.29 *et seq.*). In these cases, the individuals concerned will be deemed by law to hold the office of trustee. They have no choice in the matter.

Form of Acceptance

A. Mackenzie Stuart, *The Law of Trusts* (1932), pp. 153–154

4.07 "Acceptance may be express or it may be inferred from actings. No formal acceptance is necessary by one who has been nominated or appointed a trustee, but it is advisable to accept office in writing. The actings which will justify the inference that there has been consent to be a trustee vary indefinitely, and the reported cases are mostly illustrations and not precedents. Acceptance will usually be inferred if the person alleged to be trustee has performed the usual duties of a trustee, either personally or by directing others."

NOTE:

In *Ker v. City of Glasgow Bank* (1879) 6 R. (H.L.) 52, Ker was named as trustee in an antenuptial marriage-contract trust. He never formally accepted the office of trustee, but signed a transfer of railway stock in favour of the trust "as trustee". He never attended a meeting of trustees. It was nevertheless held that he had accepted office.

3. ASSUMPTION OF NEW TRUSTEES BY EXISTING TRUSTEES

Trusts (Scotland) Act 1921, s.3

4.08 "All trusts shall be held to include the following powers and provisions unless the contrary be expressed (that is to say)—

. . .

> (b) Power to the trustee, if there be only one, or to the trustees, if there be more than one, or to a quorum of the trustees, if there be more than two, to assume new trustees.
>
> . . .
>
> Provided that—
>
> . . .

(3) A judicial factor shall not, by virtue of this Act, have the power of assumption . . ."

NOTES:

4.09
1. This derives from the Trusts (Scotland) Act 1861, s.1. Prior to the 1861 Act, trustees had no power to assume new trustees unless such a power was explicitly conferred by the trust deed.
2. If a trust deed confers a more limited power of assumption than the statute, will this be taken to impliedly exclude the statutory power? If the trust deed predates the 1861 Act, the answer is no (*Allan's Trs v. Hairstens* (1878) 5 R. 576). With post-1861 deeds, it seems that an expressly limited power of assumption would be taken to impliedly exclude section 3 of the 1921 Act. (*Thomson's Trustee, Petitioner*, 1948 S.L.T. (Notes) 28, and see also *Thomson v. Miller's Trs* (1883) 11 R. 401, *per* Lord Young at 403: "[a]n express direction to do something else inconsistent is just the same as an express prohibition against doing the thing that is in question.")
3. *Assumption by ex officio trustees.* It might be thought that, where a truster has stipulated that his trust shall be managed by *ex officio* trustees, he is impliedly excluding the power of assumption. This is because the *ex officio* trustees will simply be replaced by their successors in office, and it might therefore be argued that there is no need for a statutory power of assumption. Because of this, some doubts were expressed (*obiter*) in *Vestry of St Silas Church v. Trustees of St Silas Church*, 1945 S.C. 110 as to whether section 3(b) of the 1921 Act applied to *ex officio* trustees. The matter arose more recently in *Winning and Others, Petitioners*, 1999 S.C. 51, where the Temporary Lord Ordinary (T.G. Coutts, Q.C.) rejected the doubts which had been expressed in *Vestry of St Silas*, holding that:

   > "As a matter of generality, it cannot in my opinion be said that *ex officio* trustees cannot appoint new trustees. The matter depends upon the particular terms of the deed under consideration and no doubt in some it may be possible to infer with clarity that such power is excluded . . . had the new implied power [s.3(b)] not been intended to apply to *ex officio* trustees, the statute could and would have said so."

4. *Charitable trusts.* In addition to the powers conferred under section 3 of the 1921 Act, trustees in a charitable trust may also invoke section 13(1) of the Law Reform (Miscellaneous Provisions) (Scotland) Act 1990, which provides that "Where a recognised body is a trust, notwithstanding anything to the contrary in the trust deed or other document constituting the trust, the trustees shall have power to appoint such number of additional trustees as will secure that, at any time, the number of trustees shall not be less than three."

4. APPOINTMENT OF NEW TRUSTEES BY TRUSTER

A. Mackenzie Stuart, *The Law of Trusts* (1932), pp. 299–300

4.10 "When the machinery of a trust breaks down owing to there being no trustee, the original truster may appoint new trustees because there is implied, at common law, a reserved right to do so when the original trustees or their successors have failed. No petition to the court is necessary to ratify the new appointment so made ... But the power is reserved by implication only in private trusts. In the case of a public trust, in the full and proper sense of the term, the person constituting the trust cannot appoint new trustees if he has not expressly reserved the power."

NOTES:

1. This principle was demonstrated in *Lindsay v. Lindsay* (1847) 9 D. 1297, where the original **4.11** trustees had all either resigned or died. The original trusters brought an action asking the court to appoint new trustees. The court declined, with the Lord Justice-Clerk (Hope) observing that he was "disposed to think that enough of radical right remains with Mr and Mrs Lindsay, under the deed, to make a nomination of new trustees themselves", while Lord Cockburn said "[a]ssuming that we have power to nominate new trustees, it would require a strong case to make us exercise it; and a strong case cannot be said to exist where the parties can do it for themselves". Accordingly, the trusters sought a declarator that they were entitled to make the appointments themselves, and this was granted. This rule has been confirmed in subsequent cases (*Tovey v. Tennent* (1854) 16 D. 866; *Newlands v. Miller* (1882) 9 R. 1104, *per* Lord Shand at 1113–1114).
2. The truster may also reserve the power to (a) appoint additional trustees or (b) to change the existing trustees.

5. APPOINTMENT OF NEW TRUSTEES BY THIRD PARTIES

Third parties may have the power to appoint trustees if the trust deed confers such power upon them.

A. Mackenzie Stuart, *The Law of Trusts* (1932), pp. 300–301

"The power to appoint new trustees may be given to the beneficiaries who are not **4.12** themselves trustees, and the terms of the power may entitle a beneficiary to add to the number of the acting trustees even against the wishes of them ...

This variety of the power is most frequently found in public trusts, where the appointment of new trustees is left in the hands of the members of the public body to be benefited or of the office-bearers. Sometimes the appointment is given to a neutral person or official outside the trust, such as a presbytery of town council as in the case of a charitable trust, or a local authority in the case of a parish trust."

NOTES:

1. For an example, see *Morison, Petr* (1834) 12 S. 307 and 547, where a trust for the erection, **4.13** maintenance and use of a church provided that "when the present number of trustees shall have been reduced to six, by death or exclusion, then an election of another trustee shall be made by the church members who are men, to complete the permanent number of seven, that the trust may be kept up; and failing the church making such election within one month after the vacancy shall be intimated to them at a church meeting, and they required to make such election, then the election shall be made by the other remaining trustees, or a majority of them, and so on during all time thereafter."
2. *Power of the Lord Advocate to appoint trustees in a charitable trust.* Section 13(1) of the Law Reform (Miscellaneous Provision) (Scotland) Act 1990 (*supra* para. 4.09) provides that the trustees in a charitable trust *always* have the power to appoint additional trustees to ensure that the trust has at least three trustees. Section 13(2) of the same Act provides that:

   "Where in the case of any trust which is a recognised body—
       (a) the number of trustees is less than three; and
       (b) it appears to the Lord Advocate that the trustees will not, or are unable to, exercise their power under subsection (1) above,
   if it appears to the Lord Advocate expedient to do so, he may exercise the power in place of the trustees."

6. APPOINTMENT OF NEW TRUSTEES BY THE COURT

A. Appointment under statute

Trusts (Scotland) Act 1921, s.22

4.14 "When trustees cannot be assumed under any trust deed, or when any person who is the sole trustee appointed in or acting under any trust deed is or has become insane or is or has become incapable of acting by reason of physical or mental disability, or by being absent continuously from the United Kingdom for a period of at least six months, or by having disappeared for a like period, the court may, upon the application of any party having interest in the trust estate, after such intimation and inquiry as may be thought necessary, appoint a trustee or trustees under such trust deed with all the powers incident to that office, and, on such appointment being made in the case of any person becoming insane or incapable of acting as aforesaid, such person shall cease to be a trustee under such trust deed . . ."

NOTE:

4.15   This provision derives, with some modifications, from the Trusts (Scotland) Act 1867, s.12. It allows the court to appoint trustees in two broad categories of case:

> (a) *Where trustees cannot be assumed under any trust deed.* According to the Lord President (Inglis) in *Graham, Petitioner* (1868) 6 M. 958 (at 958–959):

>> "the general words of the statute, 'when trustees cannot be assumed', are intended to comprehend every case where the trust cannot be kept up by means of powers within the trust-deed, and that in every such case the aid of the court may be invoked. It is, however, a matter for the discretion of the court whether to interfere or not . . ."

> This may occur in two principal situations:

>> (i) *Where all the nominated trustees have lapsed or declined office*, as in *Zoller, Petitioner* (1868) 6 M. 577.
>> (ii) *Where the truster has omitted to appoint any trustees.* In *Pattullo and Others* (1908) 16 S.L.T. 637, a testator directed in her will that certain persons were to receive the interest of her investments, and that the principal sums should not be distributed until certain persons had died. She did not appoint either trustees or executors nominate, and the beneficiaries brought a petition to have trustees appointed. Lord Salvesen granted the petition, saying:

>>> ". . . it is plain that trustees cannot be assumed under this will, and the only question is whether it can be held to be a trust deed. It is quite obvious that a will of this kind, which provides for the capital being held up for many years and only a liferent being in the first instance provided to the beneficiaries, is a deed which requires the interposition of trustees in some shape to carry it into effect, and therefore it seems to me that, construing, as I think I am entitled to construe, this statute generally, it may be described as a trust deed. If that be so, the difficulty about the competency of the appointment is removed . . ."

> (b) *Where a trustee is or has become insane or incapable, or has been absent from the U.K. for six months or has disappeared for that period.* It will be noted that the original trustee will only be automatically removed from office if they are insane or incapable. If the basis for the s.22 application is that they have been absent from the U.K. or have disappeared, then a separate application must be made under s.23 to have them removed from office. If this is not done, then they will remain in office despite the appointment of the new trustee, although they may be taken to have lost their right to be consulted before decisions are made (see *Malcolm v. Goldie* (1895) 22 R. 968). The reason for this distinction is that, where a s.23 application is

made, the court *must* remove trustees who are insane or incapable because of disability but has a discretion as to whether trustees should be removed for absence from the U.K. or disappearance.

B. Appointment at common law

The Court of Session, in the exercise of the *nobile officium*, has long had the power to appoint new **4.16** trustees regardless of any statutory provision. In *Melville v. Preston* (1838) 16 S. 457, Lord Mackenzie (sitting in the Inner House) stated (at 471): "We have ample power to appoint a trustee, wherever a necessity exists for our making such appointment." Although section 22 of the 1921 Act will be sufficient for most cases where it is necessary for the court to appoint a trustee, this residual common law power of the court is still used occasionally:

- Where two trustees were unable to work together or to agree on the assumption of a third trustee, the court used its power to appoint a new trustee to resolve the deadlock: *Aikman, Petitioner* (1881) 9 R. 213; *Taylor, Petitioner*, 1932 S.C. 1.
- Where the court removed a sole trustee as unsuitable, it exercised its common law power to appoint another trustee in his place to prevent the trust lapsing: *Lamont v. Lamont*, 1908 S.C. 1033.

The power was invoked more recently in *Coal Industry Social Welfare Organisation, Petitioners*, 1959 S.L.T. (Notes) 3, where property had been held in the name of *ex officio* trustees representing several mining organisations, all of which had ceased to exist after industrialisation. The *nobile officium* was used to appoint new trustees, although it is unclear why the power under section 22 of the 1921 Act was not felt to be applicable.

7. DEATH OF A TRUSTEE

A. Death of one of several trustees

Where one of several trustees dies, his share in the trust property passes automatically to the other **4.17** trustees. See the following case:

Gordon's Trustees v. Eglinton
(1851) 13 D. 1381

Three trustees were appointed in a *mortis causa* trust. One of them subsequently died. The two remaining trustees subsequently sold the trust's heritable property to Mr Eglinton, who sold it on to Gordon's trustees. A question then arose as to whether the original conveyance by the two trustees was valid.

LORD JUSTICE-CLERK (HOPE): "There is no such thing as a separate but *pro indiviso* right to a third in each trustee. Each has the full title along with the other two; and if they die, his title carries the whole right, to the exclusion of any others. If one dies, the title in him as trustee becomes extinct—it is absorbed by the title subsisting in the other two. He is blotted out of the title, and the infeftment of the other two is as good and perfect as if he never had been in the title."

The Court held that the original conveyance was valid.

B. Death of a sole trustee

The position is more complex where a sole trustee dies: **4.18**

A.J.P. Menzies, *The Law of Scotland Affecting Trustees* **(2nd ed., 1913), p. 83**
"It is to be noted that death in the case of one or more trustees differs in its effect upon the trust title from death in the case of a sole trustee. In the former case death divests the trustee of the title; he is, as has been said, 'blotted out of the title'. In the latter case the title still remains in him, and has to be taken out of him by process of conveyancing."

NOTE:

For the procedure required, see Wilson and Duncan, paras 20–09 *et seq.* and 22–05 *et seq.*

8. A TRUSTEE'S POWER TO RESIGN

Trusts (Scotland) Act 1921, s.3

4.19 "All trusts shall be held to include the following powers and provisions unless the contrary be expressed (that is to say)—
    (a) Power to any trustee to resign the office of trustee;
    . . .
    Provided that—
    (1) A sole trustee shall not be entitled to resign his office by virtue of this Act unless either (1) he has assumed new trustees and they have declared their acceptance of office, or (2) the court shall have appointed new trustees or a judicial factor as hereinafter in this Act provided; and
    (2) A trustee who has accepted any legacy or bequest or annuity expressly given on condition of the recipient thereof accepting the office of trustee under the trust shall not be entitled to resign the office of trustee by virtue of this Act, unless otherwise expressly declared in the trust deed, nor shall any trustee appointed to the office of trustee on the footing of receiving remuneration for his services be entitled so to resign that office in the absence of an express power to resign; but it shall be competent to the court, on the petition of any trustee to whom the foregoing provisions of this proviso apply, to grant authority to such trustee to resign the office of trustee on such conditions (if any) with respect to repayment or otherwise of his legacy as the court may think just; and
    (3) A judicial factor shall not . . . have the power by virtue of this Act to resign his office without judicial authority."

NOTES:

4.20
    1. This provision derives from the Trusts (Scotland) Act 1861, section 1.
    2. The trust deed is to be held to include a power of resignation "unless the contrary is expressed". Where a pre-1861 trust deed includes a qualified power of resignation, the provisions of section 3 are not excluded by implication (*Maxwell's Trs v. Maxwell* (1874) 2 R. 71). However, a qualified power of resignation in a post-1861 deed would probably be held to exclude the section 3 power (Mackenzie Stuart, p. 307).
    3. Section 3(1) states that a sole trustee may not resign until he has assumed "new trustees", it has been held in the sheriff court that it is sufficient for only one new trustee to be assumed (*Kennedy, Petitioner*, 1983 S.L.T. (Sh. Ct) 10). However, there is Inner House authority to the effect that it is undesirable for a trust to be in the hands of a sole trustee (*Stewart v. Chalmers* (1904) 7 F. 163) and this interpretation is perhaps questionable.
    4. Section 3(1) is designed to avoid the trust being left with no trustees to administer it. Does it, therefore, in a trust with more than one trustee, prevent all the trustees resigning simultaneously? See the comments of the Lord President (Inglis) in *Maxwell's Trustees v. Maxwell* (1874) 2 R. 71, at 74:

". . . in what form ought a body of trustees, who all want to resign, to proceed? It would be extremely improper and inconsistent with their duty if they were *de plano* to execute a deed of resignation and hand it to the beneficiaries, leaving the trust without administration. If the beneficiaries are able to act and are reasonable, there can be no difficulty in nominating new trustees. But supposing they are not, there must be some mode of proceeding, and one consistent with leaving some person to administer the trust. What better course could be followed than to present a petition for the appointment of a judicial factor or of new trustees as a preliminary step?"

5. A non-gratuitous trustee may be given authority to resign by the trust deed. For example, Wilson and Duncan note (at para. 22–21) that "[i]t is the practice of concerns such as banks who undertake trusteeships on a basis of payment for services rendered to insist that the terms of any trust in which they accept office should permit their voluntary resignation to take place at any time."

If there is no such authority in the trust deed, they may petition the court for authority to resign. Authority has been granted where a trustee was unable to fill his duties due to "delicate health" (*Dick's Trustees v. Pridie* (1855) 17 D. 835); where official duties were preventing the trustee giving due attention to the trust (*Alison and Another, Petitioners* (1886) 23 SLR 362; *Orphoot, Petitioner* (1897) 24 R. 871); where a trustee was prevented from giving due attention to the trust due to advancing age (*Alison and Another, supra*); and where a conflict of interest had arisen between the interests of the trustee personally and the trust (*Johnston, Petitioner*, 1932 S.L.T. 261; *Guthrie, Petitioner* (1895) 22 R. 879). The statute provides that the court may, in granting permission, attach conditions requiring the repayment of a legacy. In addition, the court has the option to refuse to hold the trust estate liable in the expenses of the action (*Johnston, supra*). It appears that the court will exercise its discretion to do one or both of these things where the trustee should have refused to accept office in the first instance due to the problem for which authority to seek resignation is sought (*Johnston, supra; Orphoot, supra*)

Form of Resignation

Trusts (Scotland) Act 1921, s.19(1)

19.—(1) Subject to the provisions of subsection (2) of this section, any trustee **4.21** entitled to resign his office may do so by minute of the trust entered in the sederunt book of the trust and signed in such sederent book by such trustee and by the other trustee or trustees acting at the time, or he may do so by signing a minute of resignation in the form of Schedule A to this Act annexed or to the like effect, and may register the same in the books of council and session, and in such case he shall be bound to intimate the same to his co-trustee or trustees, and the resignation shall be held to take effect from and after the date of the receipt of such intimation, or the last date thereof if more than one, and in case after inquiry the residence of any trustee to whom intimation should be given under this provision cannot be found, such intimation shall be sent by post in a registered letter addressed to the Keeper of the Register of Edictal Citations.

NOTE:

Section 19(2) provides a mechanism for a sole trustee to apply to the court for permission to resign and the appointment of new trustees or a judicial factor. Section 19(1) is not mandatory and resignation need not be in one of the forms prescribed therein to be effective. However, Wilson and Duncan (22–31) point out that there is "no authority for the effectiveness of a verbal resignation or one inferred from actings".

9. REMOVAL OF A TRUSTEE BY THE COURT

A. Removal under statute

Trusts (Scotland) Act 1921, s.23

4.22 "In the event of any trustee being or becoming insane or incapable of acting by reason of physical or mental disability or being absent from the United Kingdom continuously for a period of at least six months, or having disappeared for a like period, such trustee, in the case of insanity or incapacity of acting by reason of physical or mental disability, shall, and in the case of continuous absence from the United Kingdom or disappearance for a period of six months or upwards, may, on application in manner in this section provided by any co-trustee or any beneficiary or other person interested in the trust estate, be removed from office upon such evidence as shall satisfy the court to which the application is made of the insanity, incapacity, or continuous absence or disappearance of such trustee . . ."

NOTES:

    1. Section 23 also contains directions as to which court the application should be made in. It will be noted that the court *must* remove a trustee who is insane or incapable because of disability (confirmed in *Tod v. Marshall* (1895) 23 R. 36), but has a discretion as to whether or not a trustee who is absent from the U.K. or who has disappeared should be removed.

    2. Where an application is made to remove a sole trustee (or all trustees), it will usually be desirable to also make an application to appoint new trustees under section 22 of the 1921 Act.

B. Removal at common law

4.23 The court also has a common law power to remove a trustee for "something either equivalent to, or as bad as, malversation of office when a trustee obstinately refuses to acknowledge his legal duty and to discharge his legal responsibility, with the result of bringing the affairs of the trust into confusion" (*MacGilchrist's Trustees v. MacGilchrist*, 1930 S.C. 635, *per* the Lord President (Clyde) at 638). A trustee will not be removed simply because there has been some irregularity in the management of the trust (*Gilchrist's Trustees v. Dick* (1883) 11 R. 22). Nor is the fact that trustees are incapable of working together sufficient ground for removing one of them (*Hope v. Hope* (1884) 12 R. 27). For an example of circumstances justifying removal of a trustee by the court, see the following case:

Stewart v. Chalmers
(1904) 7 F. 163

4.24 Peter Stewart appointed three trustees under his will, two of whom subsequently died. Robert Stewart, a solicitor, was assumed as a trustee and was appointed law-agent to the trust. Another trustee was appointed but resigned shortly later. Robert Stewart subsequently wrote a letter to Thomas Chalmers, the only remaining original trustee, indicating that he wished to consult him regarding the investment of the trust estate. Thomas Chalmers wrote back, saying, "As your position and mine as trustees are now equal, I am to insist on half fees for all business to be done by you for this trust. On hearing from you that you agree to this condition, I will consider the question of investing the trust funds." The beneficiaries subsequently petitioned the Court of Session to remove Thomas Chalmers from his position as trustee.

LORD PRESIDENT (KINROSS): "He [Thomas Chalmers] insists on receiving half fees for which he had not given and was not to give any professional service, and he makes payment of this indefensible claim a condition of his attending to the business of the trust which he had accepted. It would be difficult to conceive of anything more improper than this proposal . . .

[it] was quite indefensible, and shews that the respondent is unfit to be trusted with the position of a trustee . . . he not only displayed a total disregard for the benefit of the trust, but also acted in a way contrary to its interests and calculated to bring it to a deadlock, all for the purpose of getting some of the trust funds for himself. If he thought Mr Stewart was acting wrongly with regard to the investment, it was his duty to say so, and to take steps for obtaining a proper investment, but instead of doing this he sought to prevent anything at all being done. Such an attitude on his part was quite indefensible, and it appears to me that the proper course is to remove him from the office of trustee."

The Court granted the prayer of the petition.

NOTE:

The court indicated that it would be undesirable for the trust to fall into the administration of a sole trustee, and after removing Thomas Chalmers, continued the case to allow Robert Stewart to lodge a deed assuming two other persons as trustees, which he duly did.

Chapter 5

PURPOSES OF A TRUST

This chapter considers the circumstances in which trust purposes, specified by the truster in the trust-deed, may be held to be invalid as uncertain, overly wide, or illegal.

1. PURPOSES VOID FROM UNCERTAINTY

Hardie v. Morison
(1899) 7 S.L.T. 42

5.01 David Hardie died in 1896. His will directed his trustees "to apply the whole residue of my means and estate for the purchasing of premises in the city of Edinburgh, to be used as a shop in which one of the objects is the sale of books dealing with the subject of free thought, and I direct my trustees to let said shop to a tenant who will always have for sale books dealing with such subject; Declaring always that such tenant will in nowise be bound to make this the whole of his business, and that he shall be quite at liberty to sell such other books or articles as he or she may think fit . . . ." His next of kin argued that this provision was void from uncertainty.

LORD KINCAIRNEY: "I think that a bequest for the promotion of free thought is void from uncertainty, from want of any recognised or determinate meaning of that term . . . I am not aware that it is a term with any definite or recognised meaning. In carrying out this trust it would not be possible to determine what class of books was meant . . . the mere words of the deed do not indicate whether the testator intended books favourable to free thought or adverse to it . . . Further, the testator declares that the trustees may use the shop otherwise as they please, if they only keep such books. That is not a trust power or direction capable of being enforced . . . ."

The Court held that the deed was void from uncertainty.

NOTES:

5.02
1. This decision may be compared with *McLean v. Henderson's Trs* (1880) 7 R. 601, where it was argued that a bequest "for the advancement and diffusion of the science of phrenology" was void for uncertainty. The Inner House rejected this argument, with Lord Ormidale observing that "the expression phrenology denotes a known, although not a flourishing, branch of science".
2. The question is simply whether the truster's directions are intelligible—can their meaning be understood? In *Warrender v. Anderson* (1893) 1 S.L.T. 304, Lord Kyllachy held that a direction that the residue of the testator's estate should be given to "those whom you know respects me was valid", but made the following observation:

"If there had been a simple request to the trustee to 'give to those who respected me' this would have been bad. There would have been no workable definition, nor would any means have been provided for ascertaining who were meant."

2. PURPOSES WHICH ARE TOO WIDE: TO WHAT EXTENT CAN POWERS OF SELECTION BE CONFERRED ON TRUSTEES?

A truster need not specify down to the last detail how his trustees should distribute or apply his **5.03** property. Indeed, it would be impossible and unreasonable to expect him to do so in some cases. If a trust is set up to provide funding for (for example) cancer research, or postgraduate study, it would hardly be reasonable (nor even possible) to expect the truster to specify years or decades in advance which applications for support were to be refused, and which approved. Accordingly, a truster may confer discretion upon his trustees to exercise powers of selection in such cases.

The classic formulation of this principle is found in the judgment of Lord Lyndhurst L.C. in *Crichton v. Grierson* (1828) 3 W. & S. 329, at 338–339:

"a party may, in the disposition of his property, select particular classes of individuals and objects, and then give to some particular individual a power, after his death, of appropriating the property, or applying any part of his property, to any particular individuals among that class whom that person may select and describe in his will."

Two issues arise from this principle. Firstly, how narrowly defined must the "particular class" be to be valid? Secondly, if the discretion must be conferred on a "particular individual", what is the position of a trustee who has not been appointed by the truster—but has instead, for example, been assumed by the other trustees or appointed by the court? May they also exercise discretion?

A. Defining the "particular class"

The trustee may be given powers of selection in both private and public trusts, although most of the **5.04** case law on this issue concerns public trusts. In some cases, the class is so vaguely defined as to make it impossible to say whether the trust is public or private—although the point then becomes academic, as if the class is this vague, the truster's directions will be void.

(i) Private trusts and the "particular class"

An example of powers of selection being conferred in a private trust can be found in the following case:

Smellie's Trs v. Glasgow Royal Infirmary
(1905) 13 S.L.T. 450

Thomas Smellie died in October 1900. His will provided that part of the residue of his estate **5.05** was to be distributed "to my domestic servants, old personal friends in need, employees not otherwise included in any provision by me, or others whom my trustees shall consider that I would wish to remember. A list of these with the amounts intended I purpose to supply, but, failing this, or even although such list is left by me, my trustees shall have full freedom to take into account changes by death or otherwise, and add such friends as may appear to be omitted, and modify, allocate and apportion the sums as they may see fit . . .". It was argued that this provision was void for uncertainty.

LORD DUNDAS: "'Domestic servants', 'old personal friends in need', and employees not otherwise provided for by the truster, are all, I think, sufficiently defined classes of individuals who might participate in his bounty according to the discretion of the trustees, especially with the assistance of the holograph list or memo. containing indications of the truster's intention. Some difficulty, however, is occasioned by the words which follow, 'or others whom my trustees shall consider that I would wish to remember'. But I think that this may fairly be read as meaning other persons, who, though possibly not falling accurately within any one of the classes specifically above enumerated, are so similarly circumstanced as to permit of ready assimilation to or inclusion in one or other of them, and it does not seem probable that the trustees will have any real difficulty in dealing with the money so as to accord with Mr. Smellie's intentions."

The Court held that the provision was valid.

NOTE:

5.06   Particular attention should be paid to Lord Dundas' comment that "it does not seem probable that the trustees will have any real difficulty in dealing with the money so as to accord with Mr Smellie's intentions". The key point is—do the truster's directions give sufficient guidance to the trustees to ensure that they are carrying out *his* wishes? Or are they so vague that they simply give the trustees the power to make for themselves the decisions that the truster should himself have made? To quote Lord Justice-Clerk Thomson, "The testator must make his will for himself. He cannot leave it to his trustees to make a will for him." (*Rintoul's Trustees v. Rintoul*, 1949 S.C. 297, at 299). If a testator wishes to confer an unfettered right to dispose of his property on some third party, he may, of course, simply give his property to that third party—but he cannot create a trust. The following formulations of the test to be applied provide some guidance. They look at the question from different perspectives but might be expected to lead to identical results.

- "the question . . . is whether or not the testator has described the class he means to benefit with sufficient accuracy as to enable a reasonable man to know who the persons are that he meant to benefit, leaving it only to the trustees to select among those who form that class the particular recipients of his bounty." (*Salvesen's Trustees v. Wye* 1954 S.C. 440, *per* Lord Carmont at 444).
- "The class pointed out must be definite. One test of this is whether the limits are sufficiently clear to enable the Court to say whether, at any stage, the trustees are in breach of trust." (Mackenzie Stuart, p. 109).

The following classes have been held to be too vague to be effective:

- "I give everything to her [my executrix] to share out as she knows I would wish it" (*Wood v. Wood's Executrix*, 1994 S.L.T. 563). There is, however, some suggestion in the judgment that if the executrix had been able to show that she had specific knowledge of the deceased's wishes as to the distribution of his property, then this direction might have been valid.
- "I leave and bequeath [the residue of my estate] to be disposed of by my said trustees in such manner as they may think proper." (*Sutherland's Trustees v. Sutherland's Trustee* (1893) 20 R. 925).
- "[my whole estate] shall be dealt with and disposed of by my said trustees in such way or ways as my trustees shall deem best . . . my trustees shall have full power and liberty to dispose of such residue in any manner that may approve itself to them." (*Allan and Others (Shaw's Trustees)* (1893) 1 S.L.T. 308)

The following classes have been held to be valid:

- "I hereby authorise and instruct you . . . to hold and apply the annual proceeds of these two shares for the purpose of rewarding meritorious or long service employees of our said firm, or for any other purposes of the business, as the managers may in their discretion deem expedient, and they shall be the sole judges." (*Hedderwick's Trs v. Hedderwick* 1909 1 S.L.T. 464, *appeal allowed on other grounds* 1910 1 S.L.T. 36). Lord Johnston rejected the argument that the words "for any other purposes of the business" made the direction void, stating (at 466) that: "I cannot read these words in a wide and general sense. I think that they are related to the primary purpose, which is declared to be that 'of rewarding meritorious or long service employees of our said firm', and that they must therefore be read as confined to other purposes *ejusdem generis* or of a class beneficial to the employees. Many such could be suggested, as, for instance, that of providing reading and recreation rooms at the works."

• A direction that the residue of the testator's estate should be disposed of "among any poor relations, friends or acquaintances of mine". (*Salvesen's Trustees v. Wye*, 1954 S.C. 440). In that case, it was held that "poor relations" was valid, and that "poor friends" might be, but that "poor acquaintances" was too vague—and that, therefore, the class as a whole was too vague. Lord President Cooper observed (at 447) that "the validity of the direction as a whole, must be tested on the principle that the strength of a chain is its weakest link, and that, if one of the groups is not adequately defined, the whole bequest must fall."

(ii) Public trusts and the "particular class"

This area highlights an important difference between the English and the Scottish law of trusts. In England, a trust for the public benefit is valid only if it is a "charitable trust", and charitable has a technical legal meaning (*Bowman v. Secular Society Ltd* [1917] A.C. 406, *per* Lord Parker at 441). So, in the case of *Re Astor's Settlement Trusts* [1952] Ch. 534, a number of trusts were set up, the income from which was to be applied for, *inter alia*, the "maintenance and improvement of good understanding sympathy and co-operation between nations", the "preservation of the independence and integrity of newspapers . . . [and the] promotion of the freedom independence and integrity of the press." It was held that the trusts were invalid as being neither for the benefit of individuals nor for charitable purposes. **5.07**

Scots law does not adopt this narrow approach, and a public trust need not be "charitable" in order to be valid. It does, however, attach a special status to charitable trusts, as will be seen below.

Provided the class in a public trust is reasonably well-defined, there should be little difficulty with its validity. So, for example, a direction that money be devoted "to the Bursary Fund of the Aberdeen University, to help in the education of poor and struggling youths of merit" was held sufficiently precise (*Milne's Executors v. Aberdeen University Court* (1905) 7 F. 642), as was a direction that "fifty pounds annually to be applied towards the maintenance of a nurse available for the sick poor of Galston or for some analogous purpose in such manner as my trustees may decide and direct" (*Forrest's Trustees v. Forrest's Trustees*, 1959 S.L.T. (Notes) 24).

Problems arise, however, where the truster chooses to use some vague form of words, such as "charitable purposes" or "public purposes", thus conferring a considerable amount of discretion upon his trustees. To what extent are such broadly defined classes valid? A special status is afforded to the term "charitable purposes", as is indicated by the following dictum:

Turnbull's Trs v. Lord Advocate
1918 S.C. (H.L.) 88

VISCOUNT HALDANE: "By the law of Scotland, as by that of England, a testator can only defeat the claim of those entitled by law in the absence of a valid will to succeed to the beneficial interest in his estate, if he has made a complete disposition of that beneficial interest. He cannot leave it to another person to make such a disposition for him unless he has passed the beneficial interest to that person to dispose of as his own. He may indeed provide that a special class of persons, or of institutions invested by law with the capacity of persons to hold property, are to take in such shares as a third person may determine, but that is only because he has disposed of the beneficial interest in favour of that class as his beneficiaries. There is, however, an apparent exception to the principle. The testator may indicate his intention that his estate is to go for charitable purposes. If these purposes are of the kinds which the law recognises in somewhat different ways in the two countries as charitable, the Courts will disregard a merely subordinate deficiency in particular expression of intention to dispose of the entire beneficial interest to a class, and will even themselves, by making a scheme of some kind, give effect to the general intention that the estate should be disposed of for charitable purposes." **5.08**

NOTE:

In other words "charitable purposes" is in itself sufficiently specific, and therefore "a trust for such charitable purposes as a trustee may select is valid without further definition of the purposes or of the objects to be benefited". (Mackenzie Stuart, p. 112). To quote Lord McLaren, the principle is that: **5.09**

"... bequests for charitable purposes should receive an indulgent and favourable criticism with a view, if possible, of giving effect to the testator's benevolent intentions. In the development of this principle the rule against giving effect to bequests of a wholly undefined character has been relaxed in favour of charities." (*Hay's Trustees v. Baillie*, 1908 S.C. 1224, at 1232).

The courts have not looked so favourably, however, upon other widely defined classes. Consider the following examples.

- **"Benevolent purposes"**. Some writers (Mackenzie Stuart, p. 112; Norrie & Scobbie, p. 79) have suggested that this is synonymous with "charitable purposes" and should therefore be recognised as valid. This view is not, however, justified by the authorities cited by those writers (*Hay's Trustees v. Baillie*, 1908 S.C. 1224; *Hill v. Burns* (1826) 2 W. & S. 80), which are concerned with the validity of the phrases "benevolent and charitable" or "benevolent or charitable". (See the section below on "conjunctive and disjunctive adjectives"). There is in fact clear authority to the effect that "benevolent purposes" on its own is too wide: *Caldwell's Trustees v. Caldwell*, 1920 S.C. 700, *per* Lord Skerrington at 702.

- **"Public purposes"** will not be sufficient. In *Blair v. Duncan* (1901) 4 F. (H.L.) 1, the testatrix directed that half of the residue of her estate should go to "charitable or public purposes". On the basis that the validity of this direction depended on whether "public purposes" was itself sufficiently specific, Lord Robertson remarked (at 5) that:

  "this testatrix has done nothing like selecting particular class or particular classes of objects. She excludes individuals, and then leaves the trustee at large, with the whole world to choose from. There is nothing affecting any community on the globe which is outside the ambit of his choice."

It was held that the direction was void for uncertainty. Nor does restricting the purpose to a particular area make any difference (*Turnbull's Trustees v. Lord Advocate*, 1918 S.C. (H.L.) 88 (public purposes in Lesmahagow)).

- **"Religious purposes"** was considered in the case of *Grimond v. Grimond's Trs* (1904) 6 F. 285 (Inner House); (1905) 7 F. (H.L.) 90. Lord Moncreiff (who was dissenting in the Inner House, but whose judgment was approved by the House of Lords) rejected the Lord Ordinary's view that the phrase "religious purposes" must be taken to be limited to the Christian religion, saying:

  "I apprehend that it would be within the powers of the trustees to apply the fund for the maintenance of a Unitarian or a Theistic chapel or a Jewish synagogue. But even if the Lord Ordinary were right in holding that the selection must be confined to societies professing the Christian religion, I should not be prepared to hold that such a bequest is sufficiently specific to admit of being enforced. The distinctions between different churches and denominations professing the Christian religion are sharply defined and strictly enforced. The deed gives us no clue to the truster's religious belief. He may have been a Presbyterian, yet under this power the trustees would be entitled to apply the bequest for the support of an Episcopal or Roman Catholic church. Again, he may have shared the views of the minority of the Free Church, and yet a court of law could not prevent his trustees from applying the bequest to the Sustentation Fund of the United Free Church. In short, there is not only no local limit, but no specific selection among a number of Christian churches and denominations, differing widely, not only as to church government and ritual, but as to the importance and authority of fundamental articles of faith."

Accordingly, the direction was too uncertain to receive effect. However, if a bequest to "religious purposes" is narrowed as to the type of religion in some way, it will be valid. See, for example, *Bannerman's Trs v. Bannerman*, 1915 S.C. 398 ("religious or charitable Institutions ... conducted according to Protestant principles"); *Macray v. Macray*, 1910 2 S.L.T. 74 ("Christian" purposes). Restricting the scope of the purpose to a particular locality will probably not be sufficient: see *Shaw's Trustee v. Esson's Trustees* (1905) 8 F. 52, where "religious objects or purposes within the City of Aberdeen" was held too vague. See, however, *Edgar's Trustees v. Cassels*, 1922 S.C. 395, where the Inner House (Lord Ormidale dissenting) held that a direction that the residue of the testatrix's estate be divided amongst such "benevolent, charitable, and religious institutions in Glasgow and Greenock as [the trustees] in their sole discretion may think proper" was valid. The distinction from *Shaw's Trustee* appears to be that the bequest in *Edgar's Trustees* was "confined to existing local institutions" (*per* Lord Justice-Clerk Scott Dickson at 400).

- **"Educational purposes".** In *Brough v. Brough's Trs*, 1950 S.L.T. 117, Lord Strachan reviewed the earlier authorities and concluded (at 119) that: **5.10**

> "In that state of the authorities I am not prepared to hold this bequest to be invalid because of the use of the phrase 'educational work'. In any event the word 'educational' seems to me to be sufficiently specific. It is not in my opinion open to the objection of vagueness that can be applied to such words as 'public', 'social', 'religious'."

It has been held, however, that a bequest "for the advancement of art, science or literature in the burgh of Castle-Douglas" was too vague (*Harper's Trustees v. Jacobs*, 1929 S.C. 345). In that case, however, the sum involved was less than £500, and two of the three judges (Lord Sands and Lord Blackburn) suggested that the decision might have been different if the trust had been well-funded. Lord Blackburn said (at 350):

> "If it appeared clear that the purpose of the testator was to create an educational trust for the benefit of the inhabitants of Castle Douglas, then I think we should have to treat the bequest as a charitable one, and give it such a wide construction as would enable the trustees to carry out the testator's purposes to the best of their ability. But I find it very difficult to believe that the testator intended so small a sum—and he himself realised that it might be less than it actually is—to be used as a trust for educational purposes, and it seems to me much more probable that he contemplated that his trustees should expend the sum on something which they might consider would be for "the advancement of art, science, or literature"—*e.g.* on a picture, a telescope, or books. If that was his intention, then the bequest would not fall within the definition of a charitable one, and the testator was in effect merely leaving his trustees to make his will for him instead of doing it expressly for himself. The uncertainty as to what the testator intended leads me to the conclusion that the bequest must be regarded as void . . ."

- **Conjunctive and disjunctive adjectives.** The position becomes more difficult where "charitable" is coupled with some other form of words. The crucial question becomes whether the list of adjectives is intended to be conjunctive or disjunctive. For example, if a testator makes a bequest to "charitable and religious purposes", which of the following does this mean?

   (i) Both "charitable purposes" and "religious purposes"—in which case it will be void for uncertainty. This is because such a direction would appear to give the trustee the discretion to choose between "charitable" purposes and "religious" purposes, and the latter of the two is too broad.
   (ii) Purposes which are *both* charitable *and* religious—in which case it will be valid, as "charitable purposes" is sufficiently narrow to be considered valid, and requiring the purpose to be religious *as well as* charitable is simply narrowing an already valid category.

There is, unfortunately, no simple answer to this question. The same problem arises when the word "or" is used, as "or" can sometimes be taken to indicate that the adjectives are not being used as alternatives, but are simply being used to explain or reinforce the others (referred to by Wilson and Duncan (at 14–105) as "the exegetical construction"). So, for example, in *Hay's Trustees v. Baillie*, 1908 S.C. 1224, the testatrix directed her trustees to pay over the residue of her estate "to or amongst such societies or institutions of a benevolent or charitable nature in such proportions" as they thought proper. The Inner House held that this was not void for uncertainty. Lord Kinnear explained the decision as follows (at 1234–1235):

> ". . . it is said to be an invalid bequest, because, in place of confining herself to the word 'charitable', she has used the words 'of a benevolent or charitable nature'. The real question is, whether, upon the construction of that will, that is a wider class of purposes than the word 'charitable,' taken alone, would have defined. It appears to me that the question whether this testatrix really meant, 'You are to select between two distinct classes of institutions, charitable institutions on the one hand, and a different class of institutions altogether, which I call benevolent, on the other hand,' is not a question upon which previous decisions can guide us at all. I think the question is, what the testatrix really means, and I do not think that is to be ascertained by a strict grammatical analysis of the words she has used. Taking the whole will, taking the particular directions for the distribution of the residue with reference to its context, the question is, what did this testatrix mean? And I confess that I have no doubt that by 'charitable or benevolent' she meant one thing, and not two things. The whole difficulty arises from what I think is a mere redundancy of expression, and we had cited to us several examples of a similar redundancy in the expressions, not of testators, but of learned judges who were discussing this kind of question. I do not think that, in ordinary language, when a testator describes institutions of a charitable or benevolent character, she means two different kinds of institutions which she distinguishes from one another; and, if not, I think that, as she has given a sufficiently definite description of the class of institutions which she intends to favour, she will enable trustees of requisite common sense to carry out her intention."

As Lord Kinnear suggests, previous decisions are of limited use in deciding how the words "and" and "or" are to be interpreted in individual trust deeds, although they may be of some guidance. There is a comprehensive review of the case law in Wilson and Duncan at 14–100 to 14–117.

B. The Requirement of Nomination of Trustees

5.11 If a testator wishes to select a class and confer upon his trustees the discretion to select within it, he must nominate trustees. This requirement is well shown by the following case:

Angus's Exrx v. Batchan's Trs
1949 S.C. 335

Anne Angus's will made provision for certain specific legacies, and concluded with the words: "All money after paying, please give to charities." She did not nominate a trustee or executor. It was argued that this direction was void from uncertainty. The Lord Ordinary (Lord Mackintosh) held that it was a valid direction. On appeal to the Inner House, where the case was heard by a bench of seven judges:

LORD PRESIDENT (COOPER): "No encroachment has ever yet been tolerated on the basic requirement that a testator must make his own will, and that, when he makes it by designating a class and a person to choose within that class, the designation of both must be his own act, express or plainly implied. To allow a testator to confine himself to designating the class, while deliberately leaving the choice of the individual beneficiaries to anyone who may anyhow acquire a title to administer the estate is, in my opinion, to authorise that testator to delegate the power to test—at least in a case such as the present in which the class is so vast and amorphous as to include every institution and object capable of being covered by the comprehensive term 'charity'. A *mortis causa* declaration of charitable benevolence is not a will. If a testator wishes to leave his money to others than his next of kin, it is not an unduly exacting requirement that he should take the trouble to identify, or to render identifiable, the beneficiaries whom he prefers to his intestate heirs."

The Court held that the bequest was void from uncertainty.

Notes:

1. This gives rise to a number of questions, as follows: **5.12**
2. *What happens where all the nominated trustees are dead or decline office?* This problem is unlikely to arise in an *inter vivos* trust, as the trustee could normally exercise his radical right to appoint new trustees (see Chapter 5). In a *mortis causa* trust, it would seem that the directions will be held ineffective as a result (*Macdonald v. Atherton*, 1925 S.L.T. 426). This depends, however, on the extent to which a court-appointed trustee, executor-dative or judicial factor can exercise discretion, which is discussed below.
3. *Can assumed trustees exercise discretion?* The position here is more complex. In *Angus's Exrx,* Lord Jamieson made the following observations (at 365–366):

> "In *Shedden's Trustee v. Dykes*, 1914 S.C. 106 it was held that an assumed trustee was entitled to exercise the power of selection and allocation conferred on nominated trustees. Considerable doubt was expressed by Lord Johnston, but he concurred in the judgment on a construction of the will, treating the case as a special one. We were asked to hold that the case was wrongly decided, but I am not prepared to do so.
>
> I think the judgment may be supported on the ground stated by Lord M'Laren in *Robbie's Judicial Factor* (1893) 20 R. 358 that an assumed trustee derives authority from the testator, and I think it immaterial that the will contains no express power of assumption. A testator must, I think, be assumed to be aware of the statutory power to assume new trustees, and that, especially where the trust purposes cannot be fully carried out until the lapse of a considerable period, it may become necessary to exercise such a power. I am unable, however, to agree with the Lord President's view that the residue clause contained nothing approaching *delectus personae*. In appointing trustees a testator does so because of the confidence he places in them, a point that was stressed in *Wordie's Trustees*, 1916 S.C. (H.L.) 126. It is not necessarily confidence in individuals personally, as where an appointment is made of trustees ex officio, relying on the competency of the holders of the office, and perhaps on their local knowledge, to execute the trust. A bequest to charities in the abstract is only capable of being given effect to at the hands of one or more persons empowered, expressly or by implication, to select the particular objects to be benefited. It is from the power of selection so given that 'charities' have come to be regarded as a sufficiently designated class and such a bequest derives its validity. In choosing to benefit charities rather than his heirs, a testator exercises a *delectus* in the choice of persons to whom he leaves the power of selection, although that power may only impliedly be given to his trustees. In exercising the power, the persons to whom it is committed have, in most cases, the advantage of some knowledge of the testator to guide them. I do not suggest that his wishes have actually been communicated to them. But their knowledge of the testator and his interests during his life will to some extent influence them in carrying out what they regard would have been his wishes, both as to the nature and locality of the objects they select. No such advantage is possessed by a nominee of the Court, and where, as in the present case, a judicial factor would be left to 'survey mankind from China to Peru' with a world-wide choice of charities, the bequest must, in my view, be regarded as void from uncertainty. In *Shedden's Trustee* the bequest was limited to charities in a particular locality, but the difference is only one of degree. It appears to me that in every case *delectus personae* to some extent, although not in the strictest sense, enters into the matter, and that, where a power of selection is not made personal to nominated trustees, assumed trustees may exercise it because the testator must be taken as assuming that, if necessity arises, the trustees whom he has nominated will assume persons on whom reliance may be placed to carry out his wishes."

The question, then, is whether the truster has made the power of selection "personal to nominated trustees". If the power is made personal, then assumed trustees cannot exercise discretion. This is a question of fact, the answer to which will depend on the exact terms of the trust deed and the nature of the trust. If the truster has expressly conferred a power of assumption, then that would seem to suggest that he has contemplated that assumed trustees might be appointed to exercise discretion. It would be wrong to assume the converse though, and hold that a truster who has *not* conferred a power of assumption has made the power of selection "personal to nominated trustees", since it might be argued that a truster must be assumed to know that there is a statutory power of assumption under the 1921 Act (see *Shedden's Tr. v. Dykes*, 1914 S.C. 106). There is a discussion of further factors which may be taken into account in Wilson and Duncan at 14–30. Cf. *Vollar's Judicial Factor v. Boyd*, 1952 S.L.T. (Notes) 84, where Lord Strachan interpreted *Angus's Exrx* as laying down a "rule of quite general application" that an assumed trustee could exercise discretion.

5.13   4. *Can a trustee appointed by the court, or a judicial factor, exercise discretion?* Again, the position here is rather confused. In *Vollar's J.F. v. Boyd*, 1952 S.L.T. (Notes) 84, Lord Strachan concluded (at 84) that:

> "I am of opinion that the judgments of the majority of the Judges [in *Angus's Executrix*] have the effect of formulating a rule of quite general application to the effect that where a power of selection is conferred on nominated trustees and is not made personal to them, it may be exercised by assumed trustees, but not by trustees appointed by the Court, or by a judicial factor, because there is no link between a testator and trustees appointed by the Court or a judicial factor."

However, there is some suggestion in Lord Jamieson's judgment in *Angus's Exrx* (relying on comments of Lord McLaren in *Robbie's J.F.* (1893) 20 R. 358) that, while a trustee nominated by the court could not exercise a power of selection amongst "charitable purposes generally", they could exercise a power of selection between "charities of a particular nature and in a particular locality, or [in] cases where a testator has defined the object of his bounty . . .". This is the view adopted by Wilson and Duncan (para. 14–32). Presumably the rationale of this view is that the class is sufficiently narrow that the trustee can give effect to the truster's wishes. But if this is true, it is not easy to understand *Macdonald v. Atherton*, 1925 S.L.T. 426, where it was held that, where all the nominated trustees had died or declined office, the trust purposes necessarily failed. This case, after all, involved a reasonably well-defined objective (to benefit "the nearest and most needful relatives on [the testator's] mother's side"). It may be argued that *Macdonald* concerned a private rather than public trust, but it is not clear why this distinction should be of importance.

5. *Can an executor-dative exercise discretion?* Given the confusion in the case law on trustees nominated by the courts and judicial factors, the position here is even less clear. In *Angus's Exrx* the Lord Ordinary (Lord Mackintosh) was prepared (at 339) to hold that a judicial factor could exercise discretion to select between "charitable purposes" (a decision which was reversed on appeal), but was not prepared to hold that such a power could be exercised by an executor-dative:

> "I am of opinion, however, that the discretionary powers necessary for selecting particular charitable objects cannot be held to reside in, nor could they properly be conferred upon, the pursuer as executrix-dative. She only holds that position because of the accident that the next-of-kin did not see fit to apply to be appointed, and in any case an executor-dative is appointed only for the purpose of carrying out duties which are purely executorial. Such an appointment would not cover the exercise of a discretionary power like that involved in selecting particular charitable objects out of the general class described as 'charities'. An executor-dative is not, like an executor-nominate or a judicial factor appointed by the Court on a trust estate, a trustee within the meaning of the Trusts (Scotland) Act 1921, and cannot be required to act with the discretionary powers proper to a trustee."

See now, however, section 20 of the Succession (Scotland) Act 1964:

> "An executor dative appointed to administer the estate of a deceased person shall have in his administration of such estate the whole powers, privileges and immunities, and be subject to the same obligations, limitations and restrictions, which gratuitous

trustees have, or are subject to, under any enactment or under common law, and the Trusts (Scotland) Acts, 1921 and 1961, shall have effect as if any reference therein to a trustee included a reference to such an executor dative:

Provided that nothing in this section shall exempt an executor dative from finding caution for his intromissions or confer upon him any power to resign or to assume new trustees."

This would appear to put an executor-dative in at least as good a position as a trustee nominated by the court or a judicial factor. Wilson and Duncan suggest, however, (para. 14–31) that "he cannot be in a better position than a trustee appointed by the court. He lacks, as do the trustees appointed by the court and the judicial factor, the link with the testator desiderated by Lords Jamieson and Mackay in *Angus's Exrx*". This is arguably incorrect, however, as a person "cannot be appointed an executor-dative merely on the grounds of expediency . . . [they] must have a legal title to the office." (Wilson and Duncan, para. 32–37).

In practice, an executor-dative will usually have a relatively strong link with the testator, given the order of preference for persons who are entitled to that office (see Wilson and Duncan, paras 32–49 *et seq.* for the relevant rules). That surely puts the executor-dative in a better position than the judicial factor discussed by Lord Mackay in *Angus's Exrx*, a chartered accountant who "had no element of 'link' with the testator [and could not] possibly claim other than remotely inferred power from him." (Lord Mackay was referring to *Woodard's J.F.*, 1926 S.C. 534). It is arguable that a testator should be taken to accept the legal rules governing the appointment of an executor-dative, particularly where he takes no steps at all to nominate an executor in his will.

3. ILLEGALITY OF TRUST PURPOSES

Bowman v. Secular Society Limited
[1917] A.C. 406

In his will, Charles Bowman left the residue of his estate to the Secular Society Limited. The **5.14** principal purpose of the society was "to promote . . . the principle that human conduct should be based upon natural knowledge, and not upon super-natural belief, and that human welfare in this world is the proper end of all thought and action."

His next of kin challenged the bequest, arguing that the Society's objects were illegal and that the bequest was therefore unenforceable. Joyce J. held that the bequest was valid, which was affirmed by the Court of Appeal. On appeal to the House of Lords:

LORD DUNEDIN: "[I]f money was laid out in either procuring publications or lectures in terms of the objects of the memorandum such publications or lectures need not be couched in scurrilous language and so need not be such as would constitute the crime of blasphemy at common law. Nor need they be criminal under the Blasphemy Act; for here I agree with Lord Buckmaster that the act is so framed as to make its penalties only apply when there has been what may be termed apostasy.

Criminal liability having been negatived, no one has suggested any statute in terms of which it—by which I mean the supposed use of the money—is directly prohibited. There is no question of offence against what may be termed the natural moral sense. Neither has it been held, I think, as being against public policy, as that phrase is applied in the cases that have been decided on that head. Now if this is so, I confess I cannot bring myself to believe that there is still a terra media of things illegal, which are not criminal, not directly prohibited, not contra bonos mores, and not against public policy."

Appeal dismissed.

NOTE:

Lord Dunedin's analysis indicates that trust purposes may be considered illegal if—and only if—they are:

    (i) criminal, or

    (ii) directly prohibited, or

    (iii) *contra bonos mores* (an offence against the "natural moral sense"), or

    (iv) contrary to public policy.

A. Criminal purposes

5.15 There is an almost total absence of authority on this issue, and it is doubtful that it is of much practical importance. It is clear, however, that a trust for criminal purposes is void. For example, if the submission of the appellants' counsel in *Bowman* that "it is criminal to attack the Christian religion, however decent and temperate may be the form of attack" had been upheld, there is no doubt that the bequest would have been unenforceable.

B. Directly prohibited purposes

5.16 *(i) Entails*

Scottish Law Commission,
Report on Abolition of the Feudal System
(Scot. Law Com. No. 168, 1998, footnotes omitted)

"Entails

9.8   Entails, or tailzies, were at one time commonly used to keep lands in the same family for generations. A feudal grant of land would be made in such a way that the succession to it was strictly regulated and protected. For example, the deed might provide that on the death of the owner the land was to pass to his eldest son or other male heir and so on for subsequent owners. At any one time there would often be an heir in possession and an heir apparent who could expect to succeed to the lands on surviving the heir in possession. The stipulated line of succession would be secured by provisions, called the fetters of the entail, whereby any attempt by the heir in possession to interfere with the succession or to reduce the extent or value of the estate, for example by selling or feuing or burdening the property or even, in some cases, granting leases, resulted in the lands passing immediately to the next heir.

9.9   The lawfulness of entails of feudal land was established by the Entail Act or "Act concerning Tailyies" of 1685. This Act also established a register of tailzies—later known as the register of entails.

9.10 The disadvantages of tying up land by strict entails quickly became apparent and a long succession of statutes, beginning with the Entail Improvement Act 1770, gradually increased the powers of the heir in possession to deal with the land in ways inconsistent with the fetters of the entail. In the 18th and early 19th centuries there were also numerous private Acts of Parliament to enable heirs of entail to sell or burden the entailed estates for the payment of debts. The judges were hostile to entails. The Court of Session developed a rule that the provisions of entails were to be interpreted strictly, and many lands were effectively disentailed by judicial construction.

9.11 A significant reform was introduced by the Entail Amendment Act 1848 which, with the preamble that

> "the law of entail in Scotland has been found to be attended with serious evils, both to heirs of entail and to the community at large"

introduced provisions enabling heirs in possession to disentail the lands. An heir born after the date of the entail (if the entail was dated after 1 August 1848) or after 1 August 1848 (if the entail was dated before that date) could disentail without any consent. In other cases the consent of the heir next in succession was required. The procedure was by application to the Court of Session for authority to execute, and register in the register of tailzies, an instrument of disentail. The effect was to remove the fetters of the entail. The heir in possession was placed in the same position as a full owner. The special destination in the titles remained in force but the owner could defeat it by disposing of the property or altering the succession to it.

9.12 Acts of 1875 [Entail Amendment (Scotland) Act 1875] and 1882 [Entail (Scotland) Act 1882] enabled even those heirs in possession who required consent to obtain the authority of the court to disentail without the consent of any succeeding heir provided that the value of the interest of any such heir was ascertained and paid or secured on the land. Finally, the Entail (Scotland) Act 1914 prohibited the creation of new entails after 10 August 1914.

9.13 Entails have for a long time had serious disadvantages from the point of view of tax planning. Heirs of entail will normally have been advised decades ago to take advantage of the facilities for disentail. There must be few, if any, entails still in existence. Any heir of entail in possession born after the date of the entail can now disentail without any consent or payment of compensation. Given that all existing entails must have been dated before 10 August 1914 there must be few, if any, cases where there is an heir of entail in possession who was born before the date of the entail. Even if there are any, they can disentail without the consent of the heir next entitled to succeed if the value of that heir's interest or expectancy is ascertained and secured on the land.

9.14 The result of the long history of statutory intervention in relation to entails is that there are some twenty statutes still in force to deal with an area of the law which has become obsolete. Many of these statutes contain feudal language which would have to be amended to deal with the consequences of the abolition of the feudal system of land tenure. We concluded that this would be a pointless exercise and that, rather than amend the entail statutes to remove feudal terminology, we should recommend the ending of entails and the repeal of all this obsolete legislation. We were confirmed in this view by consultation with the Keeper of the Registers, the Law Society of Scotland and some firms of solicitors known to represent large landed estates or to have acted in relation to entails in the past.

9.15 We have considered the question of compensation. For the reasons given above it seems likely that any remaining entailed estates could be disentailed under the existing law without any consents and without the need to pay compensation. Only if the heir in possession was born before the date of the entail (which must have been before 10 August 1914) could there be any question of compensation. We doubt whether any provision for compensation would be used. However, it can do no harm to err on the side of caution and to include a provision. An appropriate mechanism would be a claim to the Lands Tribunal for Scotland within two years after the appointed day. The Tribunal would have power to value the claim and to order the amount to be secured on the land for the benefit of the claimant in such manner as they might think fit. Normally the date of payment out of the lands would be the death of the current owner. If the owner chose not to alter the succession—so that the next heir succeeded in any event—the secured amount would cease to matter because it would be due to and by the same person.

9.16 The Keeper of the Registers suggested that provision should be made for the formal closure of the Register of Entails and for its transmission to the Keeper of the Records of Scotland for preservation. Otherwise there might be continuing applications for the registration of old deeds relating to entails. It appears that applications for the registration of pre-1914 deeds of entail continued to be received for decades after new entails were prohibited by the Entail (Scotland) Act 1914. We agree with this suggestion.

9.17 We therefore recommend that

58. (a) Any land held under an entail should be automatically disentailed on the appointed day.

(b) The effect of the automatic disentailing should be the same as the effect of a duly registered instrument of disentail under section 32 of the Entail Amendment Act 1848. Accordingly the heir of entail in possession should own the land free from the restrictions of the entail and should be free to alter the succession to it.

(c) Provision should be made to enable the heir next entitled to succeed to claim compensation, within two years after the appointed day, for the loss of the expectancy in any case where the consent of such an heir would have been required in the case of a voluntary disentail immediately before the appointed day. Any claim should be dealt with by the Lands Tribunal for Scotland who should be given power to value the claim and order it to be secured on the land for the benefit of the claimant in such manner as they think fit.

(d) Provision should be made for the closure of the Register of Entails and for its transmission to the Keeper of the Records for preservation."

NOTE:

5.17   These recommendations were subsequently given statutory effect: Abolition of Feudal Tenure etc. (Scotland) Act 2000, ss.50–52, although the statute had not yet been brought into force at the time of writing.

(ii) Successive Liferents

A truster might attempt to create something akin to an entail by means of a series of successive liferents: for example, directing that property is to be held on trust for his children in liferent, and his grandchildren thereafter, and his great-grandchildren thereafter, et cetera. This device has been restricted by a series of statutory provisions since 1848. The current law is as follows:

Law Reform (Miscellaneous Provisions) Scotland Act 1968, s.18

Restriction on duration of liferents

5.18   **18.**—(1) Where by any deed executed after the commencement of this Act there is created a liferent interest in any property and a person who was not living or *in utero* at the date of the coming into operation of the said deed becomes entitled to that interest, then—

(a) if that person is of full age at the date on which he becomes entitled to the liferent interest, as from that date, or

(b) if that person is not of full age at that date, as from the date on which, being still entitled to the liferent interest, he becomes of full age,

the said property shall, subject to subsection (2) of this section, belong absolutely to that person, and, if the property is vested in trustees, those trustees shall, subject as aforesaid, be bound to convey, deliver or make over the property to that person.

(2) The fact that, by virtue of subsection (1) of this section, any property has come to belong absolutely to any person shall not affect—

(a) the rights in the property of any person holding a security over the property;

(b) any rights in the property created independently of the deed by which the liferent interest in question was created;

(c) in the case of heritable property, the rights therein of the superior of the property.

(3) The expenses of the conveyance, delivery or making over of any property to any person in pursuance of subsection (1) of this section shall be borne by that person.

(4) Section 48 of the Entail Amendment Act 1848 and section 9 of the Trusts (Scotland) Act 1921 shall not have effect in relation to any deed executed after the commencement of this Act.

(5) For the purposes of this section—

(a) the date of the coming into operation of any testamentary or other *mortis causa* deed shall, subject to paragraph (c) below, be taken to be the date of the death of the granter thereof:

(b) the date of the coming into operation of any marriage contract shall, subject as aforesaid, be taken to be the date of the dissolution of the marriage;

(c) the date of the execution, or of the coming into operation, of any deed made in the exercise of a special power of appointment shall be taken to be the date of the execution, or as the case may be of the coming into operation, of the deed creating that power.

NOTES:

1. For the law relating to deeds executed prior to November 25, 1968 (the date on which the **5.19** 1968 provisions came into force), see Wilson and Duncan, paras 8–05 to 8–13.

2. Section 18 does not strike at the validity of successive liferents as such. For example, if a truster had both children and grandchildren in existence, he could create a trust whereby his children would be entitled to a liferent interest, and thereafter his grandchildren. However, the section prevents the device of successive liferents being effective in perpetuity, because, by virtue of its provisions, a liferent interest can only be validly conferred on persons who are living or *in utero* at the time when the deed is executed.

If a person who was not alive *in utero* at the time the deed was executed becomes entitled to a liferent interest under the deed, and they are of full age, they become the absolute owner of the property. If they are not of full age, then the liferent will subsist until they reach full age and they will become the absolute owner at that point.

For these purposes, "full age" is the age of 18: Age of Majority (Scotland) Act 1969, s.1.

(iii) *Accumulations of Income*

The historical background to the present law on accumulations of income is summarised by the (English) Law Commission in the following extract. (It should be noted that Scots law has never adopted the "rule against perpetuities" to which it refers: see generally Robert Burgess, *Perpetuities in Scots Law* (1979)).

Law Commission,
The Rules Against Perpetuities and Excessive Accumulations
(Law Com. No. 251, 1998, footnotes omitted)

"9.4 The rule against excessive accumulations has always been statutory. At common law, **5.20** the only restriction on a settlor's ability to direct trustees to accumulate the income of property held on trust was the rule against perpetuities. It followed that a direction to accumulate the income from some property for a period which did not exceed the perpetuity period was valid. The Accumulations Act 1800 was passed by Parliament as a direct response to the decision in the leading case of *Thellusson v. Woodford* [(1799) 4 Ves. 227; (1805) 11 Ves. 122; 31 E.R. 117; 32 E.R. 1030] in which a direction to accumulate for what was then the full perpetuity period was upheld as lawful.

9.5 By his will dated 1796, Peter Thellusson, a well-known banker, made certain generous bequests to the various members of his family. In relation to the remainder of his residuary estate which amounted to £600,000 after these bequests, he directed his trustees to accumulate the rents and profits at a compound interest. The period of accumulation was to cover the lives of all his sons, grandsons and great-grandsons living at the time of his death. On the death of the last survivor, the fund was to be divided between the three eldest male living descendants of his three sons. If there were no such descendants, the property was to pass to the Crown to reduce the National Debt.

9.6 When he died in 1797, Peter Thellusson's will, and, in particular, this direction for accumulation, was the subject of much contemporary criticism. The will was challenged by his widow and children, on whose behalf Counsel submitted—

> Mr *Thellusson's* will is morally vicious; as it was a contrivance of a parent to exclude every one of his issue from the enjoyment even of the produce of his property during almost a century; and it is politically injurious; as during the whole of that period it makes an immense property unproductive both to individuals and the community at large; and by the time, when the accumulation shall end, it will have created a fund, the revenue of which will be greater than the civil list; and will therefore give its processor the means of disturbing the whole economy of the country. [(1805) 11 Ves. 112, 114; 32 E.R. 1030, 1031]

9.7 These arguments were, however, rejected both at first instance and on appeal to the House of Lords. The trusts were valid. The testator had not postponed the vesting of the estate beyond the permissible perpetuity period. In the House of Lords, Lord Eldon LC rejected the argument that the accumulation was objectionable on the basis of what he saw as the policy of the rule against perpetuities—

> In truth there is no objection to accumulation upon the policy of the law, applying to perpetuities; for the rents and profits are not to be locked up, and made no use of, for the individuals, or the public. The effect is only to invest them from time to time in land; so that the fund is, not only in a constant course of accumulation, but also in a constant course of circulation. To that application what possible objection can there be in law?

> Furthermore, the fears that the accumulated fund might be so large so as to compromise the national state power proved to be grossly exaggerated.

9.8 However, while the courts upheld the validity of the terms of the will, Parliament was sufficiently concerned to intervene. The result was the enactment of the Accumulations Act (or 'Thellusson') Act 1800. We have already explained that the reasons for this Act were political. As the *Thellusson* case itself demonstrated, it could not be justified on economic grounds or, given the rule against perpetuities, because of the need to fetter the dead hand of a testator."

NOTE:

The Accumulations Act 1800 was applied to Scotland as well as England (for the history of the various legislative provisions, see Wilson and Duncan, 9–01 to 9–02). The current law is contained in the following two statutory provisions:

Trusts (Scotland) Act 1961, s.5

Accumulations of income

5.21   **5.**—(1) The following provisions of this section shall have effect in substitution for the provisions of the Accumulations Act, 1800, and that Act is hereby repealed.

(2) No person may by any will, settlement or other disposition dispose of any property in such manner that the income thereof shall be wholly or partially accumulated for any longer period than one of the following, that is to say—

(a) the life of the grantor; or

(b) a term of twenty-one years from the death of the grantor; or

(c) the duration of the minority or respective minorities of any person or persons living or *in utero* at the death of the grantor; or

(d) the duration of the minority or respective minorities of any person or persons who, under the terms of the will, settlement or other disposition directing the accumulation, would for the time being, if of full age, be entitled to the income directed to be accumulated.

(3) In every case where any accumulation is directed otherwise than as aforesaid, the direction shall, save as hereinafter provided, be void, and the income directed to be accumulated shall, so long as the same is directed to be accumulated contrary to this section, go to and be received by the person or persons who would have been entitled thereto if such accumulation had not been directed.

(4) For avoidance of doubt it is hereby declared that, in the case of a settlement or other disposition inter vivos, a direction to accumulate income during a period specified in paragraph (d) of subsection (2) of this section shall not be void, nor shall the accumulation of the income be contrary to this section, solely by reason of the fact that the period begins during the life of the grantor and ends after his death.

(5) The restrictions imposed by this section apply to wills, settlements and other dispositions made on or after the twenty-eighth day of July, eighteen hundred, but, in the case of wills, only where the testator was living and of testamentary capacity after the end of one year from that date.

(6) In this section "minority" in relation to any person means the period beginning with the birth of the person and ending with his attainment of the age of twenty-one years, and "grantor" includes settlor and, in relation to a will, the testator.

Law Reform (Miscellaneous Provisions) (Scotland) Act 1966, s.6

Amendment of s.5 of Trusts (Scotland) Act 1961

6.—(1) The periods for which accumulations of income under a settlement or other 5.22 disposition are permitted by section 5 of the Trusts (Scotland) Act 1961 shall include—

(a) a term of twenty-one years from the date of the making of the settlement or other disposition, and

(b) the duration of the minority or respective minorities of any person or persons living or in utero at that date,

and a direction to accumulate income during a period specified in paragraph (a) or paragraph (b) of this subsection shall not be void, nor shall the accumulation of the income be contrary to the said section 5, solely by reason of the fact that the period begins during the life of the grantor and ends after his death.

(2) The restrictions imposed by the said section 5 shall apply in relation to a power to accumulate income whether or not there is a duty to exercise that power, and they shall apply whether or not the power to accumulate extends to income produced by the investment of income previously accumulated.

(3) This section shall apply only in relation to instruments taking effect after the passing of this Act, and in the case of an instrument made in the exercise of a special power of appointment shall apply only where the instrument creating the power takes effect after the passing of this Act.

NOTES:

1. *Application of these provisions.* It has been held in England that the equivalent statutory 5.23 provisions (the Law of Property Act 1925, s.164, as amended by the Perpetuities and Accumulations Act 1964, s.13) do not apply to trusts created by legal persons (*Re Dodwell & Co Ltd's Trust Deed* [1979] Ch. 301). It was held in *Re A.E.G. Unit Trust (Managers) Ltd's*

Deed [1957] Ch. 415 that these provisions do not apply to unit trusts either, as these are not "within the mischief which the section is designed to prevent" (*per* Wynn-Parry J. at 420). They do apply to public trusts, however.

2. *Which of the periods specified in s.5(2) of the 1961 Act and s.6(1) of the 1966 Act applies?* The truster may have these provisions in mind when writing the trust deed, and select one of those periods accordingly, at the end of which accumulation is to cease. If the truster does not make any such direction, Wilson and Duncan have suggested (at 9–39) that the matter should be approached as follows. (The references to periods (e) and (f) are to sections (6)(1)(a)—(b) of the 1966 Act respectively).

> "The logical starting point is to ascertain the point of time at which accumulation is to begin. If it falls within the period between the date of the deed and the date of the testator's death, the choice is restricted to periods (a), (d), (e) and (f); if it falls within the period after death the choice is confined to (b), (c) and (d). The application of periods (c), (d) or (f) presumably requires some reference by the grantor to the minor beneficiaries. Period (e) will presumably now apply in most *inter vivos* trusts unless the deed refers to the period of the grantor's life."

3. *Directions to exceed the permitted period.* Where the trust-deed directs the trustees to accumulate for a period in excess of what is permitted by the statutory provisions, the deed must be read as if it in fact directed the trustees to cease accumulating at the end of the permitted period. (See *Elder's Trs v. Treasurer of Free Church of Scotland* (1892) 20 R. 2, *per* the Lord Ordinary (Kyllachy) at 6).

4. *Reform.* In *The Rules Against Perpetuities and Excessive Accumulations* (Law Com. No. 251, 1998), the (English) Law Commission concluded that "we do not consider that there is any case for the continued retention of the rule against excessive accumulation" (para. 10.15) and recommended that it be repealed, subject to an exception in relation to charitable trusts. In so recommending, however, the Commission noted that Scots law has no prohibition against perpetuities such as that found in English law, and that "the rule against excessive accumulations is the principal means of dead hand control in Scotland." (10.17). (The term "dead hand control" refers to the theory that prohibitions on perpetuities and accumulations are justified in the public interest, in order to restrict the power of the testator to control his property from beyond the grave). The Commission concluded that they did "not anticipate that there will be any particular pressure for abolition of the rule in Scotland in consequence of its abrogation south of the border." (10.17).

C. Purposes which are *contra bonos mores*

5.24 Trust purposes may be held invalid if they are *contra bonos mores*, or contrary to morality. The reported cases under this heading are predominantly concerned with attempts by trusters to regulate family relationships by attaching conditions to a legacy in a will. The same principles would, however, apply to conditions attached to a beneficiary's interest under an *inter vivos* trust.

(i) Conditions relating to living arrangements

Fraser v. Rose
(1849) 11 D. 1466

5.25 The testator made substantial provision for his adult daughter in his will, under the condition that she leave her mother within four weeks of his death, and that if she was "so deluded by the entreaties of her unfortunate mother, or her relatives, as to remain with her mother", she was to forfeit all but a small fraction of her rights under his will. The Lord Ordinary declared that the condition was immoral and illegal, and should be disregarded. On appeal to the Inner House:

LORD PRESIDENT (BOYLE): "This is certainly, and most happily, an unusual case; and the question is, Whether there are any legal grounds for arriving at a conclusion different from that to which the Lord Ordinary has come? I have no hesitation in concurring in the observation, that if this is not a condition *contra bonos mores*, it is impossible to say what is such a condition. It is admitted that there is not the least ground for any insinuation against the maternal conduct of the pursuer's mother. Taking it for the fact that her conduct has been perfectly irreproachable, I hold that there is not the least reason for thinking that this young lady, if left under her management, would suffer any moral contamination from her society. I think, therefore, that there cannot be the least difficulty in holding that this condition is *contra bonos mores*. I deny that any parent is entitled to dissolve the obligations under which the child lies to the other parent. A father has no title to say to his child, 'You forfeit your rights from me, if you do not cease to discharge your duties to your mother.' While there is an express command of Almighty God, 'Thou shalt honour thy father and thy mother,' I hold that such a condition as this, whatever equivalent may be held out as its reward, is directly *contra bonos mores*, and contrary to the best interests of society."

Appeal refused.

NOTE:

What if the purpose of the condition was not to encourage a child to live apart from his or her **5.26** parents, but rather to ensure that they would receive financial support if they chose to do so? Such an argument was made in *Grant's Trs v. Grant* (1898) 25 R. 929. In that case, the trustees were directed to hold a portion of the testator's estate in trust for his grandniece, who was living with his brother and daughter. They were to either use the annual income for her benefit or to make it over to her. When she turned 21 or married, she was to receive the residue. However, if she returned to live with her parents before that time, she forfeited that right. When the case was heard by the Inner House, counsel argued that this "was a direction to expend the interest for Helen Grant as long as she was in fact not resident with her father. That was not the same as a condition that she should live apart . . .". This argument was rejected, and the Lord Justice-Clerk (Macdonald) said in a terse judgment (at 930):

"I think this case may be decided upon the principle that if a sum is bequeathed to a child upon the condition that the child shall not reside with its parents—against whose character no allegation can be made—the condition does not receive effect."

This is a straightforward application of *Fraser v. Rose*. It will be noted, however, that both cases suggest that such a condition *might* be valid if there was some reason to suggest that the parent's character could be impugned in such a way as to justify the condition.

(ii) Conditions relating to marriage

Aird's Executors v. Aird
1949 S.C. 154

Robert Aird made a will in 1903, which provided that "You my brother James Aird I **5.27** bequeath my all, so long as you remain a single man. If you take unto yourself a wife, from that day I hereby give devise & bequeath to my mother . . . her heirs executors and administrators for her & their own use all my estate . . .". His brother married in 1906. Robert Aird died in 1947. James Aird argued that he was entitled to the bequest, as the condition that he should be unmarried was void.

LORD PRESIDENT (COOPER): "We had the advantage of a full and able argument with regard to the rule that an absolute and general prohibition against the marriage of a legatee is inoperative and falls to be disregarded. There is no recorded example of the operation of the rule in any reported case. All the decisions relate to cases in which exceptions to the rule were admitted. But the rule has been repeated again and again in institutional works and textbooks from Stair's Institutions to Green's Encyclopaedia until its validity is beyond challenge, though it is a matter of some difficulty to discover its precise basis in principle and precise content and limitations. What is primarily (though not universally) struck at evidently is a testamentary provision which in form or substance so operates as to require the legatee to choose between marriage and a bequest, or which holds over him *in terrorem* the threat of forfeiture of a bequest if he should thereafter marry.

Now, if this testator had died in 1904, when his brother James was still single, a different, and perhaps a difficult, question would have arisen. But he did not die in 1904. Until his death in 1947 the will was by its very nature a private, undelivered and ambulatory document, and we cannot do other than read it and consider its operation as from the date of the testator's death. In 1947, when the testator died, it seems to me that James Aird, according to the plain intendment of the will, was disqualified from taking any benefit under the bequest in question. In substance the bequest was one to James Aird, if he was unmarried, and to others if he was. There can be no objection to such a bequest. Indeed it is hardly possible in my view to maintain, with regard to a man who will shortly be celebrating his golden wedding, that he is being restrained from the free exercise of the choice whether to remain a bachelor or to marry. He has made that choice long ago, presumably in complete ignorance of the provisions of his brother's will."

The Court held that James Aird was not entitled to the bequest.

NOTE:

5.28   It appears that a testator can validly attach a condition to a bequest that the legatee should not marry a particular individual, and that he should not receive the bequest unless and until he makes a declaration that he has not and will not marry that person. (*Forbes v. Forbes's Trs* (1882) 9 R. 675).

A trustee may also provide that an individual will receive financial support only for so long as they remain unmarried: see *Sturrock v. Rankin's Trs* (1875) 2 R. 850, where the testator provided that each of his daughters should receive a share in the profits of his business (which was to be carried on by his trustees) only for so long as they remained unmarried (which meant that one daughter, who was unmarried at the date of his death, received nothing). Lord Gifford said (at 854) that:

> "the provision in this deed is not a condition in restraint of marriage, but simply a provision for unmarried daughters who, in the view of the testator, had no other means of support."

Similarly, it was held in *Kidd v. Kidds* (1863) 2 M. 227 that a liferent to the surviving spouse of the testator which would terminate upon her remarriage was valid. Lord Keith, in concurring with Lord Cooper in *Aird's Exrs*, said that "I can see cases in which the rule could be applied, but this is not, I agree, one of these." But, given the state of the authorities, it is rather difficult to imagine what such a case would look like.

(iii) Conditions relating to religion

Some testators have attempted to use their wills to regulate their family's religion from beyond the grave. In the English case of *Blathwayt v. Baron Cawley* [1976] A.C. 397, the House of Lords had to consider the validity of a condition that any beneficiary under the trust would lose his entitlement if he were to become a Roman Catholic. It was argued that this condition should be held invalid as restricting religious freedom. The House of Lords rejected this argument, with Lord Wilberforce responding to the suggestion as follows (at 426):

> "To do so would bring about a substantial reduction of another freedom, firmly rooted in our law, namely that of testamentary disposition . . . neither by express provision nor by implication has private selection yet become a matter of public policy."

There are, however, limits as to how far one can go in dictating the religion of one's beneficiaries. In *Innes's Trs v. Innes and Others*, 1963 S.L.T. 353, Lord Carmont considered (*obiter*, at 358) whether it would be valid to require beneficiaries to promise that they would "remain Protestants as long as they live", failing which they would forfeit all right to their legacies:

> "I incline to the view that it would be *contra bonos mores* for trustees to exact such a promise with reference to the future as a condition of payment of a legacy by them. There is, I think,

a plain distinction between demanding a declaration of religion as a qualification for obtaining actual payment of a legacy, and the exacting of a promise to maintain the religious qualification in the future, as a condition of taking payment and keeping the legacy. In any event, it would appear that once the legacy was paid, following on an honest declaration, no subsequent change of religion could bring about a forfeiture which could result in repayment being demandable."

(iv) What is the effect of a void condition?

John McLaren (Lord McLaren), *The Law of Wills and Succession* (3rd ed., 1894), Vol. I, para. 1094

"We proceed to consider the subject of unlawful and impossible conditions, a subject which **5.29** involves the question in what circumstances a legatee is entitled to take the bequest free from a potestative condition. On this last point our law stands clear of one element of complexity which has entered into that of England, in consequence of the Courts of law having adopted the principle that a devise of real property upon an impossible or unlawful condition is void, while the Courts of equity, in the adjudication of questions of personal succession, have adhered to the maxim of the civil law, according to which such conditions are held *pro non scriptis*. In the jurisprudence of Scotland, it is a universal rule, that a bequest, or voluntary provision, coupled with an unlawful or impossible condition, is effectual, the condition being either held *pro non scripto* or treated as satisfied because the executor or legatee has done all that is possible to satisfy the testator's requirement."

NOTE:

Norrie and Scobbie have suggested (at p. 92) that if a condition is void: **5.30**

"the trust itself will remain valid, but only if the nature of the gift and condition is not such that the one is clearly dependent upon the other. This is a matter of the intention of the truster, and if it can be shown that the truster did not intend the purpose to be given effect unless the condition were satisfied, then if the condition is contrary to public policy, so will be the purpose."

No authority is cited for this argument, and it is not entirely clear what the authors mean. The point of a condition is surely that the truster *does not* intend the purpose to be given effect unless the condition is satisfied. Take, for example, *Fraser v. Rose* (*supra* para. 5.25), where it was quite clear that the testator did not wish his daughter to receive the £3,000 pounds he had allocated to her (the purpose) unless the lived apart from her mother (the condition). Taking Norrie and Scobbie's argument literally, they appear to suggest that Fraser's bequest to his daughter should have failed entirely (in which case, the rules on intestacy would require to be applied). That seems, with respect, to be contrary to both principle and authority (and it is, of course, not what the Inner House decided in that case).

It is respectfully submitted that McLaren's position—that the validity of the condition does not (at least directly) bear upon the validity of the purpose—is the better one. Conditions and purposes must be considered separately. If a condition is void, it must be taken as *pro non scripto*, and the beneficiary will take their benefit free of the condition. It may be, of course, that *both* the condition and the purpose are *contra bonos mores*, but a purpose will not be void solely because a void condition is attached to it.

D. Purposes contrary to public policy

McCaig v. University of Glasgow
1907 S.C. 231

In his will, John McCaig directed that his heritable estate should be let to tenants, and the **5.31** income used, firstly, to erect monuments and statues of himself, his brothers, sisters and parents. Each of these was to cost not less than £1,000 and was to be erected on the top of

McCaig's Tower on the Battray Hill above Oban. Secondly, artistic towers were to be built on prominent points on his estates. He declared that his "wish and desire is to encourage young and rising artists and for that purpose prizes to be given for the best plans of the proposed statues towers &c. before building them."

Mr McCaig declared that he intended the trust to be perpetual for all time coming, and nominated the Court of Session as trustees, with the alternative of the University of Glasgow should the Court decline office. The Court did indeed decline office, but the University accepted.

Catherine McCaig, John McCaig's sister, brought an action in the Court of Session seeking a declaration that his directions were invalid and ineffectual. The Lord Ordinary dismissed the action. On appeal to the Inner House:

LORD KYLLACHY (after holding that it was unnecessary to decide whether the trust purposes were void for uncertainty): "Neither do I find it necessary to rest my opinion upon what is perhaps a wider ground than that above indicated, viz., this, that the trust purposes . . . are void as being contrary to public policy. I have, I confess, much sympathy with that argument. For I consider that if it is not unlawful, it ought to be unlawful, to dedicate by testamentary disposition, for all time, or for a length of time, the whole income of a large estate—real and personal—to objects of no utility, private or public, objects which benefit nobody, and which have no other purpose or use than that of perpetuating at great cost, and in an absurd manner, the idiosyncrasies of an eccentric testator . . .

Still, it seems to me that the pursuer is perhaps on safer ground when she appeals, not to considerations of public policy, but the definite rule of law already referred to, a rule perhaps ultimately founded on public policy, but also, and perhaps primarily, on considerations as to what is right and just as between the varied interests in a deceased's succession. Accordingly, I prefer to rest my judgment upon the doctrine which I have expressed—a doctrine which, whatever questions may arise as to its application, is itself elementary, and rests upon the cardinal principle that by the law of Scotland there can be no divestiture of a man's heirs or next of kin, except by means of beneficial rights, validly constituted in favour of third parties . . .

Taking then the question to be whether any beneficial interests are by this deed created in favour of third parties, What are the interests which are said to be so created? and who are the persons or classes of persons said to be benefited? I put that question to the defenders' counsel at the close of the argument, and the only answer I obtained was a reference to the direction in the settlement that the making of the statues or monuments was to be given to Scotch sculptors, and that in order to encourage 'young and rising artists' there should, before building the proposed statues and artistic towers, be prizes given for the best plans of the said statues, towers, &c . . .

[T]reating the matter as far as possible seriously, it seems to me to be a sufficient answer that if a trust purpose is of such a character that if, when executed, it will benefit nobody, it cannot affect the legal result that, in the course of executing the trust, there will or may be some employment of labour, or the receipt of wages or salaries by deserving persons."

The Lord Justice-Clerk (Macdonald), Lord Low and Lord Stormonth-Darling delivered concurring opinions.

Appeal allowed.

NOTE:

5.32   This case is hereafter referred to as *McCaig*. The opinions of the other three judges were to the same effect. The court was clearly reluctant to hold the directions invalid on the broad ground of public policy, and although this decision is the foundation of the modern law of public policy and trust purposes, it is probably best regarded in itself as simply an application of the rather specific doctrine of disinherison. Put simply, John McCaig was not entitled to disinherit Catherine McCaig (his heir-at-law) unless he conferred a beneficial right in his property on some other party—and he had not done so. That, of course, simply begged the question of whether John McCaig's directions would have been held invalid had there been no heir-at-law to disinherit. It was not long before the Court of Session had to consider that question—and this time, the judges found themselves considering the validity of Catherine McCaig's will.

McCaig's Trs v. Kirk-Session of United Free Church of Lismore
1915 S.C. 426

Catherine McCaig died in 1913, with no heir-at-law. She left a substantial estate, the bulk of **5.33** which had been inherited from John McCaig. In a codicil to her will, she directed that her trustees should convert the McCaig Tower in Oban into a private enclosure, and should erect bronze statues within the tower of her parents, brothers and sisters and herself, each of which was to cost not less than £1,000. The trustees were to be bound in all time coming not to sell the tower and statues, and to maintain them out of the revenue of the trust estate.

LORD SALVESEN: "For myself I am prepared to hold that the bequest is contrary to public policy on more than one ground. In the first place, I think it is so because it involves a sheer waste of money, and not the less so that the expenditure would give employment to a number of sculptors and workmen, for it must be assumed that their labour could be usefully employed in other ways. I think, further, that it would be a dangerous thing to support a bequest of this kind which can only gratify the vanity of testators, who have no claim to be immortalised, but who possess the means by which they can provide for more substantial monuments to themselves than many that are erected to famous persons by public subscription. A man may, of course, do with his money what he pleases while he is alive, but he is generally restrained from wasteful expenditure by a desire to enjoy his property, or to accumulate it, during his lifetime. The actings of the two McCaig's form an excellent illustration of this principle of human conduct. For many years they had apparently contemplated the erection of similar statues, but they could not bring themselves to part with the money during their own lifetimes. Such considerations do not restrain extravagance or eccentricity in testamentary dispositions, on which there is no check except by the Courts of law. A testator may still leave his means to be expended in stone and lime which will form a monument to his memory, provided the bequest he makes serves some useful public purpose and is not merely for his own glorification. The prospect of Scotland being dotted with monuments to obscure persons who happened to have amassed a sufficiency of means, and cumbered with trusts for the purposes of maintaining these monuments in all time coming, appears to me to be little less than appalling. What a man does in his own lifetime with his property may be removed by his successor, and no doubt will be as soon as it has ceased to serve a useful purpose. But, if a bequest such as that in Miss McCaig's codicil were held good, money would require to be expended in perpetuity merely to gratify an absurd whim which has neither reason nor public sentiment in its favour."

LORD GUTHRIE: "In this case, it seems to me that to give effect to the part of Miss McCaig's codicil concerned with the erection of eleven statues would be of no benefit to anyone except those connected with the carrying out of the work, for whose interest she expresses no concern. If anybody went to see the statues, supposing they represented faithfully the persons to be commemorated, it would not be to admire them but to laugh at them, and perhaps to philosophise on the length to which morbid family pride may drive an otherwise sensible person. These statues would not, in fact, achieve Miss McCaig's object of perpetuating an honourable memory. They would turn a respectable and creditable family into a laughing stock to succeeding generations."

The Lord Justice-Clerk (Macdonald) delivered a concurring opinion.

The Court held that the trustees were not bound to give effect to the directions in question.

NOTE:

5.34   This case is hereafter referred to as *McCaig's Trs.* It has been suggested that the two *McCaig* cases are "confused" (Wilson & Duncan, para. 14–10), but the difference between the two is simply a result of the fact that the court was unable to invoke the doctrine of disinherison in the second case (because Miss McCaig left no heir-at-law), and therefore had to fall back on a broader doctrine of public policy. The two decisions were interpreted by Lord Sands in a later case as meaning that if trust purposes "are unreasonable as conferring neither a patrimonial benefit upon anybody nor a benefit upon the public or any section thereof, the directions are invalid." (*Aitken's Trs v. Aitken*, 1927 S.C. 374, at 381, and see also Lord Ashmore at 387). An *incidental* benefit is insufficient. So, for example, tradesmen and sculptors might have been gainfully employed putting the McCaigs' schemes into effect, but the directions were still invalid because the end result would have benefited no-one.

Another way of putting it is that where there is no person "entitled to insist on the trust purposes being fulfilled" (*i.e.* because there is no person on whom any benefit has been conferred), those purposes are invalid (Mackenzie Stuart, p. 79). That does not mean that a trust which only confers a general benefit on the public rather than on specific individuals is invalid, since the Lord Advocate is entitled to intervene in the public interest in such a case (*Aitken's Trs v. Aitken*, 1927 S.C. 374, *per* Lord Ashmore at 387). It is possible, of course, that a truster may believe that his trust does confer a general benefit on the public, but this will not make the trust purposes valid if that belief is false. An example of this is *Sutherland's Tr. v. Verschoyle*, 1968 S.L.T. 43, where the testatrix directed in her will that her trustees should purchase a house "of a certain size and dignity" in St Andrews to exhibit and preserve for perpetuity her "valuable art collection". In actual fact, the "collection" was unlikely to attract any scholarly or public interest, and many of the items were simply copies. No doubt the testatrix believed that it was in the public interest for her collection to be permanently displayed, but the court disagreed, and held that her directions were invalid.

There are, however, two exceptional cases in which a trust may be valid despite there being no person entitled to insist on its fulfilment. These are trusts for memorials and trusts for animals.

(i) Trusts for Memorials

5.35   It is well accepted that a truster may make provision for a burial place and a memorial to himself (see, for example, *McCaig*, *per* Lord Kyllachy at 244), but such provision "should not be extravagant to the point of caprice" (*Lindsay's Exr v. Forsyth*, 1940 S.C. 568, *per* the Lord Justice-Clerk (Aitchison) at 572). Provision for a memorial to an immediate relative is probably also valid (*McCaig's Trs*, *per* Lord Guthrie at 437).

For an example of an extravagant memorial, see *Aitken's Trs v. Aitken*, 1927 S.C. 374, where the testator instructed his trustees to demolish a Musselburgh building and erect "a massive equestrian bronze statue of artistic merit, representing me as Champion at the Riding of the Towns Marches", which was to cost not less than £5,000. Lord Sands pointed out that the underlying objects of the direction (to commemorate the testator's ancestors, the custom of the Riding, and his own role in that custom) were not unreasonable, but that the directions would hardly be an effective way of achieving those objects: "on the contrary, [the statue's] erection would cause the memory of the testator and his family to stink in the nostrils of the community of Musselburgh." (at 382). The directions were held invalid.

A memorial to a "historical personage", even if that person is only known locally rather than nationally, will be held to confer a public benefit—so long, of course, as the public have access to the memorial. (See *McCaig's Trs*, *per* Lord Salvesen at 433). There is, therefore, nothing exceptional about such cases. (For an example, see *Campbell Smith's Trustees v. Scott*, 1944 S.L.T. 198, where a bequest of £30,000 to erect a public monument for commemorating the past services of a regiment was held valid).

(ii) Trusts for Animals

5.36   There is little difficulty with a trust for the benefit of a class of animals, or for the prevention of cruelty to animals, since such trusts are seen as conferring a public benefit (Mackenzie Stuart, pp. 69–71; *Aitken's Trs v. Aitken*, 1927 S.C. 374, *per* Lord Sands at 381). More problematic, however, is a trust for the benefit of a specified animal or animals, since there is no individual who benefits and it is difficult to see what public benefit arises out of such a trust.

In *Flockhart's Trustees v. Bourlet*, 1934 S.N. 23, the testatrix directed that "I leave all my pets an annuity of £50 each, and Cecilia to have charge of them". It was held that Cecilia was entitled to be paid this money for the purposes of looking after the pets. The situation may be more difficult where there is no individual, such as "Cecilia", who has such a right, since it is arguable that no-one would be entitled to insist on the purpose being fulfilled. However, the important issue here is perhaps that the trustees should be empowered to give effect to this sort of direction, rather than the provision of an enforcement mechanism. For further discussion of the issues involved, see Norrie, *Trusts for Animals* (1987) 32 J.L.S.S. 386.

Chapter 6

ADMINISTRATION OF THE TRUST

6.01 The manner in which a trust is administered will vary according to the nature of the trust and the terms of the trust deed. It need hardly be observed that, for example, the practical reality of administering a pension fund differs greatly from ingathering and distributing a small estate after the death of a testator.

There is, however, a common core of general principles which governs the duties of trustees, their powers, and the manner in which decisions are taken. Unless provision is made in the trust deed for the trust to be administered differently, these principles will govern. But the trust-deed must always be checked for its provisions, for, as Lord Ardmillan observed in *Goodsir v. Carruthers* (1858) 20 D. 1141, at 1145:

> "Whatever is directed or permitted by the trust-deed cannot be in breach of the trust, for the truster was entitled to direct or permit as he pleased, and the expression of his will in the trust-deed constitutes the law of the trust."

This chapter is concerned with the common core of general principles which applies where the trust-deed provides no "law" for the trust. These can be conveniently divided into three categories:
- the duties of trustees
- the powers of trustees
- the regulation of decision-making by trustees

As Norrie and Scobbie point out, however (at p. 93):

> "It is somewhat artificial to distinguish between the trustees' powers of administration and their duties to administer, because generally speaking these are interdependent, and are very often simply two sides of the same coin. For example, trustees have a duty to ingather the estate, and they have the power to do what is necessary to effect that ingathering."

Although the division into "powers" and "duties" is convenient, that caveat must be born in mind.

1. GENERAL DUTIES OF TRUSTEES

A. The Duty of Care

6.02 The most important duty on a trustee is to exercise due care in the administration of the trust, the standard of care being "the same degree of diligence that a man of ordinary prudence would exercise in the management of his own affairs". (*Raes v. Meek* (1889) 16 R. (H.L.) 31, *per* Lord Herschell at 33). This is discussed *infra*, paras 9.02 *et seq*.

B. Duty Not To Delegate The Trust

Scott v. Occidental Petroleum (Caledonia) Ltd
1990 S.L.T. 882; 1990 S.C.L.R 278

Ellen Scott's husband was killed in the Piper Alpha disaster in July 1988. She brought a **6.03**
court action against Occidental Petroleum, the operators and co-owners of Piper Alpha, as
an individual and on behalf of her two children. An extrajudicial settlement was reached in
December 1989, whereby Occidental agreed (*inter alia*) to pay Mrs Scott damages of around
£150,000 in respect of each of her children.

The Lord Ordinary was invited to interpone the authority of the court to the settlement,
and to formally approve the terms of a draft trust-deed whereby, after Mrs Scott had
received these sums in her capacity as tutrix and administratix at law for the children, she
would transfer the sums to trustees (of whom she would be one) to be held for the benefit of
the children. Expressing doubt as to the competency of such an arrangement, the Lord
Ordinary reported the matter to the Inner House for an opinion.

OPINION OF THE COURT: "In our opinion two principles of law require to be examined in this
case. One is that by which it is recognised that a tutor, as in the case of any other person
who acts in a fiduciary capacity such as a trustee, may appoint a factor or other agent to
administer the estate on his behalf. It was to this principle that counsel for the curator ad
litem drew particular attention in his submissions to the Lord Ordinary and again when he
appeared before us. But there is another principle of importance to which he also referred
and which, in the wider interest, we must consider. This is the principle that the right which
is given to a child's mother or father to act as that child's tutor or curator is not capable of
being transferred to others. This principle is analogous to that by which it is recognised that
a trustee cannot delegate his trust.

So far as the first point is concerned there is no doubt that a tutrix has power to appoint a
factor or other suitable agent to perform acts of administration on her behalf. This was
recognised by Stair in his comment at I. vi. 17 that 'tutors or their factors presume to do that
to the benefit of the pupil, which they ought to do'. Later in his discussion of the powers
which a curator may exercise he states at I. vi. 36: 'though they may intromit with the pupil's
means themselves, yet they are not obliged to be servants or factors; but may authorize such,
being liable always that they acted therein profitably'. The same point is made by Erskine, I.
vii. 16 where he says: 'When, from the great extent of the minor's estate, or other
circumstance, tutors or curators cannot conveniently undertake the whole management by
themselves, they may appoint factors or stewards under them with reasonable salaries, on
their giving security for the faithful discharge of their offices': see also Fraser on *Parent and
Child,* pp. 361–362. A power to do this now exists under statute, in view of the extended
definition which has been given to the expression 'trustee' in s.2 of the Trusts (Scotland) Act
1921, as amended by para. 4 of Sched. 1 to the Law Reform (Parent and Child) (Scotland)
Act 1986. This includes 'any trustee ex officio, executor nominate, tutor (including a father
or mother acting as tutor of a pupil), curator and judicial factor'. So the tutrix has power to
appoint factors and law agents and to pay them suitable remuneration in terms of s.4(1)(f)
of the 1921 Act. As Wilson and Duncan, *Trusts, Trustees and Executors,* [1st ed. 1975] point
out at p. 309, there are no rules of law prescribing the manner or form in which trustees
should appoint their agents or factors; and the matters committed to them may be as limited
or as extensive as the circumstances may require. Thus Menzies on *Trustees*, para. 216 states
that where the business of the trust is so extensive in nature as to require the continual
attention of someone authorised to act on behalf of the trustees, they should appoint a
competent man of business to be factor on the estate. And the more extensive the factor's
duties are the more important it is that the appointment should be made in writing so that
the terms of the engagement are made clear. These points apply equally to appointments
made by tutors or curators as they do to appointments made by trustees acting under a

formal deed of trust. The appointment of a factor would plainly be one way by which the tutrix may make provision for the proper administration from day to day of the substantial sums of money which are to be paid in this case.

But the mechanism which has been proposed in this case goes beyond what the appointment of a factor would involve. It amounts to nothing less than the delegation to the proposed trustees of all the powers and duties of the tutrix herself, including not only the power of day to day administration of the sums involved but also the taking of all decisions as to the way in which these sums are to be held and applied for the children's benefit until they are of full age. The trust is declared by cl. 5 to be revocable at the tutrix's instance until the child attains minority and at the child's own instance thereafter, and cl. 6 makes provision for what is to happen in the event of the child's death before attaining full age. It was suggested in argument that cl. 5 might be amended so as to enable one of the trustees to apply to the court for the appointment of a judicial factor if the child were to revoke the trust while still in minority. It is plain that so long as the trust in these terms exists and until it is revoked the position of the tutrix or curatrix as the case may be is entirely superseded. It is of no significance in this regard that the tutrix is to appoint herself to be one of the trustees. Clause 4 of the proposed deed of trust provides that the trustees shall have the powers, privileges and immunities of gratuitous trustees under the Trusts (Scotland) Act 1921, and one of the powers which is given to trustees by s.3 of that Act is to resign the office of trustee. So the tutrix would be able to resign office at any time, provided she was not then the sole trustee. It is not difficult to see that if this were to occur the entire responsibility for the administration of the funds on the child's behalf would then be vested in the remaining trustee or trustees, subject only to the continuing power of the tutrix to revoke the trust. There is to be a complete delegation to the trustees of the powers and duties of the widow as tutrix and curatrix of the two children, subject only to her power of revocation and then only until each child attains the age of 12 years.

Some guidance as to whether what is proposed is competent can be found from the principles about delegation by trustees. Menzies on *Trustees* begins his discussion of this matter by saying that it is a fundamental rule that a trustee cannot delegate his trust: s.156. The basis for this rule lies in the element of delectus personae which is involved in the appointment of trustees. On the other hand it is equally clear that a trustee is entitled to employ persons to do that which an ordinary man of business would do, since he is not bound to perform the whole duties of the trust personally: s.191; *Hay v. Binny* (1861) 23 D. 594. To this extent, therefore, delegation is not seen as being in conflict with the fundamental rule. The dividing line between these two propositions is to be found in the point made by Menzies in s.196 that the trustee must never surrender his own judgment in matters committed to his discretion, since the confidence of the truster was placed in his discretion and his alone. There is no doubt, therefore, that it would not be open to a trustee who had been appointed to hold and administer the funds for the children in this case with the wide discretionary powers which are set out in cl. 2(i) of the proposed deed of trust to delegate the exercise of those same powers to someone else.

6.04   In *Boylan v. Hunter*, 1922 S.L.T. 4 at p. 5, Lord President Clyde made the following observations with reference to the practice by which occasionally trust has been set up in the Outer House to administer money awarded as damages to children where the widow was thought to be unsuitable: 'Supersession of the natural guardian (either generally, or *quoad* a particular fund belonging to the ward) by the appointment of a trustee is not competent, even with the consent of the legal guardian. The right which the law accords to the father or mother to the guardianship of their children is exclusive of any right on their part to transfer their powers as guardian, either in whole or in part, to others; and the appointment of a trustee by the court, unless competent in itself, is in no way fortified by the legal guardian's consent. The Court can remove any guardian, including a legal guardian, on certain grounds; but this power does not make it competent for the Court to supersede (in relation to the whole or any part of the ward's property) the person entitled by law to the guardianship by the appointment of a trustee. The alternative and competent course is the appointment of a judicial factor *loco tutoris*'.

Provision to enable this to be done has now been made by the Rules of Court: see rule 131. So it is clear that the proper practice, in cases where the court is satisfied that the administration of damages cannot otherwise be reasonably secured, is for a judicial factor to be appointed and not for the powers of the tutor or curator to be superseded by the appointment of a trustee. If the court cannot supersede the tutrix's powers in this way even with her consent, it is equally true that she cannot do so at her own hand. But this is precisely what the tutrix would be seeking to do if she were to set up trusts in the terms proposed, by which the entire responsibility for the administration of the sums in question and the taking of all decisions as to how they are to be held and applied for the children's benefit are to be given to the trustees. It was submitted that the rule as expressed in *Boylan v. Hunter* does not exclude the setting up of a trust of this kind. In our opinion, however, the proposal goes beyond a mere delegation to agents or others of those duties which the tutrix is not bound to perform herself personally, and it is not something which it is competent for her to do. It is no answer to the problem to say that the trusts are to be revocable, because the trusts will have the effect of superseding the powers and duties of the tutrix for all purposes unless and until they are revoked.

We recognise of course that this is an exceptional case, along with all others which will have followed upon the disaster. The sums are large and there are compelling reasons why the court should lend its assistance so far as it can to the achieving of a satisfactory settlement of the claims by the relatives and to the administration of sums payable to children. But in our opinion the question of competency which we have been asked to consider must be approached as one of principle without regard to the special circumstances. Nor does it appear to us that hardship is likely to arise from this decision. The court has power to appoint a judicial factor under Rule of Court 131 if the curator ad litem considers this to be in the best interests of the children. We are not, we may say, impressed by the points made about the expense of this process, because this is no more than the price which it is necessary to pay for the administration of the funds under supervision in circumstances where their administration cannot otherwise be reasonably secured by the tutrix herself. As for her own position, the powers which she undoubtedly has to appoint an agent or factor to perform acts of administration on her behalf would enable her to be relieved of much of the burden of the day to day administration and investment of the sums involved. This would leave it to her to exercise her own judgment on those matters which are particularly within her responsibility, especially as to how the income or capital should be applied from time to time for the children's maintenance, education or benefit. It is certainly not obvious that if the tutrix is fit to act as a trustee in the trusts which it is proposed to set up the same result could not be achieved by the appointment of a suitable agent or factor to provide her with the skilled assistance which she no doubt requires.

For these reasons the Lord Ordinary was right not to give his approval to the terms of the draft deeds of trust. We shall remit the case back to the Lord Ordinary so that he can attend to the outstanding matters once the curator ad litem has had an opportunity of considering his position in the light of this opinion."

NOTES:

1. As the court makes clear, the principle that a trustee may not delegate his trust does not **6.05** mean that he is bound to undertake every act of trust administration personally. See also *Hay v. Binny* (1861) 23 D. 594, at 594:

   > "The pursuers plead that these trustees are not entitled to employ any professional agent, but are bound to do the whole duties of the trust personally, except only when the trust is engaged in litigation. This is said to be a general rule applicable to all trusts. The Lord Ordinary cannot give effect to this plea, so broadly stated. There is no authority for it in the law of Scotland, and there is a well understood and established practice to the contrary."

   A trustee may employ agents where a person of reasonable prudence would do so.

2. *Factors and law agents*. Under section 4(1)(f) of the Trusts (Scotland) Act 1921 (*infra* para. 6.31), all trusts include an implied power to "appoint factors and law agents and to pay them suitable remuneration", unless such a power would be "at variance with the terms or purposes of the trust" (for the meaning of which, see *infra* para. 6.32).

As to the scope of "factor", see *Mills v. Brown's Trs* (1900) 2 F. 1035, where it was held that a power to appoint a remunerated "factor or cashier" did not empower the trustees to employ one of their own number as manager of the testator's business. It is not clear, however, whether the decision rests on the interpretation of the word "factor", or on a special interpretation of the phrase "factor or cashier", or on the *auctor in rem suam* rule (*infra* Chapter 8) or some combination of these possibilities.

3. *Delegation explicitly sanctioned by the trust deed*. The trust deed may confer an explicit power of delegation and may even appoint a person to whom certain matters are to be delegated. Such an appointment is, however, revocable by the trustees (*Cormack v. Keith & Murray* (1893) 20 R. 977).

4. *Losses caused through the negligence or fraud of an agent employed by the trust*. Trustees will not be liable for losses caused by the negligence or fraud of an agent whom they legitimately appoint (*Thomson v. Campbell* (1838) 16 S. 560). They will, however, be liable if they fail to exercise due care in the selection or supervision of the agent (*Carruthers v. Carruthers* (1896) 23 R. (H.L.) 55).

As to what amounts to due care in supervision, see *Re Smith* (1902) 71 L.J.Ch. 411, where a trustee employed a firm of solicitors as agents. A clerk to the solicitors embezzled a portion of the trust funds by way of a forged letter requesting the trustee to sign and amend two cheques. In holding that the trustee "[had] not acted otherwise than reasonably", and was not liable for the shortfall in the trust funds, Kekewich J. observed (at 413):

> "It may be that this lady, Mrs. Thompson, did not take all the precautions which a very careful and astute person might have taken. It may be that the solicitors did not look after their clerk, in whom they trusted, as much as they ought to have done if they had acted upon the principle that no one was to be trusted. But that is a very bad principle, and one which, if adopted, would lead to great confusion from time to time."

5. *Delegation to a trustee*. The trustees may appoint one of their own number as an agent, but he may not be remunerated unless this is expressly authorised by the trust deed.

C. Duty to Take Advice

6.06 As was noted earlier (para. 6.02), trustees must administer the trust-estate to (at least) the standard that a man of ordinary prudence would exercise in the management of his own affairs. The man of ordinary prudence, of course, recognises that he is not an expert in all matters and must seek professional advice in appropriate cases. The same applies to trustees.

Martin v. City of Edinburgh District Council
1988 S.L.T. 329

6.07 Edinburgh City Council was responsible for the administration of 58 trusts. In 1984, the Labour Party won a majority of seats on the council and put into effect a policy of withdrawing investments held by those trusts in South Africa. A councillor brought an action for declarator that the council had acted in breach of its duty as a trustee.

Lord Murray: "As I have already stated I find it proved that the defenders did not in fact seek the advice of professional advisers as to whether or not it was in the best interests of the trusts and their beneficiaries to disinvest in South Africa. The question is whether this omission amounted, in the circumstances, to a breach of trust. It was not disputed, as I understand it, that under the law of Scotland a trustee's failure to apply his mind properly to a necessary decision is as much a breach of trust as failure to perform a positive duty. It may be, as Councillor Wood maintained, that in the absence of official advice to the contrary the trustees acting for the council were entitled to go forward on the assumption that what they proposed was lawful. But that would not absolve them in my view from the obvious duty of trustees to apply their minds to the best interests of the beneficiaries as a major and separate issue. It is clear from the documents, and I think from Councillor Wood's evidence also, that the trustees did not apply their minds to this as an issue which they had to decide before coming to an overall conclusion in the exercise of their discretion. Had they considered that separate matter then the need to obtain professional advice (which was essential for their decision) might well have become obvious to one or more of the trustees or to the officials in attendance. It may well be (as I think Councillor Wood intended to convey) that had this matter been explicitly considered and professional advice tendered the trustees would have exercised their discretion exactly as they did. That may be so, but the fact remains that, on the evidence, the trustees ignored or at any rate did not explicitly face a vital issue which it was their prime duty as trustees to take into account. Equally they failed to seek the necessary professional advice upon it. Accordingly I conclude that the pursuer has proved a breach of trust by the council in pursuing a policy of disinvesting in South Africa without considering expressly whether it was in the best interests of the beneficiaries and without obtaining professional advice on this matter. That is sufficient for the decision of this case and it turns entirely on the general principles of law applicable to trusts in Scotland. In short the trustees acting on behalf of the council misdirected themselves in failing to comply with a prime duty of trustees, namely, to consider and seek advice as to the best interests of the beneficiaries, and so they are in breach of trust."

NOTES:

1. *The distinction between taking and following advice.* The fact that trustees must take advice **6.08** does not mean that they are obliged to follow it. As Lord Murray explained elsewhere in *Martin* (at 334):

   ". . . it is appropriate that I should make some observations on the argument which was presented to me by counsel for the pursuer on the basis of *Cowan* [*Cowan v. Scargill* [1985] Ch. 270]. In so far as that argument may be taken to imply that the duty of trustees in seeking to secure the best interests of the beneficiaries is merely to rubber stamp the professional advice of financial advisers, I find myself unable to agree. I accept that the most profitable investment of funds is one of a number of matters which trustees have a duty to consider. But I cannot conceive that trustees have an unqualified duty, in terms of the first two propositions which counsel for the pursuer sought to draw from *Cowan*, simply to invest trust funds in the most profitable investment available. To accept that without qualification would, in my view, involve substituting the discretion of financial advisers for the discretion of trustees."

2. *Taking advice in relation to investment matters.* Section 6(2) of the Trustee Investments Act 1961 specifically requires trustees to "obtain and consider proper advice" before entering into particular types of investment. See *infra* para. 7.14. It is thought that this obligation would exist at common law regardless of the statutory provisions.

D. Duty To Secure Trust Property

A. Mackenzie Stuart, *The Law of Trusts* (1932), p. 200

"It is the duty of a trustee to take possession of the estate, and to have it transferred into the **6.09** name of the trustees to the extent that no individual trustee or third party can use it for other than trust purposes. If he allows trust estate to remain in the hands of a third party, or of the law agent, without reducing it into the possession of the trust, he incurs the risk of personal liability if it should be lost. Belief in the integrity of the party holding the property of the trust is no excuse."

Forman v. Burns
(1853) 15 D. 362

6.10 Thomas Forman died intestate in January 1845. After some doubt as to who was entitled to inherit in his estate, John Forman was ordained executor-dative in January 1847. One of the assets in the trust-estate was a promissory note for £250, payable in November 1842, granted to Thomas Forman by R.M. Connal and W. Hinds.

Two months after his appointment, John Forman wrote to Connal intimating that the debt must be paid within a few weeks and requesting Hinds' address, which Connal provided. The request was repeated several times, and in June 1847 additional security was provided in a bill signed by Connal's brother. A payment of £50 to account was made in June 1848. In January 1849, John Forman indicated that he would be obliged to use diligence to recover the debt. By this time, Hinds had died and both the Connals became bankrupt shortly afterwards.

In an action of multiplepoinding, the Lord Ordinary (Robertson) held that John Forman had "failed to exercise a reasonable and proper diligence for the recovery of this debt", and that he was therefore liable for the unpaid sum of £200. On appeal to the Inner House:

LORD IVORY: "On comparing the dates of the various proceedings in this case, and bearing in mind the nature of the debt,—which was not properly a mercantile debt, but an investment made by the deceased himself,—I am rather inclined to think that we may alter this interlocutor. No doubt the executor did not use ultimate diligence, but still he was pressing for payment, and on the whole I hardly think this is a case in which we can hold him liable in respect he has not done diligence."

LORD PRESIDENT (McNEILL): "I certainly think this is a very hard case. Probably the executor thought what he was doing was judicious enough; but we can hardly touch this interlocutor without very serious consideration. This is a process of multiplepoinding and exoneration raised in March 1848, and the claimants insist that in stating the amount of the fund *in medio*, the executor should debit himself with the amount of the bill, which they say he negligently failed to recover. The executor was active enough in making his first demand, but, after having made it, he granted repeated indulgences to the debtors. He allowed it to stand over for some months,— then he got an additional security in the shape of a bill payable in September 1847, but which was not paid; and after that, he let it stand over till January 1849, when both the Connals became bankrupt. In the meantime these parties were carrying on business, and there is no reason to presume that if they had been pressed, they would not have paid the bill. In regard to Hinds, too, the executor failed in due diligence. His address was given to the executor in the beginning of the correspondence. I am afraid we could never enforce diligence on any executor, if we did not enforce it here. It is of no consequence that he was himself a creditor; it is no excuse that he chose to risk himself as well as the executry fund."

LORD FULLERTON: "I am so sensible of the importance of the considerations urged by your Lordship, that I am not disposed to dissent; but it is one of the hardest cases I ever met. The executor, on coming into office, found this bill as an investment which the deceased himself had entered into years before his death; and I think he was entitled to exercise some discretion as to continuing the investment or enforcing payment. It is true that he gave time to the debtors, but I am hardly satisfied that he did so entirely out of tenderness for them. I think he may have been in some degree influenced by the hope, that if he did not press too hard, there would be a better chance of recovering the debt. But executors must be taught that they are bound to exercise some diligence, and on that broad principle I think the safest course is to adhere."

LORD CUNINGHAME concurred.

LORD IVORY: "Perhaps on taking a larger view of the case, and with regard to the general law, the result at which your Lordships have arrived is the safest. At the same time, looking to this as an individual case, I cannot conceive a case of greater hardship on the executor. In the first place, I think it is a mistake to hold that the executor, whose office is gratuitous, is liable in strict diligence. He is liable only in the smallest degree of diligence of a party acting for others. In the second place, this executor is to the extent of one fourth a creditor in the debt. He has done nothing for or against the others, for whom he was gratuitously acting, other than he has done for or against himself. Then he came into office in a somewhat extraordinary manner. The loan—for this was not an ordinary bill, but a loan—was taken in this way by the deceased three years before his death. After his death, there is no one to look after the estate for two years, when this party is confirmed as executor, and he immediately puts the matter into the hands of his agent. A long correspondence ensues between the agent and the debtor, and the impression the correspondence leaves on me is, that the debtor, who is stated to be a worthy man though in labouring circumstances, if he had been pressed, could not have contrived to pay. There is, besides, another important principle involved. It is not enough to say that the executor did not use due diligence, but it must also be said, that if he had done diligence, the loss would not have resulted. There is no such statement here; and I believe that the executor is willing to stand by a proof of the fact, that whatever measures he might have taken, there would have been no other result. If it can be proved that he would not have advanced matters by doing diligence, I think that to enforce his liability is the severest thing I ever heard of in practice. He demanded payment; he got corroborative security; and he also got partial payment. But further, when the multiplepoinding was raised, the document of debt was *in minibus curiae*; it constituted *in specie* part of the fund *in medio*,—it was open to the orders of Court, and the other parties might have moved that diligence should be done on it; they did not do so, and I think they were as much to blame as the executor. In short, I think Mr Forman did all that an honest man could do; and, had I the least encouragement, I would be for altering the interlocutor. But I am not so confident of my own views as to dissent from the opinion of all your Lordships, and therefore, in the hope that the punishment of one may prove the salvation of many, I concur, though with the greatest reluctance, in the general opinion."

The Court adhered.

NOTES:

1. Lord Ivory's "second thoughts" are interesting, and reflect the fact that the then common **6.11** practice of the Court of Session of judgments being given orally without the judges necessarily having advance notice of the views of their colleagues could require judges to "think on their feet" somewhat and modify their positions in the light of the other judgments. See further Rodger of Earlsferry, *The Form and Language of Judicial Opinions*, (2002) 118 L.Q.R. 226, especially 229–230.
2. See also *Donald v. Hodgart's Trs* (1893) 21 R. 246, where the trustees failed to sell off the goodwill of the testator's business, and were accordingly held liable to account to the beneficiaries for its value.
3. It should be clear that this duty is a strict one. *Forman v. Burns* illustrates that the fact the trustee has acted honestly and in good faith will not necessarily be sufficient for him to escape liability for a failure to ingather property. This is an application of the general rule that the standard of care applicable to trustees (that of the man of ordinary prudence) is an objective and not a subjective one. See *supra* para. 6.02 and *infra* para. 9.02.
4. Where a trustee has failed to take steps to ingather property, he may be able to show that even if he had taken action, it would not have been possible to ingather the property. The onus lies on the trustee to prove this, however. See *Millar's Trs v. Polson* (1897) 24 R. 1038.
5. If the beneficiaries believe that assets have not been ingathered, they can bring an action of count, reckoning and payment against the trustees. See, *e.g. Smith v. Smith* (1880) 7 R. 1013. On the action of count, reckoning and payment, see *infra* para. 9.19.

The beneficiaries cannot normally bring an action directly against the person in possession of the asset which has not been ingathered, as a creditor cannot sue his debtor's debtor (*Hinton v. Connell's Trs* (1883) 10 R. 1110; *Inglis' Tr. v. Kellar* (1900) 8 S.L.T. 323). They can, however, require the trustee to put his name to an action to ingather the asset, provided they grant him indemnity for expenses (and find caution for expenses if necessary) (*Blair v. Stirling* (1894) 1 S.L.T. 599; *Aitken v. Taylor* (1912) 28 Sh. Ct Rep. 297).

6. Exceptionally, a trustee may be given court authority not to ingather property. In *Burns' C.B. v. Burns' Trs*, 1961 S.L.T. 166, a mentally incapable man was left £300 in his wife's will. He would have been entitled to elect to claim *jus relicti* out of her estate, which would have amounted to £26,000. He had no need of the money, as his own estate was more than sufficient to maintain him for the rest of his life. His *curator bonis* was granted authority to elect to claim the £300 bequest instead of *jus relicti*. See also *B's C.B., Petr*, 1995 S.C.L.R. 671 (Sh. Ct).

E. Duties Regarding Existing Debts and Obligations

(a) Inter vivos trusts

6.12 It is unusual for an *inter vivos* trust to have existing debts and obligations, although this may be the case if the trust involves an existing business. If this is the case, the trustees are not normally personally liable to satisfy these debts or obligations (in contrast to their personal liability under contracts which they enter into on behalf of the trust—see *infra* Chapter 10). They will, however, be liable to fulfil these obligations in their capacity as trustees.

(b) Mortis causa trusts

6.13 More requires to be said, however, about *mortis causa* trusts, where the trustees will normally be required to pay off the debts of the deceased. They are not, of course, personally liable for those debts. If the deceased's liabilities exceed his assets, then his estate may be sequestrated (see section 5 of the Bankruptcy (Scotland) Act 1985, which specifically provides for sequestration of the estate of a deceased debtor).

An executor cannot be compelled to pay an ordinary debt until six months has expired from the date of death. See Act of Sederunt, February 28, 1662 ("Act anent Executors-Creditors"). The purpose of the Act of Sederunt was explained in the following case:

Sanderson v. Lockhart-Mure
1946 S.C. 298

6.14 LORD PATRICK: "It was argued for the pursuer that prescription begins to run only from the date when the creditor could take action to enforce his claim. It was said that no such action could be taken until the expiry of six months... This argument proceeds upon a misconception of the Act of Sederunt of 28th February 1662. The subject will be found fully dealt with in Bell's Commentaries (McLaren's ed.) vol. ii, pp. 82, 83. What Cromwell's laws and the Act of Sederunt were designed to prevent was the acquisition of a preference by one creditor taking action at once upon his debtor's death before other creditors of the debtor got to know of that death. The provision of the Act of Sederunt therefore is that all creditors using legal diligence *within* six months of the debtor's death by citing executors or intromitters, or by being confirmed executors-creditors, or by citing other executors-creditors, shall come in *pari passu* with other creditors. Hence it arises that an executor cannot be compelled to *pay* a debt until six months have passed from the date of the debtor's death, but nothing prevents the constitution of the debt against the debtor's estate at any time within that six months. And on page 84 Bell explains how that constitution is effected. If an executor has been confirmed, an action is raised against him by each creditor and *the citation in the action constitutes the claim*. If no executor has confirmed, or if there be only confirmation by an executor-creditor, the creditor wishing to have the benefit of the law must get himself confirmed executor-creditor, or must cited the other executor-creditor, *within the six months.* I therefore reject the argument."

NOTES:

1. *Privileged debts.* Certain debts are, however, regarded as privileged: principally confirmation, **6.15** funeral and deathbed expenses. It follows that an executor may settle these debts prior to the expiry of the six-month period and that, in the event of sequestration, they will rank above most other claims on a deceased debtor's estate. See section 51(1)(c) of the Bankruptcy (Scotland) Act 1985, and for further discussion of this complex point, McBryde, *Bankruptcy,* paras 16–73 to 16–77; Wilson and Duncan, para. 34–09; Walker, *Principles,* Vol. IV, p. 245.
2. *Payment before the expiry of the six-month period or where there are doubts as to the estate's solvency.* If the executor disburses any of the estate prior to the expiry of the six-month period, he does so at his own risk. Even after the six-month period has expired, he should not pay out legacies if he has any doubt as to the estate's solvency. So, in *Murray's Trs v. Murray* (1905) 13 S.L.T. 274, the trustees handed over a piano which was the subject of a specific bequest under a will. When it later transpired that the estate was insolvent (and the piano had since been sold), they were held liable to credit the estate with its value. The fact that they had handed over the piano after the expiry of the six-month period was irrelevant.
3. *Claims after the expiry of the six-month period.* If creditors of the deceased make claims after the expiry of the six-month period, but the executor is unable to meet them because he has already, in good faith, disbursed the estate, he will not be liable to meet the creditor's claim. See *Beith v. Mackenzie* (1875) 3 R. 185, *infra* para. 6.26. As to the possibility of recourse against the beneficiaries, see Wilson and Duncan, para. 34–15 and authorities cited there.
4. *Constitution of debts.* A trustee may "pay debts due by the truster or by the trust estate without requiring the creditors to constitute such debts where the trustees are satisfied that the debts are proper debts of the trust." (Trusts (Scotland) Act 1921, s.4(1)(l)). This is one of the implied powers of trustees under the 1921 Act, and so could be excluded by the terms of the trust deed, although that is unlikely. If the trustee is not satisfied that the debt is a proper debt of the trust, he is entitled to insist that it is properly constituted by way of court action. Where there are a number of different creditors claiming on the estate, an action of multiplepoinding may be appropriate.

F. Duties Regarding New Debts and Obligations

In most cases, in order to discharge their duties, trustees will have to enter into contracts with third **6.16** parties. The general rule is that they incur personal liability in respect of any such contracts, unless they explicitly contract out of such liability. They are, of course, entitled to be reimbursed from the trust estate for such expenses as they properly incur in the discharge of their duties as trustees. These issues are discussed further in Chapter 10.

G. Duty To Keep Accounts

(i) The general duty

Trustees must keep accounts detailing their intromissions with the trust-estate. This duty is recognised **6.17** in statute (Prescription and Limitation (Scotland) Act 1973, Sched. 3, para. e(i), where it is stated to be imprescriptible). The 1973 Act is not the source of the duty, however, which exists at common law.

Ross v. Ross
(1896) 23 R. (H.L.) 67

LORD HALSBURY L.C.: "Now, my Lords, while I say that I cannot help feeling that there are some lines which must be sharply drawn, and notwithstanding that the defender is a mother, one must not diminish, if one can help it, the obligation upon a person who is managing the estate and effects of another to be able to render an account afterwards of what he or she has done. I cannot help feeling, therefore, with respect to a great many of these things, when the mother is challenged (whether one would have expected the son to raise the point or not is another question) she has only herself to thank for the consequences of disregarding the very wise advice of those whom she had at first consulted to keep accounts. She was bound to keep accounts, and if in any respect she has suffered—and I cannot help feeling that she must have suffered very bitterly in having to defend an action of this sort against her son— she had to some extent brought it upon herself by her neglect to follow the wise advice that was given to her, by keeping accounts so as to be able to shew what in fact she had spent, and in respect to what matters she had spent it."

NOTES:

6.18
1. Where a trustee has not kept proper accounts, he is theoretically liable to a "strict accounting": "that is, he is given the benefit only of such items as the beneficiaries care to admit" (*Polland v. Sturrock's Exrs*, 1975 S.L.T. (Notes) 76, *per* Lord Guthrie at 76, quoting Mackenzie Stuart, p. 220).

2. *Auditing of trust accounts.* In England, trustees are specifically empowered "in their absolute discretion" to employ an independent accountant to audit the trust accounts. They should not do this more than once in every three years "unless the nature of the trust or any special dealings with the trust property make a more frequent exercise of the right reasonable." (Trustee Act 1925, s.22(4)). Both Wilson and Duncan (at 23–08) and Norrie and Scobbie (at p. 101), in referring to this provision as a possible source of guidance for Scottish trustees, suggest this means that English trustees are required to have the trust accounts audited every three years.

   However, that is quite clearly *not* what the statute says, nor is it the view which is taken of its terms in the English textbooks. Indeed, a standard English text explicitly rejects the view that trustees are under a duty to have accounts audited on this basis: "Apart from the case of pension trusts and charitable trusts, it is neither necessary nor, except in large and complicated trusts or where trouble with a beneficiary is foreseen, usual to have trust accounts audited." (Hanbury and Martin, p. 565).

   Indeed (in contrast to England), there appears to be no statutory power entitling Scottish trustees to employ an accountant to audit the trust accounts. It is not one of the implied powers listed in section 4 of the Trusts (Scotland) Act 1921 (*infra* para. 6.31). Nevertheless, the textbooks consistently take the view that trustees should arrange to have the trust accounts audited at regular intervals (at least in continuing *inter vivos* trusts). (See also Mackenzie Stuart, p. 221). It may be that such a power should be considered as being implied into trust deeds at common law. (*Cf. Salamon v. Morrison's Trs*, 1912 S.L.T. 499, *per* Lord Skerrington at 500: the trustees are "entitled to employ and pay solicitors for taking charge of the trust accounts and exhibiting them when necessary").

   A trust-deed may, of course, explicitly confer a power to employ an auditor, and may lay down requirements as to the frequency of audits.

   For the special position of pension trusts, see the Pensions Act 1995, s.41 and regulations thereunder. For charitable trusts, see *infra* para. 11.07.

3. *Administration by factor: accounting requirements.* If trust funds are administered by a factor, the trustees must require the production of accounts and must check these (*Sym v. Charles* (1830) 8 S. 741). If the trustees have neglected to supervise the factor properly and a loss is occasioned to the trust-estate through his conduct, the *onus* is on the trustees to show that the loss would have been occasioned even if they had supervised him properly (*Carruthers v. Carruthers* (1896) 23 R. (H.L.) 55).

(ii) The right to see the accounts

6.19   There is a useful general discussion of the beneficiary's right to see the accounts in *Murray v. Cameron*, 1969 S.L.T. (Notes) 76. Essentially, the beneficiary has a right to inspect the accounts, but not to a copy of them unless he pays the necessary expense himself. A person who is a beneficiary or potential beneficiary in a public trust has a right to see the trust accounts, but there is no general right of any member of the public to see the accounts. Charitable trusts are in a special position (for which see *infra* para. 11.07).

It was held in *Salamon v. Morrison's Trs*, 1912 S.L.T. 499 that a beneficiary's assignee was also entitled to see the accounts, but Lord Skerrington observed (at 500) that if a beneficiary made multiple assignations the assignees may be required to "either appoint a single representative to inspect the accounts on their behalf, or they must indemnify the trust by paying for the extra expense occasioned by repeated inspections of the accounts."

Does the beneficiary have any right to see trust papers beyond the accounts? See the following case:

Nouillan v. Nouillan's Exrs
1991 S.L.T. 270

LORD CLYDE: "In this action the children of the late Derek Ernest Nouillan seek an **6.20** accounting from his executors. The pursuers are beneficiaries under their father's will. Liability to account has been admitted and statements of account have been produced. Time has been allowed for objection to these accounts. The pursuers have now enrolled a motion for commission and diligence to recover certain documents. They state that they have instructed an accountant to study the accounts which have been lodged and that that accountant has reported that the accounts raise more questions than they answer and that he requires their source material in order to report on them. The pursuers have called on the defenders to make all the vouchers and supporting material available to them but the defenders have refused to provide this. The pursuers now seek a commission and diligence to recover this documentary material. Their counsel stated that without it they were unable to check the accounts or specify their objections.

Counsel for the defenders admitted their liability to account as trustees to the pursuers as beneficiaries. He argued that diligence was premature because the scope of the dispute had not been focused as no objections have yet been lodged. He described the diligence as a major fishing expedition and he stated that beneficiaries were not entitled in an action of accounting to see all the trust papers. The accounts which had been produced were sufficient and it was now for the pursuers to specify some complaint. He also submitted that in any event the specification was too wide as it would include material prepared for the purposes of the present litigation and matters which would be confidential.

Although counsel for the defenders stated that the issue raised a matter of principle, he gave to me no authority to vouch his argument that beneficiaries were not entitled to see more than the statement of accounts of the trust. The only reference which I was given was to Thomson & Middleton's *Manual of Procedure*, p. 142 which merely described the procedure of ordering the defenders to lodge the accounts in process. I took the view that in the circumstances the beneficiaries here were entitled to see the vouchers for the intromissions of the defenders in the trust in which they are beneficiaries. I received no explanation why the defenders were not willing to disclose the vouchers although their counsel stated that they had nothing to hide. They had been asked and indeed called on in the pleadings for a considerable time to produce the vouchers but they have refused to do so. The pursuers are left in a position in which they are unable to satisfy themselves that the trust has been properly administered with regard to their own direct interests in it. In general I should have thought that trustees were bound to give a beneficiary full information about their administration and let him see the vouchers as well as the accounts. The refusal to do so might well invite a sinister influence.

So far as the width of the specification was concerned I granted it subject to the exception of material prepared for the purposes of this litigation. So far as any other material might be confidential, that should be protected under the normal procedure for sealing confidential material so as to enable any issue in that regard to be resolved later if necessary. Counsel for the defenders stated that the matter raised an issue of principle and for that reason I have granted leave to reclaim."

Note:

6.21   Although not referred to in *Nouillan*, there is prior authority to the effect that beneficiaries are entitled to see the vouchers as well as the accounts themselves: *Tod v. Tod's Trs* (1842) 4 D. 1275. Quite what is meant by "vouchers" is not explained in either case, but the term presumably refers to receipts and other papers which would vouch for the expenditure noted in the accounts as being genuine. *Nouillan* should not be taken as authority for any kind of general right to see trust papers, such as minutes of trustees' meetings. There might be very good reasons why such papers should remain confidential.

(iii) Excluding the duty to keep accounts

6.22   Although the duty to keep accounts will normally be taken as implicit in any trust-deed, the truster is entitled to exclude this duty. Such exclusion may be implicit, for which see the following case:

Leitch v. Leitch
1927 S.C. 823

Lord Sands: "This is an action of accounting brought by a daughter against her mother. It appears that, under a contract entered into in 1900 between the defender and her father-in-law, he made over the whole stock, &c., on a small farm to the defender as her sole and exclusive property for behoof of herself and her family. The pursuer, as one of the family, claims an accounting against the defender for her intromissions with this estate. As originally conceived, the action contemplated what would have been an intricate accounting over a number of years, but the pursuer now limits her claim to an accounting as regards £1000, which has been accepted by the defender from her son Murdo Leitch in satisfaction of her claims—the stock, &c., having been made over to him a number of years ago. . .

In the circumstances of the present case I think it extremely improbable that, when the arrangement was entered into, there was any thought in anybody's mind of division among the children in equal shares, or anything of that kind. The defender was left with a large young family to struggle through with, and the proceeds of the holding were the only possible means of subsistence. She was to do her best to struggle along and rear the family. The idea that it was contemplated that she should keep trust accounts appears to me to be fantastic. On the other hand, I am not prepared to go so far as to hold that there was an absolute gift to the defender unfettered by any fiduciary obligation to the children. I do not think that, if she had married again, for example, she would have been entitled to make over the estate to her second husband, or, if she had died, to will it away from the family. In my view, so long as any of the beneficiaries stood in need and the supply of their need might be defeated by a division, there was no obligation to divide or to aim at equal apportionment. The pursuer, so far, concedes this, for she now admits that there is no obligation to account during the period of minority of any of the children. But the rights and interests of the defender herself were at least on a par with those of her children. The estate was to be held and administered, not 'for behoof of her family,' but 'for behoof of herself and her family.' The defender is now an elderly woman, presumably past earning a livelihood, and it is not said that she has independent estate. If, as I interpret it, the fund is an alimentary one for behoof of 'the defender and her family' as a necessitous unit, there can be no claim to division during her survivance in a state of dependence on the fund.

I am accordingly of opinion that the action, as one calling for production of an account of intromissions from the date of the agreement, and for decree of a present payment is, as the Lord Ordinary put it, 'ill-conceived'. I am of opinion that we should adhere to his interlocutor."

Lords Blackburn and Ashmore delivered concurring opinions.

NOTE:

   The fact that the truster has excluded the duty to keep accounts does not relieve the trustees of liability for breach of trust. As a practical matter, however, it will make it much more difficult for a breach of trust to be proved.

H. Duty to Pay the Correct Beneficiaries

A. Mackenzie Stuart, *The Law of Trusts* (1932), p. 221

"A trustee in distributing the estate must hand it over or pay it to the party who, under the **6.23** trust, is entitled to receive it, and he is liable to that party if he pays it to any other. He can only discharge himself of liability to account for the estate by showing that he has paid the trust funds to the right person. Money paid by a trustee to the wrong beneficiary or creditor leaves him still liable to the right one; he is not discharged. He is held in law still to have the money, and he is bound not only to account for it but to do so with interest from the date when it was payable, although he may have acted in the utmost good faith in paying it to another person."

Lamond's Trs v. Croom
(1871) 9 M. 662

LORD KINLOCH: "I consider it to be a settled principle of our law that trustees, in distributing **6.24** the trust-estate, are bound to pay it away to the party in right to receive it, and are liable to that party if they pay it away to any other. There is no hardship in trustees in so holding, for if the matter is one of difficulty, they can always have recourse to judicial authority, and refrain from paying without the warrant of a Court. The case of distribution herein differs essentially from that of realisation. I do not hold it of any moment what the precise blunder is. The payment may be to the wrong beneficiary, or may be to the beneficiary and not to the creditors, or it may be, as here, to the secondary creditors, and not the primary. In all such cases it is the rule of law that the wrong-paying trustee is responsible. Cases may undoubtedly occur in which the facts necessary to be known, in order to point out the true person entitled, may be beyond the knowledge, and fairly possible discovery of the trustees; and in such cases responsibility may be modified."

NOTE:

   In *Cross v. Cross' Trs* (1919) 1 S.L.T. 167, it was held that the defenders, as trustees, were liable to account for the sum of £2200 which they should have paid over to the pursuer, a beneficiary, in 1909. By the time the case came before the court (in 1919), the value of the trust fund had diminished substantially. It was held that this was irrelevant and that the trustees were liable to make good the shortfall personally.

(a) Liability for Improper Distribution

If trustees disburse money or other assets to the wrong person, they are generally liable to account for the assets which they have wrongly disbursed. (They may, however, be able to recover assets which have been mistakenly disbursed to the wrong person by means of the *condictio indebiti*, for which see *infra* para. 6.28)

Buttercase & Geddie's Tr. v. Geddie
(1897) 24 R. 1128

LORD KINNEAR: ". . .the trustee here has paid money belonging to the trusters to a person **6.25** who had no claim to it whatever, and the second question arises, whether in accounting with his trusters he is entitled to take credit for the money so paid. I think he is not, and I am of opinion with the Lord Ordinary that the claim cannot be stated as a good claim so as to reduce Mr Geddie's share of the surplus of the trust-estate. I agree with the Lord Ordinary that there is no room for questioning the good faith and honesty of the trustee, and the Court must always be alive to the hardship of enforcing against an honest trustee a claim which must result in his becoming personally liable to make good money which he has paid away in good faith. But then his trust was to pay to the true creditors of Buttercase & Geddie and no others, and if he has paid the trusters' money to a person not entitled to receive it, it is no answer to say that he was under an error in law; and that appears to me to be the only answer that can be made with any plausibility. . .

I think there might be circumstances in which a trustee might well be in a position to claim as against person interested in the trust that payment of a claim in error was justifiable on the ground either of some concession made by them or of some failure or neglect on their part to bring before him the true nature of the objection to the claim erroneously paid. But it is quite out of the question to suggest that we have such a state of matters here. The trustee knew perfectly well that Mr Geddie and his agent objected to the validity of the landlord's claim, and they not only objected, but they pressed upon him that it should be tried judicially. Mr Tait [the trustee] did not think the process suggested an expedient or desirable kind of action to bring, but that is of very little consequence. The material point is that Mr Geddie desired that the validity of the landlord's claim should be determined in a Court of law. I think, therefore, that in view of his knowledge of that fact, Mr Tait's action was precipitate. He received Mr White's [Mr Geddie's agent] letter on the 21st. On the 22d he was informed by Mr Balfour's agent that Mr Balfour [the landlord] would not accept Mr Geddie. On the same day he proceeded to decide the matter by sustaining Mr Balfour's claim, and on the 23d he gave effect to his decision by paying the money. Unless, therefore, he can shew that the landlord's claim was good in law he is not entitled to take credit for that payment. In the ordinary course of business, I should have thought that the proper thing to do was to intimate to Mr Geddie's agent that he had sustained the claim to a certain extent, and that within a certain time he proposed to make payment unless interpelled. Instead of doing that he decides on the 22d, and pays the money on the 23d, without giving time to Mr Geddie to interpose. I think that by doing so he took upon himself the risk of being unable to establish the validity of the claim. I fail to see that there is any very great hardship inflicted upon a trustee by requiring that if he pays away the trust money in such circumstances as to make it impossible that the objections of the parties interested, whom he knows to object, should be determined, he must be held to have taken the responsibility of a final decision upon himself, and must stand or fall according as he can justify that decision or not."

NOTE:

Where a beneficiary cannot be traced, the trustees may be able to distribute the estate to those beneficiaries who can be traced and to take out missing beneficiary insurance to protect themselves against liability should the missing beneficiary subsequently reappear: *Re Evans* [1999] 2 All ER 777.

(b) Exceptions to Liability for Improper Distribution

In what circumstances may a trustee avoid liability for having improperly distributed part of the trust estate?

Beith v. Mackenzie
(1875) 3 R. 185

6.26 LORD GIFFORD: "I think it is quite fixed in law, and the rule is in entire conformity with the plainest equity, that a trustee or trustee and executor, after reasonable time has elapsed and after reasonable enquiry has been made, is entitled and is in safety to pay away the free trust or executry funds in his hands, either to legatees for pecuniary or specific legacies, or to residuary legatees, or ultimate beneficiaries, provided he does so *in bona fide* and without knowledge that there are outstanding claims due by the estate, and that he will not be liable in repayment or in double payment to creditors whose claims were not intimated and not known at the time when such *bona fide* payments were made. The case of *Stewart v. Evans* (1871) 9 M. 810 is a strong example of the application of this rule, for there the trustee was held free and justified in having parted with the estate although he knew of the claim, because he believed it to be effectually discharged by a deed which, however, was afterwards found to be null in law. It seems to follow *a fortiori* that the trustee would have been free if he had never known of the claim at all. The principle is recognised in other cases, and indeed on no other footing would a trustee ever be safe to wind up a trust and part with the trust-funds until perhaps the lapse of forty years—the long prescription. After six months, and in a question with creditors, the trustee or executor may pay *in bona fide primo venienti*, that is, he may pay off in full the creditors who have appeared, without being answerable to creditors who may afterwards turn up; and so after six months, and after due and reasonable inquiry, he will be quite in safety to pay the free residue to legatees or beneficiaries, and if after that creditors for the first time come forward, they must look for payment not to the trustee who has honestly and in good faith handed over the funds to the beneficiaries, but only to the beneficiaries or legatees who have actually received the funds themselves."

NOTES:

1. Although Lord Gifford's comments might be taken to suggest that there is a general **6.27** exception to liability for improper distribution where the trustees have made a reasonable error, such a general exception is not recognised by most writers. (See *infra* for further discussion). A number of specific exceptions are recognised, however, and are as follows:

2. *Theft or Embezzlement of the Trust Estate.* A trustee will not be liable where his failure to pay the correct beneficiaries arises due to theft or embezzlement of the trust estate by a third party, provided he is not himself at fault (*Jobson v. Palmer* [1893] 1 Ch. 71).

3. *Personal bar.* A true beneficiary may be personally barred from bringing a claim against the trustees due to his being at fault in causing the trustees to pay out to the wrong person. See the observations of Lord Kinnear in *Buttercase & Geddie's Tr., supra* para. 6.25 and *Earl of Strathmore v. Heritors of Rescobie* (1888) 15 R. 364.

4. *Unintimated Assignations.* Both Mackenzie Stuart (at p. 225) and Norrie and Scobbie (at p. 198) suggest that there is an exception to liability for improper distribution in the case of unintimated assignations, as follows. Where the beneficiary has in fact assigned their rights to a third party, but the assignation has not been intimated to the trustees, the trustees will not be liable for wrongly paying to the original beneficiary. That is—it is respectfully submitted— right, but right for the wrong reasons. Under Scots law, assignations are not effective until intimated (see Reid, *Property*, para. 656; K.G.C. Reid, "Unintimated Assignations", 1989 S.L.T. 267). In such a case, therefore, the trustees have done nothing wrong by paying the original beneficiary and no question of an "exception" to liability arises.

5. *Distribution where the trustees are unaware of the existence of an illegitimate child.* Trustees who distribute property whilst unaware of the existence of an illegitimate child are protected from liability by section 7 of the Law Reform (Miscellaneous Provisions) (Scotland) Act 1968 (as amended by the Law Reform (Parent and Child) (Scotland) Act 1986), which provides as follows:

   > *Protection of trustees and executors*
   > A trustee or an executor may distribute any property vested in him as such trustee or executor, or may make any payment out of any such property, without having ascertained—
   >   (a) that no illegitimate person exists who is or may be entitled to an interest in that property or payment in consequence of any of the said provisions, and
   >   (b) that no illegitimate person exists or has existed, the fact of whose existence is, in consequence of any of the said provisions, relevant to the ascertainment of the persons entitled to an interest in that property or payment, and

(c) that no paternal relative of an illegitimate person exists who is or may be
entitled to an interest in that property or payment,

and such trustee or executor shall not be personally liable to any person so entitled of
whose claim he has not had notice at the time of the distribution or payment; but
(without prejudice to section 17 of the Act of 1964) nothing in this section shall affect
any right of any person so entitled to recover the property, or any property
representing it, or the payment, from any person who may have received that property
or payment.

6. *Mistake as to foreign law.* Both Mackenzie Stuart (at p. 224) and Norrie and Scobbie (at p.
198) suggest that the trustees will not be liable where they have made a mistake as to foreign
law. Norrie and Scobbie state as follows:

"the payment may be made through a mistake in foreign law. Foreign law (which of
course includes English law) is an issue of fact and it is regarded as not unreasonable
for trustees to be ignorant of this fact."

Foreign law is undoubtedly an issue of fact as far as the law of evidence is concerned (see
Walkers on Evidence, para. 16.5.1), although whether it is correct to describe it as an issue of
fact in this context is another question. However, given that neither Norrie and Scobbie nor
Mackenzie Stuart seem prepared to recognise a general rule exempting trustees for liability
for improper distribution due to mistakes of fact, it is not easy to see why describing foreign
law as an issue of fact leads to this result in the first place. Either there is a general exception
to liability where the trustees have made a reasonable mistake of fact or there is not. There is
no Scottish authority which supports the proposition that a mistake as to foreign law is in a
special category.

7. *A general exception to liability where the trustees have made a reasonable mistake?* The
observations of Lord Gifford in *Beith v. Mackenzie, supra* para. 6.26 and of Lord Kinloch in
Lamond's Trs v. Croom, supra para. 6.24 might suggest that trustees will not be liable where
they have paid out to the wrong beneficiary due to an excusable (or at least unavoidable)
error. Such an exception is not, however, specifically recognised by most writers (although
see Mackenzie Stuart, pp. 226–227). The question of whether any such exception exists at
common law is perhaps now, however, largely irrelevant given section 32 of the Trusts
(Scotland) Act 1921, which provides that the court may "wholly or partly" relieve a trustee
who has acted "honestly and reasonably" from liability for breach of trust. Trustees who
make a reasonable mistake of fact will, therefore, be able to apply to the court for relief
under this provision. For further discussion of section 32, see *infra* para. 9.30.

(c) Recovery of Payments After Improper Distribution

Armour v. Glasgow Royal Infirmary
1909 S.C. 916

6.28   THE LORD ORDINARY (LORD SKERRINGTON): "The object of this action is to obtain repetition
from the Glasgow Royal Infirmary of a payment of £2000 which they received out of the
estate of the late Mr Wright. The action is peculiar in respect that it is brought, not by the
testamentary trustees who paid the money, but by the four heirs *ab intestato* of the testator.
In the ordinary case such an action could be brought only at the instance of the trustees. In
the present case, however, the testamentary trustees have been called as defenders, and they
concur with the Infirmary in maintaining that the money was properly paid, and that the
pursuers are not entitled to insist on its repayment. In these circumstances, I think that the
pursuers have a good and sufficient title to maintain this action to the effect of demanding
that the money shall be repaid to the trustees.

The first question is as to the validity of a clause in the codicil of 4th December 1891, by
which Mr Wright directed his trustees to dispose of the residue of his estate for such
purposes of a religious, charitable, or educational character, or partly among his own
relatives, as might be specified in any writing under the hand of his wife, which failing, of his

trustees. It is, I think, clear from numerous recent decisions that this clause is void from uncertainty. It follows, in my opinion, that the deed of direction executed by Mr Wright's widow, in terms of this power, is also invalid, and that the defenders the Infirmary had no right to receive, and have no right to retain, the sum of £2000 which was paid to them by Mr Wright's trustees in obedience to this deed of directions.

It was, however, maintained by both sets of defenders, viz., the trustees and the Infirmary, that the action could not be insisted in so long as certain discharges granted by the pursuers in favour of the trustees stand unreduced. These discharges were granted by the pursuers in favour of the trustees in respect of the payment by the trustees of certain bequests made to the pursuers by Mrs Wright in the said deed of directions. I agree that these discharges preclude the pursuers from holding the trustees personally liable in respect of the latter having given effect to the directions under the deed under which the pursuers themselves took benefit; but I cannot see how these discharges prevent the trustees (or what is the same thing in the present case, the pursuers) from demanding repetition of a payment which was made in error, and which the Infirmary had no right to receive. The discharges were not intended to operate as a gift from the pursuers to the Infirmary.

The defenders further plead that the £2000 received by the Infirmary has been *bona fide* expended in the installation of a bed called 'The James Wright Bed.' The averments in regard to this are somewhat vague, but it was not maintained that the money was not still in the hands of the Infirmary. Even if the capital had been spent, I do not think that this would be a good defence. The pursuers do not claim repetition of the income.

Accordingly I propose to pronounce a decree in terms of the first, second, and third declaratory conclusions of the summons, and to decern against the defenders the Glasgow Royal Infirmary for payment to the other defenders the trustees of the late James Wright of the sum of £2000 sterling, with interest from the date of citation, and with expenses."

On appeal, the Second Division adhered without delivering any opinions.

NOTES:

1. This decision is an application of the *condictio indebiti*, which may be summarised as follows: **6.29**

> "*Condictio Indebiti* (Claim for Recovery of a Payment which is not Due)—Money paid by the pursuer under the mistaken belief that it was due to be paid under a legal obligation to the recipient can be recovered in a personal action against the recipient, unless the defender establishes factors which would make retention of the money equitable." (Gloag and Henderson, para. 28.03).

A detailed treatment of the *condictio* is outwith the scope of this text, and the reader is referred elsewhere for discussion (Stewart, *Restitution*; *Stair Memorial Encyclopaedia*, Vol. 15 (W.D.H. Sellar)). Some general observations may be made, however.

2. *The pursuer must establish that the payment was made under a mistaken belief.* It was formerly thought that the mistake must be one of fact and not of law for the *condictio* to operate (see, *e.g.*, *Grant v. Grant's Exrs*, 1994 S.L.T. 163), but it is now established that the *condictio* may be founded on a mistake of law (*Morgan Guaranty Trust Co. of New York v. Lothian R.C.*, 1995 S.C. 151).

It is not essential to show that the mistake was excusable, but the excusability or otherwise of the mistake will be taken into account by the court in deciding whether repetition would be equitable (*Morgan Guaranty*).

It appears that a mistaken belief that the trust-estate was sufficient to allow debts to be paid in full will not suffice to found the *condictio* (*Cathcart v. Moodie* (1804) Mor. App. "Heir and Executor" 1).

3. *The court will not order repetition if the defender establishes that it would not be equitable.* This is a well-established principle (for recent discussions, see *Royal Bank of Scotland v. Watt*, 1991 S.C. 48 and *Morgan Guaranty Trust Co. of New York v. Lothian R.C.*, 1995 S.C. 151). The most likely situation in which the defender will be able to establish that it would be equitable for him to retain the money is where he has changed his position in some way in

reliance on the payment. Bell, in considering cases where a true creditor has received a payment from the wrong debtor, suggests:

> "where, in consequence of such negligent proceeding by him who pays, the creditor has been led into some expenditure which may bear hard upon him if obliged to refund; or where, in consideration of the payment, he has foregone some advantage, or given up a security, or liberated his debtor—he ought to be entitled to retain what he has got." (*Principles*, s.536).

Why, then, was the court not prepared to hold in *Armour* that the defenders' good faith expenditure of the money on the installation of a bed (in, we may assume, good faith) was not a sufficient reason for declining to order repetition? Gloag and Henderson (at 28.08) cite *Armour* as authority for the principle that repetition is not available where "the recipient has spent the money on an asset". That interpretation of the decision is, however, objectionable on a number of grounds.

Firstly, there is nothing in *Armour* to suggest that this is in fact the *ratio* of the decision. Indeed, it might be argued that Lord Skerrington simply did not consider the possibility that the court might have an equitable discretion to decline to order repetition. Secondly, it is at odds with Bell's suggestion that repetition may be refused where the creditor "has been led into some expenditure which may bear hard upon him if obliged to refund". Thirdly, it is illogical to say that good faith expenditure of the money on an asset weakens the defender's case for retention. That would mean that the Infirmary would have had a stronger case for retention of the money had the action been brought earlier, before they had installed the bed—and that surely cannot be correct.

It may be, therefore, that the decision in *Armour* is to be regarded with some caution. In any event, it is submitted, it cannot be regarded as authority for the proposition for which it is cited in Gloag and Henderson.

4. *The condictio indebiti and mistaken transfer of property other than money.* Although the cases on the *condictio* are predominantly concerned with payment of money, in principle the action should be available to recover property other than money which has been mistakenly transferred to the wrong person. See Gloag and Henderson, para. 28.10.

5. *Bona fide perceptae et consumptae.* The authorities on the doctrine of *bona fide perceptae et consumptae* are somewhat confused, but the weight of authority appears to support the following statement of principle:

> Where repetition of a thing is ordered, the defender will not be required to repay any fruits of that thing (in most cases, income on an investment) which have been consumed in good faith. For this purpose, a liferent interest which is paid to the wrong person is a thing in itself and not simply a fruit. (*Darling's Trs v. Darling's Trs*, 1909 S.C. 445).

> It was suggested in *Hunter's Trs v. Hunter* (1894) 21 R. 949 that the doctrine might apply to the thing itself and not simply to the fruits. However, these suggestions were subsequently disapproved in *Darling's Trs* (but *cf. Rowan's Trs v. Rowan*, 1940 S.C. 30). The better view is probably that *bona fide* consumption is simply a factor which the court may take into account in determining whether it would be equitable to order repetition.

I. The Duty to Invest

This is discussed *infra*, Chapter 7.

2. POWERS OF TRUSTEES

A. Powers Granted in the Trust Deed

6.30 It has been said that the trust-deed "is the foundation and the measure of the powers of the trustees" (*Goodsir v. Carruthers* (1858) 20 D. 1141, *per* Lord Ardmillan at 1145). The trust-deed may confer powers upon the trustees either explicitly or implicitly.

It was formerly common to list the powers of the trustees at length in the trust-deed, but that is now normally unnecessary due to section 4 of the Trusts (Scotland) Act 1921 (*infra* para. 6.31), under which certain general powers are implied in all trust-deeds. Nevertheless, the trust-deed must be examined in all instances to determine which powers it confers upon trustees (and also whether it excludes any of the powers which are otherwise implied under the 1921 Act).

B. Powers Conferred by Statutory Provisions

(a) Statutory Powers Without Court Application

Trusts (Scotland) Act 1921, s.4

General powers of trustees.

4.—(1) In all trusts the trustees shall have power to do the following acts, where such acts **6.31** are not at variance with the terms or purposes of the trust, and such acts when done shall be as effectual as if such powers had been contained in the trust deed, viz.—

(a) To sell the trust estate or any part thereof, heritable as well as moveable.
(b) To grant feus of the heritable estate or any part thereof.
(c) To grant leases of any duration (including mineral leases) of the heritable estate or any part thereof and to remove tenants.
(d) To borrow money on the security of the trust estate or any part thereof, heritable as well as moveable.
(e) To excamb any part of the trust estate which is heritable.
(ee) To acquire with funds of the trust estate any interest in residential accommodation (whether in Scotland or elsewhere) reasonably required to enable the trustees to provide a suitable residence for occupation by any of the beneficiaries.
(f) To appoint factors and law agents and to pay them suitable remuneration.
(g) To discharge trustees who have resigned and the representatives of trustees who have died.
(h) To uplift, discharge, or assign debts due to the trust estate.
(i) To compromise or to submit and refer all claims connected with the trust estate.
(j) To refrain from doing diligence for the recovery of any debt due to the truster which the trustees may reasonably deem irrecoverable.
(k) To grant all deeds necessary for carrying into effect the powers vested in the trustees.
(l) To pay debts due by the truster or by the trust estate without requiring the creditors to constitute such debts where the trustees are satisfied that the debts are proper debts of the trust.
(m) To make abatement or reduction, either temporary or permanent, of the rent, lordship, royalty, or other consideration stipulated in any lease of land, houses, tenements, minerals, metals, or other subjects, and to accept renunciations of leases of any such subjects.
(n) To apply the whole or any part of trust funds which the trustees are empowered or directed by the trust deed to invest in the purchase of heritable property in the payment or redemption of any debt or burden affecting heritable property which may be destined to the same series of heirs and subject to the same conditions as are by the trust deed made applicable to heritable property directed to be purchased.
(o) to concur, in respect of any securities of a company (being securities comprised in the trust estate), in any scheme or arrangement—
(i) for the reconstruction of the company.
(ii) for the sale of all or any part of the property and undertaking of the company to another company.

    (iii) for the acquisition of the securities of the company, or of control thereof, by another company,

    (iv) for the amalgamation of the company with another company, or

    (v) for the release, modification, or variation of any rights, privileges or liabilities attached to the securities or any of them,

in like manner as if the trustees were entitled to such securities beneficially; to accept any securities of any denomination or description of the reconstructed or purchasing or new company in lieu of, or in exchange for, all or any of the first mentioned securities; and to retain any securities so accepted as aforesaid for any period for which the trustees could have properly retained the original securities;

    (p) to exercise, to such extent as the trustees think fit, any conditional or preferential right to subscribe for any securities in a company (being a right offered to them in respect of any holding in the company), to apply capital money of the trust estate in payment of the consideration, and to retain any such securities for which they have subscribed for any period for which they have power to retain the holding in respect of which the right to subscribe for the securities was offered (but subject to any conditions subject to which they have that power); to renounce, to such extent as they think fit, any such right; or to assign, to such extent as they think fit and for the best consideration that can reasonably be obtained, the benefit of such right or the title thereto to any person, including any beneficiary under the trust.

(2) This section shall apply to acts done before as well as after the passing of this Act, but shall not apply so as to affect any question relating to an act enumerated in head (a), (b), (c), (d), or (e) of this section which may, at the passing of this Act, be the subject of a depending action.

NOTES:

6.32

1. Section 4(1)(ee) was added by section 4 of the Trusts (Scotland) Act 1961; and sections 4(1)(o)–(p) were added by section 10 of the Trustee Investments Act 1961.
2. It should be noted that there is no implied power under the 1921 Act to grant servitudes or to purchase property (other than in order to acquire a residence for one of the beneficiaries). Such powers may, of course, be conferred expressly or impliedly by the terms of the trust-deed. It may also be possible, in exceptional cases, for the court to confer such powers in the exercise of its *nobile officium*. See *Anderson's Trs*, 1921 S.C. 315, *infra* para. 6.37.
3. *"At variance with the terms or purposes of the trust"*. It will be noted that the trustees are not entitled to exercise these powers if to do so would be "at variance with the terms or purposes of the trust". The meaning of this phrase was analysed by Lord Blackburn in *Marquess of Lothian's C.B.*, 1927 S.C. 579, at 587–588:

> "It appears to me that an act can only be 'at variance with the terms' of a trust or of an appointment when it is at variance with the express language by which the trust or appointment is created. To give the word 'terms' any wider meaning would make it difficult to distinguish it in any way from the 'purposes' of the trust or appointment. If that is so, then the performance of an act can only be at variance with the 'terms' of a trust or appointment when its exercise is expressly prohibited therein; and in that case the trustee or factor must, before exercising the power, obtain the authority of the Court under section 5 of the Act. The question whether an act will be at variance with the purposes of a trust or appointment may not be so easy to determine. The purposes can only be implied from the language by which the trust is created or from the object for which the appointment is made. The determination of the purpose rests in the first place with the trustees or appointee, but in cases of serious doubt, where they may be unwilling to decide the question on their sole responsibility, it appears to me that the proper course for them to adopt would be, as your Lordship has suggested, to present a petition under section 5 of the Act. The dismissal of the petition as unnecessary would amount to a judicial finding that the exercise of the power for the purpose for which it was craved was not at variance with the purposes of the deed or appointment; would provide the petitioner with some guidance in his future actings; and might dispense with the necessity of repeated applications to the Court."

(See also *Christie's Trs*, 1946 S.L.T. 309, where Lord Mackintosh adopts a similar analysis).
4. Where the trustees are in doubt as to whether they are entitled to exercise any one of the specified powers under section 4, they may apply to the court under section 5 for authority to exercise the power. The result may well be that the court will dismiss the petition "as unnecessary", but such a result protects the trustees and, provided they have acted reasonably in brining the petition, they will be entitled to charge their expenses against the trust-estate (see, *e.g. Cunningham's Tutrix*, 1949 S.C. 275).

(b) Statutory Powers With Court Application

Trusts (Scotland) Act 1921, s.5

Powers which may be granted to trustees by the court
  5.—It shall be competent to the court, on the petition of the trustees under any trust, to **6.33** grant authority to the trustees to do any of the acts mentioned in the section of this Act relating to general powers of trustees, notwithstanding that such act is at variance with the terms or purposes of the trust, on being satisfied that such act is in all the circumstances expedient for the execution of the trust.

  In this section the expression "trust" shall not include any trust constituted by private or local Act of Parliament, and the expression "trustees" shall be construed accordingly.

NOTES:

1. See generally Wilson and Duncan, paras 24–20 *et seq*.   **6.34**
2. It has been suggested that it may be necessary in some cases for the court to engage in "some form of enquiry by way of a remit to a man of business or otherwise" in order to decide the question of expediency: *Christie's Trs*, 1946 S.L.T. 309, *per* Lord Mackintosh at 309. It is thought that this would rarely be necessary, however, particularly where the beneficiaries (or, in the case of a public trust, the Lord Advocate for the public interest) concur in the petition.
3. One common example of where powers would be granted is where heritage has been placed in trust for a specific purpose and the property is now unsuitable for the trust purposes. In that case, the Court will grant authority to the trustees to sell the trust property, so that the proceeds can be used to acquire new, suitable, premises: *Downie* (1879) 6 R. 1013 (an application under section 3 of the Trusts Act 1867). A power to sell heritage was also granted in the following, rather unusual, case:

Tod's Trs, Petrs
1999 S.L.T. 308

Under a 1929 trust-deed, the trustees held heritable property, including a large country **6.35** house ("Tirinie House") in trust for the purpose of providing professional persons with rest and a change of air. Tirinie House was initially successful, but declined in popularity, and began to run at a loss during the 1990s. The trustees petitioned the court under section 5 of the 1921 Act for authority to sell the house.

OPINION OF THE COURT: "In light of the submissions made by counsel for the petitioners, we have been persuaded that the petitioners should be granted authority to sell the heritable subjects. The principal trust purpose was that Tirinie House should be operated as a home for rest and change of air. It was so operated for many years but latterly its popularity declined and by the 1990s it was running at a loss. In order to meet the losses the trustees sold many valuable paintings and items of furniture. In 1995 the petitioners were advised that they could not make any further sales of the home's moveable property without compromising the ambience of the property and they were obliged to sell a substantial part of the trust's investment portfolio in order to clear the bank overdraft which had arisen by virtue of the operational losses of the home. They now have liquid funds amounting to only about £30,000. In November 1995 the petitioners decided to close the home and, after taking advice from senior counsel, were of the opinion that the trust had failed. The home has been lying empty for over two years and the furniture has been put in store. The property is in a remote location and is at risk of vandalism. Further, the fabric of the house is deteriorating. We have to consider the position as it is today and we do not consider that the suggestion of counsel for the Lord Advocate that the home should be reopened under new management is a realistic one, particularly having regard to the way in which the popularity of the home deteriorated over the years and the limited funds which are now at the petitioners' disposal. That being so, it seems to us that if the petitioners are not now to be permitted to sell the property, it is likely that it will remain empty for a considerable period of time. We were also informed by counsel for the petitioners that they have made extensive inquiries with a view to ascertaining if another charity would be prepared to take over the home but they have not been able to find any charity which would be prepared to assume responsibility for the home for any purpose. Further, the probable timescale is of importance. We were informed by counsel for the petitioners that they have been advised that there is doubt as to whether the trust is a public charitable trust or there has been a private resulting trust. This is not a matter which we can determine in the present proceedings. While the trust has had charitable status for over 60 years we do not consider that we can proceed on the assumption that it is a public charitable trust and that an application for a cy pres scheme, or a scheme under s 9 or 10 of the Law Reform (Miscellaneous Provisions) (Scotland) Act 1990, would necessarily be appropriate. If a petition for directions is presented with a view to obtaining a judicial determination as to the legal status of the trust, the trust could be held to be a public charitable trust or it could be held that there is a private resulting trust. If it was held to be a public charitable trust, a cy pres scheme may well be appropriate. If, however, it was held that there was a private resulting trust, the trust assets would fall to be divided amongst the heirs, many of whom have not yet been ascertained despite the expenditure already incurred by the petitioners. On any view, it is likely that there will be considerable further delay and, as we have observed, the home has already been closed for over two years. The condition of the property is deteriorating and the liquid funds now held by the petitioners are limited. If the heritable property is now to be sold, it is proposed that the proceeds of sale should be held by the petitioners as a surrogatum for the heritage. If that were done it is, in our opinion, unlikely that the potential successors would be prejudiced. If a cy pres scheme, or a scheme under s 9 and 10 of the 1990 Act, was eventually presented, the proceeds of sale would be available for the purpose of the scheme. While Tirinie House would not be available, we consider that it is important that the petitioners should, as far as possible, preserve the value of the trust estate and, on the basis of all the information which has been made available to us, we are of the opinion that there is a substantial risk that its value will depreciate and that, even if a cy pres scheme is later approved, the funds available for that scheme will be materially reduced. We would agree that, where heritable property is held by the trustees of a trust which may be a public charitable trust, then it is, in the normal case, desirable that the heritable property should not be disposed of before the submission of a proposed cy pres scheme. However, we have taken the view that the circumstances of this case, as presented to us, are very unusual indeed and in these particular circumstances we have reached the conclusion that the proposed sale of the heritable subjects is in all the circumstances expedient for the execution of the trust and that the trustees should be given authority to sell."

(c) Common Law Powers With Court Application

Berwick
(1874) 2 R. 90

6.36 LORD PRESIDENT (INGLIS): "The powers of trustees are defined by the trust-deed, and the Court will give no higher power. The trustees are not entitled to come to the Court for advice. If they have not the power given them by the deed it is not competent for us to give it them."

This statement was quoted with approval in *Scott's Hospital Trs*, 1913 S.C. 289, *per* the Lord Justice-Clerk (Macdonald) at 290–291; see also *Hall's Trs v. McArthur*, 1918 S.C. 646. Nevertheless, it is possible for the court, in the exercise of its *nobile officium* to grant extra powers to trustees where such powers do not exist under the trust-deed and cannot be obtained under section 5 of the 1921 Act.

Anderson's Trs
1921 S.C. 315

Mr Anderson had been tenant of a farm for some time. In his will, he directed his trustees to **6.37** hold the lease of the farm and the stock in trust for his nephew, Thomas Rae, until he attained the age of 21, whereupon the whole residue of his estate (including the lease and stock) should be conveyed to his nephew. He expressed the desire that his nephew should succeed to the farm and carry on the herd of shorthorns. After the testator's death, the landlord decided to sell the farm, but gave the trustees the option of purchasing it. The trust-deed did not, however, confer upon the trustees any power to purchase heritage, or to borrow on the security of the trust-estate, which would have been necessary in order to raise sufficient funds. The trustees, accordingly, presented a petition to the *nobile officium* of the court craving authority to purchase the farm and to borrow the necessary funds.

LORD JUSTICE-CLERK (SCOTT DICKSON): "There are difficulties, of course, with regard to our granting these powers; but unless these powers are granted, the main purpose of the trust-deed will be completely frustrated. It seems to me that the facts are so special that, again, it would be almost pedantic if we were to throw difficulties in the way of enabling the petitioners to carry out what was clearly the main purpose of the truster when he executed this trust-deed. The most helpful case in this matters to which we were referred was the case of *Hall's Trs v. McArthur*, 1918 S.C. 646, especially what was said by Lord Johnston and Lord Skerrington in reference to the previous case of *Coats's Trs*. Lord Johnston said (at p. 650): 'In the matter of trusts, which are an important branch of its exercise'—he is speaking of the *nobile officium*—'resort to it has been practically confined to cases where something administrative or executive is wanting in the constituting document to enable the trust purposes to be effectually carried out, and such cases are now largely met by the provisions of the modern Trusts Acts. But, where no such executive or administrative provisions are wanting in the trust deed, the Court will not interfere, for the Court in Scotland does not undertake, as does the Court of Chancery in England, the administration of trusts. In the present case no such executive or administrative powers are wanting; on the contrary they exist in exceptionally full and carefully thought out measure.' Lord Skerrington referring to *Coats's* case, said (at p. 653): 'It was, I think, a typical illustration of the *nobile officium* that, when objection was taken to the machinery devised by the testator as not being the best in the circumstances, something better should be substituted. That, I say, is a typical illustration of the exercise of the *nobile officium*, where something is to be done which is right and necessary, and the machinery for doing it is either wanting or defective.' In that case, both Lord Johnston and Lord Skerrington referred to the fact that the machinery, or, as Lord Johnston put it, 'the administrative or executive provisions' was or were awanting. That is exactly what we have got here. There is no difficulty in understanding what the truster intended and desired to do. The only difficulty is caused by the occurrence of circumstances which he had not taken into account, and which have produced a state of facts the effect of which is that, unless the Court interferes, or unless, at any rate, the trustees do what they desire to obtain the authority of the Court to do, the whole purposes of the trust, apart from some minor purposes, will be frustrated. In these circumstances, I think we may grant the powers that the petitioners ask for, on the ground that it is only by so doing that the main purpose of the trust can be carried out, and that there could really be no doubt that, if the truster had foreseen the provision of things which has now come about, he would have made provision for it. I think that, if one may say so, this case will be, like that of *Coats*, an exceptional one, which cannot be, and certainly was not intended to be, treated as a precedent. But, however that may be, it seems to me that the petitioners have shown a case in which it would be unfortunate if, though adhering to what may be regarded as the strict letter of the law, we were to prevent them—for no good reason as far as I can see—from carrying out what was clearly and distinctly stated by the truster as the purpose which he most of all desired to have carried out.

Accordingly, while I quite recognise the delicacy of the position, I think on the whole matter, the circumstances are such that we should be well advised in granting, and have power to grant, the prayer of this petition."

Lords Dundas and Ormidale delivered concurring opinions.

NOTE:

6.38   This is closely linked to the Court of Session's power to authorise variation of a public trust (which may involve the granting of additional powers) under the *cy pres* doctrine where it can be shown that the trust purposes are incapable of fulfilment. (See *infra* Chapter 13).

In *Anderson's Trs*, the performance of the trust would have become impossible unless the additional powers were granted. As to whether the court can exercise the *nobile officium* to grant extra powers in cases of "strong expediency" (*i.e.* without impossibility or the risk of impossibility being shown), see Mackenzie Stuart, "The Nobile Officium and Trust Administration", 1935 S.L.T. (News) 1 and *Gibson's Trs*, 1933 S.C. 190, discussed *infra* para. 12.38.

(d) Statutory Powers Limited To Certain Trustees

Married Women's Policies of Assurance (Scotland) (Amendment) Act 1980, s.2(2)

Powers of trustee under policy

6.39   **2.**—(1) It is hereby declared that where a policy of assurance vests in trust by virtue of section 2 of the 1880 Act—

(a) that trust constitutes a trust within the meaning of the Trusts (Scotland) Act 1921, and

(b) any person in whom such a policy vests is a trustee within the meaning of that Act.

(2) In addition to his other powers any such trustee may, where such acts are not at variance with the terms or purposes of the trust—

(a) exercise any option under the policy, or under any deed of trust or other document constituting a trust in relation to the policy;

(b) convert the policy to a partially or a fully paid-up assurance;

(c) convert the policy into any other form of assurance on the life of the person effecting the policy;

(d) increase or reduce the amount of the annual premiums payable under the policy;

(e) alter the period during which the premiums under the policy are payable;

(f) surrender the policy.

(3) A policy of assurance is not prevented from vesting in any such trustee, by reason only that it contains a provision to the effect that a trustee may in his professional capacity charge such remuneration for his professional services as is reasonable.

NOTE:

Other trustees with special powers. Trustees in bankruptcy have certain special powers under the Bankruptcy (Scotland) Act 1985, while judicial factors may apply to the court for certain special powers under section 7 of the Judicial Factors Act 1849.

3. DECISION MAKING

A. Majority Decisions

The general rule is that trust decisions may be validly made by a majority of trustees, unless the trust-   **6.40**
deed states that the appointment of the trustees is "joint". A truster can also appoint one or more *sine quo non* trustees. Without the consent of the *sine quo non* trustee, "no act of administration shall be effectual" (McLaren, II, para. 1656). "Joint" or *sine quo non* appointments are nowadays rare, but perfectly competent.

To illustrate the rule that the majority may validly take decisions, reference may be made to *McCulloch v. Wallace* (1846) 9 D. 32, where a court action was raised on behalf of the trust by (initially) the majority but not all of the trustees. The court rejected a challenge to the competency of the action, with Lord Jeffrey observing (at 34):

> "I think the majority of the trustees could competently sue without any addition, unless the respondents could prove that a march had been stolen on the other trustees."

Conversely, a minority of trustees cannot normally bring an action on behalf of the trust (*Coulter v. Forrester* (1823) 2 S. 387; *Duncan v. Duncan* (1892) 20 R. 200, *per* Lord McLaren at 202), although an individual trustee (or, *a fortiori*, a minority) can bring an action against the other trustees in respect of a threatened breach of trust (*Ross v. Allan's Trs* (1850) 13 D. 44; *Reid v. Maxwell* (1852) 14 D. 449).

Just as a minority of trustees cannot take decision on behalf of the trust, one-half of the body of trustees (*e.g.* one of two trustees, or two of four) cannot validly act alone, at least not unless there is some suggestion of bad faith on the part of the other half of the body of trustees (*Neilson v. Mossend Iron Co.* (1885) 12 R. 499). See also the following case:

Wolfe v. Richardson
1927 S.L.T. 490

The trust property consisted largely of shares in a company. The six trustees unanimously   **6.41**
granted a mandate in favour of one of their number to act on their behalf at company meetings. Three of the trustees subsequently moved to recall the mandate, but the other three (including the mandatary) opposed the resolution.

LORD MORISON: "The complainers next maintained that, in any event, the respondent no longer held the trustees' authority to act on their behalf. It was pointed out that the effective quorum of the trustees is a majority of the number then acting, and that no quorum of the trustees had assented to the continuance of the respondent's acting on behalf of the trustees.

I think this contention is well founded. It appears to me that after the respondent received formal intimation on the 11th of October that three of the trustees had interpelled him from acting on behalf of the trust, his authority to do so necessarily terminated. Thereafter, in my view, he no longer represented the trustees. He represented only himself and the two trustees acting with him, and I think it was incompetent for him to bind the trust. I do not think he was entitled to use the mandate at the company's meeting and to vote in the unfortunate disputes which had arisen as if he had the authority of a quorum of the trustees when in fact he had not.

The truth is, that a deadlock has arisen in the affairs of the trust. In my view it cannot be solved or removed by the respondent's acting upon a mandate or authority which has been disclaimed by one-half of the trustees. I think it is now the duty of the respondent to take specific instructions of the trustees on all matters which affect the affairs of the trust of the affairs of the company which affect the trust, and if he cannot obtain the directions of a quorum of the trustees, then it is his duty to refrain from acting or attempting to act for them."

NOTE:

Where a trust is deadlocked in this fashion, it may be open to the court to appoint a new trustee (or trustees) in order to break the deadlock. See *supra* para. 4.16.

B. What Constitutes A Quorum of Trustees?

6.42   The quorum is both:

- the minimum number of trustees who must participate in trust decision-making for any decisions taken to be valid. (That does not mean that they must all agree on the decision, simply that they must all be present at the meeting where the decision is taken).
- the minimum number of trustees who must participate in a trust action (*e.g.* signing contracts on behalf of the trust, taking court action) for the action to validly bind the trust. (Note, however, that the trustees may appoint an agent—either one of their own number or a third party—with the authority to bind the trust estate).

The trust deed may contain specific provisions as to the quorum. If not, the matter is regulated by statute, as follows:

Trusts (Scotland) Act 1921, s.3

What trusts shall be held to include

6.43   **3.** All trusts shall be held to include the following powers and provisions unless the contrary be expressed (that is to say)—

. . .

(c) A provision that a majority of the trustees accepting and surviving shall be a quorum.

NOTES:

1. Where one or more of the trustees have a personal interest in the matter being decided, they should refrain from taking part in the decision (*Caldwell's Trs v. Caldwell*, 1923 S.L.T. 694). A majority of the remaining trustees will constitute a quorum (*Shanks v. Aitken* (1830) 8 S. 640).
2. Trustees may be personally liable on trust contracts even though they have not participated in the relevant actions. In *Cuninghame v. City of Glasgow Bank* (1879) 6 R. (H.L.) 98, the five trustees unanimously agreed to invest part of the trust-estate in City of Glasgow Bank stock. Three of the trustees, as a quorum, signed the deed of transfer and the names of all the trustees were entered on the register of members. All five trustees subsequently signed a mandate to draw dividends on the stock. One of the two trustees who had not signed the deed of transfer argued that he was not liable for calls on the stock after the Bank's collapse. The House of Lords rejected this argument. On the personal liability of trustees to third parties generally, see Chapter 10.
3. A majority of the quorum can validly take trust decisions, even if one or more of the quorum dissents. In that case, a dissenting trustee is obliged to take any steps which are necessary steps to give effect to the decision. See the following case:

Lynedoch v. Ouchterlony
(1827) 5 S. 358

6.44   A quorum of three trustees under Mr Kinloch's trust lent a sum of money to Colonel Kinloch on the security of a life assurance policy with the Royal Exchange Assurance Company. Mr Ouchterlony, one of the other trustees, did not concur in the loan. He alleged that he was not made aware of it at the time and disapproved of it when he was subsequently informed.

Colonel Kinloch later died, and the trustees acquired the right to uplift the sum of £2,500 from the Assurance Company. They could not do so, however, without granting a discharge to the Company. By this stage, two of the earlier trustees had died, leaving only three trustees including Mr Ouchterlony. The trust-deed declared that three was a quorum, which meant that Mr Ouchterlony's consent was necessary in order to grant a valid discharge. He refused to concur in uplifting the money, and the other two trustees brought an action to compel him to concur.

LORD PRESIDENT (HOPE): "The defender may have acted rightly in refusing to lend the money in the way in which it was done; but what he is here required to do is to consent to take the money from the Assurance Company, and so remedy that which he alleges ought not to have been done. I therefore think that he is bound to concur in doing so."

LORD BALGRAY: "By accepting of the office of trustee, the defender necessarily agreed to submit to the opinion of the majority; and indeed, if he were permitted to resist that opinion, he would just be making himself a sine quo non. If he had conceived the loan an improper transaction, he ought to have complained to this Court, but he did not do so; and the question now is, not as to the loan, but as to the repayment of the money. This cannot be accomplished without his concurrence, as there would otherwise not be a quorum; and as it is a reasonable and proper act of administration, I think he is bound to concur."

LORD GILLIES: "I am of the same opinion. The clause constituting a quorum declares that any three of those who have accepted shall form it. If he had wished not to act, he ought not to have accepted; but by accepting he is bound to act, and in doing so he is not entitled to resist the will of the majority, and to say to them, sic volo, sic jubeo. If he resisted the lending out of the money, it seems somewhat inconsistent to resist the taking of it back."

Lord Craigie concurred.

NOTE:

If a dissenting trustee believes that the decision of the majority is in breach of trust, it is open to him to take an action for interdict or declarator accordingly. Alternatively, he can resign as a trustee, assuming he has power to do so under the trust-deed.

C. The Requirement of Consultation

Where trustees act without consulting all the other trustees, even if they constitute a quorum by themselves, their actions will be void (subject to section 7 of the Trusts (Scotland) Act 1921, *infra* para. 6.49). See the following case: **6.45**

Wyse v. Abbott
(1881) 8 R. 983

LORD PRESIDENT (INGLIS): "In November 1880 the trustees upon this estate consisted of Mr Abbott, Dr Abbott, and Mr Wyse. At that time two of the three, viz. Mr Abbott and Dr Abbott, executed a deed by which they assumed two persons as additional trustees, and afterwards Mr Abbott resigned. The result was intended to be that the trust should consist of four persons, viz. Mr Abbott's wife, and Mr Macdonald, the law-agent of the trustees, Dr Abbott and Mr Wyse. Dr Abbott died, and thereafter the trust was intended to consist of three persons. Now, all this was brought about by the execution of a deed of assumption in November 1880 without any intimation to Mr Wyse, and without its being brought to his knowledge until six months after. The question we now have to decide is whether this is a good nomination, and I have no doubt that it is bad. No two trustees can do a trust act without consultation with their co-trustee. It is of the essence of the duty of a body of trustees that they should meet and exchange views on the trust affairs. The trustees were bound to see that Mr Wyse had notice of their intention to nominate co-trustees, and an opportunity of stating his views. Their excuse was that he had been disagreeable, and had refused to sign a deed of transfer. That rendered it more imperative that he should have an opportunity of stating his views. The omission of notice, and the want of consultation, are enough to make the appointment illegal. The case cited by Mr Robertson [*Reid v. Maxwell*

(1852) 14 D. 449] may, with great advantage, be referred to as of universal application. The report bears, 'At advising, it was observed by some of their Lordships, that in the administration of the trust, and especially in the exercise of so important a power as assuming new trustees, it was essential that the utmost fairness and openness should be observed towards each other, that ample time and opportunity for deliberation should be afforded, and that if any concealment or underhand dealing, or any misleading or deception, in order to carry a measure by surprise should appear, the Court, as a Court of equity, would be entitled and bound to control and restrain trustees in such abuse of their powers.' This seems to me directly applicable to the present case. If the consequence be that the trust cannot go on because Mr Wyse is the sole trustee, and he does not desire to act because some of the parties connected with the trust have not confidence in him, the only remedy seems to be the appointment of a judicial factor. It is suggested that such an appointment would be a heavy burden on the trust. That may be avoided if the parties can agree; but failing their agreeing, I fear there is no other course but the appointment of a factor."

Lords Deas, Mure and Shand concurred.

NOTES:

6.46
1. See also *Gibb v. Stanners*, 1975 S.L.T. 30, where two trustees purported to exercise a power under the trust deed entitling them to remove a third trustee from office. It was held that their actions were invalid due to their failure to consult the third trustee.
2. Where a trustee is not consulted as to a decision, he may subsequently ratify it and thereby render it valid: *Roberts v. City of Glasgow Bank* (1879) 6 R. 805.
3. Just as all trustees have a right to be consulted on matters of trust decision-making, it follows, conversely, that if a trustee fails to participate in trust decision-making, that may be considered grounds for his removal by the court: *MacGilchrist's Trs v. MacGilchrist*, 1930 S.C. 635.
4. A failure to consult may be justified on the basis that (i) circumstances of emergency necessitated immediate action or (ii) the action taken has been to the benefit of the trust estate: *Stewart v. Dobie's Trs* (1899) 1 F. 1183.
5. The principle stated by Lord Inglis in *Wyse v. Abbott* is clear: if all the trustees have not been consulted, any actions of the remaining trustees on behalf of the trust will be void. (But *cf. Cambuslang West Church Committee v. Bryce* (1897) 25 R. 322, where this principle does not appear to have been strictly adhered to). However, this does not mean that the remaining trustees cannot act where a trustee cannot be reached, is ill and cannot attend trust meetings, or simply fails to attend. Provided that the absent trustee has been given a fair opportunity to participate in the decision-making, and that the trustees' meeting is quorate, decisions may validly be taken. In exceptional cases, a trustee may go so far as to lose his right to even be consulted, as the following case illustrates:

Malcolm v. Goldie
(1895) 22 R. 968

6.47 One of five surviving trustees in a trust left Scotland to reside in Australia. The remaining trustees, acting on the narrative that the emigrant trustee "is now resident in Australia and has ceased to act", assumed two new trustees. The proposal to assume the two new trustees was not intimated to the emigrant trustee. A question later arose as to the validity of the assumption of the two new trustees.

LORD KINNEAR: ". . . the parties to the case who challenge the assumption appeal to a perfectly well-settled and very reasonable rule, by which it has been held that although trustees are entitled to act by a majority or by a quorum which may be less than a majority, that does not enable them to exclude from their deliberation any one of their number merely on the ground that there is a majority without him. It is quite manifest that so to act would be directly contrary to the intentions of the truster, because when a truster appoints a certain number of persons to act together as his trustees, he means that they are to meet together and interchange their views upon any question as to which doubt or difficulty may arise, and deliberate and come to a conclusion after consultation together. And therefore for any one or more of them to act separately to the exclusion of one or more of the others is plainly contrary to the trust. But then it is quite consistent with that doctrine to say that when a majority of trustees have come together and consulted, they may proceed to act upon their deliberate opinion although one of their number has not been able to attend the meeting, because that is just the meaning of authorising a quorum or majority to act. It is said that although they can do that, they must consult the absent trustee. I am not quite sure what is meant by that statement. If it means that trustees who are able to meet are bound by correspondence to take into consultation a co-trustee who is unable to attend their meeting, and therefore unable to interchange his views with them, I dissent from the proposition, because these matters in the ordinary course of business are not to be too strictly regulated, and trustees are not to be tied down any more than other men of business to strict technical rules. The consultation of a trustee by his co-trustees does not in strictness mean that they are to obtain his separate opinion only, but it means that they are all, like other deliberative bodies, to meet together to deliberate; and therefore I am not prepared to assent to the proposition that where a trustee cannot attend, his co-trustees are bound to obtain his opinion before they can arrive at any conclusion, they being a quorum of the trustees without him. But then I do not at all doubt that they are bound to give him an opportunity of attending the meeting, and that, I think, is the full extent of the doctrine to which the parties impugning this deed of assumption refer. If he is accessible it would be quite wrong not to give him notice of a meeting; but then if the trustees are aware that he is resident in Australia, and that he does not intend to come back, to give notice of the meeting would be a mere futile formality. I do not see any reason whatever for holding that the business and administration of the trust is to be interrupted for the sake of any such unmeaning form. . ."

Lords McLaren and Adam concurred.

The Court held that the assumption was valid.

NOTES:

1. *Cf. Kelland v. Douglas* (1863) 2 M. 150, where the court was not prepared to hold that two **6.48** trustees could act on their own without consulting the two other trustees who were resident abroad. That case, however, is rather special in that none of the four remaining trustees had acted in the trust management for some time. It was said that the two trustees who remained in Scotland "were *de facto* as much dissevered from the trust management as the two trustees who were resident abroad." (*per* Lord Cowan at 165–166). With advances in communications, it is perhaps unlikely that a modern court would reach the same result as in *Malcolm v. Goldie*, as it could rarely be said today to be impossible or impracticable for a person to participate in the administration of a trust due to residence abroad.

    However, a quorum of trustees has a statutory power under section 21 of the Trusts (Scotland) Act 1921 to assume new trustees where a trustee has been continually absent from the U.K. for more than six months. It appears to be implicit in the statute that there is no requirement to consult the absent trustee before exercising this power. Similarly, the court has a power to remove any trustee who has been continuously absent from the U.K. for six months: section 23 of the 1921 Act.

2. *Form of notice of meeting. Malcolm v. Goldie* makes it clear that trustees must normally be given notice of the fact that a meeting is to be held. They must also be given special notice of any exceptional matters which are to be discussed (*Slimon v. Slimon's Trs*, 1915 2 S.L.T. 19, *per* Lord Hunter at 21).

    Does the law require that trustees be notified in any particular way? In *Darling v. Darling* (1898) 25 R. 747, a meeting of the trustees of a church was intimated from the pulpit, as was the usual custom. A decision was taken at that meeting to raise an action against one of the trustees, George Darling, who was not present at the meeting. Darling argued that the decision to take the action was void, as the meeting had not been properly intimated and he had therefore been deprived of his right to be consulted. (He did not, however, aver that he had been unaware of the meeting). The Court rejected this argument. Lord McLaren observed (at 752):

"When trustees, a committee, directors, or members of a public body are to be called together, the question whether a meeting is properly convened must be determined primarily by the terms of the constitution of the trust. But if there is nothing written on the subject, then custom must prevail, and for all ordinary purposes I should say that if it is the custom to call together a body concerned with the administration of ecclesiastical affairs by intimation from the pulpit, then, on proof being given of the existence of such a custom, such intimation would be sufficient."

There is some suggestion in the opinions, however, that if the committee had reason to believe that Darling was in ignorance of the meeting, the proper course would have been to adjourn the meeting and to give him notice directly.

3. *Ineffective resignation of a trustee.* In *Harland Engineering Co. v. Stark's Trs*, 1913 2 S.L.T. 448 (O.H.); 1914 2 S.L.T. 292 (I.H.), a trustee had purported to resign office. Both he and his fellow trustees believed that he had done so, but a doubt was later raised as to the validity of his resignation. The question as to whether any trust acts subsequent to his purported resignation should be regarded as invalid for lack of consultation was raised but not answered. It is submitted, however, that it would be wrong to regard a trustee's blunder in failing to resign office effectually as invalidating all the subsequent actions of the remaining trustees.

4. *Ex officio trustees and vacant offices.* Where a trustee is nominated *ex officio*, and the relevant office is vacant for a period, the vacancy does not prevent the remaining trustees acting on their own provided they constitute a quorum: *Campbell v. McIntyre* (1824) 3 S. 126.

D. The Special Status of Deeds Granted by a Quorum

Trusts (Scotland) Act 1921, s.7

Deeds granted by trustees

6.49   7. Any deed bearing to be granted by the trustees under any trust, and in fact executed by a quorum of such trustees in favour of any person other than a beneficiary or co-trustee under the trust where such person has dealt onerously and in good faith shall not be void or challengeable on the ground that any trustee or trustees under the trust was or were not consulted in the matter, or was or were not present at any meeting of trustees where the same was considered, or did not consent to or concur in the granting of the deed, or on the ground of any other omission or irregularity of procedure on the part of the trustees or any of them in relation to the granting of the deed.

Nothing in this section shall affect any question of liability or otherwise between any trustee under any trust on the one hand and any co-trustee or beneficiary under such trust on the other hand. This section shall apply to deeds granted before as well as after the passing of this Act, but shall not apply so as to affect any question which may, at the passing of this Act, be the subject of a depending action.

In this section the expression "quorum" means a quorum of the trustees under any trust entitled to act in terms of the trust deed or in virtue of this Act, or of any Act repealed by this Act, as the case may be.

NOTE:

It should be noted that this section does not protect trustees, but only beneficiaries and third parties. Its effect on transactions involving heritable property is not entirely clear, as Gretton has explained:

George L. Gretton, "Problems in Partnership Conveyancing"
(1991) 36 J.L.S.S. 232, 235:

6.50   "Naturally, it is not sufficient for a minority of the infeft partners to sign a disposition or other deed. But is it necessary for all to sign, or will a majority suffice? This is a general issue for trusts of all types. The Trusts (Scotland) Act 1921, s.7, seems to say that majority execution is sufficient, and some agents accept that interpretation. But it seems to me that the precise meaning of the section is by no means clear. One point to be noted is that it makes good faith on the part of the grantee a requirement. This may mean that the deed is good only if the grantee believed that all trustees had signed. Thus suppose that A, B and C are infeft and the buyer believes that A is dead, and takes a disposition from B and C. His title will be good. But to take a disposition signed only by a majority, in the knowledge that they are only a majority, is to take a risk. The common law is that heritable deeds by trustees must be signed by all, and it is not clear to what extent s.7 modifies the common law. The present writer first raised this issue in an article at 1987 J.L.S.S. 111 at 118, and since then has seen two opinions, one agreeing and the other disagreeing. I would stress that my view is not that the law is that all trustees must sign, but rather that the law is unclear, with the result that practice should be, for safety, to insist that all sign. Whether trustees who have been assumed, but who have not completed title, fall to be included, is itself not wholly clear, so again the path of prudence is to insist that they should also sign."

NOTE:

For the common law rule that "heritable deeds by trustees must be signed by all", see *Harland Engineering Co. v. Stark's Trs*, 1913 2 S.L.T. 448 (O.H.), 1914 2 S.L.T. 292 (I.H.); *Freen v. Beveridge* (1832) 10 S. 727. It should be noted that neither case is entirely clear-cut.

E. Interference by the Courts in the Discretion of Trustees

To what extent will the court interfere in the trustees' exercise of any discretion they have been given **6.51** under the trust-deed? See the following case:

Baird v. Baird's Trs
(1872) 10 M. 482

The testator died, leaving an estate worth well over £1 million in trust for his wife and son. The court held that the sum which the trustees proposed to pay to the widow for the maintenance of the son was unreasonably low, and directed that it should be increased from between £1,000 and £2,000 to £3,000.

LORD PRESIDENT (INGLIS): "It is argued by the trustees in support of the resolution to which they have come, that the mere expense of educating a boy ten years old will not much exceed £500 a-year, and to allow more than £1500 a-year for that purpose would necessarily be extravagant. But I think this is not a fair view of the case before us. It is very true that the mere maintenance and education at school of a boy of this age may not amount to more or not much more than is thus suggested, but the education of a young man with prospects like this heir before him is to be conducted not in school only, but I think one department of his education is to be received at home much more than at school. . . He is to be a landed proprietor to a very considerable extent, and it is most desirable that he should be familiarised with the interests of his estate as he grows up. It is in the highest degree desirable that he should imbibe a taste for field sports and for other country pursuits, and it is not possible to expect that in his situation these tastes and habits should be acquired without a very liberal establishment both in stable and kennel, and that, as we know, is a very considerable expenditure. . . It appears to me, however, to be still more desirable, and indeed of paramount importance, that this young man should be early associated with those whose influence and example will engender and cultivate manly and refined tastes and sentiments, which will enable him when he enters into active life to take such part in society as his wealth and position will justify, and perhaps also to aid in advancing the civilisation of his country and the age in which he lives. I am well aware that these advantages cannot be

directly purchased by wealth alone. But we all know that the want of wealth is not
unfrequently the great obstruction to the acquisition of such tastes and habits, and the surest
way of attaining to that high cultivation is the combination of wealth with other favouring
circumstances and good personal qualities; and it is of course in the hope that such a result
may be attained that we would be justified, and in such a hope only we could be justified, in
giving to this lady such a liberal allowance as she asks, or anything approaching to it."

Lords Ardmillan and Kinloch delivered concurring opinions.

Lord Deas delivered a dissenting opinion.

The Court ordered the trustees to increase the payment to £3,000 per annum.

NOTES:

6.52

1. This case is excerpted here as much for the entertainment value it provides from a twenty-
   first century viewpoint as much as for any issue of legal principle. *Baird* represents one of the
   high-water marks of the court's jurisdiction to interfere with the discretion of trustees. By
   contrast, in *Chivas' Trs v. Stewart*, 1907 S.C. 701, it was alleged that the sum the trustees had
   set aside for a beneficiary's annuity was excessively large. The court refused to interfere, with
   Lord Low stating (at 702–703):

   > "I think that the sum retained by the trustees was very full, but it is not suggested that
   > they acted otherwise than in good faith, and I am not prepared to say that the amount
   > was so extravagant that they cannot be regarded as having exercised their discretion
   > reasonably."

   At this stage, the court appears to still assert a jurisdiction to interfere where the trustees
   have not exercised their discretion "reasonably" (see also *Train v. Buchanan's Trs*, 1907 S.C.
   517 (affd. *sub nom Train v. Clapperton*, 1908 S.C. (H.L.) 26)). Other cases, however, suggest
   that the court's discretion is more limited than that:

   > "I think it clear that, apart from some very definite and precise averments of *mala fides*,
   > or, in other words, of abuse by the trustees of the discretion vested in them, the Court
   > cannot review, or even examine, the grounds on which trustees in the defenders'
   > position have exercised a discretion, such as that here vested in them." (*MacTavish v.
   > Reid's Trs* (1904) 12 S.L.T. 404, *per* Lord Kyllachy at 405).

   Also, in *Board of Management for Dundee General Hospital v. Bell's Trs*, 1952 S.C. (H.L.) 78,
   Lord Reid stated (at 92):

   > "But by making his trustees the sole judges of question a testator does not entirely
   > exclude recourse to the Court by persons aggrieved in the trustees' decision. If it can be
   > shown that the trustees considered the wrong question, or that, although they
   > purported to consider the right question, they did not really apply their minds to it or
   > perversely shut their eyes to the facts or that they did not act honestly or in good faith,
   > then there was no true decision and the Court will intervene: but nothing of that kind is
   > alleged in this case. The appellants' case here is that, although the respondents acted
   > with deliberation and in good faith, their decision was unreasonable in the sense that
   > no reasonable man could have failed to be satisfied that the infirmary had not been
   > placed under the control of the State before the testator's death. In this case the
   > respondents have not objected to that being taken as a proper test, and I shall consider
   > the facts on that view, but I wish to reserve my opinion whether that is the proper test
   > in cases of this kind."

   It is likely that the views of Lord Kyllachy and Lord Reid would be followed by the court
   today. In a recent English case, Robert Walker J. referred to Lord Reid's observations with
   approval, adding that "to impose too stringent a test may impose intolerable burdens on
   trustees who often undertake heavy responsibilities for no financial reward; it may also lead
   to damaging uncertainty as to what has and has not been validly decided". (*Scott v. National
   Trust* [1998] 2 All E.R. 705, at 718).

2. *Trustees having an interest in the decision.* It has been observed that the court will be more ready to intervene where the trustees have an interest in the decision (Mackenzie Stuart, 252), and so the court intervened in *Thomson v. Davidson's Trs* (1888) 15 R. 719 by holding that the allowance which the trustees had made for the maintenance of certain children was too small. The trustees, as residuary legatees, had an interest in the sums allocated being as small as possible. The court was not prepared to hold that the trustees had been "actuated by their personal feelings", but the fact of the trustees' personal interest seems to have made the court more ready to intervene. (See also *Ritchie v. Davidson's Trs* (1890) 17 R. 673).

3. *Refusal to exercise discretion.* Trustees who are given a discretion must, of course, exercise it. They cannot simply refuse to apply their minds to the issue. (*Train v. Buchanan's Trs*, 1907 S.C. 517, *per* the Lord President (Dunedin) at 524–525 (affd. *sub nom Train v. Clapperton*, 1908 S.C. (H.L.) 26)).

Nor can they simply hand the administration of the trust over to the court. See *Orr Ewing v. Orr Ewing's Trs* (1884) 11 R. 600, *per* the Lord President (Inglis) at 627, where it is observed that the trustees may "throw the estate into Court" by way of a multiplepoinding, but only if "there was so much difficulty and embarrassment in the distribution of the estate that the trustees would not be in safety to act on their own judgment. . . if [the trustees] took such a proceeding without establishing its necessity, the suit would be dismissed with costs."

The court will not advise the trustees as to how they should exercise their discretion, for the court "[has] not the means of judging the circumstances which render the exercise of a discretion beneficial or the reverse to the trust." (*Earl of Stair's Trs* (1896) 23 R. 1070, *per* Lord McLaren at 1074; see also *Noble's Trs*, 1912 S.C. 1230). The court will, if necessary, advise the trustees as to what they are *required* to do, but will go no further (see, *e.g. Cuninghame's Trs v. Duke* (1873) 11 M. 543).

4. *Proper information and consultation.* The trustees must ensure that they have such information as is necessary to properly exercise their discretion (*Caldwell's Trs v. Caldwell*, 1923 S.L.T. 694). Although they must exercise their discretion for themselves, it is perfectly proper for them to discuss matters with the beneficiaries before taking a decision (*Robinson v. Fraser's Tr.* (1881) 8 R. (H.L.) 127, *per* Lord Selborne L.C. at 128–129).

5. *Must trustees give reasons for their decisions?* In *Board of Management for Dundee General Hospital v. Bell's Trs*, 1952 S.C. (H.L.) 78, Lord Normand stated (at 85):

> "It was said for the appellants that the Courts have greater liberty to examine and correct a decision committed by a testator to his trustees, if they choose to give reasons, than if they do not. In my opinion that is erroneous. The principles upon which the Courts must proceed are the same whether the reasons for the trustees' decision are disclosed or not, but, of course, it becomes easier to examine a decision if the reasons for it have been disclosed."

It would seem to follow from this that trustees are under no duty to give reasons for their decisions. See also *Scott v. National Trust* [1998] 2 All E.R. 705.

F. Who May Exercise Discretionary Powers?

Where a truster wishes to confer a dispositive power of discretion upon his trustees (*i.e.* allow his trustees to select the beneficiaries from within a class of persons), he must nominate specific trustees. (For example, if a testator leaves money in his will to "charitable purposes", the bequest will be void unless he also nominates an executor who is able and willing to accept office). This issue is discussed *supra* paras 5.11 *et seq.* **6.53**

Chapter 7

INVESTMENT DUTIES OF TRUSTEES

1. THE DUTY TO INVEST

Where trustees hold the trust estate for any period of time, they must consider investing the estate to protect its value.

Melville v. Noble's Trs
(1896) 24 R. 243

7.01 Trustees left a substantial trust fund on deposit-receipt with a bank for 19 years without considering the question of investment.

LORD JUSTICE-CLERK (MACDONALD): "The question now before us is whether the trustees are liable to bring into the trust accounting a return for funds in their hands greater than the interest on deposit-receipt with which they debit themselves. . . The question now before us is truly one of the balance to be brought out in the trust accounts, on a true accounting. Are they liable, as I have said, to bring into the accounting what are the proper profits of sums in their hands? I am of opinion that the trustees are so liable. Trustees holding trust funds should invest them so as to yield an investment return. I cannot hold that they so invest them by placing them on deposit-receipt with a bank. It is true that many private individuals often keep large sums on deposit-receipt for long periods, but this cannot be called an investment in the usual sense of that term. There is no stipulated return. The interest to be paid may fluctuate at the will of the holders of the money, and it is never equal to the amount which ordinary and recognised investment yields. But had the trustees really addressed their minds to the question of investment and given it consideration, and resolved to keep the trust funds on deposit-receipt, there would have been a great deal to say for the view that if they were wrong it was an omission from error of judgment, and that they might plausibly appeal to the indemnity clause. I do not say that would have exonerated them, but at least they would have shewn intention to do their duty. But here they did not as trustees exercise their judgment. They just let matters slide for twenty years, without giving their duty any consideration. I must therefore hold that they were in breach of the duty they had undertaken in accepting the trust to manage it for the beneficiaries so as to make the capital yield a return from investment.

This being so, the question is, what in the circumstances must be held to be the return that with such management they would have obtained. . . [His Lordship considered the question, and continued:] I would suggest to your Lordships that the justice of the case would be met by their being charged with 3 per cent interest for the whole period of the trust. . ."

LORD YOUNG (*dissenting*): "As the bank accounts shew exactly the sums paid in and drawn out by the trustees, with the interest allowed on the balances and credited to them, and as there is no dispute on the subject, I presume that the Lord Ordinary when he allowed the pursuers a proof in support of their seventh objection intended that they should have an opportunity of proving that the sums deposited could have been invested more profitably to the estate. . . His Lordship is of opinion that a loan to a bank on deposit at the current rate of interest is not an investment, and that a trustee who thus deals with trust money acts unwarrantably and in breach of his trust, and incurs the same personal liability as a trustee who himself uses the trust money, referring in support of this view to cases in which it was held (1) that a trustee who allows trust money to remain in his business as a trader (in which the deceased truster had been a partner) is personally responsible for both principal and interest, and (2) that a trustee who puts trust money to the credit of his own private bank account incurs the like liability. I differ from the Lord Ordinary, and think the authorities which he cites are not in point, but deal with another and quite different matter. A trustee who himself uses trust money or puts it to his own credit in bank acts in breach of his trust, and is personally liable accordingly for the principal, plus interest at the rate commonly allowed against anyone who retains the money of another. To say that a trustee who deposits trust money in bank property earmarked as a trust deposit thereby commits a breach of trust is, I think, quite unwarrantable.

It has not been suggested that bank deposit is objectionable as investment for trust money because it is unsafe, the bank being known as of good repute. The objection is therefore confined to the rate of interest. But the rate varies according to the rise or fall in the market value of money. At what rate then or down to what rate is bank deposit a lawful investment for trust money, and when does it cease to be? Or, if there is no rule of trust law affording an answer to the questions so put, can we announce this as the rule of law—that trustees will be held to have performed or violated their trust duty in putting and having trust money on bank deposit according to the result of a proof at large on the question whether or not they could by their diligence have invested otherwise at a higher rate of interest? I have already said that in my opinion a bank deposit at the current rate of interest is an 'investment', and we certainly know that millions of pounds sterling are thus invested by quite reasonable and prudent people. But it is, I think, immaterial whether the term 'investment' is applicable or not. It is safe and yields interest, and if the interest is as high or higher than an investment in consols would be, as it may be and certainly has been, could it be rationally maintained that the trustees were in duty bound to draw out the deposit and buy consols, the deposit not being an investment?

The Lord Ordinary is of opinion on the evidence that the trustees could have procured safe investments at two per cent more interest than the deposits yielded. Your Lordship in the chair thinks at only one per cent more. I am of the opinion that the objection is on the face of it bad in law, and that the proof is quite out of place. The objection is confessedly unprecedented, and so certainly is the proof, as indeed proof on an unprecedented objection was most likely to be."

LORD TRAYNER: "The defenders were bound to deal with the trust funds in the same way as a man of ordinary prudence would deal with his own; and I cannot think that a man of ordinary prudence would leave his fortune, or a very large part of it, lying in bank on deposit receipt for a period of about twenty years. He would certainly seek some investment which would yield a higher return than bank deposit rate. I think the trustees here neglected their duty. It was no a mere omission in management, it was a total neglect of a duty incumbent upon them, to the direct injury of the trust-estate under their charge. . ."

LORD MONCRIEFF: "I am of opinion that to leave money in bank on deposit-receipt is not a proper permanent investment for trust funds. It is an excellent temporary use to make of them pending selection of a permanent investment. There might even be circumstances which might warrant trustees if they applied their minds to the matter in leaving trust funds on deposit-receipt for a considerable period. If, for instance, it were necessary for the purposes of the trust frequently to uplift the funds, or if in the state of the market there were serious difficulty in getting safe permanent investments. Evidence that the trustees had honestly applied their minds to the matter might in such a case be held to free them from personal liability, although it might be thought that they had been unduly cautious.

But in the present case I think it is proved that during the whole currency of the trust the trustees did not apply their minds to the investment of the trust funds. They were bound from time to time to consider the question of investment with a view to getting for the beneficiaries as large a return as they could consistently with the safety of the capital. It is proved that they totally neglected this duty. . ."

NOTES:

7.02
1. See also *Clarke v. Clarke's Trs*, 1925 S.C. 693. The fault of the trustees in *Melville* seems to have been in failing to address themselves to the question of investment. If trustees consider the question of investment, and conclude in good faith that the best course is to place the trust funds on deposit-receipt, it is unlikely that they will incur any liability for breach of trust (see *Manners v. Strong's J.F.* (1902) 4 F. 829). This is consistent with the general reluctance of the courts to interfere in the discretion of trustees (see *supra* para. 6.51).
2. Mackenzie Stuart suggests (at p. 260) that there is no duty to invest where the trust "is one solely for distribution". That is no doubt true where the trustees feel able to distribute the trust-funds within a short timescale, but investment may be necessary where that is not possible.

2. DISCHARGING THE DUTY TO INVEST

7.03 Any investment entered into by the trustees must meet two criteria:

(1) It must be an *authorised* investment, *i.e.* a type of investment which the trustees are empowered to make. The trust-deed may contain provisions detailing the types of investments which the trustees are entitled to make. Otherwise, the matter is regulated by the Trustee Investments Act 1961.
(2) It must be a *proper* investment, *i.e.*, it must be one which does not expose the trust estate to excessive risk.

A. Authorised Investments

7.04 The trust-deed may (and frequently will) state the type of investments which trustees are entitled to enter into. For the case-law on the interpretation of powers of investment in trust-deeds, see Wilson and Duncan, paras 25–09 to 25–14. Otherwise, the trustees have such authorisation to make investments as is implied by law.

The fact that a testator held a particular investment before his death does not mean that his trustees are impliedly authorised to retain it:

"It appears to me that the retention by trustees after a reasonable time allowed for realisation of an investment which they had no power themselves to make is as much a breach of duty as if they had made it. While the truster is alive he is absolute master of his own estate, and he may do with it what he will. He may be of opinion that by his own superior knowledge and skill he can invest in perilous undertakings with little risk of loss or great probability of gain, or he may choose to gratify his own desire for excitement by what other people would think to be imprudent speculation, and he may even to a certain extent be justified in speculating by a well founded confidence in his own judgment and foresight. But trustees receiving a conveyance of his estate from his *mortis causa* are not entitled to deal with it as if they were owners, and the deceased owner cannot reasonably be supposed, unless he has expressly said so, to authorise them to continue his speculation. He selects them, not with that view, but because he believes them qualified for a different office and purpose altogether—for prudent administration, realisation, and distribution. The limits of the trustees' powers and liabilities as to investment must depend of course primarily on the provisions of the deed, if there be any deed, and otherwise on the rules of common or statute law, and not on the character or conduct of the truster in the management of his affairs during his lifetime, or on an inquiry how far he was a prudent and safe investor or a rash and imprudent speculator. Accordingly, I think it is well settled that to retain an unsafe and improper investment after it could be converted and realised is equivalent, as regards the duty and liability of trustees, to making the same investment by the trustees themselves. They are just as little entitled to continue the truster's imprudence as to commit it themselves." (*Brownlie v. Brownlie's Trs* (1879) 6 R. 1233, *per* the Lord President (Inglis) at 1236).

(a) Ambiguity in the trust-deed

It was held in *Warren's J.F. v. Warren's Exrx* (1903) 5 F. 890 that, where trustees had mistakenly made an unauthorised investment under a complicated trust-deed, they were not liable in respect that they had acted *bona fide*. Wilson and Duncan (at para. 25–61) express some doubts about this decision. However, a trustee in this position would now be able to apply to the court to be excused from the consequences of his breach of trust on the basis that he had acted "honestly and reasonably": Trusts (Scotland) Act 1921, s.32, *infra* para. 9.30.

(b) Investments which cease to be authorised.

Section 33 of the Trusts (Scotland) Act 1921 provides that "A trustee shall not be liable for breach of trust by reason only of his continuing to hold an investment which has ceased to be an investment authorised by the trust deed or by or under this Act."

B. Implied Powers of Investment

(a) The Common Law Position

At common law, the only impliedly authorised investments were British Government Consolidated **7.05** Stock, loans on the security of heritable property, and the placing of money on deposit-receipt. (See Menzies, paras 609 and 612). The list of authorised investments was extended by the Trusts (Scotland) Amendment Act 1884 and the Trusts (Scotland) Act 1921. (See Mackenzie Stuart, pp. 263–271).

(b) The Trustee Investments Act 1961

The matter is now regulated by the Trustee Investments Act 1961, as extended by various Orders in Council, which distinguishes between three different types of investment:

(i) Narrower-Range Investments Not Requiring Advice (Sched. 1, Part I).

This includes investments such as Defence Bonds, National Savings Certificates and bank deposits.

(ii) Narrower-Range Investments Requiring Advice (Sched. 1, Part II).

This includes investments such as government securities, debentures issued by U.K. companies, building society deposits and loans on heritable security.

(iii) Wider-Range Investments (Sched. 1, Part III).

This includes any securities issued by a U.K. company which do not fall within the category of narrower-range investments requiring advice, shares in building societies, and units in unit trust schemes.

(This is, of course, a very brief paraphrase of the statutory provisions)

Securities in companies may only be purchased if the following conditions are met: the relevant company is a U.K. company, quoted on a recognised stock exchange, the shares are fully paid up or required to be paid up within nine months of the date of issue, the company has a paid up share capital of £1million or more, and the company has, for each of the preceding five years, paid a dividend on all the shares issued by it which ranked for a dividend in those years.

C. Mix of Investment Required under the 1961 Act

7.06 Where the 1961 Act applies, the trustees may choose to invest only in narrower-range investments. If they choose to invest in wider-range investments, they must split the trust fund into two parts:

Trustee Investments Act 1961, s.2

Restrictions on wider-range investment

7.07 2.—(1) A trustee shall not have power by virtue of the foregoing section to make or retain any wider-range investment unless the trust fund has been divided into two parts (hereinafter referred to as the narrower-range part and the wider-range part), the parts being, subject to the provisions of this Act, equal in value at the time of the division; and where such a division has been made no subsequent division of the same fund shall be made for the purposes of this section, and no property shall be transferred from one part of the fund to the other unless either—

(a) the transfer is authorised or required by the following provisions of this Act, or

(b) a compensating transfer is made at the same time.

In this section "compensating transfer", in relation to any transferred property, means a transfer in the opposite direction of property of equal value.

(2) Property belonging to the narrower-range part of a trust fund shall not by virtue of the foregoing section be invested except in narrower-range investments, and any property invested in any other manner which is or becomes comprised in that part of the trust fund shall either be transferred to the wider-range part of the fund, with a compensating transfer, or be reinvested in narrower-range investments as soon as may be.

(3) Where any property accrues to a trust fund after the fund has been divided in pursuance of subsection (1) of this section, then—

(a) if the property accrues to the trustee as owner or former owner of property comprised in either part of the fund, it shall be treated as belonging to that part of the fund;

(b) in any other case, the trustee shall secure, by apportionment of the accruing property or the transfer of property from one part of the fund to the other, or both, that the value of the wider-range part of the fund is increased by an amount which bears the specified proportion to the amount by which the value of the narrower-range part of the fund is increased.

Where a trustee acquires property in consideration of a money payment the acquisition of the property shall be treated for the purposes of this section as investment and not as the accrual of property to the trust fund, notwithstanding that the amount of the consideration is less than the value of the property acquired; and paragraph (a) of this subsection shall not include the case of a dividend or interest becoming part of a trust fund.

(4) Where in the exercise of any power or duty of a trustee property falls to be taken out of the trust fund, nothing in this section shall restrict his discretion as to the choice of property to be taken out.

NOTE:

Although section 2(1) provides that the two parts must be "equal in value at the time of the division", the position has now been altered by Order in Council. See the Trustee Investments

(Division of Trust Fund) Order 1996 (S.I. 1996 No. 845), which provides that the "wider-range" part must constitute three-quarters of the trust fund, and the "narrower-range" part one-quarter.

D. Special-Range Property and the Mix of Investments

Where the trust-deed authorises the trustees to invest in property beyond that which is permitted **7.08** under the 1961 Act, such investments are regarded as "special-range property" (Trustee Investments Act 1961, s.3(3) and Sched. 2). If all the trust-estate is, by the exercise of the powers given to the trustees by the trust-deed, invested in special-range property, then the 1961 Act has no application. If, however, only some of the trust-estate is to be invested in special-range property, the proper "mix" of investments is regulated by Schedule 2 of the 1961 Act:

Trustee Investments Act 1961, Sched. 2

1. In this Schedule "special-range property" means property falling within subsection (3) **7.09** of section three of this Act.

2.—(1) Where a trust fund includes special-range property, subsection (1) of section two of this Act shall have effect as if references to the trust fund were references to so much thereof as does not consist of special-range property, and the special-range property shall be carried to a separate part of the fund.

(2) Any property which—
   (a) being property belonging to the narrower-range or wider-range part of a trust fund, is converted into special-range property, or
   (b) being special-range property, accrues to a trust fund after the division of the fund or part thereof in pursuance of subsection (1) of section two of this Act or of that subsection as modified by sub-paragraph (1) of this paragraph, shall be carried to such a separate part of the fund as aforesaid; and subsections (2) and (3) of the said section two shall have effect subject to this sub-paragraph.

3. Where property carried to such a separate part as aforesaid is converted into property other than special-range property,—
   (a) it shall be transferred to the narrower-range part of the fund or the wider-range part of the fund or apportioned between them, and
   (b) any transfer of property from one of those parts to the other shall be made which is necessary to secure that the value of each of those parts of the fund is increased by the same amount.

E. Proper Investments

Investments must not only be "authorised", but also "proper".

Henderson v. Henderson's Trs
(1900) 2 F. 1295

LORD PRESIDENT (BALFOUR): "A trustee does not adequately discharge his duty by placing **7.10** trust funds upon an investment falling within the class or classes of investments specified in an investment clause—it is also his duty 'to avoid all investments of that class which are attended with hazard.'"

NOTES:

1. In selecting investments, trustees must exercise the general standard of care required of **7.11** trustees: that of the ordinary prudent man. On the standard of care generally, see *infra* paras 9.02 *et seq.*

2. The fact that certain investments are reputed as good investments is insufficient: the trustees must examine the particular investment for themselves (*Alexander v. Johnstone* (1899) 1 F. 639). They should also periodically review the investments they have engaged in to confirm that they remain proper investments.

3. *Can the trustees be liable for being overcautious?* If the trustees avoid hazard by making overly safe investments (such as leaving a substantial trust fund in a bank account for a long period), can they be liable for the difference between the return actually received and the return which might have been received had a more appropriate investment strategy been followed? It seems that, provided the trustees have addressed their mind to the question and concluded in good faith that this method of investment is the most appropriate, they will not be liable. See *Melville v. Noble's Trs* (1896) 24 R. 243 (*supra* para. 7.01) and *Manners v. Strong's J.F.* (1902) 4 F. 829.

4. *The difficulty of establishing liability for improper investment.* Unless an investment goes disastrously wrong, it can be very difficult for the beneficiary to establish a claim for damages for breach of trust against the trustees. They must show (a) that the investment was one that no "ordinary prudent man" (this being the standard of care required of trustees) would have made, and (b) that the trustees' decision caused a loss, *i.e.* that if they had acted in accordance with their duty of care, their (hypothetical) investments would have resulted in a better return. See *Nestle v. National Westminster Bank plc.* [1993] 1 W.L.R. 1260, criticised by Gary Watt and Marc Stauch, "Is There Liability for Imprudent Trustee Investment?" [1998] Conv. 352.

    Some of this difficulty might be removed by holding that the burden should be on the trustees to show that their negligence has not caused a loss (*cf. Carruthers v. Carruthers* (1896) 23 R. (H.L.) 55), but it is not clear how the quantum of damages would be calculated if they failed to do so.

5. *Can otherwise improper investments be sanctioned by the trust-deed?* The truster may, in his absolute discretion, specify in the trust-deed which classes of investment the trustees will be authorised to make. If the truster can determine what is "authorised", can he also determine what is "proper"? See the following case:

Thomson's Trs v. Davidson
1947 S.C. 654

7.12 LORD PRESIDENT (COOPER): "The purpose of this petition for directions is to enable a body of trustees to ascertain the effect of an investment clause contained in the trust settlement, and in particular to instruct them whether they are entitled to realise some or all of the investments in which the estate was held at the date of death.

    The truster died in March 1947, and the scheme of the will is a very simple one—a liferent to one person and the fee to be divided between two charities. All the affected interests are represented before us. The relevant clause dealing with investments falls into two parts. The first branch states that 'it is my special direction to my trustees that they shall retain the marketable securities forming part of my estate at the time of my death', and the clause then proceeds to amplify that direction by conferring a power upon the trustees to continue to hold the investments 'indefinitely, as they in their sole discretion may choose to do and as though they were absolute beneficial owners thereof.' I regard that as a discretionary power to the trustees, having the effect of divesting them in this matter of the responsibilities which trustees would normally incur in holding non-trustee investments. But then the clause proceeds as follows: 'Subject to my express request that my trustees shall not sell any of "the investments" until the same shall be capable of realising such prices as shall shew a fair profit in the opinion of my trustees upon the respective prices at which I purchased them.' It is to be noted that this part of the clause is described as an 'express request' in contradistinction to the language used in the opening part of the clause which is described as a 'special direction.' It is further to be noted that it is expressed as a qualification of the very wide discretionary power conferred by the opening part of the clause. I am therefore inclined to assign weight to the argument on construction maintained before us that the direction and request are not of an absolutely imperative or peremptory character. But it is not there that I rest my decision. Even if the direction were conceived in the most imperative terms I do not think that such a direction in relation to Stock Exchange securities can ever absolutely relieve a body of trustees from their basic duty to preserve the trust estate for the benefit of the beneficiaries entitled to participate in it. In his book on the Law of Trusts the late Professor Mackenzie Stuart says this (at p. 275): 'The trustees may be directed to retain some or all of the investments of the truster although these are not ordinary trust investments. Peremptory instructions must be obeyed, but they are not absolutely binding. The fundamental condition of trust administration is the preservation of the estate, and if it is necessary for the safety of the trust to realise hazardous investments, the trustees are entitled, and probably obliged to do so, even though the truster has forbidden it.' I concur with that statement of the position, though I should like to reserve for further consideration, should necessity arise, the special factors (largely of a historical character) which affect the holding of heritage by trustees. But in a case of the kind before us the statement which I have quoted seems to me to be exactly in point. I do not think that it is legitimate for any truster to invoke our law of trusts and to confide an estate to the custody and control of a body of trustees and at the same time to attempt to prohibit these trustees from exercising the most characteristic function which falls to be discharged by every trustee—the preservation of the trust estate.

I accordingly propose to your Lordships not that we should answer the question as put to us, because, as counsel for the petitioners was constrained to admit, its phraseology is open to criticism, but rather that we should find in answer to the question that the petitioners are not bound to continue to hold the investments in question after they are convinced that to do so would imperil the safety of the trust estate. I so move your Lordships."

Lords Russell and Carmont concurred.

NOTES:

1. It should be noted that the court decided that the trustees were "not bound to continue to **7.13** hold the investments in question". It is not clear whether this means they were not *entitled* to do so. Would they have been liable for any loss which had been caused by continuing to hold these investments?

   If trustees are unhappy with the directions as to investment in a private trust, it is open to them to seek the consent of the beneficiaries to a variation of the investment powers, and, if necessary to apply to the court to consent on behalf of any beneficiaries who are incapable of doing so. (On variation of private trusts, see *infra* paras 12.02 *et seq.*). This course was not open to the trustees in *Thomson's Trs,* however, because the liferentrix opposed the sale of the investments in question. For variation of investment powers by the court in a public trust, see *infra* para. 12.42.

2. It is notable that Mackenzie Stuart's statement that the "fundamental condition of trust administration is the preservation of the estate" is accepted without question. The question must, it is submitted, depend on a proper construction of the trust-deed, and in some cases this will not be a "fundamental condition" at all, as, for example, where the main (or only) trust purpose is the disbursement of the trust funds. It is perfectly competent to set up a trust where the trustees are empowered and even directed to engage in speculative and risky investment, if that is what the truster desires.

3. THE REQUIREMENT TO TAKE ADVICE

Trustees should, where appropriate, take advice on investment matters. There is a statutory **7.14** requirement to take advice in relation to the exercise of certain investment powers under the Trustee Investments Act 1961 (see section 6 of the Act), which probably goes no further than the common law rule that trustees should take advice where a reasonably prudent trustee would do so (see *supra*, paras 6.06 *et seq.*). See also the following case:

Crabbe v. Whyte
(1891) 18 R. 1065

7.15 LORD MCLAREN: "This is a reclaiming note against an interlocutor of Lord Kyllachy, in which it is found that the defender, a curator bonis, is not entitled to take credit in his account for a sum of £2700, which the Lord Ordinary holds to have been invested on insufficient security. The security consisted of a tenement of houses, shops and workshops, which at the time of arranging the loan were being put up in a street in Dundee, which is described as being then in course of reconstruction. I cannot state the facts on which the liability of the curator bonis is said to be founded better or more shortly than by reading a few sentences from the Lord Ordinary's judgment. 'The loan was made on an estimated rental made up from the plans, and on a valuation proceeding on that rental, obtained by the borrower, and furnished by his agent to the curator. The valuation brought out a value of £4200, the rental being estimated by the valuator at about £300. The valuation was by Mr Maclaren, architect, Dundee, a gentleman of undoubted character and professional standing. The buildings themselves were not examined, except that they were visited by the valuator when in course of erection, and also by the curator's partner in business, who took charge of the transaction. The security has, in result, proved wholly inadequate. The curator has for some years been in possession, and the interest is at present in arrear to the amount of over £300. The gross rental has never exceeded £250, and is at present only £237; and the feu-duty being £73, and the taxes and repairs considerable, there is no doubt that the interest is unsecured, and that the property, if now sold, would realise considerably less than the amount of the loan.' These facts, as the Lord Ordinary observes, are undisputed.

I agree with the Lord Ordinary that the obligation of a trustee in the matter of investments is that he shall exercise ordinary care and prudence in judging of the sufficiency of the security offered. In the two recent cases in the House of Lords, *Knox v. Mackinnon* (1888) 15 R. (H.L.) 83, and *Raes v. Meek* (1889) 16 R. (H.L.) 31, the diligence required of a trustee was described as that which a prudent man of business would use in his own affairs. In applying this rule we must of course assume parallel cases. A prudent man of business may be a builder by profession, or a dealer in subjects which are more or less speculative, but which on the average of his transactions yield him a profitable return. Such an illustration is evidently not at all to the point. We must suppose a prudent man desirous of placing a sum of money in a state of safe investment, such as will produce only the ordinary interest of a loan on heritable security. The point for consideration is then the safety of the security. I shall not be thought to state the rule with undue severity against trustees when I say that a trustee will, in my view, only be personally responsible for losses when it appears that he has not made due inquiry as to the safety of the security, and that the trustee is not in fact such as a trustee ought to accept.

A trustee is not required to exercise a personal judgment in matters of professional skill; he is therefore entitled to act on the opinion of a conscientious and skilful valuator selected by himself to advise him as to the suitability of the property as a security for trust money. If he takes such advice and acts according to the best of his judgment, I should not hold him responsible for supervening loss.

But again, a trustee may have omitted to take advice, and may have acted without much consideration, and loss may result. Still, if he can satisfy the Court that the investment was such as a trustee would have been advised by competent judges to accept, or that it was such as a trustee might lawfully and prudently accept, he will not be responsible, because, in the case supposed, although the trustee was negligent, the loss was not caused by his negligence, but is due to the depreciation of property or other causes.

In the present case I agree with the Lord Ordinary that the security was not such as a trustee ought to have accepted, because it was a security of a speculative character consisting of unlet and unfinished buildings, in a new and unestablished street, the rental being calculated from plans and measurements, and not based in any fair sense on actual transactions. I am also of opinion that the defender was negligent—I do not mean that he was intentionally negligent—only that he did not take the proper means of satisfying himself as to the suitability of the security for the purposes of trust-investment. I do not overlook the fact that the defender was furnished with a valuation prepared by an architect and valuator who is admitted to be of high standing in his profession. But this was a valuation obtained by the borrower. I assume that the valuation was a fair one, just such a valuation as might guide a company or a private lender who might be willing to lend on such security, taking on himself a certain risk for which he might be indemnified by charging suitable interest. But the opinion of the architect was never asked as to the propriety of lending trust money on such security, and I am not going to assume from the statements made in the valuation that the answer to such an inquiry would have been an affirmative answer. I think it must be taken that the defender acted without due inquiry, and without taking account of the considerations which made this heritable property an unsafe investment for trust money, and that the defender may therefore be properly required to replace the money advanced on receiving an assignation to the security. It follows, in my opinion, that the reclaiming note should be refused, and the interlocutor affirmed."

Lord Kinnear and the Lord President (Inglis) concurred.

NOTE:

See also *Martin v. City of Edinburgh District Council*, 1988 S.L.T. 329, *supra* para. 6.07.

4. PROPER MOTIVATION AND ETHICAL INVESTMENT

Trustees are required to exercise their powers in the best interests of the trust beneficiaries. To what **7.16** extent, therefore, can they take into account what might be termed "ethical" considerations in making investment decisions?

Cowan v. Scargill
[1985] Ch. 270

A mineworkers' pension scheme was established under statute. There were 10 trustees. Five of the trustees were appointed by the National Coal Board, and five were appointed by the National Union of Mineworkers. From 1976 onwards, the trustees periodically drew up investment plans. The NUM trustees objected to the 1982 plan, on the basis that to invest in energies in direct competition with coal, investments overseas and acquiring land overseas was in direct conflict with policy decisions of the NUM conference. The NCB trustees applied to the court for directions as to whether the NUM trustees were in breach of their duties as trustees by refusing to concur in the 1982 plan unless amendments suggested by the NUM were made.

SIR ROBERT MEGARRY V.-C.: "I turn to the law. The starting point is the duty of trustees to exercise their powers in the best interests of the present and future beneficiaries of the trust, holding the scales impartially between different classes of beneficiaries. This duty of the trustees towards their beneficiaries is paramount. They must, of course, obey the law; but subject to that, they must put the interests of their beneficiaries first. When the purpose of the trust is to provide financial benefits for the beneficiaries, as is usually the case, the best interests of the beneficiaries are normally their best financial interests. In the case of a power of investment, as in the present case, the power must be exercised so as to yield the best return for the beneficiaries, judged in relation to the risks of the investments in question; and the prospects of the yield of income and capital appreciation both have to be considered in judging the return from the investment.

The legal memorandum that the union obtained from their solicitors is generally in accord with these views. In considering the possibility of investment for 'socially beneficial reasons which may result in lower returns to the fund', the memorandum states that 'the trustees' only concern is to ensure that the return is the maximum possible consistent with security'; and then it refers to the need for diversification. However, it continues by saying:

'Trustees cannot be criticised for failing to make a particular investment for social or political reasons, such as in South African stock for example, but may be held liable for investing in assets which yield a poor return or for disinvesting in stock at inappropriate times for non-financial criteria.'

This last sentence must be considered in the light of subsequent passages in the memorandum which indicate that the sale of South African securities by trustees might be justified on the ground of doubts about political stability in South Africa and the long-term financial soundness of its economy, whereas trustees could not properly support motions at a company meeting dealing with pay levels in South Africa, work accidents, pollution control, employment conditions for minorities, military contracting and consumer protection. The assertion that trustees could not be criticised for failing to make a particular investment for social or political reasons is one that I would not accept in its full width. If the investment in fact made is equally beneficial to the beneficiaries, then criticism would be difficult to sustain in practice, whatever the position in theory. But if the investment in fact made is less beneficial, then both in theory and in practice the trustees would normally be open to criticism.

This leads me to the second point, which is a corollary of the first. In considering what investments to make trustees must put on one side their own personal interests and views. Trustees may have strongly held social or political views. They may be firmly opposed to any investment in South Africa or other countries, or they may object to any form of investment in companies concerned with alcohol, tobacco, armaments or many other things. In the conduct of their own affairs, of course, they are free to abstain from making any such investments. Yet under a trust, if investments of this type would be more beneficial to the beneficiaries than other investments, the trustees must not refrain from making the investments by reason of the views that they hold.

Trustees may even have to act dishonourably (though not illegally) if the interests of their beneficiaries require it. Thus where trustees for sale had struck a bargain for the sale of trust property but had not bound themselves by a legally enforceable contract, they were held to be under a duty to consider and explore a better offer that they received, and not to carry through the bargain to which they felt in honour bound: *Buttle v. Saunders* [1950] 2 All E.R. 193. In other words, the duty of trustees to their beneficiaries may include a duty to 'gazump', however honourable the trustees. As Wynn-Parry J. said at p. 195, trustees 'have an overriding duty to obtain the best price which they can for their beneficiaries'. In applying this to an official receiver in *Re Wyvern Developments Ltd.* [1974] 1 W.L.R. 1097, 1106, Templeman J. said that he 'must do his best by his creditors and contributories. He is in a fiduciary capacity and cannot make moral gestures, nor can the court authorise him to do so.' In the words of Sir James Wigram V.-C. in *Balls v. Strutt* (1841) 1 Hare 146, 149:

'It is a principle in this court, that a trustee shall not be permitted to use the powers which the trust may confer upon him at law, except for the legitimate purposes of his trust;. . .'

Powers must be exercised fairly and honestly for the purposes for which they are given and not so as to accomplish any ulterior purpose, whether for the benefit of the trustees or otherwise: see *Duke of Portland v. Topham* (1864) 11 H.L.Cas. 32, a case on a power of appointment that must apply a fortiori to a power given to trustees as such.

7.17   Third, by way of caveat I should say that I am not asserting that the benefit of the beneficiaries which a trustee must make his paramount concern inevitably and solely means their financial benefit, even if the only object of the trust is to provide financial benefits. Thus if the only actual or potential beneficiaries of a trust are all adults with very strict views on moral and social matters, condemning all forms of alcohol, tobacco and popular entertainment, as well as armaments, I can well understand that it might not be for the "benefit" of such beneficiaries to know that they are obtaining rather larger financial returns under the trust by reason of investments in those activities than they would have received if the trustees had invested the trust funds in other investments. The beneficiaries might well consider that it was far better to receive less than to receive more money from what they consider to be evil and tainted sources. 'Benefit' is a word with a very wide meaning, and there are circumstances in which arrangements which work to the financial disadvantage of a beneficiary may yet be for his benefit: see, for example, *Re T's Settlement Trusts* [1964] Ch. 158 and *Re C.L.* [1969] 1 Ch. 587. But I would emphasise that such cases are likely to be very rare, and in any case I think that under a trust for the provision of financial benefits the burden would rest, and rest heavy, on him who asserts that it is for the benefit of the beneficiaries as a whole to receive less by reason of the exclusion of some of the possibly more profitable forms of investment. Plainly the present case is not one of this rare type of cases. Subject to such matters, under a trust for the provision of financial benefits, the paramount duty of the trustees is to provide the greatest financial benefits for the present and future beneficiaries.

Fourth, the standard required of a trustee in exercising his powers of investment is that he must 'take such care as an ordinary prudent man would take if he were minded to make an investment for the benefit of other people for whom he felt morally bound to provide' *per* Lindley L.J. in *Re Whiteley* (1886) 33 Ch.D. 347, 355; see also at pp. 350, 358; and see *Learoyd v. Whiteley* (1887) 12 App.Cas. 727. That duty includes the duty to seek advice on matters which the trustee does not understand, such as the making of investments, and on receiving that advice to act with the same degree of prudence. This requirement is not discharged merely by showing that the trustee has acted in good faith and with sincerity. Honesty and sincerity are not the same as prudence and reasonableness. Some of the most sincere people are the most unreasonable; and Mr. Scargill told me that he had met quite a few of them. Accordingly, although a trustee who takes advice on investments is not bound to accept and act on that advice, he is not entitled to reject it merely because he sincerely disagrees with it, unless in addition to being sincere he is acting as an ordinary prudent man would act.

[The Vice-Chancellor went on to hold that pension fund trusts 'are in general governed by the ordinary law of trusts, subject to any contrary provision in the rules or other provisions which govern the trusts. In particular, the trustees of a pension fund are subject to the overriding duty to do the best that they can for the beneficiaries. . .', and continued:]

I can see no escape from the conclusion that the N.U.M. trustees were attempting to impose the prohibitions in order to carry out union policy; and mere assertions that their sole consideration was the benefit of the beneficiaries do not alter that conclusion. If the N.U.M. trustees were thinking only of the benefit of the beneficiaries, why all the references to union policy instead of proper explanations of how and why the prohibitions would bring benefits to the beneficiaries? No doubt some trustees with strong feelings find it irksome to be forced to submerge those feelings and genuinely put the interests of the beneficiaries first. Indeed, there are some who are temperamentally unsuited to being trustees, and are more fitted for campaigning for changes in the law. This, of course, they are free to do; but if they choose to become trustees they must accept it that the rules of equity will bind them in all that they do as trustees. . .

I also reject any assertion that prior to the commencement of these proceedings the benefit of the beneficiaries was the sole consideration that the union trustees had: that also is untrue. The union trustees were mainly, if not solely, actuated by a desire to pursue union policy, and they were not putting the interests of the beneficiaries first, as they ought to have done. They were doing so deliberately and in the teeth of proper legal advice from both sides of the table as to the duties of trustees, and there has been no suggestion that at any time they obtained further legal advice, as trustees who had genuinely intended to carry out their fiduciary duties would have done when the serious conflict of views had become plain. They were adamant in their determination to impose the restrictions, whether or not they harmed their beneficiaries. In this respect I can see no difference between Mr. Scargill, who vehemently opposed investment overseas and in oil as soon as he became a trustee, and the other four union trustees, who for years before the advent of Mr. Scargill had been operating under a policy of substantial investment overseas and in oil. As soon as Mr. Scargill arrived, they promptly abandoned their previous attitude and fell in beside him.

This conclusion, however, does not end the matter. If trustees make a decision upon wholly wrong grounds, and yet it subsequently appears, from matters which they did not express or refer to, that there are in fact good and sufficient reasons for supporting their decision, then I do not think that they would incur any liability for having decided the matter upon erroneous grounds; for the decision itself was right. I must therefore turn to the 30 or 35 affidavits which, with their voluminous exhibits, made up the eight large volumes that were before me.

Some of the evidence filed by the defendants tended to show that the prohibitions would not be harmful to the beneficiaries, or jeopardise the aims of the fund, and that some pension funds got along well enough without any overseas investments. Such evidence misses the point. Trustees must do the best they can for the benefit of their beneficiaries, and not merely avoid harming them. I find it impossible to see how it will assist trustees to do the best they can for their beneficiaries by prohibiting a wide range of investments that are authorised by the terms of the trust. Whatever the position today, nobody can say that conditions tomorrow cannot possibly make it advantageous to invest in one of the prohibited investments. It is the duty of trustees, in the interests of their beneficiaries, to take advantage of the full range of investments authorised by the terms of the trust, instead of resolving to narrow that range.

[The Vice-Chancellor considered further, and rejected, the N.U.M. trustees' argument that their policy was in the interests of the beneficiaries:]

. . . on the case as a whole, in my judgment the plaintiffs are right and the defendants are wrong. The question, then, is what order should be made. The summons is cast in the form of asking the court to give directions; but I doubt whether this is the most appropriate remedy. I think that at this stage it would be more appropriate for me to make declarations, and leave it to the defendants to carry out their duties as trustees in accordance with those declarations."

NOTES:

7.18
1. The term "ethical" is used here to describe those non-financial considerations which trustees may wish to take into account in making investment decisions. The use of that term is not intended to pass any (positive or negative) judgment on the factors which trustees in the various cases referred to wished to take into account.
2. *Cowan v. Scargill* does not prevent trustees taking ethical considerations into account in making investment decisions. One passage of Megarry V.-C.'s judgment, included in the above excerpt, should be highlighted:

> "The assertion that trustees could not be criticised for failing to make a particular investment for social or political reasons is one that I would not accept in its full width. If the investment in fact made is equally beneficial to the beneficiaries, then criticism would be difficult to sustain in practice, whatever the position in theory. But if the investment in fact made is less beneficial, then both in theory and in practice the trustees would normally be open to criticism."

If a trustee has a choice between investment A and investment B, which appear to be equally good investments from the point of view of maximising the funds available for distribution to the beneficiaries, he cannot be criticised for choosing to select investment A rather than investment B on the basis of ethical factors. *Cf. Harries v. Church Commissioners for England* [1992] 1 W.L.R. 1241, *per* Sir Donald Nicholls V.-C. at 1247–1248 (considering the position of trustees in a charitable trust where there is dispute over whether a particular investment conflicts with the objects of the trust):

> "Trustees may, if they wish, accommodate the views of those who consider that on moral grounds a particular investment would be in conflict with the objects of the

charity, so long as the trustees are satisfied that course would not involve a risk of significant financial detriment. But when they are not so satisfied trustees should not make investment decisions on the basis of preferring one view of whether on moral grounds [the] investment conflicts with the objects of the charity over another. This is so even when one view is more widely supported than the other."

The stance taken by the NUM trustees in *Cowan v. Scargill* was objectionable because, if given effect to, it would have fettered the discretion of the trustees to consider whether particular investments were in the best interests of the beneficiaries. See also *Martin v. City of Edinburgh District Council*, 1988 S.L.T. 329 (*supra* para. 6.07), where trustees pursued a policy of disinvesting in South Africa without considering the best interests of the beneficiaries. A declarator to the effect that they were in breach of their duty as trustees was granted.

3. *Remedies.* Trustees who take improper considerations into account in determining investment policy will be liable in damages if any loss to the trust-estate can be shown (*Millar's Factor v. Millar's Trs* (1886) 14 R. 22). As noted earlier (para. 7.11), however, loss can be difficult to establish in cases where improper investment is alleged. Alternatively, a declarator that the policy adopted by the trustees is in breach of their fiduciary duty may be sought (as in *Martin v. City of Edinburgh District Council*, 1988 S.L.T. 329). In extreme cases, the remedies of interdict or even removal of the trustee from office by the court would be available.

4. *Considerations which appear to be ethical but which are consistent with the trust purposes.* Trustees may, of course, be explicitly authorised by the trust deed to take ethical considerations into account in selecting investments. In other cases, particularly where public trusts are concerned, the trust purposes may effectively imply a limited power to give effect to such considerations. See *Harries v. Church Commissioners for England* [1992] 1 W.L.R. 1241, *per* Sir Donald Nicholls V.-C. at 1246:

> "There will be some cases, I suspect comparatively rare, when the objects of the charity are such that investments of a particular type would conflict with the aims of the charity. Much-cited examples are those of cancer research companies and tobacco shares, trustees of temperance charities and brewery or distillery shares, and trustees of charities of the Society of Friends and shares in companies engaged in production of armaments. If, as would be likely in those examples, trustees were satisfied that investing in a company engaged in a particular type of business would conflict with the very objects their charity is seeking to achieve, they should not so invest. Carried to its logical conclusion the trustees should take this course even if it would be likely to result in significant financial detriment to the charity. The logical conclusion, whilst sound as a matter of legal analysis, is unlikely to arise in practice. It is not easy to think of an instance where in practice the exclusion for this reason of one or more companies or sectors from the whole range of investments open to trustees would be likely to leave them without an adequately wide range of investments from which to choose a properly diversified portfolio."

It may also be that a decision which at first sight appears to be motivated by such "policy" considerations is in fact in the financial interests of the beneficiaries. In *Withers v. Teachers' Retirement System of City of New York*, 447 F.Supp. 1248 (1978); affd. 595 F.2d 1210 (1979), trustees in a teachers' pension fund bought highly speculative New York City bonds in an attempt to stave off the City's bankruptcy. It was held that their actions were in fact in the best interests of the beneficiaries, because the City was a major contributor to the fund and the ultimate guarantor of the pension payments, and the pension fund would be quickly exhausted if the City's contributions ceased.

5. EXTENSION OF INVESTMENT POWERS BY THE COURT

As to the extent to which the court may extend the investment powers of the trustees beyond those **7.19** which are permitted by the Trustee Investments Act 1961 or the trust deed, see *infra* paras 12.08 and 12.42.

6. REFORM OF THE TRUSTEE INVESTMENTS ACT 1961

7.20   The Trustee Investments Act 1961 has, for some considerable time now, been regarded as outdated. The possibility of reform was recently considered by the Law Commissions:

The Law Commission and the Scottish Law Commission, *Trustees' Powers and Duties* (Law Com. No. 260; Scot. Law Com. No. 172, 1999, footnotes omitted) paras 2.16–2.34

"Criticisms of the Trustee Investments Act 1961

2.16   Although the operation of the Trustee Investments Act 1961 has been widely criticised, a number of principles upon which the Act was based are eminently sensible. It did, in fact, give trustees wider default powers of investment than they had previously enjoyed, (including power to invest in more speculative investments, such as equities), but at the same time endeavoured to ensure that trustees did not take undue risks with trust capital. It requires trustees to have regard to the need for diversification, and to obtain and consider proper advice before investing in more speculative ventures.

2.17   However, the Trustee Investments Act 1961 *has* been severely criticised—in the opinion on the two Commissions, rightly so. When enacted, it was a significant step forward. It has, however, long been out of date, a fact that has been recognised by the courts for many years. Its provisions now operate in a way which is not only needlessly restrictive, but is positively detrimental to most trusts to which it applies. In particular—

(1)   The requirement to divide the trust fund into two parts is now regarded as a crude and administratively burdensome attempt to regulate the degree of risk to which trustees may expose the trust.

(2)   The definition of 'wider-range' investments in the Trustee Investments Act 1961 is in fact quite restrictive. It does not include investments in the purchase of land, for example, and permits trustees to invest only in shares which meet certain qualifying conditions. Trustees may therefore be precluded from making investments which would be appropriate to the trust, and which appear prudent.

(3)   The frequent exclusion of the Trustee Investments Act 1961 in modern trust instruments mean that its application is now more the exception than the rule. For more than a decade, the courts have been willing to extend trustees' investment powers because the provisions of the Act are perceived to be inadequate judged by current investment practice. Nevertheless, trustees who lack adequate express powers of investment must go to the trouble and expense of applying to the court or (if a charity in England and Wales) to the Charity Commission if they do not wish to be constrained by the strict provisions of the Trustee Investments Act 1961.

2.18   In addition, the Treasury expressed the view in its Consultation Document that the Trustee Investments Act 1961 imposes unwarranted burdens affecting both beneficiaries and trustees, because—

(1)   the assets of a trust increase in value to a lesser extent than they probably would if trustees had freedom to decide in what to invest; and

(2)   the need to conform with the requirements of the Trustee Investments Act 1961 increases administrative and dealing costs.

Proposals for reform

Approach to reform

2.19 It follows from these criticisms that any proposal for reform of this aspect of the law must aim to achieve a balance between two factors—

(1) the desirability of conferring the widest possible investment powers, so that trustees may invest trust assets in whatever manner is appropriate for the trust; and

(2) the need to ensure that trustees act prudently in safeguarding the capital of the trust.

2.20 The need for reform of the Trustee Investments Act 1961 has been recognised for some time. . . [the Report then discusses whether such reform should be by primary or subordinate legislation:]

2.22 . . . **the two Commissions recommend that there should be primary legislation to reform the law governing the investment powers of trustees and that, in so far as it is practicable to do so, the Trustee Investments Act 1961 should be repealed . . .**

Proposals applicable to England and Wales and to Scotland

General power of investment

2.24 The Treasury's Consultation Document proposed that trustees would have the same power to make an investment as they would have if they were absolute owners of the trust assets. This proposal received overwhelming support from those who responded to consultation, and the two Commissions agree that it is the right approach.

2.25 In fact, a legislative precedent already exists for a trustee investment power of this kind. Section 34 of the Pensions Act 1995 makes special provision for the investment powers of the trustees of occupational pension schemes. Section 34(1) states—

> The trustees of a trust scheme have, subject to any restriction imposed by the scheme, the same power to make an investment of any kind as if they were absolutely entitled to the assets of the scheme.

This provision resulted from the 1993 Report of the Pension Law Review Committee, chaired by Professor Goode. That recommended the adoption of widely defined flexible guidelines in relation to investment by trustees of occupational pension schemes to replace the detailed rules laid down in the Trustee Investments Act 1961. Those rules were said to be 'widely regarded as excessively rigid and quite unsuited to modern investment needs and practices'.

2.26 We consider that the principle encapsulated in section 34(1) of the Pensions Act 1995 should be extended to all trusts, including charitable trusts. It has the recent sanction of Parliament and accords with the formula for conferring express investment powers which is frequently used in modern English trust deeds. Scottish trustees hold full and undivided ownership of the trust estate, so that wider investment powers are usually conferred by deeming them to be beneficial owners. It will also mean that the default investment powers of all trustees are broadly the same. Accordingly, **it is recommended that, subject to the expression of a contrary intention in the instrument creating the trust, trustees should have the same power to make an investment of any kind as if they were absolutely (or beneficially) entitled to the assets of the trust** . . .

Appropriate safeguards

2.30 Notwithstanding the above recommendations, it is clearly important not to lose **7.21** sight of the fact that trustees are *not* the absolute owners of the assets under their control. Beneficiaries need protection from the risk that the trust funds will be lost or dissipated in unwise investments. Although an absolute owner may, if he or she feels so inclined, invest heavily in some wildly speculative venture, it would seldom (if ever) be appropriate for trustees to do so. The proposals for wider powers of investment, explained above, do not affect the general duties which the law imposes on trustees to act in the best interests of the trust and to avoid any conflict between their duties as trustees and their personal interests. However, the two Commissions consider that the legislation conferring these wider default powers of investment should also set out specific duties which would apply to trustees in the performance of their investment function. We consider that two such duties should be of general application—a duty to have regard to the need for diversification and suitability of investments; and a duty to obtain and consider proper advice where appropriate. The Trustee Investments Act 1961 provides a statutory precedent for both of these safeguards. . .

2.34 The fact that we propose to move away from the idea of a list of "safe" investments means that it will no longer be possible to require trustees to seek advice in relation to particular types of investment. However, we consider that to impose an unqualified statutory requirement for trustees to take advice before making *any* investment, however small or secure, would place an unnecessary burden on trustees. There is no such requirement in relation to the exercise of express powers of investment, although there is a duty at common law to 'seek advice on matters which the trustee does not understand, such as the making of investments'. In its Consultation Document, the Treasury proposed that, notwithstanding this common law duty, any new scheme for trustee investments should include an express duty both to take advice where necessary and to review portfolios. Irrespective of whether such a duty would be implicit in any duty of care to which trustees are subject, the two Commissions consider that the need for trustees to obtain and consider advice, where appropriate, is of such importance that it should appear on the face of the statute. However, we do not believe that it is necessary to impose specific restrictions on those who should be eligible to give advice. Nor do we think it necessary to retain the present requirement for the advice to be given or confirmed in writing. Accordingly, **it is recommended that—**

(1) before exercising the proposed powers of investment, trustees should obtain and consider proper advice about the way in which those powers should be exercised, having regard to the need for diversification of investments of the trust, and the suitability to the trust of the proposed investments;

(2) whether the investments in the portfolio should be varied, again having regard to the need for diversification and to the suitability of investments;

(3) the requirement to obtain advice in (1) should not apply if the trustees reasonably conclude that in all the circumstances it is unnecessary or inappropriate to do so.

For these purposes proper advice would be the advice of a person who the trustees reasonably believe to be qualified to give it by his ability in and practical experience of financial and other matters relating to the proposed investment.''

NOTES:

7.22

1. See also Scottish Executive Central Research Unit, *Public Trusts and Educational Endowments* (2000), Chapter 8.

2. The recommendations of the Law Commission have been given effect to in English law: Trustee Act 2000, ss.3–7. The provisions of that Act were not extended to Scotland because of the creation of the Scottish Parliament. The Scottish Charity Law Review Commission has recently recommended that the Scottish Parliament legislate on the basis proposed by the Law Commissions (*CharityScotland: The Report of the Scottish Charity Law Review Commission* (2001), para. 2.20). The matter is understood to be under consideration by the Scottish Executive at the time of writing.

7. EQUALISATION AND APPROPRIATION OF INVESTMENTS

A. The principle of equalisation

As a general rule, the beneficiaries share the risks and benefits of the trust investment equally.   **7.23**

Lynch's J.F. v. Griffin
(1900) 2 F. 653

James Lynch died in 1873. His will directed that the residue of his estate should be divided into two equal shares, and that one share should be held for his son in liferent and his son's children in fee, and the other share for his daughter in liferent and her children in fee. The trustees were given certain powers to make advances.

The advances made to the son's family were considerably greater than those made to the daughter's. Four ground-annuals were purchased, two in 1880 and two in 1882, at which time the interest of the son's family, after taking account of advances, amounted to less than a quarter of the whole estate.

In 1898, a question arose as to the division of the estate. It transpired that the ground-annuals were now worth £556 more than their purchase value. The daughter's family argued that the increased value should be divided in the proportions of the interests of the beneficiaries at that date, or at the dates when the ground-annuals were purchased. The son's family argued that the £556 should be divided equally between the two families. A special case was presented to the Court of Session:

LORD ADAM: "The question we have to answer in this case is this,-'Is the profit accruing if the said ground-annuals be sold, or the enhanced value as appearing from the said valuation if they be retained, to be credited equally to the second and third parties?'

The circumstances in which the question arises are these:- The testator, after giving a liferent of one-half of the residue of his estate to this son and of the other half to his daughter, left the fee to the children of the son and the children of the daughter, one-half to each family. The estate vested in these children *a morte testatoris*, payment being postponed in respect of the liferents. The estate was in fact divisible between them long ago, but it has never been divided. It has been kept and administered as a joint trust-estate up to the present time,- first under the care of the trustees, and now under the care of a judicial factor appointed by the Court. The estate is now to be divided, and the question arises in the division of that estate, how the increase in the value of the ground-annuals, referred to in the question, is to be apportioned. . .

I think that the proper way to deal with this estate, like every other trust-estate in similar circumstances is this, when all the investments are kept together, no allocation being made of an investment to one party or to the other party, but the estate kept as a joint estate, with all the profits and losses arising on the investments of the trust-estate falling on the parties equally if they had equal shares, and proportionally if they had not—I say the proper way to state the account when a division comes to be made is to put into the account of the original undivided estate the present value of those investments—and having thus ascertained the gross amount of the joint undivided estate, then to divide it into the respective shares of the parties. Of course if one of the parties has got payment of nine-tenths of his share, then he will only now get the remaining one-tenth. Accordingly I think that in the account here to the sums of £920 and £864, which represent the purchase value of these two ground annuals, there should be added the sum of £556 of increased value, because that £556 of increased value has to that extent increased the value of the joint property which is now for division. I propose, therefore, that the question should be answered in the affirmative."

LORD TRAYNER: "I confess to feeling some sympathy with the argument offered by the second party. The ground-annuals in question were bought by the judicial factor in

December 1880, and at that time the estate held by him belonged, taking it roughly, in the proportion of one-third to the third party and two-thirds to the second party. Now, as the capital invested in the ground-annuals was furnished by the factor in this proportion, it is not unreasonable to maintain that the profit or gain (by way of increased market value) made on the investment should be divided between the parties in a like proportion. But the answer to this is, I think, that neither party was investing capital—no part of the capital of the factory estate had been appropriated or set aside for either beneficiary. In the due administration of his office the judicial factor invested part of the estates held by him, and any profit made on the investment must go to the estates generally, just as a loss (if loss had been sustained) would have been borne by the estate generally. The profit goes into the residue of the estate, and falls to be divided among the beneficiaries according to their rights in the residue. This was the view given effect to in the cases of *Teacher's Trs v. Teacher* (1890) 17 R. 303 and *Scott's Trs v. Scott* (1895) 23 R. 52, and I think the same view must be given effect to here. That leads to [the] question being answered in the affirmative."

The Lord Justice-Clerk (Macdonald) concurred.
The Court answered the question in the affirmative.

NOTES:

7.24   1. Lord Trayner's remarks about the date of purchase of the ground-annuals and the proportional interests of the beneficiaries in the trust-estate at that time are at odds with the facts narrated elsewhere in the report, but the reasoning adopted by the court means that this factual discrepancy is irrelevant.
2. A truster may, however, direct or empower his trustees to appropriate particular investments to particular beneficiaries. Where appropriation takes place, then the gain or loss on an investment held for behalf of one party will be credited to, or debited from, that part of the trust-estate only.

B. Appropriation of Investments

Duncan's Trs
1951 S.C. 557

7.25   LORD PRESIDENT (COOPER): "In the general case trustees have no power to sub-divide their trust into a number of subordinate trusts by appropriating particular investments to particular legacies (the vesting or payment of which is postponed) and so tying the fortunes of each beneficiary or group of beneficiaries to particular investments. Normally all the legatees are entitled to the security of the whole estate and of the massed trust investments, and any appreciation or depreciation in the value of these investments should enure to the benefit or prejudice of the estate as a whole and should be shared according to their several rights and interests by all the beneficiaries ultimately entitled thereto. This general rule suffers exception if, but only if, such an appropriation is either expressly or impliedly directed by the truster. I refer in support of these propositions to Mackenzie Stuart on Trusts, pp. 286–289; Menzies on Trustees, 2nd edition, section 735; and the Encyclopaedia s.v. Trustee, para. 547; and to the opinions of Lord Shand in *Teacher's Trs*, 17 R. 303, at p. 313; Lord Trayner in *Scott's Trs*, 23 R. 52, at p. 58; and Lord Mackenzie in *Colville's Trs*, 1914 S.C. 255, 1914, 1 S.L.T. 62, at p. 258. The question is: What amounts to such an implied direction?

I feel absolved from examining the earlier English decisions which were cited to us, because the doubts which were evidently entertained as to their effect had to be resolved by legislation—Lewin on Trusts, 15th edition, pp. 298 ff; Trustee Act 1925, section 15; Underhill on Trusts, 10th edition, p. 269–and because these decisions do not appear to speak with one voice—*cf.* Menzies on Trustees, section 744, note.

The leading Scottish case is *Robinson v. Fraser's Trs* (1881), 8 R. (H.L.) 127, which raised several other difficult questions in addition to appropriation. There a testatrix bequeathed to each of two daughters the liferent of £2000 and the fee to their respective issue. The trustees were expressly empowered 'to lend or place out on such security . . . as they shall consider advantageous the foresaid legacies of £2000, . . . the securities to be conceived in favour of my trustees', and the testatrix then directed her trustees 'after making provision for payment of the legacies' to divide the residue among named persons. The trustees allocated securities to each legacy with the knowledge and consent of the legatees, and then divided the residue, taking a final discharge from the residuary legatees. Thereafter they in effect administered two separate trusts for each of the two funds of £2000, and did so for a period of years. On a consideration of these facts and provisions Lord Chancellor Selborne said: 'Not only was . . . severance legally possible but it also appears to me to have been the most proper (if not the only proper) mode of fulfilling the directions of the will'; and Lord Blackburn and Lord Watson indicated that the trustees were at least empowered, if not required, to allocate securities, Lord Watson doubting whether the trustees could have declined to sever and appropriate. This decision was explained by Lord Shand in *Teacher's Trs* (*supra*), at p. 313, as one in which 'by direction of the testator or by right of the legatees, certain funds have been severed from the general funds and appropriated to particular purposes, and have, as so severed and appropriated been invested in special securities'. Lord Trayner in *Scott's Trs* (*supra*), at p. 58, explained the decision in *Robinson* (*supra*) as one of an implied direction to appropriate which might 'very reasonably be inferred, because such appropriation was necessary to enable the residue to be divided without undue delay, which was the truster's object and, indeed, direction'. This explanation was quoted with approval by Lord Dunedin in *Vans Dunlop's Trs*, 1912 S.C. 10, 1911, 2 S.L.T. 341, at p. 14. Finally, in *Colville's Trs* (*supra*), at p. 258, Lord Mackenzie said of *Robinson* that 'the terms of that settlement indicated that, in order that there might be no delay in dividing the residue, it was necessary to appropriate'.

From this it seems plain that the decision in *Robinson* would have been in the opposite sense unless the House had been able to find in the terms of the deed under consideration an implied direction to sever and appropriate; and that they found this implied direction in the provisions quoted above, and especially in the scheme of division which rendered such severance and appropriation 'necessary', or 'the only proper mode of fulfilling the directions of the will'.

In *Teacher's Trs* it was held on a consideration of the facts and of a very complicated will that there had been no such severance and appropriation as to prevent an equal distribution of losses which had arisen on investments and that the decision in *Robinson* did not apply. In *Scott's Trs* the Court found it impossible to discover in the terms of a settlement any sufficient indication that the truster contemplated an appropriation of securities of the type in fact effected, and therefore held that the trustees had acted *ultra vires*. In *Colville's Trs* the Court again failed to discover in the terms of a settlement any implied direction to appropriate, such appropriation not being necessary to facilitate the administration of the trust.

I come back to *Vans Dunlop's Trs* (*supra*), which presented some difficulty in the course of debate. The decision was to hold a specified sum for a legatee in liferent and his issue in fee, and to pay over the residue 'as it accrued and became available', to residuary legatees. There was an express direction to the trustees to divide the testator's investments among the various legatees 'or otherwise appropriate them for the purposes of this trust'. The case thus seemed to be directly covered by Robinson, if not *a fortiori* of *Robinson*, and in effect it was so held. But in giving the judgment of the Court Lord President Dunedin appears to generalise the rule to be derived from *Robinson* and the other decisions in a form which very substantially widens the previously accepted ratio. His Lordship said: 'It seems to me that when a trust is of a composite character, and is partly for holding and partly for distribution, there is of necessity an implied power upon trustees to set apart the whole at the time when they have to part with some of the trust for distribution'. Nearly every trust which contains provisions for holding also contains provisions for distribution; and Lord Dunedin cannot have meant that the bare fact of the concurrence in any trust of these very common types of provisions *per se* authorises the trustees, as soon as they pay away a penny, to appropriate securities against each and every one of the provisions for which they hold, and thus to convert the trust into a congeries of separate trusts. The *dictum* must be read in the context of the settlement under consideration and in light of the fact that Lord Dunedin immediately proceeds to refer to *Robinson* and to the explanation of that decision given by Lord Trayner in *Scott's Trs*.

7.26   I conclude accordingly that an implied direction to sever and appropriate may be inferred when the operative directions as to division of the estate are such that their fulfilment renders such severance and appropriation a necessary and proper act of trust administration which it is the duty of the trustees, so far as reasonably practicable, to carry out. I say 'duty' advisedly; for, although there are passages in the decisions which refer to a 'power' in trustees to appropriate, I do not think that the 'power' was regarded as a mere faculty or option which the trustees could at any time exercise or not at their own discretion; for it would be very difficult to infer by implication that trustees were authorised at their own hand to adopt or reject an irrevocable expedient which might have the most serious results on the benefits eventually taken by the beneficiaries, these results usually depending upon the course of future events which in the general case would be unpredictable when the decision of the trustees was taken.

With these principles before me I return to the present case. The relevant provision (which became operative whenever the estate had been ingathered) directs the trustees to divide the residue into eight equal shares and to 'apportion' five shares to a son and one share to each of three daughters. The five shares were to be made over absolutely and unconditionally to the son, who was to have a right to acquire at a valuation such part of the testator's shares in his business as he might desire. As regards the remaining three shares the direction was that 'my said trustees shall invest and hold the shares apportioned to each of my said daughters during their respective lives and pay the free annual income and produce of such shares to them for their liferent use allenarly and that at such time or times and in such proportions as my said trustees shall think proper; and on the respective deaths of my said daughters my said trustees shall pay and convey the capital of the respective shares to be so liferented by them to or for behoof of' their children and the issue of any predeceasing child as might be directed by *mortis causa* appointment, and failing appointment equally per stirpes, and failing children to such persons as the daughters might respectively appoint, and failing such appointment to their respective heirs in moveables. Vesting was postponed until payment, and there is therefore no one but the trustees to represent the eventual fiars. To my mind this factor is vital.

Such being the scheme of the will, I consider that, if a direction to sever the three shares of the three daughters and appropriate, particular securities to each falls to be inferred, that direction must have become operative in 1927 when the son's five shares were paid out. Even as at that date I feel that such an inference would be exceedingly difficult, if not impossible. To fulfil the requirements of the trust, it was necessary in 1927 to sever five-eighths of the residue from three-eighths of the residue but I cannot see that it was in the least 'necessary' or even practicable at that date to sub-divide the three-eighths into three self-contained trusts, and I do not think that this could have been done consistently with the testator's wishes. For one thing, securities had to be set aside to meet a postponed annuity (which is still being paid and may well continue to be paid for years to come), and these retained securities were directed to be brought into computation in the division of the residue into eight shares—a direction which points to a paper calculation and not to an actual severance and appropriation. Again, the testator authorised his trustees to continue his investments, recommended them to retain the bonds over his business premises, and directed them not to call up any such bonds within seven years of his death, *i.e.* before 1933. Now it appears from the petition that the three-eighths of residue is worth something in the region of £30,000, which is still represented in the hands of the trustees by two 4 $\frac{1}{2}$ per cent bonds over the business premises for £10,000 and £2000, which were unrealisable before 1933, and have not been realised even yet. Moreover the securities set aside to meet the

£100 annuity cannot be divided until the annuitant dies. It follows that the creation in 1927 of three separate trusts in respect of the daughters' shares would have involved the appropriation to at least two such trusts of *pro indiviso* shares in unrealisable investments and thereafter a good deal of complicated book-keeping. Is there any sufficient reason to suppose that the testator ever so contemplated, much less directed? I think not.

But in point of fact no severance or appropriation was made in 1927. For a quarter of a century, obviously with the knowledge and approval of the daughters, the balance of the residue has been held as a massed fund in a single trust. If severance and appropriation is now to take place I cannot see why that should be done on the basis of conditions and values as at 1951, and it is very questionable whether it is now practicable for the trustees to reconstruct the situation as it was in 1927 and to effect a belated division on that basis, upon the view that they have ever since been acting in technical breach of trust.

Nor can I ignore the single reason now alleged as justification for re-opening the matter. It has nothing to do with the rights of the fiars or a just distribution as between them, but arises solely from the fact that one of the daughters recently went to South Africa and desires the trustees to appropriate to her share part of the 3 $\frac{1}{2}$ per cent. War Stock which the trustees hold, in order that she may receive the income therefrom free of income tax, while her two sisters receive the higher rates of interest payable on the remaining investments. It is important to note that the 3 $\frac{1}{2}$ per cent. War Stock which is the occasion of the present controversy did not come into existence until 1932.

Upon the assumption that the trustees are still 'empowered' to sever and appropriate, I do not envy their task, least of all if, as I think, they would require to divide up the five securities which they hold on the basis of the state of matters as they were in 1927. But the true question is not whether these trustees were vested with a continuing option at any time to sever and appropriate, and whether, if they so wish, they can at any time determine to exercise it. Such a view would make the trustees (however anxiously they tried to do their duty) the arbiters of the fate of the contingent fiars, and on no possible view of the settlement can I find any warrant for the suggestion that the truster ever contemplated such a result. The true question is whether the trustees ought to have severed and appropriated in 1927 and whether they could have been compelled to do so. For the reasons already indicated, I can find no sufficient indication of an implied direction to that effect; but, as they did not then do so, I am clearly of opinion that they cannot sever and appropriate now."

Lords Carmont and Russell concurred.
Lord Keith delivered a dissenting opinion.

NOTES:

1. *What will amount to a direction to appropriate? Duncan's Trs*, along with *Lynch's J.F. v. Griffin* (1900) 2 F. 653, makes it clear that a reference to dividing an estate into shares is likely to be construed as simply requiring trustees to make a paper calculation rather than to make an actual appropriation. **7.27**

   Although, as Lord Carmont suggests in *Duncan's Trs*, "it is difficult to lay down definite general principles as to the powers of trustees to allocate portions of an estate to the beneficiaries", some guidance may be taken from the following two cases:
   - *Robinson v. Fraser's Tr.* (1881) 8 R. (H.L.) 127: a direction to hold "legacies of £2,000 and £2,000 respectively", which could be lent out on security at the trustees' discretion, was held to imply at least a power to appropriate. The House of Lords did not find it necessary whether the direction actually required an appropriation (but see the subsequent interpretations of this decision noted in *Duncan's Trs, supra*, which suggest that this direction should be taken as requiring an appropriation.)
   - *Grosset v. Birrell's Trs*, 1920 S.C. 231: a direction that a sum should be "invested, held or set aside and retained and administered" for one beneficiary was held to be a direction to appropriate.

2. *Discretionary appropriation*. Lord Cooper expresses hostility in *Duncan's Trs* to the suggestion that trustees might be given a discretionary power to appropriate. There seems no good

reason, however, why such a power, if explicitly conferred by the terms of the trust-deed, should not be valid. Such a power was conferred by the trust-deed in *Macfarlane's Tr. v. Macfarlane* (1903) 6 F. 201, and its validity was not questioned by the court. It was suggested, however (*per* Lord Kyllachy at 205) that where the trustees exercise a discretionary power of appropriation, the appropriation must be intimated to the beneficiaries concerned in order to be valid. See also *Warrack's Trs v. Warrack*, 1919 S.C. 522.

3. *The effect of appropriation.* See *Grosset v. Birrell's Trs*, 1920 S.C. 231, *per* Lord Anderson at 227–228:

> "It is well settled, by cases such as *Robinson v. Fraser's Tr.* (1881) 8 R. (H.L.) 127, *Scott's Trs v. Scott* (1895) 23 R. 52, and *Vans Dunlop's Trs v. Pollok* 1912 S.C. 10, that the effect of allocation is to create a special trust, whereby the investments allocated are held and administered on behalf of the beneficiaries whose interests are to be secured. The result is that, if the allocated investments appreciate in value, the beneficiaries reap the benefit of the appreciation; if they depreciate in value, the beneficiaries must bear the loss. In short, allocation operates a satisfaction of the beneficiaries' claims against the trust-estate."

In *Robinson v. Fraser's Tr.* (1881) 8 R. (H.L.) 127, one beneficiary's share of the trust-estate included stock in the City of Glasgow Bank. This stock was subject to heavy calls which exceeded the value of her share of the trust-estate. It was held that the trustees could not use the remainder of the trust-estate to satisfy those calls. See also *Gordon v. Gordon's Trs* (1868) 41 Sc. Jur. 43.

Chapter 8

CONFLICT OF INTEREST: AUCTOR IN REM SUAM

It has been said that trustees "must not be governed by caprice", and must exercise their powers "in **8.01** good faith in the presumed interest" of the beneficiaries (*Train v. Buchanan's Trs*, 1907 S.C. 517, *per* Lord Pearson at 527). The law of trusts seeks to ensure that trustees act only in the interests of the beneficiaries, and not to advance their own interests, by a strict application of the rule against a trustee being *auctor in rem suam*.

Auctor in rem suam may be translated as "actor in his own cause". The rule prohibits a trustee from placing himself in a position where his interests as trustee and his interests as an individual conflict.

The consequences of breaching the rule are severe: if a trustee enters into a transaction in breach of the rule, the transaction is voidable regardless of whether he was acting in good faith. If he profits from a breach of the rule, he must hand over those profits to the trust-estate regardless of whether the trust-estate has in fact suffered any loss. As Menzies points out (at para. 437), the rule "is a penal rule, not a merely remedial one".

A trustee may, however, be permitted to be *auctor in rem suam* by virtue of the provisions of the trust-deed, or by the sanction of the beneficiaries.

This chapter considers the following issues:
- the basis of the principle;
- its practical applications;
- the consequences of a transaction in breach of the principle;
- whether trustees should resign where a conflict of interest arises;
- the circumstances in which a trustee may be permitted to be *auctor in rem suam* because of the sanction of the trust-deed or the beneficiaries;
- whether transactions by a former trustee are struck at by the *auctor in rem suam* principle.

1. *AUCTOR IN REM SUAM*: THE GENERAL PRINCIPLE

Hamilton v. Wright
(1842) 1 Bell 574

James Hamilton executed a trust-deed for the benefit of his creditors in 1815. Thomas **8.02** Wright became a trustee under that deed in 1818.

In 1817, Hamilton had become cautioner for Mr Bowes (who subsequently became the Earl of Strathmore) in a bond for the payment of an annuity to Mr Telford. In 1822, Wright obtained an assignation of the bond. Wright later died, and his trustees attempted to obtain payment of the annuity from Lord Strathmore. When this failed, they attempted to pursue Hamilton for the debt. By this stage, the assignation was worth more than the price which Wright had paid for it.

The Lord Ordinary (Cockburn) held that Wright had not been entitled to purchase the annuity for his own benefit, and that the benefit of the assignation should accrue to the trust-estate, subject to credit being given for the price which Wright had paid for it. The First Division allowed an appeal by Wright's trustees. On appeal to the House of Lords:

LORD BROUGHAM: "There cannot be a greater mistake to suppose, as seems to have been done below, that a trustee is only prevented from doing things which bring an actual loss upon the estate under his administration. It is quite enough that the thing which he does has a tendency to injure the trust, a tendency to interfere with his duty. The trustee cannot purchase the trust-estate, though at a sale, without leave of the Court, and yet he might, probably would, if at an auction, give as good a price as any one else. So he cannot purchase outstanding debts. Glen *v.* Pearson, *Fac. Coll.* March 6, 1817.

Then if it be said that the creditors are not actually injured, or that the fund, either to pay them, or to hand over by way of reversion to the maker of the trust-deed, cannot be lessened by such purchases, inasmuch as the debts must be satisfied whether payment is made to the original creditor, or to the trustee who takes an assignment, the answer is, that he shall not avail himself of rights so purchased by him, although these rights might have come in competition with the trust had he not purchased. And so it has been decided, Wright, *Mor.* 16193; Anderson, 1740, Nov. 21, *Elchies*.

Nor is it only on account of the conflict between his interest and his duty to the trust that such transactions are forbidden. The knowledge which he acquires as trustee is of itself a sufficient ground of disqualification, and of requiring that such knowledge be not only used to the detriment of the trust, but be not used for his own benefit, because it may, by possibility, injure the trust, rather than because it may give him an undue advantage over others.

In *ex parte* Lacey, 6 *Ves.* 625, and *ex parte* Jones, 8 *Ves.* 328, Lord Eldon denied the doctrine supposed to have been delivered by Lord Loughborough in Whichcote *v.* Lawrence, 3 *Ves.* 740, that a trustee must make some advantage of his purchase before it can be set aside; because, in ninety-nine cases out of every hundred, he held that it might be impossible for the Court to examine into this matter. So the conduct of the trustee not being blameable in the purchase, is nothing to the purpose; for the Court must act, his Lordship said, upon the general principle, and unless the policy of the law make it impossible for the trustees to do any thing for their own benefit, it is impossible for the Court to see in what cases the transaction is morally right, and in what cases it is not.

The ordinary case has been, where the question arose upon a purchase of debts owing at the time of the trust being created. But the purchase of a debt subsequently incurred, if that be relied on as taking the present case out of the general rule, gives the trustee, whose duty it is to keep the residue as large as possible for the debtor, an interest in cutting it down, at least, by the amount of his own debt. It also gives him an interest in keeping as large a fund as possible free from the operation of debts prior to his own, in order that his own may be the more surely and speedily satisfied, and this is an interest directly in conflict with his duty under the trust to the prior creditors.

The interlocutors appealed from must be reversed so far as to restore the interlocutor of the Lord Ordinary. . ."

Lord Lyndhurst L.C. and Lord Campbell concurred.

The House of Lords remitted the case back to the Court of Session with instructions to adhere to the Lord Ordinary's interlocutor.

NOTES:

1. See also the similar decision in *Gillies v. Maclachlan's Reps.* (1846) 8 D. 487.
2. Three general points regarding the *auctor in rem suam* principle should be noted:

(1) The fairness of any transaction entered into in violation of the auctor in rem suam *principle is irrelevant.*

Aberdeen Railway Co. v. Blaikie Bros.
(1854) 1 Macq. 461

8.03 LORD CRANWORTH L.C.: "So strictly is this principle adhered to, that no question is allowed to be raised as to the fairness or unfairness of a contract entered into.

It obviously is, or may be, impossible to demonstrate how far in any particular case the terms of such a contract have been the best for the interest of the cestui que trust, which it was possible to obtain.

It may sometimes happen that the terms on which a trustee has dealt or attempted to deal with the trust estate or interests of those for whom he is a trustee, have been as good as could have been obtained from any other person,— they may even at the time have been better.

But still so inflexible is the rule that no inquiry on that subject is permitted."

NOTE:

See also *Cherry's Trs v. Patrick*, 1911 2 S.L.T. 313, *infra* para. 8.08.

(2) The question of whether the trust-estate has suffered any loss is irrelevant. The liability of the trustee may be far greater than any loss suffered by the trust.

Wilsons v. Wilson
(1789) Mor. 16376; June 26, 1789 F.C.

James Wilson, the defender, was appointed tutor of the pursuers, who were then infants, **8.04** their father having died in the possession of a considerable farm. He then entered into a bargain with the farm's owner, whereby he renounced the existing lease (which had two years left to run) and obtained a new lease for 15 years in his own name. When there were four years left of this lease, he obtained another lease for 13 years. The pursuers brought an action claiming that the defender was obliged to pay to them the profits which had arisen from those leases.

OPINION OF THE COURT: "Some of the Judges were of opinion, that the defender should only be obliged to pay over to the pursuers the surplus rents, this being the only advantage they could have reaped from the farm, without such a degree of personal industry and exertion on his pert as he was not called to bestow on their affairs. And all the Judges seemed to be of opinion, that, in accounting for the profits, he would be entitled to an ample recompence for his labour and attention in cultivating the lands.

The Lords, after advising memorials, found, 'That the defender was obliged to account to the pursuers for the profits arising from the farm in question during the two years which were not run of their fathers lease, at the time of his death, and also during the remaining thirteen years of the first tack, and during the whole years of the second tack obtained by him.'

A reclaiming petition was preferred for the defender, insisting, that he should only be liable for the surplus rents.

After advising this petition, which was followed with answers, the Lords adhered to their former interlocutor."

NOTE:

For a full discussion of the consequences of breaching the *auctor in rem suam* principle, see *infra* paras 8.18 *et seq*.

(3) A trustee may only be auctor in rem suam *if this is sanctioned by the truster in the trust deed, or by the beneficiaries.*

Dale v. I.R.C.
[1954] A.C. 11

LORD NORMAND: ". . .it is not that reward for services is repugnant to the fiduciary duty, but **8.05** that he who has the duty shall not take any secret remuneration or any financial benefit not authorized by the law, or by his contract, or by the trust deed under which he acts, as the case may be."

Inglis v. Inglis
1983 S.C. 8

LORD HUNTER: "It is well settled that a person in a fiduciary position is not allowed by law to put himself in a position where there may be a conflict between his interest as an individual and his duty as a trustee. This principle has been applied in a great variety of circumstances. If a person by putting himself in such a position has made a profit he must account for it to the person to whom he stands in the fiduciary relationship. It is immaterial whether or not the transaction can be shown to have been fair. The fact, if it be a fact, that the transaction was entered into bona fide or even that it was done for the benefit of the beneficiary does not provide a defence. The only ground upon which a claim against the person in a fiduciary position to account for a profit can in such circumstances be defeated is that the person in the fiduciary position made that profit with the knowledge and assent of the other person".

NOTE:

For a full discussion of the possibility of sanction by the truster or the beneficiaries, see *infra* paras 8.25 *et seq.*

2. PRACTICAL APPLICATIONS OF THE *AUCTOR IN REM SUAM* PRINCIPLE

8.06 The *auctor in rem suam* principle has three main consequences (see the classification adopted by Norrie and Scobbie at pp. 128–133, which is similar to that used by Mackenzie Stuart at pp. 167–168):

(1) trustees may not enter into transactions with the trust estate
(2) trustees may not use their position to obtain a personal advantage
(3) trustees may not charge fees for work done for the trust

A. Transactions with the Trust Estate

University of Aberdeen v. Town Council of Aberdeen
(1876) 3 R. 1087
(affirmed *sub nom Magistrates of Aberdeen v. University of Aberdeen*
(1877) 4 R. (H.L.) 48)

8.07 In 1613, funds were transferred to the Aberdeen council to be held on trust (by deed of mortification), primarily for the purpose of funding two professorships. In 1704, the council invested the funds (along with other trust funds under their management) in the purchase of the lands and barony of Torry. In 1797, the council's master of mortifications sold the property to Gavin Hadden, treasurer of the burgh of Aberdeen, "for the use and behoof of the provost, bailies, council, and community of the burgh", in consideration of a feu-duty of £50 per year.

In 1801, the town council petitioned the Lords of the Treasury for a grant of the salmon-fishings pertaining to the land, and a charter of salmon-fishings was granted. From thereon, the council paid the feu-duty of £50 each year for the purposes of the mortifications, while drawing the rents of the land and salmon-fishings, which greatly increased in value. Almost three-quarters of a century later, the University, with consent of the two relevant professors, brought an action for declarator that the land was held in trust for their benefit, and also an action for accounting.

LORD PRESIDENT (INGLIS): "The first question we have to determine is, Whether that is a valid sale, and, if so, what is the effect of it? Now, I do not think that is a question that admits of any doubt at all. The town of Aberdeen, acting through the provost, magistrates, and council, were trustees for the parties entitled to benefit by these mortifications, and they were not, as such trustees, entitled to purchase the trust-estate. Yet that is the very thing they did by this sale in 1797. The master of mortification was merely their representative in holding the land under the title beginning in 1704, and the treasurer, on the other hand, was merely their hand and instrument in holding the property for their own behoof—I do not say for behoof of the community, because I am speaking of the corporation or community itself in saying that they were trustees. And therefore this is nothing short of a direct sale of the estate by the trustees to themselves for their own behoof, and as such it is plainly an illegal sale, or, in other words, the estate continues to belong to the beneficiaries under the trust just as if no such transaction had ever taken place. We were told indeed that the title which was acquired by the treasurer of the burgh in 1797 had been fortified by prescription; but that admits, I think, of a very short answer. No trustee of such an endowment as this can by any course of time prescribe a right to perpetuate a breach of trust. I hold that to be clear in legal principle and settled on authority, and therefore it is needless to dwell further upon the plea of prescription.

Then, if these lands do truly belong to this trust, just as much as if this transaction had never taken place, the next question comes to be whether the fishings which were acquired by a separate title by these trustees also belong to the beneficiaries under the trust. That raises a question of much greater nicety and difficulty. At the time that this illegal sale took place the community of Aberdeen did not, as trustees, possess those fishings. They were acquired after the illegal sale had taken place, in a manner which needs to be very carefully followed and described, but not until after four years after the sale which is said to be illegal, and which, in my opinion, is manifestly illegal. But although that length of time elapsed between the illegal sale of the lands and the acquisition of the fishings, I think it is pretty clearly established by some evidence to which I am about to refer that the very object of the illegal sale by the trustees to themselves was to give an opportunity of acquiring these fishings. One thing is quite clear, that without the title to the lands which they acquired by the illegal sale, they would not have obtained these fishings in the way in which they did obtain them. Whether they could have obtained them in any other way is a different matter; but I think it is pretty clear that without the title to the lands which they acquired by the illegal sale they could not have proceeded to acquire the fishings in the manner they did. . .

Now, it has been contended with great force that whatever may be said of the way in which this right of salmon-fishing was obtained, or the representations which were made to the Crown as the reasons for asking this grant, the crown-charter is granted to the town of Aberdeen expressly on account of the favour which the Crown bears to the town, and that it is impossible to get the better of that grant,— to have that grant recalled and another grant made in favour of the town as trustees of this charity. I think there is a great deal of force in that, but it does not appear to me that this is the form of the question we have to consider. The question we have to consider is whether, although the town of Aberdeen has got a grant out and out in its own favour of these salmon fishings, it is not bound to hold them in trust for the beneficiaries under the mortifications in question. It is not proposed, and does not require to be proposed, that any alteration shall be made in this crown-grant. The only question is whether, though being *ex facie* an absolute grant in favour of the town for its own behoof, the town is not under a legal obligation to communicate the benefit of that grant to the beneficiaries under the mortifications. I have felt that to be a question attended with very considerable difficulty, but upon a full consideration of the matter I have come to be of the opinion that the beneficiaries under the mortifications are entitled to the benefit of the crown-grant. . .

Then we come to consider whether there is not applicable to the circumstances of such a case this important legal principle, that a trustee can never use either the property of the trust or the title of that trust to advance his own private interests, and if he does so, and is successful in advancing his own private interests, he must communicate that benefit to the trust-estate. Now, it appears to me that that principle is clearly applicable to the circumstances of the case, as disclosed in the evidence to which I have referred. Without the land they could have got no salmon-fishing; by reason of their possession of the property in the lands they did get the salmon-fishing; but they were bound to hold that land which they so used for the purpose of procuring the benefit to themselves for the purposes of the trust, and for no other purpose whatever, and they were not entitled to use it in any way for their own benefit. And yet they did use it for their own benefit, to the effect of obtaining this grant of salmon-fishing. It appears to me that it is very difficult, if not impossible, to resist the conclusion that, acting upon that well-known principle in the law of trusts, the town are bound to communicate the benefit of the fishings so obtained to the persons interested in the trust-estate. . ."

Lords Deas and Mure delivered concurring opinions.

Lord Ardmillan concurred.

The Court held that the trustees continued to hold the land in trust for the mortifications, and were bound to communicate the benefit of the salmon-fishings to the trust.

The House of Lords affirmed the judgment, but remitted the case back to the Court of Session on a question of accounting.

NOTES:

8.08
1. A trustee may not take a loan from the trust-estate (*Croskery v. Gilmour's Trs* (1890) 17 R. 697; *Ritchies v. Ritchie's Trs* (1888) 15 R. 1068), even if security is given (*Perston v. Perston's Trs* (1863) 1 M. 245).
2. See also *Cherry's Trs v. Patrick*, 1911 2 S.L.T. 313. In that case, Mr Patrick was appointed one of the trustees under Mr Cherry's will. The trustees carried on Mr Cherry's retail business, and Mr Patrick continued to supply beer and spirits to the business, as he had done before. In an action of accounting later brought by his co-trustees, Mr Patrick was held liable to make over the profit which he had made on these sales to the trust. This was so despite Lord Ormidale's observation (at 314) that:

   "There seems no reason to doubt that the arrangement whereby Mr Cherry got his whiskies and beers through Mr Patrick was a good arrangement for Mr Cherry. Forty per cent. discount [the discount given by Mr Patrick on beer] was about the largest discount from the invoice prices given to the trade, and the price charged by Mr Patrick for the whisky supplied by him, viz. 3s. a gallon, was not excessive, probably less than Mr Cherry would have had to pay, had he got it from any other wholesale dealer."

   This serves to demonstrate that the fairness of the transaction concerned is irrelevant.
3. It has also been held to be a violation of the principle for the trust-estate to enter into a transaction with a firm of which a trustee is a partner (*Lord Gray and Others* (1856) 19 D. 1), or with a company of which he is a managing director (*Dunn v. Chambers* (1897) 25 R. 247). On the purchase of a beneficiary's interest in trust property by a trustee, see *Dougan v. Macpherson* (1902) 4 F. (H.L.) 7, noted *infra* para. 8.30.

B. Obtaining of Personal Advantage

8.09 A trustee may not use his position as trustee to obtain any personal advantage. So, if he is given a discretion, he may not exercise it in his favour (*Inglis v. Inglis*, 1983 S.C. 8). The consequences of this rule may be unfortunate, but they can be avoided by the trustee refusing office or resigning. (On the question of whether the *auctor in rem suam* principle strikes at the acts of a former trustee, see *infra* para. 8.32).

(a) Indirect advantage?

A trustee is not prohibited by this rule, however, from acting as a remunerated adviser to persons with an interest in the trust. So, in *Pott v. Stevenson*, 1935 S.L.T. 106, it was held that it was not a breach of the principle for one of the trustees to be law-agent to a lender to the trust. The fact that the practice was "firmly established" appears to have influenced the decision.

See also *Sleigh v. Sleigh's J.F.*, 1908 S.C. 1112, where it was held that it was not a breach of the principle for a judicial factor to be a law-agent to the beneficiaries, nor for part of the trust funds to be loaned on security to clients of his firm. Nor was he obliged to repay the funds received by his firm from those borrowers to the trust.

The fact that such transactions do not breach the *auctor in rem suam* principle (which has been doubted—see Menzies, paras 437 and 440) is not to say that they are necessarily sensible, however. *Cf.* the Solicitors (Scotland) Practice Rules 1986, r. 5 and the Law Society Guidelines on Conflict of Interest. (These do not specifically deal with the position of solicitor-trustees, but may nevertheless provide some guidance on the proper approach in such cases).

(b) Trustees and partnerships

In *Lawrie v. Lawrie's Trs* (1892) 19 R. 675, D.L. had been in partnership with the testator (J.L.) before his death. He was appointed a trustee under J.L.'s will. The trustees continued to carry on J.L.'s retail spirit business, and D.L., as partner, continued to receive half the profits. It was held that this was acceptable and that the trustees were bound to pay over half the profits to D.L. Lord McLaren observed (at 683) that:

> ". . .under the deed of trust there was a power to the trustees to carry on any business in which the truster might be engaged, either alone or in partnership. Therefore if at the time of his death it was found that there was a subsisting partnership between him and his brother, the trustees were not under any disability in consequence of the ordinary rules of trust administration from continuing to leave the truster's money in its then state of investment. . . There are many cases in the books in which the question of the propriety of trustees entering into partnership with one of their own number has been discussed; but I know of no case where it has been held objectionable to continue the partnership arrangement where there was a power given to the trustees to invest money in trade, and no greater interest given to the deceased's partners than they had before."

(c) Directors' fees

Where trustees hold shares as part of the trust property, those shares may enable them to become company directors. Are they required to communicate any directors' fees which they receive to the trust? The English position is that remuneration must be communicated to the trust where the trustee "[acquired] the position in respect of which he drew the remuneration by virtue of his position as trustee" (*Re Macadam* [1946] Ch. 73, *per* Cohen J. at 82; quoted with approval in *Re Gee* [1948] Ch. 284, *per* Harman J. at 295). They are not, therefore, obliged to communicate the remuneration where the votes of the trust were irrelevant to the question of appointment as directors (*Re Gee* [1948] Ch. 284), or *a fortiori* where they were already directors when they became trustees (see, *e.g. Re Orwell's Will Trusts* [1982] 1 W.L.R. 1337).

The only Scottish authority on the issue is *Elliot v. Mackie & Sons*, 1935 S.C. 81, where it was suggested that there is no requirement to communicate directors' fees. It should be noted, however, that the court purported to be following English law in that case (see *per* Lord Moncrieff at 87, referring to *Re Dover Coalfield Extension Ltd* [1907] 2 Ch. 76; [1908] 1 Ch. 65, which may have been misinterpreted by the court). It should not, therefore, be assumed that Scots law takes a different approach from English law on this issue.

C. The Charging of Fees By Trustees

A trustee is not, unless authorised by the trust-deed, entitled to be remunerated for the work he **8.10** performs for the trust. Up until the early nineteenth century, however, Scots law recognised an exception to this rule, whereby a quorum of trustees could contract with another trustee (so long as he did not form part of the quorum) and therefore employ him as a remunerated agent for the trust. See Erskine, *Inst.,* i, 7, 19 and the following case:

Montgomery v. Wauchope
June 4, 1822, F.C.

8.11 Opinion of the Court: ". . . we are of opinion that it is consistent with the law and practice of Scotland for tutors, curators, and trustees to nominate one of their number, especially one who has been the family agent of their constituent, to act as their agent and cashier; that, while officiating in such capacity, he is entitled to the usual remuneration of an ordinary agent and cashier. . ."

Note:

See also the observations of Lord Neaves in *Aitken v. Hunter* (1871) 9 M. 756, at 761–763. It was not long before this exception was rejected by the courts:

Home v. Pringle
(1841) 2 Rob. 384

8.12 Lord Chancellor: ". . .it is said that there is a difference between the law of England and of Scotland. In England, the appointment by trustees of one of their body, to act exclusively in any part of the trust, under the authority of all, would, as to the others, have the effect of making the trustees appointing responsible for the act of the one appointed; that is, they could not treat acts done, or sums received by such appointee, in the character so conferred upon him, as the acts or receipts of a co-trustee, for which they, as co-trustees, would not be liable, but as acts and receipts of their agent, for which they would, or would not, be liable, as there might be proof of culpable neglect in their dealings with such agent. The allowance of a salary to such appointee would clearly be a breach of trust, and would therefore be disallowed.

But it is said, that the practice, if not the law of Scotland, sanctions such appointment, and the case of *Montgomery v. Wauchope,* June 4, 1822, F.C., is referred to in proof of that proposition. Nothing was decided in that case upon that point, but the Judges stated, that such appointments were not inconsistent with the law of Scotland, and that a trustee, appointed by his co-trustees, was entitled to the usual remuneration of an agent or cashier. This is the real question, because it is not necessary to hold that the appointment is illegal, in order to maintain the principle, that the party who, having accepted the office of trustee, which, unless otherwise provided for by the trust, must be performed gratuitously, accepts another office inconsistent with that of trustee, shall not be permitted to derive any emolument out of the trust-property, in respect of such employment. That the office of trustee, and of factor or cashier to the property, are inconsistent, cannot be disputed. If the execution of the trust require such appointments, it becomes the duty of the trustee to exercise his discretion and judgment in the selection of the officers, and his vigilant superintendence of their proceedings when appointed, all of which is lost to the trust when a trustee is appointed to the execution of those duties. Therefore the Courts of Equity in England, in such cases, refuse to the trustee any remuneration, which would come to others from the appointment, which produces the salutary effect of deterring trustees from making such appointment when not actually required; and when such necessity exists, preserves to the trust the superintendence and control of the trustees over the officer they may appoint. I should be sorry to give any sanction to a contrary practice in Scotland. There can be no reason for any difference in this rule upon this subject in the two countries. The benefit of the rule, as acted upon in England, is not disputed, and as there is no decision to the contrary, there cannot be any reason for sanctioning a contrary rule in Scotland."

Notes:

8.13   1. The comments of the Lord Chancellor in *Home v. Pringle* were, like those in *Montgomery v. Wauchope, obiter.* Without casting doubt on the soundness of the principle which was being stated, it may be noted that they contain some unfortunate traces of Anglicisation for

Anglicisation's sake (which was, perhaps, not unusual for the House of Lords during this period: see further A.D. Gibb, *Law from Over the Border* (1950)).

They were, however, swiftly accepted by the Scottish courts. Within months of the decision in *Home v. Pringle*, Lord Justice-Clerk Boyle was at pains to say that "I wish, in passing, to be understood to say, that I never shall be prepared to sanction the legality of a payment of a salary or profit to one of the trustees to be factor." (*Seton v. Dawson* (1841) 4 D. 310, at 319), and a few years later that "[I] have often seen the evils that have arisen from the whole management [of] trusts falling into the hands of an agent trustee. The object of the rule laid down by the House of Lords is to prevent the possibility of such abuse." (*Bon-Accord Marine Assurance Co. v. Souter's Trs* (1850) 12 D. 1010, at 1013–1014. See also *Cullen v. Baillie* (1846) 8 D. 511, *per* the Lord President (Boyle) at 517).

The Lord Chancellor's comments were soon accepted as correctly representing the law of Scotland, and the principle was quickly firmly established. (See *Bon-Accord Marine Assurance Co., supra*; *Wellwood's Trs v. Hill* (1856) 19 D. 187; *Aitken v. Hunter* (1871) 9 M. 756). The Court of Session declined to apply the principle in *Miller's Trs v. Miller* (1848) 10 D. 765, however, with the Lord President (Boyle) observing (at 785):

> "Considering the practice and understanding of the country at the commencement, and I may say down to the close of this trust-management, I think it would be giving a retrospective effect to a judicial view, which ought to guide in future only."

The actual result in *Miller* on this point is, of course, of no interest today now that the principle has stood for the best part of two centuries. The decision is, however, interesting as a rejection of the fiction that judges only declare and never make the law.

2. *The rationale for the rule.* The rationale for the rule has been said to be as follows:

> "It is the duty of an executor and a trustee to be the guardian of an estate, and to watch over the interests of the estate committed to his charge. If he be allowed to perform the duties connected with the estate, and to claim compensation for his services, his interest would then be opposed to his duty, and, as a matter of prudence, the Court does not allow the executor or trustee to place himself in that situation. If he chooses to perform those duties or services on that estate, he is not entitled to receive compensation." (*Lord Gray and Others* (1856) 19 D. 1, *per* the Lord Justice-Clerk (Hope) at 5, quoting *New v. Jones* (1833) 1 H. & Tw. 632; 47 E.R. 1562, *per* Lord Lyndhurst C.B. at 634–635, 1564).

3. *The extent of the rule.* Just as a trustee may not personally perform work for the trust for remuneration, he may not employ a firm of which he is a partner to carry out such work (*Lord Gray and Others* (1856) 19 D. 1). But a trustee is still entitled to the expenses and outlays incurred in undertaking professional work for the trust: *Henderson v. Watson*, 1939 S.C. 711, *per* Lord Mackay at 722.

4. *Sanction by the court.* The court has no power to permit a trustee to receive remuneration (or **8.14** to sanction remuneration already received) on the grounds that it would be fair or equitable for the trustee to be remunerated: *Fegan v. Thomson* (1855) 17 D. 1146, *per* the Lord Justice-Clerk (Hope) at 1148: "We cannot allow a great principle to be frittered away by looking merely to the special circumstances of each particular case."

5. *Sanction or acquiescence by the truster or beneficiaries.* See *Ommaney v. Smith* (1854) 16 D. 712, *per* the Lord President (McNeill) at 726:

> "We must look not only to the general law, but to the particular circumstances of the trust; and if the truster himself has said that the agent appointed by him trustee shall also act as agent for the trust, or if the beneficiaries say it, that would be the law of the trust. If the residuary legatee says so, that also would be a case in which objection would be removed, and especially where the party having the interest in the trust is a party who cannot be supposed to be ignorant of the rules applicable to it."

For acquiescence to operate, however, it must be shown that the beneficiary was aware of their legal right to object to remuneration (*Lauder v. Millars* (1859) 21 D. 1353). *Cf. Scott v.*

Handyside's Trs (1868) 6 M. 753, where proof of awareness of the right to object does not appear to have been insisted on.

In *Mackie's Trs v. Mackie* (1875) 2 R. 312, it was stated (*per* Lord Neaves at 316 and Lord Gifford at 317) that where a beneficiary's interest is postponed (as in that case, where two beneficiaries were not to receive trust property until they attained the age of 25), they could nevertheless consent to remuneration before they had acquired a vested interest.

On sanction generally, see *infra* paras 8.25 *et seq.*

6. *Trust-deed: terminology implying the sanction of remuneration.* In *Goodsir v. Carruthers* (1858) 20 D. 1141, the trust-deed conferred a power on the trustees "to appoint agents and factors, either of their own number or other fit persons, for managing said trust". It was held that because "the office of factor, or of agent, is not in its nature gratuitous" (*per* Lord Ardmillan at 1146), this implied an intention on the part of the testator that a trustee who was appointed should be entitled to remuneration. So does a direction that the trustees should be given the "sole management" of a business (*Cameron's Trs v. Cameron* (1864) 3 M. 200). On the extent of a power to appoint a "factor or cashier", see *Mills v. Brown's Trs* (1900) 2 F. 1035

7. *Exercising the power to appoint a trustee to a remunerated position.* See *Lewis's Trs v. Pirie,* 1912 S.C. 574, *per* Lord Dundas at 578:

> "Where the trust-deed contains no power to appoint him [a trustee] to be law-agent, he cannot, as already stated, recover any remuneration. Where there is such power, and the trustees resolve to appoint him to the agency, his appointment ought to be minuted; but though that correct and business-like step be neglected, I think he may yet recover his remuneration if it is proved that in fact he did proper professional work for the trust on the instructions of the trustees, or with their knowledge and approval."

It was held in *Turner v. Fraser's Trs* (1897) 24 R. 673 that, where a trustee is appointed law-agent to the trust, he will not generally be entitled to charge law-agent fees for attending trustees' meetings, since he has a duty of attendance as trustee. It was observed, however, that this "must to a certain extent depend on the circumstances of each case, and, in particular, on the subject-matter of the business before the meeting" (*per* the Lord President (Robertson) at 676).

8. *Certain special trustees.* It is recognised in statute that a trustee in bankruptcy is entitled to remuneration (Bankruptcy (Scotland) Act 1985, s.51(1)(a)–(b), which gives claims for remuneration a priority in the distribution of the debtor's estate). The Married Women's Policies of Assurance (Scotland) Amendment Act 1980, s.2(3) provides that a policy of assurance is not prevented from vesting in a trustee "by reason only that it contains a provision to the effect that a trustee may in his professional capacity charge such remuneration for his professional services as is reasonable".

D. Possible further consequences of the *auctor in rem suam* principle

(a) Indirect transactions with the trust-estate

8.15 Does the *auctor in rem suam* principle prevent indirect transactions with the trust estate? For example, if A is a trustee, and the trust sells trust property to B, a third party (or distributes trust property to C, a beneficiary), is A prohibited from subsequently purchasing that property from B or C?

In *Clark v. Clark's Exrx*, 1989 S.L.T. 120, the trustees agreed to sell heritable property to a Mr and Mrs Millar. Missives were concluded with between the trustees and the Millars. The Millars did not pay the purchase price, however. Rather than resile from the contract, the executors agreed that the Millars could assign their rights under the missives to Mrs Clark, one of the trustees. They did so. Lord Mayfield held that the beneficiaries were entitled to have the assignation reduced as a violation of the *auctor in rem suam* principle. Two features of this case should be noted. Firstly, because no disposition had ever been granted to the Millars, the property had not been alienated from the trust estate (*per* Lord Mayfield at 607). Secondly, Mrs Clark had entered into an agreement with the trustees whereby they agreed to consent to the assignation, and she agreed to pay any interest that was due for late payment of the purchase price, but at a lower rate (two per cent above bank base rate) than the Millars were obliged to pay under the missives which they had concluded. Lord Mayfield observed (at 607–608):

> "It is clear that the first defender [Mrs Clark] was bound to have regard to the best interests of the estate. In my view at the date of entering into the assignation Mrs Clark had an interest as an individual to acquire the property as cheaply as possible. On the other hand it was stated she was bound to have regard to the best interests of the estate. Accordingly she had placed herself in the position where there was a possible conflict between her duties as an individual and as trustee. In referring to the missives relating to the assignation, counsel for the pursuers pointed out cl. 1 relating to interest from the Millars and cl. 5 referred to above and that if there was any interest left after deduction of interest the Millars would receive the benefit. It is also clear that in the agreement between the first defender as an individual and as an executor and the executors dated 22 August 1986, and the reply date 25 August 1986, in cl. 3 of the latter document referred to above in connection with the missives between the executors and the Millars, interest by the first defender was to be at 2 per cent above bank base rate, in other words less than the 5 per cent payable by the Millars as stated (15 April 1986) in the original missives. Accordingly there is a conflict between the individual rate of 2 per cent and her duties as an executrix of 5 per cent. In my view accordingly the first defender was in breach of her duties as an executrix. She was auctor in rem suam."

The difference between the rates of interest to late payment should probably be treated as merely demonstrative of the conflict of interest rather than a necessary element of it, as no prejudice to the trust-estate is required in order for the *auctor in rem suam* principle to be breached (see *Hamilton v. Wright* (1842) 1 Bell 574, *supra* para. 8.02.

The fact that reliance was placed on the property not having been alienated from the trust estate is more interesting, however. Does this mean that, if the sale between the executors and the Millars had been completed, and Mrs Clark had subsequently purchased the property directly from the Millars, that transaction would not have been open to challenge? In *Clark v. McCash and Hunter*, 1993 G.W.D. 36–2366, Mrs Clark brought an action against her solicitors for damages, arguing *inter alia* that they should have advised her to proceed in this fashion instead. Her averments on this issue were held irrelevant, however, in part on the ground that this method of proceeding would have been "open to challenge. . . as an illegitimate and circuitous transaction."

The limited Scottish case-law on this point is concerned only with the scenario where the trustee has had the re-purchase of the property in mind at the time when the trust property was sold to the third party. It is likely that, where the sale to the third party was genuine and not undertaken with a view to the trustee acquiring the trust property personally, there will be no impediment to a subsequent purchase of the property by the trustee personally. See the English cases of *Baker v. Peck* (1861) 4 L.T. 3 and *Re Postlethwaite* (1888) 60 L.T. 514.

(b) Transactions between the trust-estate and parties connected to a trustee

Burrell v. Burrell's Trs
1915 1 S.L.T. 101

LORD DUNDAS: "We have here reclaiming notes by the same pursuer in two actions which **8.16** were heard of and disposed of together in the Outer House. The reclaiming noted have similarly been heard together at our bar, and will be disposed of together now. In each case the pursuer seeks to set aside the purchase of certain ship shares, forming part of the trust estate of his deceased mother, the purchase in each instance having been made from the trustees by the wife of one of the trustees. . .

I shall state in brief words what I consider to be the gist of the evidence. I think it is clear enough upon the proof in each case that there was no bargaining of any sort between the wife and the trustees; that the wife made her purchase on her own initiative, and neither at the instigation nor under the advice of her husband; that both ladies were capable business women accustomed to manage their own ample means; that payment was made in each case out of the wife's separate estate; and that the price was an adequate, and even a full one. It further appears that the transfers bore *ex facie* the exclusion of the husband's *jus mariti* and right of administration. I do not say that the production of the transfers in itself must be conclusive proof of that as a fact, but in the absence of counter evidence of any sort, I do not see how the pursuer can maintain that the contrary is the fact. If these be the facts of the case, I cannot see how the pursuer can succeed unless we are to lay down as an absolute principle or rule of law that the purchase of trust estate from trustees by the wife of one of the trustees is illegal. No authority for such a proposition has been cited, and I know of none, and I am not prepared to lay down any such broad proposition. . ."

LORD MACKENZIE: "I am of the same opinion. . . [His Lordship referred to the English authorities, and continued:] I venture to remark that in all cases of this class the Court will seek to be certain, by vigilant scrutiny, of the true nature of such a transaction; because one can readily see that the close relationship between husband and wife may, unless explained, give rise to the not unnatural inference that the husband was truly the party intervening in the case, and that not without benefit to himself. Subjecting everything that was done in this case to that scrutiny, I am unable to imagine any case which would well be stronger for sustaining the transaction which the pursuer seeks to challenge."

Lord Cullen concurred.

NOTES:

8.17
1. As Lord Mackenzie indicates, such a transaction will be regarded with suspicion by the courts. A trustee may not, therefore, employ a third party to purchase trust property for him in order to evade the rule. See *Silkstone and Haigh Moor Coal Co. v. Edey* [1900] 1 Ch. 167.
2. A trustee may not employ a firm of which he is a partner to undertake work for the trust (*Lord Gray and Others* (1856) 19 D. 1; *Henderson v. Watson*, 1939 S.C. 711; see *supra* para. 8.13), nor may such a firm purchase trust property. It seems, however, that this prohibition is not based on the connection between the trustee and the firm, but rather on the fact that the trustee, as a partner, is entitled to a share of the firm's profits and therefore personally benefits from such a transaction. It is not clear, therefore, whether a trustee is prohibited from employing a firm of which he is a salaried employee to perform trust work, although it would seem prudent to avoid such a course.

3. THE CONSEQUENCES OF BREACHING THE *AUCTOR IN REM SUAM* PRINCIPLE

A transaction entered into in breach of the *auctor in rem suam* principle is not void, but merely voidable (*Fraser v. Hankey & Co.* (1847) 9 D. 415).

A. Who may challenge a transaction?

8.18 In most cases, a challenge will be brought by the beneficiaries. A challenge can, however, be brought by trust creditors (*Bon-Accord Marine Assurance Co. v. Souter's Trs* (1850) 12 D. 1010), co-trustees (*Wilson v. Smith's Trs*, 1939 S.L.T. 120), or (probably) the truster (*Ashburton v. Escombe* (1892) 20 R. 187).

A person who has consented to or acquiesced in the breach of trust is not entitled to challenge it (see the authorities cited *supra* para. 8.14 with regard to remuneration, the cases *infra* para. 8.25 regarding sanction in the trust-deed or by the beneficiaries, and see also *Corsar v. Mathers* (1887) 3 Sh. Ct Rep. 75 as regards acquiescence by a co-trustee. *Cf.*, however, *Davis v. Davis* (1908) 16 S.L.T. 380).

Third parties may not challenge the transaction (*Aberdein v. Stratton's Trs* (1867) 5 M. 726).

B. Bringing a challenge timeously and personal bar

8.19 It has been said that a challenge must be brought timeously to be successful (*Mackie's Trs v. Mackie* (1875) 2 R. 312, *per* Lord Neaves at 316), but it is thought the passage of time will only be relevant if it gives rise to a plea of personal bar.

C. The result

What is the result of a successful challenge?   **8.20**

> "[It] seems clear that where a trustee has acted as auctor in rem suam, and restitutio in integrum can be achieved, the appropriate remedy is reduction, and parties will be returned to the position in which they were before the transaction complained of took place. In addition there may be a good claim against the trustee for an accounting. On the other hand, where restitutio in integrum cannot be achieved, the remedy of reduction is not available. In such a case the trustee may be made the subject of a claim for accounting. If the trustee has obtained a profit, then he must account to the executors for that profit." (*Sarris v. Clark*, 1995 S.L.T. 44, *per* the Lord Justice-Clerk (Ross) at 49).

> "Whenever it can be shewn that the trustee has so arranged matters as to obtain an advantage, whether in money or in money's worth, to himself personally through the execution of his trust, he will not be permitted to retain it, but be compelled to make it over to his constituent." (*Huntingdon Copper Co. v. Henderson* (1877) 4 R. 294, *per* the Lord President (Inglis) at 308, approving a statement by the Lord Ordinary (Young) at 299).

The beneficiaries can, however, elect either to have the transaction reduced or for the trust to take the benefit of the transaction. So, for example, in *Taylor v. Hillhouse's Trs* (1901) 9 S.L.T. 31, the trustees converted the trust business into a limited company (which they were allowed to do) and allotted shares to themselves (which they were not allowed to do). It was held that the beneficiaries were entitled to demand that they transferred the shares to the trust upon reimbursement of the purchase price which they had paid. (For another example of the trust taking the benefit of the transaction, see *Hamilton v. Wright* (1842) 1 Bell 574, *supra* para. 8.02).

D. Prescription

Prescription is unlikely to provide an effective defence for a trustee who has acted as *auctor in rem* **8.21** *suam*. Under the Prescription and Limitation (Scotland) Act 1973, Sched. 3, para. e(iii), "any obligation of a trustee. . . to make forthcoming to any person entitled thereto any trust property, or the proceeds of any such property, in the possession of the trustee, or to make good the value of any such property previously received by the trustee and appropriated to his own use" is imprescriptible. See further Johnston, *Prescription and Limitation*, paras 3.39 *et seq.* So, in *University of Aberdeen v. Town Council of Aberdeen* (1876) 3 R. 1087, *supra* para. 8.07, the passage of three-quarters of a century did not protect the Town Council from having to account to the beneficiaries for their breach of trust.

It should not be thought that this rule only applies to cases involving the sale of trust property. Where a trustee has acquired property from a third party in breach of the principle, he will be taken to have acquired that property on behalf of the trust. The property is therefore trust property, and the beneficiary's right to challenge the transaction is therefore imprescriptible.

E. Removal of a trustee from office

The fact that a conflict of interest has arisen may provide grounds for an application to the court to **8.22** have a trustee removed from office. See *supra* para. 4.23.

4. CONFLICTS AND TRUST DECISION-MAKING

Should a trustee resign if a conflict of interest arises? Wilson and Duncan state (at pp. 26–25) that "Normally, when a conflict arises, the trustee must resign". It is submitted, however, that this overstates matters somewhat. The question was explored by Lord Inglis in the following case:

Perston v. Perston's Trs
(1863) 1 M. 245; 35 Scot. Jur. 166

Mathew Perston senior died in 1833, leaving a trust-deed under which his three sons, **8.23** Mathew, James and Andrew were appointed trustees. In 1847, the trustees advanced a loan of £5000 to Mathew, upon the security of heritable property which he owned, having obtained a valuation of the property. Mathew became bankrupt immediately afterwards. When the property was sold, it brought only £3250. A number of the beneficiaries later brought an action of count, reckoning and payment against the trustees.

LORD JUSTICE-CLERK (INGLIS): "It is quite true, as your Lordships have observed, that it has never yet been, in express terms, decided, that a loan by trustees to one of their own number, of a part of the trust-funds, is an illegal transaction; and the circumstance that the question thus possesses a certain novelty gives it a degree of importance, which, in any other view, appears to me not to belong to it; because, I think, the determination of the question depends upon a principle of very clear application.

Trustees are not entitled individually to separate themselves from the body of trustees, for the purpose of dealing or transacting with the trustees or the trust-estate upon their own account, under any pretence whatever. This rule depends upon more considerations than one. It is clearly inexpedient that a trustee should be allowed to place himself in a position adverse to the interests of the trust which he has undertaken to manage. That is one view. But it is also a clear dereliction of duty upon the part of the trustee, that in any transaction into which the trust and the trustees are about to enter, he should withdraw himself from the administration, and deprive them of the weight of his authority, and the benefit of his advice. And, therefore, the general rule depends upon such a broad and clear principle, that I think it is quite impossible that its application should be doubted to transactions of any kind in which one of the trustees separates himself from the other trustees, for the purpose of dealing upon his own account with the trust-estate and the trustees.

It is no doubt perfectly true, that occasions may arise when it is impossible to prevent transactions between one of the trustees, as an individual, and the rest of the trustees, as representing the trust-estate. That must always occur where any of the trustees are beneficiaries under the trust; because, in settling with the trustees in regard to their own beneficial interest under the trust, they are maintaining their own individual interest necessarily, and acting, to a certain extent, adversely to the general body of trustees and to the trust-estate.

It is very easy to figure other cases where the trust must be left in the hands of a quorum of the trustees, and where the remaining trustees may be acting adversely to the trust and the trust-estate—as, for example, where rights come to individual trustees by inheritance or marriage after they have accepted the office of trustee. They cannot be expected to reject such successions, merely for the purpose of enabling them rightly to perform their duties as trustees; and just as little, on the other hand, are they entitled to resign their office of trustees, merely because they have succeeded to such a right as may bring them in one particular case into a position of antagonism to the trust-estate and its interests.

But it is only where these necessities arise, that the withdrawal of any trustees from taking a part in the trust-management, and from giving the full benefit of their assistance to the other trustees, can be justified. Wherever, therefore, any trustee voluntarily puts himself in a position of withdrawing from the side of the trust, the transaction which he enters upon with the trust-estate is necessarily illegal.

Now, the application of that principle to the case of loan is too clear to require almost any observation. In what way is it possible to distinguish between the case of loan and the case of sale? In one view, in the case of sale, equally as in the case of loan, there is no conflicting interest between the trust-estate and the party with whom the trust-estate is dealing. The one desires to sell, and the other desires to buy, and there is no antagonism between these two objects—none whatever. And, in the case of loan, the one desires to lend, and the other desires to borrow; and there is no antagonism, but perfect harmony, between these views. But in the case of loan equally as in the case of sale, the antagonism of interests arises in adjusting the terms of the transaction,— the price, the term of entry, the title, in the case of sale; the security, the rate of interest, the term of payment, in the case of loan. What is the difference in principle between these? The parties are dealing at arm's length, as it has often been expressed, in both the one case and the other, and that is the true test as to whether the transaction is legal or illegal as between the trustees and one of their number.

Therefore upon the general question I entertain no doubt whatever. And in regard to the specialities of the present case, I take them as stated by the defenders themselves, and I import nothing into the case adversely to them except what they themselves have stated. In the 2d article of their condescendence they admit, that they made the loan of £5000 in 1843 to Mr Mathew Perston, one of their own number. They say that they believed they were taking ample security for that loan over certain house property which he had at Largs. They say, further, that they believed him to be prosperous, and they say that they not only took valuations of the property, but that the trustees did deliberate maturely upon the whole matter, and after having done so, lent this £5000.

I presume that means that the whole body of trustees deliberated maturely, and that Mr Mathew Perston, the borrower, was in the counsels of the trustees in deliberating upon this loan. If that were so, I think it makes the case all the worse; but even if it were not, what is the consequence? That out of five trustees, four are left to conduct this transaction upon their own discretion and responsibility, and the fifth not only withdraws from them the benefit of his assistance and advice, but puts himself in a position to have an interest to obtain the loan upon terms not favourable to the trust-estate. It is said, no doubt, that there is here the specialty of the trustees having taken heritable security for the loan, and that was the circumstance that was most strongly founded upon in the argument before us.

Well, if the taking of heritable security afforded an absolute protection against all loss, one could understand the force of the argument; but we know unfortunately that it is not so, and it is just because some heritable securities are good, and other heritable securities are bad, that it becomes a matter of discretion and judgment upon the part of trustees to determine what heritable security they will take for their money. Now, in the consideration of that very question, they not only lost the benefit of Mathew Perston's assistance and advice, but they found him in a position adverse to them, magnifying, of course, the value of his own security, and endeavouring to persuade them, as much as he could, that it was sufficient for the sum which they were going to advance to him.

And what is the result? That it turns out to be insufficient. Is that not the best practical illustration of the soundness of the principle which I have already announced, that this was one of the very matters on which a single trustee is not entitled to put himself in a position of adverse interest to the trust-estate? If this loan could have been justified, as was also attempted, by reference to a power conferred on the trustees by the settlement under which they act, it would have made a very special case indeed, and might have entirely prevented the application of the principle which we have been engaged in expounding, but I agree with all your Lordships that it is quite impossible to find in the settlement any justification of the allegation made upon this point."

Lords Neaves, Cowan and Benholme delivered concurring opinions.

The Court sustained the third plea-in-law for the pursuers, *viz.* "The loan to Mathew Perston being a loan to one of the trustees was illegal, and any loss sustained thereby cannot be debited to the pursuers."

NOTES:

1. It should be noted that Lord Inglis' judgment appears unparagraphed in the Session Cases **8.24** report (although not in the Scottish Jurist version). Paragraphing has been introduced here for the purposes of readability.

2. See also *Dunn v. Chambers* (1897) 25 R. 247, where, in view of Lord Inglis' observations, Lord McLaren reserved his opinion as to the extent of a duty on a curator bonis to resign where a conflict of interest arose.

3. *Entitlement and duty to resign.* Lord Inglis' discussion is phrased in terms of a trustee's "entitlement" to resign rather than any question of a duty to resign. This is because *Perston's Trs* predates the introduction of a statutory power of resignation (Trusts (Scotland) Act 1861, s.1). The question of whether a conflict of interest gives rise to a power to resign where none exists under the trust-deed has never been authoritatively decided (although see *Maclean* (1895) 22 R. 872). The question is, however, now largely irrelevant because remunerated

trustees (who do not have an implied power to resign under the section 3 of the Trusts (Scotland) Act 1921) can always apply to the court for authority to resign, and it is unlikely that anyone would accept office as a gratuitous trustee under exclusion of the power.

4. *The extent of the conflict.* Lord Inglis states that trustees are not entitled to resign (and are, it may be assumed, under no duty to do so) simply because events have put them in "one particular case into a position of antagonism to the trust-estate and its interests". It may be, however, that the "position of antagonism" is so serious that it would be impossible for the trustee to remain in office, as in *Maclean* (1895) 22 R. 872 where the testator and trustee were partners in the same company, and a dispute arose after the testator's death as to the value of his share in the company, which may well (although it is not entirely clear from the report) have formed a very substantial part of the trust assets.

Otherwise, it seems the proper course is simply for the trustee to refrain from participating in those decisions where a conflict arises. For example, in *Caldwell's Trs v. Caldwell*, 1923 S.L.T. 694, one of the trustees, as the testator's next of kin, was involved in a challenge to the validity of a residuary bequest to "charitable and benevolent institutions". It was held that he should not take part in meetings concerning the distribution of funds under this clause. It does not, however, appear to have been suggested that he should resign. Resignation may nevertheless be the most prudent course where a conflict of interest arises, particularly as acting in good faith is no defence where a trustee has been *auctor in rem suam*.

5. SANCTIONING OF ACTS WHICH ARE *AUCTOR IN REM SUAM*

A. Sanction in the Trust-Deed

8.25   It has long been understood that a trustee may be *auctor in rem suam* where this has been sanctioned by the truster in the trust-deed. (See the authorities quoted *supra* para. 8.14 and also *Maclean* (1895) 22 R. 872, *per* Lord McLaren at 875).

The court will, however, strictly construe any wording in a trust deed which it is claimed sanctions a trustee being *auctor in rem suam*. In *Johnston v. Macfarlane*, 1987 S.L.T. 593, it was held that a power to sell trust property to "any beneficiary" did not include a power to sell to a beneficiary who was also a trustee. In reaching this conclusion, the court took the view that as the truster had specifically excluded the application of the *auctor in rem suam* principle at other points in the deed (for example, by allowing the trustees to charge remuneration), he could not be held to have impliedly excluded it elsewhere.

Some of the *dicta* in *Jamieson* suggest that an authorisation of *auctor in rem suam* must be express to be effective. However, there are a number of earlier authorities which suggest that such authorisation may be implied (*Goodsir v. Carruthers* (1858) 20 D. 1141; *Cameron's Trs v. Cameron* (1864) 3 M. 200, both noted *supra* para. 8.14). The issue was considered more fully in the following case:

Sarris v. Clark
1995 S.L.T. 44

8.26   James Clark executed a will in November 1985, by which he bequeathed his whole property equally among his wife and his three children. His wife was named as one of the executors under the will. In December 1985, he entered into a contract of copartnery with his wife, which narrated that he and his wife had for some time been carrying on business as farmers and that their agreement was now being reduced to writing. On the same day, he granted leases of the three farms to himself and his wife as partners of the firm, and to the survivors and survivor of them as individuals.

He died the next day, with the result that his wife became entitled as an individual to the tenancies of the three farms which he had owned. His wife accepted office as one of the executors, but subsequently resigned office in September 1986. In September 1989, the executors entered into an agreement with her whereby she agreed to give up the tenancies of the holdings in consideration of the sum of £476,300.

Mr Clark's children subsequently raised an action claiming that Mrs Clark had been *auctor in rem suam* in concluding the September 1989 agreement and that the sums which she had received were trust property which fell to be distributed among the beneficiaries.

LORD JUSTICE-CLERK (ROSS): "The principle that a trustee is not allowed to enter into transactions in which he has or can have a personal interest which conflicts or may conflict with the interests of those whom he is bound by fiduciary duty to protect is well established: 'It appears to me that from first to last the rule of the law of Scotland has been that any one holding a fiduciary character, whether that of guardian or trustee, cannot lawfully become *auctor in rem suam*' (*Aitken v. Hunter* (1871) 9 M. 757, per Lord Neaves at p 762).

However, there are a number of dicta which make it clear that what is objectionable is a trustee putting himself into a position where his duty and his interest may conflict. This is recognised in Menzies on *Trustees* (2nd ed.), at para. 451: 'As the law requires that the trustee shall act as trustee only, it will not allow him to put himself in a position where his duty and his interest may conflict; for it is presumed that in such a position he will sacrifice his duty to his interest.'. . .

In the present case it was the deceased himself who appointed the first defender as an executrix, and also acknowledged her as a partner and conferred upon her a sole right of tenancy of the farms at his death. In these circumstances, it cannot be asserted that the first defender 'so arranged matters as to obtain an advantage', nor can it be maintained that she put herself in a position where her duty and her interest might conflict.

It was at one stage suggested by counsel for the pursuers that since there was such a conflict, the first defender should have declined to accept office as executor, or at least should have resigned sooner than she did. That argument was effectively dealt with by Lord Shaw of Dunfermline in *Hordern v. Hordern* [1910] AC 465 at p 475:

'It is no doubt true that the conflict between duty and interest may arise, but it is also true that that conflict is brought about entirely by the action of [the testator], who appointed [the executor] his executor in the full knowledge that he would have to exercise on survivance the rights, and come under the obligations, stipulated in regard to the surviving partner by the articles of association. The idea that, in consequence of that possible conflict, [the executor's] duty was to decline the trust reposed in him by his brother is out of the question.'

I have already referred to the fact that the doctrine *auctor in rem suam* will not apply where the conduct complained of was specifically authorised by the truster. Junior counsel for the pursuers contended under reference to *Johnston v. Macfarlane*, 1987 S.L.T. 593 that express authorisation of the truster was required. However, as counsel for the first defender pointed out under reference to the report in the Outer House, it appears to have been conceded in that case that only express provisions would do. At 1985 S.L.T., p 340 the Lord Ordinary said: 'Although, as counsel for the pursuer properly maintained, this is a jealously guarded principle of law, it will nevertheless give way to express provisions in the trust deed to the contrary, and I understood this to be conceded by counsel.'

In his opinion in the Inner House, 1987 S.L.T. at p 598F, Lord Hunter observed: 'Counsel for the parties were in complete agreement as to the principle of law which must, according to a wealth of authority, be applied. The principle is that a person in a fiduciary position is not, unless otherwise expressly provided, allowed to put himself in a position where his interest and duty conflict.'

It is accordingly clear that in *Johnston v. Macfarlane* the court were not invited to consider whether anything other than express authorisation would do. As I understood it counsel for the pursuers in the present case accepted that the exception might be established if authorisation could be implied. In my opinion counsel were correct to make that concession. In The Laws of Scotland: Stair Memorial Encyclopaedia, Vol. 24, para. 173, it is stated: 'In certain circumstances authorisation may be implied from the terms of the deed which constitutes a fiduciary relationship.'

This is clear from cases like *Goodsir v. Carruthers* (1858) 20 D 1141 at p 1146, where Lord Ardmillan expressed the view that authorisation might come 'from the express words of the trust-deed, or from its plain meaning, ascertained by necessary implication'.

I am accordingly satisfied that an exception to the general rule *auctor in rem suam* may arise if the truster has expressly or impliedly authorised the conduct alleged to constitute the breach of fiduciary duty. So far as implied authorisation is concerned, another way of expressing this may be to say that the truster has appointed the trustee in the knowledge that there will or may be a conflict of interest between his duty as trustee and his own interest. In *Maclean* (1895) 22 R. 872, pp 875–876 Lord McLaren said:

'When, therefore a trustee, having originally found it consistent with his duty to take up a trust, finds that he is disabled from acting by personal conflicting interests, as in the present case, he must necessarily withdraw absolutely from the management. Of course this would not apply to cases where a truster having foreseen such a conflict of interests has yet appointed a trustee. It is a common occurrence for a son or partner of the truster to be appointed for the express purpose of carrying on a business, where there must be adverse interests in his capacity as partner and trustee existing at the time of the constitution of the trust. But such a conflict cannot be held to disable him from acting when he has been appointed especially for the purpose of carrying on the business.'

The foregoing decision led to the author of Menzies on *Trustees* saying at para. 451: 'There is an important exception to the general rule. It does "not apply to cases where a truster, having foreseen a conflict of interest, has yet appointed a trustee".'

It was this aspect of the matter which led Nourse LJ in *Sargeant v. National Westminster Bank plc* (1991) 61 P. & C.R. 518 at p 523 to say:

'But the conclusive objection to the application of the absolute rule in which Mr. Romer [counsel for the appellants] relies is that it is not they who have put themselves in that position. They have been put there mainly by the testator's grant of the tenancies and by the provisions of his will and partly by contractual arrangements to which Charles himself was a party and of which his representatives cannot complain. The administrators cannot therefore complain of the trustees' continued assertion of their rights as tenants.'

8.27 *Inglis v. Inglis*, 1983 S.C. 8 was a different type of case; the defender was an executor dative and not an executor nominate. He was under no obligation to seek confirmation as an executor of the deceased, and thus had placed himself in the position of conflict (see Lord Hunter at 1983 S.C., p 17).

Counsel for the first defender reminded us that the aim must always be to discover the intention of the truster. Counsel for the pursuers accepted that the intention of the deceased was to be found not merely in his will, but also having regard to the terms of the contract of copartnery and the lease. Junior counsel for the pursuers had stressed that the will had been executed before the contract of copartnership and the lease had come into existence, but senior counsel for the pursuers conceded, in my opinion properly, that it was proper to have regard to all three deeds when determining whether there was express or implied authorisation of the truster for what had occurred. The context in which that issue had to be determined was that there had been three deeds executed by the deceased during the 14 days from 20 November to 4 December 1985. Counsel for the pursuers maintained that there was plainly no express authorisation for the transaction complained of, and they further maintained that there was no necessary implication of authorisation. Counsel pointed out that after the death of the deceased there was no need for the first defender to renounce the tenancy; she could have retained the tenancies and left the trustees to sell the farms subject to tenant's rights, or alternatively she could have resigned. It therefore could not be contended that the deceased impliedly authorised her to transact with the trustees as she did.

Counsel for the first defender on the other hand maintained that they had averred sufficient to support a case to the effect that the deceased must have intended that the first defender would be able to transact with the trustees as she did.

The averments bearing upon this matter appear in ans 8 for the first defender and in ans 8 for the second and third defenders. In ans 8 for the first defender it is averred inter alia as follows:

'It was a necessary step in the administration of the executry estate to realise the major assets. The major assets were the farms. To realise the farm it was necessary that the tenancies thereof be renounced. Any sale subject to the (then) existing tenancies of the first defender would, having regard to her age and her intention to continue farming, have been achieved, if at all, only at a price disadvantageous to the executry estate.'

No challenge was taken to the relevancy of the foregoing averments. In ans 8 for the first defender there follow other averments to which objection was taken by the pursuer. These are in the following terms:

'The deceased was aware before his death that he had nominated as an executrix of his estate this defender who was also, by virtue of the terms of the partnership, the person entitled to the tenancy of his farms on his death. He was also aware of the illiquid nature of his estate and the potential conflict which would arise between the need of the executry to realise assets and the interest of this defender as tenant of said farms. Despite this knowledge he so nominated this defender as executrix. Accordingly there was no duty on this defender to withdraw from acting as an executor although, in the event, she did so withdraw.'

In ans 8 for the second and third defenders it is inter alia averred as follows:

'Explained and averred that when the said bargain was concluded the first defender was not an executor. In order properly to perform their duties as executors, the said farms had to be realised. The best price could only be achieved by sale with vacant possession. The first defender was the tenant of the said farms. Her tenancy was a secure agricultural tenancy the existence of which substantially reduced the market value of the farms. In order to sell the farms at the best possible price, it was a prudent act of administration to bring to an end the first defender's said tenancy. Her interest as tenant had a substantial capital value. The executors could not have secured vacant possession of the farms other than by negotiating the renunciation of the first defender's interest as tenant.'

In my opinion in the foregoing averments the first defender, and the second and third defenders, have averred sufficient to go to inquiry upon the question of whether the transaction complained of does not fall within the rule *auctor in rem suam*. Whether the defence is regarded as amounting to implied authorisation by the deceased, or whether it is treated as within an exception to the general rule in respect that the deceased must have foreseen the conflict of interests and had yet appointed the first defender as executrix, I am satisfied that the first defenders and the second and third defenders have averred sufficient to go to inquiry. If they establish what they have averred, it would be open to the court to hold that the conduct complained of had been impliedly authorised by the deceased or that the deceased had made the appointment after foreseeing that conflict of interest would arise. In either event, it would be open to the court to hold that the conduct complained of was not struck at by the doctrine *auctor in rem suam*.

The deceased made the first defender both tenant of the holdings after his death and an executor. The deceased must be taken to have been aware that his assets would require to be realised after his death, and that his estate was of an illiquid nature. He must therefore have appreciated that some at least of the farm assets would require to be sold. Executors have a duty to exercise reasonable prudence and to obtain the best price possible for any sale of the executry estate. The first defender offers to prove that a sale subject to the existing tenancies of the first defender would have been disadvantageous to the executry. If the farms or any of them were to be sold with vacant possession, it was inevitable that there would require to be negotiations between the executors and the first defender. This would inevitably give rise to a conflict of interest since the first defender's interest as executor would differ from that of the first defender as tenant. This must have been known to the deceased, and accordingly, there appears to me on the first defender's averments to be a basis for a defence to the pursuers' assertion that the first defender was acting as *auctor in rem suam*. I am accordingly satisfied that the Lord Ordinary was well founded in concluding that a proof before answer should be allowed on this issue."

Lords Murray and Morison delivered concurring opinions.

NOTES:

1. For earlier steps in this saga, see *Clark v. Clark's Exrs*, 1989 S.L.T. 665; *Clark v. McCash & Hunter*, 1993 G.W.D. 36–2366.   **8.28**

2. It is not clear why any question of *auctor in rem suam* arose in this case, since Mrs Clark resigned as trustee three years before the agreement to give up the tenancies of the farms. One might question, therefore, whether the pursuers' averments were sufficient to support an allegation that she had been *auctor in rem suam*, but this is not the approach taken by the court. Indeed, the opinions delivered suggest that, if Mrs Clark were to escape an obligation to repay the money which she had received to the trust, she could only do so on the basis of authorisation of a conflict of interest by the truster and not on the basis that she had resigned before the September 1989 agreement. On the general issue of whether a trustee can enter into a transaction with the trust estate after resigning as trustee, see *infra* para. 8.32.

B. Sanction by the Beneficiaries

Buckner v. Jopp's Trs
(1887) 14 R. 1006

8.29   LORD YOUNG: "The acquisition by trustees of the trust-estate under their control has always been regarded by the Court with the greatest jealousy, and if it appears that the trustees have made a profit out of it, it will not be difficult, as a general rule, for the beneficiary, coming timeously into Court to have it set aside; although even if such challenge is timeously made the trustee would according to law, as I understand it, uphold an arrangement with the beneficiaries upon satisfying the Court that they had been quite fairly dealt with and had full information in regard to everything; and the case would be all the stronger if, besides having full information, the beneficiaries being *sui juris* desired the bargain which was made betwixt them and the trustees, the trustees taking no advantage of the position of the beneficiaries. That is all that the Court requires, and the burden of shewing that would be on the trustees, in order to uphold such a transaction betwixt them and beneficiaries *sui juris*."

NOTES:

8.30
1. See also *Taylor v. Hillhouse's Trs* (1901) 9 S.L.T. 31, *per* Lord Kincairney at 33: "When trustees in defence of a breach of trust, especially when it is one by which they profit, plead the consent of the beneficiaries, I think they must show that the beneficiaries were aware of the breach of trust and the legal wrong, and condoned it."
2. A trustee who proposes to purchase a beneficiary's interest in trust property must "give the beneficiary full information as to his position in entering into [the] transaction" (*Dougan v. Macpherson* (1902) 4 F. (H.L.) 7, *per* Lord Shand at 10). So, in that case, a trustee did not disclose to the beneficiary that he had obtained a valuation of the beneficiary's interest in the trust (which valued it at substantially more than he was to pay) before purchasing it. It was held that the beneficiary was entitled to have the transaction reduced.
3. In a sequestration, neither the debtor nor "a person who holds an interest opposed to the general interests of the creditors" may be appointed as permanent trustee: Bankruptcy (Scotland) Act 1985, s.24(2). This pre-empts the possibility of certain possible conflicts of interest.

C. Sanction by the Court

8.31   The court cannot give sanction to a trustee to enter into a transaction in breach of the *auctor in rem suam* rule. See *Hall's Trs v. McArthur*, 1918 S.C. 646 (explaining *Coats's Trs, Petrs*, 1914 S.C. 723). The court does, however, have an *ex post facto* power to relieve a trustee from personal liability for a breach of trust where he has acted "honestly and reasonably". See section 32 of the Trusts (Scotland) Act 1921, discussed *infra* paras 9.31 *et seq*.

6. CAN A FORMER TRUSTEE FALL FOUL OF THE *AUCTOR IN REM SUAM* PRINCIPLE?

There are a number of dicta which suggest that a trustee may enter into contracts with the trust-estate **8.32** after resignation, and that such contracts will not be invalid by virtue of the ex-trustee's former status (*Brown v. Burt* (1848) 11 D. 338, *per* Lord Moncrieff at 342; *Dunn v. Chambers* (1897) 25 R. 247, *per* Lord McLaren at 251; *Mills v. Brown's Trs* (1900) 2 F. 1035, *per* Lord Young at 1039).

However, the courts have not always taken such a lenient view. In *Halley's Trs v. Halley*, 1920 2 S.L.T. 343, it was held that a trustee who had resigned could not enter into a lease of property which had previously been leased to the trust, even though the proprietors had refused to renew the trust's lease. In reaching this conclusion, Lord Ashmore observed (at 344–345):

> "the respondent's counsel founded on these facts: that the respondent had resigned his trusteeship before the lease could come into operation, and further had resigned before this application was presented.
>
> In my opinion, the considerations referred to are immaterial. The respondent before his resignation on 11th March, while still a trustee, had negotiated with the proprietors for a lease, and, in the words of his solicitors' letter of 8th March, had 'already arranged' with them for a lease as from the ensuing term of Whitsunday. Moreover, his resignation before the date of commencing these proceedings could not cancel or undo the breach of trust duty which he had committed and which it was the object of the interdict to prevent him from making effectual."

It seems, therefore, that the decision might well have been different had the trustee refrained from entering into any negotiations with the proprietors before his resignation. (*Cf.,* however, the interpretation of this case in Wilson and Duncan at 26–06). See also *Sarris v. Clark*, 1995 S.L.T. 44, *supra* para. 8.26 where it seems to be assumed that agreements entered into after the resignation of a trustee, but based on negotiations which took place before resignation, will fall foul of the *auctor in rem suam* principle. But *cf. Mills v. Brown's Trs* (1900) 2 F. 1035, *per* Lord Young at 1039, where it seems to be assumed that negotiations prior to resignation will not invalidate a subsequent transaction.

A slightly different approach is suggested by Lord Cranworth L.C. in *Aberdeen Railway Co. v. Blaikie Bros.* (1854) 1 Macq. 461 (although it is not referred to in his opinion), to the effect that a former trustee who enters into a transaction with the trust-estate "should be permitted to show fairness in the transaction".

It will be seen that the *dicta* on this issue are not easy to reconcile. Overall, however, the cases seem to support the view that a former trustee may enter into a transaction with the trust provided that no negotiations relating to this transaction took place prior to his resignation. Where prior negotiations have taken place, the transaction will not necessarily be voidable, but the court will regard it with suspicion. The *onus* will probably lie on the former trustee to establish that the transaction was a fair one.

Where a trustee resigns after entering into a contract with the trust-estate and subsequently renegotiates the terms of the contract, the renegotiation will not cure the defect in the original contract (*Aberdeen Railway Co. v. Blaikie Bros.* (1854) 1 Macq. 461).

7. THE REQUIREMENT OF PROPER MOTIVATION

Trustees must exercise their powers under the trust in the best interests of the beneficiaries and should **8.33** not allow their decision-making to be motivated by considerations which are irrelevant to those interests, at least where that leads them to act in a way which is prejudicial to the beneficiaries. This issue has arisen most commonly in the context of investment decisions by trustees—although it is not limited to that context—and is therefore discussed *supra* at paras 7.16 *et seq.*

Chapter 9

LIABILITY OF TRUSTEES TO BENEFICIARIES

9.01 This chapter considers the liability of trustees to beneficiaries for breach of trust. Firstly, it considers the standard of care which is incumbent upon trustees. (It should be noted, however, that a trustee may be in breach of trust without having breached the duty of care, by breaching another relevant duty—for example, the duty to pay the correct beneficiaries. See *supra* Chapter 6 for the duties of trustees). It then considers the various remedies which are open to beneficiaries where a trustee has acted in breach of trust. Finally, it considers the defences which may be open to a trustee who has acted in breach of trust, either in the form of an immunity clause in the trust-deed itself or in certain statutory provisions contained in the Trusts (Scotland) Act 1921.

1. THE DUTY OF CARE

A. What is the standard of care?

Rae v. Meek
(1888) 15 R. 1033

9.02 LORD PRESIDENT (INGLIS): "It is said that a trustee must under all circumstances shew in the conduct of trust affairs all the prudence and intelligence that a prudent man would shew in the management of his own affairs. I am not quite sure that that is either a very definite or a very satisfactory statement of the ground of liability of a trustee—that he has failed to exercise that amount of prudence which a prudent man would use in the conduct of his own affairs—because there are many degrees of prudence. One man is a great deal more prudent than another, and one man is a great deal more intelligent than another, and it must depend a good deal on the prudence and intelligence of the particular trustee whether he is to blame or not. If he brings to the consideration of the question before the trustees all the mental capacity with which he is endowed, can he be expected to do more? I rather think that the rule of liability in such a case is better stated by Lord Stair than by any of the more recent cases. He says, Stair, i. 12, 10,—"By the nature of the contract, mandators, seeing their undertakings are gratuitous, ought to be but liable for such diligence as they use in their own affairs, and the mandant ought to impute it to himself that he made not choice of a more diligent person, which our custom follows, but still there must be *bona fides*." Now, if we apply that rule to the present case we must not demand of Mr Meek any more prudence or diligence or knowledge than he actually possesses and uses in the management of his own business. For that purpose we must consider what Mr Meek is."

LORD SHAND (DISSENTING ON THIS POINT): "It has been suggested that a new principle for determining the liability of trustees should be adopted—perhaps I am wrong in calling it new, as it is founded on the passage from Lord Stair which your Lordship has read. The suggestion, as I understand it, is that responsibility for improper investments should depend on the capacity of the trustee, so that one trustee, if a person of intelligence and ability, might be held responsible, while another of less business capacity would not be so. If the trustee is able to say, 'Well, it is quite true I have made a very bad investment, but I am a very stupid man', it is said that he shall be free from responsibility. I do not think a principle of that kind can receive effect in the administration of the law of trusts. If it were to be introduced now, and made a foundation for legal decision, the issue in each case would come to be, what was the capacity of the trustee? and it is easy to see that this would open up a very curious inquiry, and leave the Court with no settled rules or principles to be applied as cases occurred. We must, I think, keep to the much broader rule, and the only rule which we can proceed upon is that which has been recognised for years, namely, that a trustee shall be responsible if he does not in the transaction challenged shew the reasonable care which a man of ordinary prudence shews in the conduct of his own affairs."

Raes v. Meek
(1889) 16 R. (H.L.) 31
(on appeal from *Rae v. Meek, supra*)

LORD HERSCHELL: "The law bearing upon the liability of trustees has been recently **9.03** considered by your Lordships in the cases of *Whiteley v. Learoyd*, August 1, 1887, L.R. 12 App. Ca. 727, and *Knox v. Mackinnon*, August 7, 1888, 15 R. (H. L.) 83, the one coming from the English, the other from the Scottish Courts. I think these cases establish that the law in both countries requires of a trustee the same degree of diligence that a man of ordinary prudence would exercise in the management of his own affairs. The Lord President in the present case did not adopt this as the test. 'We must not demand,' he said, 'of Mr Meek any more prudence or diligence than he actually possesses or uses in the management of his own business. For that purpose we must consider what Mr Meek is.' As a result of this consideration he came to the conclusion that Mr Meek was not a man of business habits, or of great intelligence or discretion. I do not think that the inquiry thus entered upon was a relevant one. The test which the Lord President applied was rejected as erroneous by this House in *Knox v. Mackinnon*. Lord Watson there said,— 'It was seriously argued that according to the law of Scotland the responsibility of a gratuitous trustee must (apart from any special dispensation by the truster), be tested by reference not to an average standard but to the degree of care and prudence which he uses in the management of his private affairs. The rule, which is quite new to me, would be highly inconvenient in practice. In every case where neglect of duty is imputed to a body of trustees it would necessitate an exhaustive inquiry into the private transactions of each individual member, the interest of the trustee being to shew that he was a stupid fellow, careless in money matters, and that of his opponents to prove that he was a man of superior intelligence and exceptional shrewdness.'

I think therefore that the ground upon which the Lord President, and the learned Judges who concurred with him, rested their judgments upon this part of the case cannot be supported."

NOTES:

1. *The ordinary prudent "man" or "man of business"?* The standard of care required by Scots **9.04** law is objective, and not subjective. *Raes v. Meek* makes that perfectly clear. But is the standard that of the "ordinary prudent man", or the "ordinary prudent man of business"? The latter standard would seem to be a more exacting one, and it is the one which is required by English law (*Learoyd v. Whiteley* (1887) 12 App. Cas. 727). Scots law is unclear on this point.

   In *Crabbe v. Whyte* (1891) 18 R. 1065, Lord McLaren suggested that the House of Lords had adopted the "prudent man of business" standard in *Raes v. Meek* (*supra*) and *Knox v.*

Mackinnon (1888) 15 R. (H.L.) 83. However, these cases simply refer to the "ordinary prudent man", although the reference to *Learoyd v. Whiteley* in *Raes* suggests that their Lordships thought that Scots and English law were at one as to the standard of care. More recently, in *Tibbert v. McColl*, 1994 S.L.T. 1227, the Inner House has endorsed the "prudent man" standard of *Raes* with no reference to the "man of business".

2. This question is important, because it has been suggested that the standard required by English law is too high (see, *e.g.* Dennis R. Paling, "The Trustee's Duty of Skill and Care" (1973) 37 Conv. 48). Why should an executor of a small estate, perhaps acting on a gratuitous basis, be held to the standard of a man of business, when he may have no experience whatsoever of business? Why is such a standard necessary? Why, if the testator has specifically selected him as executor, should he be expected to exercise skills he clearly does not possess? It is not as if the "ordinary prudent man" is a dangerously low standard. This hypothetical man, after all, is presumably capable of knowing when he is out of his depth and requires to take specialist advice.

This, of course, simply raises the question of whether those who undertake trusteeship on a professional, remunerated basis should be held to a higher standard of care.

B. Should non-gratuitous trustees be held to a higher standard of care?

Dennis R. Paling, "The Trustee's Duty of Skill and Care"
(1973) 37 Conv. 48, 55–56

9.05 "The traditional view stated by Underhill and by the editors of subsequent editions of his textbook up to and including the tenth edition [*The Law Relating to Trusts and Trustees,* 1950] was that the same standard should be demanded of a trustee whether he acts gratuitously or receives payment. Romer J. in *Jobson v. Palmer* [[1893] 1 Ch. 71] expressed the same view. He thus held that a paid trustee, who had selected a servant with the same degree of prudence as an ordinary man of business would exercise in his own affairs, was not liable when the servant stole trust property.

But it is preferable to distinguish between the standards imposed upon paid and unpaid trustees, because the status of paid and unpaid trustees is different. The paid trustee is frequently a banker or actuary who advertises for business and has no personal relationship with the settlor. The unpaid trustee is frequently a personal friend of the settlor.

The editors of the eleventh edition of *Underhill* adopt this view, [11th ed. 1959, p323] and this is supported by Harman J. in *Re Waterman's Will Trusts* [1952 2 All E.R. 1054, 1055]: 'I do not forget that a paid trustee is expected to exercise a higher standard of diligence and knowledge than an unpaid trustee and that a bank which advertises itself largely in the public press as taking charge of administration is under a special duty.' This was in fact *obiter*, because Harman J. decided that an exclusion clause had effectively excluded liability. It is noteworthy that in the case before Harman J. the paid trustee was in fact a bank. Though it is possible for a private individual to be paid for his services, the paid trustee will usually be a bank or other commercial institution, and the difference in status makes desirable a difference in the degree of skill and care.

However, if there are different standards, and if the standard of skill and care expected of an unpaid trustee is that of an ordinary prudent man in the conduct of his own affairs, the higher standard to be imposed upon a paid trustee must be oppressively high. This may make the trustee excessively cautious, and because he chooses the safest investments the income produced will often be relatively less. Moreover, unless the court is prepared to examine the adequacy of the payment, it may enable the settlor to impose the higher standard of liability by making a token payment.

The distinction between paid and unpaid trustees could however be retained and these unfortunate consequences could be avoided if the standard of skill and care demanded of an unpaid trustee were to be that which he is accustomed to exercise with regard to his own private affairs, whilst the standard of skill and care demanded of a paid trustee was henceforth that which the ordinary prudent man would exercise in the management of his own affairs if he were regardful of the pecuniary interests in the future of those having claims upon him."

Bartlett v. Barclays Bank Trust Co Ltd (No. 1)
[1980] Ch. 515; [1980] 2 W.L.R. 430; [1980] 1 All E.R. 139

BRIGHTMAN J: "So far, I have applied the test of the ordinary prudent man of business. **9.06** Although I am not aware that the point has previously been considered, except briefly in *Re Waterman's Will Trusts* [1952] 2 All ER 1054, I am of opinion that a higher duty of care is plainly due from someone like a trust corporation which carries on a specialised business of trust management. A trust corporation holds itself out in its advertising literature as being above ordinary mortals. With a specialist staff of trained trust officers and managers, with ready access to financial information and professional advice, dealing with and solving trust problems day after day, the trust corporation holds itself out, and rightly, as capable of providing an expertise which it would be unrealistic to expect and unjust to demand from the ordinary prudent man or woman who accepts, probably unpaid and sometimes reluctantly from a sense of family duty, the burdens of a trusteeship. Just as, under the law of contract, a professional person possessed of a particular skill is liable for breach of contract if he neglects to use the skill and experience which he professes, so I think that a professional corporate trustee is liable for breach of trust if loss is caused to the trust fund because it neglects to exercise the special care and skill which it professes to have. The advertising literature of the bank was not in evidence (other than the scale of fees) but counsel for the bank did not dispute that trust corporations, including the bank, hold themselves out as possessing a superior ability for the conduct of trust business, and in any event I would take judicial notice of that fact. Having expressed my view of the higher duty required from a trust corporation, I should add that the bank's counsel did not dispute the proposition."

Kenneth McK. Norrie and Eilidh M. Scobbie, *Trusts* (1991), p. 141

"In the English first instance decision of *Bartlett v. Barclays Bank Trust Co. (No. 1)*, the **9.07** judge stated *obiter* that a corporate trustee carrying on a specialised business of trust management, which holds itself out as being skilled as a trustee, will be subject to a higher standard of care and diligence than a non-corporate trustee. There is no authority for this proposition in Scots law, and certainly the high authority from last century laying down the standard of the ordinary prudent man makes no such qualification. It is suggested that the approach in *Bartlett* ought to be resisted. The standard of care required is designed to protect the beneficiaries, and from their point of view, it is wholly fortuitous whether or not the trustee is corporate or non-corporate, professional or non-professional. The corporate trustee does not hold itself out to the beneficiary, but to the truster. Also, there is authority in the delict cases for suggesting that an amateur performing a function requiring skill and competence will be subject to the same standard as that expected from the professional, for the standard is determined by the nature of the task rather than by the competence of the performed. This is as it should be in trust law also."

NOTES:

1. In *Lutea Trs Ltd v. Orbis Trs Guernsey Ltd*, 1997 S.C.L.R. 735, the Inner House reserved **9.08** opinion on whether "the standard of care required of professional trustees might be different from and higher than that required of gratuitous trustees". Lord McCluskey took the view that the breach of trust in that case was "so gross that it amounts to *culpa lata* regardless of whether the trustees are professional or gratuitous". Accordingly, it was unnecessary to decide the point. *Cf. Fales v. Canada Permanent Trust Co.* [1977] 2 S.C.R. 302, where the Canadian Supreme Court avoided resolving the issue on similar grounds.
2. It should be noted that there are two separate issues here, which are linked and often conflated, but which should, strictly speaking, be separated out. One is the *Bartlett* principle:

that a trustee who is selected because he professes to possess a particular care and skill should be held liable for breach of trust if he fails to exercise that ability. (It is arguable that this principle has nothing to do with the fact that the trustee is remunerated and should not be limited to remunerated trustees, although Brightman J. did appear to limit it in this fashion in *Bartlett*).

The second is the *Waterman* principle: that a trustee who is remunerated is to be held to a "higher standard of care" than a gratuitous trustee. This is more difficult than the *Bartlett* principle, because it is far from clear what it means. Wilson & Duncan refer (at 28–17) to a "higher standard of diligence and knowledge" but, with respect, this is close to meaningless without some further guidance as to what this standard is. Perhaps, if the normal Scottish standard is the "ordinary prudent man", the higher standard is the "ordinary prudent man of business"?

3. It is interesting that while, in *Bartlett*, Brightman J. justifies holding the professional trustee to a higher standard of care by reference to principles of contract law, Norrie & Scobbie oppose it by reference to principles of delict. Why the delictual analogy is to be preferred to the contractual one is unclear, particularly as Norrie & Scobbie (at p. 140) adopt Walker's view that liability for breach of trust is "an obligation *sui generis* and not wholly analogous either to a contractual or delictual obligation" (in contrast to the view of Wilson & Duncan, who assert (at 28–15) that the liability is "*ex delicto* or *ex quasi delicto*"). (For further discussion of the nature of liability for breach of trust, see *Ross v. Davy*, 1996 S.C.L.R. 369)

In some ways, the contractual analogy seems more apposite, as the obligation of trusteeship is normally voluntarily undertaken (like a contractual obligation) and not imposed by law (like a delictual obligation). (This is not always true, of course, as the law relating to legally implied trusts (*supra* paras 2.29 *et seq.*) illustrates. But the *Bartlett* principle would presumably not apply in such a case, as the trustee in a legally implied trust has not been selected because he professes to possess certain skills, nor is he remunerated.)

4. Norrie & Scobbie's opposition to differential standards of care also rests on the statement that "[t]he standard of care required is designed to protect the beneficiaries, and from their point of view, it is wholly fortuitous whether or not the trustee is corporate or non-corporate, professional or non-professional". But if the truster can vary the standard of care required of the trustees by the protection of an immunity clause (see *infra*, para. 9.25), why should he not also be able to vary the standard required by deciding whether or not the trustees should be remunerated?

Additionally, one might respond that the standard of care is also designed to protect the trustee (by limiting the potential scope of his liability for losses to the trust estate). Is a gratuitous trustee not perhaps deserving of more protection than a professional one? It might be noted that Scots law did formerly draw a distinction of this sort between gratuitous and non-gratuitous trustees: see, for example, section 3(d) of the Trusts (Scotland) Act 1921 (*infra*, para. 9.23), which in its previous incarnation as section 1 of the Trusts (Scotland) Act 1861 extended only to gratuitous trustees.

5. Norrie & Scobbie's objections notwithstanding, the principle stated by Brightman J. in *Bartlett* appears to be gaining in acceptance. It has been referred to with approval in a number of first instance Australian and Canadian decisions: *Gill v. Eagle Star Nominees Ltd.*, Supreme Court of New South Wales, September 22, 1993, unreported; *Australian Securities Commission v. AS Nominees Ltd.* (1995) 133 A.L.R. 1; *Wilkinson v. Feldworth Financial Services Pty Ltd*, Supreme Court of New South Wales, November 30, 1998, unreported; *Ford v. Laidlaw Carriers Ltd* (1993) 44 A.C.W.S. (3d) 243.

2. INTERDICT

A.J.P. Menzies, *The Law of Scotland Affecting Trustees* (2nd ed., 1913)

9.09 "The first remedy of a beneficiary against a trustee is naturally a preventive one. Where the beneficiary desires to interfere with the action of a trustee who proposes to do anything that the beneficiary thinks *ultra vires*, the proper legal process for the purpose is that of suspension and interdict.

Where fraudulent abuse of their position as trustees is alleged against a majority who have resolved upon a line of conduct, a petition for their removal, and not an interdict, is the proper remedy."

NOTES:

1. Interdict has been defined as follows: **9.10**

> "a remedy, by decree of court, either against a wrong in course of being done, or against an apprehended violation of a party's rights, only to be awarded on evidence of the wrong, or on reasonable grounds of apprehension that such violation is intended." (*Hay's Trs v. Young* (1878) 4 R. 398, *per* Lord Ormidale at 401)

The order prohibits the defender from doing the act specified. Although Menzies refers to "suspension and interdict", "interdict is now deemed competent to stop wrongs in progress as well as wrongs apprehended, and the element of suspension is being forgotten." (Walker, *Civil Remedies*, p. 214). It is now normal to simply refer to "interdict".

2. Note that the wrong must be "apprehended", or "in course of being done". Interdict is useless where the wrong has already occurred, and will not be granted in such a case. A past breach of trust may of course, in appropriate circumstances, be grounds to apprehend that a future violation is likely.

3. An interim interdict may be sought pending the outcome of a full court action. Breach of interdict can have serious consequences, including imprisonment, although this is unusual. For a full treatment of the law of interdict, see Scott Robinson, *The Law of Interdict* (2nd ed., 1994); Walker, *Civil Remedies*, Chapter 11.

3. DAMAGES

Town and County Bank Ltd. v. Walker
(1904) 12 S.L.T. 411

LORD KYLLACHY: "there may be varieties in breaches or alleged breaches of trust. A breach **9.11** of trust may consist of embezzlement, or it may arise simply from failure to account, or it may consist, as alleged here, of some act or default which amounts only to some irregularity or error of judgment for which, nevertheless, there may be personal liability. But in all such cases the result is simply to create a liability by the trustee to make good to the trust estate the loss which he has caused. And that liability is just like any other debt due to the estate that has to be enforced by the existing trustees. . ."

NOTES:

1. *The nature of the remedy.* Although this remedy is commonly referred to in the textbooks as **9.12** "damages", in *Tibbert v. McColl*, 1994 S.L.T. 1227, the Inner House expressed some doubt as to whether this was the correct way of characterising the remedy.

2. *Quantifying the loss.* Usually, quantifying the loss to the trust will be a straightforward question of fact. So, in *Forman v. Burns* (1853) 12 D. 362 (*supra* para. 6.10), an executor failed over a period of two years to do diligence to recover a debt of £250 due to the estate. The debtor did, however, make a payment to account of £50 during that period. The executor was therefore liable to make good the balance of £200.

   A more difficult case is *Whyte v. Burt* (1851) 13 D. 679. In that case, trust property was exposed for sale at auction at an upset price of £6,500. There were only two bidders, a Mr Anderson and the trustee (Mr Burt). Anderson bid up to £6,690 (his first bid being £6,505), but the trustee bid £6,700. The "sale" to the trustee was never implemented, and the lands were exposed for sale a second time, when they were purchased by Burt (who had, by now, been removed as a trustee) for £5,580. It was held that Burt was liable to the trust-estate for the sum of £1,110, this being the difference between what Anderson was willing to pay at the first auction (£6,690) and the sum which the land was eventually sold for. It is difficult to understand the logic of this decision. If Burt had not improperly participated in the first auction, Anderson would never have made an offer as high as £6,690 and the trust would have received only £6,505 (or perhaps only the upset price of £6,500) for the property. The effect of Burt paying £1,110 in damages would, therefore, be to put the trust-estate in a better position than it would have been had he not participated in the first action.

3. *Causation and the inaction of subsequent trustees*. In *Duncan v. Newlands* (1882) 20 S.L.R. 8, trustees improperly continued to hold City of Glasgow Bank stock which had been owned by the testator. One of the trustees died, and the other continued in office. The bank later collapsed. It was held that the deceased trustee's representatives were liable in damages despite the surviving trustee's failure to sell the bank stock. Lord Kinnear stated (at 9):

> "But it is maintained that since the failure of the bank did not take place until nearly three years after Mr Newlands' death, the consequent loss to the trust-estate is not directly attributable to any failure of duty with which he is chargeable, but to neglect or breach of duty on the part of his co-trustee, who survived him, and who failed to realise investments improperly made or continued by him within a reasonable time after his death. I am unable to give effect to that contention. The loss which has occurred is the direct and natural consequence of the mal-administration for which Mr Newlands is admittedly responsible. It may be true that after his death the surviving trustee might have obviated the ill consequences of his breach of duty by selling the bank stock; in other words, by undoing what he and his colleague had wrongly done. But I am unable to see that the failure of one trustee to rectify the error of another should relieve that other of responsibility. The deceased trustee might have been relieved of investments made or sanctioned by him had they been altered after his death. But he or his representatives must, in my opinion, remain responsible for a course of administration with which his surviving colleague has not interfered."

A. Showing that the breach of trust did not cause the loss

Millar's Trs v. Polson
(1897) 24 R. 1038

9.13 LORD PRESIDENT (ROBERTSON): "There is no controversy as to the material facts of this case; and I accept unreservedly the evidence of the defender, which is perfectly candid and distinct.

It appears then, that in the beginning of February 1895 it came to the knowledge of the defender that Mr Elliot, his sole co-trustee, had not lodged in bank on deposit-receipt a sum of £150 of trust money, which had been entrusted to him for that purpose. This information did not come from Mr Elliot. The defender at once went to Mr Elliot and asked for explanations. He got none that satisfied him. Admittedly, Mr Elliot had not put the money in bank, and he gave no account of what he had done with it. Some words were used about a five per cent investment, but they did not deceive the defender. He says, frankly, 'I thought he was keeping the money in his possession and using it for his own purposes, and was offering to pay five per cent upon it or something of that kind.'

From February onwards then the defender knew that this £150 of trust money was in Mr Elliot's hands, contrary to express instructions, and that it was applied to his own uses. It admits of no doubt that, *prima facie*, it was the duty of the defender to take immediate steps to compel the replacement of the money. Beyond vague promises that the money would be repaid, the defender got nothing to re-assure him. The fact of Elliot's default could only be accounted for by his being desperately in want of money. The defender does not profess to have at first abstained from action for any politic reason, in the belief that some temporary difficulty was to be tided over; and, as time passed, things looked worse and worse, and called more and more clamantly for decisive action. By midsummer the defender knew, apart from the default in question, that Elliot was in difficulties. In October he saw Elliot's brother-in law, Mr Stevenson, and his suspicions were confirmed. Yet from February to November the defender allowed himself (to use his own phrase) to be trifled with by Elliot. He clung to the hope that the money would be repaid, and took no legal action.

The true state of Elliot's finances and his inability to pay anything were not known to the defender, or indeed to anyone outside Elliot's own office; and accordingly are not advanced by the defender as accounting for his inaction.

It seems to me that these facts constitute a clear, and I may say, a strong case of *culpa lata*. The defender was one of two trustees; his co-trustee appropriates to his own uses £150 of trust money, which he had been entrusted with for investment, and conceals the fact, which was only accidentally discovered; no presentable excuse is made, nor is any real prospect given of the money being replaced, if time is given. It is, of course, disagreeable to take a co-trustee by the throat, but if a man undertakes to act as trustee he must face the necessity of doing disagreeable things when they become necessary in order to keep the estate intact. A trustee is not entitled to purchase a quiet life at the expense of the estate, or to act as good-natured men sometimes do in their own affairs, in letting things slide and losing money rather than create ill-feeling.

If it be asked what ought the defender to have done, the answer is obvious. Owing to the default of his sole co-trustee, the defender was placed in the position of a sole acting trustee, deprived of the legal assistance of his co-trustee. His duty was clear. He ought without delay to have instructed a lawyer to recover the missing £150, and he ought to have seen to it (by himself or through the lawyer) that the rest of the trust-estate was safe, and did not get into the hands of Elliot. A lawyer so instructed would naturally have written Elliot, intimating that unless the £150 was replaced within a given number of days a summons would be served, and steps would have been taken to prevent the Whitsunday rent from getting into Elliot's hands.

The latter precaution as well as the former was omitted by the defender, and the Whitsunday rent of Bellevue was allowed to be uplifted by Elliot. It is nothing to say that the defender did not know that Elliot was uplifting these rents. Once he knew that his sole co-trustee was intercepting trust funds and applying them to his own uses, the defender ought to have taken alarm about the whole trust-estate, and to have seen where it was and where it was going.

The next defence is that, even assuming the defender has made himself liable for the loss resulting to the trust-estate through his omissions, yet no loss has in facto occurred, because nothing could have been recovered from Elliot. It is necessary to observe that, in the view which I take, this defence does not apply to the Whitsunday rent, for, if the defender had done his duty, it would have been intercepted and would never have got into Elliot's hands at all. Of the two sums which I have mentioned, this defence can only apply to the £150.

Now, it is clear that the burden of proof is on the defender. It is for the defender to prove that if he had done his duty the loss would equally have resulted. The defender has recognised this, and has placed before us very full information about the financial position of Elliot. He has proved that in and for long prior to 1895 Elliot was hopelessly insolvent. Now, where a trustee states the defender which we are now considering, I should not in every case be content with proof that the debtor's own means were exhausted. Some men, after their own means are exhausted, have other resources,— they can appeal to their friends. Take the case of a young merchant, the son of a rich and liberal man. If he were indebted to a trust-estate the circumstances might be such that, even if it were proved that his own means were exhausted, the trustee might not have negatived the likelihood that, if action had been raised, the debt would have been recovered, especially if it touched the honour of the debtor. But the present case is in strong contrast to that which I have figured. The sequestrated estate of Elliot is not expected to pay any dividend at all. He is about seventy years of age. He had been in pecuniary straits for years. He had borrowed from friends, but seems to have come to an end of his resources in that quarter before 1895, and to have betaken himself to less defensible methods. The witness Steadman says,— 'He paid pressing creditors by taking from one client to pay another.'

Now, on this evidence, I am prepared to hold that the defender has made out his case. The only suggestion to the contrary which is at all consistent with the facts comes to be that if the defender had sued Elliot for the £150, Elliot would have stolen the money from some third party and have paid it to the defender. I own that there is great plausibility in this conjecture. But in such a surmise, I feel myself to be out of the region of legitimate inference.

The only other suggestion of possible aid coming from friends arises from the fact that in November 1895 some claim by people called Purvis' trustees was bought off at 5s. per £ by General Boswell, a brother-in-law of Elliot. We do not know anything but the fact, and I am unable to infer from this that General Boswell would have intervened, or that any other General Boswell was available. The *onus* on the defender cannot impose on him the necessity of negativing such remote conjectures.

My opinion on the whole case is that, in February 1895, and certainly before Whitsunday 1895, it was the duty of the defender to take steps for the recovery of the £150 and for the interception of the Whitsunday rent of Bellevue, that his omission to do so constitutes *culpa lata*, that he is liable for the Whitsunday 1895 rent of Bellevue, with interest from that date, and that no loss has been sustained by the trust-estate through the omission of the defender in the matter of the £150. The pursuers claimed from the defender another half-year's rent of Bellevue due at Martimas 1894. As that rent fell due and was ingathered by Elliot before the defalcation of the £150 and its discovery, some *culpa lata* must be found to support this demand other than that which I hold proved. I have only to say that I think the pursuers' case on this head has entirely failed, but even if it had not, the same defence would avail the defender as I sustain regarding the £150. In my view, the Lord Ordinary's interlocutor must be recalled and decree granted for the Whitsunday rent of Bellevue, with interest, the defender being *quoad ultra* assolzied."

Lords Adam and Kinnear concurred.

NOTE:

9.14   Dicta to the effect that the *onus* is on the trustee to show that his breach of trust has not caused the loss can also be found in *Carruthers v. Carruthers* (1896) 23 R. (H.L.) 55, and *Crabbe v. Whyte* (1891) 18 R. 1065, *per* Lord McLaren at 1069 (where it is said that a trustee who makes a negligent investment may be able to escape liability by satisfying the court that "the loss was not caused by his negligence, but is due to the depreciation of property or other causes").

It should not be thought that this is an exception to the rule that the burden of proof is on the pursuer in a civil case. Rather, it indicates that a pursuer, by proving (for example) that (a) the trustee negligently failed to take steps to recover a debt, and (b) that the debt was never recovered by the trust, then that is sufficient to discharge the persuasive burden of proof, and a provisional burden then falls upon the defender (the trustee) to rebut the presumption which has been raised by the pursuer's evidence. (See further *Walkers on Evidence*, paras 2.6 *et seq.*).

B. The problem of set-off

9.15   Not every breach of trust will cause a loss to the trust estate. Indeed, some breaches of trust might even be very profitable for the trust. How are damages quantified, therefore, where a trustee engages in multiple breaches of trust—some profitable; others not? Is he entitled to ask that the profit occasioned by one breach be set off against the loss created by another when damages are quantified? The traditional view is stated by Mackenzie Stuart:

A. Mackenzie Stuart, *The Law of Trusts* (1932), p. 375

"A trustee cannot, where there are two separate transactions in breach of trust on one of which there has been a gain and on the other a loss, set the gain on the one against the loss on the other. The profit is part of the trust estate, while the loss is a personal liability. Still less can he set off his beneficial administration generally against a specific breach of trust which has caused loss. But a trustee is only liable for the actual loss on each complete transaction. When there are losses and gains on various items in that transaction, he is entitled to have it taken as a whole and to benefit if the total of the gains equal the losses."

NOTES:

9.16   1. See also Menzies, p. 1083, which is to similar effect. English law has consistently taken the
              same position (*Dimes v. Scott* (1824) 4 Russ. 195; 38 E.R. 778; *Wiles v. Gresham* (1854) 2
              Drew. 258; 61 E.R. 718).

2. Note Mackenzie Stuart's statement that "a trustee is only liable for the actual loss on each complete transaction". The obvious question is, how is it to be determined whether two items are separate or constituent parts of a "complete transaction"? Sometimes, this will be straightforward, as in *Henderson v. Henderson's Trs* (1900) 2 F. 1295, where trustees improperly guaranteed debenture stock for a commission of £80. As a result, they subsequently became liable to take up stock to the value of £1,285. It was held that they could set off the commission of £80 against that loss and were therefore only liable to the trust-estate for the sum of £1,205.

The following case, however, is more difficult:

Bartlett v. Barclays Bank Trust Co Ltd (No. 1)
[1980] Ch. 515; [1980] 2 W.L.R. 430; [1980] 1 All E.R. 139

Trustees negligently failed to prevent a company, in which the trust held a controlling interest, from engaging in a speculative property development transaction involving property opposite the Old Bailey in London, which resulted in a substantial loss.   **9.17**

BRIGHTMAN J. (after holding that the trustees were liable to make good the loss): "There remains this defence, which I take from para. 26 of the amended pleading:

'In about 1963 the Old Company purchased a site at Woodbridge Road, Guildford, pursuant to the policy pleaded in paragraph 19 hereof, for the sum of £79,000, and re-sold the same for £350,000 to MEPC Ltd. in 1973. The net profit resulting from such sale was £271,000. If, which is denied, the Defendant is liable for breach of trust, whether as alleged in the amended Statement of Claim or otherwise, the Defendant claims credit for such sum of £271,000 or other sum found to be gained in taking any accounts or inquiries.'

The general rule as stated in all the textbooks, with some reservations, is that where a trustee is liable in respect of distinct breaches of trust, one of which has resulted in a loss and the other in a gain, he is not entitled to set off the gain against the loss, unless they arise in the same transaction: see *Halsbury's Laws of England*, 3rd ed., vol. 38 (1962), p. 1046; *Snell's Principles of Equity*, 27th ed. (1973), p. 276; *Lewin on the Law of Trusts*, 16th ed. (1964), p. 670 and *Underhill's Law of Trusts and Trustees*, 12th ed. (1970), p. 634. The relevant cases are, however, not altogether easy to reconcile. All are centenarians and none is quite like the present. The Guildford development stemmed from exactly the same policy and (to a lesser degree because it proceeded less for) exemplified the same folly as the Old Bailey project. Part of the profit was in fact used to finance the Old Bailey disaster. By sheer luck the gamble paid off handsomely, on capital account. I think it would be unjust to deprive the bank of this element of salvage in the course of assessing the cost of the shipwreck. My order will therefore reflect the bank's right to an appropriate set-off."

NOTES:

1. It is submitted that this decision should not be understood as undermining the prohibition on set-off. It is probably best understood as holding that the two transactions were *not* truly separate, as they were part of the same speculative investment policy. Accordingly, as they were not separate transactions, set-off was available.   **9.18**
2. Norrie & Scobbie argue (at p. 144) that *Bartlett* suggests "that English law adopts a slightly different position" from Scots law on this point. But why should this be the case? They justify this position with reference to Walker's *Civil Remedies*: "Walker suggests [at 1072] that gains must be accounted for and losses must be reimbursed whether they come from distinct and separate breaches of trust, or from the same breach." The relevant paragraph from Walker's text contains two relevant propositions, which are worth quoting in full:

- "A trustee who has incurred liability to make good the loss occasioned by a breach of trust in respect of one portion of the trust funds may not set off against this liability any gain which has accrued to another portion of the trust funds through the same or a distinct and unconnected breach of trust." Walker cites no authority for this point, and insofar as it suggests (as do Norrie & Scobbie) that set-off may not be invoked even where the gain and loss are attributable to the same breach of trust, it is inconsistent with *Henderson v. Henderson's Trs* (*supra*) and the passage in Mackenzie Stuart's text quoted above.
- "Each distinct transaction must be looked at, and if it is in breach of trust, the trustee must make good any loss thereon." All of the authorities cited by Walker for this point are English—the same cases which were considered by Brightman J. in *Bartlett*. A statement by a Scottish author based solely on nineteenth century English decisions provides no grounds for asserting that a twentieth century English decision is inconsistent with Scots law. But in any case, the transactions in *Bartlett* were not "distinct": they were part of the same speculative investment policy.

3. It is submitted that there is no reason in principle why Scots law should reject the approach of Brightman J. in *Bartlett*. Indeed, it is submitted that it would be wrong in principle to do so. Had set-off not been permitted in *Bartlett*, then the trust-estate would have been put in a *better* position than it would have been had the trustees not negligently allowed the company to engage in speculative property investment. To deny set-off in such a case would mean that the negligent trustee would not be required to do *more* than make good the loss which he has caused to the trust. Such a "windfall" effect seems inappropriate and unnecessary.

4. COUNT, RECKONING AND PAYMENT (ACCOUNTING)

D.M. Walker, *The Law of Civil Remedies in Scotland* (1974), p. 304

9.19 "A claim for count, reckoning and payment is appropriate where there is a right to demand and a liability to render an account, where the pursuer believes that money is due to him and he wishes to exact payment but he cannot state precisely how much is due, and accordingly in the first place calls on the defender to count and reckon, or account for his intromissions, and to pay the balance found justly due. The main conclusions are for the production of accounts, and for payment of a sum as stated in the balance, or such other sums as may be ascertained to be the true balance. It is a mixture of an action *ad factum praestandum*, to produce accounts, with an action for payment."

NOTES:

9.20
1. An action of count, reckoning and payment is based in part on the legal duty of the trustee to keep accounts. It follows, therefore, that in the exceptional cases where there is no such duty on the trustee, an action of count, reckoning and payment is likely to be inappropriate. See *Leitch v. Leitch*, 1927 S.C. 823, *supra*, para 6.22.
2. Where a trustee has not kept proper accounts, he is theoretically liable to a "strict accounting": "that is, he is given the benefit only of such items as the beneficiaries care to admit." (*Pollard v. Sturrock's Exrs*, 1975 S.L.T. (Notes) 76, *per* Lord Guthrie at 76, quoting Mackenzie Stuart, p. 220). See *supra*, para 6.17.
3. An action of count, reckoning and payment should generally have the same practical result as an action for damages. However, it has two advantages in appropriate cases. Firstly, it provides a means of ascertaining the quantum of damages where this cannot be otherwise done. Secondly, it may remain available where an action for damages is barred by prescription. See *Hobday v. Kirkpatrick's Trs*, 1985 S.L.T. 197, but *cf. Ross v. Davy*, 1996 S.C.L.R. 369.

5. REMOVAL OF A TRUSTEE

One remedy for a breach of trust may be to petition the Court to remove the offending trustee(s) (and, **9.21** if appropriate, appoint a new trustee or trustees). See *supra*, Chapter 5 for the relevant rules.

6. REPORTING THE MATTER TO THE APPROPRIATE AUTHORITIES

9.22

If the breach of trust is a particularly serious one, it may be appropriate to report the matter to the police (if a crime is suspected) or (if, for example, the breach involves illegal dealing in securities) a regulatory body such as the Financial Services Authority, the Department of Trade and Industry or Stock Exchange if appropriate. If the trustee is a professional such as a solicitor or accountant, complaints may also be made to the relevant professional body. Representations could also be made to the Lord Advocate in respect of maladministration of a public trust.

For the regulatory regime relating to charitable trusts, see *infra*, Chapter 11.

7. LIABILITY FOR CO-TRUSTEES, PREDECESSORS AND OMISSIONS

Trusts (Scotland) Act 1921, s.3(d)

What trusts shall be held to include

3.—All trusts shall be held to include the following powers and provisions unless the **9.23** contrary be expressed (that is to say)—

[. . .]

    (d) A provision that each trustee shall be liable only for his own acts and intromissions and shall not be liable for the acts and intromissions of co-trustees and shall not be liable for omissions. . .

NOTES:

1. This provision derives from section 1 of the Trusts (Scotland) Act 1861, although the **9.24** protection under that section only extended to gratuitous trustees. It is generally stated that s.3(d) is "declaratory of the common law" (Wilson & Duncan, 28–41; Norrie & Scobbie, p. 147), but the position is not quite so simple. Those authors cite McLaren, 2267 for this point, but McLaren was concerned with the 1861 Act—which only protected gratuitous trustees. So, does this mean that non-gratuitous trustees were not so protected at common law? And, if so, does this lend weight to the argument that a non-gratuitous trustee is to be held to a higher standard of care than a gratuitous one? (See *supra*, para. 9.05).

2. As to the effect of s.3(d) on the liability of trustees for the acts and intromissions of their predecessors, see *Mackenzie's Exr v. Thomson's Trs*, 1965 S.C. 154, *per* Lord Cameron at 156:

> "By [this section] trustees are liable only for their own acts and intromissions and are not liable for the acts and intromissions of co-trustees, nor are they liable for omissions. From this it is to be inferred that trustees in office are, *prima facie* at least, not liable for the acts and intromissions of their predecessors, unless they have knowingly adopted or approved them, in which event they, in effect, make them their own. But in the absence of exceptional circumstances the only obligation of existing trustees is to account to the beneficiaries, and, while this includes an obligation to account for the intromissions of previous trustees, it does not make the existing trustees liable for those intromissions. . ."

See also *Scott v. Gray* (1862) 1 M. 57.

8. IMMUNITY CLAUSES

9.25 It is common for trust deeds to contain provisions which purport to limit the scope of the trustee's liability for breach of trust. The trust deed in *Knox v. Mackinnon* (1888) 15 R. (H.L.) 83 contained the following immunity clause (at 86):

> The trustees "shall not be liable for omissions, errors, or neglect of management, nor *singuli in solidum*, but each shall be liable for his own actual intromissions only".

As might be expected, such clauses have grown more complex and legalistic. The immunity clause in the trust deed in *Lutea Trs Ltd. v. Orbis Trs Guernsey Ltd*, 1997 S.C.L.R. 735, at 740, may be more reflective of modern practice:

> "The trustee shall not be in any way liable for any loss suffered as a result of the exercise of any of the powers given to them by these presents or for any fall in value of or for the validity and sufficiency of investments, securities and others held by them or on their account whether made or retained by the trustees or for omissions or for neglect in their management or for one another or for factors, attorneys, solicitors, accountants, stockbrokers, agents or others appointed or employed by them except that they were habit or repute responsible at the time of their appointment or employment but each for his or her own actual personal intromissions only."

> In *Inglis and Ors, Petrs*, 1965 S.L.T. (Notes) 326, Lord President Clyde suggested that the use of such clauses "only creates a false sense of security in the minds of the trustees". How much protection do they actually provide to trustees? In *Knox v. Mackinnon* (1886) 15 R. (H.L.) 83, Lord Watson (at 86) had the following to say about the immunity clause quoted above:

> "I see no reason to doubt that a clause conceived in these or similar terms will afford a considerable measure of protection to trustees who have *bona fide* abstained from closely superintending the administration of the trust, or who have committed mere errors of judgment whilst acting with a single eye to the benefit of the trust and of the persons whom it concerns; but it is settled in the law of Scotland that such a clause is ineffectual to protect a trustee against the consequences of *culpa lata*, or of gross negligence on his part, or of any conduct which is inconsistent with *bona fides*. I think it is equally clear that the clause will afford no protection to trustees who, from motives however laudable in themselves, act in plain violation of the duty which they owe to the individuals beneficially interested in the funds which they administer. I agree with the opinion expressed by Lords Ivory, Gillies and Murray in *Seton v. Dawson*, 4 D. 318, to the effect 'that clauses of this kind do not protect against positive breach of duty'."

It seems that it is still accepted that such clauses do not excuse trustees from liability for gross negligence (*Lutea Trustees*). Given that the reported cases seem to be uniformly ones in which it was held that the clause did *not* excuse liability for the negligence in question (see Wilson & Duncan, paras 28–42 to 28–48), one might wonder exactly what they do excuse. Lord Watson suggests that they may excuse "mere errors of judgment", but it is not clear that "mere errors of judgment" are negligent in the first place—and if they are not negligent, then reliance on an immunity clause to escape liability is unnecessary.

It might be argued that the issue is a simple one: without an immunity clause, trustees will be liable for negligence—while with an immunity clause, they will only be liable for *gross* negligence. But that rests on the assumption that there is a distinction between "negligence" and "gross negligence", which is far from obvious. As Rolfe B. stated in *Wilson v. Brett* (1843) 11 M. & W. 113, at 115–116; 152 E.R. 737, at 739, "I can see no difference between negligence and gross negligence—it is the same thing with the addition of a vituperative epithet." This observation seems to have been of importance to the Inner House in the medical negligence case of *Hunter v. Hanley*, 1955 S.C. 200, where the concept of "gross negligence" was effectively rejected as part of the law of delict. The Inner House did note that "gross negligence" appeared to remain of importance in the law of trusts, but made no attempt to explain how this might be distinguished from ordinary negligence.

If there is no difference between "gross" and "mere" negligence, and immunity clauses do not exclude liability for "gross" negligence, then they logically cannot exclude liability for "mere" negligence either, and are clearly of limited use (particularly given the protection of section 3(d) of the

Trusts (Scotland) Act 1921, discussed *infra* at para. 9.24). But perhaps that is no bad thing. As Lord President Clyde observed in *Clarke v. Clarke's Trs*, 1925 S.C. 693, at 707:

> "It is difficult to imagine that any clause of indemnity in a trust settlement could be capable of being construed to mean that the trustees might with impunity neglect to execute their duty as trustees—in other words, that they were licensed to perform their duty carelessly."

A rather different approach (and a different interpretation of these cases) can be found in the English case of *Armitage v. Nurse* [1998] Ch. 241, where it was held that a clause which excluded liability for anything short of "actual fraud" was valid. In reaching this decision, Millett L.J. opined (at 255) that:

> "Each of the Scottish cases contains dicta, especially in the speeches of the Scottish members of the House of Lords, which have been taken by academic writers to indicate that no trustee exemption clause in a Scottish settlement could exonerate a trustee from his own *culpa lata*. But in fact all the cases were merely decisions on the true construction of the particular clauses under consideration, which were in common form at the time."

He did, however, make the following observations (at 256):

> "At the same time, it must be acknowledged that the view is widely held that these clauses have gone too far, and that trustees who charge for their services and who, as professional men, would not dream of excluding liability for ordinary professional negligence should not be able to rely on a trustee exemption clause excluding liability for gross negligence. Jersey introduced a law in 1989 which denies effect to a trustee exemption clause which purports to absolve a trustee from liability for his own 'fraud, wilful misconduct or gross negligence'. The subject is presently under consideration in this country by the Trust Law Committee under the chairmanship of Sir John Vinelott. If clauses such as [the one under consideration] are to be denied effect, then in my opinion this should be done by Parliament, which will have the advantage of wide consultation with interested bodies and the advice of the Trust Law Committee."

See also Gerard McCormack, "The Liability of Trustees for Gross Negligence" [1998] Conv. 100.

9. STATUTORY PROTECTIONS FOR TRUSTEES

A. Section 30 of the 1921 Act

Trusts (Scotland) Act 1921, s.30

Trustee not to be chargeable with breach of trust for lending money on security of any property on certain conditions

30.—(1) Any trustee lending money on the security of any property shall not be **9.26** chargeable with breach of trust by reason only of the proportion borne by the amount of the loan to the value of the property at the time when the loan was made, provided that it shall appear to the court that in making such loan the trustee was acting upon a report as to the value of the property made by a person whom the trustee reasonably believed to be an able practical valuator instructed and employed independently of any owner of the property, whether such valuator carried on business in the locality where the property is situated or elsewhere, and that the loan by itself or in combination with any other loan or loans upon the property ranking prior to or *pari passu* with the loan in question does not exceed two equal third parts of the value of the property as stated in such report, and this section shall apply to a loan upon any property on which the trustees can lawfully lend.

(2) This section shall apply to transfers of existing securities as well as to new securities, and in its application to a partial transfer of an existing security the expression "the amount of the loan" shall include the amount of any other loan or loans upon the property ranking prior to or *pari passu* with the loan in question.

Notes:

9.27

1. This provision derives from the Trusts (Scotland) Amendment Act 1891, s.4. The corresponding English provision is the Trustee Act 1925, s.8 (which derives from the Trustee Act 1893, s.8 and the Trustee Act 1888, s.4). The English provision includes the additional requirement that "the loan was made under the advice of the surveyor or valuer expressed in the report".

2. Historically, the protection offered by this provision would have been of considerable importance, because loans on the security of heritable property in Scotland were one of the very few implied powers of investment which trustees had at common law. (See *supra* para. 7.05). It is doubtful that this type of investment would be attractive to many trusts today, given the competitive nature of the market in lending on the security of heritable property. A trust would normally be unable to compete with commercial lenders without taking a degree of risk which would generally be considered unacceptable for the investment of trust property.

3. Trustees are not *required* to follow these provisions when lending money on the security of property, but this section protects them if they do. The fact that they have not followed these provisions does not necessarily mean that they have breached their duty of care, nor that they are barred from seeking relief under s.32 of the 1921 Act if necessary. (*Palmer v. Emerson* [1911] 1 Ch. 758, and see *infra*, para. 9.30). It might well, in an appropriate case, be reasonable for trustees to lend money notwithstanding that the conditions of s.30 are not met. In *Lutea Trs Ltd v. Orbis Trs Guernsey Ltd*, 1997 S.C.L.R. 735, counsel for the pursuers suggested (at 744) that "there might be circumstances in which trustees acting under this trust deed could lend without security—for example, to a highly reputable bank", and that would seem correct in principle.

B. Section 31 of the 1921 Act

Trusts (Scotland) Act 1921, s.31

Power of court to make orders in case of breach of trust

9.28   **31.** Where a trustee shall have committed a breach of trust at the instigation or request or with the consent in writing of a beneficiary, the court may, if it shall think fit, make such order as to the court shall seem just for applying all or any part of the interest of the beneficiary in the trust estate by way of indemnity to the trustee or person claiming through him.

Notes:

9.29

1. This provision derives from the Trusts (Scotland) Amendment Act 1891, s.6. The corresponding English provision is the Trustee Act 1925, s.62, which itself derives from the Trustee Act 1888, s.6. For the definition of the expression "the court", see s.32(2), reproduced *infra* para. 9.30.

2. A trustee in this position may receive some protection by virtue of the doctrine of personal bar. Wilson & Duncan state (at 28–57) that "[a] beneficiary at whose request or instigation the trustee committed a breach of trust cannot claim against the trustee in respect of the breach". That is probably too narrowly stated, as a beneficiary who acquiesces in a breach after it has taken place may be similarly barred: see *dicta* in *City of Glasgow Bank v. Parkhurst* (1880) 7 R. 749. It is unclear whether the beneficiary must know that what he is acquiescing in or instigating amounts to a breach of trust for personal bar to operate. In *Re Pauling's Settlement Trusts* [1962] 1 WLR 86, Wilberforce J. reviewed the English authorities and concluded (at 108):

> "the court has to consider all the circumstances in which the concurrence of the *cestui que* trust was given with a view to seeing whether it is fair and equitable that, having given his concurrence, he should afterwards turn round and sue the trustees: that, subject to this, it is not necessary that he should know that what he is concurring in is a

breach of trust, provided that he fully understands what he is concurring in, and that it is not necessary that he himself should have directly benefited by the breach of trust."

(See also *Holder v. Holder* [1968] Ch. 353). There would appear to be no Scottish authority in point, however.

3. Personal bar, of course, does not protect the trustee against claims by *other* beneficiaries (or, indeed, claims brought by co-trustees on behalf of the trust estate). See, for example, *Raes v. Meek* (1889) 16 R. (H.L.) 31, where trustees under a marriage contract (including the spouses) committed a breach of trust. It was held that the children of the marriage were entitled to apply to the court to have their contingent interest protected, but the court had to frame its order in such a way as to prevent their parents benefiting. It is in relation to such claims that s.31 may be of value to the trustee, there being no such right to indemnity at common law (*cf. City of Glasgow Bank v. Parkhurst, supra*).

4. *The beneficiary's state of knowledge and section 31.* For s.31 to be applicable, the beneficiary must be aware of the facts which make the proposed action a breach of trust. It is not necessary for the beneficiary to know that it is, in law, such a breach. A consent to a particular type of investment is not a consent to a want of care in making that investment. (See *Cathcart's Trs v. Cathcart* (1907) 15 S.L.T. 646; *Henderson v. Henderson's Trs* (1900) 2 F. 1295; *Re Somerset* [1894] 1 Ch. 321).

5. It is only a consent that need be in writing for s.31 to operate; an instigation or request need not be: *Griffith v. Hughes* [1892] 3 Ch. 105.

C. Section 32 of the 1921 Act

Trusts (Scotland) Act 1921, s.32

Court may relieve trustee from personal liability

32.—(1) If it appears to the court that a trustee is or may be personally liable for any breach of trust, whether the transaction alleged to be a breach of trust occurred before or after the passing of this Act, but has acted honestly and reasonably, and ought fairly to be excused for the breach of trust, then the court may relieve the trustee either wholly or partly from personal liability for the same.   **9.30**

(2) In this section and in the two immediately preceding sections the expression "the court" shall mean any court of competent jurisdiction in which a question relative to the actings, liability, or removal of a trustee comes to be tried.

NOTES:

1. The corresponding English provision is the Trustee Act 1925, s.61, which derives from the Judicial Trustees Act 1896, s.3. See Dennis R. Paling, "The Trustee's Duty of Skill and Care", (1973) 37 Conv. 48; F.H. Maugham, "Excusable Breaches of Trust" (1898) 14 L.Q.R. 159.   **9.31**

2. Judging from the reported English cases, the section is most likely to be of application where the trustees have acted under a *bona fide* mistake of law. The section has rarely been invoked in reported Scottish cases (see, for examples, *Clarke v. Clarke's Trs*, 1925 S.C. 693; *Breckney v. Nicol* (1942) 58 Sh.Ct.Rep. 133).

3. A number of issues arise from the wording of section 32(1), which are as follows:

4. *"Is or may be personally liable"*. In *Re Mackay* [1911] 1 Ch. 300, Parker J. observed (at 306) that "in order to give relief. . . it is not necessary for the Court to decide that the trustee is under any personal liability. It is enough that in the opinion of the Court he may be under some personal liability. It will be convenient, therefore, to deal first with the question whether the Act applies to the present case." But the words "may be" do not give the court the power to grant relief in advance for an anticipated breach of trust: *Re Tollemache* [1903] 1 Ch. 457, *per* Kckcwich J. at 465–466, affd [1903] 1 Ch. 955.

5. "Honestly and reasonably". Questions of reasonableness are more likely to arise than questions of honesty: "relief is seldom claimed by trustees whose honesty is in doubt" (Keeton & Sheridan, 473).

What is the standard of reasonableness required under the section? It has been suggested that "acting reasonably means acting with such a degree of prudence as a person of ordinary intelligence and diligence may be expected to act with in the conduct of his own affairs." (*Re Mackay* [1911] 1 Ch. 300, *per* Parker J. at 306) But this would mean that s.32(1) can be of no application where the pursuer's case requires proof of breach of the general duty of care (*supra*, para. 9.02), and it is arguable that the standard of reasonableness should in fact be "whether the trustee has acted with the same skill and care as he is accustomed to in the conduct of his own affairs" (Paling, *supra*, at 54; see also *Re Stuart* [1897] 2 Ch. 583, but see *Lord De Clifford's Estate* [1900] 2 Ch. 707, *per* Farwell J. at 716). The question awaits authoritative resolution.

Factors relevant to reasonableness may include (i) any uncertainty or obscurity in the terms of the trust deed (*Re Mackay* [1911] 1 Ch. 300); (ii) the size of the sum involved, as where a small sum is involved it might be disproportionate to seek judicial guidance (*Re Grindley* [1898] 2 Ch. 593); (iii) any uncertainty or obscurity as to the state of the law (*cf. Home v. Pringle* (1841) 2 Rob. App. 384). The fact that the truster would have acted in the same way with the property does not show reasonableness (*Khoo Tek Keong v. Ch'ng Joo Tuan Neoh* [1934] A.C. 529).

Keeton & Sheridan (at 474, considering the equivalent English provisions), have suggested that where a trustee could have availed himself of the protection of section 30 of the 1921 Act and have thereby avoided being found in breach of trust, he cannot be entitled to relief. However, this is a misreading of the authority cited (*Re Stuart* [1897] 2 Ch. 583) and is, with respect, incorrect (see also *Palmer v. Emerson* [1911] 1 Ch. 758).

6. *"Ought fairly to be excused"*. It is clear that a trustee who has acted honestly and reasonably is not automatically entitled to relief (otherwise, section 32(1) would state that the court "shall relieve the trustee", rather than "may relieve the trustee"). The court clearly has a discretion as to whether or not the trustee should be relieved. Because, in the few reported Scottish cases on section 32(1), it has been held that the trustees did not act "honestly and reasonably", the Scottish courts have so far not been required to consider the effect of the "fairness" requirement. Guidance can, however, be sought from decisions on the equivalent English provisions.

Firstly, the decision as to whether or not to grant relief is within the discretion of the trial court, and an appellate court will be slow to interfere (*Marsden v. Evans* [1954] 1 W.L.R. 423).

Secondly, it will be assumed that it is fair to grant relief unless there are special considerations which suggest otherwise. (See *Perrins v. Bellamy* [1898] 2 Ch 521, *per* Kekewich J at 528, affd [1899] 1 Ch. 797).

Thirdly, the fact that the trustee has acted on legal advice is relevant, but will not automatically result in relief being granted (*Marsden v. Evans* [1954] 1 W.L.R. 423).

In *National Trustees Co. of Australasia v. General Finance Co. of Australasia* [1905] A.C. 373, the trustees, relying on incorrect legal advice, paid out money to the wrong parties. The Privy Council held that, although they had acted "honestly and reasonably", they were not entitled to relief, for two reasons: (i), they were professional, remunerated trustees and it hardly seemed "fair" that another party with clear title to the trust property should suffer a loss in order to relieve the trustees from the consequences of their error, and (ii), they had not taken any steps to recover the property or to seek redress from their legal advisers, and had advanced no reason for their inaction in this respect.

Although the Privy Council treated both of these factors as going to "fairness", the second is probably more properly seen as going to the question of whether the trustees had acted reasonably. The Privy Council seems to have approached the question in this way due to an unwillingness to disturb the finding of the courts below that the trustees had acted "honestly and reasonably". The "fairness" requirement is important, because any relief which is granted will generally be at the expense of the beneficiaries, and the court is therefore faced with the difficulty of allocating loss between two (or more) largely "innocent" parties. If the trustee's management of the trust estate has otherwise been of a high standard, and this is reflected in the value of the estate, it may be easier for the court to conclude that it would be fair to grant relief (see *Fogo's J.F. v. Fogo*, 1929 SC 546, *per* Lord Anderson at 555).

7. *"Fairness" and the position of non-gratuitous trustees*. Mackenzie Stuart (at pp. 382–383) appears to have misinterpreted *National Trustees* as holding that non-gratuitous trustees are never entitled to benefit from statutory relief (*i.e.* even if such trustees have acted "honestly

and reasonably", it would never be "fair" to grant relief). The Privy Council, in fact, expressly declined to take that view (*National Trustees*, at 381, but *cf. Re Windsor Steam Coal Co. (1901) Ltd* [1929] 1 Ch 151, *per* Lawrence L.J. at 164–165). The court will, however, be less willing to grant relief to a non-gratuitous trustee (*National Trustees; Re Pauling's Settlement Trusts* [1964] Ch. 303). This is because it would seem unfair to excuse a professional trustee (who can, it might be observed, take out indemnity insurance) at the expense of the beneficiaries (see also *Bartlett v. Barclays Bank Trust Co. Ltd* [1980] Ch 515, *per* Brightman J. at 537–538). But where a number of trustees are in breach of trust, and the question is one of relieving one trustee at the expense of the others, rather than at the expense of the beneficiaries, different considerations might apply.

8. *"Wholly or partly"*. The reported cases are generally concerned with whether or not it would be proper to grant full relief to the trustees, but the statute clearly permits the court to grant relief in part only, and this approach to allocating liability between a blameless trustee and a blameless beneficiary may have much to commend it in appropriate circumstances. In *Re Evans* [1999] 2 All E.R. 777, a trustee who was in breach of trust continued to hold a property derived from the trust estate. It was held that she was entitled to relief to the extent that the plaintiff's claim could not be satisfied out of the proceeds of sale of that property.

Chapter 10

TRUSTEES AND THIRD PARTIES

10.01 Trustees will commonly, in order to discharge their responsibilities as trustees, enter into contracts with third parties. In some cases, they may even become involved in litigation with third parties. This chapter considers the extent to which trustees can be personally liable to third parties in contract and delict, their right to reimbursement from the trust estate, and their rights and liabilities in litigation. It also considers the protection which the law affords to third parties who transact in good faith with trustees who later transpire to have acted in breach of trust.

1. PERSONAL LIABILITY UNDER CONTRACT

A. Mackenzie Stuart, *The Law of Trusts* (1932), p. 358

10.02 "Trustees who enter into contractual obligations with third parties are personally liable on them unless there is an agreement express or implied that the trust estate only is to be held bound.

The fact that a transaction is one which is known to concern a trust does not of itself restrict the third party to accepting the trust only as his debtor. The act of a trustee is not the act of an agent but of the owner of the trust estate, and the knowledge of a third party that the person with whom he is contracting is a trustee, does not exclude the personal liability of the latter in the same way as if he were known to be acting as an agent. Another reason is that trustees know the value of the estate against which they have a right of relief, but of this the other party is generally very imperfectly informed. The presumption, therefore, is that a third party, in entering into contracts with trustees, is relying on the credit of the trustees as individuals."

Brown v. Sutherland
(1875) 2 R. 615

10.03 The trustees of an unregistered joint stock building association employed Sutherland to execute the plaster work required for the buildings which they were erecting. On the September 23, 1874, the association's architect certified that Sutherland was entitled to payment of £200 on the basis of the work he had completed thus far. The trustees then granted a bill of exchange for £200 in Sutherland's favour. There was no reference to their status as trustees in the bill. The trustees were subsequently charged upon the bill, and presented a note of suspension of the charge, arguing that "under the articles of association [they] were appointed trustees to grant deeds on behalf of the association, and these deeds were to be binding on the whole association; this bill had been granted by the trustees as trustees, and the association was bound by it, not the trustees personally". The Lord Ordinary held that the trustees were personally liable. The trustees appealed to the Inner House:

LORD JUSTICE-CLERK (MONCREIFF): ". . .the subscription of this bill by the suspenders was not *factorio nominee*, as trustees for this association, but actually as individuals. Wherever signatures to documents of this sort are not expressly qualified they must be held to bind the parties as individuals. . .

The obligation here is not a company obligation, it is a personal obligation by individuals who purposely did not qualify their signatures, and that for the excellent reason that the creditor would not have accepted the bill if so qualified. They undertook an individual obligation to pay this charger £200, and they must now implement it."

LORD NEAVES: "The parties here can never have intended to grant this bill as a nullity. Certainly Sutherland never would have given his plaster work for a piece of moonshine. It is incredible that people would enter into a document of debt knowing it to be useless. The intention of the parties, as shewn by the probabilities of the case and confirmed by the oath of the charger, was that this should be an additional guarantee to Sutherland for payment of his work. It is not stated that there are no funds of the association.

The most favourable view for these suspenders is, that they have powers under which they are entitled to borrow money in order to finish the buildings. They undertook to borrow and pay Sutherland, and if they have not done so or are not prepared with an explanation why they have not done so, that is enough to enable us to decide the case.

This is a personal obligation by these trustees. If they have funds they can pay, but if not they should explain why they have not.

If they are compelled to make this money forthcoming out of their own pockets they can get relief against the association in an action of count and reckoning. *Hoc statu*, and on the face of this document, I think it seems one on which a charge is justified."

LORD GIFFORD: "It is admitted that the bill would be good to a bank, and would create a personal obligation against the suspenders in favour of the bank. Indeed this was the very purpose for which it was granted. It was meant to be discounted on the credit of the granters; but if the granters were to be only liable as trustees, and *in valorem* of the trust-funds, no bank would have discounted the bill, knowing nothing of the state of the trust. Now, if the bill would bind the suspenders personally and individually to the bank, it must have the same effect to the drawer. Its terms are the same, and the obligation arises from its terms. If the drawer had discounted it the bank could have made these acceptors pay, because they had not limited their liability on the face of the document itself. Whenever a man means to bind another and not himself he should take care to say so. I think this is never to be implied. Even if a trust character is mentioned it will be held in general that this is merely descriptive of the obligant, but does not exempt him from personal liability. A trustee who does not mean to be personally bound should take care to use words which will exclude his personal liability,— for example, 'I bind not myself, but the trust-estate;' 'I bind not myself, but my constituent, or my client, for whom I act.' If he binds 'himself' it will not in general limit his responsibility that he adds, 'as agent for so and so,' or 'as trustee.' This may indicate that he claims relief, but, in general, he himself will be liable in the first place."

Lord Ormidale delivered a concurring opinion.

NOTES:

1. *The context in which personal liability arises.* Where trustees have validly entered into **10.04** contracts on behalf of the trust, and the trust funds are sufficient to meet the contractual obligations, no issue of personal liability should normally arise. Personal liability should not normally become an issue unless the trust itself becomes insolvent. For this reason, a great number of the reported cases on personal liability arose in the context of the disastrous collapse of the City of Glasgow Bank in 1878. It appears that many trust funds included stock in the Bank, which had previously been in good repute. The Bank was one of unlimited liability, and the stock was subject to heavy calls. (For example, the trust fund in *Cunningham v. Montgomerie* (1879) 6 R. 1333 included £1,000 of bank stock, on which calls of £27,500

were made). In many cases, the calls on the stock exceeded the value of the trust estate, with the result that the liquidators pursued the trustees personally for the shortfall—often bankrupting the trustees as well as the trust itself.

2. *The rationale for personal liability.* Why should trustees be held personally liable for trust debts where the person(s) with whom they are contracting know that they are acting on behalf of the trust? The rationale for this rule has been explained as follows:

> "in regard to debts contracted by the trustees themselves, although it may be *bona fide* for the trust purposes, they will be personally bound to third parties, unless it appear clearly from the terms of the transaction that the creditor expressly took the trust-estate, as distinct from the individual trustees, as his debtor. In such cases it is held, and justly held, that the trustees who are supposed to know their own trust-affairs, are bound to warrant the sufficiency of the trust-funds to the persons with whom they deal, and who have no such means of information." (*Cullen v. Baillie* (1846) 8 D. 511, *per* Lord Fullerton at 522)

> "as the trustees must know whether there are funds to answer the purpose, they, when they contract with others who do not know, act as if representing that they had a fund applicable to the object, and are then personally bound to pay funds to the contractors." (*Higgins v. Livingstone* (1816) 4 Dow. 341, *per* Lord Eldon L.C. at 355–356)

3. *Incurring personal liability through an agent.* Trustees may incur personal liability through the actions of an agent, at least where it is clear that (a) the other party was relying on the credit of the trustee (*Ford & Sons v. Stephenson* (1888) 16 R. 24) or (b) the trustees have negligently failed to implement the bargain struck by their agent (*Thomas v. Walker's Trs* (1832) 11 S. 162). Wilson and Duncan appear to suggest (at 29–04) that personal liability applies more broadly to any contract entered into by an agent, but the two additional cases which they cite for this proposition (*Murray v. McGregor & Campbell* (1827) 6 S. 147 and *Macphail & Son v. Maclean's Tr.* (1887) 15 R. 47) seem to be concerned only with whether an agent's actions were binding on the trust-estate, and not whether they bound the trustee(s) personally. Indeed, counsel for the pursuers in *Macphail* specifically undertook that decree would not be enforced against the trustee personally.

Trustees may also become personally liable through the acts of a co-trustee, provided that he was authorised to act on behalf of the trustees as a whole, or that his acts are subsequently homologated (ratified) by the trustees (*Higgins v. Livingstone* (1816) 4 Dow. 341). Where trustees are personally liable, they are liable joint and severally (*Oswald's Trs v. City of Glasgow Bank* (1879) 6 R. 461, *per* the Lord President (Inglis) at 466).

10.05   4. *Judicial factors and personal liability.* It appears that a judicial factor who acts in good faith and gives notice of his appointment to those with whom he contracts does not incur personal liability for trust contracts: *Scottish Brewers Ltd. v. J Douglas Pearson & Co.*, 1996 S.L.T. (Sh. Ct) 50.

5. *Personal liability to an individual who knows the state of the trust.* Trustees will generally not be personally liable on a contract with the solicitors to the trust:

> ". . .whatever may be the rights of ordinary persons contracting with a trustee without notice of any limitation of his (the trustee's) powers to pledge the credit of the trust-estate, the law-agents of the trust are, and are necessarily, in an exceptional position. For they have notice of everything. They are, or are presumed to be, conversant not only with the terms of the trust-deed, but with the whole circumstances of the trust-estate, its amount, the claims upon it, actual or anticipated, and the results, probable or possible, of unsuccessful litigations. They are not, therefore, in the position of tradesmen or other persons employed in the ordinary course of the trust management. Unlike such ordinary employees, they cannot, if the trust funds prove inadequate, proceed against the trustee personally on the ground of his implied warranty as to the adequacy of the trust funds. On the contrary, knowing all that the trustee knows, they are held, with respect to their charges, to take their chance of recovering from the trust-estate. That, I think, must be held as settled by the authorities mentioned. And that being so, it seems to me to follow by parity of reasoning that if employed, as here,

to conduct and advise as to a litigation which may or may not be successful, they take their risk of such contingencies as may be involved; including, in particular, the contingency that as the result of the litigation the trust-estate, or a large part of it, may not be available for their costs." (*Ferme, Ferme and Williamson v. Stephenson's Tr.* (1905) 7 F. 902, *per* Lord Kyllachy at 905)

For similar reasons, where a trustee himself becomes a creditor of the trust, his co-trustees cannot be held personally liable to him (*Cullen v. Baillie* (1846) 8 D. 511). *Cf. Brown v. Sutherland, supra* para. 10.03, where trustees were held personally liable to a person who was a partner in the association of which they were trustees.

6. *Personal liability and the death of a trustee.* The personal liability of a trustee for trust contracts ceases on death:

> "I hold that persons who enter their names on the register of a bank, though describing themselves as trustees, are personally responsible for the debts of the bank incurred during their lives, but it is not in the least inconsistent with the view that they are personally responsible, and jointly and severally responsible, for the debts of a bank, to hold that liability ceases upon death. The liability ceases, for this reason, that the title and interest in the stock is thereby transferred to the other joint holders of the stock." (*Oswald's Trs v. City of Glasgow Bank* (1879) 6 R. 461).

However, this rule may not apply to sole trustees, because title to the trust assets remains with a sole trustee even after his death (there being no co-trustees for it to automatically devolve to). See para. 4.18.

7. *Personal liability on pre-existing contracts.* A trustee may become personally liable on a continuing contract to which the truster was a party, but only if he adopts the contract. See Wilson and Duncan, paras 29–18 *et seq.*

8. *Contracts for the sale of heritable property and warrandice.* Where trustees contract to sell heritable property, they will normally only be required to grant warrandice from fact and deed in the disposition. (*Forbes's Trs v. McIntosh* (1822) 1 S. 535). But if they have contracted as individuals (even if the purchaser knows that they are trustees), the purchaser will not be bound to accept their disposition unless it includes a clause granting absolute warrandice (*Mackenzie v. Neill* (1899) 37 S.L.R. 666). It is an open question as to whether a clause in the terms "I grant warrandice" or even "I grant warrandice as trustee" renders a trustee liable in absolute warrandice, but it at least binds him in warrandice from fact and deed. (*Horsburgh's Trs v. Welch* (1886) 14 R. 67).

2. EXCLUDING PERSONAL LIABILITY UNDER CONTRACT

Mackenzie Stuart (*supra,* para. 10.02) observes that trustees may escape personal liability if there "is an agreement express or implied that the trust estate only is to be held bound". Wilson and Duncan make a very similar statement (29–05). However, it is submitted that it is highly doubtful whether it is possible to impliedly exclude personal liability. There appears to be no reported decision where such an exclusion was held to be implicit, and there are strong *dicta* to the effect that any exclusion must be express: *Lumsden v. Buchanan* (1865) 3 M. (H.L.) 89, *per* Lord Westbury L.C. at 93 (exclusion of personal liability "must be the result of express stipulation"); *Brown v. Sutherland* (1875) 2 R. 615, *per* Lord Gifford at 621 ("Whenever a man means to bind another and not himself he should take care to say so. I think this is never to be implied.") **10.06**

What words will serve to exclude personal liability? It is clear that simply designating oneself as a trustee will not suffice. The court may conclude that the word "trustee" has simply been used descriptively, and so trustees who signed a bill in the terms "we, trustees of the late Colin McLachlan, promise to pay" were held personally bound by its terms (*Thomson v. McLachlan's Trs* (1829) 7 S. 787; see also *Lumsden v. Buchanan* (1865) 3 M. (H.L.) 89 and the Bills of Exchange Act 1882, s.26(1)). Similarly, the fact that the other party knew that he was contracting with a trustee does not exclude personal liability (*Mackenzie & Ors. v. Neill* (1899) 37 S.L.R. 666, *per* Lord Kincairney at 667).

Signing "as trustee", however, will normally be sufficient to exclude personal liability (*Gordon v. Campbell* (1842) 1 Bell 428). This is not a fixed rule, however:

"It is urged that the necessary import of a contract in Scotland 'as trustees' is to exclude unlimited personal liability. . . the premiss is not correct. The authorities cited at the bar (*Gordon v. Campbell* (1842) 1 Bell 428; *Thompson v. McLachlan's Trs* (1829) 7 S. 787) shew that there is no fixed rule in Scotland as to the effect of such words, but that it must always depend upon the context and upon the nature and circumstances of the contract in which they occur. If they are open to either of two constructions, the one consistent with the context and with the substance of the contract, the other repugnant to and destructive of it, the former ought certainly to prevail." (*Muir v. City of Glasgow Bank* (1879) 6 R. (H.L.) 21, *per* Lord Selborne at 41–42).

In *Muir*, the fact that trustees had registered their shares in the City of Glasgow Bank as trustees was held not to exclude personal liability, largely on the basis that to allow shareholders to limit their personal liability by taking shares "as trustees" would have been to create an impermissible class of limited liability shares. See also, to similar effect, *Lumsden v. Peddie* (1866) 3 M. 34.

   Not all contracts, of course, are reduced to writing in this fashion, but it may be correct to say that the general principle is that trustees will be personally liable on trust contracts unless they have given "due notice" to the contrary (*Johnston v. Waddell*, 1928 S.N. 81). The considerations relevant to applying this test have been outlined as follows:

"Whether in any particular case the contract of an executor or trustee is one which binds himself personally, or is to be satisfied only out of the estate of which he is the representative, is, as it seems to me, a question of construction, to be decided with reference to all the circumstances of the case, the nature of the contract, the subject-matter on which it is to operate, and the capacity and duty of the parties to make the contract in one form or the other." (*Muir v. City of Glasgow Bank* (1879) 6 R. (H.L.) 21, *per* Lord Cairns L.C. at 22–23)

A trustee may, of course, explicitly *include* rather than exclude personal liability. (See, *e.g. Commercial Bank of Scotland v. Sprot* (1841) 3 D. 939, where trustees obliged themselves "as trustees, and individually" to repay money advanced by a bank to the trust). An undertaking in such terms may be necessary where a third party is unwilling to rely on the credit of the trust funds alone.

3. PERSONAL LIABILITY IN DELICT

10.07   There is very little authority indeed on the question of personal liability of trustees in delict. If a trustee commits a delict himself, there is no doubt that he is personally liable for his actions. A more difficult question arose in *Mulholland v. Macfarlane's Trs*, 1928 S.L.T. 251, where the trustees carried on the truster's motor-hire business for a period after his death. Mulholland subsequently brought an action against the trustees, alleging that he had been run down by a bus driven by an employee of the business. Lord Moncrieff observed (at 252):

"The sum sued for is claimed as due in respect of the action of the trustees themselves in the conduct of the truster's business as carried on by them after the truster's death. To make payment of such a claim trustees are *prima facie* liable as individuals."

Lord Moncrieff's observation that the case concerned "the action of the trustees themselves" is rather difficult to understand given that the case appears to be (although the report is unclear) one of vicarious liability. It would seem unproblematic to say that trustees are vicariously liable *as trustees* for the actions of trust employees, but it is not clear how *personal* liability is to be justified. One does not, after all, expect company directors to be personally liable for delicts committed by employees of the company. The point, however, was rendered moot in *Mulholland* by the fact that the pursuer had designed the defenders "as trustees acting under" Macfarlane's will in the initial writ in his action, which (it was held) meant that damages could only be awarded against them as trustees and they could not be personally liable. Beyond *Mulholland*, there appears to be no other case which bears on this issue.

4. The Right to Reimbursement

A. Mackenzie Stuart, *The Law of Trusts* (1932), p. 358

"It is of the nature of the office of a trustee, as between him and the beneficiaries, that he **10.08** shall receive out of the trust estate all the proper charges and expenses incurred in him in the execution of the trust. This is implied in every deed of trust."

Notes:

1. *"Proper charges and expenses".* The expenditure must have been properly incurred by the trustee; *i.e.* he must have been acting within his powers as a trustee in incurring it. A trustee who acts outwith his powers will generally not be entitled to reimbursement, except perhaps where he has acted in circumstances of emergency (*Stewart v. Dobie's Trs* (1899) 1 F. 1183, *per* Lord McLaren at 1187), or where the trust-estate has been enriched by his unauthorised actions (*cf. Brown v. Meek's Trs* (1896) 4 S.L.T. 46).
2. *From where should reimbursement be sought?* In *Robinson v. Fraser's Tr.* (1881) 8 R. (H.L.) 127, the trustees had lawfully appropriated the trust fund into two parts; one part consisting of investments for the behoof of beneficiary A, and the other consisting of investments for the behoof of beneficiary B. The investments held for A included City of Glasgow Bank stock. When the Bank failed and calls were made on the stock, it was held that the trustees were not entitled to seek reimbursement from that part of the trust fund which had been appropriated for behoof of B. *A fortiori*, the trustee cannot seek reimbursement outside of the trust-estate.

5. The Interaction Between Personal Liability and Liability as a Trustee

Although trustees generally incur personal liability on trust contracts, and are entitled to reimburse- **10.09** ment for trust expenditure, this does not mean that they are bound to make all payments necessary for the trust out of their own pockets and then claim reimbursement from the trust funds. They may (and normally will) apply the trust funds directly to those purposes. See the following case:

Cunningham v. Montgomerie
(1879) 6 R. 1333

Roger Montgomerie and John Cunningham, the trustees under a marriage-contract trust, **10.10** purchased £1,000 stock in the City of Glasgow Bank. The Bank failed in 1878. Calls of £27,500 were made upon the stock, for which the trustees were found personally liable. The liquidators agreed to give the trustees a discharge if they surrendered their whole means and estate, and made over the whole of the trust-funds in their hands, which were between £12,000 and £13,000.

Lord President (Inglis): "The defenders, Montgomerie and others, are trustees under the marriage-contract of Mr and Mrs Charles Arthur Cunningham, the pursuers of the action, and the object of this action, as I understand it, is to prevent the trustees from applying any part of the trust-funds towards payment of calls upon certain stock of the City of Glasgow Bank, which forms part of the trust-estate.

[The Lord President rejected the pursuers' argument that investment in the City of Glasgow Bank stock had not been authorised by the terms of the trust deed, and continued:]

But there is a second, and I think a much more important question raised by this reclaiming note. It is said that the trustees are not able out of their own funds to meet the whole calls that have been made in respect of this stock, and that they are not entitled to use the trust funds for the purpose of paying calls to any greater extent than they have themselves actually paid money out of their own funds. Now, here again I agree with the Lord Ordinary. I think that contention proceeds upon an entire misapprehension of the relation of trusters and trustees under a deed of this kind. Scientifically considered, the position of trustees under such a deed is this, that they are depositaries of the trust-estate and mandataries for its administration. This is a combination of two well-known contracts in the civil law, and the character and quality of these contracts is perfectly well fixed both in the civil law and in modern jurisprudence. There can be no doubt whatever that the mandant is bound to relieve his mandatary not only of all expenses incurred by him in the execution of his mandate, but of all liability incurred by him in the exercise of his powers as mandatary, and in the administration of the affairs of the mandant, and this obligation of relief on the part of the mandant may be enforced not merely upon the occasion of each payment that the mandatary is compelled to make on behalf of the mandant, but if any liability has been incurred by the mandatary in the due execution of his power, and if liability is threatened to be enforced against him, he is quite entitled to fall back upon the mandant's obligation of relief and demand that he shall stand between him and the creditor who is demanding the performance of this obligation. It is not mere reimbursement of money spent that the mandatary is entitled to have, but it is relief of obligation, and therefore before any call had been made at all upon the failure of this bank, when it became perfectly obvious that these trustees would be made personally answerable for the payment of the calls that were certain to be made, they were in a condition at once to say to the trusters, 'You must stand between us and this liability; we must be protected, and protected at the expense of the trust-estate.' Therefore it seems abundantly clear, I think, upon principle, that the trust-estate must stand between the liquidators and the parties who are sought to be made liable as registered owners of this stock, because they have become registered owners of this stock in fulfilment of the duty and power conferred upon them by the trusters. To come to any other conclusion upon a question of this kind would involve something very like a practical absurdity, as I think the Lord Ordinary has very well explained. The liability of the trust-estate according to the view developed in this alternative conclusion of the declarator would be that the liability of the trust-estate would be measured entirely by the solvency or insolvency, total or partial, of the trustees. If the trustees were men of wealth the trust-estate would be answerable for every shilling, because then the money would be disbursed in the first place by the trustees, and they would have a direct claim of reimbursement from the trust-estate. But if they happened to be men of no personal means, then if they could pay nothing the trust-estate would escape altogether, and if they could pay only a small portion of the calls demanded by the liquidators, then the trust-estate would only be liable to the extent to which the trustees were able to pay out of their own means. Now, that is one of those absurd results which is a very good test of the unsoundness of the doctrine of which it is a result. But there is another view also, which completely exposes, I think, the untenable character of this proposition. If the trustees are not able, either out of their own means, or out of the trust-estate, by reason of the trusters' intervention, to pay more than, we shall say, one-fifth part of the calls made upon them by the liquidators, what would be the consequence? The consequence would be that the trustees would then, at all events, at the very lowest view of this alternative, be entitled to be reimbursed by the trust-estate to the extent of which they had paid money. Well, then, that would put the trustees in funds again, and as they have not been discharged by the liquidators, and as the liquidators certainly would not in such circumstances discharge them, the result would just be that the liquidators would come upon them for the payment of the new funds which they had got; and that operation would be performed successively, according to the various sums that are received by the trustees out of the trust-estate as indemnity, until in the end the trust-estate would be exhausted, just in the same manner as it would be according to the sounder doctrine for which the Lord Ordinary has pronounced. I therefore think on the whole matter that he has come to a perfectly sound conclusion, and that the conclusions of this summons cannot to any extent be entertained."

Lords Deas and Sands delivered concurring opinions.
Lord Mure concurred.

6. LITIGATION

A. Form of summons or interlocutor

In *Mulholland v. Macfarlane's Trs*, 1928 S.L.T. 251, an action was brought against trustees in delict. The **10.11**
trustees were designed in the initial writ "as trustees acting under Macfarlane's will". It was held that
damages could therefore only be awarded against them as trustees and they could not be made
personally liable. Lord Moncrieff observed (at 252):

> "If the pursuer had convened the defenders as individuals they would have had an opportunity of
> consulting with the beneficiaries before lodging defences and of obtaining from them an
> immunity if so advised. Finding themselves convened only as trustees, they had no occasion to
> take any such step for their protection. I am of opinion that the pursuer is entitled to decree
> against the defenders only in the capacity in which he has convened them."

In such a case, however, the court is entitled to hold the trustees personally liable in expenses despite
the fact that the action has only been brought against them as trustees (*Mulholland, supra*; *Kay v.
Wilson's Trs* (1850) 12 D. 845).

Similarly, where an interlocutor is pronounced decerning against a trustee "as trustee" or "*qua*
trustee*", or holding him liable in expenses in similar terms, he cannot be held personally liable (*Craig
v. Hogg* (1896) 24 R. 6; *Beadie v. Carr* (1850) 12 D. 1069).

B. The right to be reimbursed for expenses incurred in litigation

Wemyss v. Kennedy
(1906) 14 S.L.T. 237

Kennedy and other members of the Easter Wemyss Kirk-Session, as trustees of the **10.12**
"Wemyss Catechist Fund", acting on the advice of counsel, raised an action against
Randolph Wemyss. In this action, they sought to have it declared that he was bound to pay
them £64, 14s. annually for behoof of a catechist, and that he should either find security for
this payment or pay over to them the funds belonging to the office of catechist. They were
granted decree to the effect that he was bound to pay the sum of £64, 14s. annually, but
Wemyss was assoilzied from the other conclusions of the action. The trustees took their
expenses out of the trust-fund. Thereafter, Wemyss sought a declarator that the trustees had
not been entitled to do this, and decree that they should restore the amount of their
expenses to the fund.

LORD ARDWALL: "I do not think there is any difficulty in this case, and I am quite clear that
the defenders here are entitled to absolvitor, with expenses. They litigated an action, and
although it may be true that there were a number of conclusions in that action which were
not given effect to, every one knows that often when an action is brought in the Court
parties take the opportunity of raising all possible points that may emerge, or anticipate any
difficulty being raised, by inserting a number of conclusions in the summons besides the
main one on which they depend.

The question is whether the trustees pursued that action in the *bona fide* discharge of
their duty as trustees. I think there can only be one answer to that, because their duty was to
maintain the fund at what they believed to be its proper position, namely a fund yielding £64
a year instead of £22 a year. It was no answer to say that £64 had formerly been paid *ex
gratia*; trustees are not bound to be satisfied with *ex gratia* payments if they are payments to
which they are legally entitled, and they were wholly successful in their conclusions on that
point, whatever became of the minor conclusions. They having thus litigated for the benefit
of the trust and in the discharge of their duty, and the Lord Ordinary having found no
expenses due to or by either party, of course meaning neither party as against the other,

what I am asked for here is a declaration that the trustees are not entitled to take their own expenses out of the trust funds.

The question accordingly is whether the trustees are to pay the expenses of that action, amounting to £269, 9s. 11d., out of their own private pockets. I think that trustees are, as a rule, very much harassed and bullied by beneficiaries and courts of law and everybody else, but fortunately they have this decided in their favour that if they expend money in litigation in the discharge of their duty as trustees, they are entitled to take their expenses out of the trust if they are successful, or even if they are unsuccessful. In the case of *Sarah Knight* (1883) 26 Ch. D. 82, it was laid down that the Courts had really no discretion in the matter unless the trustees had been guilty of misconduct, and in *Gibson v. Caddall's Trs* (1895) 22 R. 889; *Anderson v. Anderson's Tr.* (1901) 4 F. 896; and *Cameron v. Anderson* (1844) 7 D. 92, it was perfectly clearly laid down beyond all cavil that if the trustees were in discharge of their duty they were entitled to repay themselves out of the funds under their charge. . .

On the whole matter I have no difficulty in holding that the trustees are entitled to absolvitor, with expenses as against the pursuer."

NOTES:

10.13

1. As a general rule, trustees should be entitled to be reimbursed for expenses incurred in connection with litigation unless they have "acted unreasonably or recklessly, or otherwise than in accordance with their duty". (*Gibson v. Caddall's Trs* (1895) 22 R. 889, *per* the Lord President (Robertson) at 892). See also *Graham v. Marshall* (1860) 23 D. 41, *per* the Lord Justice-Clerk (Inglis) at 43. Trustees are entitled to be reimbursed for expenses incurred in litigation properly conducted in a foreign court, even though that court may have made no judgment on the question of expenses (*Johnstone v. Beattie* (1856) 18 D. 343).

2. *The right to reimbursement and success in the litigation.* As Lord Ardwall observes, trustees may be entitled to reimbursement of expenses incurred in litigation even though they have been unsuccessful. In *Cameron v. Anderson* (1844) 7 D. 92, Lord Cockburn observed (at 103–104):

   "I should be sorry to give any opinion which, on the one hand, should expose gratuitous trustees to excessive risk; or should, on the other hand, encourage their negligence or litigiousness. The general rule is, that they are never to litigate with such gross unreasonableness as implies a disregard of their duty. But, in judging whether they have actually done so or not, we can rarely determine merely from the result. A reasonable action may have an unfortunate issue. We must look to the whole circumstances. And where a trustee, though not perhaps proceeding with perfect wisdom, appears, upon the whole, to have acted substantially according to his warrant, and with a sincere desire to do right, a court is not called upon to visit him personally with loss which his honest and reasonable view of his duty may have occasioned to the estate."

   See also *Gibson v. Caddall's Trs* (1895) 22 R. 889, *per* Lord McLaren at 893; *Buckle v. Kirk* (1908) 15 S.L.T. 1002.

3. *The right to reimbursement and fault on the part of the trustee.* Two related points may be noted:
   (a) Trustees will not be entitled to be reimbursed for their expenses where they have been forced to resort to litigation because of their own fault or lack of attention to trust matters. (*Fothringham v. Salton* (1852) 14 D. 427; *Hill v. Tait* (1856) 18 D. 316).
   (b) Similarly, trustees will not be entitled to be reimbursed for expenses incurred in defending an action where the litigation arose as a result of their own fault or lack of attention to trust matters. (*Jackson v. Jackson's Trs*, 1918 1 S.L.T. 119, where the beneficiaries in a trust had been forced to resort to an action of accounting due to "inexcusable delay" on the part of the trustees). See also *Thomson v. Dalrymple* (1865) 3 M. 336.

4. *The right to reimbursement and fault on the part of the beneficiaries.* In *Fothringham v. Salton* (1852) 14 D. 427, Lord Dundrennan held that a trustee should be entitled to the expenses of

a multiplepoinding out of the trust estate "in the circumstances, and looking generally to the vacillating and inconstant conduct of the beneficiaries").

5. *Overly litigious conduct on the part of the trustee.* It may be a ground for refusing to find the trustee entitled to expenses out of the trust estate that he has conducted litigation in an "over-scrupulous or obstinate" fashion (*Smith v. Telford* (1838) 16 S. 1233). Similarly, expenses were refused where the trustees' conduct of the litigation "displayed an animus unnecessary for any legitimate object which they could have in view" (*Morrison v. Morrison's Trs* (1848) 11 D. 297, *per* Lord Jeffrey at 300). See also *Cruickshank's Exr v. Cruickshank's Trs* (1907) 14 S.L.T. 761.

Trustees will not normally be entitled to the expenses of an appeal against a judgment at first **10.14** instance (*Munro v. Strain* (1874) 1 R. 1039). This is because the compliance with the decision of the court of first instance will itself protect them from liability for breach of trust (see *Stewart v. Bruce's Trs* (1898) 25 R. 965, *per* Lord Moncrieff at 984). Trustees who are considering appealing against a judgment at first instance may wish to ask the beneficiaries for whose benefit they are litigating if they are prepared to indemnify them against the costs of an appeal.

6. *Apportioning expenses to a particular portion of the trust fund.* Where expenses are chargeable against a testamentary trust fund, they should come out of the residue and cannot be set against the special legacies, unless the residue is insufficient: *Cameron v. Anderson* (1844) 7 D. 92. In *Easson's Trs v. Mailer* (1901) 3 F. 778, testamentary trustees unsuccessfully brought an action against one of the residuary legatees for the return of money paid by the testator to her during her lifetime. It was held that she was entitled to a finding that no part of the expenses of the litigation should be paid out of her share of the residue.

Where the trustee is litigating for the benefit of only *some* (not all) of the beneficiaries, it may be appropriate to direct that the expenses should be met out of their share of the trust property. So, in *Anderson v. Anderson's Tr.* (1901) 4 F. 96, where the trustee in a testamentary trust had unsuccessfully defended a claim by the deceased's widow and was held liable to her in expenses, it was held that her share of *jus relictae* should be calculated before deduction of the expenses (both those due to her and those for which he was entitled to be reimbursed), which should then come out of the remainder of the estate. It was inappropriate that he should effectively be able to make her pay her expenses back.

On trusts for liferent and fee, see *Baxter and Mitchell v. Wood* (1864) 2 M. 915, *per* the Lord President (McNeill) at 917:

> "A still further question remains, how this expense is to be taken out of the trust estate? Is it to come entirely out of the interest of Mrs Smith [the liferenter] in that estate, or is it to be taken in such a way that the burden will fall on the fiars and the liferenter equally? In ordinary matters of management the expenses are borne by those entitled to the current benefit of the trust; and if this had been an action of that kind, that would be the proper course. But I do not regard this as an action of that kind. The proceedings which were resisted by the trustee were of the nature of a blow directed against the existence of the trust, and the interests of the fiars and liferenter were alike involved, if it were material to uphold the trust at all. It was, therefore, not an ordinary or a current, but an extraordinary expense; and therefore I think that the trust, which got the benefit of the proceedings, and has been maintained, should bear the expense out of the capital, and that, of course, will have the effect of diminishing the liferent."

7. *Where a party loses the character of trustee as a result of the action.* A court action such as one for the reduction of a will may have the result of depriving a party of his position as trustee. Nevertheless, the court is still entitled to make a ruling that he should be entitled to receive his expenses out of the trust estate. (See, *e.g. Ross v. Ross's Trs* (1898) 25 R. 897).

8. *Imputations on the character of a trustee.* In *Ross v. Ross's Trs* (1898) 25 R. 897, Donald Ross sought reduction of his brother's will, alleging that it had been obtained by the fraud and circumvention of the trustees. The jury unanimously exonerated the trustees of those allegations, but nonetheless held (by a majority) that the will was not the deed of William Ross, as he was of weak mind. On the question of expenses, the Lord President (Robertson) observed (at 898):

> "The jury have given a special verdict. On the first issue they find in general terms for the pursuer; but on the second issue they do not find for the pursuer, but 'find that the

deceased William Ross was of weak mind, but unanimously exonerate the defenders from all charges contained in the second issue'. It seems to me that we must give at all events equal, if not greater, deference to the special finding upon the question of fact, more especially when the question is one of conduct. Now, on the assumption of the soundness of the jury's verdict, the position is that these gentlemen, the defenders, acted honestly and rightly in relation to this will, and it follows that they were right in accepting the trusteeship purported to be imposed upon them by the will. The facts are peculiar in this respect, that the charges from which these gentlemen are exonerated are exactly the charges which apply to the inception of the will, and to the accepting of the trusteeship, and we could not hold that the views of the jury were correct, and at the same time that the trustees were blameworthy, and were not entitled to be indemnified out of the estate from the consequences of this action. I must own that I have some difficulty in harmonising, or conjecturing any harmony between the jury's finding in fact and the implications contained in their findings in favour of the pursuer on the two issues, but I am disposed to think that they may have considered there was some strain of insanity in the testator, which, though occult, none the less disabled him from executing a valid testament. I do not say that that is my own view of the facts, but state the theory, because some such theory is necessary as a condition of the argument upon the question of expenses. On the other hand, my own view, as well as that of the jury, is that these gentlemen acted rightly, and accordingly I am of opinion that they are entitled to be indemnified out of the estate."

See also *Stewart v. Morrison* (1892) 19 R. 1009; *Crichton v. Henderson's Trs* (1898) 1 F. 24. Where the imputations on character only form a small part of the action, it may be appropriate to award the defenders expenses only insofar as referable to that point: *Sutherland v. Hamilton's Trs*, 1917 2 S.L.T. 173.

C. Liability for the expenses of the other party

Mulholland v. Macfarlane's Trs
1928 S.L.T. 251

10.15 LORD MONCRIEFF: "Counsel for the defenders. . . admitted that, apart from exceptional circumstance, it was now the settled practice of the Court to find trustees who had litigated liable for expenses as principals. He claimed, however, that the circumstances of this case afforded two separate grounds for relieving the trustees from such liability as individuals. *First*, the defence had been justified and shewn to be a reasonable and proper one by the award of the jury, which gave damages of only one-half of the amount of the sum sued for. I do not think that this circumstance affords ground for varying the general rule. *Second*, the defenders were called in the action to account for a liability arising under the doctrine *respondeat superior*. There was exceptional difficulty in measuring or estimating any eventual liability under such a claim. In my opinion this circumstance may also be disregarded. I shall accordingly apply the general rule, and as regards expenses shall grant decree *simpliciter* against the three named persons convened as defenders. A decree in this form, which will be a joint and several decree, will leave open all questions of right to relief against the trust estate."

Jeffrey v. Brown
(1842) 2 Shaw 349

10.16 LORD CRINGLETIE: "The Lord Ordinary cannot assent to the proposition, that a trustee is not liable for the expense of a law-suit in which he embarks. It is his duty to lay by a sum to meet a contingent claim, and if he do not lay it by, he is answerable. He alone knows who his constituents are, and what the funds under his management. If, therefore, he engage in a law-suit, from which money is to be recovered from his constituents, the burden ought to lie on him who knows who they are, and who ought to have provided for it before commencing the law-suit, and not the opposing party, who neither knows who are the constituents of the trustee, nor the funds under his care."

Notes:

1. The case for holding the trustees personally liable in expenses will obviously be even stronger **10.17** where it has been shown that they acted excessively in defending the action. In *Kay v. Wilson's Trs* (1850) 12 D. 845, testamentary trustees unsuccessfully opposed an action for damages for seduction. The Lord President (Boyle) observed (at 847):

> "If the defenders had read the letters produced in process, and taken the slightest trouble to investigate the circumstances, they would have seen that their opposition to the pursuer's claim was hopeless. Such being the complexion of the case, I am of opinion that the decree [for expenses] should go out against them, both as executors and personally."

2. *Trustees in bankruptcy.* Where a party in a court action becomes bankrupt during proceedings, the trustee in bankruptcy may sist himself in the party's place. By doing so, however, he incurs "all the risks of an ordinary litigant" (*Sturrock v. Robertson's Tr.*, 1913 S.C. 582, *per* Lord Salvesen at 587), and so may be held personally liable to the other party in expenses, including those expenses incurred before he sisted himself. (*Torbet v. Borthwick* (1849) 11 D. 694; *Scott v. Patison* (1826) 5 S. 172).

D. Action rendered necessary by an ambiguity in the trust-deed.

Court action may occasionally be necessary to determine the true effect of an ambiguous will, or the **10.18** validity of a will which is not in proper form. In such a case, the general rule is that the expenses of all parties should come out of the trust estate. Although this effectively means that the successful parties (*i.e.* those who the court holds are entitled to benefit under the will) will be required to bear all the costs of the action, the rule is justified on the basis that the testator has himself "caused a litigation on the subject by leaving such a document in his repositories" (*Whyte v. Hamilton* (1881) 8 R. 940, *per* Lord Fraser at 946. See also *Sinclair v. The Royal Bank of Scotland Ltd*, 1983 S.L.T. 256, *per* Lord Ross at 258; *Grieve's Trs v. Bethune* (1830) 8 S. 896, at 898; *Rigg v. Ramsay* (1836) 14 S. 472; *Hickling's Trs v. Garland's Trs* (1898) 1 F. (H.L.) 7, *per* Lord Halsbury L.C. at 22).

Even where there is no fault on the part of the testator, trustees may be justified in bringing a court action for guidance, on the basis that they would not be safe in administering the estate without such guidance. In such a case, they should normally be entitled to expenses out of the estate (*cf. Fairbairn v. Neville* (1897) 25 R. 192, *per* Lord McLaren at 211).

E. Miscellaneous issues regarding litigation

(a) Trustees who dissent from the action

Where a majority of trustees choose to initiate litigation or to lodge defences in an action, the law- **10.19** agent is only entitled to lodge pleadings in the names of the majority (*Fairlie v. Fairlie's Trs* (1903) 11 S.L.T. 51). This means that the dissenting trustees cannot be held personally liable in the result or the expenses of the action. If the agent wrongly enters pleadings in the names of all the trustees, the minority should lodge a minute of disclaimer to avoid personal liability (*Fairlie*).

(b) Trustees who resign during the course of litigation

Can a trustee who resigns office during the course of court proceedings escape personal liability? See *Mulholland v. Macfarlane's Trs*, 1928 S.L.T. 251, *per* Lord Moncrieff at 251–252:

"A special point was taken in favour of the defender John Macfarlane. It was stated that he had resigned office as trustee by a letter addressed to his co-trustees which was dated 2nd November 1927. Reference was made to a minute of the trustees in which this resignation was accepted as of its date. The minute itself, however, was not dated. The warrant to cite the defenders in the action is dated 13th September, and defences were due to be lodged on or before 29th September 1927. The cause was remitted to the Court of Session on the pursuer's requisition dated 28th October 1927 and was received on 1st November. On a review of these dates it is clear that the defences were instructed and were *in initio* maintained by all three trustees alike. The defender John Macfarlane took no steps to intimate to the pursuer that he had resigned office as trustee, and did not at any time disclaim the defences. I doubt whether a disclaimer of the defences which he had instructed would have availed him; but I am of opinion that in the absence of any such disclaimer he, in any event, continued liable in a question with the pursuer for the expenses occasioned by the defences which he had instructed and had purported to maintain (see *Bennett v. Maclellan* (1891) 18 R. 955)."

(c) Formal appearance or observation of proceedings

Where trustees appear simply to state their position in an action involving the trust estate, they will normally be entitled to their expenses out of the trust estate (*Edminston v. Miller's Trs* (1871) 9 M. 987). In *Martin & Co. v. Hunter's Tr.* (1897) 25 R. 125, M unsuccessfully petitioned for recall of a sequestration. The petition was opposed by the bankrupt and a concurring creditor, and the trustee simply watched the case and attended the proof so that he could consider whether he ought to intervene. It was held that the petitioner was liable to meet his expenses in doing so.

7. PROTECTION FOR THIRD PARTIES

10.20 Where a trustee, acting in breach of trust, sells trust property to a third party, that third party will acquire a good title to the property provided that he purchased the property in good faith and for value.

Hume, *Lectures* (1821–1822)
(Stair Society Vol. 17, 1952, ed. G.C.H. Paton), Vol. IV, p. 315

"Suppose this case: that John means to buy certain lands, but he does not wish to appear or be known as purchaser, at the time. He concerts it, therefore, with his friend, James, that he, James, shall purchase the lands as for himself,— and that the disposition and infeftment shall be taken in James's name, as absolute and unlimited owner of the lands. He takes, however, a separate back bond from James, binding him to accompt for the profits, and to dispone the lands to him, John, when he shall be required, or in a certain specified event. Feudal titles are accordingly made up in James's person; and afterwards, taking advantage of this situation, James fraudulently sells the lands for a price to William, who knows nothing of this secret trust. William is here secure of his purchase. There is, you observe, in these circumstances no fundamental defect of real right on the part of James. He had an absolute and unlimited conveyance and seisin of the lands, proceeding from the last owner, and made up with the knowledge and privity, nay by the contrivance and direction of John, who now insists in challenge of his powers. In making such an arrangement, John trusted entirely to the personal faith and honour of James, that he would not deceive him. The case was at bottom the same, as if John himself had been previous owner of those lands, and had disponed them to James in the like absolute terms. There was, therefore, nothing hollow, or false,—nothing vitious, or defective,—in the first concoction of James's investiture. He had the will of the last owner to convey in property, and delivery of the subject made, in pursuance of their contract, and the property must therefore have been his. It is obvious, accordingly, that John could not have challenged a title—could not have impeached a title as null and void, or as irregular and unwarrantable—which was made up by James in these very terms, by his own direction, and in execution of the previous concert between them. So standing the case, his claim against James is purely personal and peculiar: it does not in any wise attach upon the feudal right of property, regularly and fairly vested in James: nor, of consequence, does it all concern William, who is not partaker of James' wrong, and to whom that real right has been duly, and with *bona fides* on his part, transferred."

NOTES:

1. As Hume explains, the third party acquires a good title by virtue of the fact that the trustees **10.21** are the owners of the trust property and may therefore validly transfer ownership of that property. Their obligations to the beneficiaries do not in themselves affect the validity of that transfer. Although Hume's comments are concerned directly with heritable property, the principle is a general one and applies equally to moveable property.

2. Where a third party acquires trust property *mala fide* or gratuitously, his title may be reduced. Both points are illustrated by *Macgowan v. Robb* (1864) 2 M. 943. While the facts of the case are rather complex, the essential points can be summarised as follows. By virtue of an antenuptial marriage-contract with her husband, William Jaffray, Margaret Jaffray held heritable property in trust for the children of her husband's prior marriage and any children who might be borne of their own. They had one child, William Jaffray junior. After William Jaffray's death, Margaret Jaffrey granted a disposition of the property concerned in favour of William Jaffray junior. He later sold that property to John Robb. Ann Macgowan, the sole surviving child of William Jaffray's first marriage, subsequently brought an action for reduction of John Robb's title to one-half of the property. The action was successful. Lord Curriehill observed (at 951):

   > "In so far as the conveyance by Mrs Jaffray affected the half of the subjects to which the pursuer had a right under the marriage contract, it was *in fraudem* of the pursuer's right, and the conveyance being gratuitous the pursuer would have been entitled to challenge the disponee's title. The disponee, however, conveyed the subjects to the defender by a deed which we must assume to be onerous. If the defender had been a *bona fide* purchaser, he would have been safe, but he tells us on record that at the time of the purchase he was in the knowledge of the marriage contract, so that he was not in *bona fides*. This being the case, the pursuer is entitled to reduce the defender's title to one-half of the subjects."

   See also *Bertram, Gardner & Co.'s Tr. v. King's Remembrancer*, 1920 S.C. 555, *per* Lord Skerrington at 562. The onus of proving *mala fides* rests on the beneficiary who is seeking to have the transaction reduced (*Thomson v. Clydesdale Bank* (1893) 20 R. 59).

3. For a third party to be held to have acted in bad faith, he must not only have known that the property is subject to a trust, but also have been aware (at the point when the transfer took place) that it would be a breach of trust for the property to be transferred to him. In *Thomson v. Clydesdale Bank* (1893) 20 R. (H.L.) 59, a stockbroker sold shares on behalf of trustees. He was under instructions to invest the funds received, but instead paid it into his overdrawn bank account. In holding that the bank was not obliged to repay the funds concerned to the trustees, Lord Shand observed (at 62–63):

   > "I am of opinion that the same principle which applies to third parties generally is equally applicable to the case of dealings between stockbrokers and their bankers, and that the only circumstances in which money misapplied by a broker in payment to the banker of a debt due to him can be recovered from the banker by the principal to whom the money belonged, is where it can be shewn directly, or by inference from the facts proved, that the banker or his representative in the transaction knew that the money was being misapplied. It has been shewn in the present case, and indeed is notorious, that a stockbroker is often in advance for his customers, and that on settlement days and at other times he may require temporary advances, which will in due course be repaid shortly afterwards, when the broker receives payment of the price of stocks sold and delivered by him. Accordingly the knowledge of a banker that money paid in by which a broker reduces or extinguishes an overdraft on his account consists

of the prices received for customers' stocks delivered, or of the price of stock belonging to a particular customer, is nothing more than knowledge of what is constantly occurring in the ordinary course of business. The broker may or may not owe the price to his principal. In the general case he does, but in others he may have already advanced the amount; or his principal and he may have had other stock transactions which leave a balance in the broker's favour; or the arrangement between the parties may be that the broker is to retain the fund for an interval of more or less time for the purpose of reinvestment or otherwise. It would be impossible that such business could be carried on if it were held to be obligatory on a banker, in order to save himself from the consequences of a possible breach of duty or obligation, or of the fraud of an agent to his principal, that the bankers should examine into the particulars of the various transactions resulting in the payments by brokers or agents to the credit of their accounts, on each occasion on which such payments are made; and the only rule that can be applied in practice, and which, as I think, rests on sound principle, is that liability for repayment of funds which can be traced or followed into the banker's hands, and which has been applied in payment of the agent's debt, shall arise only where it can be shewn that there was knowledge on the banker's part, not merely that the fund was received from the broker's principal, but knowledge also that the payment was a misapplication of the fund, made in violation of the agent's duty and obligation. . .

I can see nothing suspicious in the state of the broker's account, and nothing to indicate to the bankers that any funds to be now paid in to wipe out the balance, in whole or in part, were being obtained by any violation of duty or fraud; and I agree with the Lord Chancellor in thinking that there is no evidence whatever here of facts which put the bankers on inquiry, or which can be founded on as shewing that they must have believed or known that this was a misapplication of funds."

10.22   4. *Section 2 of the Trusts (Scotland) Act 1961.* Some further protection for third parties can be found in this provision, which states as follows:

> "(1) Where after the commencement of this Act, the trustees under any trust enter into a transaction with any person (in this section referred to as "the second party"), being a transaction under which the trustees purport to do in relation to the trust estate or any part thereof an act of any of the descriptions specified in paragraphs (a) to (ee) of subsection (1) of section 4 of the Act of 1921 (which empowers trustees to do certain acts where such acts are not at variance with the terms or purposes of the trust) the validity of the transaction and of any title acquired by the second party under the transaction shall not be challengeable by the second party or any other person on the ground that the act in question is at variance with the terms or purposes of the trust:
>
> Provided that in relation to a transaction entered into by trustees who are acting under the supervision of the accountant of court this section shall have effect only if the said accountant consents to the transaction.
>
> (2) Nothing in subsection (1) of this section shall affect any question of liability between any of the trustees on the one hand and any co-trustee or any of the beneficiaries on the other hand."

Subsections 4(1)(a)—(ee) of the Trusts (Scotland) Act 1921 empower trustees to sell, feu, lease or excamb (swap) or borrow money on the security of the trust estate (or any part thereof), or to acquire an interest in residential accommodation for occupation by the beneficiaries, except where the act in question would be at variance with the terms or purposes of the trust.

The protection granted by section 2(1) is very strong indeed. It appears to go further than the common law rule protecting *bona fide* third parties, by closing down any question of *mala fides* whatsoever. The transaction simply cannot be challenged on the ground of bad faith. That would not, however, as section 2(2) makes clear, prevent the beneficiaries taking action against the trustees for breach of trust if the act in question was in fact at variance with the terms or purposes of the trust.

Where a transaction protected by section 2(1) relates to heritable property, section 12(3)(j)(i) of the Land Registration (Scotland) Act 1979 excludes any possibility of the beneficiary being entitled to indemnity from the Keeper of the Registers of Scotland.

5. *Section 7 of the Trusts (Scotland) Act 1921.* This section protects third parties where a deed granted by the trustees might otherwise be challenged on the grounds of certain procedural irregularities. See *supra* para. 6.49.
6. *Section 17 of the Succession (Scotland) Act 1964.* This section provides as follows:

> **Protection of persons acquiring title**
> Where any person has in good faith and for value acquired title to any interest in or security over heritable property which has vested in an executor as aforesaid directly or indirectly from—
> (a) the executor, or
> (b) a person deriving title directly from the executor,
> the title so acquired shall not be challengeable on the ground that the confirmation was reducible or has in fact been reduced, or, in a case falling under paragraph (b) above, that the title should not have been transferred to the person mentioned in that paragraph.

Where a transaction protected by section 17 relates to heritable property, section 12(3)(j)(i) of the Land Registration (Scotland) Act 1979 excludes any possibility of the beneficiary being entitled to indemnity from the Keeper of the Registers of Scotland.

7. *Third parties and indemnity under the Land Registration (Scotland) Act 1979.* Where an interest in land is transferred to a third party "by trustees in purported implement of trust purposes", the third party has no entitlement to indemnity under section 12 of the 1979 Act in respect of that interest: section 12(3)(j)(ii).

Chapter 11

ADMINISTRATION AND SUPERVISION OF CHARITABLE TRUSTS

11.01 Charity law is a complex subject and a comprehensive treatment is well outwith the scope of this book. For more detailed discussion, the reader is referred to the following sources:
- Christine R. Barker (ed.), *Charity Law in Scotland* (1996)
- Scottish Executive Central Research Unit, *Scottish Charity Legislation: An Evaluation* (2000)
- *CharityScotland: The Report of the Scottish Charity Law Review Commission* (2001).

Charity law is not part of the law of trusts, but there is a significant interaction between the two areas. In a Scottish Executive study, *Scottish Charity Legislation: An Evaluation* (2000), as many as four in five of the charities surveyed appeared to be either trusts or unincorporated associations (paras 2.17–2.18). The law of trusts is applicable to both categories, because an unincorporated association has no legal personality, and its assets must, therefore, be held by trustees on behalf of the association. For a discussion of the implications of this principle, see Barker, *Charity Law in Scotland*, paras 3.2.9 and 3.3.31–3.3.39.

Scottish charity law was recently the subject of a comprehensive review by the Scottish Charity Law Review Commission and it is expected that the current legal regime will be comprehensively overhauled by the Scottish Parliament in the near future. Accordingly, this chapter simply sets out briefly the current regulatory framework and notes the current proposals for reform.

1. GENERAL

11.02 The principal regulatory framework for Scottish charities is contained in the Law Reform (Miscellaneous Provisions) (Scotland) Act 1990.

Christine R Barker, Robert C Elliot and Susan R Moody, "The Impact of the New Regulatory Framework on Scottish Charities"
1994 S.L.T. (News) 331

"The Law Reform (Miscellaneous Provisions) (Scotland) Act 1990 establishes a regulatory framework with particular functions for a new agency, the Scottish Charities Office, which was established as a division of the Crown Office in April 1992 in order to exercise powers of investigation and supervision on behalf of the Lord Advocate. Under the 1990 Act the Lord Advocate is given powers to carry out investigations into alleged mismanagement or misconduct, to suspend trustees and to bring actions in the Court of Session as well as the power to investigate bodies which represent themselves as charities. It is to the Scottish Charities Office that application for waivers of disqualification for criminal offences or bankruptcy is made. It does not have the dual advisory and investigatory roles of the Charity Commission, and its investigative powers are essentially reactive, in response to complaints from members of the public. The Scottish Council for Voluntary Organisations (SCVO) and other bodies representing charities would have liked to have see the establishment of an office with far more sweeping powers, more akin to those of the Charity Commission in England and Wales".

2. WHEN IS A TRUST A "CHARITABLE" TRUST?

The 1990 Act refers to charities as "recognised bodies". A body is a "recognised body" if the **11.03** Commissioners of Inland Revenue have granted it relief from tax in respect of "income of the body which is applicable and applied to charitable purposes only". For the 1990 Act to apply, the body must either be established under the law of Scotland, or managed or controlled wholly or mainly from Scotland. (See section 1(7) of the 1990 Act and section 505 of the Income and Corporation Taxes Act 1988).

A "recognised body" is entitled to describe itself as "a Scottish charity" (section 1(7) of the 1990 Act). Where a body which is neither entitled to describe itself as a charity under the 1990 Act or the relevant English legislation does so, the Lord Advocate is entitled to apply to the Court of Session for an interdict to prevent that body describing itself in this way (section 2 of the 1990 Act).

In determining charitable status, the Scottish courts must apply the English law of charities:

Inland Revenue v. Glasgow Police Athletic Association
1953 S.C. (H.L.) 13; 1953 S.L.T. 105

The City of Glasgow Police Athletic Association claimed exemption from liability to income **11.04** tax on the profits of their annual sports meeting. The Commissioners for the Special Purposes of the Income Tax Acts held that they were entitled to this exemption, and the Inland Revenue appealed to the First Division of the Court of Session, which refused the appeal. On appeal to the House of Lords:

LORD NORMAND: "The stated case came before the First Division of the Court of Session. Their Lordships did not address themselves to a discussion and decision of the question of law submitted for their opinion, 'whether the City of Glasgow Police Athletic Association is, within the meaning and for the purposes of section 30 of the Finance Act, 1921 (as amended by section 24 of the Finance Act, 1927) a charity, namely a body of persons established for charitable purposes only'. The Lord President pointed out that *Pemsel's* case, [1891] A.C. 531, decided that the words 'charity' and 'charitable' in the Income Tax Act, 1842, must be construed in their technical meaning according to English law. The words which have to be construed under the Acts now in force are the same. *Pemsel's* (*supra*) case also disapproved of *Baird's Trs*, 15 R. 682, in which Lord President Inglis had held that the words 'charitable purposes' in the Act of 1842 were to be interpreted in their popular signification as meaning the relief of poverty. Plainly, *Pemsel's* case laid down the rule for construing 'charity' and 'charitable' as one to be observed both by the Courts in England and by the Court of Session. The advantage for Scottish taxpayers of this rule over the construction accepted in *Baird's Trs* (*supra*) is obvious and considerable. The Lord President proceeds to say that the general law of charities has progressed in England and Scotland since *Pemsel's* case was decided and that there is a considerable and growing divergence. His conclusion is that the Court of Session cannot invest itself with the unique attributes of the Chancery Division or perform the functions which belong to the system of law there administered and that the difficulty in which the Court of Session finds itself, hitherto evaded, must now be faced. His solution of the problem is that the English law of charities is foreign law and a matter of fact for the Court of Session, and therefore that the only course open to him was to take the determination of the Special Commissioners as a finding of fact for the Scottish Courts. With this mode of disposing of the stated case the other members of the Court agreed. They professed a sense of incapacity to deal with the case in any other way.

My Lords, I will not disguise that I have a certain sympathy with the Scottish Judges, who feel embarrassed at having to administer as part of the law of Scotland a difficult and technical branch of English law. For I have had in the Court of Session some, though not a large, experience of this jurisdiction, and I felt the embarrassment. Nevertheless, I must at once say that there has been here a failure to exercise a jurisdiction which the Court had a plain duty to exercise.

My Lords, in *Pemsel's* case it was decided authoritatively that it was part of the jurisdiction of the Court of Session as Court of Exchequer in Scotland to administer this branch of English law in claims for exemption by charities. Since then the Finance Act, 1925, section 19, has provided that claims for exemption by charities were in future to be made to the Commissioners of Inland Revenue and were to be determined by the Special Commissioners in like manner as an appeal made to them against an assessment under Schedule D, and that all the provisions of the Income Tax Acts relating to such an appeal (including the provisions relating to the statement of a case for the opinion of the High Court on a point of law) shall apply accordingly with any necessary modifications. For Scottish subjects the appeal on law is, of course, to the Court of Session (Income Tax Act, 1918, section 235 and section 149 (3)). The Court of Session has, therefore, a statutory duty to decide any question of law that may come before it in a claim to exemption, and the law which it must administer is the English law of charity.

The necessary effect of *Pemsel's* case and now also of the provisions of section 19 of the Act of 1925 is that the English law of charity has, for income tax purposes and for them alone, to be regarded as part of the law of Scotland and not as a foreign law. The practical difficulties for a Scottish lawyer are considerable, but I would not have them exaggerated. These difficulties spring mainly from the nature of charity and from the way in which the law of charity has grown up. I need not enlarge on this for it is an aspect of the English law which has been recently sufficiently commented on with special authority by Lord Simonds, as he then was, in *Gilmour v. Coats*, [1949] A.C. 427 at 449, and in *Oppenheim v. Tobacco Securities Trust Company Limited*, [1951] A.C. 297, at 307. I venture, however, to say that many of the difficulties felt by Scottish lawyers in administering this law, are scarcely less felt by English equity lawyers, and that the general Scots law of charities likewise has difficulties of its own. It has never yet, for example, been found possible to define in generally accepted terms what is the precise meaning of charity in Scottish law, and one reason is that the Scots law of charities owes nothing to the great institutional writers, and much of it, like its counterpart in England, has been built up piecemeal by the decisions of the Courts.

The duty of the Court of Session to apply the English law of charities in Income Tax cases has been expressly recognised in *Jackson's Trs*, 1926 S.C. 579, 1926 S.L.T. 358, by Lord President Clyde and Lord Sands. In that case the limits of the rule were defined. It was also recognised and applied in *Trustees for the Roll of Voluntary Workers*, 1942 S.C. 47, 1942 S.L.T. 102. Among the consequences of the action taken by the First Division in this case is to cast some doubt on these cases and to deprive Scottish claimants of an effective right to appeal from the determination of the Commissioners.

In certain respects the jurisdiction is less embarrassing than their Lordships seem to have supposed. They are technically not bound by the decisions of the English Courts in the matter of charities and it is not improper for them to discuss or criticise English decisions. The Court of Session is not reduced to the role of an obsequious follower of decisions either of a Judge of first instance or of the Court of Appeal, though it is only good sense to pay special regard and respect to the decisions and opinions pronounced by the English Courts on a branch of the law built up by English Judges, and familiar to them by long training and experience."

The House of Lords then considered the merits of the appeal and reversed the interlocutor of the First Division.

NOTE:

11.05 The English law of charities (which, by virtue of the decision in *Inland Revenue v. Glasgow Police Athletic Association*, must be applied in Scotland for the purposes of taxation—and, therefore, determining whether a body is a "recognised body" within the meaning of the 1990 Act) contemplates four broad categories of charitable purpose:

> "'Charity' in its legal sense comprises four principal divisions: trusts for the relief of poverty; trusts for the advancement of education; trusts for the advancement of religion; and trusts for other purposes beneficial to the community, not falling under any of the preceding heads." (*Income Tax Special Commissioners v. Pemsel* [1891] A.C. 531, *per* Lord Macnaghten at 583).

As to the meaning of the fourth of these divisions, see the following extract:

CharityScotland: The Report of the Scottish Charity Law Review Commission (2001), paras 1.23–1.24

"Other charitable purposes for the benefit of the community   **11.06**
   1.23 This category has been described as a 'residual grouping'. Examples of purposes which benefit the community and are considered to be charitable include:
- the relief of old age, sickness, or disability, even where there is no financial need
- the promotion of racial harmony
- the resettlement and rehabilitation of offenders and drug abusers
- the provision of help for victims of natural or civil disasters
- the provisions of recreational facilities which are open to everyone (for example, a sports centre)
- the provision of recreational facilities for particular beneficiary groups such as a people with disabilities or the elderly
- the promotion of the arts
- the promotion of industry and business for the public benefit
- the welfare of animals

   1.24 The following are examples of organisations which are often assumed to be charitable, but in fact are not:
- sports clubs set up to benefit only their members (as distinct from sports facilities open to everyone or specifically provided for special groups of people, such as elderly people)
- the promotion of political or propagandist purposes, or the promotion of a particular point of view
- purposes which include arrangement where the people who manage the organisation receive significant personal benefit
- raising funds for other charities where the organisers do not have any say over how the funds are spent
- purposes which promote friendship or international friendship, for example, town twinning
- organisations such as Amnesty International and Greenpeace."

4. DUTIES IMPOSED BY THE 1990 ACT

A. Duty to keep accounting records

Law Reform (Miscellaneous Provisions) (Scotland) Act 1990, ss.4–5

Duty to keep accounting records
   4.—(1) The persons concerned in the management or control of every recognised body   **11.07** shall ensure that there are kept in respect of the body, accounting records which are sufficient to show and explain the body's transactions and which are such as to—

(a) disclose with reasonable accuracy, at any time, the financial position of the body at that time; and

(b) enable them to ensure that any statement of accounts prepared under section 5 of this Act complies with the requirements of that section.

(2) The accounting records shall in particular contain—

(a) entries showing from day to day all sums of money received and expended by the body, and the matters in respect of which the receipt and expenditure takes place; and

(b) a record of the assets and liabilities of the body.

(3) The accounting records which are required by this section to be kept in respect of a recognised body shall be preserved, without prejudice to any requirement of any other enactment or rule of law, for six years from the date on which they are made.

(4) The Secretary of State may, by regulations—

(a) prescribe requirements as to the places where and the persons by whom the accounting records of recognised bodies, including bodies which have been wound up or have ceased to be active, are to be kept; and

(b) provide that such class or classes of recognised body as may be prescribed shall be exempt from such requirements of this section and section 5 of this Act as may be prescribed.

Annual accounts and report

5.—(1) The persons concerned in the management or control of every recognised body shall ensure that, in respect of each financial year of the body, there is prepared a statement of accounts.

(2) Subject to subsection (3) below, the statement of accounts of every recognised body shall comprise—

(a) a balance sheet as at the last day of the year;

(b) an income and expenditure account; and

(c) a report as to the activities of the body, having regard to its charitable purposes.

(3) As regards such class or classes of recognised body as the Secretary of State may, by regulations, prescribe a recognised body may elect that in respect of any financial year its statement of accounts shall, instead of the requirements of subsection (2) above, comprise—

(a) a statement of balances as at the last day of the year

(b) a receipts and payments account; and

(c) a report as to the activities of the body, having regard to its charitable purposes.

(4) The balance sheet shall give a true and fair view of the state of affairs of the body as at the end of the financial year; and the income and expenditure account shall give a true fair view of the surplus or deficit of the body for the financial year.

(5) The Secretary of State may, by regulations, prescribe—

(a) the form and content of the statement of accounts;

(b) any additional information to be provided by way of notes to the accounts; and

(c) such requirements as to auditing of the balance sheet, statement of balances, income and expenditure account and receipts and payments account and any notes thereon and as to the consideration of the report as he considers appropriate, and different provision may be prescribed for different bodies or classes of bodies.

(6) The Lord Advocate may require any recognised body to furnish him, without payment therefor, with a copy of its statement of accounts.

(7) Every such body shall—

(a) make available to any person who requests it, on payment of such reasonable charge in respect of copying and postage as the body may stipulate, a copy of its most recent statement of accounts;

(b) inform any person who requests it of its accounting reference date.

(8) Where any recognised body fails, within 10 months, or such longer period as the Lord Advocate may allow, after the end of a financial year, to have prepared a statement of

accounts, the Lord Advocate may require that such fact shall be noted for the purposes of section 1(3) of this Act.

(9) Where a body has failed to have prepared a statement of accounts as mentioned in subsection (8) above, the Lord Advocate may require the persons concerned in the management or control of the body to have prepared a statement of accounts, by such date as he may require.

(10) In any case where the statement of accounts has not been prepared by the date specified under subsection (9) above, the Lord Advocate may appoint a suitably qualified person to prepare a balance sheet and income and expenditure account or, in the case of a body which belongs to a class to which subsection (3) above applies if it appears to such person more appropriate to do so, a statement of balances and receipts and payments account; and a person so appointed shall be entitled, for that purpose—

(a) on giving prior notice in writing, to enter, at all reasonable times, the premises of the body;

(b) to take possession of any document appearing to him to relate to the financial affairs of the body;

(c) to require any person concerned in the management or control of the body to give him such information as he may reasonably require relating to the activities of the body,

and the persons concerned in the management or control of the body shall be personally liable jointly and severally for the expenses incurred in the performance of his functions under this section by any person so appointed.

(11) A person appointed under subsection (10) above shall make a report to the Lord Advocate as to the affairs and accounting records of the body and shall send a copy of the report to any person appearing to him to be concerned in the management and control of the body.

(12) Where any such body, within one month of its being requested to do so by any person—

(a) fails to provide to that person a copy of its most recent statement of accounts as mentioned in subsection (7) above; or

(b) fails to inform that person of its accounting reference date,

the Lord Advocate, on a compliant being made to him by such person, may direct that the fact of such failure shall be noted for the purposes of section 1(3) of this Act.

(13) Where in the case of any recognised body, there has been a failure such as is mentioned in subsection (9) or (12) above the court may, on an application being made by the Lord Advocate, interdict the body and any person concerned in its management or control from engaging in any activity specified in the application until the Lord Advocate intimates to the court that he is satisfied that the failure has been rectified.

[Subsection 14 deals with the application of certain of these provisions to companies].

NOTES:

1. When the Lord Advocate requires that a fact be "noted for the purposes of section 1(3)" **11.08** (see sections 5(8) and (12)), that means that it will be communicated to any person who requests the name and address of the charity from the Commissioners of Inland Revenue. See section 1(1)(b) and (3) of the 1990 Act.

2. Regulations have been made under this section: see the Charities Accounts (Scotland) Regulations 1992 (S.I. 1992 No. 2165). These provide, *inter alia*, that s.5(3) applies to charities "the gross receipts of which in the financial year in question do not exceed £25,000 per annum and the founding deed of which contains no requirement that its statement of accounts shall be audited." (reg. 3). The regulations make further provision for the form and content of accounts. Under reg. 7, where a charity's gross income or expenditure exceeds £100,000 per annum, or where its founding deed states that its accounts must be audited, its accounts must be audited in accordance with the procedures and requirements specified in

the Regulations. Where an audit is not required, an "independent examiner" must examined the accounts. A pilot study of the effect of the 1990 Act by the University of Dundee revealed the following:

> "The accounting aspects of the new regulatory framework have given rise to a number of problems and a considerable amount of confusion. For example, there was confusion amongst the interviewees about the date from which the new Accounting Regulations came into effect. . . Secondly, many small charities had used the term "audit" in their constitutions and had to incur the cost of a professional audit regardless of the level of their income or go to the expense of having their constitution rewritten. Thirdly, those charities which are not obliged to have a professional audit must have their accounts examined by an "independent examiner", but again there is confusion and uncertainty about who is qualified to act in this role. Fourthly, the Scottish Accounting Regulations were introduced before SORP2 was adopted by the Charity Commission as represent-ing "best recommended practice" for accountants and auditors in England and Wales, and the mainly presentational differences between these accounting requirements seems likely to make charities operating throughout the whole of the UK produce two different sets of accounts." (Christine R Barker, Robert C Elliot and Susan R Moody, "The Impact of the New Regulatory Framework on Scottish Charities", 1994 S.L.T. (News) 331, at 332).

"SORP2" refers to in the (English) Charity Commissioners' *Accounting by Charities: Statement of Recommended Practice* (1995). In 1996, the Accounting Regulations were understood to be under review by the Scottish Office in light of this document (See Barker *et al, Charity Law in Scotland* (1996), para. 8.4.5). They remain in force at the time of writing, however.

3. *Exemption from accounting requirements under s.4(4)(b)*. The relevant regulations are the Charities (Exemption from Accounting Requirements) (Scotland) Regulations 1993 (S.I. 1993 No. 1624), as amended by the Charities (Exemption from Accounting Requirements) (Scotland) Amendment Regulations 1995 (S.I. 1995 No. 645) and the Charities (Exemption from Accounting Requirements (Scotland) Amendment Regulations 2000 (S.S.I. 2000 No. 49). These regulations exempt Scottish charitable corporations, local authority trusts and registered housing associations from section 4 and specified subsections of section 5.

5. SUPERVISION OF CHARITABLE TRUSTS UNDER THE 1990 ACT

A. Supervision by the Lord Advocate

Law Reform (Miscellaneous Provisions) (Scotland) Act 1990, s.6

Powers of Lord Advocate to investigate charities and to suspend trustees

11.09   6.—(1) The Lord Advocate may at any time make inquiries, either generally or for particular purposes, with regard to—

(a) a recognised body;

(b) a registered, or non-registered, charity operating as such in Scotland; or

(c) a non-recognised body which appears to him to represent itself or hold itself out as a charity and—

(i) is established under the law of Scotland;

(ii) is managed or controlled wholly or mainly in or from Scotland; or

(iii) has any moveable or immoveable property situated in Scotland,
    or with regard to any class of any such bodies.

(2) Where it appears to the Lord Advocate—

(a) in the case of a body referred to in paragraph (a) or (b) of subsection (1) above—

(i) that there is or has been any misconduct or mismanagement in its administra-tion; or

(ii) that it is necessary or desirable to act for the purpose of protecting its property or securing a proper application of such property for its purposes; or

(b) in any other case, that a body is a non-recognised body which appears to him to represent itself or hold itself out as a charity, he may, if the body is managed or controlled wholly or mainly in or from Scotland, suspend any person concerned in its management or control from the exercise of his functions (but not for a period longer than 28 days), and may make provision as respects the period of the suspension for matters arising out of it.

(3) The Lord Advocate may from time to time nominate officers for the purpose of making inquiries such as are mentioned in subsection (1) above.

(4) A nominated officer may by notice in writing require any person who he has reason to believe has relevant information to answer questions or otherwise furnish information with respect to any matter relevant to inquiries being made under this section at a specified place and either at a specified time or forthwith.

(5) A nominated officer may, for the purpose of making inquiries under this section—

(a) require any person having in his possession or control any records relating to a body which is the subject of inquiries under this section to furnish him with copies of or extracts from any such records; or

(b) unless it forms part of the records of a court or of a public body or local authority, require such a person to transmit the record itself to him for inspection, either by a specified time or forthwith.

(6) If any person fails or refuses to comply with a requirement made under subsection (4) or (5) above, the nominated officer may apply by summary application to the sheriff for an order requiring that person to—

(a) attend and to answer such questions or to furnish such information at a time and place specified in the order;

(b) furnish the nominated officer with copies or extracts of such records as are specified in the order and by such time as is specified in the order;

(c) transmit to the nominated officer such records as are specified in the order by such time as is specified in the order,

and the sheriff shall, if he considers it expedient to do so, make such an order.

(7) A person shall not be excused from answering such questions as he may be required to answer by virtue of subsection (6) above on the ground that the answer may incriminate or tend to incriminate him, but a statement made by him in answer to any such question shall not be admissible in evidence in any subsequent criminal proceedings against him, except in a prosecution for an offence under section 2 of the False Oaths (Scotland) Act 1933.

(8) A person who fails to comply with an order under subsection (6) above shall be guilty of an offence and liable on summary conviction to a fine not exceeding level 5 on the standard scale.

(9) Any person who wilfully alters, suppresses, conceals or destroys any record which he may be required to furnish or transmit under this section shall be guilty of an offence and liable on summary conviction to a fine not exceeding level 5 on the standard scale or to imprisonment for a term not exceeding 6 months or to both.

(10) Subject to subsections (11) and (12) below, there shall be paid to any person who complies with a requirement under subsection (4) or (5) above such expenses as he has reasonably incurred in so complying.

(11) A nominated officer shall, for the purpose of making inquiries under this section, be entitled without payment to inspect and take copies of or extracts from records in respect of which no requirement can be made under paragraph (b) of subsection (5) above.

(12) A nominated officer shall, for the purpose of making inquiries under this section, be entitled without payment to keep any copy or extract furnished to him under this section; and where a record transmitted to him for his inspection relates only to one or more recognised body and is not held by any person entitled as trustee or otherwise of such a body to the custody of it, the nominated officer may keep it or may deliver it to the trustees of such a body or to any other person who may be so entitled.

(13) In this section, "record" means a record held in any medium and includes books, documents, deeds or papers; and, in this Part of this Act—

"registered charity" means a body which is registered as a charity in England and Wales under section 4 of the Charities Act 1960; and

"non-registered charity" means a charity which, by virtue of sub- section (4) of section 4 of that Act, is not required to register under that section.

B. Supervision by the Court of Session

Law Reform (Miscellaneous Provision) (Scotland) Act 1990, s.7

Powers of Court of Session to deal with management of charities

11.10   7.—(1)Where it appears to the court, in the case of a recognised body or a registered, or non-registered, charity which is managed or controlled wholly or mainly in or from Scotland, that—

(a) there is or has been any misconduct or mismanagement in its administration; or

(b) it is necessary or desirable to act for the purpose of protecting its property or securing a proper application of such property for its purposes,

it may, on the application of the Lord Advocate, exercise any of the powers specified in paragraphs (a) to (f) of subsection (4) below.

(2) Where the court is satisfied, in the case of such a body as is mentioned in subsection (1) above, that—

(a) there is or has been any misconduct or mismanagement in its administration; and

(b) it is necessary or desirable to act for the purpose of protecting its property or securing a proper application of such property for its purposes,

it may, on the application of the Lord Advocate, exercise any of the powers specified in paragraphs (f) to (j) of subsection (4) below.

(3) Where the court is satisfied that a non-recognised body—

(a) represents itself or holds itself out as a charity; and

(b) is established under the law of Scotland or is managed or controlled wholly or mainly in or from Scotland or has moveable or immoveable property situated in Scotland,

it may, on the application of the Lord Advocate, exercise any of the powers specified in subsection (4) below.

(4) The powers which may be exercised under this subsection by the court are—

(a) to interdict ad interim the body from representing itself or holding itself out as a charity or from such other action as the court, on the application of the Lord Advocate, thinks fit;

(b) to suspend any person concerned in the management or control of the body;

(c) to appoint ad interim a judicial factor to manage the affairs of the body;

(d) to make an order requiring any bank or other person holding money or securities on behalf of the body or of any person concerned in its control and management not to part with the money or securities without the court's approval;

(e) to make an order, notwithstanding anything in the trust deed or other document constituting the body, restricting the transactions which may be entered into, or the nature or amount of the payments which may be made, in the administration of the body without the approval of the court;

(f) to appoint a trustee, and section 22 of the Trusts (Scotland) Act 1921 shall apply to such a trustee as if he had been appointed under that section;

(g) to interdict the body from representing itself or holding itself out as a charity or from such other action as the court, on the application of the Lord Advocate, thinks fit;

(h) to remove any person concerned in the management or control of the body;

(j) to appoint a judicial factor to manage the affairs of the body.

(5) Where the court is satisfied, in the case of such a body as is mentioned in subsection (1) above, that—

(a) there has been in its administration any misconduct or mismanagement;

(b) it is necessary or desirable to act for the purpose of protecting its property or securing a proper application of such property for its purposes;

(c) it is not practicable nor in the best interests of the body to retain its existing administrative structure and, if appropriate, trustee body; and

(d) in its opinion, the body's purpose would be achieved better by transferring its assets to another such body,

or where the court is satisfied as mentioned in subsection (3) above in the case of a non-recognised body, it may approve a scheme, presented to it by the Lord Advocate and prepared by him in accordance with regulations made by the Secretary of State, for the transfer of any assets of the body to such body as the Lord Advocate specifies in the scheme, being a recognised body or a registered, or non-registered, charity which is managed or controlled wholly or mainly in or from Scotland.

(6) In the case of a registered, or non-registered, charity which is managed or controlled wholly or mainly outside Scotland but on behalf of which a bank or other person in Scotland holds moveable property, the court may, on the application of the Lord Advocate acting on information received from the Charity Commissioners for England and Wales, make an order requiring the bank or person not to part with that property without the court's approval and such an order shall be subject to such conditions as the court thinks fit.

(7) Where the court has made an order under subsection (6) above and is satisfied, in the case of such a charity, that—

(a) there has been in its administration any misconduct or mismanagement; and

(b) it is necessary or desirable to act for the purpose of protecting its property or securing a proper application of such property for its purposes,

it may, on the further application of the Lord Advocate, make an order confirming the order made under subsection (6) above and such an order shall be subject to such conditions as the court thinks fit.

(8) Where the court has made an order under subsection (6) above and it is satisfied as to the matters specified in subsection (7) above in respect of such a charity, if in its opinion the moveable property would not be applied for the purposes of the charity, it may, on the further application of the Lord Advocate, transfer that property to such body as the Lord Advocate specifies in the application, being a body—

(a) which is a recognised body or registered, or non-registered, charity the purposes of which closely resemble the purpose of the charity whose moveable property is transferred; and

(b) which has intimated that it will receive that property.

(9) The court shall have power—

(a) to vary or recall an order made under paragraph (d) or (e) of subsection (4) above or under subsection (6) or (7) above;

(b) to recall the suspension of a person under paragraph (b) of subsection (4) above

(c) to approve a scheme under subsection (5) above subject to such modifications as it thinks fit;

(d) subject to subsection (10) below, to award expenses as it thinks fit in any proceedings before it under this section.

(10) In a case where, but for the provisions of this subsection, the court would have awarded expenses against the body which is the subject of the proceedings, the court—

(a) shall have regard to the desirability of applying the property of the body for the charitable purposes of that body, or the charitable purposes which are purported to be the purposes of that body, and

(b) may award expenses against a person concerned in the control or management of the body, or against any such persons jointly and severally.

(11) Where the court exercises in respect of a recognised body any power specified in subsection (4) or (5) above, the Lord Advocate may require that exercise to be noted for the purposes of section 1(3) of this Act.

(12) In this section "the court" means the Court of Session.

6. CAPACITY TO BE A TRUSTEE IN A CHARITABLE TRUST

11.11 The same rules which apply to capacity to be a trustee generally (*supra*, Chapter 3) are also applicable to charitable trusts. However, there are a number of additional categories of persons who are disqualified from being trustees in a charitable trust.

Law Reform (Miscellaneous Provisions) (Scotland) Act 1990, s.8

Disqualification of persons concerned in the management or control of recognised bodies
    8.—(1)A person who—
    (a) has been convicted of an offence involving dishonesty;
    (b) is an undischarged bankrupt;
    (c) has been removed, under section 7 of this Act, from being concerned in the management or control of any body; or
    (e) is subject to a disqualification order or disqualification undertaking under the Company Directors Disqualification Act 1986 or to a disqualification order under Part II of the Companies (Northern Ireland) Order 1989,
shall, subject to the provisions of this section, be disqualified from being concerned with the management or control of a recognised body.

    (2) A person shall not be disqualified under subsection (1) above if—
    (a) the conviction mentioned in that subsection is spent by virtue of the Rehabilitation of Offenders Act 1974; or
    (b) the Lord Advocate has thought fit to grant in writing a waiver of that disqualification in respect of that person,
but the Lord Advocate shall not grant a waiver where to do so would prejudice the operation of the Company Directors Disqualification Act 1986.

    (3) A person who is concerned with the management or control of a recognised body whilst disqualified by virtue of this section shall be guilty of an offence and liable—
    (a) on summary conviction, to imprisonment for a term not exceeding 6 months or to a fine not exceeding the statutory maximum or to both; and
    (b) on conviction on indictment, to imprisonment for a term not exceeding 2 years or to a fine or to both.

    (4) The acts, in relation to the management or control of such a body, of such a person as is mentioned in subsection (1) above shall not be invalid only by reason of his disqualification under that subsection.

[Subsection (5) specifies time limits for the commencement of a prosecution for the offence under s8(3)]

[Subsection (6) defines "undischarged bankrupt"]

NOTES:

11.12   1. An "offence involving dishonesty" is not defined, and this disqualification is not limited to any particular offences. It is probably capable of applying to a conviction for an offence which does not necessarily involve dishonesty provided it does so in the particular case.
         2. These grounds are broadly similar to those which apply in England by virtue of the Charities Act 1993, s.72. It may be noted, however, that while a person who is removed from the

management or control of a charity under section 7 of the 1990 Act is disqualified from being a charitable trustee in England (section 72(1)(e) of the 1993 Act), the reverse does not apply—there is no such provision for reciprocal disqualification in the 1990 Act. This would appear to represent a lacuna in the provisions.

3. These provisions, of course, do not apply solely to trustees. It is possible that someone could be concerned in the "management or control" of a trust (for example, a manager employed by the trust) without actually being a trustee.

4. For the avoidance of doubt, it is desirable that the trust deed for a charitable trust should specify that a trustee will automatically cease to hold office if he becomes disqualified by virtue of s.8(1).

7. REFORM

As noted earlier, the Scottish Charity Law Review Commission submitted its report (*CharityScotland: The Report of the Scottish Charity Law Review Commission*) to the Scottish Executive in 2001. The following extract summarises some of the major recommendations. **11.13**

Jean McFadden, "The Modernisation of Charity Law in Scotland: The Report of the Scottish Charity Law Commission" (2001) S.L.P.Q. 215

"The Remit of the Commission
The Commission's remit was as follows:

'To review the law relating to charities in Scotland and to make recommendations on any reforms considered necessary.'

In carrying out its remit the Commission was asked to:

- consider the structure of regulation and support for the charitable sector in Scotland;
- consider the operational effects of Scottish legislation on charities of all types and size, bearing in mind the need to encourage voluntary and charitable activity and the contribution which the voluntary sector makes to the social economy;
- consider how best to protect the public, ensure high standards among charities but at the same time avoid over-burdensome administrative requirements;
- consider whether in addition to reform, the law should also be consolidated. . .

The main recommendations of the Commission

After the consultation ended in the autumn of 2000, the Commissioners entered into a period of intensive discussion and debate and carried out a rigorous examination of the present legal framework. We have made 114 recommendations which are designed to enhance both charitable activity and public confidence in it. One of the recommendations is that the law should be consolidated into a new Charities (Scotland) Act, containing some of the existing law and a substantial volume of new legislation.

The following paragraphs give a broad summary of our main conclusions.

The definition of charities in Scotland

We concluded that the concept of charity had changed dramatically in the years since Lord Macnaghten set out the four heads of charity discussed above [see *supra* para. 11.05]. People who give their time and money are no longer the Lady Bountifuls of the nineteenth century who gave their money for the conversion of heathens or the marriages of poor maids. Charities now play an important part in fields of social welfare, health, housing, the environment, education, the arts and are recognised as a third force, along with the public and private sectors in the delivery of services. Charity law in Scotland has not kept up with the pace of change. The current definition of charitable purpose is not inclusive enough and does not match the modern perception.

We decided to attempt to define some basic principles for determining charitable status in Scotland which go beyond the current legal categories of charitable purpose in the technical English sense. We recommend the following defining principles.

A Scottish Charity should be an organisation:
- whose overriding purpose is for the public benefit;
- which is non-profit-distributing;
- which is independent; and
- which is non-party political.

. . .

The legal form of charities

Incorporation is becoming increasingly important to charities, particularly as a means of limiting trustee liability. At present charities choose from a variety of methods to achieve this, all of which are designed for other purposes and all of which present their own problems.

In the course of a fundamental review of company law launched in 1998 by the Department of Trade and Industry, the Company Law Review Steering Group concluded that there should be a new vehicle for incorporating charities which would be used exclusively by charities and would offer all the benefits of incorporation, including limited liability, without the need for separate regulation. The Department of Trade and Industry have proposed that this new vehicle should be called the Charitable Incorporated Organisation (CIO) and that this vehicle should be open to all charities to adopt but should not be mandatory. We endorsed these proposals and have recommended to the Scottish Executive that proposals for CIO be progressed for Scotland at the same time as in England and Wales. The Scottish Executive has accepted that recommendation. . .

The registration and regulation of Scottish Charities

11.14 It was clear from the responses to our consultation that there is a perceived deficit in Scotland in that there is no body similar to the Charity Commission in England and Wales which can *inter alia* pursue a programme of modernisation of charity law and policy. The definition of a Scottish charity has effectively changed as a result of decisions taken in England. Scotland has been unable to set the agenda for change. In addition, over three-quarters of our respondents favoured the establishment of a Scottish Charity Registrar and regulator. One of the three options for change discussed in the Dundee research paper [*Scottish Charity Legislation: An Evaluation*] was a Charity Commission for Scotland and an adaptation of that option is the one which we favour.

We recommend the establishment of a body (which we have called CharityScotland) which would have the general function of promoting the effective use of charitable resources by encouraging the development of better methods of administration, by giving charity trustees information and advice and by investigating and checking abuses. CharityScotland would have the following powers:
- the determination of charitable status;
- the maintenance of a register of charities
- the ensuring of the public accountability of charities;

- the monitoring of Scottish charities;
- the provision of a support service; and
- the protection of the public

The Scottish Executive and the Scottish Parliament would retain political responsibility for charity law; the Lord Advocate would retain a residual role as guardian of the public interest and the Scottish courts would retain final jurisdiction in relation to discipline and charity reorganisation. The Inland Revenue would retain its function of deciding entitlement to and administration of tax reliefs.

There are various options for setting up such a body. It could be established as an agency of the Scottish Executive, as a non-departmental body, or as a body established by Royal Charter. We concluded that its form was less important than its function. Whatever form is decided upon, the organisation must be as independent as possible to have the confidence of the public and the voluntary sector.

CharityScotland would determine an organisation's eligibility for status as a Scottish Charity with a right of appeal against refusal to a Scottish Charity Review Tribunal. CharityScotland would establish and maintain a Scottish Charity Register which would contain the following documents which would be available for public inspection:

- the founding documents of the charity;
- a statement of the charity's aims and objectives;
- a list of the charity's trustees [meaning those involved in the management or control of the charity]; and
- the charity's last two sets of accounts

We believe that all charities which operate in Scotland, including UK-wide charities, should be formally registered with CharityScotland. Double registration might be unnecessarily bureaucratic and we thus recommend that charities which are registered with the Charity Commission should normally be regarded to undergo a simplified registration process with CharityScotland. We also recommend a formal protocol between CharityScotland and the Charity Commission regarding organisations which operate in both jurisdictions. There are also some Scottish Charities which, because of the work in which they are involved, have other regulatory regimes. To avoid the burden of double or triple registration, we recommend that CharityScotland should be empowered to exempt from its reporting and accounting arrangements those Scottish Charities which appear to it to be sufficiently well-regulated elsewhere.

To improve public accountability, we recommend that all Scottish Charities should submit an annual return to CharityScotland which should contain *inter alia* information on their annual activities and various financial information. To minimise the cost of compliance for smaller Scottish Charities, we recommend that those with assets of less than £100,000, with an annual income of less than £25,000 or which employ no staff should be required to complete an abridged version of the annual return.

None of the Scottish supervisory institutions is presently expressly charged with the function of routine monitoring of Scottish Charities to check for abuses. We recommend that the annual returns should be used by CharityScotland to undertake preventative and systematic monitoring of Scottish Charities. . .

The provision of support for Scottish Charities

. . .

Our consultation revealed that it can be difficult for a Scottish Charity to reorganise. Trustees may want to reorganise when:

- the purposes for which the charity was set up have become outmoded or ineffective;
- a merger with another charity is desired;
- a change in administrative arrangements and/or powers is desired.

Reorganisation may be difficult and expensive if the founding document of the body does not provide an adequate mechanism for this.

We believe that powers to assist Scottish Charities to reorganise should be vested in CharityScotland, as part of its role in providing support for charities, and that these powers should extend to tax-exempt charities operating in Scotland which fall outwith the new definition of Scottish Charity and to non-charitable public trusts. There should be a right of appeal to the courts from CharityScotland's decisions by the charity, the Crown Office or by anyone with a demonstrable interest. In appropriate cases CharityScotland should also have the power to initiate and submit to the court for approval schemes for the reorganisation of a charity where the trustees fail or refuse to carry this out themselves. . .

The protection of the public

The governance of Scottish Charities

11.15 Many people give voluntarily of their time and money to charities and it is important that the integrity of charities is preserved. Our consultation process revealed that there is growing concern that the flow of individuals willing and able to volunteer their time and expertise is dwindling. Smaller organisations find it particularly difficult to secure the service of trustees. We were urged to consider ways of encouraging people to become involved.

Our recommendations include the production of a standard code of best practice for trustees to be devised by CharityScotland in collaboration with appropriate umbrella bodies. We also consider that all those serving on management committees should be encouraged to undertake training to help them discharge their duties.

It was clear from our consultation that limited liability is very important to trustees. The introduction of a new legal form for charities, the proposed Charitable Incorporated Organisation, will offer protection for trustees, but we recommend that CharityScotland should, as well as advising on appropriate organisational forms which offer limited liability, investigate new ways of achieving affordable insurance for trustees.

There was overwhelming support from consultees for the establishment of a register of trustees. However, the Commissioners felt that, in the short term, this might not be a simple task. We do recommend that CharityScotland should keep the establishment of such a register under review. However, we recommend that trustees of Scottish Charities should be required to sign a declaration that they are not disqualified from serving as trustees and that the making of a false declaration should be a criminal offence, leading to automatic disqualification. We also recommend that CharityScotland should maintain a register of disqualified trustees against which interested parties, who show just cause, should be able to check individual names. The Lord Advocate's power to grant a waiver of disqualification should be transferred to CharityScotland. . .

Other key issues

Public trusts

Many public trusts are charities but some are not, as the concept of a public trust in Scots law is different from that in English law. In Scots law, a trust is valid provided it is for the public benefit. In England and Wales a trust for the public benefit is valid only if it is a charitable trust. In Scotland it is quite competent to have a public trust which does not have charitable status and which is not therefore a Scottish Charity within the meaning of s.1(7) of the 1990 Act. The law relating to the reorganisation of public trusts is complex and reorganisation can be expensive.

If our recommendations as to the definition of a charity are accepted, we expect that many more public trusts will be registered as Scottish Charities. How many will remain outwith the new Scottish Charity umbrella will not become clear until the Scottish Charities register is established. We do not recommend the immediate establishment of a register of public trusts but recommend that CharityScotland should keep this issue under review.

The 1990 Act contains simplified procedures for the reorganisation of public trusts, but we believe that these procedures could be further simplified and made less expensive. We therefore recommend that public trusts which are not charities should be able to use CharityScotland to facilitate reorganisation. . .

What next?

The Commission completed its work and reported to the Justice Minister in May 2001. The Scottish Ministers issued a statement welcoming the work of the Commission and stating that they would want to consider the 114 recommendations carefully before moving towards implementation. As part of the process, the Ministers embarked on a consultation exercise both on the broad principles of the report and on the specific recommendations. The Commission's report has been made widely available, both in paper and in electronic form and the consultation period ended on 30th September 2001. The Report has attracted much favourable comment from the voluntary sector in Scotland and from elsewhere in the UK.

New charity legislation does not feature in the list of 18 Bills unveiled by the First Minister as the Executive's legislative programme for 2001–2. Indications from within the Scottish Executive suggest that a Green or White Paper, perhaps with a draft Bill, will be produced at the beginning of 2002. Reform of charity law in Scotland is very high on the agenda of the charitable and voluntary sectors. No doubt politics will dictate whether legislation will come forward in the last year before the next Scottish Parliamentary election in May 2003 or appear as a flagship commitment in the Labour and Liberal Democrat election manifestos for the new Parliament."

Chapter 12

JUDICIAL VARIATION OF TRUSTS

12.01 A trust, by its very nature, severely limits the manner in which the property which is subject to it may be held and applied. The relevant limitations, have, of course, been selected by the truster, and doubtless because, when establishing the trust, he considered that they would represent the most appropriate and expedient set of rules for governing the trust.

Circumstances change, however, and what appears appropriate when the trust is established may cease to be appropriate with the passage of time. The following examples illustrate some of the possibilities, but this list is in no way exhaustive:

- Changes in the law of taxation may mean that the trust property is no longer being managed in the most tax-efficient way possible.
- The truster may have laid down restrictions as to the way in which trust property may be invested which are no longer applicable in a changed economic climate.
- A public trust may be established for a purpose which is subsequently satisfied by government action without the expenditure of the trust funds.
- The trustees may be able to fulfil all the trust purposes without having to expend all of the trust capital.
- A testator may, in a will, have left money to an institution which no longer exists or never existed.
- It may be impossible to give effect to the trust purposes due to a lack of funds.
- Some or all of the beneficiaries in a private trust may decide amongst themselves that they would prefer the trust to be administered differently.

It is not, of course, open to the truster (unless the trust is revocable, on which see *infra,* paras 13.01 *et seq.*) to amend the trust to render it more effective or appropriate to changed circumstances. That would be to defeat the very essence of the trust, which is that the truster has alienated his property and put it beyond his control. (Even if he is a trustee as well as a truster, his powers as trustee are limited by the conditions he laid down as truster). So what scope exists for varying the terms of the trust?

The answer differs according to whether the trust is private or public. In a private trust, the court has certain very limited powers to extend the powers of the trustees or to authorise the trustees to make advances to beneficiaries. Beyond that, the underlying principle is that variation is competent only by the consent of all the beneficiaries. Because it will not always be possible to obtain the consent of all the beneficiaries (some of whom may be legally incapable or unascertained), the court now has a statutory power to grant consent on behalf of certain beneficiaries under certain conditions.

In a public trust, variation is almost always by court application. The court has a common law power to vary trust purposes by approving what is known as a *cy-près* scheme where the performance of the trust has become impossible (and, where the trust has never taken effect, the truster had what is termed a "general charitable intention"). More recently, these powers have been extended by the Law Reform (Miscellaneous Provisions) (Scotland) Act 1990 to cover certain cases which fall short of the "impossibility" requirement. The statute also provides a procedure whereby small public trusts may be varied without the need to apply to the court.

That is the position in summary. The remainder of this chapter considers the position in more depth.

1. PRIVATE TRUSTS

A. Variation prior to the Trusts (Scotland) Act 1961

(a) Variation at common law

At common law, "[i]f all those who are beneficially interested in the trust estate concur in asking the **12.02** trustees to denude, and if they are legally capable of giving their consent, the trustees must terminate the trust on being exonered and discharged." (Mackenzie Stuart, p. 346). It follows, therefore, that if the beneficiaries, by unanimous consent, may terminate the existing trust and establish a new one, they may equally vary the terms of the trust.

The obvious practical problem with this approach is that not all the beneficiaries may be capable of consenting. In particular, the beneficiaries may include children, or it may even be that the trust deed makes provision for persons who are not yet born (and who may never be). Nonage and non-existence obviously preclude giving consent to a variation. Also, where a trust deed makes provision for various contingencies (for example, by stating that property is to be held in liferent for A and in fee for B, and going on to make provision for who is to be entitled to the fee should B predecease A), it is quite possible that the number of possible beneficiaries could become extremely large indeed, making it practically impossible to secure the consent of all the beneficiaries. A second problem is that, if the trust includes an alimentary liferent, the alimentary beneficiary cannot lawfully renounce that liferent.

The Court of Session does have a very limited jurisdiction at common law to authorise variation or termination without all the necessary consents being obtained, such as where the trust would become unworkable without additional powers being granted or where the trustees were only prevented from obtaining the consent of all the beneficiaries by virtue of the fact that unborn children who were, in fact, unlikely ever to be born, would be entitled to benefit under the trust. (See Mackenzie Stuart, pp. 254–259 and 349–353 and *Coles*, 1951 S.C. 608). The trustees might be required to effect insurance to meet the claims of any children who might subsequently be born (*McPherson's Trs v. Hill* (1902) 4 F. 921). The jurisdiction was very limited, however.

A limited variation might also be achieved by way of a beneficiary assigning his or her right in the trust property to a third party (or to one of the other beneficiaries).

(b) Variation under statute

Prior to 1961, there was scope under the Trusts (Scotland) Act 1921 for the court to authorise certain limited variations, as follows.

Section 4 of the 1921 Act lists a number of "general powers of trustees" which all trustees have unless they are "at variance with the terms or purposes of the trust" (see *supra*, para. 6.31). Where any of the section 4 powers are excluded by the trust deed, it is open to the trustees to petition the court under section 5 of the 1921 Act for authority to exercise that power. The court may grant such authority if it is "satisfied that such act is in all the circumstances expedient for the execution of the trust".

Secondly, section 16 of the 1921 Act provides as follows:

"The court may, from time to time under such conditions as they see fit, authorise trustees to advance any part of the capital of a fund destined either absolutely or contingently to beneficiaries who at the date of the application are not of full age, if it shall appear that the income of the fund is insufficient or not applicable to, and that such advance is necessary for, the maintenance and education of such beneficiaries or any of them, and that it is not expressly prohibited by the trust deed, and that the rights of such beneficiaries, if contingent, are contingent only on their survivance."

Although this section only empowers the court to authorise future advances, past advances may be approved by the Inner House under the *nobile officium* (*Christie's Trs*, 1932 S.C. 189).

B. The Trusts (Scotland) Act 1961

12.03 As Wilson and Duncan point out (at 13–08), the common law and 1921 Act powers "are related to keeping private trusts in being by making good defects in the trust machinery. They do not enable the court in any way to innovate upon the basic trust purposes. Most important of all they do not enable the court to improve the position of beneficiaries by varying the trust so as to avoid part of the burden of taxation."

Law Reform Committee for Scotland
Ninth Report: The powers of trustees to sell, purchase or otherwise deal with heritable property; and the variation of trust purposes
(Cmnd. 1102, 1960)

12.04 "30. We understand the scope of our inquiry to be set against the background of an English Bill which has, since the remit to us was made, become an Act of Parliament—The Variation of Trusts Act, 1958, 6 & 7 Eliz. 2, c. 53, designed 'to extend the jurisdiction of Courts of law to vary trusts in the interests of beneficiaries and sanction dealings with trust property. . . the question at issue is whether facilities corresponding to those provided thereby for England should, with or without modification, be incorporated by statute into the law of Scotland. . .

32. For many years it has become increasingly apparent that the traditional type of trust settlement, particularly of a testamentary character, is too inflexible for modern conditions. The primary object generally was to preserve the trust estate for successive generations, the range of investment was severely restricted, there was often no provision for capital payments to beneficiaries during the currency of the settlement, while a very common feature was an alimentary liferent, or successive liferents. Where all the beneficiaries are of full legal capacity it has often been possible for them here, as in England, to 'break' the trust by agreement. But potential beneficiaries, alimentary beneficiaries, persons under age and persons of mental incapacity at present create insuperable obstacles in Scotland because they cannot themselves give legally effective consent and there is no jurisdiction on the part of the Scottish courts to approve schemes on their behalf. . .

35. As already mentioned, the Variation of Trusts Act, 1958, was designed to 'extend' the jurisdiction of the English courts to vary trusts. The genesis of this Act merits explanation. Such jurisdiction had existed in England previous to the Act, but the decision of the House of Lords in *Chapman v. Chapman*, [1954] A.C. 429, disclosed an awkward legal limitation, not previously apprehended, on the general jurisdiction of the English courts to sanction on behalf of persons under age and potential beneficiaries schemes involving an alteration in the rights of such persons, though the Court might consider the same to be for their benefit. The House of Lords held that the jurisdiction of the Court, *quoad* such persons, was confined to cases where the rights of the beneficiaries were in dispute. It was pointed out in the report of the [English] Law Reform Committee (paragraph 10 thereof) that in the result such beneficiaries might be better off if the governing settlement had been badly drawn than if it had been well drawn. . .

38. The Variation of Trusts Act, 1958, restores the English law substantially to what it was apprehended to be until *Chapman* intervened.

39. The variation of trusts by sanction of the Court is thus no new thing in English law. In Scotland, on the other hand, the idea that the Court should have power to sanction variation of the substantive provisions of trusts, as distinct from the mere powers of trustees, is a conception foreign to our jurisprudence and would require a fundamental innovation.

40. Nevertheless we are satisfied that the innovation should be adopted in Scotland. Indeed there is a clamant professional and public demand therefore, partly on the ground that it is quite unreasonable that such facilities should be available in England and denied to Scotland.

41. As pointed out in paragraph 32, the provisions of the old fashioned settlement were designed to preserve the settled property for successive generations. Under modern conditions, particularly looking to the impact of taxation, such provisions, so far from preserving settled property, may have the opposite effect. If capital can be invested only in 'trustee' securities, heavy depreciation may emerge in a period of inflation; if the income be substantial and payable over to a single liferenter, it may be largely absorbed by tax; if capital cannot be paid over to beneficiaries, but must be retained until the death of a liferenter, it may be largely swallowed up by estate duty, with the principle of aggregation swelling the exaction in many cases. Moreover, in the case of a moderate sized estate, a widow liferenter may have a nett income insufficient, gauged by the standard of living while her husband was alive, for the needs of herself and young children, while, in the absence of a power to advance capital with the liferenter's consent, the children may be deprived of education and training for which capital payments at a future and problematical date may be a poor substitute.

42. If an adult *sui juris* can so arrange his affairs within the law as to minimise the impact of Income Tax, Surtax and Estate Duty, or otherwise for his benefit, there is no reason why such facilities should be impossible of extension to a person under age or otherwise incapax. . .

45. As stated in paragraph 31, the English Act of 1958 also empowers the Court to approve of an arrangement enlarging the powers of trustees of managing or administering any of the property subject to the trust concerned. This goes further than any corresponding statutory provision in Scotland. It would cover, for instance, the investment powers of trustees, or their power to sell the trust property and any case of management or administration where the trustees are prohibited by the terms of the trust from exercising powers normally enjoyed by trustees. We consider that the question whether or not a similar facility should be available in Scotland is governed by the same considerations as apply to the power to vary the substantive provisions of trusts. We understand that there is in existence a proposal to extend the investment powers of trustees but, even if implemented, this does not affect the general principle.

46. We accordingly recommend legislation for Scotland empowering the Court, upon the lines and under the limitations indicated later in this Report, to approve the variation and revocation of trust purposes, and arrangements enlarging the powers of trustees in managing or administering any of the property subject to the trust."

Legislation was subsequently enacted in the following terms:

Trusts (Scotland) Act 1961, s.1

Jurisdiction of court in relation to variation of trust purposes

1.—(1) In relation to any trust taking effect, whether before or after the commencement **12.05** of this Act, under any will, settlement or other disposition, the court may if it thinks fit, on the petition of the trustees or any of the beneficiaries, approve on behalf of—

(a) any of the beneficiaries who because of any legal disability by reason of nonage or other incapacity is incapable of assenting, or

(b) any person (whether ascertained or not) who may become one of the beneficiaries as being at a future date or on the happening of a future event a person of any specified description or a member of any specified class of persons, so however that this paragraph shall not include any person who is capable of assenting and would be of that description, or a member of that class, as the case may be, if the said date had fallen or the said event had happened at the date of the presentation of the petition to the court, or

(c) any person unborn,

arrangement (by whomsoever proposed, and whether or not there is any other person beneficially interested who is capable of assenting thereto) varying or revoking all or any of the trust purposes or enlarging the powers of the trustees of managing or administering the trust estate:

Provided that the court shall not approve an arrangement under this subsection on behalf of any person unless it is of the opinion that the carrying out thereof would not be prejudicial to that person.

(2) For the purposes of the foregoing subsection a person who is of or over the age of 16 years but has not attained the age of eighteen years shall be deemed to be incapable of assenting; but before approving an arrangement under that subsection on behalf of any such person the court shall take such account as it thinks appropriate of his attitude to the arrangement.

(3) [Repealed by the Age of Legal Capacity (Scotland) Act 1991, Sch. 2 para. 1]

(4) Where under any trust such as is mentioned in subsection (1) of this section a trust purpose entitles any of the beneficiaries (in this subsection referred to as "the alimentary beneficiary") to an alimentary liferent of, or any alimentary income from, the ftrust estate or any part thereof, the court may if it thinks fit, on the petition of the trustees or any of the beneficiaries, authorise any arrangement varying or revoking that trust purpose and making new provision in lieu thereof, including, if the court thinks fit, new provision for the disposal of the fee or capital of the trust estate or, as the case may be, of such part thereof as was burdened with the liferent or the payment of the income:

Provided that the court shall not authorise an arrangement under this subsection unless—

(a) it considers that the carrying out of the arrangement would be reasonable, having regard to the income of the alimentary beneficiary from all sources, and to such other factors, if any, as the court considers material, and

(b) the arrangement is approved by the alimentary beneficiary, or, where the alimentary beneficiary is a person on whose behalf the court is empowered by subsection (1) of this section or that subsection as extended by subsection (2) of this section to approve the arrangement, the arrangement is so approved by the court under that subsection

(5) Nothing in the foregoing provisions of this section shall be taken to limit or restrict any power possessed by the court apart from this section under any Act of Parliament or rule of law.

(6) In this section the expression "beneficiary" in relation to a trust includes any person having, directly or indirectly, an interest, whether vested or contingent, under the trust.

Notes:

12.06

1. For an overview of the statutory provisions, see Colin Tyre, "Variation of Trusts in Scotland" (1997) 3 Priv. Client Bus. 184. See also J.W. Harris, *Variation of Trusts* (1975), a detailed study of the English legislation which takes into account the Scottish position as well as the approach in other jurisdictions.

2. *The nature of a petition under section 1 of the 1961 Act.* The 1961 Act empowers the court to consent to a variation on behalf of certain persons. It does *not* empower the court to rewrite the terms of the trust. See *Colville, Petr*, 1962 S.L.T. 45, *per* the Lord President (Clyde) at 51–52:

> "If the petitioner's liferent had not been made alimentary, and if the fee of this part of the estate had already vested indefeasibly in ascertained persons who were all over twenty-one years of age, there would, of course, have been nothing to prevent the parties making some arrangement *inter se* to distribute the funds otherwise than as provided by the testator. But under our law as it stood prior to the coming into force of the 1961 Act, such a rearrangement was impossible in the present case because, firstly, the petitioner was enjoying an alimentary liferent which he was in law disabled from renouncing, and secondly, because the persons interested in the fee include a child under twenty-one years of age and, possibly, other children, or remoter issue, of the petitioner yet to be born. It was to meet these obstacles, and to make it possible to surmount them that section 1 of the 1961 Act was enacted. The main purpose of

subsection (1) (a) and (c) is to enable the Court to grant on behalf of a child under twenty-one, or a child not yet born, that approval to a variation of a trust purpose which otherwise could not be obtained, and in terms of subsection (4) the Court may authorise an arrangement which involves varying or revoking an alimentary liferent and making new provisions in place of that liferent. Section 1 does not enable the Court to make a new will or a new purpose in a will which would completely supersede the old and be effective against all possible claimants. It merely affords machinery for giving effective approval to a variation on the part of beneficiaries who owing to age or incapacity, or because they cannot discharge an alimentary liferent, could not otherwise approve."

3. *From whom is consent (or consent "on behalf of" by the court) necessary?* Where a trust provided that the trust property might, in certain circumstances, pass to a wife's testamentary disponees, it was held that because a testamentary provision was revocable no consent (or consent on behalf of) was required: *Law, Petrs*, 1962 S.C. 500.

See also *Phillips, Petr*, 1964 S.C. 141, *per* the Lord President (Clyde) at 150–151:

"This is a petition for the approval and authorisation of an arrangement under section 1 of the Trusts (Scotland) Act, 1961, in connection with the will and codicils of the late Mr James Currie. Under that will and codicils provision is made in certain remote events for the estate passing to certain distant relations of the testator and also certain charitable organisations. The number of persons or bodies that fall within that class is very substantial and service has not been effected upon those members of this class among those who are under twenty-one years of age. Those who are older and the charities mentioned in the testamentary writings have not received intimation of the present proceedings. In order to make provision for the interest of this group of persons, some of whom are represented by a curator and others of whom are not parties to the application, provision has been inserted in the arrangement for insurance cover to protect these ultimate beneficiaries. In our view, however, their interest is so remote and so negligible that they do not qualify as beneficiaries within the meaning of the Act, and need not be therefore provided for in the scheme. That subsection must be given a reasonable construction, and it can never have been intended to include persons whose interest is so remote as to be negligible. If parties choose to make an arrangement outside the scheme for the protection of these parties they are of course free to do so, but in our view article 2 of the arrangement should not be included in the arrangement which the Court approves."

It may be notable that the wording of this passage in the Session Cases report differs from that found in the Scots Law Times, suggesting that Lord Clyde may have had some second thoughts before revising his opinion for publication. In particular, the sentence "That subsection must be given a reasonable construction. . ." does not appear in the Scots Law Times report. It is difficult to see why so much stress is laid on the interpretation to be given to the word "beneficiary" in the statute (and Lord Clyde's interpretation has been disputed: see Wilson and Duncan, para. 13–35). The statute only addresses the question of whom the court is entitled to consent on behalf of. That is a logically separate issue from the question of from whom the trustees must obtain consent in order to be entitled to put a variation into effect. It may be that *Phillips* should be properly regarded as an application of the common law principle that the court might permit a variation where the only thing standing in the trustees' way is the difficulty of obtaining consent from remote beneficiaries who are highly unlikely to ever be entitled to benefit under the trust (*supra*, para. 12.02 and see also *Morris, Petr*, 1985 S.L.T. 252)—but that is certainly not the way in which Lord Clyde rationalizes the decision in *Phillips*. For further discussion of the problems raised by *Phillips*, see Wilson and Duncan, paras 13–35 *et seq*.

On s.1(1)(b), see *Buchan, Petr*, 1964 S.L.T. 51 and *Allan, Petrs*, 1991 S.L.T. 202.

4. *What factors are to be taken into account in the exercise of discretion?* The court has a **12.07** discretion as to whether or not to grant consent. It certainly does not follow that just because it has been shown that a beneficiary will not be prejudiced by the proposed variation, that the court will necessarily grant consent on that beneficiary's behalf (*Lobnitz, Petr*, 1966 S.L.T. (Notes) 81, *infra*, para. 12.08). The fact that the proposed variation may defeat the intention

of the truster in certain respects is not necessarily a bar to granting consent (*Goulding v. James* [1997] 2 All E.R. 239, but see *Re Steed's Will Trusts* [1960] Ch. 407). In *Re Van Gruisen's Will Trusts* [1964] 1 W.L.R. 449, Ungoed-Thomas J. observed (at 450):

> "It is shown that actuarially the provisions for the infants and unborn persons are more beneficial for them under the arrangement than under the present trusts of the will. That, however, does not conclude the case. The court is not merely concerned with this actuarial calculation, even assuming that it satisfies the statutory requirement that the arrangement must be for the benefit of the infants and unborn persons. The court is also concerned whether the arrangement as a whole, in all the circumstances, is such that it is proper to approve it. The court's concern involves, inter alia, a practical and business-like consideration of the arrangement, including the total amounts of the advantages which the various parties obtain, and their bargaining strength."

It has been suggested that there is no need to consider whether a beneficiary who is capable of granting consent himself, and does so, might be prejudiced by the variation: *Colville, Petr*, 1962 S.L.T. 45, *per* the Lord President (Clyde) at 52.

5. *"Exporting" the trust.* Although the terms of s.1 are wide enough to permit the court to approve an arrangement which involves taking the trust funds out of the jurisdiction of the Scottish courts (for example, amalgamating a Scottish and an English trust into one English trust), "such a course is not one which this court would be prepared to follow unless it were clearly warranted by the circumstances of the particular case, since it involves a transfer of the trust estate out of our jurisdiction." (*Baroness Lloyd, Petr*, 1963 S.C. 37, *per* the Lord President (Clyde) at 45). The English courts have been prepared to consent to a transfer out of the jurisdiction where the beneficiaries have emigrated (*Re Seale's Marriage Settlement* [1961] Ch. 574). In one case, an English court was prepared to approve a transfer of the trust funds to Guernsey (proposed for tax reasons) despite the beneficiaries having no connection with that jurisdiction. (*Re Chamberlain* (1976) unreported, but see J.B. Morcom, "Trust Exporting" (1976) 126 N.L.J. 1034).

6. *What constitutes "prejudice" under section 1(1)?* Under s.1(1), the court cannot grant approval on behalf of any person "unless it is of the opinion that the carrying out thereof would not be prejudicial to that person". This is a notable difference from the English legislation, which states that the court shall not grant approval unless the variation "would be for the benefit of that person" (s.1(1) of the 1958 Act). It is not clear why the Scottish legislation was worded differently. The concept of "prejudice" was considered in *Pollok-Morris, Petrs*, 1969 S.L.T. (Notes) 60. In that case, P had established a trust for the benefit of his wife, lawful issue, mother and two named sisters. It was unlikely that there would be any children of his existing marriage and he and his wife adopted a child. Approval was sought for a variation so that adoptive children and their issue would fall within the class of beneficiaries. The court refused to approve the proposed variation on behalf of any unborn children, observing (*per* the Lord President (Clyde)):

> "The application is formally opposed by the trustees in order to secure a determination from the Court as to whether these lawful issue, if there ever are any, would be prejudiced. In my view, we cannot affirm that there would be no prejudice to them. If the group of persons among whom the estate may be divided is increased to include some other person not originally in it, that does, in my view, constitute a possible prejudice to those in the group and makes it impossible for this Court to hold that the carrying out of this arrangement would not be prejudicial to the lawful issue of the truster."

Pollok-Morris is a rather harsh decision, and adopts what might be considered to be an unduly narrow interpretation of "prejudice" by measuring the concept in purely financial terms. Is it not arguable that the "spectral" unborn child might, if born, actually benefit from an arrangement which treated all the children in the family equally and thus avoided the possibility of family dissension? See *Re Remnant's Settlement Trusts* [1970] 1 Ch. 560, *per* Pennycuick J. at 566 and *Re Zekelman* (1971) 19 D.L.R. (3d.) 652. *Pollok-Morris* is worth comparing with *Stanbrook v. Perpetual Trustees WA Ltd* [1998] WASC 229, where the Supreme Court of Western Australia was asked to consent to a trust variation on behalf of children who might potentially be born to a 51 year old woman, who had deposed that she had no intention of having or of adopting a child. The proposed variation would, as in *Pollok-Morris*, have reduced the "spectral" child's share of the trust estate. Nevertheless, it was held that "the risk of any possible detriment is so remote that it should not be allowed to stand in the way of the generally beneficial arrangement proposed." Note, however, that this decision rested on the slightly different terms of the Western Australian legislation, which provides as follows:

> "the Court shall not approve an arrangement on behalf of any person if the arrangement is to his detriment; and, in determining whether any such arrangement is to the detriment of a person, the Court may have regard to all the benefits that may accrue to him directly or indirectly in consequence of the arrangement, including the welfare and honour of the family to which he belongs." (Trusts Act 1962 (WA), s.90(2)).

Whether under the Australian or the Scottish legislation, however, the point is still problematic. It is arguable that a variation is not to a person's prejudice if there is only a minor risk of prejudice occurring. Consider the following *dicta* from two English cases (bearing in mind that the English legislation requires a "benefit" rather than simply the absence of prejudice):

> "if people ask the court to sanction this sort of scheme they must be prepared to have some sort of risk and if it is a risk that an adult would be prepared to take, the court is prepared to take it on behalf of the infant." (*Re Cohen's Will Trusts* [1959] 1 W.L.R. 865, *per* Danckwerts J. at 868)

> "I have not got to consider whether the scheme is bound to confer a benefit on every one who may become interested in the trusts in every event, but whether in the probable events it is calculated to confer a benefit." (*Re Michelham's Will Trusts* [1964] Ch. 550, *per* Buckley J. at 557)

However, given that the "spectral" child in *Pollok-Morris* would necessarily, if born, be entitled to a smaller share of the trust estate if the variation had taken place than he would under the status quo, it would seem rather odd to justify granting consent on the basis that the "spectral" child is only taking a "risk" of prejudice or detriment. The point is a difficult one.

Although the English courts have, as noted above, tended to view it as acceptable for a beneficiary to be put at a minor risk of not benefiting (or, in Scottish terms, being prejudiced), the Scottish courts have indicated that they may require the trustees to effect an insurance policy against the contingency which would result in prejudice. For example, in *Colville, Petr*, 1962 S.L.T. 45, the other beneficiaries might have been prejudiced by the proposed variation if the petitioner had died within five years, because of the death duty which would be payable. Accordingly, as part of the variation, the trustees proposed to effect a policy of assurance which would pay out a sum equal to the estimated death duty if this were to happen. The proposed variation was approved. The court may refuse to grant approval for a variation unless provision is made for insurance: *National Commercial Bank of Scotland Ltd, Petr*, 1962 S.L.T. (Notes) 65. It appears, however, that it is becoming more difficult as a matter of practice to obtain the type of insurance required in such cases: see Colin Tyre, "Variation of Trusts in Scotland" (1997) 3 Priv. Client Bus. 184, who discusses the alternative of retaining an actuarially valued fund.

It has been said that "a curator *ad litem* [will] always be appointed to beneficiaries of nonage whose interests [are] liable to be affected by the proposed arrangement." (*Tulloch's Trs, Petrs*, 1962 S.C. 245)

7. *When will the court authorise variation of an alimentary liferent?* The court will take into account considerations such as the liferenter's other assets and income and the provision which will be made for them under the varied trust: *e.g. Findlay, Petr*, 1962 S.C. 210. In *Colville, Petr*, 1962 S.L.T. 45, taxation meant that C derived "little, if any, benefit from a large part of the alimentary liferent payable to him", and extremely heavy estate duty would be payable on his death at current rates. A variation (substitution of a right in fee for his

liferent) was approved. It should be noted that where it is still open to the party concerned to renounce an alimentary liferent, there is no need to seek the court's authority to do so: *Findlay, Petr*, 1962 S.C. 210; *Smillie, Petr*, 1966 S.L.T. 41. See also the following case:

Lobnitz, Petr
1966 S.L.T. (Notes) 81

12.08 L, an alimentary beneficiary, sought the court's permission to vary his liferent in the trust property.

LORD PRESIDENT (CLYDE): "The [proposed] arrangement takes the now familiar form of an enlargement of the petitioner's liferent into a right of fee of a portion of the capital presently liferented by him, the remainder being held in trust for the petitioner's children and remoter issue. For the purposes of this opinion it is unnecessary to consider the detailed provisions for the children and their issue. These appear adequately to protect them *inter se*.

The matter which has caused us some difficulty is the method adopted of apportioning the capital of the trust fund between the liferenter on the one hand and his children and remoter issue on the other. The ordinary method of doing this in a case of this kind is to ascertain what proportion of the total trust funds in question is represented by the actuarial value of the liferent, what proportion is represented by the saving in estate duty consequent on the application being granted and what proportion is left for the fiars. The saving in estate duty is then allocated proportionately between the liferenter and fiars.

The figures in the present case were not arrived at on this basis. What the petitioner has done is to allocate to the children and issue the proportion of the trust fund representing what they would get if no arrangement were made and estate duty payable on the trust fund on his death were deducted. The balance of the trust fund is then allocated to himself. The argument in favour of this method of fixing the allocation is that no prejudice within the meaning of section 1(1) of the Act could thereby be suffered by the children and remoter issue on whose behalf our approval is asked, since they will get now at least as large a slice of capital as they could get if no arrangement were made. In such circumstances it is immaterial, so it is argued, what is the amount the liferenter gets, provided only, as is demonstrated in this case, that having regard to his income from all sources the capital sum he is to get involves no material reduction in his financial position.

But in our view this does not involve adequate compliance with section 1(4)(a) of the Act. In order to justify us in authorising a variation of the alimentary provision we must be satisfied not merely that the arrangement is reasonable having regard to the income of the liferenter from all sources, but 'after taking into account such other factors as the Court considers material'. In our view it is necessary in order to determine this question of reasonableness that the actuarial value of the liferenter's interest should be placed before the Court. The value of the liferenter's interest is obviously a material circumstance and therefore to enable us to carry out our statutory duty in granting authority we require to know from an actuary what proportion of the trust fund represents the actuarial value of the liferent.

We shall therefore continue this case to enable the petitioner to produce the usual report by an actuary."

> 8. *The importance of taking actuarial advice.* In *National Commercial Bank of Scotland Ltd, Petr*, 1962 S.L.T. (Notes) 65, it was proposed that G's alimentary liferent should be revoked as insufficient for his needs and that a capital payment in lieu thereof should be made to him. An actuary's opinion was lodged with the petition "setting forth the proper apportionment of the trust capital between the liferenter and the fiars". The Lord President (Clyde) observed (at 65): "It is of importance in these cases that an actuary's apportionment should be adhered to by the parties because any adjustment or compromise upon it might introduce an element of gift by the liferenter to the fiars and thus possibly attract death duty. If the

actuary's figure as produced is to be challenged the only proper way to do it would be to lodge another actuary's certificate bringing out a different apportionment and the Court would then have to decide between the two. In the present case we shall abide by the actuary's apportionment which therefore excludes any question of gift by the liferenter to the fiars or vice versa."

9. *Can the court authorise an extension to the investment powers of the trustees?* In *Inglis, Petr*, 1965 S.L.T. 326, the Inner House took the view that "the petitioner may seek to clear up ambiguities in the investment powers of the trustees but, in my opinion, the petition cannot competently be used to extend the investment powers beyond (1) what the truster has authorised and (2) what parliament has sanctioned in the Trustee Investment Act, 1961." (*per* the Lord President (Clyde) at 327). However, a Full Bench, having been referred to *Inglis*, allowed such an extension in 1981 (*Henderson, Petr*, 1981 S.L.T. (Notes) 40).

Although no opinions were issued in that case, it has since been observed that *Inglis* has effectively been overruled by *Henderson* (*University of Glasgow, Petrs*, 1991 S.L.T. 604, *per* the Lord President (Hope) at 606). That seems correct in principle, given, first, that the Law Reform Committee, in its 1960 report, had clearly envisaged that such an extension would be competent (see para. 45 of the Report, *supra* para. 12.04); second, that section 15 of the Trustee Investments Act 1961 explicitly preserves the power of the court to "confer wider powers of investment on trustees", and thirdly, that the powers conferred by the 1961 Act are now considered to be outdated (see *British Museum Trs v. Attorney-General* [1984] 1 W.L.R. 418).

10. *Procedure*. It has been observed that proceedings in an application under section 1 of the 1961 Act "are to some extent administrative and the Court is not bound to adhere to strict rules of evidence. If essential facts are disputed inquiry by way of remit or even by allowing a proof may be necessary, but this must be rare. If documents are produced to vouch material averments and actuarial or other reports produced to support material calculations, and if these are either accepted or not disputed by the trustees and the respondents or minuters who appear in the process they may be accepted by the Court without further proof." (*Colville, Petr*, 1962 S.L.T. 45, *per* the Lord President (Clyde) at 51). See further Wilson and Duncan, paras 13–57 *et seq.* and the relevant Rules of the Court of Session (RCS r. 14.3(g) and Chapter 63, Part I).

2. PUBLIC TRUSTS

A. Variation under the Trusts (Scotland) Act 1921

As was noted earlier in the context of private trusts (*supra,* para. 12.02), section 4 of the Trusts **12.09** (Scotland) Act 1921 lists a number of "general powers of trustees" which all trustees have unless they are "at variance with the terms or purposes of the trust". Where any of the section 4 powers are excluded by the trust deed, it is open to the trustees to petition the court under section 5 of the 1921 Act for authority to exercise that power. The court may grant such authority if it is "satisfied that such act is in all the circumstances expedient for the execution of the trust". This provides some limited scope for the court to extend the powers of trustees in a public trust.

B. The common law power of the Court of Session to provide machinery

Where the truster has specified a public purpose, but has failed to specify the machinery by which this **12.10** purpose is to be given effect, the Court of Session may make up the deficiency in the trust deed. This is an exercise of the *nobile officium*.

Gibson's Trs
1933 S.C. 190

LORD PRESIDENT (CLYDE): "[If] a settlor has clearly manifested an intention to establish some specific kind of charitable institution, but has failed to provide his trustees with the powers and machinery to establish and work it, the endowment will not only not be allowed to fail, but the Court will take it upon itself to carry out the establishment of the specific institution by creating the powers and machinery, and placing them in the hands of the trustees—*Magistrates of Dundee v. Morris* (1858) 3 Macq. 134."

Lindsay's Trs v. Lindsay
1938 S.C. 44

12.11 LORD PRESIDENT (NORMAND): "This is a peculiar case. It is peculiar in its facts and it is peculiar in its procedure.

The testator, Mr Archibald Macneil Lindsay, merchant, Dalbeattie, by his trust-disposition and settlement, directed his testamentary trustees to make over the residue of his estate to 'the trustees of the John Lindsay Memorial Hospital, Dalbeattie (known as the Lindsay Memorial Trustees) whether that hospital be then erected or no, said residue to be held by said last-mentioned Trustees as an endowment for said hospital when erected, and the annual income and produce from such endowment shall be applied by them towards the cost of maintaining and running said hospital in such way and manner as said last-mentioned Trustees may consider proper and in accordance with the terms of the Declaration of Trust executed by them of even date with my execution of these presents and of the constitution which they are authorised to frame under the eighth article of said Declaration of Trust.'

The petitioners aver that the testator had in mind to provide funds for the erection of a hospital at Dalbeattie to be known as the John Lindsay Memorial Hospital, that a deed of trust had been prepared and approved by him, and was to be executed by certain trustees who had agreed to act in the administration of the trust fund, and it was the intention of the testator that his will and this deed of trust should be executed at the same date. Before the deed of trust could be executed by the trustees who were to act under it he should I have handed over to them certain securities which were to be held by them subject to the declaration. Now, the testator was taken ill and he sent for his solicitor in order that he might sign his will. His will was accordingly duly executed on 1st February 1937. He died very shortly after the execution of his will, the fund was never handed over by him, and the trustees or the gentlemen who had agreed to act as trustees have never executed the deed of declaration. These are the averments.

The petitioners, who are the testamentary provide trustees, now come forward and apply to the Court, laying before the Court a *cy pres* scheme of administration and asking the Court to authorise that scheme... [Lord Normand expressed doubts about the mode of procedure adopted, and continued:] But, since parties have joined issue, I think that the question at any rate may be settled in this process, and the answer to that question will go a considerable distance towards solving the dispute between the parties.

The next-of-kin, the respondents, maintain that the only matter which is relevant for the consideration of the Court is the will itself, with perhaps in addition the admissions made by the testamentary trustees that no declaration of trust had been executed, that there are in fact no Lindsay Memorial Trustees in existence, and that there is at present no fund for the erection of the hospital at Dalbeattie. Their contention is that, as the residuary fund was given by the will to the trustees of the John Lindsay Memorial Hospital who do not exist, and as no provision exists for creating the hospital, the whole trust purpose has failed.

That is not the view which I take of the residuary purpose. As I read it, it evinces a clear intention to endow a John Lindsay Memorial Hospital at Dalbeattie. I am satisfied that that is a charitable purpose, and while it directs his testamentary trustees to hand over the residue for endowment purposes to the Lindsay Memorial Trustees, that provision is a provision which relates to trust machinery for carrying the purpose into operation and is not a controlling purpose of the testator in disposing of his residue. It has to be noted that the testator expressly provides that the endowment is to be used for a hospital and is to be handed over when the time of payment arrives whether that hospital be then erected or not.

It is therefore a provision for the endowment of a hospital which may be only a prospective hospital. When the endowment has been handed over it is directed that it shall be applied by the trustees who receive it towards the cost of maintaining and running the hospital in such way and manner as they may consider proper, and in accordance with the terms of the declaration of trust. It is perfectly true that that machinery has failed, but failure of machinery does not have the effect, in my opinion, of invalidating the purpose for which the machinery was to have been created. Accordingly, I think that we are left with an endowment of a prospective hospital and a failure of machinery to carry that endowment into effect, and in these circumstances it is the duty of the Court to provide the trust machinery which is requisite to enable the testator's intention to be carried into effect. If trustees are appointed to receive the residue and to administer it under the terms of the testator's will, it will be for them to consider whether it is possible to carry out the testator's will according to its terms. It may or may not be possible for them to do so. If it is not, they will then have to consider whether the case is one in which they can properly approach the Court and ask the Court to authorise a scheme of administration by virtue of its *nobile officium*.

In the meantime all we can decide is that the trust purpose has not failed merely because the trustees named in it do not exist, or merely because there is, as far as is known, no fund available for the immediate erection of a John Lindsay Memorial Hospital. Accordingly, I think the proper method of disposing of the petition is to appoint trustees, and I should propose that we appoint as trustees the persons who are named in the first paragraph of the draft scheme put forward by the petitioners, viz. the President of Dalbeattie and District Nursing Association *ex officio*, the Provost of Dalbeattie *ex officio*, the agent of the Union Bank of Scotland in Dalbeattie *ex officio*, and Dr William David Gillespie, medical practitioner, Dalbeattie. These are proper persons to carry on the administration of a trust such as the testator intended to create, and we are assured that these gentlemen are willing to act.

It remains to consider the precise terms of their appointment and to consider what should be done with the petition itself. I do think we should not appoint them, using the same terms as the testator, as the Lindsay Memorial Trustees, but that we should appoint them simply as trustees to receive the residue of the testator's estate and to administer the same in terms of the last purpose of his trust disposition and settlement. It would be of little utility to retain the petition in the Court, for, as I have pointed out, the persons who will have to consider whether the scheme embodied in the last purpose of the testator's will is a really workable scheme according to its terms are not the testamentary trustees. The trustees now appointed are the persons who will be concerned with that question, and if a *cy pres* scheme ultimately becomes necessary, or if it becomes necessary to consider whether a *cy pres* scheme is appropriate, it is they who should apply to the Court, and their opponents may be, for aught I know, the present respondents. If the testamentary trustees have no proper title to bring the petition, the petition has now exhausted its usefulness.

For that reason I propose that, apart from the appointing of trustees such as I have described, and thus giving a certain effect to the prayer of the petition, the petition should be dismissed."

Lords Fleming and Moncrieff delivered concurring opinions.
Lord Carmont concurred.

NOTES:

1. The trustees won the battle, but they lost the war: the hospital was never constructed due to **12.12** a lack of funds and the bequest failed after the creation of the National Health Service, whereupon the duty of providing hospital services devolved upon the Secretary of State for Scotland. The *cy-près* jurisdiction was unavailable because of the absence of a general charitable intention (see *infra*, paras 12.21–12.23), and so Mr Lindsay's heirs became entitled to the trust fund. See *Lindsay's Trs v. Lindsay*, 1948 S.L.T. (Notes) 81.

2. It is only in truly exceptional cases that the Court will be required to provide machinery. In the normal case, if the truster appoints trustees in the trust-deed, and valid trust purposes are

stated, that will normally be sufficient. The trustees are then empowered to exercise their discretion in constructing the trust machinery. (See *Tait's J.F. v. Lillie*, 1940 S.C. 534, *per* the Lord Justice-Clerk (Aitchison) at 541: "If it is a mere deficiency in the testator's direction as to administration, such as might be supplied by a trustee or a judicial factor applying his mind to the question to be solved, the gift would not be imperilled".)

The truster may have neglected to specify the powers of the trustees, but in such a case the powers which are implied under section 4 of the Trusts (Scotland) Act 1921 should normally be sufficient. If additional powers are required, however, but are not clearly implied by the terms of the trust deed, it may be possible for the court to provide them. In *Caird* (1879) 1 R. 529, the testator created a trust for the management of a school. The trustees petitioned the court for the power to delegate questions of admission to the committee of management, on the basis that it was impracticable for the whole body of trustees to deal with this point. The court granted the power sought. See also *Gibson's Trs*, 1933 S.C. 190.

3. It may be, however, that the machinery provided by the truster fails at a later date. See *Thomson's Trs*, 1930 S.C. 767, where a testator provided that his trust should be administered by three *ex officio* trustees. Two of the relevant offices were subsequently abolished by legislation. The Court of Session exercised its *nobile officium* to appoint two new *ex officio* trustees who held corresponding offices. See also *Rosyth Canadian Fund Trs*, 1924 S.C. 352.

4. It was noted earlier (paras 5.11 *et seq.*) that where a truster wishes to confer a power of selection upon his trustees, he should nominate trustees in order for the trust to be valid. So, for example, a trust for "charitable purposes" will not be valid unless trustees are appointed (*Angus's Exrx v. Batchan's Trs*, 1949 S.C. 335). However, it appears that if the purposes are somewhat more precisely stated (although still requiring the exercise of some discretion), but no trustees are appointed, the court may exercise the *nobile officium* to provide machinery and prevent the trust from failing. See, in this respect, *Ballingall's J.F. v. Hamilton*, 1973 S.C. 298 (residue to be equally divided between "Heart Diseases and Cancer Research"). Quite how the line is to be drawn between purposes which the court may "save" by providing machinery and purposes which are so broad that they must fail if trustees are not appointed is unclear.

C. Variation by private Act of Parliament

12.13 It is, exceptionally, possible to vary a trust by means of a private Act of Parliament. For example, the Court of Session felt unable to grant extended powers of investment to a trust in *Scott's Hospital Trs*, 1913 S.C. 289, but the powers requested were subsequently granted by statute: Alexander Scott's Hospital and the North of Scotland College of Agriculture Order Confirmation Act 1914 (4 Geo. 5). There are, indeed, a significant number of private Acts relating to that particular trust, spanning 81 years (see also 31 & 32 Vict., c. 1 (1868); 5 Edw. 7, c. lxv (1905); 21 & 22 Geo. 5, c. xxv (1931); 26 Geo. 5 & 1 Edw. 8, c. xxxii (1936) and 12, 13 & 14 Geo. 6, c. xii (1949)). While such Acts appear to have been quite common historically, they are unlikely to be a practical option today for all but the largest of public trusts.

D. The *cy-près* jurisdiction and section 9 of the Law Reform (Miscellaneous Provisions) (Scotland) Act 1990

12.14 What is *cy-près*? Broadly speaking, it is the power of the Court of Session to sanction a variation of the terms of a public trust where it is impossible to fulfil the purposes of the trust.

First Scottish Standing Committee, July 5, 1990, Law Reform (Miscellaneous Provisions) (Scotland) Bill cols 480–481 and 483

"**Mrs. Fyfe**: On a point of order, Mr Knox. Could someone tell us what a *cy-près* scheme is?

Lord James Douglas-Hamilton: I shall do my best. The hon. and learned Member for Fife, North-East (Mr. Campbell) described *cy-près* as an approximation. The principle applies in

Scotland where there is an impossibility in performance of the trust purposes. For example, someone left a large sum for the restoration of the abbey at Holyrood palace, the funds left were too small for that and were used to build the Thistle chapel at St Giles cathedral in Edinburgh.

Sir Nicholas Fairbairn: Hideous thing.

Lord James Douglas-Hamilton: My hon. and learned friend expressed a doubt about the *cy près* procedure. . .

Sir Nicholas Fairbairn:. . . I did not know that the funds that were subscribed to restore the glorious abbey of Holyrood had been set to build the dreadful Lorimar chapel as a carbuncle on St Giles. All I can say is that if that was done under the *cy près* scheme—I do not think that it was—all the members of the Inner House must have been asleep, as has perhaps not been unknown on previous occasions."

NOTE:

The circumstances in which the *cy près* jurisdiction may be exercised must be distinguished into two **12.15** cases (Wilson and Duncan, 15–01). The first is "where the truster's directions cannot be carried out but it is possible to find in the settlement a general charitable intention" (initial failure), and the second is "where there is a bequest to a particular public object and that object has failed after the bequest has taken effect." (subsequent failure). The distinction is important, because a "general charitable intention" must be shown before the *cy-près* jurisdiction can be exercised in cases of initial failure (*infra*, para. 12.21), but this is not necessary in cases of subsequent failure.

The *cy-près* jurisdiction must, however, be read in conjunction with section 9 of the Law Reform (Miscellaneous Provisions) (Scotland) Act 1990, which provides as follows:

Law Reform (Miscellaneous Provisions) (Scotland) Act 1990, s.9

9.—(1) Where, in the case of any public trust, the court is satisfied—   **12.16**
    (a) that the purposes of the trust, whether in whole or in part—
        (i) have been fulfilled as far as it is possible to do so; or
        (ii) can no longer be given effect to, whether in accordance with the directions or spirit of the trust deed or other document constituting the trust or otherwise;
    (b) that the purposes of the trust provide a use for only part of the property available under the trust;
    (c) that the purposes of the trust were expressed by reference to—
        (i) an area which has, since the trust was constituted, ceased to have effect for the purpose described expressly or by implication in the trust deed or other document constituting the trust; or
        (ii) a class of persons or area which has ceased to be suitable or appropriate, having regard to the spirit of the trust deed or other document constituting the trust, or as regards which it has ceased to be practicable to administer the property available under the trust; or
    (d) that the purposes of the trust, whether in whole or in part, have, since the trust was constituted—
        (i) been adequately provided for by other means; or
        (ii) ceased to be such as would enable the trust to become a recognised body; or
        (iii) ceased in any other way to provide a suitable and effective method of using the property available under the trust, having regard to the spirit of the trust deed or other document constituting the trust,
the court, on the application of the trustees, may, subject to subsection (2) below, approve a scheme for the variation or reorganisation of the trust purposes.

(2) The court shall not approve a scheme as mentioned in subsection (1) above unless it is satisfied that the trust purposes proposed in the scheme will enable the resources of the trust

to be applied to better effect consistently with the spirit of the trust deed or other document constituting the trust, having regard to changes in social and economic conditions since the time when the trust was constituted.

(3) Where any of paragraphs (a) to (d) of subsection (1) above applies to a public trust, an application may be made under this section for the approval of a scheme—

    (a) for the transfer of the assets of the trust to another public trust, whether involving a change to the trust purposes of such other trust or not; or

    (b) for the amalgamation of the trust with one or more public trusts,

      and the court, if it is satisfied that the conditions specified in subsection (2) above are met, may approve such a scheme.

. . .

(7) This section shall be without prejudice to the power of the Court of Session to approve a *cy-près* scheme in relation to any public trust.

NOTE:

12.17   *"Purposes" and "original purposes".* A glance at section 9 of the 1990 Act and its English equivalent (section 13 of the Charities Act 1993) will reveal that the English legislation repeatedly refers to the "original purposes of the trust", while the Scottish legislation merely refers to the "purposes of the trust". This should not be taken to indicate any difference in approach. The adjective "original" was initially included in the 1990 Bill but was removed in order to make it clear, for the avoidance of doubt, "that in the case of any trust that had been reconstituted under these provisions and in later years wished to reorganise or amalgamate further, the requirement will not be to return to the original trust deed or document but to the deed or document formulated at the time of reorganisation" (First Scottish Standing Committee, July 5, 1990, Law Reform (Miscellaneous Provisions) (Scotland) Bill, col. 477 (Lord James Douglas-Hamilton, Parliamentary Under-Secretary of State for Scotland)).

(a) What is the interaction between section 9 of the 1990 Act and the cy-près jurisdiction?

12.18   Section 9 of the 1990 Act is modelled on section 13 of the (English) Charities Act 1960 (now re-enacted as section 13 of the Charities Act 1993), which explicitly replaced the circumstances in which *cy-près* was exercisable at common law with a new set of criteria which are largely identical to those in the 1990 Act. By contrast, the 1990 Act purports to run in tandem with the existing *cy-près* jurisdiction of the Court of Session (see s.9(7)).

Why the difference? Originally, it was proposed that the 1990 legislation would simply extend the *cy-près* jurisdiction rather than create a new variation jurisdiction. When first introduced into Parliament, the Bill contained the following provision:

> "In addition to any ground upon which the Court of Session could, before the commencement of this section, have granted a petition for the approval of a *cy-près* scheme in relation to any public trust, the Court may grant such a petition if it is satisfied that, having regard to social and economic changes which have taken place since the constitution of the trust and any other circumstances which, in the opinion of the Court, may be relevant to the functioning of the trust, the purposes of the trust are obsolete or are lacking in usefulness."

However, the Lord Advocate subsequently moved an amendment which replaced this clause with one which (subject to further minor amendments) became the current section 9 (H.L. Debs, March 27, 1990, col. 764). In doing so, the government seems to have attempted to address two separate issues at once. Firstly, it was felt that the current *cy-près* jurisdiction (being limited to impossibility or failure of the trust purposes) was too narrow and required to be extended. Secondly, it was felt that applying to the Inner House (as was then required for the *cy-près* jurisdiction to be exercised) was generally too cumbersome and expensive. Accordingly, section 9 provides that applications under that section for variation may be brought in the Outer House or, if the Lord Advocate makes an appropriate order (which he has not yet done) in the sheriff court.

Presumably, because the *cy-près* jurisdiction is an exercise of the Court of Session's *nobile officium*, it was felt that it would be inappropriate (if not impossible) to confer a *cy-près* jurisdiction on the sheriff court. This has the odd result that, while we now have two separate jurisdictions for the variation of public trusts (one common law and one statutory), these two jurisdictions run in tandem, because a *cy-près* petition may now be presented in the Outer House and is subject to the same provisions of the Rules of the Court of Session as applications under section 9 of the 1990 Act (RCS rr. 63.7–63.9).

The provisions of the 1990 Act are considerably wider than the common law jurisdiction and will, in many cases, render the common law rules irrelevant as a matter of practice. It is necessary, therefore, to consider the two jurisdictions together. (It is, of course, appropriate—even necessary—to make reference to the common law rules when considering the proper application of this legislation; and it is also appropriate to make reference to English authority given the origins of the statutory provisions).

To return to the distinction between cases of initial and subsequent failure (*supra*, para. 12.21), it is suggested that the common law position has been modified (or not modified) as follows:

(i) Initial failure of the trust purposes.

In England, such a case would now fall under the statutory provisions. However, section 9 of the 1990 Act is stated at the outset to apply "in the case of any public trust", which suggests that the trust must have come into existence (*i.e.* taken effect) before section 9 can be applied. While the English legislation may be applied where the purposes "cannot be carried out" (s.13(1)(a)(ii) of the Charities Acts 1960 and 1993), the equivalent Scottish provision applies when the trust purposes "can no longer be given effect to" (s.9(1)(a)(ii) of the 1990 Act). The use of the words "can no longer" instead of "cannot" suggests that the 1990 Act may only be invoked when the trust has actually taken effect. It follows that cases of initial failure must be dealt with under the common law *cy-près* jurisdiction and not the 1990 Act.

(ii) Subsequent failure of the trust purposes.

Such a case would clearly now fall under the 1990 Act (although it would still be competent to present a *cy-près* petition in such a case). More importantly, the 1990 Act has the effect of considerably widening the court's jurisdiction in cases where the trust has actually taken effect. Consequently, it is submitted that the 1990 Act is the proper starting point for considering variation of a public trust which has already taken effect. That is not to say, however, that the *cy-près* jurisdiction is now entirely redundant in such cases. There may be rare instances where variation is impossible under the 1990 Act but possible under *cy-près*. (See *infra*, para. 12.38).

(b) *Distinguishing Between Initial and Subsequent Failure: Has the Trust Taken Effect?*

Davidson's Trs v. Arnott
1951 S.C. 42

Thomas Davidson died in 1924. His will provided that the residue of his estate should be **12.19** held in trust and that the income thereof should be applied for the benefit of the Davidson Cottage Hospital. The hospital was subsequently taken over under the National Health Service (Scotland) Act 1947, and it was held that the object of Mr Davidson's bequest had accordingly failed. It was also held that there was no general charitable intention in his part.

Accordingly, the court had to determine whether the trust had taken effect or not. If it had not taken effect, then the case would be regarded as one of initial failure, and the *cy-près* jurisdiction would be unavailable because of the absence of a general charitable intention. The trust funds would therefore fall to Mr Davidson's heirs. If the bequest had taken effect, then the case would be one of subsequent failure. In that case, the absence of a general charitable intention would be irrelevant and a *cy-près* scheme could be devised in respect of the trust fund.

LORD JAMIESON: "The reclaimers accepted the principle of *Anderson's Trustees v. Scott*, 1914 S.C. 942 that in the case of a charitable or public trust which has taken effect the trust funds will, on the subsequent failure of the objects of the trust, fall to be administered *cy-près*. They maintained, however, in the present case that as regards the capital sum and the unexpended and accumulated income in the hands of the trustees the bequest had not taken effect and that these funds have fallen into intestacy. The test which they sought to apply was that of vesting, and they argued that, as the trustees were given a discretion as to what sums were to be applied for the benefit of the hospital, vesting took place only in the sums which from time to time were so applied.

In the case of a simple legacy to a particular charitable institution, just as in the case of a legacy to an individual, if the institution is not in existence at the date of the testator, the legacy lapses and falls into residue, unless the testator has in his will evinced a general charitable intention, in which case the legacy may be applied to charity *cy-près*. On the other hand, if the institution is in existence at the death of the testator, it takes a vested right to the legacy and it becomes its absolute property. If, in such a case, the institution ceases to exist before payment is made, the amount of the legacy does not fall to be made over to the residuary legatees, but in England to the Crown to be applied to some analogous purpose of charity, and that is so although the will discloses no general charitable intention—*In re Slevin* [1891] 2 Ch. 236. In Scotland the fund would be administered by trustees under a *cy-près* scheme approved by the Court. But the present is not a case of a simple legacy. What was in contemplation was a continuing trust. The testator directed his trustees to hold the residue of his estate as a capital fund, and I agree with the construction placed on the direction by the Lord Ordinary that the capital fund, as well as the income, was to be held for the benefit of the Davidson Cottage Hospital. It is true that the trustees were given a discretion, but it was not an unlimited discretion whether or not to apply the residue for the benefit of the hospital. Reading the clause as a whole, they were bound to hold the residue as a capital fund in accordance with and for the purposes indicated by the testator, and the only discretion which was left to them was as to how much of the income should be expended in each year in rendering the administration of the hospital more efficient, and whether any encroachment should be made on the capital for structural extensions. Once the amount of the residue was ascertained, it was earmarked or dedicated for the benefit of the hospital. The trustees could not have used it for any other purpose, unless perhaps to a small extent for the maintenance of the family lair, and they could have been restrained from any attempt to do so.

The trustees have carried out the testator's directions and have from time to time in their discretion applied so much of the income as they thought expedient in supplement of the income of the hospital. That the immediate requirements of the hospital did not in their view call for the expenditure of the whole income is immaterial. It was conceded that they were not bound to expend the whole income of each year in that year, and that any surplus in any one year might be expended in future years. That applied whether any surplus happened to be large or small, and at any time until the hospital was taken over under the National Health Service (Scotland) Act the trustees were entitled to apply the accumulated income and the capital in accordance with the testator's directions. The whole fund having been dedicated by the testator and held and administered by the trustees for the purposes of the hospital, there is, in my view, no room for a resulting trust in favour of the heirs.

The reclaimers attempted to draw a distinction between funds in the hands of testamentary trustees and funds made over to and held by trustees administering a charity. It was said that it was only when the funds were made over to the latter that the charitable bequest took effect. I can see no room for any such distinction. There are innumerable cases where no vesting takes place in the beneficiaries of a charity, but the funds are held by testamentary trustees and administered by them for behoof of the beneficiaries. Here the funds were vested in the trustees for behoof of the hospital.

I am of opinion, therefore, that the pursuers and real raisers fall to be ranked and preferred to the whole fund *in medio* to be administered by them in accordance with a *cy-près* scheme to be approved by the Court."

The Lord Justice-Clerk (Thomson) and Lord Patrick delivered concurring opinions.

Lord Mackay delivered a dissenting opinion.

Notes:

1. *Davidson's Trs* can be contrasted with two cases where testators left funds for the establishment of a hospital (*Lindsay's Trs v. Lindsay*, 1948 S.L.T. (Notes) 81) and for a maternity hostel (*Cameron's Trs v. Edinburgh Corp.*, 1959 S.L.T. (Notes) 32). In those cases, no such facilities existed and the trust funds never proved sufficient to establish any. It was held, therefore, that the trusts had never taken effect. **12.20**

2. In *Cuthbert's Trs v. Cuthbert*, 1958 S.L.T. 315 a testator left funds to establish a holiday home for nurses in 1936. In an action of multiplepoinding in 1938, his next-of-kin argued that this purpose had failed because the income for the fund was insufficient for the upkeep of the home and it was impracticable to run it as a holiday home for nurses. Lord Keith directed that "the trustees should be allowed further time to consider the possibility of carrying out this bequest". The trustees attempted to give effect to the bequest and did succeed in providing accommodation for a period of five years, but ultimately failed to make the trust work. They argued, however, that the fact that accommodation had been provided for a period of time meant that the trust had "taken effect" and that the rights of the next-of-kin were therefore excluded despite the absence of any general charitable intention. Lord Guthrie rejected that contention, observing (at 318):

   > "They [the trustees] now admit that the experiment has failed, and that the impracticability of running Badcall as a holiday home has been demonstrated. Is it to be held that because the attempt has been made and has failed, the rights of the next-of-kin have been defeated? If that is the result, experience has demonstrated that they [the next-of-kin] were right in their contention in the original action that the fourteenth purpose was incapable of fulfilment but their success has destroyed their own claims. The proof of the impossibility of fulfilment of the purpose has ousted the next-of-kin who were entitled to succeed if the bequest could not be fulfilled. It is a paradoxical conclusion. In my opinion it is also unjust and unsound."

(c) Initial Failure of the Trust Purposes

In a case of initial failure, two things must be established in order for the *cy-près* jurisdiction to be invoked: firstly, a general charitable intention on the part of the truster; and secondly, failure of the trust purposes (impossibility). **12.21**

(i) Is there a general charitable intention?

There is no single accepted test for identifying a general charitable intention, but the following tests have been suggested:

- "Was the testator's object here to establish a charity for the benefit of a certain class, with a particular mode of doing it? Or was the mode of application such an essential part of the gift that it is not possible to distinguish any general purpose of charity?" (*Burgess' Trs v. Crawford*, 1912 S.C. 387, *per* Lord Mackenzie at 398. See also *Tait's J.F. v. Lillie*, 1940 S.C. 534, *per* the Lord Justice-Clerk (Aitchison) at 539: "no more concise statement of the distinction can be found".)
- "a general charitable intention may be inferred where it is possible, taking the instrument as a whole, to say that, notwithstanding the form of the gift, the paramount intention, according to the true construction of the instrument, is to give the property in the first instance for a general charitable purpose rather than a particular charitable purpose, and to graft on to the general gift a direction as to the desires or intentions of the donor as to the manner in which

the general gift is to be carried into effect." (*Tait's J.F. v. Lillie*, 1940 S.C. 534, *per* Lord Mackay at 546, quoting with approval from *Lewin on Trusts* (14th ed., 1939) p. 473. The language used in *Lewin* is in substance that found in *Re Wilson* [1913] 1 Ch. 314, *per* Parker J. at 320–321).

Hay's J.F. v. Hay's Trs
1952 S.C. (H.L.) 29

12.22 A testatrix directed that her trustees should maintain a mansion-house "under the style and designation of 'The Hay Memorial' either as a home for aged and infirm Shetland seamen, a surgical hospital, or a convalescent hospital, whichever the said trustees may consider most beneficial for the islands of Shetland." The funds available under the trust-deed were insufficient to maintain the house for any of the three alternatives. The question arose as to whether a general charitable intention could be shown, in which case the *cy-près* jurisdiction would apply.

LORD REID: "I cannot avoid the conclusion that the foundation of a permanent memorial was as essential an element in the testatrix's intention as the conferring of benefits on the people of Shetland. The direction to maintain the house in all time under the style and designation of 'The Hay Memorial' is clear and imperative, and the money is given as a fund to be held in all time for the upkeep and maintenance of the house and other subjects comprising 'The Hay Memorial'. It is true that the testatrix adds 'and in connection with the conduct thereof for the object and purpose before mentioned,' and that must refer back to whichever of the three specified methods of using the house the trustees have adopted; but 'the conduct thereof' is the conduct of the house, and it appears to me that the testatrix cannot be held to have intended the money to be used for any other purpose than one in connexion with the house.

It was argued that the fact that the testatrix did not limit herself to a single charitable purpose but authorised her trustees to select one of three purposes indicates that, as she had no preference for any particular method, she must have had a general charitable intention and the three specified alternatives were merely methods of achieving her general objective of benefiting the people of Shetland. I think that there is some force in this argument; but, even if it is right, it does not carry the respondent very far. All the specified methods are methods of using the house as a memorial, and, if it was an essential part of the testatrix's intention that the house should be so used, any general intention could only be a general intention that the house should be used for whatever form of charity might be most suitable. It would be necessary to decide this question if there were any ground for supposing that, although the house cannot be used for any of the three specified purposes, it could be used for some other charitable purpose. But counsel for the respondent frankly admitted that this would be impossible with the funds which will be available, and I think that your Lordships can accept that admission in view of the detailed facts stated in the petition. To repair and equip the house for any purpose would obviously require at least a very large part of the total funds available, and the house could not then be maintained for any purpose without a large amount of assistance from some other source. There is nothing to suggest that such assistance could be expected.

In my opinion, it is clear that the subjects bequeathed can only be applied to charitable purposes if it is permissible to sell the house and add the proceeds of sale to the sums bequeathed. Counsel for the respondent argued that the testatrix's desire that there should be a Hay Memorial would be sufficiently fulfilled if the name Hay Memorial were attached to whatever purpose might be authorised under a *cy-près* scheme for the administration of the fund so realised. In my opinion, this would be essentially different from the intention of the testatrix as that appears from the terms of her trust-disposition and settlement. In my judgment, therefore, the bequest must be held to have failed, the appeal should be allowed and the question submitted in the petition should be answered in the affirmative."

LORD TUCKER: "The language used [in the trust-disposition and settlement] appears to be clearly to indicate an intention on the part of the testatrix that the maintenance of Hayfield House as a memorial should be an essential element in the charitable disposition. It seems to me impossible to spell out a general charitable intention to benefit the people of Shetland except in so far as this can be achieved by means of the use and maintenance of Hayfield House as a memorial.

Once it has been made to appear—as I agree it has on the facts and admissions in this case—that it is impossible with the funds available to use Hayfield House for any charitable purpose, the bequest fails and nothing remains as a basis for any *cy-près* scheme."

Lord Normand delivered a concurring opinion.
Lord Cohen concurred.

NOTES:

1. It is extremely difficult to lay down any general rules, beyond the guidance given by Lord Mackenzie in *Burgess's Trs* and Lord Mackay in *Tait's J.F.* (*supra*, para. 12.21) on when a general charitable intention will be found to exist. Some observations may be made, however. **12.23**

2. The more specific and precise the truster's directions, the less likely the court is to find a general charitable intention. So, where the truster directed that particular heritable property should be run as a medical facility, and there were insufficient funds to fulfil that purpose, there was no general charitable intention (*Hay's J.F., supra; Tait's J.F. v. Lillie*, 1940 S.C. 534; see also *Lindsay's Trs v. Lindsay*, 1948 S.L.T. (Notes) 81). Similarly, in *McRobert's Trs v. Cameron*, 1961 S.L.T. (Notes) 66, where the truster had directed that his trustees should establish a private ward at a local hospital, to be named after him, it was held that no general charitable intention had been shown. In *Pennie's Trs v. Royal National Lifeboat Institution*, 1924 S.L.T. 520, the testatrix left money for a lifeboat to be named after her late husband and stationed on or near the Island of Bressay. The R.N.L.I. was unable to accept the bequest on the terms specified because the sum was too small, there were no funds to operate a lifeboat station, and there was no sufficient reason to justify stationing a lifeboat at Bressay. Lord Murray held that "locality" was the essence of the gift and that there was therefore no general charitable intention.

3. Where a testator leaves property to an organisation for a specified purpose, and that organisation declines to accept the bequest, the court is likely to hold that the organisation was only "an agency selected to carry out that purpose", and will sanction a *cy-près* scheme in order to give effect to the testator's general charitable intention (assuming that it is possible to do so): *National Bible Society of Scotland v. Church of Scotland*, 1946 S.L.T. (Notes) 26.

4. In *Forrest's Trs v. Forrest's Trs*, 1959 S.L.T. 24, the testator directed that an annuity from his estate should "be applied towards the maintenance of a nurse available for the sick poor of Galston or for some analogous purpose in such manner as my trustees may decide or direct". The first purpose (the maintenance of a nurse) failed due to the establishment of the National Health Service. Lord Mackintosh held that the alternative of "some analogous purpose" was not void from uncertainty, that it evinced a general charitable intention, and that the *cy-près* jurisdiction could therefore be applied. It is difficult to see why it was necessary to invoke *cy-près* in this case, however. If the alternative purpose was not void from uncertainty, then there was no failure of the trust purposes, and the trustees should have been empowered to apply the trust property in their discretion without resort to a *cy-près* scheme. The fact that there was no failure of purpose should have rendered a *cy-près* scheme incompetent.

5. *What if a general charitable intention is only shown in respect of some, but not all, of the trust purposes?* The answer depends on whether the relevant property can be separated out into distinct funds. Compare *MacTavish's Trs, infra* with *Shorthouse's Trs v. Aberdeen Medico-Chirurgical Society*, 1977 S.L.T. 148. In the latter case, a testator directed that certain heritable property should be used as "homes of rest, recreation and convalescence" for "sick, disabled, aged or retired doctors" who met certain conditions. The free income of the residue was to be used for annuities, gifts to or maintenance of such doctors, but they did not have to be residents of the homes. The bequest failed and a question arose as to whether the trust property could be applied *cy-près*. Lord Maxwell held that a general charitable intention had been shown by virtue of the provision relating to the free income of the residue, and that

therefore *cy-près* could be applied. He rejected the argument that because a general charitable intention had only been shown in respect of part of the trust property, *cy-près* could only be applied in respect of that part, observing as follows (at 151):

> "Counsel for the society suggested, as an alternative and second-best argument, that a different result could be arrived at for the heritage and the residue respectively, the residue to be applied cy-près and the heritage going on intestacy. Had I been against him or his main submission I would not have sustained this alternative. Unlike the situation for example in *Hay* [*Hay's J.F., supra*], there are not here two or more distinct charitable trusts. The provisions for residue are closely related to the provisions for the heritage. By sub-clause 28(b) the income of the residue is primo loco devoted to the upkeep of the heritage, and sub-clause 28(c) envisages that part of the free balance of income of residue is to go to maintenance of the inmates of the heritage. I do not think that the trust can be dissected for present purposes. In my opinion the proper approach is to consider whether any part of the provisions indicates a general charitable intention and, if so, to apply the cy-près jurisdiction to the whole."

6. *The problem of bequests to defunct or non-existent institutions.* Where a testator leaves money to a supposed charitable institution which has never existed, the court will normally find a general charitable intention in respect of the bequest, provided that the name of the institution (or other language in the trust deed) makes it clear what purpose the testator intended the funds to be applied to.

A general charitable intention was found in the following cases: *Tod's Trs v. The Sailors' and Firemen's Orphans' and Widows' Society*, 1953 S.L.T. (Notes) 72 ("The Society for Old and Infirm Officers of the Mercantile Marine"); *MacTavish's Trs v. St Columba High Church*, 1967 S.L.T. (Notes) 50 ("The Scottish Convalescent Home for Children, Edinburgh"); *Pomphrey's Trs v. Royal Naval Benevolent Trust*, 1967 S.L.T. 61 ("Royal Navy Benevolent Fund"); *Cumming's Exrs v. Cumming*, 1967 S.L.T. 68 ("Aged Peoples Home, Glasgow" and "School for Blind Children, Glasgow").

In *MacTavish's Trs,* a general charitable intention was held *not* to exist in respect of a purported bequest to the "Merchant Navy Fishing Fleet", on the basis that it was not possible to ascertain what the testatrix had in mind, the Merchant Navy and the Fishing Fleet being two distinct bodies.

Where the institution did previously exist, however, but is now defunct, the court is unlikely to find a general charitable intention. See the *obiter* comments of the Lord President (Dunedin) in *Burgess' Trs v. Crawford*, 1912 S.C. 387, at 395, and of Lord Sorn in *Tod's Trs, supra.* This rule appears to have been applied in *Laing's Trs v. Perth Model Lodging House*, 1954 S.L.T. (Notes) 13 and *Fergusson's Trs v. Buchanan*, 1973 S.L.T. 41. The distinction has been heavily criticised by Norrie and Scobbie (pp. 180–182), and appears inconsistent both with the general tests which have been formulated for identifying a general charitable intention (*supra,* para. 12.21) and the principle applied in *National Bible Society of Scotland, supra.* It is thought that the testator will normally only have named a specific institution as the agency for giving effect to his intention. It would seem inappropriate that his underlying intention should be defeated by the fact of the institution having ceased to exist when it would be possible to give it effect by way of a *cy-près* scheme.

For a more detailed discussion of some of these problems, see J.M. Thomson, "A Question of Identity—The Problem of Bequests to Non-Existent Institutions in Scots Law", 1973 J.R. 281.

(ii) Have the trust purposes failed?

Marquess of Bute's Trs v. Marquess of Bute
(1904) 7 F. 49

12.24 In his will, the third Marquess of Bute directed that his trustees should expend two sums of £20,000 upon the erection of two Roman Catholic churches. He made a provision of £10,000 for the endowment of one, but made no other provision for endowment. The trustees were directed to convey the buildings after construction, on certain specified conditions, to trustees to be appointed by the appropriate Bishops. After the Marquess' death, the Bishops stated that they would be unable to accept the bequests on the conditions specified, because the conditions could not be implemented owing to the lack of endowment. The Lord Ordinary (Kyllachy) held that the bequests had not failed. On appeal:

LORD JUSTICE-CLERK (MACDONALD): "I am unable to agree with the interlocutor of the Lord Ordinary, as my view is that the claimant the Marquess of Bute is entitled to judgment. The bequest of the late Marquess which is in dispute is quite clear in its terms, that his trustees are authorised and directed to provide church buildings at Whithorn and Oban, at an expense of not more than £20,000 at each place, it being further expressed as his intention that if on the buildings being completed the whole sum of £20,000 has not been expended, the remainder is to revert to his estate, his 'intention being merely' to have the buildings completed, although 'at a less cost than £20,000'.

He affixed to the bequest the conditions that a conveyance of the buildings to trustees was not to be given by his testamentary trustees except upon certain conditions, two of which were that the buildings should be consecrated within eight days, and that the 'Divine Office' should be said or sung in the building every day.

The ecclesiastical authorities by whom these conditions could alone be carried out, viz., the Roman Catholic Bishops in Argyll and Galloway, state their inability to fulfil either of these conditions if the buildings are erected in terms of the bequest, because of the want of any endowment by which the conditions could be fulfilled.

The trustees accordingly have not proceeded with the erection of the buildings, and propose, with the acquiescence of the Bishops, to hold the funds so that by accumulation they may increase and thus provide for endowment as well as building.

I can find no authority for this being done. The late Marquess nowhere indicates that his estate is to provide any endowment, except one which he specifies, viz., £10,000 for the Oban Cathedral which he intended to be built. It seems to me to be very plain that he did not intend to provide any other endowment, and that to keep up the money he left to raise an endowment fund would be to do what he has given no authority for doing.

Thus his purpose in the bequest for building has failed, as the circumstances are such that those to whom it would fall to consecrate the buildings and to carry on the services decline on the ground of inability to undertake that these conditions of the gift shall be fulfilled.

I feel constrained, therefore, to hold that the sums bequeathed fall back into the residue of the late Marquess, to be dealt with as the residue is required to be dealt with, and that the interlocutor of the Lord Ordinary should be recalled and the claim of the present Marquess sustained."

Lord Young concurred.
Lord Trayner delivered a concurring opinion.

NOTES:

1. Where there is insufficient property in the trust fund to carry out the specified purposes, this **12.25** will clearly amount to failure. (See, *e.g. Tait's J.F. v. Lillie*, 1940 S.C. 542; *Hay's J.F. v. Hay's Trs*, 1952 S.C. (H.L.) 29). But the fact that the trust fund is below a minimum value specified by the testator does not necessarily constitute failure. In *Donaldson's Trs v. H.M. Advocate*, 1938 S.L.T. 106, the truster had directed that his estate should be accumulated until it reached a value of at least £1,000, and then applied to purchase annuities for "humble heroes", but that the value of the estate should never be allowed to fall below £1,000. Twenty-one years after the testator's death—the maximum accumulation period permitted by law—the estate had only reached the value of £850. Lord Russell held that although the accumulation provision was no longer valid, it did not necessarily follow that the trust funds were inadequate for carrying out the specified purpose. Failure had therefore not been established. (See also *Ogilvie's Trs v. Kirk-Session of Dundee* (1846) 8 D. 1229).

2. The fact that the trust purposes cannot be given effect to immediately does not in itself amount to failure, provided there is the possibility that they can be given effect to in the

future: *Templeton v. Burgh of Ayr*, 1910 2 S.L.T. 12 (*supra*, para. 2.33). Nor does the fact that the manner in which the trust can be given effect to is "probably very much smaller and poorer than the testator dreamed of" amount to failure: *Ness v. Mills's Trs*, 1923 S.C. 344, *per* the Lord President (Clyde) at 354.

3. Where the trust purposes can be given effect to, but the terms of the trust deed mean that the trust will inevitably (or is very likely to) fail at some point in the future, this may be treated as equivalent to impossibility and therefore justifying the exercise of the *cy-près* jurisdiction. (See *Glasgow Young Men's Christian Association*, 1934 S.C. 452, *per* Lord Blackburn at 458: "to save a charitable trust from wreckage it is not necessary for the Court to hesitate until the trust is actually upon the rocks.") But, of course, if the trust can at least initially be given effect, then the wider grounds for variation under section 9 of the 1990 Act will become available. (See *infra*, paras 12.26 *et seq.*).

4. As to what action it is open to the court to take once the *cy pres* jurisdiction has been triggered, see *infra*, paras 12.39 *et seq.*

(d) Variation of the Trust Purposes After the Trust Has Taken Effect

(i) Applying the 1990 legislation

12.26 Each of the alternative grounds for variation under section 9 of the 1990 Act will be considered in turn.

s.9(1)(a)(i): "the purposes of the trust, whether in whole or in part, have been fulfilled as far as it is possible to do so"

Scotstown Moor Children's Camp
1948 S.C. 630

12.27 The Scotstown Moor Children's Camp was established "to provide for needy and ailing children a short holiday at Scotstown Moor, near Aberdeen". The camp was initially under canvas, but buildings were later erected and expanded as and when funds became available. The camp was discontinued in 1939 due to the Second World War and the buildings were partially requisitioned by the Air Ministry in 1944, and were not derequisitioned until 1947. One of the dormitory buildings was destroyed by fire in 1945. The camp was no longer able to obtain donations of food from shopkeepers due to rationing and its income from donations had dropped considerably due to the camp having been discontinued. The camp trustees presented a petition to the Court of Session seeking approval of a *cy-près* scheme whereby the assets of the camp would be transferred to the Aberdeen battalion of the Boys' Brigade.

LORD PRESIDENT (COOPER): "I wish once again to emphasise the point taken by Lord President Clyde in *Glasgow Domestic Training School*, 1923 S.C. 892, that the jurisdiction which this Court exercises in relation to charitable trusts is not a general discretionary jurisdiction to divert the funds of charities from one object to another as we may think appropriate. We are not a charitable endowments commission clothed with subordinate legislative powers. The exercise of our *cy pres* jurisdiction is conditional and dependent upon our ability in the first instance to determine that the object or purpose of the charity has failed, or, where particular methods have been prescribed for the achievement of the object, that those methods have in altered circumstances become impracticable.

Now in this case, as I said, the object which is prescribed for this organisation is to provide for needy and ailing children a holiday in the country, and no methods are prescribed for the achievement of that object. It would manifestly be competent for the association to achieve it in any practicable method they care to select. The question accordingly comes to be whether the petitioners can satisfy us that the object of their association has in a substantial sense failed, and I am bound to say that that seems to me to be an exceedingly difficult onus for them to undertake. For one reason, it is, I think, a matter of judicial knowledge that similar organisations with similar objects are operating to this day in many parts of the country. We know that in the Camps Act of 1939 provision was made for the carrying on of enterprises of this kind under official auspices, and in the latest Education (Scotland) Act of 1946, section 3, one of the duties imposed upon education authorities is to establish, maintain and manage, or assist the establishment, maintenance and management of, camps and holiday classes and various other *quasi*-educational and recreational institutions of that kind. In addition, I would note that from one paragraph of the report which is before us it appears that there is at the moment in Aberdeen another organisation which, so far as appears, is still carrying on the very object for which the present petitioners exist.

What, then, is said in favour of the *prima facie* unacceptable view that the object of this charity has failed? It is said, in the first place, that the food-rationing regulations are fatal to the whole enterprise. I am afraid that I fail to understand that argument. It is not possible to determine whether, in terms of sundry regulations to which reference was made, this organisation could or could not obtain a special licence for the Scotstown Moor Camp. What seems abundantly plain is that the children who may be invited to go to the Scotstown Moor Camp are just as much entitled to their individual rations as they would be if they remained at home, or went on holiday to any other place whether with their parents or otherwise; and while the rationing regulations may well introduce into the life of this organisation, as into the life of other citizens of the country, a good deal of worry, I cannot understand why that feature in isolation, or even in combination with the other factors relied upon, should be regarded as fatal to the enterprise. It is said, in the second place, that there are financial difficulties because, during the nine years throughout which the enterprise has been dormant, the public support has fallen off. Such a result, as our reporter points out, was only to be expected; and I do not see why a revival of activity at Scotstown Moor Camp should not elicit a revival in some measure of the local public support previously attracted by this scheme. But, apart from that, the association is not bankrupt, but on the contrary has substantial assets which places it far beyond immediate financial difficulties. It was said, in the third place, that owing to disuse and to the requisitioning, and owing to a fire which destroyed one of the buildings, the premises would require to be reconditioned at considerable expense. I do not know how much money would be necessary, and it appears that no estimates have been obtained; but this at least is clear, that the buildings are no essential part of the object for which this organisation was formed. Indeed, until comparatively recent, times, the organisation had no buildings at all, but relied upon canvas; and if the trustees prefer to recommence operations on a more modest scale than obtained in 1939 there is no reason why they should not do so. The mere fact that they may have to do so is, as is shewn by the case of *Ness*, 1923 S.C. 344, no reason for regarding their primary object as one which is now incapable of achievement.

I forbear making any reference to the alternative project advanced in the petition, because in my view that question has not arisen. We are still at the stage of having to satisfy ourselves that we have jurisdiction to intervene at all, and, for aught yet seen in the petition, the report, and the oral arguments addressed to us, I am not satisfied that we possess the indispensable basis for the exercise of the Court's jurisdiction.

My motion accordingly would be that the appropriate course, with a view to avoiding unnecessary expense to the petitioners, would simply be to continue this case upon the footing that, if and when they have exhausted further efforts to resuscitate this enterprise even on a more modest scale, the case might be open in the light of new circumstances to be reviewed a second time."

NOTES:

1. *Scotstown Moor* indicates that the court will construe the "impossibility" criterion narrowly. **12.28** This is particularly so where the trustees have not even attempted to give effect to the trust, as was the case in *Scotstown*. The court may be inclined towards a more liberal approach

where the trustees have tried to give the trust effect with little success, although that may depend on the nature of the trust. To illustrate this point, the cases of *Glasgow Domestic Training School*, 1923 S.C. 892 and *Edinburgh Corporation v. Cranston's Trs*, 1960 S.C. 244 may be compared. In the first case, the trustees ran a domestic training school and hostel for young girls who wished to enter domestic service. The School, however, had considerable difficulty in finding girls who wished to receive domestic training, and the numbers had dropped from 26 in 1904 to 8 in 1922. The court sanctioned a *cy-près* scheme. In the second case, a trust was established in 1892 for the purpose of paying annuities to 12 poor tailors who fulfilled certain conditions. In 1960, the City of Edinburgh, after administering the trust for a number of years, had succeeded in only finding two qualifying beneficiaries. The court refused to hold that impossibility had been demonstrated.

The reason for the differing results in the two cases may be found in an observation made by Lord Sorn in the *Edinburgh Corporation* case (at 254):

> "Here, there is no heritage to be kept up out of inadequate funds, and no other incidental drain upon the funds. All that is to be done is that the fund is held for such qualified beneficiaries as may emerge. During the trial period, two such qualified beneficiaries had in fact emerged, and, although the case seems to be a narrow one, I think we cannot say in the face of this fact that this is a bequest which failed and never took effect."

By contrast, one cannot maintain a hostel or school (see also *Anderson Female School*, 1911 S.C. 1035) indefinitely in the hope that beneficiaries might emerge. For that reason, the court will be more willing to find impossibility in cases where the trust fund is subject to "incidental drains" such as maintaining facilities which are required for the trust purposes.

2. Although the court still does not have the "general discretionary jurisdiction" referred to by Lord Cooper in *Scotstown*, its jurisdiction is no longer restricted to cases of impossibility. This is made clear by the provisions of the 1990 Act, particularly s.9(1)(c)(ii) (*infra*, para. 12.33) and s.9(1)(d)(iii) (*infra*, para. 12.37) which enable the court to vary trust purposes which are no longer "suitable or effective". It is doubtful, however, that the court would be persuaded that this condition had been established in a case such as *Scotstown Moor* where no attempt had been made to re-open the camp.

s.9(1)(a)(ii): "the purposes of the trust, whether in whole or in part, can no longer be given effect to, whether in accordance with the directions or spirit of the trust deed or other document constituting the trust or otherwise"

12.29 The language "can no longer be given effect to" does not seem to give the court any broader power to authorise a variation than section 9(1)(a)(i). The reference to "directions", however, suggests that this provision gives the court an additional power to strike out impossible or impractical conditions attached to a trust. The English courts clearly had this power at common law and it has been held that the English equivalent of section 9(1)(a)(ii) simply restates this power in statutory form (*Re J.W. Laing Trust* [1984] Ch. 143, *per* Peter Gibson J. at 151–153).

The English courts have taken a wide view of when conditions may be said to be impossible or impractical. See in particular *Re Dominion Students' Hall Trust* [1947] Ch. 183, where a condition that only students "of European origin" could stay in a hostel was removed as being impossible. Evershed J. stated (at 183):

> "I have, however, to consider the primary intention of the charity. At the time when it came into being, the objects of promoting community of citizenship, culture and tradition among all members of the British Commonwealth of Nations might have been attained by confining the Hall to members of the Empire of European origin. But times have changed, particularly as a result of the war; and it is said that to retain the condition, so far from furthering the charity's main object, might defeat it and would be liable to antagonize those students, both white and coloured, whose support and goodwill it is the purpose of the charity to sustain. The case, therefore, can be said to fall within the broad description of impossibility illustrated by *In re Campden Charities* [(1881) 18 Ch. D. 310] and *In Re Robinson*. [[1923] 2 Ch. 332]"

The Court of Session has not, however, taken such a broad approach:

Grigor Medical Bursary Fund Trs
(1903) 5 F. 1143

LORD PRESIDENT (KINROSS): "The material facts in this case are, that the late Dr John Grigor **12.30** died on 18th October 1886, leaving a trust-disposition and settlement dated 20th November 1880, and a codicil dated 30th December 1885, so that he was considering his testamentary arrangements down to a period of less than a year prior to his death. He left a sum of money to his trustees for the purpose of founding the 'Grigor Medical Bursary,' and he declared that the recipient of the bursary was to be 'a young man, a native of the county of Nairn, whose parents are unable to defray the cost of a medical education, to enable such young man to pursue his medical studies at the University of Edinburgh, to be tenable during the curriculum of study'. The object of his bounty is unequivocally declared to be 'a young man'.

In 1893, owing to the difficulty experienced by the trustees in getting 'natives' of the county of Nairn to come forward as applicants for the bursary, the benefits of the bequest were extended by this Court so as to include residents in, as well as natives of, the county. The proposal now is, that the benefits should be further extended, so as to include young women, either, I suppose, natives of or residents in, the county of Nairn, to assist them in pursuing their medical studies in Edinburgh. That is a great change, for if Dr Grigor had intended that the benefit of his bequest should be extended to young women, he had the opportunity of saying so before his death, and we find that he did not do so. I cannot think that the difficulty of getting young men to come forward as candidates is a sufficient reason to justify us in authorising so great a change as is here proposed. The trustees only state that they experience difficulty in getting suitable male candidates; there is no allegation that male candidates cannot be obtained, or that no more young men from the county of Nairn contemplate entering the medical profession.

I suppose that if this petition is refused, and in consequence of the dearth of male candidates the bursary remains vacant for a time, the result will be that the income of the trust fund will be accumulated and added to the capital, and that thereby the value of the bequest, when an eligible male candidate appears, will be increased. It is not as if our refusal of the prayer of the petition would cause the scheme to become nugatory or inept. On the whole matter, I do not think that any sufficient reasons have been laid before us to induce us to sanction the drastic change which is here proposed."

NOTES:

1. It is somewhat difficult to follow the logic of this decision. Lord Kinross appears to be **12.31** unperturbed by the fact that the class of persons entitled to benefit under the trust was extended from "natives" to "residents" of Nairn in 1893 on the ground that the trustees experienced "difficulty" in finding applicants, but is at the same time wholly opposed to the class of potential beneficiaries being extended from men to include both men and women on the basis of "difficulty". How could "difficulty" be held to justify one change but not the other? Much stress is laid on the presumed intentions of the testator, but one could fairly respond that Dr Grigor had the opportunity to extend the benefit of his bequest to residents of Nairn, but specifically chose not to do so. At the risk of being unfair to the truster, one might suggest that the court was assuming (but on what basis?) that Dr Grigor's parochialism was of a milder form than his sexism.

   A similar result to that in the *Grigor Medical Bursary* case was reached in *Duart Bursary Fund Trs*, 1911 S.C. 9. However, the Court did remove a similar restriction in *Clark Bursary Fund (Mile-end) Trs* (1903) 5 F. 433, seemingly on the basis that the bursary had been established before women were permitted to enter the classes to which the bursary applied, and that it should not therefore be taken from the reference to "sons of Protestant parents" that the testator had actually intended to exclude female students. A restriction as to nativity was removed in *Kirk-Session of Dunbar*, 1908 S.C. 852, where it was shown that no application for the bursary had ever been made in the 19 years since it had been established.

   These decisions suggest that the Scottish courts may not be as quick as the English courts have been in declaring that conditions attached to trusts are impossible of fulfilment. That will not, of course, prevent the trustees from seeking permission for a variation under s.9(1)(d)(iii), on the basis that the trust purposes are no longer "suitable and effective" (*infra,* para. 12.37). But that condition requires the court to have regard to the "spirit of the gift", and where it is clear that a restriction on the class of beneficiaries was of importance to the truster, it will not be easy to justify variation under that provision either. However, a more liberal approach is perhaps suggested by the case of *Pollock, Petr*, 1948 S.L.T. (Notes) 11. In that case, a testator left a sum of money to the Presbytery of Ayr, directing that the income should be used to provide a bursary for a student from within the Presbytery to study divinity at Edinburgh University. The trustees experienced difficulty in finding qualified candidates "owing to the general desire of Ayrshire divinity students to study at Glasgow University". The Court approved a variation whereby, in any year where there was no suitable candidate studying at Edinburgh, the income might "be applied for the use of qualified persons studying divinity in any University in Scotland". The case is not fully reported, but it is notable that "difficulty" appears to have been considered a ground for removal of a restriction on the class of beneficiaries, unlike in the earlier decisions.

2. Lord Kinross referred in the *Grigor Medical Bursary* case to the fact that the trust income could simply be accumulated if no qualified candidate came forward. That suggests that where accumulation is not possible due to the nature of the trust (for example, where the trust provides accommodation to beneficiaries in property owned or operated by the trust), or may be of limited benefit due to annual calls on the trust fund, the court will be quicker to hold that a restriction on the class of beneficiaries should be struck out as impossible of fulfilment: *cf. Governors of Mitchell's Hospital, Petrs* (1902) 4 F. 582.

s.9(1)(b): "the purposes of the trust provide a use for only part of the property available under the trust"

12.32 This appears to simply restate the position at common law. A section 9(1)(b) situation will generally arise in one of two ways:

Where the trust funds are excessive for the specified purposes. In *Trs of Carnegie Park Orphanage* (1892) 19 R. 605, a testator left certain lands and the residue of his estate to trustees for the purpose of founding an orphanage for orphans between the ages of eight and fourteen in a specified area. The residue of the estate was much greater than the testator had envisaged, and the trust received far fewer applications for admission than it was capable of supporting. The court granted approval for a variation whereby the age limit would be reduced to five years, but preference would be given to children of eight or older. The Lord President (Robertson) observed (at 607) that:

> "this appears to me to be a legitimate proposal, because it will merely lead to the application of the scheme to a larger number of the same class as the truster desired to benefit, and the restriction prevents any violence being done to the intentions of the testator. . . the salient feature of the petitioners' proposal, in my view, is that it only applies to the surplus funds remaining after the testator's intentions, as these are specifically expressed, have been fully carried out."

If the trust funds are vastly in excess of the level the truster had anticipated, it is possible that to apply all those funds to the specified purposes might be self-defeating: see *University of Aberdeen v. Irvine* (1869) 7 M. 1087, where a restriction on the number of students who could benefit from a bursary fund meant that the bursars would receive excessively large sums of money if the restriction were not varied. According to the University, this would have been counterproductive: "experience shews that students enjoying allowances much beyond what is required for the payment of their ordinary expenses are apt to fall into habits seriously detrimental both to themselves and their fellow students". The Court authorised the university to double the number of bursars.

Where the trust purposes have come to an end and surplus funds remain. In *Clarke v. Ross*, 1976 S.L.T. (Notes) 62, a sum of almost £8,000 was raised for the purpose of relieving hardship to miners and their families during the miners' strike, and to promote the interests of the striking miners before and immediately after the strike. After the strike had ended, almost £3,000 remained unspent. The court approved a *cy-près* scheme whereby the remaining funds were to be held in trust to promote the interests of miners and alleviate hardship during any subsequent strikes *s.9(1)(c)(i): "the purposes of the trust were expressed by reference to an area which has, since the trust was constituted, ceased to have effect for the purpose described expressly or by implication in the trust deed or other document constituting the trust".*

This might apply if, for example, the trust purposes were expressed by reference to local government **12.33** boundaries which have since changed due to reorganisation (*Tudor on Charities*, p. 428). However, it should be noted that where trust purposes are expressed by reference to existing boundaries, it does not necessarily follow that a change in those boundaries is effectual insofar as the trust is concerned. See *St Nicholas Kirk-Session v. St George's-in-the-West Kirk-Session*, 1915 S.C. 834, where a trust was established in 1851 for the benefit of the residents of the West Parish of St Nicholas in Aberdeen. The Parish of St George's-in-the-West was disjoined from the West Parish of St Nicholas in 1880. The court held that, despite this fact, the residents of St George's had not ceased to be beneficiaries under the trust.

s.9(1)(c)(ii): "the purposes of the trust were expressed by reference to a class of persons or area which has ceased to be suitable or appropriate, having regard to the spirit of the trust deed or other document constituting the trust, or as regards which it has ceased to be practicable to administer the property available under the trust".

Peggs v. Lamb
[1994] Ch. 172

A trust for grazing land had been established from time immemorial, the income from which **12.34** was distributed to the freemen of the borough of Huntingdon and their widows. By 1991, the number of freemen and the income of the trust was such that the annual benefit to the freemen was more than the Charity Commissioners considered consistent with the application of charitable funds. At their suggestion, the trustees applied for a *cy-près* scheme.

MORRITT J.: "I have concluded that the original purposes were and are general charitable purposes for the benefit of qualifying freemen and their widows. These are presumed to be the purposes laid down in the middle ages. In those days there can be little doubt that the freemen of a borough were a substantial section of the public both numerically and in their social, economic and political importance. As such the class of freemen was then and for several centuries thereafter entirely suitable as a class by reference to which the charitable purposes should be laid down. But I am satisfied that that is no longer so. The effect of the Municipal Corporations Act 1835 was to destroy the political importance of the freemen and thereby to undermine their social and economic importance too. But, of more importance, membership of the class was thereby restricted, in the case of these charities, to those who were the sons of freemen and born in the ancient borough. The inevitable consequence after over 150 years is that the class has dwindled very considerably. There will come a time, if it has not arrived already, when the class of freemen ceases to be a section of the public at all. It is not necessary to decide whether that time has passed so that a case for a scheme can be made out under section 13(1)(e)(ii) of the Act of 1960 [equivalent to s.9(1)(d)(ii) of the Scottish legislation] because I think it is clear that a sufficient case is made out under paragraph (d) [equivalent to paragraph (c) of the Scottish legislation].

   The original basic intention or spirit of the gift was the benefit of the borough of Huntingdon. It would, in my judgment, be entirely consistent with that, that in 1993 the class of persons by reference to which the charitable purposes are laid down should be enlarged from the freemen to the inhabitants as a whole. Accordingly I will direct the settlement of a scheme. I will hear further argument on what other provisions it should contain or principles it should observe."

s.9(1)(d)(i): "the purposes of the trust, whether in whole or in part, have, since the trust was constituted, been adequately provided for by other means".

12.35 It has been suggested that this condition "may be illustrated by a *cy-près* scheme where the original benefits of the trust are now provided for by the statutory services of public or local authorities, for example, a charity for the upkeep of a road or bridge" (*Tudor on Charities* (8th ed., 1995), p. 429). Again, variation for this reason would have been competent at common law. In the *Glasgow Royal Infirmary* cases, trusts were set up with the purpose of establishing a fever convalescent home in Glasgow. However, before these purposes could be effected, the local authority subsequently constructed a fever hospital, thus removing the need for a fever convalescent home. The Court of Session approved *cy-près* schemes in respect of the trusts. (*Glasgow Royal Infirmary, Petitioners* (1887) 14 R. 680 and *Glasgow Royal Infirmary v. Magistrates of Glasgow* (1888) 15 R. 264)

s.9(1)(d)(ii): "the purposes of the trust, whether in whole or in part, have, since the trust was constituted, ceased to be such as would enable the trust to become a recognised body".

12.36 This provision is likely to be applicable in three limited circumstances. Firstly, if the definition of "charity" were to be amended by legislation (as has been recently suggested: see *CharityScotland: The Report of the Scottish Charity Law Review Commission* (2001)), then a trust which was previously entitled to the status of a "recognised" (*i.e.* charitable) body might have to seek a variation of its purposes in order to retain charitable status. Secondly, it is possible that a judicial decision might alter the previously understood interpretation of what is considered "charitable". (See, *e.g. National Anti-Vivisection Society v. Inland Revenue Commissioners* [1948] A.C. 31). In such a case, again, a trust might have to seek a variation of its purposes in order to retain charitable status. Thirdly, the passage of time may have resulted in the class of potential beneficiaries and the size of the funds available for distribution becoming (taken together) inconsistent with charitable status: see *Peggs v. Lamb* [1994] Ch. 172 (*supra* para. 12.34).

s.9(1)(d)(iii): "the purposes of the trust, whether in whole or in part, have, since the trust was constituted, ceased in any other way to provide a suitable and effective method of using the property available under the trust, having regard to the spirit of the trust deed or other document constituting the trust."

12.37 This provision is probably the most radical extension to the *cy-près* jurisdiction contained within the 1990 Act. In some cases, it will allow the court to vary the trust where the directions given by the truster can no longer fulfil his underlying intention due to circumstances such as a change in the value of money (*Re Lepton's Charity* [1972] Ch. 276) or other surrounding circumstances (see, *e.g. Re Steele* [1976] N.I. 66). It will also enable the court to sanction "pre-emptive" variation in order to avoid failure of the trust purposes. (Such variation would have been competent at common law in the exercise of the *cy-près* jurisdiction, at least where it could be shown that there was a "grave risk" of failure if variation were not sanctioned: *Gibson's Trs*, 1933 S.C. 190; *Glasgow Young Men's Christian Association*, 1934 S.C. 452).

The section can also be used to lift restrictions imposed by the truster which are no longer necessary: see *Forrest v. Attorney-General* [1986] V.R. 187, where the truster had limited the class of charities who could benefit from a trust set up by his will for taxation reasons, but the restriction concerned was no longer necessary due to changes in the law of taxation.

The courts have probably not yet pushed this power to its limits. The Court of Appeal has, however, recently adverted to the "concern that potential donors should not be deterred by a belief that their intentions will be overridden by a too ready use of the *cy-près* jurisdiction", but suggested that this must be "set beside the equal but opposite problem that in circumstances unforeseen by the donor his or her bounty may not achieve all that was intended or was reasonably feasible". (*Varsani v. Jesani* [1999] Ch. 219, *per* Morritt L.J. at 235)

(ii) Amalgamating trusts on the ground of expediency: a residual role for *cy-près* outwith the statutory provisions?

12.38 In *Mining Institute of Scotland Benevolent Fund Trs, Petrs*, 1994 S.L.T. 785, the trustees of two public trusts applied under section 9 of the 1990 Act for permission to amalgamate. It was held that the trustees had not demonstrated in their averments that any of the criteria laid down in section 9 applied. However, the Lord President (Hope), sitting in the Outer House, opined that:

"It is a matter for the Inner House of the Court of Session to define the limits of its *cy-près* jurisdiction in the exercise of the *nobile officium*. Recent decisions of the court have demonstrated that, while at one time a strict approach was taken to this matter, the court is now willing to exercise its power in cases of strong expediency falling short of impossibility of performance. The flexibility of approach which is inherent in the *nobile officium* enables the Inner House to take full account of the circumstances of each case and to act in accordance with principle as each case requires. . . [His Lordship considered the trustees' averments and continued:]

In my opinion therefore the court does not have power to approve of this scheme under s.9 of the 1990 Act. This is because the petitioners are unable to satisfy me that any of the requirements set out in paras (a) to (d) of subs (1) apply to the two trusts. On the other hand, it is clear that the petitioners are in a position to say that it is expedient, in view of the social and economic changes to which they refer and in the interests of the better management of the trust funds, that the schemes which were approved in 1971 should now be varied and the funds amalgamated into a single trust. It is a question of degree whether cases of this kind are sufficiently compelling to justify the approval of a *cy-près* scheme. Such cases cannot be dealt with, however, under the statutory jurisdiction for the reorganisation of public trusts under s.9 of the 1990 Act."

A *cy-près* petition was subsequently granted by the court, but it is not clear on exactly what grounds. Nor is it clear which authorities Lord Hope had in mind when stating that "recent decisions" of the court had indicated that the *cy-près* jurisdiction was now available in cases of "strong expediency falling short of impossibility of performance". The use of the phrase "strong expediency" suggests that he may have *Gibson's Trs*, 1933 S.C. 190 in mind, but in that case it was observed that "if the petitioners are not given some wider powers of investment, there is a grave risk of the trust becoming insolvent and the carrying on of the truster's main purpose becoming impossible." (*per* Lord Blackburn at 218). (See also *Glasgow Young Men's Christian Association*, 1934 S.C. 452).

"Strong expediency" may, therefore, be a ground for sanctioning a *cy-près* scheme in order to avert a grave risk of impossibility of performance, but *Gibson's Trs* does not provide any authority for the use of the *cy-près* jurisdiction in cases where no risk of supervening impossibility is demonstrated. (Lord Blackburn does appear, in *Gibson's Trs*, by referring to *University of Aberdeen v. Irvine* (1869) 7 M. 1087, to suggest that mere expediency without a risk of impossibility is sufficient, but this suggestion appears, with respect, to be ill-founded as *Irvine* itself should properly regarded as a case of impossibility: see the dissenting opinion of the Lord President (Clyde) in *Gibson's Trs* at 200–201).

These criticisms notwithstanding, the result in the *Mining Institute* case does, however, suggest that the court may exercise the *cy-près* jurisdiction in order to permit two public trusts to be amalgamated where it would be expedient to do so. In this context, it is worth noting that section 13(1)(c) of the Charities Act 1993 (which re-enacts section 13(1)(c) of the Charities Act 1960) specifically gives the English courts the power to make a *cy-près* scheme in the following circumstances:

"where the property available by virtue of the gift and other property applicable for similar purposes can be more effectively used in conjunction, and to that end can suitably, regard being had to the spirit of the gift, be made applicable to common purposes".

For reasons which are not clear, no equivalent provision was included in section 9 of the 1990 Act. Lord Hope's comments (and the eventual result in the *Mining Institute* case) notwithstanding, there does not appear to be any prior authority which explicitly supports the proposition that the Court of Session may use the *cy-près* jurisdiction to sanction the amalgamation of public trusts on the ground of expediency. Support might be found, however, in the case of *Clutterbuck, Petr*, 1961 S.L.T. 427. In that case, two infantry regiments were amalgamated into one by the Army Council. A voluntary benevolent association existed in respect of each regiment, and the trustees of the two associations petitioned the Inner House for approval of a *cy-près* scheme involving amalgamation of the two associations. The court granted approval, with the Lord President (Clyde) observing as follows (at 428):

"the underlying charitable purpose of [each association] is to promote the welfare and esprit de corps of the existing members and past members of each regiment and keep up the contact between each regiment and its past and present members. The financial help given is merely the practical means taken to achieve this underlying charitable purpose.

In my view, it can be affirmed that in the light of the amalgamation of the two regiments this underlying charitable purpose, which is the whole basis for these two Associations, has now become impossible of achievement. Existing members of the new regiment could not qualify for the benefits under either of the existing Associations and past members of either of the old regiments, although they might continue if no change were made to get financial help from the existing Associations, would necessarily be getting it not from the Royal Highland Fusiliers but from an Association related to a regiment which has ceased to exist. The creation of the new regiment, therefore, and the disappearance of the two older regiments has rendered impossible the underlying purpose of both the existing Associations in regard, not only to past members of the old regiments, but also to existing and future members of the new one.

In these circumstances, it seems to me that the underlying object of each of these Associations can be given practical effect today by a scheme on the lines proposed. This is not a mere amalgamation of two voluntary Associations. . . but a proper matter for the exercise by this Court of its *nobile officium* where owing to supervening events a charitable trust has become unworkable."

Although the exercise of the *cy-près* jurisdiction was justified on the ground of impossibility, this argument is extremely difficult to support. Firstly, Lord Clyde was probably incorrect in saying that members of the new regiment would not qualify as beneficiaries of the existing Associations (*Mailler's Trs v. Allan* (1904) 7 F. 326). That observation might, however, have depended on the specific provisions of the trust deeds concerned, which are not reproduced in the report. But secondly, even if members of the new regiment were unable to benefit from the existing Associations, this hardly amounts to impossibility given that there were other potential beneficiaries in existence. Thirdly, even if that did constitute impossibility, it would hardly have been necessary to go so far as amalgamating the two Associations to remove that impossibility. Although the decision in *Clutterbuck* is clothed in the language of necessity, it is difficult to justify the result on the basis of anything other than expediency.

Read together, therefore, *Mining Institute* and *Clutterbuck* suggest that *cy-près* does have a residual role outwith the statutory provisions, permitting the court to sanction the amalgamation of trusts on the ground of expediency. (It should be noted that section 9(3)(b) of the 1990 Act specifically allows the court to sanction amalgamation if one of the conditions set out in section 9(1) is satisfied; expediency, however, is not one of those conditions, which is why the section 9 application in *Mining Institute* failed).

(e) What can the court do once the variation jurisdiction is triggered?

(i) The principle of approximation

12.39 Once the *cy-près* jurisdiction, or the statutory variation jurisdiction under the 1990 Act, has been triggered, the court may approve a scheme for the variation of the trust. What is the court then entitled to do? The fact that the jurisdiction has been triggered does not give the court an unlimited scope to apply the trust funds in whatever way it feels to be appropriate.

Rather, the principle of approximation must be applied. The court must ensure that "the objects of the proposed scheme approximate as closely as may be to those which the testatrix originally selected" (*Stranraer Original Secession Corporation*, 1923 S.C. 722, *per* the Lord President (Clyde) at 725). In cases of initial failure, the court must ensure that the *cy-près* scheme remains within the scope of the truster's general charitable intent.

Clephane v. Magistrates of Edinburgh
(1869) 7 M. (H.L.) 7, at 15

12.40 LORD WESTBURY: "Now, it is perfectly true that you cannot substitute one charity for another. You may substitute for a particular charity, which has been defined and which has failed, another charity *ejusdem generis*, or which approaches it in its nature and character; but it is quite true that you cannot take a charity which was intended for one purpose, and apply it altogether to a different purpose."

Glasgow Royal Infirmary v. Magistrates of Glasgow
(1888) 15 R. 264

LORD PRESIDENT (INGLIS): "The funds in question here were raised by a society called the **12.41** Royal Infirmary Dorcas Society of Glasgow, the purpose for which they were raised being to establish a house for the reception of patients recovering from fever, and also a children's hospital. The latter object is provided for, and the only question is what is to be done with the remainder of the funds. At the time the money was raised the Royal Infirmary received all the fever patients who fell to be treated in the hospitals of Glasgow. Since that time it has ceased to receive any fever patients in consequence of the Local Authority having established a fever hospital for fever patients. That is no doubt a great improvement as regards the interests of public health, but it has created a difficulty as regards these funds, for it is idle to suppose that we can authorise the establishment of a home for patients recovering from fever in the Royal Infirmary when there are no patients of that class in the infirmary at all.

The question we have now to dispose of is how in these circumstances we can fulfil most nearly the wishes and intentions of those who raised the fund. The case resolves into a competition between two claimants. The Royal Infirmary, on the one hand, maintain that as they were the original objects of the charity (or rather that as the Dorcas Society, which was in connection with them, was) and were intended to be its recipients, and to employ it in a certain way, they have the best claim to it now, and what they propose to do is to expend it in providing a home for nurses employed in the infirmary. That certainly is not very near the object of the original charity. It has nothing to do with fever patients or convalescent patients.

On the other hand answers have been lodged for the Magistrates of Glasgow and the Dorcas Society in connection with the Belvidere and other hospitals. They say that in consequence of the new arrangement by which fever patients are now treated in a separate hospital, a meeting was held of parties interested, in Glasgow, and they now state that their principal object is to provide warm clothing for the fever convalescents on leaving the hospital. They further state that since December 1871 they have been in use to employ their funds for that purpose. There is now one fever hospital in Glasgow, the other hospitals in which the respondents are interested not being within the city, and that one hospital in Glasgow no doubt has taken the place of the Royal Infirmary, which was also in Glasgow, in treating fever patients. The contention of these respondents is that the fund will be disposed of in the way most nearly approaching to the wishes of the original donors if it is given to them to assist the convalescent fever patients in the Glasgow Fever Hospital.

My opinion is that the claim of these latter respondents ought to be sustained. Their charity comes very naturally in the place of the charity originally contemplated. The same class of persons will be benefited in the same way as was intended, but I do not see my way to saying that this Dorcas Society should be allowed to use these funds for the relief of patients out of Glasgow. That would be an extension of the charity which I do not think is justified in view of the original purpose of the donors. Subject to that restriction, I think their proposal is just and proper."

Lord Mure and Lord Adam concurred.

NOTES:

1. *Maintaining a local connection.* Lord Inglis indicates that, because the trust was originally **12.42** intended to benefit patients in Glasgow, the court would not authorise a variation which would benefit patients from elsewhere. This is consistent with the general approach of the courts. Where the trust was intended to benefit a specific area, the proposed variation should normally ensure that the trust will continue to benefit that area (and that area alone), unless (a) that is impossible or (b) in the case of variation after the trust has taken effect, that area is no longer "suitable or appropriate" (s.9(1)(c)(ii) of the 1990 Act). See *Milngavie District Nursing Association*, 1950 S.L.T. (Notes) 45; *Pentcaitland, Saltoun and Humbie District Nursing Association*, 1954 S.L.T. (Notes) 28.

The court will not normally sanction a variation which involves transferring trust funds to a body outwith the jurisdiction of the Scottish courts, at least where there is a suitable body in Scotland to whom the funds can be transferred: *Glasgow Society for Prevention of Cruelty to Animals v. National Anti-Vivisection Society*, 1915 S.C. 757; *Goodman and Ors, Petrs*, 1959 S.L.T. 254.

2. *Services which are provided by central or local government.* The court will not approve a variation whereby the trust funds will be used to provide services or facilities which central or local government agencies are obliged to provide. See *Governors of Jonathan Anderson Trust* (1896) 23 R. 592, *per* the Lord President (Robertson) at 594:

> "If some educational or charitable purpose be one for which it is lawful to impose rates, or to the accomplishment of which public moneys are already dedicated, then it is plain that to give the money of a charitable trust to that purpose is not to further the purpose, which is already provided for, but to relieve the ratepayer or the taxpayer, as the case may be, who is by statute made the debtor in an obligation. The Court, if it were to make such application of trust money, would, under the guise of promoting a purpose which once depended on charity, be ignoring the facts that by legislation that purpose had passed out of the region of charity into that of obligation on the ratepayers, and that a charity devoted to the recipients of education is misapplied, if devoted to the givers of education, whether voluntary or compulsory."

This principle, however, only applies to expenditure which is mandatory upon central or local government, and not expenditure to which the government has a discretion to contribute: *Campbell Endowment Trust*, 1928 S.C. 171.

In *Arbroath Female Home Mission*, 1966 S.C. 1, where a *cy-près* scheme was approved which involved winding up a charitable trust and distributing its funds to various other appropriate organisations, the Lord President (Clyde) observed (at 3) "that it is usual and advisable to include in schemes of this kind a provision declaring its benefits supplementary to and not in substitution for any benefit which could otherwise be provided by the central or local authority", and an appropriate provision was inserted before approval of the scheme.

3. *Transferring the trust funds to another body.* The court may, in approving a variation scheme, authorise the trust to transfer its funds to another body. Such a course of action may be attractive as minimising the administrative expenses which will have to come out of the trust fund. (*Murray and Anr, Petrs* (1891) 29 S.L.R. 173). Although considerable hostility was expressed in *McLean* (1898) 1 F. 48 to the suggestion that the court might grant permission for a transfer where the trustees hold office *ex officio* rather than as private individuals, it appears that such a transfer is competent where it can be shown that the transfer would be expedient and provide a more effective means of giving effect to the trust purposes: *Aberdeen Servants' Benevolent Fund* 1914 S.C. 8.

The transfer may be to a new body of trustees specifically established for the purpose: *Clyde Industrial Training Ship Association*, 1925 S.C. 676.

Where a testator has left funds to a body for particular purposes and that body is unwilling or unable to accept the trust, the court may authorise the funds to be paid over to an alternative body for the same purposes: *Glasgow Society for Prevention of Cruelty to Animals v. National Anti-Vivisection Society*, 1915 S.C. 757.

As regards statutory variation, transfer is specifically permitted under section 9(3)(a), but the funds must be transferred to "another public trust". There seems to be no good reason for this restriction, particularly given that not all Scottish charities take the form of public trusts, but it must nevertheless be observed. It should also be noted that this section refers to "another public trust" in the singular. This appears to rule out a scheme whereby the assets might be distributed amongst a number of other public trusts (which has been done in the exercise of the *cy-près* jurisdiction—see *e.g. Arbroath Female Home Mission*, 1966 S.C. 1). This limitation probably results from bad drafting rather than a policy decision, and is, it is submitted, regrettable, given that distribution amongst a number of trusts might be more consistent with the spirit of the trust deed than simply transferring all the assets to one single other trust.

4. *Increasing the class of beneficiaries.* The court can increase the class of beneficiaries by removing restrictions as to the qualifications of potential beneficiaries (age, sex, race etc.), or by removing a restriction as to the number of beneficiaries. See, *e.g. Trs of Carnegie Park*

Orphanage (1892) 19 R. 605; *University of Aberdeen v. Irvine* (1869) 7 M. 1087 and *supra*, para. 12.29 on the removal of impossible or impractical conditions.

5. *Extending the trustees' powers.* The court may approve an extension of the trustees' powers as part of a scheme of variation: *McCrie's Trs*, 1927 S.C. 556. An extension of investment powers was refused in *Scott's Hospital Trs*, 1913 S.C. 289, but that was on the basis that impossibility (which was then the only ground on which variation could be approved) had not been established. (The powers sought in that case were subsequently granted by a Private Act of Parliament: Alexander Scott's Hospital and the North of Scotland College of Agriculture Order Confirmation Act 1914 (4 Geo. 5)).

It has been said, however, that the Court will not authorise an extension of powers of investment beyond those permitted by the Trustee Investments Act 1961: "No considerations of expediency or convenience can entitle the Court to authorise trustees operating under an existing scheme to invest their funds in securities which Parliament has impliedly prohibited them from holding. For, were the Court to do so in one case, it would inevitably follow that the Court would require to do so for all, and the Act of Parliament would cease to be effective." (*Mitchell Bequest Trs*, 1959 S.C. 395, *per* the Lord President (Clyde) at 398–399). It is unlikely, however, that this principle would be followed today. It is inconsistent with the modern position in relation to variation of private trusts (*supra*, para. 12.08) and is probably no longer appropriate given that the 1961 Act is now somewhat outdated (see also *British Museum Trs v. Attorney-General* [1984] 1 W.L.R. 418; *Steel v. Wellcome Trs Ltd* [1988] 1 W.L.R. 167).

In *Stranraer Original Secession Congregation*, 1923 S.C. 722, property was left to a congregation to be held on trust under a trust-deed which specifically prohibited alienation of the property. The congregation ceased to exist and the trustees sought approval for a *cy-près* scheme which involved selling the trust property and applying the income for the benefit of two other funds. The Inner House remitted the petition to a reporter, who recommended that the court should approve the scheme under deletion of the power to sell the trust property, and that the trustees could subsequently apply in the Outer House for a power of sale under section 5 of the 1921 Act (*supra*, para. 12.09). The Inner House approved the scheme without making the deletion. The Lord President (Clyde) observed (at 726) that "a general power to sell and to hold the proceeds and administer the revenue arising from such proceeds must be incorporated in the new scheme, unless it is to prove abortive and inoperative".

E. Variation of small public trusts without court application

(a) Section 10 of the Law Reform (Miscellaneous Provisions) (Scotland) Act **12.43**
1990.

Law Reform (Miscellaneous Provisions) (Scotland) Act 1990, s.10

10.—(1) Where a majority of the trustees of any public trust having an annual income not exceeding £5,000 are of the opinion—

[The remainder of this subsection lays down preconditions for variation which are identical to those set down in section 9(1) for variation of the trust by approval of the court. See *supra*, para. 12.16 for these conditions]

(2) Where this subsection applies in respect of a trust, the trustees may determine that, to enable the resources of the trust to be applied to better effect consistently with the spirit of the trust deed or other document constituting the trust—
  (a) a modification of the trust's purposes should be made;
  (b) the whole assets of the trust should be transferred to another public trust; or
  (c) that the trust should be amalgamated with one or more public trusts.

(3) Where the trustees of a trust determine as mentioned in subsection (2)(a) above, they may, subject to subsections (4) to (6) below, pass a resolution that the trust deed be modified by replacing the trust purposes by other purposes specified in the resolution.

(4) The trustees shall ensure that, so far as is practicable in the circumstances, the purposes so specified are not so far dissimilar in character to those of the purposes set out in the original trust deed or other document constituting the trust that such modification of the trust deed would constitute an unreasonable departure from the spirit of such trust deed or other document.

(5) Before passing a resolution under subsection (3) above the trustees shall have regard—

    (a) where the trust purposes relate to a particular locality, to the circumstances of the locality; and

    (b) to the extent to which it may be desirable to achieve economy by amalgamating two or more trusts.

(6) As regards a trust which is a recognised body, the trustees shall ensure that the purposes specified as mentioned in subsection (3) above are such as will enable the trust to continue to be granted an exemption from tax by the Commissioners of Inland Revenue under section 505(1) of the Income and Corporation Taxes Act 1988 (exemption from tax for charities).

(7) Subject to subsection (14) below, a modification of trust purposes under this section shall not have effect before the expiry of a period of two months commencing with the date on which any advertisement in pursuance of regulations made under subsection (13) below is first published.

(8) Where the trustees determine as mentioned in subsection (2)(b) above they may pass a resolution that the trust be wound up and that the assets of the trust be transferred to another trust or trusts the purposes of which are not so dissimilar in character to those of the trust to be wound up as to constitute an unreasonable departure from the spirit of the trust deed or other document constituting the trust to be wound up.

(9) Before passing a resolution under subsection (8) above, the trustees shall—

    (a) where the trust purposes relate to a particular locality, have regard to the circumstances of the locality;

    (b) where the trust is a recognised body, ensure that the purposes of the trust to which it is proposed that the assets be transferred are such as will enable the trust to be granted an exemption from tax by the Commissioners of Inland Revenue under section 505(1) of the Income and Corporation Taxes Act 1988 (exemption from tax for charities); and

    (c) ascertain that the trustees of the trust to which it is proposed to transfer the assets will consent to the transfer of the assets.

(10) Where the trustees determine as mentioned in subsection (2)(c) above, they may pass a resolution that the trust be amalgamated with one or more other trusts so that the purposes of the trust constituted by such amalgamation will not be so dissimilar in character to those of the trust to which the resolution relates as to constitute an unreasonable departure from the spirit of the trust deed or other document constituting the last mentioned trust.

(11) Before passing a resolution under subsection (10) above, the trustees shall—

    (a) where the trust purposes relate to a particular locality, have regard to the circumstances of the locality;

    (b) where any of the trusts to be amalgamated is a recognised body, ensure that the trust purposes of the trust to be constituted by such amalgamation will be such as to enable it to be granted an exemption from tax by the Commissioners of Inland Revenue under section 505(1) of the Income and Corporation Taxes Act 1988 (exemption from tax for charities); and

    (c) ascertain that the trustees of any other trust with which it is proposed that the trust will be amalgamated will agree to such amalgamation.

(12) Subject to subsection (14) below, a transfer of trust assets or an amalgamation of two or more trusts under this section shall not be effected before the expiry of a period of two months commencing with the date on which any advertisement in pursuance of regulations made under subsection (13) below is first published.

(13) The Secretary of State may, by regulations, prescribe the procedure to be followed by trustees following upon a resolution passed under subsection (3), (8) or (10) above, and such regulations may, without prejudice to the generality, include provision as to advertisement of the proposed modification or winding up, the making of objections by persons with an interest in the purposes of the trust, notification to the Lord Advocate of the terms of the resolution and the time within which anything requires to be done.

(14) If it appears to the Lord Advocate, whether in consideration of any objections made in pursuance of regulations made under subsection (13) above or otherwise—

    (a) that the trust deed should not be modified as mentioned in subsection (3) above;

    (b) that the trust should not be wound up as mentioned in subsection (8) above; or

    (c) that the trust should not be amalgamated as mentioned in subsection (10) above,

he may direct the trust not to proceed with the modification or, as the case may be winding up and transfer of funds or amalgamation.

(15) The Secretary of State may, by order, amend subsection (1) above by substituting a different figure for the figure, for the time being, mentioned in that subsection.

(16) This section shall apply to any trust to which section 223 of the Local Government (Scotland) Act 1973 (property held on trust by local authorities) applies.

NOTES:

1. The requirements for advertising and notification to the Lord Advocate are laid down in the **12.44** Public Trusts (Reorganisation) (Scotland) (No. 2) Regulations 1993 (S.I. 1993 No. 2036).
2. As argued earlier in relation to variation by the court, the wording of section 10(2)(b) is regrettable in that it excludes the possibility of the trustees distributing the trust assets among a number of other appropriate public trusts. Nor is it easy to see why the trustees should be restricted from transferring the trust assets to a registered charity that is not a trust. (See *supra,* para. 12.42).

(b) Removing a prohibition on expenditure of capital

Section 11 of the Law Reform (Miscellaneous Provisions) Act 1990 applies to any public trust with an **12.45** annual income not exceeding £1,000 where the trust deed prohibits the expenditure of any of the trust capital. It empowers trustees to proceed with the expenditure of capital where they:

> "(a) have resolved unanimously that, having regard to the purposes of the trust, the income of the trust is too small to enable the purposes of the trust to be achieved; and
> (b) are satisfied that either there is no reasonable prospect of effecting a transfer of the trust's assets under section 10 of this Act or that the expenditure of capital is more likely to achieve the purposes of the trust."

They must, in accordance with the Public Trusts (Reorganisation) (Scotland) (No. 2) Regulations 1993 (S.I. 1993 No. 2036), advertise their intention to do so and notify the Lord Advocate. The Lord Advocate is entitled to apply to the court for an order prohibiting the expenditure.

(c) Dormant bank accounts of charities

Under section 12 of the Law Reform (Miscellaneous Provisions) Act 1990, the Scottish Charities **12.46** Nominee is entitled to investigate dormant accounts held by banks or building societies for charities and may take steps to transfer the funds to another Scottish charity if no one concerned in the management or control of the company can be traced.

(d) Educational endowments

It should be noted that there are special provisions relating to the variation of educational **12.47** endowments, although these will not be dealt with further here due to limitations of space. See further Wilson and Duncan, paras 16–21 *et seq.*, and the Education (Scotland) Act 1980, Part VI, as amended by the Education (Scotland) Act 1981, s.115 and Sched. 6.

Chapter 13

REVOCATION AND TERMINATION OF TRUSTS

This chapter considers the circumstances in which trusts may be revoked or terminated.

1. REVOCATION BY THE TRUSTER: *MORTIS CAUSA* TRUSTS

13.01   Because a *mortis causa* trust does not take effect until the death of the truster, there is, strictly speaking, no question of such a trust being revoked by the truster. There is, however, a related (but separate) question, which is to what extent a testator may revoke a testamentary deed during his lifetime.

C de B Murray, *The Law of Wills in Scotland* (1945), p. 45

13.02   "A will does not operate until the testator's death. Consequently he may revoke it at any time, if he wants to. This power to revoke flows from the very nature of a testamentary deed, which is the voluntary exercise of a testator's right to leave his property as he chooses, subject only to those provisions in favour of wife and children imposed under the common law or by statute. Menzies, in his Lectures on Conveyancing (Sturrock's edition), p. 425, states the law thus: 'A testament. . . takes effect only at the testator's death; and as it is held to express his mind as at his death, so he may revoke it at any time before that event; and so strong is this principle that that right of revocation continues even though it may have been renounced.' The will, however, must *be* a voluntary settlement, and in cases where a settlement has been made for an onerous consideration the power to revoke may be barred."

NOTES:

1. Even where a will contains a clause stating that it is irrevocable, the testator retains the power to revoke the will. The declaration of irrevocability is ineffective, as it is merely part of a revocable deed. (See the *Stair Memorial Encyclopaedia*, Vol. 25, para. 736).
2. Murray states that "where a settlement has been made for an onerous consideration the power to revoke may be barred". Is the rule really so narrow, or would the courts give effect to a gratuitous promise not to revoke? See the following case, which is generally cited as the leading authority on binding oneself not to revoke a will:

Paterson v. Paterson
(1893) 20 R. 484

13.03   On October 12, 1889, Margaret Paterson executed a minute of agreement with her son, John Paterson. The minute narrated that the son had advanced a sum of over £800 to his mother and her late husband, which was more than the value of the heritable property in Linlithgow now wholly owned by the mother. Under the minute, the mother agreed to execute a will under which the son would be entitled to the entirety of her estate on her death. This will was to be regarded as irrevocable and the mother bound herself not to alter or revoke it to any extent. The son was granted the management and control of the heritable property during the mother's life. He agreed to take over responsibility for a bond and disposition in security for £150 which affected the heritable property, and to "pay all taxes or assessments leviable on account of the same", and to pay to the mother the full rents which he received for the heritable property, "without any deduction whatever".

On the same date, the mother executed a will which left her entire estate to her son. On the June 26, 1891, she executed another will, which purported to revoke the 1889 will and dispose of her property equally among her three sons, John, James and Andrew, and appointing James sole trustee. She died on the July 27, 1891. In December 1891, John Paterson brought an action for reduction of the 1891 will.

LORD KINCAIRNEY: "I do not hold the prior settlement irrevocable on the ground that it is declared to be so in the deed itself. I agree that it is settled that such a declaration in a testamentary deed is itself revocable along with the rest of the deed—*Dougal v. Dougal*, 1789, M. 15, 949; and further, that a *mortis causa* deed will not be protected or rendered irrevocable by delivery—*Somerville v. Somerville*, May 18, 1819, F.C.; *Millar v. Dickson*, July 11, 1825, 4 S.D. 822; M'Laren on Wills, i. 249. Further, I think it may be held at least doubtful whether a bare obligation in a separate deed not to revoke a testament or legacy if undelivered would not be equally revocable with the testament or legacy, as suggested by Lord Ivory in his note 575 to Ersk. 3,9,6. But revocation of the will appears to me in this case to be barred by the agreement which I must hold to be irrevocable. It was argued, indeed, that the agreement was a mere pretence, not a true agreement at all, but at most a unilateral obligation. I must hold that the deed is what it purports to be, a bilateral agreement, and as such a delivered deed, or, as binding without delivery, equivalent to a delivered deed. I see no reason why it should not be held to be, as it purports to be, irrevocable.

The authority of Stair, iii. 8, 28–33, on this point is explicit. In the latter passage he says that legacies may be taken away by a derogatory deed, 'unless the defunct be obliged by contract *inter vivos* not to alter the same, in which case contract and paction doth so far overrule the power of testing that posterior deeds, whether expressly or impliedly altering, would be ineffectual.'

And Erskine states the law in similar terms, 3,9,6. It is true that Lord Ivory, in his note already referred to, questions whether the law so stated be warranted by the case of *Houston*, quoted by Stair, and that may certainly be open to doubt. But I doubt whether either Stair or Erskine meant to rest their statement of the law on that case, which is mentioned by Stair rather as an illustration than as an authority, and is not quoted by Erskine at all. I take it that the doctrine may be rested on the authority of Stair and Erskine independently of that case.

[Lord Kincairney reviewed the following authorities: *Curdy v. Boyd* (1775) Mor. 15948; *Duguid v. Caddall's Trs* (1831) 9 S. 844; *Murison v. Dick* (1854) 16 D. 529; McLaren i., 250; *Turnbull v. Tawse* (1825) 1 W&S 80. He continued:]

These authorities appear to establish that an *inter vivos* agreement to make a testament or grant a legacy will bar revocation of a will or legacy made in implement of it.

It was contended that the agreement between Mrs Paterson and the pursuer was not obligatory on Mrs Paterson, because it was gratuitous. It was said that the obligations on the pursuer were merely nominal. I do not think that these obligations are wholly nominal, although they are certainly not burdensome. The obligation to pay the rents without deduction of taxes amounts to something, if not to much. Further, the deed is not gratuitous in the sense of being without any good reason, and granted for mere favour and affection; for the statement that the pursuer had spent on the heritable subjects more than they were worth is certainly some reason for agreeing to leave the property to him.

But according to our law it is of no importance in this question whether a deed is binding or is revocable to consider whether the deed is gratuitous or onerous. The one is just as irrevocable as the other if meant to be so, and containing nothing to the contrary. In *Duguid v. Cadell's Trustees* the letter founded on was gratuitous, and yet was held irrevocable. . ."

The Lord Ordinary granted decree of reduction.

The defenders reclaimed to the Inner House:

Lord President (Robertson): "I think that the Lord Ordinary has arrived at the right conclusion in holding that this agreement is not open to challenge. The agreement appears to me to be on the face of it onerous, and that in two respects. This lady begins by admitting that her son has advanced to her and her husband sums amounting to something over £800, which had been expended on property belonging to her, and accordingly she treats him as her creditor for that amount. She then goes on to bind herself to execute an irrevocable settlement in favour of her whole property. Taking it even so far therefore, it cannot, I think, be said that this agreement is wholly gratuitous on the part of this lady; but the onerous character of the deed becomes much clearer when we proceed to its third article, for she there in effect says to her son 'I am debtor in a bond for £150, and if you will either discharge that bond or take an assignation to it, and if you will also pay me the rents of my property in full without any deduction for taxes or insurance, then I bind myself to give you my whole estate at my death.' It is admitted that the son did relieve his mother of the bond in one or other of the forms suggested, and I think that having done so he could not have distressed her for payment of the amount of the bond. His obligation, I think, was to let the bond lie during her lifetime and take no interest. This agreement, purporting as it does to be onerous, and having been implemented on his part by the pursuer, it seems to me that he is in the position of having given value for the counter obligation which his mother bears to have come under to him, and that he is now entitled to have that obligation enforced. I think that it is not the less to be enforced because it in its nature could be implemented only after her death. I think, therefore, that we should adhere."

Lords Adam, McLaren and Kinnear concurred.

The Court adhered.

Notes:

13.04
1. Although the Lord President appears at first to simply uphold Lord Kincairney's reasoning, there is a subtle difference between the two approaches. Lord Kincairney seems to tend towards the view that the agreement not to revoke is onerous rather than gratuitous, but that whether it is one or the other makes no difference and it is still effective. The Lord President seems to take the view that the agreement is onerous, and says nothing as to whether a gratuitous promise would be effective. The fact, however, that he lays weight on the agreement between the Patersons being onerous seems to suggest that a gratuitous promise might not be effective.

     This may explain Murray's suggestion that the agreement not to revoke must be onerous. However, given that Scots law recognises the enforceability of gratuitous promises, there would seem no justification for such a requirement. The better view is probably that of Mackenzie Stuart, who states (at 133):

> "The reported cases deal with onerous contracts, but there seems no reason why a gratuitous promise should not be given effect to if sufficiently proved."

The reference to "sufficient proof" by Mackenzie Stuart relates to the special rules of proof which applied to gratuitous promises prior to section 11 of the Requirements of Writing (Scotland) Act 1995. See further *Walkers on Evidence*, paras 25.1 and 25.15.

2. The agreement not to revoke must be explicit. As Mackenzie Stuart points out (at 133), "[t]here is a presumption against anyone depriving himself of free testamentary power, and a contract which is alleged to have this effect is read strictly."

3. A testator may revoke a will in one of two ways—either by destroying the will, or by executing a new will. For further discussion, see the *Stair Memorial Encyclopaedia*, Vol. 25, paras 736 *et seq.*; Macdonald, *Succession*, Chapter 7.

2. REVOCATION: *INTER VIVOS* TRUSTS

It is possible that a truster may wish to revoke an *inter vivos* trust which he has created. Even if the **13.05**
truster himself does not wish to revoke the trust, the question of revocability may arise in a number of
other ways, *e.g.*:

- Upon the death of the truster, a question may arise as to whether the trust property formed
  part of his estate at the time of his death. If the trust is a revocable one, the trust property
  may be subject to claims for prior or legal rights by his spouse or children, or subject to the
  provisions of his will. (See, *e.g. Montgomery's Trs v. Montgomery* (1895) 22 R. 824).
- If the truster becomes insolvent, his creditors may seek to have the trust revoked so that the
  trust property can be applied to payment of his debts. (See, *e.g. Lawson's Tr. v. Lawson*, 1938
  S.C. 632).

It is convenient to approach the question of revocability in a reverse fashion, by asking whether the
trust in question is to be considered irrevocable. The conditions for irrevocability have been set out by
Wilson and Duncan:

W.A. Wilson and A.G.M. Duncan, *Trusts, Trustees and Executors* (2nd ed., 1995), para. 11–03

"A trust is irrevocable if the following conditions are satisfied:

(1) the granter must have been solvent at the date of the divestiture and must not have
    been made insolvent by the divestiture. Provided that this condition is satisfied, the
    alienation can be gratuitous. If the granter was insolvent, a gratuitous alienation
    may be reduced at the instance of his creditors but not at the instance of his wife
    and children.

(2) the trust-deed must have been delivered to the creditors and the estate conveyed to
    them. The conveyance must be absolute and unqualified by any back bond or other
    similar reservation. A provision that the truster was to be a necessary consenting
    party to acts of trust administration was held not to affect the divestiture. The fact
    that the truster is one of the trustees does not prevent irrevocability.

(3) there must be in existence an ascertained beneficiary. There is an exception in the
    case of an antenuptial marriage-contract trust.

(4) the beneficiary must have a *jus quaesitium*—an immediate beneficial interest—and
    not merely a *spes successionis* under a testamentary provision. The beneficial
    interest may be vested or contingent. If it is contingent, it does not matter that
    emergence of the maturity of the interest can occur only on the granter's death."

NOTE:

Each of these conditions can be dealt with in turn.

A. Solvency

Strictly speaking, the first condition stated by Wilson and Duncan is a rule of insolvency law rather **13.06**
than a rule of trust law. Where a truster is insolvent at the time of the trust's creation, or was rendered
insolvent by its creation, the creation of the trust may be challengeable by his creditor or by the office
holder administering the insolvent estate (such as a trustee in bankruptcy or a receiver) as a gratuitous
alienation. Insolvency would not (provided the other three conditions outlined by Wilson and Duncan
were satisfied) give the truster a right to revoke the trust himself.

It is a defence to any challenge that (a) the truster was absolutely solvent (*i.e.* his assets exceeded his
liabilities) immediately after the alienation or at any time thereafter; (b) that the alienation was made
for adequate consideration, or (c) that the alienation was a permitted gift. See the Bankruptcy
(Scotland) Act 1985, s.34 and the Insolvency Act 1986, s.242. On the statutory provisions generally
(and also the common law right to challenge a gratuitous alienation), see McKenzie Skene, *Insolvency*,
Chapter 30.

B. Property must have passed to the trustees

13.07 A trust cannot be created without delivery of the trust property to the trustees, or some equivalent of delivery. See *supra*, Chapter 2. Although it is usually said that a trust remains revocable until property passes, it would be more correct to say that the trust simply does not exist until this takes place.

C. An ascertained beneficiary must exist

13.08 If the only ascertained beneficiary is the truster himself, the trust remains revocable. See the following case:

Bertram's Trs v. Bertram
1909 S.C. 1238; 1909 2 S.L.T. 86

Norman Bertram created a trust for the benefit of himself, his wife (if he were to marry) and his children (if he were to have any). He did not marry, nor have children, and desired to revoke the trust. A special case was presented to the Inner House of the Court of Session.

LORD LOW: "It is not easy to reconcile all the decisions which have been given on the question whether a trust deed is revocable or not, but there are certain principles which may be gathered from the decisions, and they have been nowhere better stated than by Lord Dundas in the case of *Walker v. Amey* (1906, 8 F. 376). He says: 'The question must always be one of intention, whether, on the one hand, the granter intended the trust to be one merely for the administration of his affairs, he retaining the radical and beneficial interest in the estate conveyed, and being entitled to revoke the deed at pleasure; or whether, on the other hand, he must be held to have truly divested himself of the estate so as to enable the trustees to hold it against him.' That being the general principle the precise provisions of this deed must be considered. It is clear that the principal objects for which Mr Bertram granted the trust deed were (first) that he should be protected against himself by being limited to an alimentary liferent, and (second) to provide for his wife and children in the event of his being married. It is certain that the first of these purposes will not render the deed irrevocable. A man may think it prudent to protect himself against his own facility or improvidence, and for that object may convey his estate to trustees, but if he changes his mind he is entitled to revoke the deed and to call on the trustees to denude.

    As to the second object, if Mr Bertram had married and had children, that might have rendered the deed irrevocable. But then he did not marry, and there is no person in existence who has acquired an interest or jus quaesitum which entitles him to found on this part of the deed. So far as regards the two main objects of the deed, therefore, I am of opinion that Mr Bertram was not debarred from revoking."

Lords Ardwall and Dundas concurred.

The Court answered the question in the special case accordingly.

NOTES:

13.09   1. See also *Watt v. Watson* (1897) 24 R. 330, where a woman set up a trust for the benefit of herself, her husband and the children of their marriage. The Inner House held that, as there were no children of the marriage, she could revoke the trust with the consent of her husband.
        2. It follows from this principle that a truster cannot create an alimentary liferent in his own favour, and thereby put his estate beyond the reach of his creditors.

The beneficiary need not be in existence at the time of the trust's creation. The question is whether there is a beneficiary in existence at the point in time when the truster seeks to revoke the trust. See the following case:

Lyon v. Lyon's Trs
(1901) 3 F. 653; (1900) 8 S.L.T. 489

In 1883, in contemplation of marriage, Mr Lyon executed a bond of annuity in favour of Mrs **13.10** Lyon, to provide for her in the event of him predeceasing her. At the same time, Mrs Lyon conveyed "the whole property which should accrue and pertain and belong to her during the subsistence of the intended marriage" to trustees, for various purposes, including the maintenance of any children that might be born of the marriage. A daughter was born to the Lyons in 1885. In 1901, Mrs Lyon sought to revoke the trust.

LORD PRESIDENT (BALFOUR) (after considering, and rejecting, various other grounds for permitting revocation or reduction of the trust deed): "The most important question therefore appears to me to be the third, viz.:—Whether the conveyance contained in the trust disposition and assignation is revocable by Mrs Lyon? It was maintained by the defender that it is not so revocable, (1) because it is one of two deeds which in effect constitute a marriage settlement, the other being the bond of annuity by Mr Lyon. Both of these deeds were executed intuitu matrimonii, and each contains a provision by one spouse in favour of the other, so that there is some mutuality between them, and they seem to me to come very near to constituting a marriage contract. They were prepared by the same agent on the same instructions, and drafts of both were sent together for consideration and revisal by Mrs Lyon, her mother, and her brother-in-law. Mr Lyon does not appear to have seen the draft of the trust assignation and settlement, but he made material alterations on the draft of the bond of annuity, and effect was given to these alterations. Two deeds became necessary in consequence of the refusal of Mr Lyon to be a party to a settlement, as he desired to retain the control of the property which he had at the time of the marriage, or which he might afterwards acquire. While I think that a marriage contract might be constituted by two deeds as well as by one, it does not appear to me to be necessary to express an opinion upon the question whether the two deeds in question did or did not make a contract, as I consider that there are sufficient grounds for a decision apart from this point. Mrs Lyon's disposition and assignation was, as already stated, delivered to the trustees, who still hold the property settled under it (except the £1,000 withdrawn by her in exercise of the reserved power to do so), and a child of the marriage is in existence. The trustees are thus holding the fee of the trust estate under a delivered deed, for a person in existence. This, it seems to me, makes an essential distinction between the present case and that of *Watt v. Watson* (24 R. 330), and other cases referred to in the argument. Farther, the deed to which the case of *Watt v. Watson* related was not declared to be irrevocable, as Mrs Lyon's trust disposition and assignation is, and in that case, no deed was granted by the husband which could introduce the element of mutuality. It was maintained on behalf of the pursuers that the trustees cannot be said to be holding the estate for their daughter, in respect that she has not a vested interest in the settled fund, as she will not become entitled to it unless she shall survive her mother, or at all events the dissolution of the marriage. It is true that she has not as yet an indefeasible right to the fee, but I think that she has such a right as it is not within the power of her parents by any act of theirs to defeat. One of the leading objects of the trust disposition and assignation was to provide for children, and it seems to me that the daughter has at all events a right to have the trust maintained, so that if she shall survive the dissolution of the marriage (and possibly also her mother), the settled funds shall be available for her. I think that upon principle her right is of such a character as to bar revocation of the trust disposition and assignation, and I am not aware of any authority for holding such a deed to be revocable where (as here) the following conditions exist concurrently—(1) the deed was executed in immediate contemplation of marriage and for the purposes of the marriage; (2) marriage followed upon it; (3) the deed was declared irrevocable; (4) it was delivered, the estate was handed over to the trustees and is still held by them; and (5) a child born of the marriage is in existence."

Lords Adam, McLaren and Kinnear concurred.
The Court held that Mrs Lyon was not entitled to revoke the trust.

NOTES:

13.11   1. As Norrie and Scobbie point out (at 192):

> "It follows that a trust may start out as revocable and then become irrevocable (*e.g.* by the birth of beneficiaries); or it may be irrevocable and then become revocable (*e.g.* by the death of beneficiaries)."

2. *Antenuptial marriage-contract trusts.* The provisions of an ante-nuptial marriage contract trust are presumed to be contractual and therefore irrevocable, even with the consent of the spouse. However, such a trust may contain a power of revocation, which will be effective. For further discussion, see Mackenzie Stuart, pp. 141–149.

D. The beneficiary must have a *jus quaesitium*

13.12 There are two questions which must be addressed here:
(a) Did the truster intend to confer a beneficial interest on the beneficiary, or did he simply intend to make a testamentary provision?
(b) If the beneficial interest is only contingent, can it nevertheless be irrevocable?

(a) Beneficial interest or testamentary provision?

Bertram's Trs v. Bertram
1909 S.C. 1238; 1909 2 S.L.T. 86

13.13 For the facts of this case, see *supra*, para. 13.08.

LORD LOW (immediately after the part of his judgment quoted *supra*, para. 13.08): "But then it is said that he cannot revoke because he has given an interest which he cannot take away to his brother David Stanley Bertram and to his step-sister Dorys Jessie Bertram. That contention can only be well founded if it appears from the deed that the granter's intention was to confer a present right on these beneficiaries, although subject, it may be, to contingencies.

Now the way in which this matter comes into the trust deed is as follows: By the fourth purpose the trustees are directed to hold the capital for the lawful issue of the truster, and by the fifth purpose it is provided that 'in the event of there being no lawful issue who shall acquire a vested right to the capital of the said trust estate . . . my trustees upon the death of the survivor of me and my widow shall assign dispone, convey, and make over (First) one half of the capital of the said trust estate to my brother the said David Stanley Bertram and to his heirs and assignees whomsoever; and (Second) the other one-half to Dorys Jessie Bertram my step-sister, and to her heirs and assignees whomsoever.' Now that appears to me to be a provision of a purely testamentary nature intended to prevent the estate falling into intestacy in the event of the truster marrying and being predeceased by all his children."

NOTES:

13.14   1. The question is always one of the truster's intention. If he intended simply to make a testamentary provision, then such provisions will normally be revocable. (For the circumstances in which testamentary provisions may be held to be irrevocable, see *supra*, paras 13.01 *et seq.*).

2. If, however, the truster intended to confer a beneficial interest, then the trust will be irrevocable—provided, of course, that the other conditions of irrevocability are satisfied. A declaration of irrevocability will be of no effect where there is no beneficiary—as in such a case, no beneficial interest has been conferred on anyone. (See *Mackenzie v. Mackenzie's Trs* (1878) 5 R. 1027).

3. An declaration of irrevocability is, however, of considerable importance. In *Torrance v. Torrance's Trs*, 1950 S.C. 78, the Lord Justice-Clerk (Thomson) made the following observations (at 90):

> "If the truster says that the trust is irrevocable, that is usually an end of the matter. Indeed, it was agreed that there was no case in which the Court had found for revocation where there was such a clause, although the cases show that the Courts have not proceeded on this feature alone and have usually discovered other elements pointing towards irrevocability."

4. For a discussion of the factors which may be taken into account in determining the truster's intention, see Wilson and Duncan, paras 11–10 to 11–25.

(b) Contingent interests and revocation

Bulkeley-Gavin's Trs v. Bulkeley-Gavin's Trs
1971 S.C. 209

LORD JUSTICE-CLERK (GRANT): "The provisions of the trust deed which was executed by the **13.15** late Dr Bulkeley-Gavin on 20th May 1955, and which it falls to our lot to construe, are odd and, if not unique, are at any rate highly unusual and refreshingly original—hence largely the need for this special case. The difficulties which are raised by the provisions which are made in the deed are, moreover, in no way lessened by the number of contingencies for which no provision is made at all. In essence, purpose (Second) is the income-disposing clause and purpose (Third) is the capital-disposing clause. Even on a most benignant interpretation, however, neither clause achieves a high legal rating in the role which each was apparently designed to fulfil. . . [His Lordship considered the purpose (Second), and continued]

Going on to purpose (Third), one finds that it is conditional upon the occurrence of one or other of two events, neither of which may ever happen. The first is the nationalisation of land in this country: the second is the acquisition of the estate of Craigengillan and Barbeth by the County Council. On the occurrence of either of these events the trustees are directed to hold the trust estate for behoof of and ultimate payment to Alastair Gavin, whom failing his issue *per stirpes*, whom failing, Gavin Burton, whom failing his issue *per stirpes*, under declaration that the capital shall not be paid over until the beneficiary or beneficiaries attain the age of 25, but with provision for the payment or application of income before their attaining that age. Accordingly, not only may neither of the conditions upon which alone purpose (Third) could take effect ever be purified, but, even if one or other is purified at some future date, there may be no person then in existence who comes within the specified class of beneficiaries.

The truster then goes on to 'declare the conveyance'—*i.e.* of the trust estate—'before written and this deed to be irrevocable' and to oblige himself that he 'shall do no act inconsistent with these presents'. It may be noted here that the trustees to whom the trust estate was conveyed were in the first place the truster, then other named trustees, including the truster's secretary, and, *inter alios*, 'such other person or persons as I may thereafter appoint . . . to act in the trust'. The situation on the execution of the deed was accordingly this, that the truster was the first named trustee, that he had unlimited power to appoint further trustees, and that purpose (Second) directed that the trust income be utilised (during the period therein specified) solely for the upkeep of an estate of which the truster was then the heritable proprietor. In fact the income has never been so utilised nor has there been any encroachment on capital.

The basic issue between the parties is whether by the trust deed, and in the events which have happened, the truster validly and effectively divested himself of the trust estate in such manner as to place it irrevocably beyond his own reach. If he did not, it is common ground that the trust estate is carried by his trust disposition and settlement (*Byres' Trustees v. Gemmell* (1897) 23 R. 332, *per* Lord M'Laren at 337). In contending that he did so divest himself, the first and third parties founded strongly on the declaration of irrevocability mentioned above. Such a declaration may well be conclusive, particularly where, as here, the deed has been delivered (*Byres' Trustees, per* Lord Kinnear at 339). As Lord President Clyde pointed out, however, in *Scott v. Scott* 1930 S.C. 903, at 917, the importance of a declaration of irrevocability must depend on the nature of the provisions of the deed and there may be circumstances (of which he gives examples) in which such a declaration is of no effect. This brings us back to the terms of the deed, which I have already summarised, and to the test which I understood parties to accept as valid, viz. whether there has been divestiture in favour of third party beneficiaries with the intention that the divestiture shall not be revocable. (Cf. Mackenzie Stuart on Trusts, p. 134). It is not disputed that, if the beneficial interests of the third parties are immediate, the test may be satisfied even if those interests are contingent and unvested; but a mere spec successionis is not enough. (*Cf. Torrance v. Torrance's Trustees* 1950 S.C. 78, *per* Lord Patrick at 99).

In their written contentions the second parties contend in essence that the truster did not by the deed effectively create any beneficial interest in anybody other than himself. As I understood him, Mr Keith went further than this in argument and argued that the deed created no beneficial interest even in the truster. Whether or not this latter argument be valid, there is, I think, no doubt that, on the execution of the deed, no third party had any beneficial interest under purpose (Second) thereof. If such an interest was created in favour of any person, that person was the truster and such an interest could have been attached by his creditors. So far as there was any divestiture of the truster, that divestiture was plainly revocable, despite the irrevocability provision, and at best purpose (Second) created no more than a mere trust for administration.

The first and third parties, however, pray in aid the provisions of purpose (Third) and the conveyance of Craigengillan by the truster to the third party in 1960. So far as purpose (Third) is concerned, they argue that its provisions created an immediate beneficial interest in the two persons named therein. Clearly no vested right was created (or had come into existence by the time the truster died in 1967). It is said, however, that a contingent interest was created by this purpose in favour of those named persons so as to preclude revocation of the provisions in their favour. If that be right, and assuming for the moment that the truster had remained infeft in the estate of Craigengillan, the situation would seem to have been this, that the provisions of purpose (Second) were revoked by the truster's trust disposition, but that the first parties remained bound to hold the trust estate in their hands until the occurrence of the earliest of one of three events: (a) the nationalisation of land in the lifetime of one or more of Alastair, Gavin or their respective issue; (b) the acquisition of Craigengillan by the county council during such lifetime; and (c) the death of the last survivor of Alastair, Gavin and their respective issue. On the occurrence of (a) or (b) prior to the occurrence of (c), purpose (Third) would operate: on the occurrence of (c) prior to the occurrence of (a) or (b), it would fail. None of these three events, however, may ever happen, and, if the first and third parties are right, the capital of the trust estate may be held in perpetuity for a purpose which can never be fulfilled, yet never fails.

In my opinion, however, that is not the true situation, for in purpose (Third), as in purpose (Second), I may find no irrevocable divesture in favour of any third party beneficiary. The 'interests' purporting to be conferred on Alastair and Gavin are hypothetical and extremely remote. This is not the case of an interest which, although contingent and unvested, depends merely on the beneficiary surviving a *diem certum*. In order to take any benefit, Alastair must survive one or other of two events which may never occur; Gavin must not only similarly survive but must survive Alastair and the latter's issue. One or both may have had a *spes successionis*, but in my opinion neither had anything more. Here again we have provisions which, I think, amount to no more than a revocable trust for administration, which may be explicable possibly and in part by the fact that they were executed at a time when the general election campaign of 1955 had reached its height."

NOTE:

It does not follow, however, that a trust is revocable simply because the interest created is "merely" **13.16** contingent. As Lord Justice-Clerk Grant suggests, an interest which "depends merely on the beneficiary surviving a *diem certum*" (a specified date) could be protected by means of a trust. See, for example, *Robertson v. Robertson's Trs* (1892) 19 R. 849, where the truster assigned certain life assurance policies to trustees. He directed them, *inter alia*, to pay £500 to a nephew upon receiving payment of the proceeds of the policies. He later purported to revoke this direction. The Inner House held he could not. Lord Adam stated (at 853):

"One of the trust purposes was the payment of £500 to the pursuer out of the proceeds of the policies, if he should survive the period of payment. The pursuer has survived that period; the trustees have received the proceeds of the policies, and I think they are bound to fulfil that purpose."

E. A further condition of irrevocability?

Norrie and Scobbie have suggested that there is one further condition of irrevocability. See the **13.17** following extract:

Kenneth McK. Norrie and Eilidh M. Scobbie, *Trusts* (1991), pp. 192–194

"the question of whether [an *inter vivos*] trust is irrevocable is determined by the satisfaction of all of the following conditions. Failure to satisfy any of these conditions results in the trust remaining revocable.
    1. Property must have passed. . .
    2. Beneficiaries must exist. . .
    3. The beneficiaries must have a beneficial interest. . .
    4. The truster must intend the deed to be irrevocable
In a sense this is the most important condition, for all the above must be satisfied compatibly with the intention of the truster being that the trust is irrevocable."

NOTE:

With respect, it is submitted that this is *not* a separate condition of irrevocability. A truster cannot confer a beneficial interest on a beneficiary and at the same time retain the right to revoke the trust. That would seem self-contradictory. Either the truster has conferred a beneficial interest (in which case the trust is irrevocable), or he has retained the right to revoke the trust (in which case the beneficiary only has a *spes successionis*, or a "hope" of benefiting). The intention of the truster is an important factor in determining whether a beneficial interest has been created. It is submitted, however, that it is wrong to treat it as a separate condition of irrevocability in this fashion.

3. TERMINATION BY THE TRUSTEES

The trustees may bring the trust to an end by fulfilling the trust purposes and distributing the trust **13.18** estate. If they do not fulfil the trust purposes, or distribute the estate to the wrong beneficiaries, they may be liable for breach of trust (see *supra*, Chapters 7 and 10). Trustees are entitled to receive a discharge before denuding office, which should generally be granted by the person entitled to the residue of the trust estate. See *infra* paras 13.29 *et seq.* for further discussion of discharges.

4. TERMINATION BY THE BENEFICIARIES

13.19 Two principles require to be considered here. They are:
(1) the rule whereby all the beneficiaries may compel the termination of a trust;
(2) the rule in *Miller's Trustees v. Miller* (1890) 18 R. 301, whereby a beneficiary who has acquired a right in fee to property is entitled to insist that the trustees denude in his favour.

A. Termination by consent of all the beneficiaries

Mackenzie Stuart, *The Law of Trusts* (1932), p. 346

13.20 "If all those who are beneficially interested in the trust estate concur in asking the trustees to denude, and if they are legally capable of giving their consent, the trustees must terminate the trust on being exonered and discharged. The concurrence may be given by all the beneficiaries acting together, or it may happen that all interests come to be held by one person, as where a liferenter becomes entitled also to the fee, and no other interests are concerned. There are two chief exceptions to the exercise of this right: it must not prejudice the trustees in their proper administration of the trust, and it must not interfere with the protection of any alimentary rights created by the truster."

NOTES:

13.21 1. *Legally capable of giving their consent.* This must be read subject to the power of the court (under section 1 of the Trusts (Scotland) Act 1961) to approve a variation of trust purposes on behalf of those who are not legally capable of doing so. See *supra*, paras 12.02 *et seq*.
2. *Prejudicing the proper administration of the trust.* In *De Robeck v. Inland Revenue*, 1928 S.C. (H.L.) 34, D's husband, in his will, left his estate to trustees for certain purposes. The heritable estates were found to be heavily mortgaged, and considerable death-duties applied. To avoid a forced sale, the trustees elected to pay these duties by 16 half-yearly instalments. At a later date, a question arose as to whether, for taxation purposes, D was to be treated as the owner of the estate. The House of Lords held that she was not, with Viscount Dunedin making the following observations (at 40–41):

"I do not doubt that the Inland Revenue could not be defeated by the trustees simply holding on to the estate without making the disposition as directed, which disposition, when executed, would undoubtedly make her a proper liferenter. Accordingly, the Lord Advocate urged that she was all along in a position to compel the trustees to execute the disposition, and that being so, it must be held as if done. *Quod fieri debet infectum valet.* I do not think that she was in such a position. The trustees were executors, and under the provisions of the settlement the whole estate was under their control; and therefore under section 6, subsection (2), of the Finance Act, 1894, they were in a position, if they chose, to elect to pay the estate duty on the heritable property, and having done so, they became accountable. They chose the alternative of settling the duty by sixteen half-yearly instalments, as is found by the special case. Under these circumstances they were, in my opinion, entitled to keep the estates until the duties were paid off and they were free of further liability. That the course of administration was beneficial to all concerned cannot be denied. Any other course would have entailed a forced sale, which in the position of the heritable debt would have led to disastrous results. That, however, is not the question. The question is whether the respondent could have compelled a disposition at an earlier date. I am of opinion she could not."

In other words, D, as beneficiary, could not force the trustees to terminate the trust because that would have prejudiced the proper administration of the trust. However, as Mackenzie Stuart points out (at 346–347): "whether administrative arrangements made by trustees will entitle them to refuse to denude when all the beneficiaries concur in making the demand will depend on the circumstances of each case."

3. *Protection of alimentary rights.* This restriction on the right of the beneficiaries to terminate the trust is a consequence of the principle that an alimentary right, once accepted, cannot be renounced. But a beneficiary is not bound to *accept* an alimentary right. The distinction is well brought out in the following case:

Douglas-Hamilton v. Duke and Duchess of Hamilton's Trs
1961 S.C. 205; 1961 S.L.T. 305

LORD PRESIDENT (CLYDE): "The only issue in this reclaiming motion is whether during the **13.22** lifetime of the spouses a wife is entitled to disclaim or renounce all interest in a contingent alimentary annuity payable to her, in the event of her surviving her husband, out of funds made over by him to their ante-nuptial marriage contract trustees. The Lord Ordinary has held that she cannot do so.

The matter arises in this way. By an ante-nuptial marriage contract, entered into on 30th November 1937, a trust was set up, the trust estate being contributed by the husband, the Duke of Hamilton. Under the marriage contract the Duchess is entitled during the Duke's lifetime to an annuity, which is not declared alimentary and which admittedly she could discharge and has discharged. The balance of the income of the trust funds after meeting this annuity was to be paid over during his lifetime to the Duke. This provision he could and has discharged. The clause in the marriage contract, in regard to which the present question arises, provides for an alimentary annuity or jointure in favour of the Duchess payable upon the death of the Duke survived by the Duchess. The annuity is to be 'such sum as after deduction of income tax at the rates current from time to time and all other Government duties which may be payable in respect thereof (other than surtax) shall yield in each year a sum of £3,000', or in certain events £4,000. Under the marriage contract provision is made for certain capital sums being available for the younger children of the marriage, divisible among them in such shares as the spouses or the survivor may appoint. There are certain further provisions for other eventualities, but in no case is any part of the capital under the trust destined to pass to the Duchess. She has in the marriage contract accepted the provisions in her favour as in full satisfaction of her legal rights. There are five sons of the marriage.

By two deeds of renunciation, dated 6th November 1959 and granted respectively by the Duke and by the Duchess, they each irrevocably released and renounced the whole provisions in their respective favours contained in the ante-nuptial contract of marriage, including, so far as the Duchess was concerned, 'the said alimentary annuity of £3,000 or of £4,000 free of income tax and other duties as aforesaid to which I am prospectively entitled' but only to the extent of the capital and income of a block of Mexican Eagle Oil Company shares, which forms a part of the trust estate. By deed of appointment and supplementary deed of appointment the spouses thereafter jointly executed an appointment declaring that the capital of these shares should vest in their second son immediately. This son is the pursuer in the present action, and the first defenders are the trustees under the said marriage contract. It is not now disputed that, as the Lord Ordinary held, these shares have indefeasibly vested in the pursuer if the renunciation by the Duchess of her prospective alimentary annuity is effectual. I turn, therefore, to consider the question whether or not it is effectual.

The doctrine of an alimentary annuity is a survival from an age when the *ius mariti* and the *ius administrationis* gave a husband virtual control over his wife's property. Without some such provision the weaker partner in the marriage could be compelled to hand over to her husband, to pay his personal debts, moneys which were intended for her benefit and use. The provision of an alimentary annuity under a trust, however, enabled funds to be put beyond the reach of matrimonial importunity (see Lord Justice-Clerk Moncrieff in *Menzies v. Murray* (1875) 2 R. 507, at page 511). For the existence of the trust and the alimentary nature of the annuity placed a restriction on the wife, disabling her from anticipating the termly payments and getting them into her hands before they were due. For once in her hands they were subject to her husband's control. But, as the time has gone on, the basis upon which this whole doctrine was founded has been undermined. 'The restricted capacity of the married woman in relation to property rights has passed into legal history. She is now "a free agent". Her will and mind are no longer "in abeyance". Her husband is no longer her guardian. She can contract, and sue or be sued, as if she were unmarried. The *ius mariti* and the *ius administrationis* have been abolished' (see Lord President Cooper in *Beith's Trustees v. Beith*, 1950 S.C. 66, at page 71, 1950 S.L.T. 70). The circumstances in which an alimentary liferent is required have, therefore, gradually been narrowed and the whole doctrine has become eroded, since its justification is largely based upon a situation which no longer today exists in law. It follows, therefore, that existing decisions, in so far as based on a fundamentally different legal concept of the rights of a married woman, have been superseded, just as if they had been based on a statute which has since been repealed (see Lord President Cooper in *Beith's Trustees* (supra), at page 73). Today the Courts have a duty to approach the question of the capacity of a wife to renounce an alimentary liferent in the light of the present position and status of a married woman in the eyes of the law. But, even today, the doctrine of an alimentary liferent has not disappeared altogether.

13.23   It has long been settled that a liferentrix in current enjoyment of an alimentary liferent constituted by a trust cannot, by a renunciation of her alimentary provision or by an arrangement with other beneficiaries, secure to herself an unfettered right to the capital or income of the fund. It is unnecessary, for present purposes, to consider whether this is based on the doctrine of approbate and reprobate or upon the principle that the recipient of a gift must enjoy it on the terms on which it is given. This latter view gains some support from Lord Deas in *Smith & Campbell, Petitioners* (1873) 11 M. 639, at page 646 where he says: 'A legacy must be taken on the conditions on which it is given or rejected altogether'. (Compare *White's Trustees v. Whyte* (1877) 4 R. 786, per Lord Deas, at page 791.) The same principle is illustrated in *Duthie's Trustees v. Kinloch* (1878) 5 R. 858. In that case a testator conferred an alimentary liferent in his trust disposition and settlement on a lady to whom, under a later codicil, he also gave the fee of his estate. She did not discharge or renounce her claim to the alimentary liferent, but contended that it was swallowed up in the gift of the fee to her. The Court rejected this contention and held that the only benefit she could immediately enjoy in the estate was the alimentary liferent.

The same results have followed in the cases of alimentary liferents enjoyed under marriage contracts. In *Hughes v. Edwardes* (1892) 19 R. (H.L.) 33, under an ante-nuptial contract of marriage a trust was duly constituted, under which a surviving husband was enjoying an alimentary liferent payable to him on his wife's death out of funds contributed by her. He sought to make an arrangement with the fiar of the fund whereby he ceased to enjoy his alimentary liferent of the funds, and thereafter secured a different interest in them. The House of Lords negatived his right to do so. As Lord Watson said at page 35: 'The learned judges of the Inner House . . . do not suggest that a trust duly constituted for payment of an alimentary annuity can be brought to an end by the joint action of the annuitant and the parties having beneficial right to the fee. A rule to the contrary has long been settled, and was recently enforced in *White's Trustees v. Whyte* and *Duthie's Trustees v. Kinloch*. In both instances the parties entitled to the fee had a vested interest, which is not the case here; and in *Duthie's Trustees v. Kinloch* the alimentary liferenter and the beneficial fiar were one and the same person. Yet it was held that the combined action of all parties interested could not defeat the settlor's intention to make the annuitant's right alimentary, a result which could not be attained except by continuing the trust.' In this case, Lord Watson was considering a case of an existing alimentary liferent being enjoyed by the liferenter, which he was seeking to end in the course of its existence, and for which he sought to substitute a different interest in the trust estate. In *Eliott's Trustees v. Eliott* (1894) 21 R. 975, 2 S.L.T. 164 and *Main's Trustees v. Main*, 1917 S.C. 660, 1917, 2 S.L.T. 35, the Court decided that a predeceasing spouse cannot by a testamentary settlement revoke the alimentary protection provided for a liferent in favour of the other spouse in a marriage contract. These were both cases in which the surviving spouse sought to acquire an interest in the marriage contract funds freed of the alimentary restriction. In *Kennedy v. Kennedy's Trustees*, 1953 S.C. 60, 1953 S.L.T. 131, the spouses had jointly requested their ante-nuptial marriage contract trustees to denude in their favour, after it was clear that there would be no issue of the marriage. Under the contract each spouse had contributed funds for payment of an alimentary liferent for each (and the survivor). Each was enjoying the alimentary liferent at the time of their request. The fee of the funds was to go to the issue of the marriage, whom failing the spouses or their heirs. The Court refused to give effect to their request. As the Lord President said at page 64: 'The weight of opinion is, I think, in favour of the view that "the combined action of all parties interested will not avail to cancel an alimentary restriction or to terminate the trust upon which its efficacy depends"—Dobie, *Liferent and Fee*, page 235'. In *Chrystal's Trustees v. Haldane*, 1960 S.C. 127, 1961 S.L.T. 25, a renunciation by a wife of an alimentary liferent interest while it was being enjoyed was again regarded as being invalid.

It appears from these decisions, accordingly, that once an alimentary provision is being enjoyed the beneficiary can only enjoy it subject to the alimentary condition. The wife enjoying an alimentary annuity under a marriage contract cannot, either at her own hand or by arrangement with the other beneficiaries, convert it into an ordinary liferent or secure from the trust estate some interest in the estate of a different kind. For to do so would be quite inconsistent with the very nature of an alimentary provision. She would be converting a gift subject to a restrictive condition into a gift of a different kind which had no such restriction imposed on it.

There are, however, two features in the present case which, in my opinion, take it outside the ambit of these decisions. In the first place, the alimentary annuity which the Duchess is renouncing or discharging is not at present being enjoyed by her. She may never enjoy it. Her enjoyment is dependent upon her survivance of her husband. Her right to it is therefore purely contingent. In the second place, she is not seeking to convert her right or interest in this contingent annuity into an interest or right of any other kind in the trust funds. On the contrary, she is gratuitously surrendering now her whole personal interest in the shares provided to meet the annuity.

These two features seem to me to constitute a clear distinction between these cases and the present one. Here the Duchess is not seeking to continue to enjoy the gift but to free it of a fetter, nor is she seeking to substitute a different gift from the marriage trust in place of the alimentary liferent to which she is contingently entitled under the marriage contract. She is repudiating the contingent gift before she has any right to enjoy it. I can see no justification for the law forcing her to take in the future a gift which is not hers now and which she does not wish at all.

It has never been contended that, merely because a wife is left an alimentary liferent under her husband's trust disposition and settlement, the law will compel her to take it, and will deny her the right to repudiate it and claim her legal rights in his estate instead. Similarly it seems to me that if a wife is entitled under a marriage contract to an alimentary liferent from the husband's funds on his death if she survives him, it would follow that she can, during his lifetime, repudiate that gift, and decide in advance not to take it. In both cases a trust has been deliberately set up to place the alimentary funds beyond the control of the beneficiary. This factor, however, in the case of the gift under the trust disposition and settlement, is not fatal to her repudiating it: the same factor cannot, therefore, prevent her repudiating the gift under the marriage contract. It might be suggested that there is a distinction between an alimentary liferent given under a trust disposition and settlement, and one given under a marriage contract by one spouse to the other on the death of the former. For in the case of a marriage contract an element of contract is involved on the wife's part. But nowadays wives are free to contract on their own. The mere fact that a wife has contracted in certain events to take a certain interest in the funds of another is today no necessary barrier to her renouncing that interest before it emerges.

Of the many cases quoted to us there are only two in which any reference was made to a contingent alimentary liferent. The first of them is *Kennedy v. Kennedy's Trustees* (*supra*). What was fatal to the denuding requested of the trustees in that case was the fact that the **13.24** wife was then enjoying an alimentary liferent which she had not discharged or renounced. But there was in the marriage contract in that case a further provision for a contingent alimentary liferent for the wife, if she survived the husband, out of his fund. The Lord President (at page 64) does indicate that this also precluded renunciation as, in his view, it was immaterial that this interest was deferred and contingent upon the wife's survivance of the husband. But this view is obiter, it is not adopted by the other members of the Court and was not necessary for the decision of the case. There is, in my opinion, no warrant for it in principle nor in authority. The only other case in which the matter of a renunciation of a contingent right to an alimentary liferent is mentioned is *Chrystal's Trs v. Haldane* (*supra*) where the point is left open. In this situation, therefore, the Duchess, in my opinion, in the present case was entitled to renounce her contingent alimentary liferent, particularly as she did not seek to substitute any other right in the trust's funds in place of it.

It was argued for the marriage contract trustees that the criterion of the irrevocability of an alimentary provision was not whether the beneficiary is enjoying the benefit, but whether the beneficiary has accepted the benefit. Once this has taken place, so it is contended, the benefit is irrevocable. The Duchess's signature to the marriage contract constituted her acceptance of the benefit.

This argument appears to me to be wrong in principle. An alimentary liferent is merely an ordinary liferent with a restriction on the anticipation of its benefits. If a liferentrix takes the benefit, she must accept the conditions, and cannot evade them by unilateral action on her own or by some arrangement with the other parties to the deed conferring the liferent. But I am unable to see why she should not be able on her own to say to the trustees before she is entitled to any liferent payments: I do not want this liferent at all. The mere fact that she has signed the deed under which the alimentary liferent is conferred cannot, in itself, preclude her from subsequently renouncing it while matters are still entire. If the marriage contract confers upon her a contingent liferent after her husband's death, the mere acceptance of this contingent right will not preclude her renouncing it (see *Lord and Lady Strathmore's Trustees v. Lord Glamis*, 1932 S.C. 458, 1932 S.L.T. 301). For no one can be forced to take a benefit under a contract where his own interest only is involved. The same result must apply whether the benefit is an unqualified one (an ordinary liferent) or a qualified one (an alimentary liferent).

The Lord Ordinary appears to have taken the view that he was precluded from reaching the conclusion to which I have come by the decision in *Kennedy v. Kennedy's Trs*. He did so because (1961 S.L.T. at page 215) 'a request by the parties to the trustees to denude is, in my view, equivalent to a disclaimer'. With this conclusion I do not agree. The request by the parties in that case on the trustees to denude involved no disclaimer or renunciation by the wife, but an attempt on her part jointly with her husband to bring the trust to an end and get some other rights in place of her alimentary interest in the trust estate. This is just what Lord Watson in *Hughes v. Edwardes* (1892) 19 R. (H.L.) 33, at page 35 said could not be done. In the present case the Duchess is taking no such course. She is now seeking gratuitously to renounce a right (to an alimentary liferent) which she may never enjoy, and she is asking nothing in return. In my opinion she can do so, and her doing so does not run counter to anything decided in *Kennedy v. Kennedy's Trustees*. . .

Secondly, an argument was founded on a clause in the alimentary liferent provision for the Duchess in the event of her surviving her husband. The clause in question provides that 'the payment is to be for her alimentary use allenarly and for the maintenance during pupillarity and minority of the children and issue if any of the said intended marriage but without any obligation on the second party (*i.e.* the Duchess) to account for the manner in which she may expend the said annuity or jointure'. The argument was that this clause showed that the alimentary annuity was not simply for the Duchess herself, but that third parties (*i.e.* the children) had rights in this alimentary provision. Consequently it was said the existence of these rights precluded the Duchess from herself renouncing the annuity.

But in my opinion this is not so. The exclusion of any liability on her part to account for the way in which she expends the annuity gives her a complete discretion as to what she does with it, and deprives the children of any right or interest in anything connected with the annuity, except what payments she may choose to give to them. The existence of this clause, therefore, does not prevent her discharging or renouncing the annuity. As Lord Keith said in *Sturgis's Trs v. Sturgis*, 1951 S.C. 637, at page 648 (1952 S.L.T. 37): 'To confer on children any right or interest in the maintenance of a widow's liferent as alimentary, such a right or interest would have, in my opinion, to be manifest in the language of the marriage-settlement.' In my opinion, the clause in question here, so far from making that right manifest, deprives it of any content at all, by excluding the Duchess's liability to account for the way in which she expends the annuity.

On the whole matter, accordingly, the pursuer is, in my opinion, entitled to succeed. The Lord Ordinary's interlocutor should be recalled and decree granted in terms of the first four conclusions of the summons. I should add that, in reaching this result, I have assumed that the liferent in question, substantial as it appears to be, is not merely alimentary in name, but falls within the legal conception of a true alimentary liferent. No argument on this matter was presented to us, and there are no figures or facts in the case upon which we could determine whether the liferent conferred was, in the circumstances, more than sufficient for the maintenance of the Duchess. If it was, this would constitute an additional reason for the conclusion to which I have come."

NOTES:

It should be noted that, by virtue of section 1(4) of the Trusts (Scotland) Act 1961 (*supra*, para. **13.25** 12.05), the court has power to authorise an arrangement varying or revoking an alimentary provision in a trust. Section 1(4) provides, however, that the court shall not authorise such an arrangement unless:

"(a) it considers that the carrying out of the arrangement would be reasonable, having regard to the income of the alimentary beneficiary from all sources, and to such other factors, if any, as the court considers material, and

(b) the arrangement is approved by the alimentary beneficiary, or, where the alimentary beneficiary is a person on whose behalf the court is empowered by subsection (1) of this section or that subsection as extended by subsection (2) of this section to approve the arrangement, the arrangement is so approved by the court under that subsection."

See further *supra* paras 12.05 *et seq*.

B. The *Miller's Trustees* principle

According to the case of *Miller's Trs v. Miller* (1890) 18 R. 301, where a beneficiary has acquired a right **13.26** in fee to property he is entitled to insist that the trustees denude in his favour, even if they have instructions to the contrary. This differs from the principle discussed above, as it need not necessarily entail complete termination of the trust. The trust may well continue in existence in relation to other property and/or beneficiaries. The *Miller's Trustees* principle is not unqualified, however, and is subject to certain exceptions, which are discussed below.

Miller's Trs v. Miller
(1890) 18 R. 301

In his will, Sir William Miller directed his trustees to "manage, as absolute proprietors" **13.27** certain properties for the benefit of his second son, John Miller. The trustees were to denude in his favour once he reached the age of 25. It was further stated that the property was to vest in him once he reached the age of 25, or if he were to marry after the age of 21 with the consent and approbation of the trustees, whichever happened first.

After attaining the age of 21, John Miller married with the consent and approbation of the trustees. Being dissatisfied with the allowance made to him by the trustees, he claimed that he was entitled to have his share in his father's estate conveyed to him. The trustees maintained that they were not entitled to do so, and a special case was presented for the opinion of the Court of Session.

Lord President (Inglis): "There is, in my opinion, a general rule, the result of a comparison of a long series of decisions of this Court, that where by the operation of a testamentary instrument the fee of an estate or parts of an estate, whether heritable or moveable, has vested in a beneficiary, the Court will always, if possible, relieve him of any trust management that is cumbrous, unnecessary, or expensive. Where there are trust purposes to be served which cannot be secured without the retention of the vested estate or interest of the beneficiary in the hands of the trustees, the rule cannot be applied, and the right of the beneficiary must be subordinated to the will of the testator. But I am not aware of any case in which the mere maintenance of a trust management without any ulterior object or purpose has been held to be a trust purpose in the sense in which I have used that term. In this case the testator has directed his trustees to hold the estate of Barneyhill for behoof of his second son John Alexander and a series of heirs substituted to him, subject to a liferent use of the mansion-house in favour of his widow. The trustees are to manage the estate as absolute proprietors till the party entitled attain the age of twenty-five. But the testator further declares that no part of the estate shall vest in the party entitled thereto until he attain the age of twenty-five, or be married after attaining the age of twenty-one with the consent and approbation of the trustees, "whichever event shall first happen." This declaration though expressed in a negative form is a negative-pregnant, and involves a corresponding affirmative that the estate shall vest on the beneficiary either attaining twenty-five years of age or being married after twenty-one with the consent of the trustees. Marriage with consent after twenty-one (the event which has happened) is thus made precisely equivalent in its effect to attaining the age of twenty-five. But on the heir attaining the age of twenty-five the trustees are expressly directed to denude in his favour. I am of opinion that the same effect must follow the equivalent event of the heir marrying after twenty-one with the consent of the trustees. . ."

Lord McLaren: "My opinion may be expressed very shortly.
   Ever since I knew anything of the law of trusts I have considered it to be a settled and indeed an elementary proposition that where trustees hold property for a person in fee, that is a simple trust which the Court will execute by divesting the trustees at the suit of the person interested. It seems to me that a beneficiary who has an estate in fee has by the very terms of the gift the same right of divesting the trustees, and so putting an end to the trust, which the truster himself possessed, because under a gift in fee the grantee acquires all the right in the property which the truster had to give. It seems to be not only an unsound proposition in law, but a logical impossibility, that a person should have an estate in fee, and that some other person should at the same time have the power of withholding it. This I understand to be a well-settled principle. . .
   There are only two exceptions, so far as I know, to the operation of this general rule, as I understand it, and these are founded upon civil disability—I mean the case of marriage and the case of minority or mental incapacity. The case of minority or mental incapacity is only an apparent exception, because the trustees are only possessors in the character of guardians of the estate of a beneficiary who is not in the position to manage the property for himself. . ."

Lords Rutherfurd Clark and Adam delivered concurring opinions.
Lords Young delivered a dissenting opinion, in which Lord Trayner concurred.
The Court answered the questions in the special case accordingly.

Notes:

13.28   1. If the trust deed had simply stated that the estate would not vest in the beneficiary until he attained the age of 25, he would not have been entitled to lay claim to it until he reached that age. If the trustees were to pay it over to him before that date, they would be acting to the prejudice of whoever was to become entitled to the estate if he died without reaching that age.

2. The *Miller's Trs v. Miller* principle has been confirmed in a number of subsequent cases (see *e.g. Yuill's Trs v. Thomson* (1902) 4 F. 815; *Macculloch v. McCulloch's Trs* (1903) 6 F. (H.L.) 3). There are three principal exceptions to the principle, which are as follows:

3. *Civil disability.* Marriage is, of course, no longer regarded as a disability. As for minority, see now the Age of Legal Capacity (Scotland) Act 1991, s.1(1). Under the 1991 Act, a person over the age of 16 now has "legal capacity to enter into any transaction", but this is subject to the court's power under section 3 of the Act to set aside prejudicial transactions entered into by a person between the ages of 16 and 18. Trustees may, therefore, be entitled to refuse to denude where the beneficiary is under 18 and they believe that payment to the beneficiary might amount to a prejudicial transaction. It may be necessary to seek judicial guidance if a dispute arises.

4. *Prejudicing the proper administration of the trust.* Mackenzie Stuart takes the view (at 354–355) that the *Miller* principle cannot be invoked where the trustees would be prejudiced in the proper administration of the trust by its application, in accordance with the decision in *De Robeck v. Inland Revenue*, 1928 S.C. (H.L.) 34 (*supra* para. 13.21). There is no direct authority on this point, but Mackenzie Stuart's view seems right in principle.

5. *Prejudicing other trust purposes.* Lord Inglis states in *Miller's Trs* (at 305) that:

> "Where there are trust purposes to be served which cannot be secured without the retention of the vested estate or interest of the beneficiary in the hands of the trustees, the rule cannot be applied, and the right of the beneficiary must be subordinated to the will of the testator."

An example of this rule being applied can be found in *Graham's Trs v. Graham* (1899) 2 F. 232, where the Second Division declined to apply the principle in *Miller's Trustees*, stating as follows:

> "[John Graham] maintains that the provision in his favour vested *a morte*, and that when he attained twenty-five years of age both capital and interest on the provision became his indefeasibly, and that therefore he may insist on payment now without awaiting the arrival of the more postponed term of payment fixed by the testator. The case of *Miller's Trustees* was cited as an authority for this contention. I deem it unnecessary to consider whether this question is ruled by the case of *Miller's Trustees*, because it appears to me that there is sufficient ground for refusing effect to the contention of the third party in the fact that there are purposes of the trust yet to be fulfilled which forbid the trustees paying to the third party just now the provisions in his favour under the testator's settlement. The ground I refer to is this: The trustees are directed (and are bound) to pay certain beneficiaries interest on the amount of their bequests at the rate of 4 per cent for some years to come. We are informed that the income of the estate will not suffice for this, and that to some extent this direction will require to be met out of capital. It is at present impossible to say how far this application of the capital may reduce the amount of the legacy or provision to each beneficiary, and (as was observed by the Lord President in *Miller's* case) 'where there are trust purposes to be served which cannot be secured without the retention of the vested estate or interest of the beneficiary in the hands of the trustees. . . the right of the beneficiary must be subordinated to the will of the testator.' The fifth question therefore should be answered in the negative."

What if the "purpose" in question is simply to accumulate income for the benefit of the beneficiary? Mackenzie Stuart takes the view (at 355–356) that the beneficiary is still entitled to require the trustees to denude, and this is supported by English authority (*Saunders v. Vautier* (1841) Cr. & Ph. 240; 41 E.R. 482), and by the observations of Lord Moncrieff in *Miller Richard's Trs v. Miller Richard* (1903) 5 F. 909, at 913:

> "In the cases of *Miller's Trustees* and *Yuill's Trustees* it was conceded that notwithstanding a gift in fee the trustees would be entitled to withhold payment if retention of the

capital were required for the fulfilment of other trust purposes. Unfortunately there is no precise definition of 'trust purposes' which will warrant such retention. But I am disposed to think, on a consideration of the opinions of the majority in the two cases, that we must now hold that in order to warrant retention where a fee is given, the trust purposes must be connected with other objects and persons than the beneficiary whose share is in question; and that if the purposes are concerned solely with the management of the estate or bequest and the protection of the beneficiary against his own improvidence, they must be entirely disregarded, and immediate payment must be made to the fiar free of all restrictions."

5. DISCHARGE OF THE TRUSTEES

13.29 A. J. P. Menzies, *The Law of Scotland Affecting Trustees* (2nd ed., 1913), pp. 575–576
"Though the trustee may at any time during the currency of his period of office obtain from the beneficiaries, or other person empowered to discharge him, a discharge of his actings and intromissions with the estate, in whole or in part, the usual time for a general discharge is when the trust comes to an end or he has divested himself of the office, and wishes finally to sever his connection with the trust. At such a time, while divesting himself of his powers, he usually takes occasion to free himself from all his responsibilities in connection with his office, by being validly discharged and exonered of all his actings and intromissions in that office."

NOTES:

1. "The effect of the discharge is to protect the trustees from any further claims against them in respect of their intromissions with the trust estate" (Mackenzie Stuart, p. 343). A trustee is not bound to denude until he has received a discharge: *Elliot's Trs v. Elliot* (1828) 6 S. 1058.
2. As to the extent of the discharge which the trustee is entitled to insist upon, see the following case:

Mackenzie's Exr v. Thomson's Trs
1965 S.C. 155; 1965 S.L.T. 410

13.30 Kenneth Mackenzie, executor of the late Jane Mackenzie, raised an action against the trustees of the late John Thomson. The action called for payment and delivery of Jane Mackenzie's share of the trust estate. The trustees admitted that payment was due, but that they were entitled to receive a discharge not only in respect of their own intromissions with the trust estate, but also in respect of those of the predecessors.

LORD CAMERON: "The sharp question of law which arises for decision is this: whether the defenders, as the present trustees, are entitled to insist on a discharge, not only in respect of their own intromissions with the trust estate, but also in respect of their predecessors? The point is not academic, because the pursuer makes it clear that he may desire to raise proceedings for reparation against the estate of a former trustee, now deceased, in respect of his intromissions over a period for which it seems the defenders are not able to produce any, or at least any adequate accounts. In addition it appears to be the fact that the first defender is the representative of that deceased trustee.

There is nothing in the pleadings to indicate that in the case of this trustee any discharge was granted to him or his representatives by the trustees then in office; it may be inferred that none was. By section 3(D) of the Trusts (Scotland) Act, 1921 trustees are only liable for their own acts and intromissions and are not liable for the acts and intromissions of co-trustees nor are they liable for omissions. From this it is to be inferred that trustees in office are, prima facie at least, not liable for the acts and intromissions of their predecessors unless they have knowingly adopted or approved them, in which event they, in effect, make them their own. But in the absence of exceptional circumstances the only obligation of existing trustees is to account to the beneficiaries, and while this includes an obligation to account for the intromissions of previous trustees it does not make the existing trustees liable for those intromissions (see Mackenzie Stuart on *Trusts*, page 370). In the present case, of course, it is not suggested that the defenders have any responsibility for the acts or intromissions of their predecessors and, in particular, for those of the deceased trustee whose conduct has been called in question. If, therefore, they receive a discharge of their own acts and intromissions, as the pursuer offers, and has offered, they are themselves fully protected from any claim at the instance of the pursuer. In these circumstances it is difficult to see what interest the defenders can legitimately have in insisting upon a blanket discharge which would cover all the acts of their predecessors and themselves. In any case the protective value of such a discharge would seem to be at least open to doubt.

The matter is put thus by Mackenzie Stuart at page 345: 'The beneficiary, when granting a discharge, is only bound by it if he has all the facts before him or deliberately waives all enquiry and he must know what he is doing.' Counsel for the pursuer, in his careful address, drew my attention to certain authorities which, as he said, touched at least the fringe of the matter. The case of *Elliott's Trustees v. Elliott* (1828) 6 S. 1058 was a case in which the Court held they had no power to compel the trustees to denude unless, at the same time, they could pronounce a decree of exoneration and discharge. A similar decision was reached in the case of *Davidson's Trustees v. Cooper*, 3 S.L.T. 28. In the case of *Fleming v. Brown* (1861) 23 D. 443 the view was expressed, though obiter, that in the case of a residuary legatee a receipt for the residue implies adoption of the administration of the trust. This expression of opinion, however, was made in a case where the question which arises here was not before the Court and it would appear that all the Court there had in mind was the administration by the existing trustees. Counsel for the pursuer also cited the cases of *Edmond v. Dingwall's Trustees* (1860) 23 D. 21 and *Davidson's Trustees v. Simmons* (1896) 23 R. 1117, 4 S.L.T. 80, but I do not think that there is anything in these cases which materially advances the pursuer's argument beyond *Elliott's Trustees* (*supra*) and *Davidson's Trustees v. Cooper* (*supra*).

Counsel for the pursuer summarised his argument by submitting that a residuary beneficiary is bound to discharge the trustees presently in office of their whole acts and intromissions in return for receiving his share of residue, but at the same time is entitled to reserve any question of liability against former trustees. In the present case, therefore, the pursuer was entitled to payment and delivery in return for the discharge which he had already offered, reserving always his right against a former trustee. In these circumstances, as it was not denied that such a form of discharge had been offered, the pursuer was entitled to have the defences repelled as irrelevant and decree pronounced de plano on his conclusions as they are to be amended.

Counsel for the defenders in addition to taking the preliminary point on the form of the conclusions with which I have already dealt, contended that it was competent to receive a discharge covering the intromissions of all trustees, past and present, and their representatives. He referred to a form in the *Scots Style Book*, volume 7, page 309 as illustrative of such a discharge. There was, therefore, nothing incompetent in the position which the defenders were taking up, though he conceded that it was not easy to see what additional measure of protection such a discharge could afford the existing trustees or what interest they had to obtain such protection as such a discharge could give for their predecessors in this case. Counsel for the defenders was not, however, able to point to any authority which laid down that existing trustees were entitled to demand such a discharge as a matter of right when called upon to denude in favour of a residuary beneficiary. In my opinion, the pursuer's principal contention here is correct. The obligation of the defenders is to account and the right of the defenders in return for an accounting, is to be protected against claims which can competently be made against them in respect of their own acts and intromissions, no more and no less.

As regards accounting, the pursuer accepts the scheme of division referred to on record and indeed bases his claim upon it, so that the matter of the defenders' liability to account is settled.

I am therefore of opinion that the defenders here are bound to denude in the pursuer's favour on receiving a discharge in respect of their own acts and intromissions. This is the discharge which the pursuer offers on record, and I do not think he is obliged to do more.

Various attempts have been made since the case was called in debate roll before Lord Kilbrandon to adjust a suitable and agreed form of discharge and these attempts have failed, partly, it would seem, because of disagreement between parties as to how expenses are to be dealt with. The question of expenses, however, is obviously one which is now separate from the legal issue which has divided parties, and it is one which will have to be decided after I have had an opportunity of hearing parties on the point.

In these circumstances, I will, at this stage, limit my decision to a finding on the point of law which was argued before me, so that parties may have an opportunity of themselves adjusting the requisite form of discharge in light of that finding. My finding is that the defenders are, in law, bound to denude in the pursuer's favour on receiving from the pursuer a discharge in respect of their own acts and intromissions with the trust estate."

NOTES:

13.31   1. This decision is perfectly logical. If trustees are not liable for the acts and intromissions of their predecessors, then it would be illogical and unnecessary to discharge them from liability for those acts and intromissions. As Lord Cameron points out, trustees may "knowingly adopt and approve" the actions of their predecessors, and, in this way, "make them their own". But as it is their own actions which have made them responsible for those of their predecessors, a discharge in respect of their own actions would be sufficient to relieve them of responsibility for those of their predecessors.
       2. Although trustees are not liable for the acts and omissions of their predecessors as such, they might be in breach of trust if they failed to seek redress from former trustees who had been in breach of trust and caused loss thereby.

A. Methods of discharge

(a) Regulation in the trust deed

13.32 The method of discharge may be regulated by the trust deed. For example, the trust deed in *Bunten v. Muir* (1894) 21 R. 370 provided that, if a trustee resigned and accounted for his intromissions with the trust estate, the remaining trustees or trustee (or, if there were none, the beneficiaries) were "empowered and shall be bound to discharge" the remaining trustee.

A perhaps more unusual, but perfectly competent, method was found in *Tod v. Tod's Trs* (1842) 4 D. 1275, where the trust deed provided that accounts should be kept, which:

"shall be annually produced to, and examined by, an accountant of character and experience, to be chosen by the said trustees or trustee; and after being examined and passed by him, shall be fitted and docqueted by the said trustees or trustee, and which shall operate as a complete exoneration to them or him. . ."

The Lord Justice-Clerk (Hope) commented upon this system in the following terms (at 1279–1280):

"The plan and system of trust enquiry and examination here provided for are complete, and carried out to the extent of exoneration. There is nothing awanting or imperfect in the system thus laid down, so far as I have quoted the clause. Accounts are to be kept by the cashier and the trustees. These accounts are to be annually produced to, and examined by, an accountant of character and experience. That accountant is to be chosen by the trustees. Then he is to examine the accounts, and to pass the same; and when so examined, and passed, and docqueted by the trustees, in acknowledgement that they have no more to say, such audited accounts shall operate as a complete exoneration. The system is thus in itself perfect and complete. Whether expedient, was a point for the truster."

The Lord Justice-Clerk did observe, however, that an improper choice of accountant might leave the discharge open to challenge. Presumably this would be through an action for reduction of the discharge (*infra* para. 13.37).

Where the trust deed makes no provision as to who is empowered to grant a discharge, a discharge may generally be sought from either the beneficiaries or from co-trustees. Alternatively, if necessary, a discharge may be sought from the court.

(b) Discharge by the beneficiaries

13.33 Trustees cannot require a discharge from a legatee who has received a specific legacy. They are entitled to a receipt, however, which will act as a sufficient discharge in respect of that obligation. A residuary legatee is in a different position, however:

> "He is not in the same position as a party who receives a definite legacy of say £50, because the residue depends on the administration of the trust, and the parties may then require exoneration as trustees in reference to the management of the trust, which is a totally different thing from a receipt of a sum of money." (*Fleming v. Brown* (1861) 23 D. 443, *per* the Lord President (McNeill) at 445).

(c) Discharge by co-trustees

Trusts (Scotland) Act 1921, s.4

General powers of trustees

13.34 **4.**—(1) In all trusts the trustees shall have power to do the following acts, where such acts are not at variance with the terms or purposes of the trust, and such acts when done shall be as effectual as if such powers had been contained in the trust deed, *viz.*—

. . .

> (g) To discharge trustees who have resigned and the representatives of trustees who have died.

NOTES:

1. **13.35** What is the effect of a discharge granted under this section? It has been argued that a discharge granted in the exercise of this power is of limited effect:

> "it can scarcely be held that discharge from co-trustees would protect a man from a claim made against him by beneficiaries under the trust, in respect of maladministration, to which he was a party before his resignation. If such a discharge were to be held good, it would be easy for dishonest trustees, in expectation of trouble, to grant discharges to such of their number as were men of substance, and leave no one but men of straw to answer to the beneficiaries for the maladministration of the trust." (C.R.A. Howden, "Discharge of a Resigning Trustee" (1895) 3 S.L.T. (News) 139, at 140).

However, the accepted view is that such a discharge is as valid and effective as one granted by the beneficiaries. (Menzies, 932; Wilson and Duncan, 27–33). Mackenzie Stuart, however, appears to take a slightly different view, stating (at p. 345):

> "The power given to trustees to discharge resigning trustees and representatives of deceased trustees does not deprive the beneficiaries of their right to challenge any such discharge if it should not have been given. If trustees grant such a discharge to a trustee when there are claims existing against him, the discharge does not bind the beneficiaries or prevent the discharged trustee from having to account."

Mackenzie Stuart appears to be pointing out that, in such cases, the beneficiaries may have grounds for seeking reduction of the discharge (*infra*, para. 13.37), which answers the concern raised by Howden. But if a discharge granted by co-trustees is as effective as one granted by the beneficiaries, then it surely must bind the beneficiaries until it is reduced, even if there are claims existing against the trustee.

2. What happens where the existing trustees have wrongly granted a discharge to a former trustee? Unless this discharge can be reduced (see *infra*, para. 13.37), it would seem the former trustee has no liability, but the existing trustees may be liable for breach of trust in having fraudulently or negligently granted the discharge. (Menzies, p. 932; Wilson and Duncan, 27–33).

(d) Discharge by the court

Trusts (Scotland) Act 1921, s.18

Discharge of trustees resigning and heirs of trustees dying during the subsistence of the trust

13.36 **18.** When a trustee who resigns or the representatives of a trustee who has died or resigned cannot obtain a discharge of his acts and intromissions from the remaining trustees, and when the beneficiaries of the trust refuse or are unable from absence, incapacity or otherwise to grant a discharge, the court may on petition to that effect at the instance of such trustee or representative and after such intimation and inquiry as may be thought necessary, grant such discharge.

NOTE:

See *Matthews' Trs, Petrs* (1894) 2 S.L.T. 122, which confirms that the court will not grant a discharge unless it is "impossible for the resigning trustee to obtain a valid discharge either from the remaining trustees or from the beneficiaries".

B. Reduction of discharge

Mackenzie Stuart, *The Law of Trusts* (1932), pp. 344–345

13.37 "A discharge may be reduced or refused effect on the usual grounds of fraud or misrepresentation. It would also fail as being void if it was granted under essential error, as where, unknown to both parties, another deed existed which materially affected the beneficiary's right in the trust estate; or where it was granted on express condition that something was to be done which has become impossible.

A discharge is usually a gratuitous deed which may be set aside on the ground of the granter's error on some essential however that error has arisen, so long, at least, as the rights of third parties are not affected. The beneficiary, when granting a discharge, is only bound by it if he has all the facts before him or deliberately waives all enquiry, and he must know what he is doing."

Chapter 14

PRIVATE INTERNATIONAL LAW

This chapter briefly sets out the rules of private international law relating to trusts. For a fuller **14.01** discussion, the reader should consult a specialist text on private international law, such as A.E. Anton with P.R. Beaumont, *Private International Law* (2nd ed., 1990), Chapter 25.

The principal rules of private international law relating to trusts can be found in the Recognition of Trusts Act 1987, which gave effect to the Hague Convention on the Law Applicable to Trusts and their Recognition.

1. THE HAGUE CONVENTION ON THE LAW APPLICABLE TO TRUSTS AND THEIR RECOGNITION

A.E. Anton, "The Recognition of Trusts Act 1987"
1987 S.L.T. (News) 377

"Reasons for the Convention

While the concept of trust is a familiar one in Scots law, in English law, and in systems **14.02** derived from English law, it is conspicuous by its absence in most civil law systems. (The qualifying term 'most' is introduced because institutions modelled upon the trust have been created in some civil law systems, such as those of Liechtenstein, Louisiana, Sri Lanka, South Africa, and of several Latin American countries. See Dyer and van Loon, 'Report on trusts and analogous institutions', *Proceedings of the Fifteenth Session of the Hague Conference on Private International Law*, Vol. II, pp. 27–35; W. F. Fratcher, *International Encyclopaedia of Comparative Law*, Vol. VI, Chap. 11, esp. pp. 84–118). But the wide use of trusts of an international character in common law countries forced even civil law systems to come to grips with the implications of foreign trusts. (See Dyer and van Loon, above, pp. 35–40 and various articles in W. A. Wilson (ed.), *Trusts and Trust-Like Devices* (1981).) Those systems tended to deal with the problem not by recognising the trust as such with its normal incidents but by applying by analogy to trusts the institutions of their own law which appeared most apt to secure results similar to those which would have been achieved by the application of the rules of the foreign law of trusts. The results were seldom entirely satisfactory. In consequence, at the request of the United Kingdom, the subject of trusts was placed upon the agenda of the Hague Conference on Private International Law with a view to securing the wider and direct international recognition of United Kingdom and other common law trusts.

Obstacles to the drafting of the Convention

The absence of the trust concept in the legal systems of so many other states presented the draftsmen of the Convention with formidable practical and theoretical difficulties. Systems of private international law normally resolve legal problems by allocating them to familiar branches and categories of law, such as those of contract, delict, succession, etc. But what is the judge to do when he is faced with a branch or category of law which is entirely unknown to his own system and with which he is unfamiliar? The Hague Convention tackles this problem in a novel way. It describes in Art. 2(1) the general nature of the legal institution—a trust—which the Convention is intended to cover and states in Art. 2(2) and (3) some of the characteristics of this institution. (Although the paragraphs of each Article are not numbered in the Convention, it is convenient to express them as 'Art. 2(1)', 'Art. 2(2)', etc.) The Convention then asks civil law countries to recognise and give effect in their own laws to the—to them—unfamiliar institution of a trust with all its incidents and not merely to transmute the trust relationship into the most nearly analogous categories of their own law. If the Convention is accepted by a significant number of civil law countries it will represent a remarkable advance. It was signed by Italy, Luxembourg and the Netherlands on 1 July 1985 and by the United Kingdom on 10 January 1986. The bringing into force of the Recognition of Trusts Act 1987 will permit its ratification by the United Kingdom."

NOTES:

14.03
1. At the time of writing, the Convention had been ratified by the following countries: Australia, Canada (but only in relation to certain provinces, of which Quebec is a notable exception), China (in relation only to Hong Kong), Italy, Malta, the Netherlands, and the United Kingdom. It has been signed—but not ratified—by the following countries: Cyprus, France, Luxembourg and the United States of America. (The Hague Conference website, at http://www.hcch.net, may be consulted for up to date information as regards signatures and ratifications).
2. For discussion of the Convention, see Alfred E. von Overbeck, *Explanatory Report*, in *Proceedings of the Fifteenth Session of the Hague Conference* (1984), Vol. II, 370 (hereafter the "*von Overbeck Report*"); A.E. Anton, *The Recognition of Trusts Act 1987*, 1987 S.L.T. (News) 377; David Hayton, *The Hague Convention on the Law Applicable to Trusts and on Their Recognition* (1987) 36 I.C.L.Q. 260; Emmanuel Gaillard and Donald T. Trautman, *Trusts in Non-Trust Countries: Conflict of Laws and the Hague Convention on Trusts* (1987) 35 Am. J. Comp. L. 307; Maurizio Lupoi, *Trusts: A Comparative Study* (1997, English tr. by Simon Dix, 2000), Chapter 6.

2. APPLICATION OF THE CONVENTION IN THE UNITED KINGDOM

Recognition of Trusts Act 1987, s.1

Applicable law and recognition of trusts
14.04   **1.**—(1) The provisions of the Convention set out in the Schedule to this Act shall have the force of law in the United Kingdom.

(2) Those provisions shall, so far as applicable, have effect not only in relation to the trusts described in Articles 2 and 3 of the Convention but also in relation to any other trusts of property arising under the law of any part of the United Kingdom or by virtue of a judicial decision whether in the United Kingdom or elsewhere.

NOTES:

14.05
1. By virtue of section 1(2), the Convention rules govern not only the recognition by the Scottish courts of trusts created outwith the U.K., but also of trusts created within the other U.K. jurisdictions—as Anton suggests, "presumably because it was thought inconvenient to have one set of rules for those questions in relation to purely 'foreign' trusts and another set of rules for the recognition of 'United Kingdom' trusts." (1987 S.L.T. (News) 178).
2. However, while the Convention only applies to trusts within the definition specified in Article 2 (*infra* para. 14.06) and which are "created voluntarily and evidenced in writing" (Article 3),

section 1 of the 1987 Act extends the application of its provisions to "United Kingdom" trusts and trusts arising "by virtue of a judicial decision" which do not meet these criteria.

3. THE APPLICABLE LAW

A. The Convention concept of the trust

Hague Convention on the Law Applicable to Trusts and their Recognition (1985)

Article 2

14.06 For the purposes of this Convention, the term 'trust' refers to the legal relationship created—inter vivos or on death—by a person, the settlor, when assets have been placed under the control of a trustee for the benefit of a beneficiary or for a specified purpose.

A trust has the following characteristics—

    (a) the assets constitute a separate fund and are not a part of the trustee's own estate;

    (b) title to the trust assets stands in the name of the trustee or in the name of another person on behalf of the trustee;

    (c) the trustee has the power and the duty, in respect of which he is accountable, to manage, employ or dispose of the assets in accordance with the terms of the trust and the special duties imposed upon him by law.

The reservation by the settlor of certain rights and powers, and the fact that the trustee may himself have rights as a beneficiary, are not necessarily inconsistent with the existence of a trust.

NOTE:

As explained by Anton (*supra* para. 14.02), it was felt necessary to define the institution of the trust in the Convention by reason of the fact that the concept of the trust is unknown to many jurisdictions. (*Cf.,* however, Maurizio Lupoi, *Trusts: A Comparative Study* (1997, English tr. by Simon Dix, 2000), at p. 329: "the condescending attitude [of the common lawyers] found its institutional home in the transformation of the Convention into a textbook for civilians").

B. Which law applies?

Hague Convention on the Law Applicable to Trusts and their Recognition (1985)

Article 6

14.07 A trust shall be governed by the law chosen by the settlor. The choice must be express or be implied in the terms of the instrument creating or the writing evidencing the trust, interpreted, if necessary, in the light of the circumstances of the case.

Where the law chosen under the previous paragraph does not provide for trusts or the category of trust involved, the choice shall not be effective and the law specified in Article 7 shall apply.

Article 7

Where no applicable law has been chosen, a trust shall be governed by the law with which it is most closely connected.

In ascertaining the law with which a trust is most closely connected reference shall be made in particular to—

    (a) the place of administration of the trust designated by the settlor;

    (b) the situs of the assets of the trust;

(c) the place of residence or business of the trustee;
(d) the objects of the trust and the places where they are to be fulfilled.

NOTES:

14.08   The applicable law may therefore be determined in three ways:
1. *Express choice of the truster (settlor).* The Convention does not limit the truster's freedom of choice in selecting the applicable law.
2. *Implied choice of the truster.* Hayton has commented that:

> "An implied choice of law will most readily be found where the settlor's trust instrument excludes, qualifies or extends expressly mentioned provisions of a particular State's trust law, *e.g.* in England sections 23 and 30 to 33 of the Trustee Act 1925, or the Trustee Investments Act 1961. It might also be found where a particular technical clause in the trust instrument could only have been inserted to deal with a problem otherwise arising under the law of a particular State, though no express reference is made to such law. It would then be necessary to bring this circumstance to light to illuminate the choice implicit in the terms of the instrument." (David Hayton, "The Hague Convention on the Law Applicable to Trusts and on Their Recognition" (1987) 36 I.C.L.Q. 260, 270).

(The Trustee Investments Act 1961, which applied both north and south of the border in 1987, is perhaps not the best example, however!)
3. *Law of the state most closely connected to the trust.* This law will apply where (a) the truster has not selected an applicable law or (b) the applicable law selected by the truster does not provide for trusts. This concept is similar to the common law concept of the "domicile of the trust". The order in which the various factors which are to be taken into account are listed has been described as an "implicit hierarchy" (*von Overbeck Report*, para. 77), which reflects the fact that the U.S. and Canadian delegates to the Hague Conference considered the place of administration to be a particularly important factor (see Anton, 1987 S.L.T. (News) 377, 380). The court is, of course, not precluded from taking other factors into account.

C. What does the applicable law govern?

Hague Convention on the Law Applicable to Trusts and their Recognition (1985)

Article 8

14.09   The law specified by Article 6 or 7 shall govern the validity of the trust, its construction, its effects and the administration of the trust.
In particular that law shall govern—
(a) the appointment, resignation and removal of trustees, the capacity to act as a trustee, and the devolution of the office of trustee;
(b) the rights and duties of trustees among themselves;
(c) the right of trustees to delegate in whole or in part the discharge of their duties or the exercise of their powers;
(d) the power of trustees to administer or to dispose of trust assets, to create security interests in the trust assets, or to acquire new assets;
(e) the powers of investment of trustees;
(f) restrictions upon the duration of the trust, and upon the power to accumulate the income of the trust;
(g) the relationships between the trustees and the beneficiaries including the personal liability of the trustees to the beneficiaries;
(h) the variation or termination of the trust;

(i) the distribution of the trust assets;

(j) the duty of trustees to account for their administration.

NOTE:

The applicable law, however, does not govern questions of general capacity (particularly, capacity to create a trust) (*von Overbeck Report*, para. 85), nor does it govern formal validity (*von Overbeck Report*, para. 82).

D. *Dépeçage*

Hague Convention on the Law Applicable to Trusts and their Recognition (1985)

Article 9

In applying this Chapter a severable aspect of the trust, particularly matters of **14.10** administration, may be governed by a different law.

Article 10

The law applicable to the validity of the trust shall determine whether that law or the law governing a severable aspect of the trust may be replaced by another law.

NOTE:

These provisions allow for *dépeçage*, "the practice of subjecting certain elements of the trust to different laws" (*von Overbeck Report*, para. 91). The proposal to provide for *dépeçage* was met with some hostility by the representatives of civilian jurisdictions at the Hague Conference, but was pressed for by the common law jurisdictions, particularly the United States and Canada. However, it seems to have been accepted that "it may be desirable to apply to the administration of the trust a law other than that which governs its validity; the law of the place where the administration of the trust is located will particularly come to mind. Also, it is possible to envisage as severable aspects of a trust issues concerning property which is situated in different countries or beneficiaries domiciled in different countries." (*von Overbeck Report*, para. 91).

E. Consequences of Recognition

Hague Convention on the Law Applicable to Trusts and their Recognition (1985)

Article 11

A trust created in accordance with the law specified by the preceding Chapter shall be **14.11** recognised as a trust.

Such recognition shall imply, as a minimum, that the trust property constitutes a separate fund, that the trustee may sue and be sued in his capacity as trustee, and that he may appear or act in this capacity before a notary or any person acting in an official capacity.

In so far as the law applicable to the trust requires or provides, such recognition shall imply, in particular—

(a) that personal creditors of the trustee shall have no recourse against the trust assets;

(b) that the trust assets shall not form part of the trustee's estate upon his insolvency or bankruptcy;

(c) that the trust assets shall not form part of the matrimonial property of the trustee or his spouse nor part of the trustee's estate upon his death;

(d) that the trust assets may be recovered when the trustee, in breach of trust, has mingled trust assets with his own property or has alienated trust assets. However, the rights and obligations of any third party holder of the assets shall remain subject to the law determined by the choice of law rules of the forum.

F. Limitations to the sphere of the applicable law

A.E. Anton, "The Recognition of Trusts Act 1987"
1987 S.L.T. (News) 377

"Limitations to the sphere of the applicable law

14.12 There are, however, important limitations in the Convention to the operation of the applicable law under it. The most important of these limitations are contained in Art. 15, which provides: 'The Convention does not prevent the application of provisions of the law designated by the conflicts rules of the forum, in so far as these provisions cannot be derogated from by voluntary act, relating in particular to the following matters—(*a*) the protection of minors and incapable parties; (*b*) the personal and proprietary effects of marriage; (*c*) succession rights, testate and intestate, especially the indefeasible shares of spouses and relatives; (*d*) the transfer of title to property and security interests in property; (*e*) the protection of creditors in matters of insolvency; (*f*) the protection, in other respects, of third parties acting in good faith.

'If recognition of a trust is prevented by application of the preceding paragraph, the court shall try to give effect to the objects of the trust by other means.'

It has been suggested that the primary purpose of this provision was to preserve the mandatory rules of the forum in relation to the matters which Art. 15 specifies and other relevant matters; but the provision is wider in its effect because it extends also to protection of the substantive laws of other countries which may be indicated by the choice of law rules of the forum (von Overbeck Report, p. 401). An important subsidiary purpose of this rule is clearly that of delimiting the respective spheres of trust law and of other branches of law in the complex issues which arise in international situations. In this context the limitation to mandatory rules is possibly unfortunate. It will not always be an easy matter to determine whether the provisions of a foreign system are such that they 'cannot be derogated from by voluntary act'.

Article 15, as we have seen, looks to the mandatory rules of systems of law designated by the conflict rules of the forum. Article 16(1) looks to the mandatory rules of the internal law of the forum 'which must be applied even to international situations, irrespective of rules of conflict of laws'. These rules are often referred to by continental lawyers as 'rules of immediate application'. They are rules which discharge the ordinary conflict rules of their normal role and must be applied irrespective of the latter. They include rules which are intended to preserve the treasures of art and antiquity and rules protecting certain economic interests. One would have thought that these problems would be covered in practice by the concept of public policy and that Art. 16(1) is something of a fifth wheel on the coach. In the Convention, Art. 16(1) is complemented by another provision, Art. 16(2), which allows the application in exceptional circumstances of the 'rules of immediate application' of another state closely connected with the case. Article 16(3), however, permits Contracting States by reservation not to apply Art. 16(2) and the United Kingdom, it may be assumed, has made or intends to make such a reservation since Art. 16(2) has been excluded from the provisions of the Convention as scheduled to the Act. Article 16(2) introduces an element of uncertainty into the recognition of trusts and it is to be hoped that most states will not avail themselves of this provision.

The Convention contains in Art. 18 the usual rule that: 'The provisions of the Convention may be disregarded when their application would be manifestly incompatible with public policy (ordre public).' Though the continental concept of ordre public is arguably wider than the United Kingdom concept of public policy, those words have been omitted from the text of Art. 18 as scheduled to the Act."

NOTE:

The United Kingdom did, indeed, declare that it would not apply Article 16(2). Other states, however, have not followed suit.

INDEX